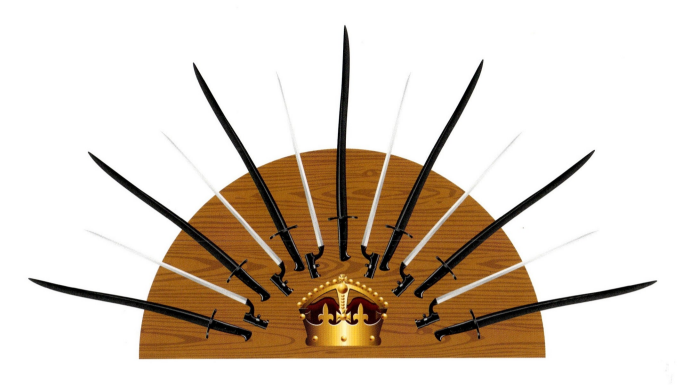

PRESERVING OUR PROUD
HERITAGE

The Customs and Traditions of the Australian Army

L.I. TERRETT & S.C. TAUBERT

BIG SKY PUBLISHING

Editorial Preface

The Board of Management accepted the view that as much information as was able to be discovered in the writing and publication timeframe should be included in this first edition. To a large degree this has been accommodated. However, this brought its own set of issues, not the least of which is that many readers will have differing perspectives and experiences of their time in or with the Australian Army. This is a contentious topic about which many views will and should exist.

Shortened forms for organisations and ranks have been used throughout and a full listing of all such abbreviations, acronyms and initialisms has been provided for the reader's information.

All proposals for new material and amendments for inclusion in future editions will be considered if accompanied by supporting evidence. Readers are invited to provide their evidence-based proposals for change or inclusion by accessing the Australian Army History Unit Enquiries page on the web at AHU. Enquiries@defence.gov.au or by writing to:

Australian Army History Unit
PO Box 7911
CANBERRA BC 2610 ACT

All accepted inclusions will be acknowledged and documents will be returned to the sender.

Preserving our Proud Heritage

This book has been written about the Australian Army in general; efforts have been made to avoid Corps-specific customs and traditions but this has not always been possible. Readers wishing to find more detailed information on Corps and their customs and traditions should search specific Corps publications. The first chapter of this work is taken almost in its entirety from the book, 'The Australian Army - A Brief History'[1], edited by Major Geoff Lever of the Australian Army History Unit (AAHU). Our thanks are extended to the AAHU for permission to amend and use this work.

Originally, the authors of this book worked independently to produce a definitive work on the various aspects of the customs and traditions of the Australian Army.

Major Les Terrett began work on a book on Australian Army Customs and Traditions in 2003. On transitioning to the Army Reserve in 2007, he joined the AAHU where he was given the opportunity to further develop his work. He used as his starting point the books 'Military Traditions and Customs and How They Began 1870-1975', and 'Customs and Traditions 1996', both of which had been published by the Warrant Officer Wing, School of Infantry, Singleton having been developed over the years from the original 'Ceremonial Drill 1-13' produced at the Infantry Centre, Ingleburn in February 1962.

Stephen Taubert, working independently since 2001, prepared several original works covering his areas of interest including customs and traditions, army lineages and mottoes, regimental march music, standards, guidons, colours and banners as well as Australian honours and awards. The drafts were enhanced with graphical depictions of army flags, badges and other military icons especially developed by the author for those books and many of his depictions are used in this publication.

In 2007, Dr Roger Lee, the Head of the AAHU, invited Stephen to team up with Les to produce this book, the first fully-referenced work on the subject. This first edition, a culmination of that work, provides the reader with an understanding of the evolution of the Australian Army and its Customs and Traditions. Whilst every effort has been made to confirm the accuracy of the content, errors in understanding and context are regrettably almost certain to occur.

---

1   Lever GO. (editor). *The Australian Army A Brief History, 4th Edition.* Sydney, Big Sky Publishing: 2011

Foreword

Preserving Our Proud Heritage
The Customs and Traditions of the Australian Army

The Australian Army's customs and traditions represent the symbols and substance of much of our character and have been adopted from Army's forebears and developed over the previous 113 years to where we are today. They shape (led by our badge of honour, the Rising Sun) our 'family recognition' and to an extent our collective personality, which provide, along with our members both past and present, the Army's beating heart. The Army will survive as a respected National institution for the eons, building on the customs and traditions we take for granted today.

Much can be learnt from the past and the Army is constantly validating the importance of our comparatively young but rich history. These origins have provided the forms for our badges, insignia and symbols of office; the way we demonstrate our respect through our formal functions and dinners, the way we address our people and the way we wear the uniform. These tangible links to our past, like the weft and warp of a rich historical tapestry, set us well for our future. If we respect the past, we will respect today and tomorrow.

I acknowledge the very hard, long and dedicated work of Major Les Terrett and Mr Stephen Taubert, the authors of this comprehensive work. Their legacy for this important effort will be an enduring compilation of the customs and traditions of our great Army.

I join with the Regimental Sergeant Major of the Army in commending this work to all who have a professional interest and passion in our customs and traditions. This must be every one of us.

DL Morrison, AO
LTGEN
CA

DM Ashley, AM
WO
RSM-A

The Diggers

Yet at heart even the oldest Australian soldier was incorrigibly civilian. However thoroughly he accepted the rigid army methods as conditions temporarily necessary, he never became reconciled to continuous obedience to orders, existence by rule, and lack of privacy. His individualism had been so strongly implanted as to stand out after years of subordination. Even on the Western Front he had exercised his vote in the Australian elections and in the referendums as to conscription, and it was largely through his own act in these ballots that the Australian people had rejected conscription and that, to the end, the AIF consisted entirely of volunteers. He was subject to no death penalty for disobedience or failure to face the enemy.

His outlook contrasted sharply with that of most English soldiers of that time, whose discipline was largely founded on the social division of their nation into upper, middle and lower classes. English officers were mainly drawn from the two former, and their troops accepted the principle that the general business of the great world was the affair of their superiors alone rather than of themselves; if action outside routine was called for, they looked to their officers to tell them what to do and how to do it. In Australia the distinction into social classes was so resented that it was difficult to get born Australians to serve as officers' batmen and grooms, who by the English tradition were servants. Those Australians who did so serve regarded themselves as their officers' guardians or helpers; they would look after the boss in those matters in which he was deemed incapable of looking after himself.

From early childhood the average Australian had regarded himself and everyone around him as masters of their own lives. He was accustomed to make decisions; and was always ready to run risks for an object in which he was interested - whether the saving of a mate, the securing of a souvenir or an unlicensed trip to Paris (or, after the war, to Cologne). He was less affected than most men by risk of punishment, but was bound to his fellows, and to the Old Country and the Allies, by a tense bond of democratic loyalty - a man must 'stand by his mates' at all costs; and as he knew only one social horizon, that of race, most of his officers came within that category. He was the easiest man in the world to interest and lead, but was intolerant of incompetent or uninteresting leaders.

Except for a few demoniac spirits, one immersion in a great battle more than satisfied the eagerness that had led many to enlist, and left in almost all minds an often sub-conscious but never-absent dread. Most Australians yearned for return to their country with an intensity of longing of which they had not believed themselves capable, but which was remarked by most other soldiers who met them; so much so, that their word-pictures of their dry, sunlit, war-free land freely sketched by them to their British friends amid the smoke and vin rouge of the estaminets, or to their girl admirers on English leave, not infrequently determined their hearers to seek homes there after the war.[2]

CEW Bean[3]

---

2   Bean CEW. *The Australian Imperial Force in France during the Allied Offensive, 1918.* Sydney, Angus and Robertson: 1942
3   Dr. Charles Edwin Woodrow Bean, BA, BCL, MA; barrister; military historian, journalist, Official War Correspondent AIF,
     Chairman AWM 1952; born, Bathurst NSW 18 Nov 1879 – died, Concord Repatriation General Hospital, NSW 30 Aug 1968.

Military Tradition

The Concise Oxford Dictionary[4] defines 'Custom' as *'a traditional and widely accepted way of behaving or doing something that is specific to a particular society, place, or time'* and 'Tradition' as *'an oral transmission of knowledge or belief from generation to generation, or the fact of being so passed on.'*

Oral transmission of any form of knowledge passed down through the ages would suffer some degree of distortion and because of this there are certain 'grey' areas in any consensus of military writing dealing with customs and traditions. Fortunately, by in-depth research and utilising many authoritative original documents and books in the United Kingdom and elsewhere, it has been possible to produce this book. It should be remembered that by its very definition, tradition is not something which can be established overnight. Few of our military traditions are native in origin. Those present in everyday barracks life have been passed down over the years, having been adopted by the soldiers of the colonial and later Australian Military Forces from those developed in the British and other Armies.

One of the hardest things in writing this book was to decide; what is a custom and what is a tradition within the Australian Army and where do they meet? To compound this dilemma, what is the truth? There are many truths: my truth; your truth; their truth; our truth; and the truth. What comes to mind is that, in the fog of war, there are many truths and many myths and it has been known to happen that they cross and join. Regardless, it is hoped that this book provides an accurate and useful source of information to those readers within and without our Army.

The veteran soldier does not need to be 'sold' on the importance of traditions and customs. But he occasionally re-examines them and does away with ones that no longer serve any purpose or that interfere with military efficiency. But before we condemn a custom, we owe our predecessors the courtesy of realising that the custom once made sense. We must be sure our refusal to accept a custom is not based on poor judgment or ignorance.

Colonel James A. Moss[5]
United States Army, 1929

Every trifle, every tag or ribbon that tradition may have associated with former glories of a regiment should be retained, so long as its retention does not interfere with efficiency.

Colonel Clifford Walton[6]
British Army

---

4   Pearsall J. (editor) *The Concise Oxford English Dictionary (10th edition revised)*. Oxford University Press: 2002
5   Colonel James A. Moss, US Army, wrote the 'Officer's Manual, and Origin and Significance of Military Customs': born 12 May 1872 – died 23 April 1941.
6   Colonel Clifford Elliot Walton, British Army, wrote the 'History of the British standing army: A.D. 1660-1700': born Jul 1839 – died unknown.

Contents

Acknowledgements

Many people have given generously of their time and knowledge to help in the production of this publication; special thanks must also go to our respective wives Robyn Taubert and Vikki Terrett for without their moral support, assistance and patience this project would not have been possible.

Particular note of sincere recognition, appreciation and thanks goes to:

Dr Roger Lee
Professor Allan Terrett
CAPT Rod Mason, OAM
Dr Andrew Richardson

Further sincere appreciation is extended to:

The Steering Group:

    MAJGEN (Retd) Ian Gordon, AO
    LTCOL David Cran
    MAJ Cathy McCullagh

Heads of Corps of the Australian Army
MAJGEN (Retd) Gordon Maitland, AO, OBE, RFD, ED
MAJ Geoff Lever
MAJ Stephen Ward, OAM - Ex RSM of the Army
WO Dave Ashley, AM - RSM of the Army
WO1 Danny Brookes
WO1 Ian D'Arcy, OAM
WO1 John Franklin
WO1 David Lehr, OAM - Ex RSM Ceremonial - Army
WO1 Philip Matthysen
WO1 Gary Mychael, OAM
MRS Gillian Heard, Staff Officer Ceremonial - Army
MR Jason Silsby, DPS Canberra
MR Peter Tait, DMO
MR Doug Fothergill
MR Graham Wilson
MR Ian Kuring
MR Russell Sams
Staff at the Australian Army History Unit
Staff of the Defence Library Service
Musicians, audio engineers and arrangers of the Australian Army Band Corps in recording the music for this project

We also wish to sincerely thank the editor, Neil Churches, for his technical and literary skills.

Dedication

*This book is dedicated to the soldiers who created the traditions of our Army
and to those who will carry them forward.*

Chapter One

Evolution of the Australian Army

The Beginning

Australia's military history began in 1788 when four companies of the Marine Corps arrived with the convicts of the First Fleet. The Marines soon clashed with Governor Arthur Philip[7], refusing to supervise convicts or undertake judicial duties. On 8th June 1789, the British Government issued an order to raise a new regiment, the New South Wales Corps, a British Army unit specifically recruited to serve in the new Colony. The first 183 men of the New South Wales Corps arrived in Sydney Cove in June 1790. Between June 1790 and February 1792 the Marines were gradually replaced by the New South Wales Corps, later redesignated the 102nd Regiment. Major (MAJ) Francis Grose[8] arrived in Sydney in 1792 to take command and also assume the role of Lieutenant-Governor of the Colony.

The British Garrison

The New South Wales Corps proved little better than its predecessor and it soon raised the indignation of the colonial administration for the irregular trading activities of some of its officers. Constant bickering with a succession of naval governors culminated in the deposing of Governor William Bligh[9] in 1808. The Corps' military efficiency was unquestioned as during the March 1804 Castle Hill Rebellion (known as the Battle of Vinegar Hill) involving about 200 escaped convicts, a company of the Corps marched from Sydney to Parramatta in about three hours and after a short rest, spent the remainder of the day subduing the convicts.

In 1809, Colonel (COL) Lachlan Macquarie[10] arrived as Governor and the New South Wales Corps was replaced by his own regiment, the 1/73rd, which was a regular regiment of the British Army. Thus began a succession of 26 British infantry regiments and a number of smaller artillery and engineer units that garrisoned the Australian Colonies until the last was withdrawn in 1870.

Governor Macquarie needed to bring his own Battalion (Bn) up to strength, and he achieved this by selecting private soldiers of the 102nd with long service, getting to within 19 of his full entitlement. An additional 100 men were enlisted as a 'veteran' or 'invalid' company for garrison duty in New South Wales. This company, although incorporated into and commanded by an officer of the 73rd, was distinguished from the 73rd by the blue facings on their uniforms which were otherwise the same as the uniforms worn by the 1/73rd, with dark green facings. By 1817 its members were well beyond their prime, having been attached to each regiment of foot stationed in New South Wales, before being disbanded in 1823.

The garrison force discharged a broad variety of responsibilities. Apart from their duties as guards and administrators of convicts, both afloat and ashore, the garrison soldiers also established and maintained the Mounted Police in New South Wales between 1825 and 1850. Troops constructed fortifications, attended fires and executions and assisted the police in keeping the peace between rioting sailors, rival election parties and squabbling sectarians. They provided guards for wrecks, goldfields, colonial treasuries, quarantine stations, Government Houses, the opening and closing of legislatures and mounted escorts for gold in transit. They manned coastal defences and fired ceremonial artillery salutes. They also operated in their infantry role against indigenous resistance in the Colonies. Some regiments also saw active service in New Zealand during the Maori Wars. Two were deployed to assist the Victorian Government during the uprising by gold miners at Ballarat in 1854 (The Eureka Stockade). They were called on again in 1861 by the New South Wales Government during six anti-Chinese riots by gold miners at Lambing Flat (later renamed Young) over a 10-month period.

---

7   Admiral Arthur Phillip; Navy Lieutenant 1761, Post Captain 1781, appointed the first Governor of New South Wales 1786, returned to England due to ill health and resigned in 1793: born London 1738 – died Bath England 1814.

8   Lieutenant General Francis Grose; Ensign 1775, Lieutenant-Governor of New South Wales and Commandant of the New South Wales Corps 1789, Acting Governor NSW 1792-1794: born about 1758 England – died Surrey England 1814.

9   Vice-Admiral William Bligh; Royal Navy, Master of HMS *Resolution* 1776, Commander and Purser of HMS *Bounty* 1787, Captain 1790, Governor New South Wales 1806, replaced by Lachlan Macquarie 1809: born Devon England 1754 – died Kent England 1817.

10   Major General Lachlan Macquarie; Ensign 84th Regiment 1777, Lieutenant 71st Regiment 1781, Captain-Lieutenant 1788, Major of Brigade 1791, Governor of Colombo and Point de Galle 1796, Brevet Major 1796, Commanding Officer 86th Regiment Bombay 1801, Commanding Officer 73rd Regiment 1805, Governor New South Wales 1809, Colonel 1810, Brigadier General 1811, Major General 1813: born Ulva Scotland 1762 – died London 1824.

The Colonial Armies

In the early years of the Colony, the professional military presence was small. To supplement the full-time military, a number of governors, and later, colonial governments, turned to the local community to provide part-time soldiers, either for short-term local defence or in response to international developments that appeared to threaten local interests. There were two forms of local military service: the 'militia'; and the volunteer forces. In the early years of the 19th century, in both England and the Australian Colonies, militia forces were recruited for a specific purpose by a ballot of men of specified ages drawn from within the local population. These forces could not be used outside defined, usually local, areas. They were fully outfitted, equipped and paid by the Government and operated under a form of military discipline. The volunteer forces on the other hand, provided their own uniforms and were not paid, thus providing a military force at minimum expense to the Government, which supplied only weapons and ammunition. Consequently, a volunteer unit usually enjoyed certain privileges such as the right to elect its own officers, frame its own regulations, and remain exempt from militia service. Historically, few groups of either type lasted very long or were well-trained, and the military value of both groups was questionable.

The first example of locally-raised forces was a group known as the Loyal Associations or Loyal Volunteers. This group appeared in September 1800 when Governor Hunter[11] asked 100 free male citizens in Sydney and Parramatta to form a military unit to safeguard against riots and rebellions by the large, disaffected Irish convict community. In addition to, and in support of the Loyal Volunteers, the first full-time locally-raised military force in Australia was formed about 1803 when the third governor of the Colony of New South Wales, Philip King[12], raised a mounted bodyguard of six ex-convicts as his personal escort. The professional military, particularly the officers of the New South Wales Corps, objected to the presence of these locally-raised forces, although they quickly drafted them to help suppress the 1804 convict uprising near Parramatta. Both the Loyal Volunteers and Governor King's bodyguard were made redundant by the arrival in 1810 of the first of the British regular regiments that would garrison in Australia until 1870. Interest in forming local military units continued to wax and wane throughout the entire colonial period. Only five years elapsed between the demise of the Loyal Associations in 1810 and renewed calls for the raising of a colonial force in 1815. In 1830, a so-called mounted volunteer party was raised to assist the Mounted Police in suppressing bushrangers near Bathurst.

However, it was not until 1840 that the first official colonial force, with the confusing title of the Royal South Australian Volunteer Militia, was raised to assist with local security. Never a success, it was quietly disbanded five years later.

The imperial ambitions of France in the Pacific, culminating in the annexation of New Caledonia in 1853, raised colonial suspicions and promoted renewed interest in local defence. However, it was not until the following year, with the outbreak of the Crimean War and the threat of Russian maritime raids, that volunteer units were first raised in New South Wales, Victoria and South Australia. Tasmania and Western Australia considered the Russians too distant to pose a threat and did not rush to raise any local defence units. The cost of a paid force, the militia, was such that most colonial governments preferred to rely on volunteers. By the mid-1800s, there were sufficient British Army veterans within the community to provide a nucleus of competent military support. However, South Australia doubted the willingness of its citizens to volunteer, so a *Militia Act* was passed which could be used if compulsory enlistment became necessary to augment the volunteers. Most of the Volunteer Corps raised were rifle companies, populated by prosperous British immigrants and trained to fight as skirmishing infantry. These soldiers regarded themselves as auxiliaries who would fight in support of the regular forces.

With the end of the Crimean War in 1856, interest in volunteer forces declined. However, with the emergence of a threat from Napoleon III, including the assessment that he planned to invade England in 1859, there was yet another revival; again, this was more focused on volunteer service than paid militia and many volunteer units appeared in suburbs and towns of the various Colonies. Other world events, including the American Civil War, Russia's actions in Poland, the Balkans and Asia, the ever-present fear of an advance of

---

11 Vice Admiral John Hunter; Navy Midshipman 1764; Lieutenant 1765, Captain 1786, appointed Governor of New South Wales 1794, replaced 28 Sep 1800 returned to England, Rear Admiral 1807, Vice Admiral 1810: born Edinburgh 29 Aug 1737 – died London England 1821.

12 Philip Gidley King; Navy Midshipman 1775, Lieutenant 1778, Commander 1791, Lieutenant Governor Norfolk Island 1791, post Captain 1798, Governor New South Wales 1802-1806: born Cornwall 23 Apr 1758 – died London 3 Sep 1808.

*Above: AWM Neg No ART94391
Courtesy of the Australian War Memorial.
The Eureka Stockade, Ballarat.*

*Right: AWM Neg No 04590 Courtesy
of the Australian War Memorial.
Captain HEW Preston - 50th Regiment
of Foot (West Kent) about 1869[13]*

Russia through Afghanistan to India, and later the Franco-Prussian War, maintained a healthy level of interest in defence matters within the colonial communities. The upsurge in volunteering was also replicated in Britain and Canada and continued beyond the end of the immediate threat. During the early 1860s, almost every town and suburb in Australia possessed its own volunteer unit, usually a Rifle Corps.

With the end of the French threat to England, volunteer numbers declined, although many of the formed units remained. Both the Imperial Government and the colonial legislatures realised that Volunteer Corps could be a double-edged sword. They were essentially an ¬armed force that existed outside the control of the Government. While no volunteer unit ever degenerated into an armed mob, the potential for them to use their military skills against the Government existed. Also, the professional military began to question their military value, particularly their value for money, even the small amount spent solely on weapons and ammunition. At the same time, there appeared little option but to continue to encourage volunteer service. Over the next 40 years, all British and colonial governments began to recognise their increasing vulnerability to the rising new military powers of Europe. They also realised that they could not fund the necessary permanent forces. As democracies, these Governments were reluctant to embrace the use of conscription fully, even for militia service. Thus, volunteers presented the only real option.

Over the same period, changes in British foreign policy priorities (a greater focus on India and the European continent) and concerns raised by the British Treasury over escalating costs, provided a growing impetus to reduce the British garrison obligation in all Britain's Colonies. The Australian Colonies remained aware of the need to provide some contribution to their own defence, raising volunteer units in Tasmania (1859), Queensland (1860) and Western Australia (1861).

The strategic and political realities of the time were also accompanied by attitudinal changes amongst those in the community who traditionally served in a volunteer capacity, leading to major fluctuations in volunteer unit size and numbers. Many volunteers became impatient with the Government's attempts to improve the organisational and operational base of the volunteer units to make them more 'military'. Recruiting was not helped by a gradual but serious decline in the discipline and efficiency of the troops. The causes of this were many and varied and included: the constant debate over their 'right' to elect their own officers; lobbying for advancement by volunteers who were also members of parliament; and a lack of a cohesive command and training structure. In addition, a migratory population, newspaper

opposition, legislatures which had no understanding of their defence obligations and needs, obsolete weapons, the heavy financial burdens on volunteers of only moderate means and Government financial stringency and indifference by legislatures in the lulls between international crises, combined to degrade the morale and enthusiasm of the volunteer units.

The Colonies reacted in different ways, and the recommendations of parliamentary committees and commissions were not always adopted. Tasmania, perceiving no immediate threat in 1863, disbanded its volunteer infantry component, although it increased that of the artillery, and between 1870 and 1878 completely discontinued the 'volunteer vote'. In 1863, Western Australia also withdrew the right of volunteers to elect their own officers. In the same year, Victoria amalgamated all mounted troops into the Prince of Wales's Victorian Volunteer Light Horse. In 1865, South Australia introduced the concept of partly-paid volunteers, thereby heralding the end of the purely volunteer system, a model that was ultimately adopted by all colonial Governments. In one colony, free land grants were offered in return for five years' efficient voluntary service.

Over the years, the terms 'volunteer' and 'militia' became confused, and the status of the local military forces of the Australian colonies prior to Federation in 1901 remains ambiguous. Some volunteer units were paid or received token gratuities, thus losing their right to elect officers. While compulsory service was possible under some colonial acts, these powers were never invoked, and voluntary enlistment was used by both volunteer and militia units. Despite this, volunteer units continued to exist and, following Federation, a number of these units were among the colonial forces that amalgamated to form the new federal Army.

---

13 Captain Henry Evelyn Woodville Preston; obtained his commission (by purchase) as Ensign in the 50th (Queen's Own) Regiment of Foot, served in New Zealand, 50th Regiment (NSW), and India, he returned to Australia in 1877: born unknown – died Waverley Sydney 1905.

Left: New Zealand Medal – reverse

Right: AWM No. ART50235 Courtesy of the Australian War Memorial. Storming the Rifle Pits at Te Ranga, 21st June 1864

The Second Maori (Taranaki) War – 1863-1866

The Second Maori War in New Zealand, in the 1860s, saw the British 40th Regiment withdrawn from Victoria for active service with local colonial volunteers assuming their duties. Three years later the New Zealand Government recruited men, mainly from Victoria, to serve as militia in the 1st, 2nd, 3rd and 4th Battalions of the Waikato Regiment. This is likely to have been the first occasion where formed bodies of Australian military volunteers served on active service outside Australia (even though Australian-born volunteers had been recruited into British regiments from the early 1800s), and were the first recorded Australian-born casualties of war. Although the identity of the first casualty cannot be verified beyond doubt, the action in which he was killed occurred on 23rd October 1863, when at Wheeler's Farm, Titi Hill, members of the 9th Company, 1st Waikato Regiment, fought a pitched battle against Maori tribesmen at Wheeler's Farm, resulting in the death of seven men, four of whom were Victorians. The Australian men killed were Lieutenant (LT) John Spencer Perceval, Corporal (CPL) Michael Power, Private (PTE) William Beswick and PTE William Williamson.[14] LT Perceval was a retired Imperial Army officer born in England; however, the other three were likely to have been natural-born citizens of Australia from the Bendigo region of Victoria.

The major New Zealand campaign was the Waikato War (1863-1864), where 39,000 soldiers were in the field against a confederation of Waikato tribes. About 2,500 Australians[15] travelled across the Tasman Sea, lured by the promise of land confiscated from the Maori. Although most of these men joined the Waikato Militia regiments, others became scouts and bush guerrillas in the Company of Forest Rangers.

14 Barton LL. *Australians in the Waikato War, 1863-1864*. Sydney, Library of Australian History: 1979, pp. 22-23

15 Dennis P, Grey J, Morris E, Prior R. *The Oxford Companion to Australian Military History (Second Edition)*. Australia, Oxford University Press: 2008, p. 395

Regular Colonial Forces

Small regular colonial forces were first raised in Victoria in 1870, and in New South Wales the following year, to fill the vacuum caused by the departure of the Royal Artillery which had been manning the coastal defences of New South Wales from 1856 and Victoria from 1861. Two regular (but seriously under-strength) infantry companies were also raised in New South Wales in 1871, but were disbanded the following year. Apart from a small detachment, the Victorian regular artillery was disbanded in 1880, only to be re-established two years later.

Towards Federation: 1870-1900

After the withdrawal of the British garrison in 1870 following the reforms of Edward Cardwell, Secretary of State for War, the Colonies began to recognise that defence was not a matter of individual effort. To be effective, defence had to be coordinated at the national level. In 1877, at the insistence of New South Wales, Major General (MAJGEN) Sir William Jervois[16] (who later became Governor of South Australia) and Lieutenant Colonel (LTCOL) Peter Scratchley[17] of the Royal Engineers were engaged to act as advisers to the Colonies on defence matters. A series of inter-colonial conferences aimed at considering the defence of Australia were held from the early 1880s. These initiatives illustrate the importance of the defence debate as a factor in the overall impetus for Federation.

While a gradual process, the training and efficiency of the colonial forces improved over time. The introduction of higher defence structures and the posting of British officers and warrant officers to appointments in these higher headquarters and within the various units introduced an air of reality into colonial defences and did much to improve the efficiency of colonial regiments.

While the colonies believed the defence of the Torres Strait, New Guinea and King George's Sound was a British responsibility, they also recognised the strategic importance of these regions. A small detachment of Royal Marines was stationed at Port Albany, on Cape York, between 1865 and 1867. Following their withdrawal, Queensland maintained a tenuous local military presence there until the garrison was eventually moved to Thursday Island.

The threat of German annexation of New Guinea led Queensland, supported by the other colonies, to annex Papua in April 1883, to the consternation of the British Government which was firmly opposed to further colonial

AWM Neg AWM 100953 Courtesy of the Australian War Memorial. New South Wales troops of the Australian Infantry marching from the Camp of Suakin during the Sudan Campaign of 1885

expansion. Resolute action by the colonies finally secured a British Protectorate over southern New Guinea (Papua) in October 1884. Much to the irritation of the Australian colonies, Germany annexed the north-eastern portion two weeks later. In 1887, the defence of Thursday Island and King George's Sound was discussed at a London conference; by 1893, both were fortified and garrisoned.

At the same time, railway communications within Australia had developed rapidly. In spite of the different gauges of the various colonies, it was now possible to transfer troops rapidly from one colony to another, with the exception of Western Australia, the Northern Territory[18] and of course, Tasmania. In 1889, MAJGEN Brian Edwards, who had recently completed a survey of colonial military forces, noted that it would be possible to mobilise a force on a standard brigade basis and move the troops in the direction of the threat. In his view, this would 'prevent the unseemly scares which take place (in Australia), whenever the relations of the mother country with a foreign power are somewhat strained'. He added his belief that purely volunteer units were unsatisfactory and that paid or partly-paid forces would better suit Australia's needs. While neither Britain nor Australia fully endorsed MAJGEN Edwards' views, the concept of mobile defence, rather than static defence based on coastal forts, gradually gained acceptance.

---

16 Lieutenant General Sir William Jervois, KCMG, CB; Governor of South Australia 1877-1882: born Isle of Wight England 1821 – died Surrey England 1897.

17 Major General Sir Peter Scratchley, KCMG; military engineer, Colonial administrator: born Paris France 1835 – died at sea 1885.

18 A rail link between Sydney and Perth existed from 1917 but travel required several changes of gauge; the standard gauge Sydney to Perth rail-link was completed in 1970, whilst the Adelaide to Darwin railway did not open until 2003.

AWM No. A04402 Courtesy of the
Australian War Memorial. Troops of
the New South Wales Contingent –
Sudan 1885

The Sudan Campaign – 1885[19]

In February 1885, as implementation of the Jervois-Scratchley recommendations in New South Wales were almost complete, news was received of the death of General (GEN) Charles Gordon[20] at Khartoum during the Dervish revolt in the eastern Sudan. The New South Wales Government immediately offered two batteries of its regular artillery, a battalion of infantry and a small ambulance detachment, to serve with the British forces. Within three weeks, the force of 768 was enlisted, equipped, and dispatched in two ships, although only one artillery battery embarked. A total of 809[21] Australian personnel are recorded as having served in the Sudan during the conflict.

Within a month of embarkation, the contingent saw action at Tamai. By May 1885, the campaign had been reduced to a series of skirmishes and the troops returned to Sydney in mid-June. Three soldiers were wounded during the campaign, although not seriously, and a total of nine members[22] of the contingent died of disease.

GEN Lord Wolseley[23], commander of the Nile Expedition, commented that 'the result was so satisfactory that I trust the noble and patriotic example set by New South Wales may, should the occasion arise, be followed by other Colonies'. The opportunity arose a mere 14 years later. The Sudan contingent was the first army contingent to be raised and dispatched by an Australian colony. In 1907, the Battle Honour 'Suakin 1885' was awarded to the New South Wales infantry regiments of the Australian Army descended from those colonial forebears who had contributed volunteers to the infantry battalion that served in the Sudan. This became Australia's first 'Battle Honour', despite the fact that the Australian Army had not been created at the time it was won.

---

19 Stanley, P. (editor) *But Little Glory.* Military Historical Society of Australia, Canberra: 1984

20 Major General Charles George Gordon, CB: born Woolwich London 1833 – died Khartoum Sudan 1885.

21 The Australian War Memorial. http://www.awm.gov.au/research/people/nominal_rolls/pre _first _ world _war/?Name=&ServiceNumber=&Unit=&Co nflict=Sudan&page=1: 1 Aug 13

22 Australian War Memorial. https://www.awm.gov.au/encyclopedia/war_casualties/

23 Field Marshall Garnet Joseph Wolseley 1st Viscount Wolseley, KP, GCB, OM, GCMG, VD, PC; soldier, Commander in Chief of the Forces 1895-1900: born Ireland 4 Jun 1833 – died France 25 Mar 1913.

NO 219 TROOPER VICTOR STANLEY JONES.

THE FIRST AUSTRALIAN SOLDIER TO BE KILLED IN WAR.

BORN IN CLERMONT ON 24TH DECEMBER, 1872,
SON OF EDWARD AND ANNA JONES.

IN SEPTEMBER 1899 HE VOLUNTEERED TO GO TO THE BOER WAR.

HE WAS KILLED IN ACTION AT SUNNYSIDE, SOUTH AFRICA,
ON 1ST JANUARY, 1900, AGED 27 YEARS.

TROOPER VICTOR STANLEY JONES, B COMPANY, 1ST QUEENSLAND
MOUNTED INFANTRY, COLONY OF QUEENSLAND, WAS THE FIRST
AUSTRALIAN SOLDIER TO LOSE HIS LIFE IN ACTION ON A
FOREIGN BATTLEFIELD.

Aid to the Civil Power

During the late 1880s and early 1890s, the worldwide depression saw Australia's economy deteriorate, reducing the funding available for the colonial armies and increasing the possibility of internal unrest. In 1890, during the Great Maritime Strike, the Victoria Police anticipated rioting on a scale beyond their control. 600 troops, including 200 from the Victorian Mounted Rifles, were called out, and their presence at Victoria Barracks provided an effective deterrent to would-be rioters.

The following year, the Queensland shearers withheld their labour when the pastoralists, refusing to recognise the Shearers Union, began importing non-union labour from other colonies. The ensuing confrontation was deemed sufficiently serious to call out 1,442 members of the Queensland Defence Force and send them to centres where the unionists were concentrated. By May 1891, the strike was virtually over, without the employers having conceded freedom of contract to the strikers. The troops received the thanks of the Queensland Parliament, but earned the long-held suspicion of several sections of the Australian community. It is significant that the Defence Act 1903 prevented the raising of regular infantry and fostered a citizen army for the defence of Australia which could not be used in industrial disputes or serve beyond the nation's borders.

The 2nd Boer War – 1899-1902

The 2nd Boer War erupted in October 1899, when forces from the Boer Republics of Transvaal and the Orange Free State attacked British troops in Natal and the Bechuanaland extension of the Cape Colony. The 2nd Boer War reflected the Boer Republics' resistance to British interference and followed almost directly from the 1st Boer War of 1881. The first Australian Colonial contingent (NSW Lancers) arrived in Cape Town from England on 2nd November 1899 where they had attended Queen Victoria's Diamond Jubilee celebrations. The 2nd Boer War involved three distinct phases: from November 1899 to January 1900 involving a series of defeats inflicted on British forces by Boer mounted infantry operating as commandos; the second phase featured the resurgence of bolstered British forces resulting in the annexation of the Boer Republics by August 1900; and the final phase was characterised by the Boer's use of mounted guerrilla warfare tactics and continued until May 1902 when the war finally ended.

In October 1899, following an 'encouraging' telegram from the Imperial Government, all Australian colonies began to organise and raise volunteers for military service in South Africa. Elements of the Victorian, Tasmanian, South Australian and Western Australian contingents were embarked in one ship for Cape Town. These detachments, later converted from infantry to mounted infantry, were initially combined as 'The Australian Regiment' on deployment in South Africa. The colonists were at last to see active service abroad as a united force.

The British defeats in the first phase of the war prompted increased recruiting in Australia. The first two Australian contingents comprised mainly part-time volunteers and militia, while the later contingents were primarily recruited from experienced horsemen with shooting skills but no previous military training. Later contingents formed prior

Left: Note - Australian-born soldiers had served and died in other conflicts prior to Trooper Jones' death (the Maori Wars) but it is believed he may have been the first serving member to die as a result of enemy action whilst serving with an Australian Colonial contingent

Above: AWM Neg No A04337 Courtesy of the Australian War Memorial. Troops of the 2nd New South Wales Mounted Rifles crossing the Orange River while on service in South Africa

to Federation were identified as 'Bushmen's Contingents', while those raised after Federation were organised into eight battalions of 'Australian Commonwealth Horse'.

Colonial, and later Australian, troops saw much fighting, including actions at Graspan, Modder River, Sunnyside, Slingersfontein, Pink Hill, the Relief of Kimberley, Paardeburg, the siege of Eland's River, Rhenosterkop and Haartebeestefontein. A total of 16,378 men (this figure includes volunteers who embarked twice), left Australia in 38 contingents to serve in South Africa.[24] Casualties amounted to 282 killed in action or died of wounds, 286 died of disease and 38 died of accidents and other causes.[25] Five Victoria Crosses (VC) were awarded to members of the Australian colonial and national contingents. A sixth VC was awarded to Sergeant (SGT) James Rogers, an Australian serving with the South African Constabulary. After his return to Australia SGT Rogers joined the Australian Commonwealth Horse, and went on to serve in South Africa, later joining the AIF[26] and went to Gallipoli. The Battle Honour 'South Africa' was awarded in 1908 to light horse and infantry units descended from the contingents that served in the 2nd Boer War.

Unique awards occurred during the Boer War including the promotion of soldiers to the ranks of 'King's Corporal' and 'Kitchener Sergeant' (see Chapter 2) and the awarding of 'The Queen Victoria Scarf' (see Chapter 14).

Federation

Prior to Federation, the various military commandants of the Australian colonies had successfully lobbied their Governments and the Colonial Office to allow their respective artillery formations to combine into a single unit that was formed on 24th August 1899.

On 9th July 1900, Royal Assent was granted to the *Commonwealth of Australia Constitution Act*. An Order in Council on 17th September approved a proclamation which declared that the union of New South Wales, Victoria, South Australia, Queensland, Tasmania and Western Australia should take effect from 1st January 1901.

A total of 28,923 colonial soldiers, comprising 1,457 permanent, 18,603 militia and 8,863 unpaid volunteers, were transferred to the new Commonwealth Military Forces on 1st March 1901. However, until the *Defence Act* of 22nd October 1903, these troops continued to be administered under the relevant State acts.

AWM Neg No P03875.002 Courtesy of the Australian War Memorial. Major General ETH Hutton

MAJGEN Sir Edward Hutton[27], commander of New South Wales Military Forces from 1893 to 1896, assumed command of the Commonwealth Forces on 26th December 1901. His recommendations for the structure of the new force were accepted by the Federal Government and, shortly before he relinquished his command in 1904, a Council of Defence, a Military Board of Administration, and an Inspector-General were established by the *Defence Act 1903*, which came into force on 1st March 1904. The Act was further amended in 1908 to increase membership of the Military Board and to reallocate duties among its members.

While compulsory military training had been debated since 1902, it was not until December 1909 that the necessary amendments were made to the *Defence Act 1903* to allow its introduction. Before these amendments could be implemented, however, Field Marshal (FM) Lord Kitchener[28] was invited to report on the state of Australian defences. His recommendations were embodied in further amendments to the Act in December 1910, one of which established the Royal Military College - Duntroon (RMC-D) in June 1911. Kitchener's recommendations also saw the introduction of a system of universal military training for junior and senior cadets aged from 12 to 18 and thereafter, in the Citizen Forces (CF), to age 26. In 1911, some 155,000 youths were registered, of whom 90,000 were in training, with 20,000 inducted each year until the outbreak of World War One (WWI).

24 Dennis P, Grey J, Morris E, Prior R. *The Oxford Companion to Australian Military History (Second Edition). Australia*, Oxford University Press: 2008, p. 94

25 Australian War Memorial. https://www.awm.gov.au/atwar/boer/: 8 Jan 15

26 Note: The AIF is frequently and incorrectly referred to as the 1st AIF or First AIF – technically, officially and historically there is not and has never been an organisation called the 1st AIF or First AIF. The AIF was formed in 1914 and the 2nd AIF was formed in 1939.

27 Lieutenant General Edward Thomas Henry Hutton, KCB, KCMG, psc; British Regular Army GOC 21 Div (Brit): born Torquay England 6 Dec 1848 – died England 4 Aug 1923.

28 Field Marshal Horatio Herbert Kitchener, 1st Earl Kitchener, KG, KP, GCB, OM, GCSI, GCMG, GCIE, ADC, PC: born Ireland 24 June 1850 – died at sea 5 June 1916.

AWM Neg No ART08007 Courtesy of the Australian War Memorial. The incident for which Lieutenant FH McNamara, AFC, was awarded the VC

World War I – 1914-1918

The origins of the war that erupted in Europe on 4th August 1914 were numerous and complex. For Australia, the broader international issues were perhaps less important than the simple fact that the British Empire was at war. As the Australian Government had been warned of the likely commencement of hostilities, Australia's defences were already being prepared when war was declared. Imperial defence plans assumed that the Royal Australian Navy (RAN) would operate as an integral part of the Royal Navy (RN) wherever required; however, such an assumption could not be applied to the Australian Army. The *Defence Act 1903* restricted the Australian Army to service within Australian territory for home defence purposes. To allow Australian participation in a European land war, a separate all-volunteer force had to be recruited specifically for overseas service.

Following the declaration of war in August 1914, the Fisher Government's pledge of full support for Britain led to the raising of what became known as the Australian Imperial Force (AIF). The name 'Australian Imperial Force' was the suggestion of MAJGEN Sir William Throsby Bridges[29], who also coined the term 'AIF'. Recruiting began on 10th August 1914, and by November 1914 almost 20,000 members of an infantry division and a light horse brigade, under the respective commands of MAJGEN Bridges and COL Harry Chauvel[30], were on their way to Egypt, accompanied by a contingent of troops from New Zealand.

It is believed that the first rounds fired by any army of the British Empire in WWI were from the six-inch Mark VII guns at Fort Nepean situated at the entrance to Port Phillip Bay, Victoria. The Fort fired one round to prevent the German freighter 'PHALZ' escaping from Port Phillip a few hours after the declaration of war.

Before the AIF could embark for foreign shores, another all-volunteer force was already in action. The strategic importance of German wireless stations in New Guinea and the surrounding islands led British authorities to ask the Australian Government to destroy them as a matter of urgency. To perform this task, the Australian Government raised a force of 1,500 men, the 'Australian Naval and Military Expeditionary Force' (AN&MEF) commanded by COL William Holmes.[31] By October 1914, this mixed force of naval reservists and soldiers had forced the surrender of the garrison and taken possession of German New Guinea and the neighbouring islands of the Bismarck Archipelago.

Australian Flying Corps

The Australian Flying Corps (AFC) was established in 1912. It was not until 1914 that it began flight training at the newly-established military aviation base, the Central Flying School, at Point Cook, with two flying instructors and five training aircraft. From this modest beginning, Australia became the only British dominion to set up a Flying Corps for service during WWI.

During WWI approximately 4,640 personnel served in the AFC and 175 lost their lives. During 1920, the AFC was replaced by the Australian Air Corps, which in turn became the Australian Air Force on 31st March 1921. The 'Royal' title was officially appended on 31st August 1921 (Royal Assent had been granted in June 1921).

Subsequently, the Australian Army Aviation Corps (AAAvn) was formed on 1st July 1968 when the need for closer air support within Army was acknowledged.

---

29 Major General Sir William Throsby Bridges, KCB, CMG; Commanded 1st Aust. Div and AIF – 1914-1915: born Greenock, Scotland, 18 February 1861 – died of wounds 18 May 1915.

30 General Sir Henry George 'Harry' Chauvel, GCMG, KCB; Comd Desert Mtd Corps 1917-1919, Inspector General AMF 1919-1920, CGS 1922-1930, Inspector-in-Chief Volunteer Defence Corps 1940: born Tabulam Clarence River NSW 16 April 1865 – died Melbourne 4 Mar 1945.

31 Major General William Holmes, CMG, DSO, VD; Commander 1st NSW Infantry Regiment, AN&MEF, 5th Brigade AIF, GOC 4th Australian Division: born Sydney 1862 – died of wounds 2 July 1917.

World War I – Gallipoli

While still training in the Egyptian desert late in 1914, the 1st Australian Division and the New Zealand and Australian Division, which later included the 1st Light Horse Brigade, were formed into the Australian and New Zealand Army Corps (ANZAC[32]), under the command of Lieutenant General (LTGEN) William Birdwood.[33] The ANZAC forces had been based in Egypt because of a lack of training and accommodation facilities in England. Later, these forces helped protect the Suez Canal following Turkey's entry into the war in October 1914.

Late in 1914, when fighting on the Western Front in France had deteriorated into stalemate, the British War Council suggested that Germany could best be defeated by attacks on her weaker allies, Austria-Hungary and Turkey. Initially, the attack on Turkey was planned as a naval operation. However, following several abortive attempts to force the Dardanelles in February and March, the British Cabinet agreed that land forces could be used. A combined international force (the Mediterranean Expeditionary Force) was assembled under the command of British General Sir Ian Hamilton[34], and a three-pronged landing was planned to clear the Turkish defenders from the straits. Once the straits were

clear, the Allied fleet would steam through to Constantinople where, it was believed, the threat of the fleet's guns would cause mass panic and force Turkey to surrender. At dawn on 25th April 1915, the Anzacs landed north of Gaba Tepe (the landing area later named Anzac Cove) while the British forces landed at Cape Helles on the Gallipoli Peninsula. The aim of these two landings was to capture the Turkish forts commanding the narrow straits. French forces attacked the Turkish positions on the Asia Minor side of the Dardanelles as a diversion and later landed and took over part of the Helles front line alongside the British. Later reinforcements included the dismounted Australian Light Horse (ALH) and New Zealand Mounted Brigades at Anzac Cove. In August a new British Corps landed at Suvla Bay, to the north of Anzac Cove, in support of an attempt by the Allies to break out of the ANZAC beachhead.

The campaign was a heroic but costly failure and by December plans were drawn up to evacuate the entire force from Gallipoli. On 19th and 20th December, the evacuation of Anzac and Suvla was completed with the last British troops leaving Cape Helles by 8th January 1916. The well-executed operation evacuated 142,000 men with only a handful of casualties. Australian casualties from the Gallipoli campaign amounted to 26,111; of these, 8,141 were killed in action, died of wounds or succumbed to disease. Nine VCs were awarded to soldiers in Australian units.[35]

While the campaign is considered a military failure, Gallipoli became a household word in Australia and with it the Anzac tradition was created. Gallipoli became the common tie forged in adversity that bound the colonies and people of Australia into a nation, a nation that still commemorates the 25th of April each year as Anzac Day, when the sacrifices of all Australian and New Zealand Servicemen and women in all conflicts are remembered.

32 Note: 'ANZAC' with or without full stops is a military acronym, standing for the 'Australian and New Zealand Army Corps'. 'Anzac' on the other hand, is an accepted Australian English word, which came into regular use as early as May 1915. The fact that 'Anzac' is a proper word is confirmed by the '*Protection of the Word Anzac Regulation*', made under the *War Precautions Act Repeal Act 1920*; this Act and Regulation are still in force.

33 Field Marshal Lord William Riddle Birdwood, GCB, GCSI, GCMG, GCVO, CIE, DSO; Commander A. & N.Z. Corps (later Australian Corps) 1914-1918, Dardanelles Army 1915-1916 (3 months), 5th Army 1918-1919, and GOC AIF 1915-1920, Commander-in-Chief of the Army in India 1925-1930: born Poona India 13 September 1865 – died Hampton Court Palace 17 May 1951.

34 General Sir Ian Standish Monteith Hamilton, GCB, GCMG, DSO, TD; Lieutenant 1871, Captain 1882, Major 1884, Lieutenant Colonel 1886, Colonel 1891, Major General 1902: born Corfu 16 January 1853 – died London 12 October 1947.

35 Dennis P, Grey J, Morris E, Prior R. *The Oxford Companion to Australian Military History*. Australia, Oxford University Press: 1995, p. 261

Left: AWM Neg No P00035.001 Courtesy of the Australian War Memorial. Landing at Anzac Cove 25th April 1915

Above: AWM No ART 02436 Courtesy of the Australian War Memorial. Roll Call - taken after the charge on Sunday night, 9th May 1915

Battalion Numbering[36,37]

To the uninitiated, the unit numbers used by the current Army Reserve battalions can be very confusing; for instance why is there a 9th Battalion in Queensland and a 10th Battalion in South Australia or why was there a 40th Battalion in Tasmania and a 41st Battalion in New South Wales. The reason for the present numbering of the Army Reserve battalions can be traced to the original formation of the AIF.

Unlike the regular Army battalions of today, Reserve battalions have always been a locally-recruited force with strong ties to the local area and community. It is still not unusual for a soldier of a Reserve battalion to explain the reason they joined the battalion is because both their father and/or grandfather were in the unit and it is a tradition within their family to serve with that unit.

How battalions of the AIF were enlisted from each State initially, and as the Force developed, is described below.

36 **Authors' Disclaimer:** While every effort has been made to ensure accuracy of information on Battalion, Brigade and Division Numbering, no effort has been attempted on other units or organisations (such as the Light Horse) as this is a significant task in itself and beyond the scope of this book. Defence, and in particular the Army, has always been and will continue to be an evolving organisation; the information provided on 'Organisational' numbering, structure and naming conventions throughout this book should be used as a guide only. Further research should be conducted on individual units and organisations to confirm accuracy against discrete requirements and timelines.

37 This information is reproduced with permission of Mr Graham McKenzie-Smith: 2009

Organisation of the AIF[38]

In August 1914, the AIF consisted of the 1st Division, comprising:

1st Inf Bde formed in NSW	1st Bn, 2nd Bn, 3rd Bn, 4th Bn
2nd Inf Bde formed in Vic	5th Bn, 6th Bn, 7th Bn, 8th Bn
3rd Inf Bde	9th Bn ex Qld, 10th Bn ex SA, 11th Bn ex WA, 12th Bn ex Tas/WA/SA (composite)

A fourth brigade was raised in September 1914, as a separate contingent:

4th Inf Bde	13th Bn ex NSW, 14th Bn ex Vic
	15th Bn ex Qld/Tas, 16th Bn ex WA/SA

Note: The 4th Inf Bde was allocated to the newly-raised New Zealand and Australia Division and remained part of that organisation until the end of the Gallipoli Campaign.

The 2nd Division was formed in Egypt in July 1915. The division embarked for Gallipoli in August 1915. After being withdrawn from Gallipoli the division returned to Egypt for reorganisation. The division sailed for France in March 1916, comprising:

5th Inf Bde formed in NSW	17th Bn, 18th Bn, 19th Bn, 20th Bn
6th Inf Bde formed in Vic	21st Bn, 22nd Bn, 23rd Bn, 24th Bn
7th Inf Bde	25th Bn ex Qld, 26th Bn ex Qld/Tas
	27th Bn, ex SA, 28th Bn ex WA

Raised in October 1915 in Australia, as a separate contingent:[39]

8th Inf Bde	29th Bn ex Vic, 30th Bn ex NSW
	31st Bn ex Qld/Tas, 32nd Bn ex WA/SA

The 3rd Division was formed in Australia in February 1916, the personnel for its three infantry brigades being drawn from all six States:

9th Inf Bde formed in NSW	33rd Bn, 34th Bn, 35th Bn, 36th Bn
10th Inf Bde formed in Vic	37th Bn, 38th Bn, 39th Bn, 40th Bn ex Tas
11th Inf Bde	41st Bn ex Qld/NSW, 42nd Bn ex Qld, 43rd Bn ex SA, 44th Bn ex WA

---

38 Bean CEW. *Official History of Australia in the War of 1914-1918 Volume I.* Sydney, Angus & Robertson: 1941, Chap 3
39 Bean CEW. *Official History of Australia in the War of 1914-1918 Volume III. The Australian Imperial Force in France 1916.* Sydney, Angus & Robertson: 1941, Chap 1 p. 8

Doubling of the AIF

After the withdrawal from Gallipoli it was decided to reorganise the AIF and, as there were many unallocated reinforcements in Egypt, it was decided to raise a 4th and 5th Infantry Division, by splitting the battalions of 1st Infantry Division and 4th Infantry Brigade to form the 12th, 13th, 14th and 15th Brigades.[40]

The 4th Infantry Division comprised:

4th Inf Bde as above with	16th Bn becoming a fully-WA unit
12th Inf Bde	45th Bn formed from 13th Bn ex NSW
	46th Bn formed from 14th Bn ex Vic
	47th Bn formed from 15th Bn ex Qld/Tas
	48th Bn formed from 16th Bn ex SA
13th Inf Bde	49th Bn formed from 9th Bn ex Qld
	50th Bn formed from 10th Bn ex SA
	51st Bn formed from 12th Bn ex Tas/Qld
	52nd Bn formed from 11th Bn ex WA

The 5th Infantry Division comprised:

	8th Inf Bde as above
14th Inf Bde all NSW	53rd Bn formed from 1st Bn
	54th Bn formed from 2nd Bn
	55th Bn formed from 3rd Bn
	56th Bn formed from 4th Bn
The 15th Inf Bde (Victorian)	57th Bn formed from 5th Bn
	58th Bn formed from 6th Bn
	59th Bn formed from 7th Bn
	60th Bn formed from 8th Bn

These five divisions fought throughout WWI; although a 6th Division was raised as a headquarters, it never progressed beyond an embryonic stage due to the shortage of reinforcements caused by troop losses on the front. Consequently, the Division was broken-up to provide front-line reinforcements.

---

40 Bean CEW. *Official History of Australia in the War of 1914-1918 Volume III. The Australian Imperial Force in France 1916.* Sydney, Angus & Robertson: 1941, Chap 2

World War I – Western Front

By early 1916, recruiting in Australia had raised sufficient troops to replace the Anzac losses. The AIF in Egypt was expanded to four divisions before being transferred to the Western Front, with a fifth division raised in Australia. On arrival in France, the divisions were organised, initially, into I ANZAC Corps (1st and 2nd Australian Divisions, and the New Zealand Division) and II ANZAC Corps (4th and 5th Australian Divisions). The 3rd Division did not arrive in France until November 1916. The composition of the two Corps changed significantly in response to operational needs and for most of the war, I ANZAC Corps included the 1st, 2nd, 4th and 5th Divisions, while II ANZAC Corps included the Australian 3rd Division, the New Zealand Division and one or two British divisions.

In March 1916 the AIF moved to France and by July and August the Australians were heavily involved on the Western Front. The 5th Division was the first to encounter the Germans on 19th July 1916 in a small but bloody engagement at Fromelles in northern France. Shortly after, the 1st, 2nd and 4th Divisions became embroiled in the Somme offensive, at Pozieres and Mouquet Farm. In six weeks of operations, the Australian divisions suffered approximately 28,000 casualties.

In November 1916 the 3rd Australian Division arrived in France from England where it had been training since arrival from Australia in July. The 3rd Division was sent to the 'nursery' sector around Armentières as part of II ANZAC Corps. The other four Australian divisions, now all in I ANZAC Corps, had returned to the trenches in the final phase of the Somme campaign, which ended in November, and spent the terrible winter of 1916-1917 consolidating the forward positions near Bapaume.

In March 1917, the Australians were again heavily engaged in battle at Bapaume, in May and June at Bullecourt, and at Messines from September to November in the great battles of the Ypres offensive (Menin Road, Polygon Wood, Broodseinde, Poelcapelle and Passchendaele). The casualties

sustained made it difficult to maintain the strength of the Australian divisions and a partially-formed 6th Australian Division was disbanded in order to provide reinforcements. In November 1917, the five divisions were formed into the Australian Corps, although it would not be until May 1918 that this amalgamation was complete and LTGEN Sir John Monash[41], (previously GOC 3rd Australian Division) was appointed to command it.

In March and April 1918, the Australian Corps played a prominent part in the defence of Amiens, Hazebrouck and Villers-Bretonneux during a massive German multi-pronged attack in France and Belgium, known to history as the *Kaiserschlacht* or the Spring Offensive. The German offensive was halted and the Allies mounted their own offensive from July. Following a successful Allied attack just east of Amiens in August, with the Australian and the Canadian Corps operating side by side, the Australians were engaged in a number of battles as the Allies drove the Germans back towards eventual defeat. During this period known as 'The Hundred Days', the AIF was engaged at Mont St Quentin, St Quentin Canal and Montbrehain. The Australian Corps, which had been fighting almost continuously since March, was then placed in reserve, rebuilding for the next offensive when the Armistice was signed on 11th November 1918.

While the AIF strength in France varied in response to battle casualties and shortfalls in recruiting, it never fell below 117,000 men. Its battle casualties for the three years of trench warfare between 1916 and 1918 amounted to 182,250 men of whom 46,960 died, 131,406 were wounded, 16,496 gassed and 4,044 taken prisoner.[42] In terms of total deaths per 1,000 men mobilised, the AIF figure was 145, one of the highest of all the British Empire armies.

---

41 General Sir John Monash, GCMG, KCB, VD; Commanded 3rd Aust. Div, 1916-1918, Aust. Corps 1918. Director-General Repatriation and Demobilisation Department, London *1918-1919*, Chairman of Commissioners and General Manager State Electricity Commission of Victoria 1920-1931: born: Flagstaff Hill, Melbourne 27 June 1865 – died Melbourne 8 October 1931.

42 Beaumont J. *Australian Defence: Sources and Statistics*. Melbourne, Oxford University Press: 2001, p. 275

AWM ART 02927 Courtesy of the Australian War Memorial. Polygon Wood

World War I – Sinai, Palestine and Syria

In March 1916, the ANZAC Mounted Division was formed in Egypt from the 1st, 2nd and 3rd Light Horse Brigades and the New Zealand Mounted Rifles Brigade, with MAJGEN Harry Chauvel as the GOC. In August, the division helped defeat the Turkish advance to Romani and by March 1917 had forced the enemy back to the Gaza-Beersheba line. Participation in the initial battles for Gaza then followed. In August 1917, the Desert Mounted Corps (formerly the Desert Column) was formed, consisting of the ANZAC Mounted Division (less the 3rd Light Horse), the Australian Mounted Division (3rd and 4th Light Horse and 5th Yeomanry Brigades) and the Yeomanry Division. The strategic town of Beersheba was captured on 31st October 1917 by the 4th Light Horse Brigade in what is popularly, but erroneously, believed to be one of the last great cavalry charges in history, the Light Horsemen being armed only with rifles and bayonets.

The Desert Mounted Corps also played a prominent role in the capture of Jerusalem in December 1917. In March 1918 many of the British troops, including the Yeomanry Division, were withdrawn and redeployed to France to shore up Allied resistance to the German Spring offensive. Despite the loss of many experienced troops, the Corps defeated a determined attack by the German Asia Corps at Abu Tellul in April 1918. In September, the Corps played a significant role in the advance to Haifa and Semakh, entering Damascus on 1st October. Turkey signed an armistice at the end of that month, by which time Corps units had reached Aleppo.

The total battle casualties for the AIF in this campaign were 4,062 all ranks, with 1,282 men dying from wounds and disease.[43]

---

43 Beaumont J. *Australian Defence: Sources and Statistics.* Melbourne, Oxford University Press: 2001, p. 277

AWM No ART 09230 Courtesy of the Australian War Memorial. Camel Corps at Magdhaba

Between the Wars

The years between the First and Second World Wars were difficult for the Australian Army. The public's reaction to the immense cost of the Great War varied from exhaustion to apathy, compounded by economic problems (the Great Depression 1929-1939). Widely referred to as 'the war to end all wars', worldwide popular perception was that little was achieved by military means, and there was a strong international call for disarmament. The League of Nations, which existed until 1947 as the predecessor to the United Nations, was established to resolve international differences with the aim of preventing international differences escalating into military conflict.

The AIF disbanded on 1st February 1921. In the same year, the Citizen Military Forces (CMF) was reorganised along the same lines as the old AIF, adopting AIF unit numbers, colour patches and, in due course, inheriting AIF battle honours.[44] A planned restructure was envisaged comprising two cavalry and four infantry divisions, troops for local defence equating to a fifth division, with supporting Corps and Army troops. The militia was reorganised to mirror the unit numbering system and organisation of the AIF; units with titles such as 2nd Battalion 13th Infantry Regiment were retitled and became the 2nd Battalion, Australian Military Forces (AMF). Although seemingly a superficial change, this formalised the unit's entitlement to the Battle Honours[45] applicable to the AIF unit. The units were allocated as follows:

HQ 1st and 2nd Infantry Division formed in NSW with 1st Infantry Brigade (Inf Bde), 5th Inf Bde, 8th Inf Bde, 9th Inf Bde and 14th Inf Bde

HQ 3rd and 4th Infantry Divisions formed in Victoria with 2nd Inf Bde, 4th Inf Bde, 6th Inf Bde, 10th Inf Bde and the 15th Inf Bde

3rd Inf Bde formed in SA

7th Inf Bde in Brisbane

11th Inf Bde in North Qld

12th Inf Bde in Tasmania

13th Inf Bde in WA

Battalion numbers were allocated by State generally, but not always in line with those of the AIF:

New South Wales:	1st Bn, 2nd Bn, 3rd Bn, 4th Bn, 13th Bn, 17th Bn, 18th Bn, 19th Bn, 20th Bn, 30th Bn, 33rd Bn, 34th Bn, 35th Bn, 36th Bn, 41st Bn, 45th Bn, 53rd Bn, 54th Bn, 55th Bn and 56th Bn
Victoria:	5th Bn, 6th Bn, 7th Bn, 8th Bn, 14th Bn, 21st Bn, 22nd Bn, 23rd Bn, 24th, Bn, 29th Bn, 32nd Bn, 37th Bn, 38th Bn, 39th Bn, 46th Bn, 49th Bn, 52nd Bn, 57th Bn, 58th Bn, 59th Bn and 60th Bn
Queensland:	9th Bn, 15th Bn, 25th Bn, 26th Bn, 31st Bn, 42nd Bn and 47th Bn
South Australia:	10th Bn, 27th Bn, 43rd Bn and 48th Bn
Western Australia:	11th Bn, 16th Bn, 28th Bn and 44th Bn
Tasmania:	12th Bn, 40th Bn, 50th Bn and 51st Bn.

In 1922, a reduction in the peacetime establishment to 37,000 meant the restructuring goal was unachievable due to a lack of political interest. A severe cutback in funds saw compulsory training reduced to cover only the populous areas, and annual training camps were cancelled.

Strategic concerns over Japanese imperialist intentions were muted during the war years but re-surfaced in the 1920s, despite the limitations placed on Japan by the 1921-1922 Washington Naval Conference. These concerns provided the impetus for Australia's support for the establishment of a British naval base in Singapore. Australia's own coastal defences remained little touched since Kitchener's recommendations of 1910 and various later attempts to improve them failed, with little improvement being achieved until the period 1934-1937.

---

44   Military Order 172/1921
45   Australian Army Order (AAO) 91-9/3/1927. *Battle Honours*: 1927

Each battalion had a regimental territorial title associated with their recruiting area or some other relevant historical/colonial connection.[46] The allocation of units in each State by 1927[47] was:

New South Wales

1st Bn City of Sydney's Own Regt	2nd Bn City of Newcastle Regt
3rd Bn Werriwa Regt	4th Bn Australian Rifles
13th Bn Macquarie Regt	17th Bn North Sydney Regt
18th Bn Kuring-Gai Regt	19th Bn South Sydney Regt
20th Bn Parramatta and Blue Mountains Regt	30th Bn NSW Scottish Regt
33rd Bn New England Regt	34th Bn Illawarra Regt
35th Bn Newcastle's Own Regt	36th Bn St George's English Rifle Regt
41st Bn Byron Scottish Regt	45th Bn St George Regt
53rd Bn Western Sydney Regt	54th Bn Lachlan–Macquarie Regt
55th Bn NSW Rifle Regt	56th Bn Riverina Regt

Victoria

5th Bn Victorian Scottish Regt	6th Bn Royal Melbourne Regt
7th Bn NW Murray Borderers	8th Bn City of Ballarat Regt
14th Bn Prahran Regt	21st Bn Victorian Rangers
22nd Bn Richmond Regt	23rd Bn City of Geelong Regt
24th Bn Kooyong Regt	29th Bn East Melbourne Regt
32nd Bn Footscray Regt	37th Bn Henty Regt
38th Bn Northern Victorian Regt	39th Bn Hawthorn–Kew Regt
46th Bn Brighton Rifles	52nd Bn Gippsland Regt
57th Bn Merri Regt	58th Bn Essendon, Coburg, Brunswick Regt
59th Bn Hume Regt	60th Bn Heidelberg Regt

Queensland

9th Bn Moreton Regt	15th Bn Oxley Regt
25th Bn Darling Downs Regt	26th Bn Logan and Albert Regt
31st Bn Kennedy Regt	42nd Bn Capricornia Regt
47th Bn Wide Bay Regt	49th Bn Stanley Regt

South Australia

10th Bn Adelaide Rifles	27th Bn SA Scottish Regt
43rd Bn Hindmarsh Regt	48th Bn Torrens Regt

Western Australia

11th Bn City of Perth Regt	16th Bn Cameron Highlanders of WA
28th Bn Swan Regt	44th Bn WA Rifles

Tasmania

12th Bn Launceston Regt	40th Bn Derwent Regt
50th Bn Tasmanian Rangers	51st Bn Field of Mars Regt

Note: By 1937[48] 51st Bn had been transferred to Queensland and given the territorial title 'Far North Queensland Regiment'

---

46   Festberg AN. *Australian Army Guidons and Colours*. Melbourne, Allara Publishing: 1972
47   Australian Army Order (AAO) 132/1927, *Territorial Titles and Mottoes – Regiments and Battalions*, AMF: 1927
48   Australian Army Order (AAO) 175/1937. *Territorial Titles and Mottoes – Australian Military Forces* 1937

Some militia battalions were linked during the 1930s but most were reformed early in World War Two (WWII) except the 23rd/21st Bn and 57th/60th Bn in Victoria, the 12th/50th Bn in Tasmania and the 61st Bn (Cameron Highlanders) in Queensland.

In the decade prior to 1929, opposition to the compulsory training scheme began to grow and the Australian Labor Party (ALP), elected on a platform that included the abolition of universal training, terminated the scheme in November 1929. Henceforth, Australia was to have an all-volunteer, primarily part-time, 35,000-strong Army. The part-time element was renamed the 'Militia'. Within 12 months of the election, the Army's strength had fallen to 27,000. In 1931, despite Japan's invasion of Manchuria and an escalation in international tension, unit strengths were reduced even further. The Government favoured a strategy based on naval and air power, in part because the British Government shouldered most of the cost.

In 1932, the newly-elected United Australia Party Government, led by Prime Minister Joseph Lyons[49], faced severe budgetary concerns with the deepening of the Great Depression. All available funding was allocated to critical programs for basic services. Few resources remained and very few defence improvements were initiated. Indeed, many defence activities were cut back severely or halted altogether. The RMC-D was moved to Victoria Barracks in Sydney for four years. There was no new intake and the entire cadet population remained at an unsustainable 31. It was not until 1937 that the Government finally approved the return to Duntroon and an increase in cadet numbers. Given the ongoing war commitment in Europe and Asia, in 1943, the Government attempted to redress the consequences of these years of neglect by shortening the duration of the officer training to one year.

---

49 Joseph Aloysius Lyons, CH; teacher, politician, Premier Tasmania 1923-1928, Prime Minister 1932-1939: born Stanley Tasmania 15 September 1879 – died Sydney 7 April 1939.

In 1935, an increase in Militia strength was authorised, but sufficient funding to allow the commencement of the difficult process of building an army to meet the looming challenge was not made available until 1937.

While the strategic situation in Europe continued to deteriorate, the improving economic situation in Australia allowed the commencement of a three-year program of expenditure on defence commencing in 1937. Given this increased expenditure, a recruiting campaign that began in 1938 had, by mid-1939, increased the Militia strength from 35,000 to 80,000.

The Darwin Mobile Force (DMF) was the first regular (permanent) Australian Army infantry unit raised during peacetime. The DMF only had a short life, existing from November 1938 to 20th August 1940; the unit came into being as a result of the Imperial Defence Conference in 1937 and from a study by MAJGEN JD Lavarack[50] completed in September 1936. In July 1938 the Government announced its intentions to station 750 military personnel from the three Services in Darwin to improve defences in Northern Australia. Due to the restrictions of the *Defence Act 1903*, only artillery and a small number of other specialists could be enlisted for full-time duty in the permanent force. For this reason, even though a significant portion of the 12 officers and 245 other ranks that comprised the DMF Army element were infantry soldiers, the men were enlisted into the Artillery as 'gunners'.

In June 1938, a British officer, LTGEN Ernest Squires,[51] was appointed Inspector-General of the AMF. LTGEN Squires recommended the formation of a small regular army of 7,500 men, organised into two brigades, to bolster the Militia in the event of war and to assist in its peacetime training. Early in 1939, the Government agreed in principle to this proposal. However, following the death of Prime Minister Lyons in April, the new Prime Minister, Robert Gordon Menzies,[52] cancelled this project. Prime Minister Menzies hoped that war might be avoided and was opposed to the permanent nature of the proposed new force.

Left: AWM Neg No. P02307.026 Courtesy of the Australian War Memorial. Militia Unit about 1930

Right: AWM Neg No P01449.047 Courtesy of the Australian War Memorial. Darwin Mobile Force on parade at the 1939 Anzac Day ceremonies in Darwin

In March 1933, Japan withdrew from the League of Nations following the League's condemnation of Japan's attack on China. In October that year, Germany also withdrew. By 1937 Italy had annexed Abyssinia, and the Chancellor of Germany, Adolph Hitler, had repudiated the Treaty of Versailles. The Rome–Berlin Axis was established and civil war erupted in Spain. Japan used the volatile situation in Europe to defy world opinion and continued her undeclared war on China.

By 1935 the growing threat posed by imperialist Japan forced the Australian Government to begin directing some priority to Defence. However, given the poor state of the Army following its years of Government neglect, priorities were focused on fixed defences and vulnerable locations. Thus, while the defences of Darwin were strengthened, there was very limited upgrading of the Army overall. Most equipment was surplus WWI stock and few items of modern equipment reached the hands of the Militia until the outbreak of WWII.

50 Lieutenant General Sir John Dudley Lavarack, KCMG, KBE, CB, DSO; Commander First Army, I Corps, 7th Division, Royal Military College, Chief of the General Staff, Governor of Queensland 1946-1957: born Brisbane 19 December 1885 – died Buderim Queensland 4 December 1957.

51 Lieutenant General Ernest Ker Squires, CB, DSO, MC; Royal Engineers 1903, Captain 1914, Major 1918, Brigadier 1932, Major General 1935, Lieutenant General 1938, Inspector General AMF 1938, CGS AMF 1939: born Poona, India 18 December 1882 – died Melbourne 2 March 1940.

52 Robert Gordon Menzies, KT, AK, CH, FAA, FRS, QC; Attorney-General 1935-1939, Prime Minister and Minister for Defence 1939-1941, Prime Minister 1949: born Jeparit Victoria 20 December 1894 – died Melbourne 15 May 1978.

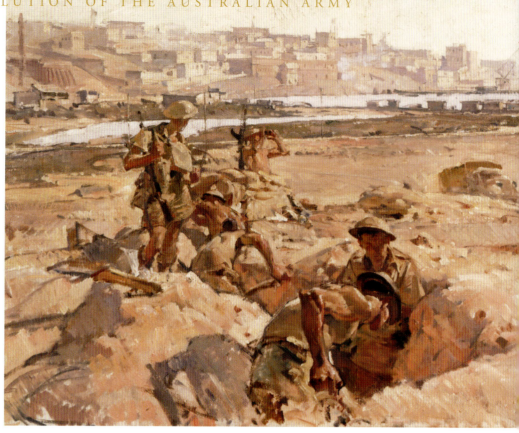

World War II – 1939-1945

Germany invaded Poland on 1st September 1939. Given their treaty obligations to support Poland, Britain and France responded by serving Germany an ultimatum to withdraw within two days, under threat of retaliation. By 3rd September, Germany had not responded and war was declared, first by Britain and soon after by France. Prime Minister Menzies addressed the Australian nation on the evening of 3rd September to announce, as a consequence of Britain's declaration of war, Australia was also at war.

Australia went to war with an ill-equipped and poorly-trained army, still restricted to home defence within Australia's borders by the provisions of the *Defence Act 1903*. To support the Empire with troops, Australia again had to follow the WWI procedures and raise an all-volunteer force for overseas service. The Second Australian Imperial Force (2nd AIF)[53] was raised in a remarkably similar fashion to the original AIF; from former soldiers, civilians and volunteers from Militia units. The new Army was also structured along the same lines as its predecessor with a four-battalion brigade in a three-brigade division.

It is interesting that the first round fired by Britain and the Dominions once again erupted from the Fort Nepean battery south of Melbourne, Victoria. A freighter ignored repeated requests to identify herself and attempted to enter Port Phillip Bay at 1.50am on 4th September 1939, only five hours after the declaration of war. One round was sufficient for the Australian freighter 'SS WONIORA' to establish her friendly intentions.

The outbreak of the war posed a number of difficulties for the Australian Government. With uncertainty over Japan's intentions and an Opposition opposed both to the raising of an expeditionary force and to conscription for home defence, the contribution Australia should and could make to the war effort in Europe in terms of soldier numbers and composition was a contentious issue. The same problem did not affect the RAN or the RAAF which were not bound to home service by the *Defence Act 1903* and already had personnel serving overseas.

On 15th September 1939 the Government announced the raising of an infantry division (later to become the 6th Division) for 'service at home or abroad as circumstances permit'. By late November, the 6th Division was preparing to leave for the Middle East, and the first elements finally departed in January 1940. In February, the Government approved the raising of the 7th Division and provided an Australian Corps.

The Germans' successful invasion of France and the Low Countries in May 1940 left Britain and the Dominions standing alone. The continuing uncertainty over Japanese

intentions in the Pacific changed both the Government's and the people's attitude to the war from that of total opposition (albeit many Unions continued their disapproval) to generally one of total commitment. This also saw the raising of another AIF formation, the 8th Infantry Division.

By May, one brigade of the 6th Division was already in Palestine, and two more convoys carrying the rest of the division were on their way. Following discussions between the British and Australian Governments, one convoy continued to the Middle East while the other was diverted to England to bolster Britain's anti-invasion preparations. This force was subsequently reorganised into two infantry brigades, eventually re-joining the other Australians in Egypt as the nucleus of the new 9th Division. At the same time, the 7th Division was sent to join the 6th Division, while the 8th Division readied itself for service in Malaya to bolster the Singapore and Malaya garrison forces in case of a Japanese southward thrust (Japan was not yet at war when this decision was taken). When Australia followed the British decision to reduce the number of battalions in a brigade from four to three, the resulting re-organisation provided sufficient resources to form a fourth AIF Infantry Division. The 9th Division was formed from those troops stationed in Britain, along with others in the Middle East. As a result of the European experience, an armoured formation, 1st Armoured Division, was raised in Australia at the beginning of 1941, but it was destined never to serve as a complete division outside Australia. At the same time, Japan continued her 'peaceful penetration' of South East Asia by moving into or intimidating neutral states such the Vichy French territories of Vietnam, Cambodia and neutral Siam (modern-day Thailand).

Above: AWM ART 22233 Courtesy of the Australian War Memorial. Tobruk

53 Military Board Instruction (MBI) No.59 of 18 October 1939

World War II – the Middle East

Italy declared war on Britain and France on 10th June 1940 and in September, began an advance into Egypt. Initial successes enabled them to reach Sidi Barrani, an advance of about 50 kilometres. On 10th December, however, British and Indian troops counter-attacked and forced the Italians back to Bardia. On 3rd January 1941 the Australian 6th Division attacked and quickly captured Bardia for the loss of 130 killed and 326 wounded.[54] Two days later, the 6th Division was outside Tobruk, well into Cyrenaica (the eastern region of modern-day Libya). Tobruk, a major Italian fortress, was attacked on 21st January 1942 and captured the next day, with 49 Australians killed and 306 wounded. The retreating enemy was pursued relentlessly and by 6th February, the 6th Division had reached Benghazi. On 9th March, the 9th Division began its relief of the 6th Division. In two months, an Italian Army of 10 divisions, some 1,300 guns and 400 tanks had been destroyed, with tens of thousands taken prisoner.

The situation changed rapidly, when advance elements of the German *Afrika Korps* landed in North Africa during late February 1941. Their advance forced the withdrawal of British and Dominion troops from most of their recently-captured

Below: AWM ART 27776 Courtesy of the Australian War Memorial. Battle of Retimo, Crete [56]

---

54 Long G. *Greece, Crete and Syria (1st edition).* Canberra, Australian War Memorial: 1953, p. 203n

territory in Cyrenaica. By 11th April, the 9th Division, 18th Australian Infantry Brigade and British armoured and artillery units were besieged in Tobruk, with German forces as far forward as the Egyptian frontier. Tobruk was heavily attacked on 30th April but, although a salient (an incursion by an attacking force into an adversary's position) was forced into the defences, the garrison held firm. Another attack on 16th May was similarly defeated while the salient was steadily reduced by intense patrolling. During September and October the Australians were relieved and left Tobruk for a well-earned rest. Over 3,000 Australian casualties had been sustained, including 559 killed, 2,450 wounded and 941 taken prisoner.[55]

Further east, following a coup d'état by Rashid Ali al-Gaylani (former Prime Minister of the Kingdom of Iraq) in early May, Iraq abrogated its treaty with Britain. The Iraqi Army was quickly defeated by British and Kurdish troops and the internal situation stabilised. However, the risk of German intervention, not just in Iraq but in areas under Vichy French control, made it strategically necessary to take control of Syria as well.

Syria was invaded on 8th June 1941 by the 7th Division (less the 18th Brigade which was in Tobruk), together with one Indian and two Free French brigades. The attack followed three routes: the direct road to Damascus, the route through the mountains to the Damascus-Beirut road at Zahle, and the coast road to Beirut. The Vichy French fought courageously but by 15th June the Allied force had reached the Kiswe–Merdjayoun–Jezzine–Sidon line. Despite a strong Vichy counter-attack in the vicinity of Merdjayoun, Damascus was captured on 21st June.

Fighting continued until 12th July when the Vichy French were granted an armistice. This campaign resulted in 1,552 Australian casualties, including 416 killed in action and 1,136 wounded.[56]

In addition to their military reverses in North Africa in February and March 1941, the Italians were in danger of being driven out of Greece. On 1st March 1941 German forces had entered Bulgaria and had taken Yugoslavia by 6th April. Allied troops had been ordered to Greece and a British armoured brigade and the ANZAC Corps (most of the 6th Australian Division and the New Zealand Division) arrived at Port Piraeus in Greece by 3rd April. On 10th April elements of this force made contact with the Germans some 15 kilometres south of the Yugoslav border. Outnumbered, and with the enemy in total control of the air, the Allied forces were pushed back through the Aliakmon and Thermopylae lines to the Athens area. Resistance finally collapsed, but the skill and resolution of the Navy ensured that, by 28th April, almost every fighting unit had been evacuated to Egypt or Crete.

---

55 Australian War Memorial. http://www.awm.gov.au/encyclopedia/ tobruk/retrieved 24 Aug 2012

56 Australian War Memorial. https://www.awm.gov.au/units/event_295. asp retrieved 24 Aug 2012

AWM No ART 27821 Courtesy of the Australian War Memorial. El Alamein

On 20th May 1941 Germany launched a parachute and airborne attack on Crete. Awaiting the German troops was an ad hoc force of British, New Zealand, Australian and Greek troops. These primarily comprised recent evacuees from Greece with little heavy equipment and almost no air support. By 26th May the Allied position was deemed hopeless and an evacuation was ordered. Despite crippling losses, the Royal Navy saved 15,000 troops. A further 12,000, including 3,102 Australians, could not be evacuated and were taken prisoner; Australian casualties included 274 killed and 507 wounded.[57]

Japan entered the war on 7th December 1941, and in early 1942 the 6th and 7th Divisions returned to Australia. The 9th Division remained in the Middle East. Late in May 1942, reinforced Axis forces under Field Marshal Erwin Rommel began to advance in the Western Desert and by 21st June had recaptured Tobruk. They were finally halted after three days of intense fighting at the El Alamein defensive positions, only 90 kilometres west of Alexandria. The 9th Division, then in Syria awaiting transport to Australia, was hurried forward to El Alamein. On 30th August the Axis forces again attacked, but were defeated at Alam el Halfa. German General Friedrich von Mellenthin was later to describe this action as the turning point in the Desert War.

On 23rd October 1942 the British 8th Army (which included the Australian 9th Division) attacked at El Alamein (the Second Battle of El Alamein), the battle reaching a climax a week later. An attack by the 9th Division north towards the sea gained ground and successfully held out against heavy German counter-attacks. After an intense effort, British armoured forces broke out through the corridor originally secured by the 9th Division and by 9th November the Axis forces were in full retreat. This success released the 9th Division to return to Australia where it arrived in February 1943. Australian casualties for the whole period of the El Alamein operations from 7th July to November amounted to 5,794, including 1,177 dead, 193 missing, 3,629 wounded and 795 taken prisoner.[58]

World War II – Asia Pacific 1941-1942

The Japanese Army had been fighting in and had occupied Manchuria since 1931, but when Japanese forces entered northern Indochina in September 1940, the Australian Government became gravely concerned about the security of Singapore. From October 1940 the British and Dominion garrison in Singapore was steadily strengthened, particularly by the arrival of the Australian 8th Division (less one brigade) in February 1941. In an agreement with the Netherland East Indies (now Indonesia) made in early 1941, Australian battalion groups were landed at Ambon, a Dutch colony; Rabaul in New Guinea, controlled by Australia; and Timor, a Portuguese colony by mid-December 1941.

Japan's attack on the United States (US) base at Pearl Harbor on 7th December 1941 was not the only Japanese operation at that time. Japanese forces also landed in Thailand and Malaya and attacked the Philippines. They advanced, quickly capturing Rabaul in New Guinea (by 23rd January 1942) and forced the surrender of Singapore (on 15th February 1942). Both Timor and Ambon were

---

57 Long G. *Greece, Crete and Syria (1st edition)*. Canberra, Australian War Memorial: 1953, p. 316

58 Johnston M, Stanley P. *Alamein: The Australian Story*. South Melbourne, Victoria, Oxford University Press: 2005, p. 265

overrun by the Japanese by 23rd February 1942, although some 300 Australians continued to harass the Japanese forces in Timor until withdrawn in February 1943. By 12th March the Japanese had taken Java.

A significant effect of the defeat of Singapore was the surrender of more than 130,000 British Empire troops to the Japanese Army, more than one-third died in captivity. Initially the Japanese held these prisoners in Singapore in a camp at Changi, which was a British Army Barracks before the war. A total of 15,384 Australian prisoners[59] were marched to Changi and housed there while the Japanese decided what to do with them.

The Changi Camp remained active throughout the war and continued to house a significant number of prisoners, including Australians. Approximately 51,000 allied prisoners of war, including 9,500 Australians[60] and about 270,000 Asian conscripts, were used as slave labour by the Japanese Army to build a 420 kilometre railway to link Thanbyuzayat in Burma with Bampong in Thailand (the Burma-Thailand Railway). This was a very ambitious undertaking with a planned completion date of August 1943. The Japanese Army intended to use the railway to launch an attack on India, which was under British control.

The conditions the prisoners and civilian workers endured were extremely harsh and appalling. The Japanese were totally focused on speed and treated prisoners with brutality. A combination of working conditions and a shortage of food soon led to malnutrition, disease and death. It was only through the heroic efforts of extremely dedicated, innovative and brave military doctors and medical assistants that some prisoners were able to recover from a wide range of injuries and diseases. 2,646 Australians died on the railway[61], as well as approximately 10,000 other Allied prisoners and 70,000 Asian workers. The railway was completed on 16 October 1943 and the surviving prisoners were returned to Changi.

Elsewhere in the Pacific, the Japanese advance was equally dramatic, reaching Lae and Salamaua in New Guinea by 8th March 1942. Following a Japanese landing in the Philippines on 10th December 1941, Bataan surrendered on 9th April, followed by Corregidor on 6th May 1942. In the decisive Battle of the Coral Sea from 4th to 8th May 1942, the US Navy, supported by ships of the RAN, turned back a Japanese convoy headed for Port Moresby. The Japanese Army then attempted an overland attack against Port Moresby across the rugged Owen Stanley Range.

AWM ART 26492 Courtesy of the Australian War Memorial. Interior View of 100 Metre Hut, Changi

In December 1941, Australia's seven Militia divisions were mobilised and in early January 1942, Australia recalled I Australian Corps (6th and 7th Divisions) from the Middle East to ready them for service in the Asia Pacific Region. The Port Moresby garrison was strengthened by two Militia battalions and other units. The final destination of I Australian Corps, en route to the Netherland East Indies in February 1942, was the subject of heated exchanges between the British Prime Minister, Winston Churchill and the Australian Government. Churchill attempted to divert the Australian troops to Rangoon to assist in the defence of Burma. The Australian Prime Minister, John Curtin[62], acting on advice from the Australian Chief of the General Staff (CGS), LTGEN Vernon Sturdee[63], insisted on the return of these experienced divisions so that they would be available for the defence of Australia. As a concession, Curtin allowed two brigades of the 6th Division to help garrison Ceylon (now Sri Lanka) for four months before they also returned to Australia.

59 Wigmore L. *The Japanese Thrust*. Canberra, Australian War Memorial: 1957, p. 511

60 Australian War Memorial. https://www.awm.gov.au/encyclopedia/pow/general_info/retrieved 24 Aug 2012

61 Australian War Memorial. https://www.awm.gov.au/encyclopedia/pow/general_info//retrieved 24 Aug 2012

62 John Joseph Curtin; Prime Minister and Minister for Defence 1941-1945: born Creswick Victoria 8 January 1885 – died Canberra 5 July 1945.

63 Lieutenant General Sir Vernon Ashton Hobart Sturdee, KBE, CB, DSO; Commands - Chief of the General Staff First Army, 8th Division, Eastern Command, 4th Pioneer Battalion, 8th Field Company, Officer in charge – Military Mission Washington 1942-1944: born Frankston Victoria 16 April 1890 – died Melbourne 25 May 1966.

In March-April 1942, the USA formed the South West Pacific Command and with Australia's agreement, GEN Douglas MacArthur was appointed Supreme Commander South West Pacific Region, with GEN Sir Thomas Blamey[64] as his Commander Allied Land Forces.

The Japanese continued their campaign to seize New Guinea and on 21st-22nd July 1942 landed two infantry regiments (approximately 7,700 soldiers) with supporting troops at Gona and quickly moved inland to the northern end of the Kokoda Track. They planned to advance across this tortuous path and take Port Moresby from the north.

The small Australian Militia force in the Buna/Gona area and later, the 39th Battalion, advanced up the Track to fight a desperate rear-guard action, but were pushed all the way across the mountains to Isurava. On 23rd August, the 21st Brigade of the 7th Division 2nd AIF was sent into action on the Kokoda Track. Fierce fighting ensued and after a desperate struggle, the Australians withdrew closer to Port Moresby.

By this time, Milne Bay had been reinforced by Army and RAAF units under the command of MAJGEN Cyril Clowes,[65] who anticipated an attempt by a Japanese landing force to capture the bay as an additional base from which

---

64 Field Marshal Sir Thomas Albert Blamey, GBE, KCB, CMG, DSO; 1st Australian Division 1916-1917, Australian Corps 1918, 2nd AIF GOC 6 Div 1939-1940, I Australian Corps 1940-1941, Deputy C-in-C ME 1941, GOC-in-C AMF 1942-1946: born Wagga Wagga NSW 24 January 1884 – died 27 May 1951.

65 Lieutenant General Cyril Albert Clowes, CBE, DSO, MC; Battalion Major 2 Div Arty 1918, I Corps 1940-1941 and HQ 2nd AIF 1941, GOC 1 Div 1942, Comd Milne Force 1942, GOC 11 Div 1942-1943, Comd Vic L of C Area 1943-1945: born Warwick Queensland 11 March 1842 – died Melbourne 19 May 1968.

to advance on Port Moresby. The Army and RAAF worked together to defeat this Japanese amphibious force. Two weeks after landing, the Japanese withdrew. This was the first time in the Asia Pacific War that a Japanese amphibious force had been defeated.

By 2nd November 1942, the reinforced Australians had retaken Kokoda, and on 11th November, Japanese fighting units were forced to abandon Oivi. By 13th November, the Australians had reached the Kumusi River. The battle for the Kokoda Track was over, although Japanese units continued to give strong resistance in the extremely difficult terrain adjoining the coast around Buna, Gona and Sanananda until mid-January 1943.

World War II – Asia Pacific 1943-1945

Allied plans for 1943 included the recapture of the Solomon Islands as far as southern Bougainville; the New Guinea coast as far as Madang; the west coast of New Britain; and the establishment of airfields on Kiriwina and Woodlark Islands. Defences were readied for a possible attack against northern Australia from the Merauke-Torres Strait area.

As in WWI, Australia was facing an acute manpower shortage commensurate with maintaining an Army of 12 divisions, a far larger number in proportion to population than Britain, America or Japan. Battle casualties and the high incidence of tropical diseases, particularly malaria and dysentery, had reduced the Army by the equivalent

of a division. The provisions of the *Defence Act 1903* that prevented conscripts from serving outside Australian territory compounded the manpower problem as, by this stage, most ground operations were in northern New Guinea and the islands to the north which were not formally Australian territory. Many Militia units were already designated as AIF since three-quarters of their members had volunteered for overseas service. In February 1943, legislation was passed allowing the Militia (AMF, as distinct from the AIF) to serve anywhere in the South West Pacific Area below the equator.

By early 1943 the Japanese had heavily reinforced the Lae–Salamaua area in New Guinea and were advancing in the south-east through Mubo to Wau, before being forced back to Mubo. In early March, enemy attempts to reinforce Lae were defeated in the Battle of the Bismarck Sea. By 14th July, the 3rd Division had cleared Mubo and laid siege to Salamaua, held by the substantially-reinforced Japanese 51st Division. Salamaua fell on 11th September followed closely by Lae on 16th September, both taken in operations by the 7th and 9th Divisions to the west and east. Lae was the first Australian amphibious assault since Gallipoli.

The 7th Division continued the offensive, moving up the Markham Valley and the Ramu River to occupy Dumpu by 4th October. Heavy fighting on Shaggy Ridge in the Finisterre Mountains to the north saw Japanese resistance collapse by the end of January 1944.

Above: AWM ART 27543 Courtesy of the Australian War Memorial. Taking Old Vickers Position, Bobdubi Ridge, 28th July 1943

Right: AWM Neg No 092562 Courtesy of the Australian War Memorial. Troops of 31/51 Infantry Battalion landing on the beach at Soraken Peninsula - Bougainville

On 22nd September 1943, the 9th Division had made a further landing north of Finschhafen. Bitter fighting followed, particularly for possession of Sattelberg which remained in enemy hands until 24th November. By 8th December, the Japanese were in retreat, with Sio falling on 15th January 1944. The three AIF divisions were withdrawn for rest and retraining, and were replaced by the 3rd, 5th and 11th Militia Divisions.

Allied successes now opened the way for a US invasion of the Philippines. As Australia's national strategy was focused on clearing Japanese forces from New Guinea, Australian forces were used to relieve the US garrisons in those territories. Due to manpower difficulties, the relieving Australian forces were much smaller than their US predecessors.

From October 1944 onwards, the 3rd Division and two independent brigades were moved to the Solomon Islands, the 5th Division allotted to New Britain and the 6th Division to Aitape, while the 8th Brigade continued its operations in the Madang-Sepik River area. Plans for 1945 committed I Corps (the 7th and 9th Divisions) to operations south of the American invasion of the Philippines, to capture areas in Borneo suitable as naval and air bases for future operations. They were also tasked with the capture of Borneo's oil installations and the re-establishment of the Netherlands East Indies Government in Borneo.

On 29th November 1944, the unofficial ceasefire between the American and Japanese forces on Bougainville was broken by the 3rd Division offensives to the north, across the centre and in the south of the island. These continued in the face of sporadic resistance and counter-attacks by the Japanese through the first half of 1945. On New Britain, operations against the main Japanese positions across the Gazelle Peninsula were launched by the 5th Division, initially from Jacquinot Bay where the Division landed in early November 1944. From mid-March, the Australians effectively decimated the Japanese garrison and operational requirements were reduced to active patrolling forward of the secured areas. In New Guinea, the 6th Division further developed its operations eastward along the coast from Aitape and through the Torricelli Ranges towards Wewak, which was secured by the end of May. Operations continued against the Japanese forces, which had withdrawn into the Prince Alexander Mountain Range, until fighting ended in August 1945.

Operations on Borneo commenced eight days before the fighting in Europe ended. On 1st May 1945, the 26th Brigade of the 9th Division landed at Tarakan and secured the airfield against heavy opposition. Obstinate resistance by the Japanese continued around Tarakan until enemy forces withdrew on 14th June, pursued relentlessly into the island's interior until the ceasefire in August. On 10th June, the bulk of the 9th Division was committed to capturing Brunei, following landings at Labuan, Muara Island and Brunei Bluff. On 1st July, on the other side of the island, the 7th Division landed at Balikpapan in the largest amphibious assault ever undertaken by Australians. After heavy fighting, the enemy withdrew on 21st July. Japanese forces surrendered in August 1945 following Emperor Hirohito's admission of defeat.

Organisation of 2nd AIF [66]

Initially a single division, the 2nd AIF was raised with the 6th Infantry Division, comprising the 16th, 17th and 18th Infantry Brigades. These names followed on from the five existing Militia divisions and the battalions of this new organisation were numbered sequentially from 1 with the prefix 2/x added later to differentiate between existing Militia battalions and units of the 2nd AIF.

16th Inf Bde formed in NSW with: 2/1st Bn, 2/2nd Bn, 2/3rd Bn and 2nd/4th Bn

17th Inf Bde formed in Vic with: 2/5th Bn, 2/6th Bn, 2/7th Bn and 2nd/8th Bn

18th Inf Bde formed from other States: 2/9th Bn ex Qld, 2/10th Bn ex SA, 2/11th Bn ex WA and 2/12th Bn ex Tas/Qld.

In February 1940, the 2nd AIF was expanded to a corps of two divisions, but brigades were reduced to three battalions in accordance with British doctrine. The 7th Infantry Division comprised 19th, 20th and 21st Infantry Brigades as follows:

- The 19th Infantry Brigade comprised the excess battalions of 6th Infantry Division[67], 2/4th Bn ex 16th Bde, 2/8th Bn ex 17th Bde and 2/12th Bn ex 18th Bde; with an additional six new battalions required, they were allocated two battalions from NSW and one from Qld to form the 20th Bde, and one each from Vic, SA and WA to form the 21st Inf Bde

- The next Militia numbers associated with NSW were 13 and 17 while the next number in Qld was 15 so the 20th Inf Bde comprised 2/13th Bn, 2/15th Bn and 2/17th Bn

- The next Militia numbers in the other States were 14 in Vic, 27 in SA and 16 in WA, so accordingly the 21st Inf Bde comprised 2/14th Bn, 2/16th Bn and 2/27th Bn.

---

66 Long G. *Australia in the War of 1939-1945, Series 1, Army, Volume I, To Benghazi*. Adelaide, The Advertiser Printing Office: 1961, p. 51
67 Long G. *Australia in the War of 1939-1945, Series 1, Army, Volume I, To Benghazi*. Adelaide, The Advertiser Printing Office: 1961, p. 82

In May 1940 the Government authorised the raising of the 8th Infantry Division which comprised the 22nd, 23rd and 24th Inf Bdes:

- The 22nd Inf Bde formed in NSW with the next Militia numbers being 18, 19 and 20; thus the 22nd Inf Bde comprised 2/18th Bn, 2/19th Bn and 2/20th Bn.

- The 23rd Inf Bde formed in Vic/Tas with the next Militia numbers being 21 and 22 in Vic and 40 in Tasmania; the 23rd Inf Bde accordingly comprised 2/21st Bn, 2/22nd Bn and 2/40th Bn

- The 24th Inf Bde was formed using the next lowest militia numbers being 2/25th Bn ex Qld, 2/28th Bn ex WA and 2/43rd Bn ex SA.

The 16th Inf Bde moved to the Middle East on the 'First Convoy' with four battalions.

The 17th Inf Bde moved to the Middle East in the 'Second Convoy' with four battalions while 2/11th Bn went home to WA on leave and instead of returning to NSW to join the 'Third Convoy' went to the Middle East in the 'Second Convoy'.

The 18th Inf Bde (less 2/11th Bn) left on the 'Third Convoy' along with reinforcements and Corps technical units, but was diverted to the United Kingdom, landing there just after Dunkirk. The reinforcements and technical troops were formed into 25th Inf Bde with 70th Bn, 71st Bn and 72nd Bn. The two brigades became part of Australforce[68] and were given roles in the defence of the United Kingdom.

The 19th Inf Bde was formed in the Middle East from the units already there 2/4th Bn, 2/8th Bn and 2/11th Bn and joined 6th Infantry Division to replace the diverted 18th Inf Bde Group.

The 26th Inf Bde was formed in Australia to replace 19th Inf Bde of the 7th Infantry Division with Victoria's 2/23rd and 2/24th Bn and SA's 2/48th Bn.

The Government next decided to make Australforce permanent as 9th Infantry Division and reinforced the two brigades in the United Kingdom with 24th Inf Bde from 8th Infantry Division which was replaced by the newly-recruited 27th Inf Bde. This new brigade was to have 2/26th Bn ex-Qld, 2/29th Bn ex-Victoria and 2/30th Bn ex-NSW, all numbered after the next Militia numbers in each State. The battalions of the 25th Inf Bde were renumbered as 2/31st Bn, 2/32nd Bn and 2/33rd Bn.

Whilst the 6th, 7th and 9th Divisions concentrated in the Middle East the ill-fated 8th Infantry Division was ordered to Malaya. After the Western Desert Campaign, I Australian Corps was to go to Greece with the 6th Infantry Division and 7th Infantry Division. Blamey wanted to have the most experienced and well-trained brigades in the 7th Infantry Division, so the 18th Inf Bde and 25th Inf Bde were reassigned to 7th Infantry Division and the newly-formed 26th Inf Bde went to the 9th Infantry Division along with 20th Inf Bde.

In the final organisation, the 2/25th Bn was delayed in Darwin when the rest of the 24th Inf Bde left for the Middle East. When the brigade was sent to Tobruk, the 2/32nd Bn was allocated to replace the 2/25th Bn which then joined the 25th Inf Bde on their eventual arrival in the Middle East.

The final allocation of brigades of the 2nd AIF comprised:

6 Inf Div	16th Inf Bde	2/1st Bn	2/2nd Bn	2/3rd Bn
	17th Inf Bde	2/5th Bn	2/6th Bn	2/7th Bn
	19th Inf Bde	2/4th Bn	2/8th Bn	2/11th Bn
7 Inf Div	18th Inf Bde	2/9th Bn	2/10th Bn	2/12th Bn
	21st Inf Bde	2/14th Bn	2/16th Bn	2/27th Bn
	25th Inf Bde	2/25th Bn	2/31st Bn	2/33rd Bn
8 Inf Div	22nd Inf Bde	2/18th Bn	2/19th Bn	2/20th Bn
	23rd Inf Bde	2/21st Bn	2/22nd Bn	2/40th Bn
	27th Inf Bde	2/26th Bn	2/29th Bn	2/30th Bn
9 Inf Div	20th Inf Bn	2/13th Bn	2/15th Bn	2/17th Bn
	24th Inf Bde	2/28th Bn	2/32nd Bn	2/43rd Bn
	26th Inf Bde	2/23rd Bn	2/24th Bn	2/48th Bn

68   Long G. *Australia in the War of 1939-1945, Series 1, Army, Volume I, To Benghazi*. Adelaide, The Advertiser Printing Office: 1961, p. 310

In the initial reductions in manpower of 1942 and 1943, units were linked to form 1st/45th Bn, 10th/48th Bn, 12th/40th Bn, 13th/33rd Bn, 14th/32nd Bn, 20th/34th Bn, 29th/46th Bn, 31st/51st Bn, 37th/52nd Bn, 41st/2nd Bn, 55th/53rd Bn and 58th/59th Bn.

Post-World War II – 1945-1951

The Army continued to experience a high level of activity in the years following the end of WWII, although it never regained the same extraordinary momentum. A post-war agreement between the British Commonwealth and the US saw the raising of a British Commonwealth Occupation Force (BCOF), comprising Australia, British, Indian and New Zealand formations, to serve as an occupying force in Japan. BCOF's primary tasks were demilitarisation, demobilisation and policing the regulations set by the Military Government. As some acknowledgement of the level of Australian commitment to the Pacific theatre during the war, the appointment of GOC BCOF was filled by Australian Army officers; this also demonstrated the building-up of a regular Army in peace and the wish to be independent of the United Kingdom. The Australian Army's contribution to BCOF was the 34th Infantry Brigade with its three battalions – the 65th, 66th and 67th. This formation was raised at Morotai and drawn from infantry units spread across the South West Pacific Area at the cessation of hostilities. An armoured car squadron, a general hospital and a number of smaller units also joined the force.

Two years later, the bulk of the Commonwealth's Forces had been withdrawn, although Australia still maintained a presence in Japan. The three battalions of the 34th Infantry Brigade formed the nucleus of the post-war Regular Army and were designated the 1st, 2nd and 3rd Battalions of the Australian Regiment in 1948. The following year the Australian Regiment was re-designated The Royal Australian Regiment (RAR). Of the original three battalions, only the 3rd Battalion (3 RAR) remained in Japan. A Depot Training Battalion of the Regiment was raised in Australia in 1952 (renamed 4 RAR in 1954), but disbanded before the end of the decade. The occupation of Japan ended with the signing of the Treaty of San Francisco in September 1951.

The Australian Regular Army (ARA) was formed in September 1947 and in 1948 the CMF was re-raised to augment the ARA of 19,000 with its field force component of a regular brigade group including an armoured element. The CMF was to comprise two infantry divisions and other units, to a strength of 50,000. However, by 1949-1950 the CMF numbered only 23,000 troops.

The Australian Army's involvement in multinational peacekeeping commenced in 1947 with the contribution of military observers to what was initially titled the United Nations (UN) Good Offices Commission (GOC). The Commission was tasked with delineating and supervising the ceasefire between the Netherlands forces trying to re-establish Dutch rule in the East Indies and Indonesian forces fighting for an independent republic. The GOC was later retitled the United Nations Commission for Indonesia (UNCI) and its mission concluded in 1951. The Australian Army also contributed observers to the UN Military Observer Group in India and Pakistan (UNMOGIP) from 1950 until 1985, and one observer to the UN Commission on Korea (UNCOK) in 1950, although this commitment ceased with the outbreak of the Korean War that same year.

In mid-1949, the Federal Government responded to the New South Wales and Queensland coal strike by sending troops into the mines to maintain production. The strike was broken in August when the railway unions decided to move the coal mined by the Army, leaving the mining union isolated within the trade union movement.

In December 1949 a new Federal Government was elected on a platform based broadly on reducing communist influence in Australia and its further spread throughout South East Asia. To deter the spread of communism, the Government worked to build regional confidence against external pressure, to encourage regional security and defence force development, and to maintain Australia's own defence capability. The Australian Government considered the structure of its Army ill-suited to meet this challenge, and introduced National Service (NS) through the *National Service Act* in 1951. All 18-year old males were now drafted for compulsory military service, with an obligation to serve 176 days, 98 of which were to be full-time. This effectively boosted the strength of the CMF to over 87,000 by 1956 but only provided partially-trained soldiers; this was a major drain on the Regular soldiers who had to train and administer the National Servicemen who then went off to the CMF. This NS scheme continued until 1959, and it was officially abolished in 1960. 1951 also saw the raising again in Papua New Guinea of the Pacific Islands Regiment (PIR). This unit had served with distinction from 1941 to 1946; in the initial years the unit relied on Australian commanders and also provision of specialist support.

The Korean War – 1950-1953

On 25th June 1950, the Korean People's Army (North Korea) invaded the Republic of Korea (South Korea). The invasion was regarded as a challenge to the Western democracies, a consequence of the growing Cold War tensions between east and west. The United Nations Security Council (UNSC) invited UN member States to send forces to repel the North Korean Army under the auspices of United Nations Command – Korea (UNC-K).

Reproduced Courtesy of 3 RAR.
Battle of Kapyong

By October 1951, Australia had succumbed to US pressure and agreed to send a second battalion to Korea. Several other members of the Commonwealth increased their contribution and a British Commonwealth Division was formed with an Australian officer commanding one of its brigades.

A UN offensive in October 1951 saw the newly-formed 1st Commonwealth Division involved in Operation COMMANDO when UN forces extended their positions along the Jamestown Line. During this operation, 3 RAR took the strongly-defended Chinese positions on Maryang San. In November 1951, the Korean War entered its static phase which lasted until a ceasefire was agreed on 27th July 1953. A formal end of hostilities treaty has never been signed.

In April 1952, 3 RAR was joined by 1 RAR, the brigade having been re-designated the previous year as 28th Commonwealth Brigade. Australian brigadiers commanded the brigade, which included two RAR battalions, from July 1952 until the end of hostilities. In March 1953, 1 RAR was relieved by 2 RAR while 3 RAR, with its system of individual, rather than unit replacement, remained committed until the ceasefire.

The static phase of the war saw the RAR battalions involved in extensive patrolling and trench raids, as well as in the major actions of Hill 355 and the Hook. In April 1954, 1 RAR relieved 2 RAR and 3 RAR returned to Australia in November 1954, leaving 1 RAR as a component of a reduced Commonwealth commitment to the UN force in Korea.

Australian casualties numbered 1,584, of whom 340[69] were killed, Army casualties totalled 276 killed in action or died of wounds, 1,210 wounded in action and 23 taken prisoner.[70] The highest decoration for bravery awarded to an Australian during the war was to Horace William Madden of 3 RAR who was awarded the George Cross for extreme courage whilst a prisoner of war.

In late September 1950, 3 RAR joined the 27th British Commonwealth Brigade in Korea. The Brigade advanced into North Korea, and, in October, saw action close to the Yalu River, which formed the Korean-Chinese border. With the entry of massed Chinese forces into the conflict in November, the Commonwealth Brigade began a long withdrawal which ended when the Brigade consolidated behind the 38th Parallel.

In April 1951, a determined Chinese offensive saw 3 RAR, the 2nd Battalion, Princess Patricia's Canadian Light Infantry (2PPCLI) and A Company of the US 72nd Heavy Tank Battalion, committed to a hard-fought defensive battle at Kapyong to halt the advance of a Chinese division. For this action these battalions and A Company were awarded the Distinguished Unit Citation (DUC), renamed the US Presidential Unit Citation in 1966.

69   Australian War Memorial. http://www.awm.gov.au/atwar/korea/
70   Beaumont J. *Australian Defence: Sources and Statistics.* Melbourne, Oxford University Press: 2001, p. 327t

Regional Security – 1951-1955

For some years, Australia had been seeking a 'more comprehensive system of regional security in the Pacific area.' To a degree, this was met by the Australian, New Zealand and United States Treaty (ANZUS), which was signed in September 1951. A further step towards regional security occurred in September 1954 with the signing of the South East Asia Collective Defence Treaty by the US, Australia, New Zealand, France, Britain, Pakistan, Thailand and the Philippines, establishing the South East Asia Treaty Organisation (SEATO). Any attack on a member State, or on protocol States (South Vietnam, Laos and Cambodia) was deemed a matter of common danger inviting a common response, although the US specified that the treaty could only be invoked in relation to a communist attack. A more localised security arrangement for Australian, New Zealand and British interests was created with the formation of ANZAM – Anglo-New Zealand-Australia-Malaya (Britain being the governing power of what was then the Federation of Malaya). In 1955, the British Commonwealth Far East Strategic Reserve (FESR) was formed in Malaya. The Australian Army component was a battalion group, based on an RAR battalion, which formed part of the 28th Commonwealth Brigade Group.

The primary role of FESR was 'to provide a deterrent to, and be available at short notice to assist in countering further communist aggression in South East Asia.' Its secondary and related role was to assist in maintaining the security of Malaya by participating in operations against communist terrorists. A communist insurrection to seize control of Malaya had commenced in 1948 and was to become known as the Malayan Emergency.

Malayan Emergency – 1955-1960

At the peak of the Malayan Emergency, several years before the FESR commitment, there were some 8,000 communist terrorists and an estimated 50,000 sympathisers within the Malayan population. The communist terrorist movement was primarily Chinese-based and was pitted against the security forces which included 23 infantry battalions, over 60,000 police and 250,000 home guards.

In October 1955, 2 RAR, with its supporting artillery battery, was deployed to Malaya until October 1957 when it was relieved by 3 RAR and its battery. October 1959 saw 1 RAR and its battery deployed to Malaya, as 3 RAR returned to Australia. Except for short periods of leave, the battalions were used almost continually on patrolling, ambushing, food denial and cordon and search operations in northern Malaya. Approximately 7,000 members of the Australian Army served in this theatre during the Emergency. Losses amounted to 169 in total which included 13 killed in action and 24 wounded, with 21 non-operational deaths and 111 cases of non-operational casualties.[71] The Emergency officially ended on 31st July 1960.

The Pentropic Organisation – 1960-1965

With the end of the NS scheme in November 1959, the Army looked to modernise and restructure to allow better integration into operations with the forces of Australia's main ally, the US. The Army was reorganised around a new structure known as the Pentropic division. The US Army had experimented with a Pentomic divisional structure based on five battle groups. The core element of each was a significantly enlarged infantry battalion, to which were added elements of supporting arms. In effect, the Pentropic Organisation eliminated the intermediate-level brigade headquarters. Implementation of the Pentropic divisional structure commenced in 1960.

The restructuring of the Army, particularly the CMF infantry battalions, to form the new Battle groups, involved the disbanding of many old units with historical links going back to the Sudan, South Africa and the two World Wars, and the severing of traditional ties with their local communities. This caused a great deal of resentment within the CMF and was perceived as a pernicious tactic by the Regular Army to assert its authority over the CMF and reduce its influence over senior figures in Government and society.

The new Pentropic blueprint presented a complex and challenging command and staff organisation and created a number of difficulties at lower levels. The US Army abandoned its experiment in 1961; however, the Australian Army persevered with its Pentropic structure until November 1964.

To maintain some semblance of tradition the individual Militia companies of these larger battalions adopted the territorial titles of their former units as follows:[72]

71 Beaumont J. *Australian Defence: Sources and Statistics.* Melbourne, Oxford University Press: 2001, p. 328

72 Festburg AN. *The Lineage of the Australian Army.* Melbourne, Allara Publishing: 1972, pp. 26-33

New South Wales

2nd Bn RNSWR

A Coy NSW Scottish Coy	B Coy North Shore Coy
C Coy City of Newcastle Coy	D Coy Macquarie Coy
E Coy Mounted Rifles Coy	Sup Coy Kuring-Gai Coy

3rd Bn RNSWR

A Coy St George Coy	B Coy Illawarra Coy
C Coy Werriwa Coy	D Coy Aust Rifles Coy
E Coy Riverina Coy	Sup Coy St George Coy

Victoria

1st Bn RVR

A Coy Vic Scottish Coy	B Coy Merri Coy
C Coy Melbourne Coy	D Coy Essendon Coy
E Coy Footscray Coy	

2nd Bn RVR

A Coy Geelong Coy	B Coy Ballarat Coy
C Coy Sunraysia Coy	D Coy Bendigo Coy
E Coy Goulburn Valley Coy	

Queensland

1st Bn RQR

A Coy Moreton Coy	B Coy Darling Downs Coy
C Coy Gatton College Coy	D Coy Wide Bay Coy
E Coy Byron Scottish Coy	

2nd Bn RQR

A Coy Far North Qld Coy	B Coy Far North Qld Coy
C Coy The Kennedy Coy	D Coy The Capricornia Coy
E Coy The Capricornia Coy	

South Australia

1st Bn RSAR

A Coy South East Coy	B Coy River Coy
C Coy Mid North Coy	D Coy Adelaide Coy
E Coy Port Adelaide Coy	

Western Australia

1st Bn RWAR

A Coy City of Perth Coy	B Coy Cameron Coy
C Coy Swan Coy	D Coy WA Rifle Coy
E Coy North Coast Coy	

Tasmania

1st Bn RTR

A Coy Launceston Coy	B Coy Derwent Coy

Papua New Guinea

1st Battalion PIR[73]

Formation Sign 1st Division Pentropic

73   Dennis P, Grey J, Morris E, Prior R. *The Oxford Companion to Australian Military History (Second Edition)*. Australia, Oxford University Press: 2008, p.404 (The 1st Bn PIR was the only Australian reserve unit not placed on the new Pentropic Establishment)

One significant complication for the Army was the requirement to maintain an RAR battalion with British Commonwealth Far East Strategic Reserve (FESR) in Malaya (Malaysia after 1963) based on the standard British Commonwealth battalion structure, while all other battalions conformed to the enlarged Pentropic structure. This resulted in constant reorganisation of those battalions preparing to deploy for service with FESR. Reversion to the previous tropical warfare divisional (and battalion) structure was effected in 1965, with some restoration of the old identities of the original CMF battalions.

When the Army was again reorganised, returning to the standard battalion model, initially the new, smaller battalions were numbered sequentially within the State-based regiments. These units were soon renumbered to mirror the former Militia battalion numbers, thus establishing historical links to the battalions of the AIF; however the traditional territorial titles were not restored.[74]

Indonesian Confrontation – 1964-1965

In 1964, Indonesia launched a campaign of confrontation against the newly-created Federation of Malaysia, seeking to destabilise and ultimately destroy it. Most incursions occurred in Sarawak and Sabah, with a few incursions into mainland (Western) Malaysia. By the end of 1964 there were 21 British, Gurkha and Malaysian battalions, with supporting arms, serving in Borneo. The Malaysian Government requested military support from Australia in January 1965, and 3 RAR and 102nd Field Battery RAA (then with the FESR), 1st SAS Squadron and a number of field and construction squadrons were deployed to Borneo. In addition, 111th Light Anti-Aircraft Battery, relieved later by 110th Battery, was deployed to the Butterworth Air Base in Western Malaysia in case of Indonesian air attack.

Sarawak and Sabah Regions, Malaysia

At the same time, several brigades of Indonesian regular troops had been moved from Java to Kalimantan, opposite Sarawak and Sabah. Ultimately, 22,000 regular Indonesian Army troops, including 12 infantry battalions, 4,000 irregulars and 2,000 Clandestine Communist Organisation (CCO) operatives with some 24,000 Chinese sympathisers, were involved in the confrontation. The Indonesian incursions into Sarawak and Sabah were predominantly the work of relatively small groups, often less than platoon size.

The Commonwealth security forces were deployed primarily in company bases within mutually supporting gun range, with patrols mounted to gain intelligence, set ambushes and force the Indonesians back behind their own border. From March to July 1965, 3 RAR served on operations while 4 RAR was deployed from April to August 1966. The SAS squadrons likewise served in turn with 1st SAS Squadron deployed from April to August 1965 and 2nd SAS Squadron from March to July 1966.

As well as operations in Borneo and the mainland of Malaysia, Australian troops, mainly from the PIR, were engaged in intensive patrolling along the Territory of Papua New Guinea land border between Indonesian and Australian territory. The demands of patrolling in such difficult terrain imposed a considerable drain on the available pool of Australian officers, warrant officers and non-commissioned officers. Confrontation formally ended in August 1966 and Australian Army casualties amounted to seven killed and six wounded, with 10 non-operational deaths and 14 other non-operational casualties.[75]

National Service – 1965-1972

A NS scheme was reintroduced in 1965 primarily because of Australian Government concerns over the Army's capacity to deal effectively with direct security concerns in the region. The Government harboured misgivings over the Army's ability to deal with simultaneous deployments such as a commitment in Vietnam, the Indonesian confrontation in Malaysia, and a conflict in PNG along the common border with Indonesia. The Army's preference was to increase recruiting, but Treasury vetoed the necessary budget increases.

This period of NS was different from the 1950s version and generally involved two years full-time duty. Selection was not universal but based on a ballot, and the *National Service Act* allowed conscripts to serve overseas. National Servicemen saw service in Malaysia and Singapore, as well as Vietnam.

---

74 In 2009 the Regimental Council of the RNSWR introduced Territorial Titles, refer to Chap 14.

75 Beaumont J. *Australian Defence: Sources and Statistics*. Melbourne, Oxford University Press: 2001, p. 329t.

Vietnam War – 1962-1972

Following the defeat of the French Army at Dien Bien Phu in May 1954 in the First Indochina War, Vietnam was partitioned at the 17th Parallel. The communist Democratic Republic of Vietnam (DRV) took control in the northern half of the country and the non-communist Republic of Vietnam (RVN) maintained control in the south. From the late 1950s, a civil war developed in South Vietnam between the communist-supported National Liberation Front (NLF) with its military arm, the Viet Cong (VC), and the US-backed Government of Ngo Dinh Diem. The war intensified in 1963 following the assassination of Diem and the replacement of his administration by a series of unstable 'revolving door' governments.

On 3rd August 1962, following negotiations with the US and at the request of the RVN, 30 Australian Army training advisers arrived in South Vietnam to join US Army advisers in what later became Military Assistance Command Vietnam (MACV). Their tasks were primarily to assist in training RVN ground forces in jungle warfare, village defence and related activities. The Australian Army Training Team Vietnam (AATTV) increased in strength throughout the war to reach 215 by mid-1970.

In late 1964 and early 1965, the US proposed the introduction of sizeable ground forces in response to the deteriorating military situation in South Vietnam.

With RVN agreement, 1 RAR was deployed to Bien Hoa, north-east of Saigon, in May 1965, joining the US 173rd Airborne Brigade as the third battalion of the Brigade. Australian and New Zealand artillery batteries, as well as other supporting arms and services units, arrived later. In addition to its responsibilities for the security of the Bien Hoa air base, the 173rd Airborne Division conducted a number of important operations against VC forces throughout the III Corps Tactical Zone. This tactical zone included the RVN capital city, Saigon, which lay between the II Corps Tactical Zone of the Central Highlands and the IV Corps Tactical Zone incorporating the Mekong Delta.

In May 1966, the size of the Army's combat element was significantly increased. Having completed its 12-month tour, 1 RAR was replaced by 1 Australian Task Force (1ATF). This was a brigade-sized formation comprising a headquarters, two infantry battalions (5 RAR and 6 RAR) and elements from all supporting arms and services. It was based at Nui Dat in Phuoc Tuy Province located on the coast, east of Saigon, within the III Corps Tactical Zone.

In essence, 1ATF was handed tactical responsibility for the security of the province, excluding the populated areas, working in close coordination with RVN forces. Logistic support for the 1ATF units was provided by 1st Australian Logistic Support Group (1ALSG), located at Vung Tau, a coastal town and port immediately south of Phuoc Tuy. While both 1ATF and 1ALSG (and the AATTV, RAN and RAAF units) were under national command of Headquarters

AWM ART 40758 Courtesy of the Australian War Memorial. Battle of Long Tan

43

BEL_69_0556_VN Courtesy of the Australian War Memorial. Long Tan, South Vietnam – Memorial Service, 18th August 1969

Australian Force Vietnam located in Saigon, 1ATF was under operational control of the equivalent of a US Army Corps Headquarters (Headquarters II Field Force Vietnam) located at Long Binh, east of Saigon. No. 9 Squadron, RAAF, equipped with Iroquois (UH-1H) helicopters and based at Vung Tau, supported 1ATF operations, as did the Caribou-equipped No. 35 Squadron, RAAF, albeit to a lesser extent.

Infantry battalions, artillery batteries, and RAAC and SAS squadrons were rotated on a yearly basis, with the remainder of the force relieved by individual replacement. Additional battalions were raised to give the RAR a total strength of nine battalions, and other supporting arms and services units were also raised. At its peak strength in 1969, the Australian Army in Vietnam numbered more than 7,000 personnel.

Initially, 1ATF met little serious opposition but, on 18th August 1966, D Company 6 RAR, on a fighting patrol to clear suspected recoilless rifle and mortar sites, encountered a large enemy force in the Long Tan rubber plantation east of Nui Dat. During a number of bitterly-fought attempts to overrun D Company, a large force of VC and North Vietnamese suffered heavy casualties from artillery fire, small arms fire of the company and machine guns of the armoured relief force. A US Presidential Unit Citation was awarded to D Company, 6 RAR for this action.

Over the next 18 months, 1ATF extended its control over Phuoc Tuy Province with a range of task force and battalion operations. Some were undertaken in cooperation with US and RVN forces, and covered the full range of mission types from jungle patrolling to cordon and search operations in various towns and villages. A Civil Affairs unit was added to 1ATF in March 1967 to conduct and coordinate a vast range of construction, resettlement, medical and dental, education and welfare activities for the civil population of Phuoc Tuy. The New Zealand Army infantry companies were integrated into an RAR battalion which was then designated the 'ANZAC' Battalion. In December 1967, 1ATF was augmented by a third RAR battalion and a squadron of Centurion tanks.

Three key operations to protect the major bases of Long Binh, Bien Hoa and the capital Saigon, from VC and North Vietnam Army (NVA) offensives, involved 1ATF operating as a formation (less one battalion and other elements securing its base) outside Phuoc Tuy Province. These comprised Operation COBURG in January/February 1968, THOAN THANG I in May 1968, and FEDERAL in February 1969. The first two operations involved significant clashes with large enemy forces. May 1968 also saw large-scale enemy attacks on Australian positions in the battles of Fire Support Base (FSB) Coral and FSB Balmoral, and at the village of Binh Ba.

In 1969, growing disenchantment with the war, along with US attempts to reduce casualties and prepare for disengagement, led to a change in operational focus

COM/69/0250/VN Courtesy of the
Australian War Memorial. Phuoc Tuy
Province, South Vietnam, 1969

to 'pacification' involving enhancing the security of the populated areas of the RVN, combined with the upgrading of the effectiveness of RVN forces. Notwithstanding this commitment, 1ATF offensive operations in Phuoc Tuy ensured that by 1971 there were few incursions by major VC and NVA units.

From 1968, public opinion in both Australia and the US became stridently anti-war. Exacerbated by the propaganda disaster of the communists' 1968 'Tet' Offensive, the combination of the unpopularity of conscription and the rising casualty rates, public opposition in both the US and Australia forced the political leaderships to announce the withdrawal of Allied forces. In November 1970, 8 RAR was withdrawn and not replaced.

12 months later, 1ATF withdrew from Phuoc Tuy, followed shortly after by 1ALSG. The AATTV, having been gradually reduced in strength, concentrated in Phuoc Tuy Province with the departure of 1ATF, and continued training RVN forces until the withdrawal of the last Australian elements in December 1972.

Prime Minister John Gorton[76] had begun the process of reducing Australia's commitment to Vietnam by December 1970, a process that continued when William 'Billy'

McMahon[77] became Prime Minister in March 1971. On 7th November 1971, the Australians handed over control of Nui Dat to the Army of the Republic of Vietnam's (ARVN) 946 Regional Force Company and relocated to Vung Tau. The last Australian infantrymen left Vung Tau in February 1972, and by 5th March, there were only 128 Australian Servicemen remaining in Vietnam. Following the Australian federal election on 2nd December 1972, the new Prime Minister, Gough Whitlam[78] ordered the remaining troops out of South Vietnam. Prime Minister Whitlam also suspended NS and announced that currently serving National Servicemen could seek discharge.

Over the 10 years of the war, more than 50,000 Army, RAAF and RAN personnel served in Vietnam. There is a popular misconception held by Australian society that the war was predominately fought by National Servicemen; in fact, the 17,424 National Servicemen who served in the Vietnam War represented less than half the total number of Australians who served. Of those young Australians called up for NS during the period 1965-1972, only 27.3% served in Vietnam.

---

76 John Grey Gorton, GCMC, AC, CH; politician, Senator 1950-1968, Prime Minister 1968-1971: born Melbourne 9 September 1911 – died Sydney 19 May 2002.

77 William "Billy" McMahon, GCMC, CH; politician, privy councillor, Prime Minister 1971-1972: born Sydney 23 Feb 1908 – died 31 Mar 1988.

78 Edward Gough Whitlam, AC, QC; barrister, politician, Prime Minister 1972-1975: born Melbourne 11 Jul 1916 – died Sydney 21 Oct 2014.

For the Australian Army, the withdrawal from Vietnam represented the end of 33 years of continuous operations (1939-1972), which had commenced with WWII and continued through the occupation of Japan, the Korean War, the Malayan Emergency, the Indonesian Confrontation and finally the Vietnam War.

Army casualties in Vietnam amounted to 415 killed or died of wounds, 2,348 wounded, and 79 who died from non-operational causes.[79] Two soldiers[80] were added to the official casualty list in the 1990s when their deaths, although in Australian hospitals, were deemed to be directly attributed to their service in Vietnam. Four soldiers were also listed as missing in action until 2007-2009 when their remains were recovered and repatriated to Australia for burial. A total of four VCs were awarded to members of the Australian Army during the Vietnam War.

The 1971-1977 Period

In 1967, the United Kingdom had announced that half of its forces in Malaysia and Singapore would be withdrawn by 1971 and the remainder within the following five years. In 1971 a new defence agreement, the Five Power Defence Arrangements (FPDA), was negotiated to provide for consultation on the response to any threats or external attacks on Malaysia and Singapore. This involved the formation of an Australian, New Zealand and United Kingdom (ANZUK) force which was based in Singapore. This force included an RAR battalion with a supporting field battery (similar to 1955 when Australia committed a battalion to FESR's 28th Commonwealth Brigade) as well as support elements. The ANZUK force was disbanded in 1975 when first the Australian, and then the British Government, withdrew its ground forces.

With the completion of the withdrawal from Vietnam and the disbandment of the NS scheme, the Army required a new direction and focus. The new Australian defence and military policy was based on a withdrawal from the previous policy of 'forward defence' and a judgement that there was no credible short-term threat to Australia's security. A further significant change in defence commitments occurred in 1976 when the last SEATO exercise was held. The organisation formally disbanded on 30th June 1977.

In 1972, following a major review under the chairmanship of LTGEN FG Hassett[81], the Australian Government agreed

to a complete reorganisation of the Army along functional lines. This involved disbanding the geographical commands and creating Field Force, Logistic and Training Commands, leaving smaller geographically-based Military Districts with predominately supporting administrative roles. In May 1973, the Defence Minister, Lance Barnard, announced a reduction in the number of regular infantry battalions from nine to six. This resulted in the linking of six of the RAR battalions to become 2/4 RAR, 5/7 RAR, and 8/9 RAR. The other three battalions of the ARA comprised 1 RAR, 3 RAR and 6 RAR.

In anticipation of the granting of independence to PNG, the Papua New Guinea Defence Force was established in 1973, based largely on the battalions of the PIR (became The Royal Pacific Islands Regiment in 1985). With independence, an Australian Defence Advisory Group, primarily manned by the Australian Army, was located at Port Moresby to assist in the development of the PNGDF.

In 1974, the Committee of Inquiry into the CMF (the Millar Report) published its findings. In the years following its reforming in 1948, the CMF had suffered a number of setbacks through the impact on volunteers of the two NS schemes and the Pentropic reorganisation. The Millar Committee had been commissioned in 1973 to address perceived problems such as lack of a role, poor morale and organisational issues. A number of changes were recommended and implemented including a change in title to 'Army Reserve'; a major reorganisation affecting the status of the two infantry divisions; the amalgamation of under-strength units; improved conditions of service and the adoption of the 'One Army' concept.

A history of confusion and duplication of effort in the provision of defence aid to the civil community in time of major disasters prompted the Whitlam Government to create the Natural Disasters Organisation (NDO) within the Department of Defence in 1974. The NDO coordinated the defence efforts to support the civil defence organisations in the States and Territories. The first major Army commitment under the new organisation was the relief of Darwin following the devastation of Cyclone Tracy on 25th December 1974. Other major commitments have included bushfire, flood and earthquake relief, the provision of emergency shelter, evacuation of medical emergency cases and making dangerous ordnance safe, all performed in a range of locations throughout Australia.

In 1975, the *Defence Force Reorganisation Act* was passed as a result of the *Tange Report*, a review led by the Secretary of Defence, Sir Arthur Tange. The Act abolished the three Service Boards, designating the three Service chiefs of staff as the professional heads of their Services with full powers of command under higher defence direction. The position of Chief of the Defence Force Staff (CDFS) was redesignated

---

79 Dennis P, Grey J, Morris E, Prior R. *The Oxford Companion to Australian Military History (Second Edition)*. Australia, Oxford University Press: 2008, p. 557

80 Sgt R.T.R. Parker RAA, and Chaplain N.R. Mills.

81 General Sir Francis George Hassett, AC, KBE, CB, DSO, LVO; Commanding Officer 1st Bn RAR 1951, Commanding Officer 3rd Bn RAR 1951, Comd 28th Comm. Inf Bde 1960, DCGS 1963, GOC Nth Comd 1968, VCGS 1971, CGS 1973: born Marrickville NSW 11 Apr 1918 – died Canberra 11 Jun 2008.

AWM P04111.010 Courtesy of the Australian War Memorial. Rwanda 1995, Australian soldiers evacuating wounded civilians from Kibeho refugee camp

Chief of the Defence Force (CDF) in 1986; the CDF's prime task being to command the Defence Force and act as the principal military advisor to Government. The reorganisation of the Defence group of departments (Defence, Navy, Army, Air Force and Supply), combining all five within an enlarged Department of Defence, was completed.

During that period (1971-1977), the Army suffered heavily from financial cutbacks that were renewed with every successive Federal Government. These cutbacks slowly reduced the effectiveness of the Army and culminated in the early 1990s with the introduction of military redundancy packages designed to further reduce the size of the force. This was a time of continual restructuring to achieve the necessary financial economies required by Government budgets and in vesting increased power and influence in the Public Service element within Defence.

Peacekeeping – 1947-today

Australian Army commitments to international peacekeeping operations began in 1947 and continue to the present day. Australia has contributed forces of varying sizes to over 20 UN missions in Africa, the Middle East, and Asia. Australia has also assisted operations outside the control of the UN such as the Commonwealth Monitoring Force (CMF) in Rhodesia, the Multinational Force and Observers (MFO) in the Sinai and the Bougainville Peace Monitoring Group which was replaced in July 1998 by a UN mission.

One of the most important UN operations was the United Nations Transitional Authority in Cambodia (UNTAC), which was tasked with overseeing the disarming of 250,000

Cambodians and the restoration of a democratic government. The Australian Army provided both the commander of the UN force, LTGEN John Sanderson[82], and the 500 strong Force Communications Unit (FCU). Unified Task Force (UNITAF) (Somalia) saw 1 RAR deployed with supporting arms elements to provide protection to humanitarian aid in south-western Somalia. In Rwanda, a medical unit of 100 with a rifle company from 2 RAR and supporting troops provided medical support primarily for the UN force as part of United Nations Assistance Mission for Rwanda (UNAMIR).

The First Gulf War – 1990-1991

On 2nd August 1990, Iraq invaded Kuwait, initiating the First Gulf War. The UN-sanctioned operation to liberate Kuwait was launched on 17th January 1991, with the land offensive following on 24th February. A ceasefire was declared on 28th February, with a formal end to hostilities on 12th April 1991.

The RAN provided the main Australian contribution in the form of RAN Task Group 627.4 comprising two frigates and an underway replenishment ship. Because the replenishment ship had no air defence capability, a missile-launcher detachment from the Army's 16th Air Defence Regiment was also deployed. Two Australian surgical support teams comprising Army medical personnel were based aboard US Navy hospital ships in the area while other Army personnel served with a joint intelligence detachment and on individual exchanges with US and other Allied armies.

Following the ceasefire, Kurdish dissidents in Iraq staged an unsuccessful revolt against the regime of Saddam Hussein. Operation HABITAT was launched to assist Kurdish refugees in northern Iraq, with over 70 Army personnel deployed to provide engineering, medical, dental and logistic support. The Army also provided engineer officers to assist the UN Special Commission in the inspection of Iraqi chemical, biological and nuclear weapons capabilities.

East Timor – 1999-2013

Australia's involvement in East Timor dates from WWII when Australian soldiers fought the occupying Japanese. Following the Indonesian support for the anti-Fretilin Apodeti group in the chaos that followed the collapse of the colonial administration and the subsequent Indonesian invasion in December 1975, East Timor became a source of considerable strain on the Australia–Indonesia relationship. Fretilin waged a protracted guerrilla campaign for independence which, following the end of the Suharto regime in 1998, culminated

---

82 Lieutenant General John Murray Sanderson, AC; Comd 1st Field Engineer Regt 1975, Comd 1st Brigade 1987, Comd UNTAC 1991-1993, Chief of the General Staff 1995, Chief of the Army 1997, Governor of Western Australia 2000-2005: born Geraldton Western Australia 4 November 1940.

AWM ART91105 Courtesy of the Australian War Memorial. East Timor 1999-2000

in a UN-sponsored plebiscite on self-determination. The 1999 United Nations Assistance Mission to East Timor (UNAMET) was supported by Australian Defence Force (ADF) transport resources and included some military observers.

The plebiscite resulted in a 'pro-independence' result which not being accepted by many East Timorese with connections to Indonesia ushered in a period of civil chaos. Widespread violence by East Timorese militias threatened Australian nationals, and in September 1999, under Operation SPITFIRE, the ADF evacuated a large number of Australians and other nationalities (including many East Timorese) caught up in the violence.

Worldwide condemnation of the violence prompted the UN to commit a peacekeeping force to restore order. The UN agreed to the establishment of the Australian-led International Force East Timor (INTERFET) to stabilise the situation and hand over to the subsequent United Nations Transition Authority East Timor (UNTAET) to oversee the country's transition to independence. INTERFET (Operation WARDEN for the Australian component) was the largest deployment of Australian troops since the end of the Vietnam War. Liaison between Australia and Indonesia, especially at the military level, ensured there was no major opposition to the deployment of the INTERFET Forces on 20th September 1999. Having secured the capital Dili, Australian troops moved

out to occupy the remainder of the country. The key task was to protect the local population from violence at the hands of the local militia and some Indonesian military elements.

By early February 2000, INTERFET had pacified the country sufficiently to permit UNTAET to take responsibility. The Australian troop commitment (Operation TANAGER) continued under UNTAET, albeit reduced in size. UNTAET responsibilities included training local East Timorese in politics, administration and security until 23rd May 2002. Its role ended with the successful election of an East Timorese Government. UNTAET was replaced by the United Nations Mission to East Timor (UNMISET) which performed a purely advisory role, with some security responsibilities on the border. The remaining Australian battalion group took responsibility for the entire Tactical Control Line (the border with Indonesian West Timor) until the situation improved sufficiently to permit its withdrawal in May 2004. Training teams and support elements remained in Timor after the battalion group departed.

In 2006, internal unrest saw Australian troops return to East Timor, under UN sponsorship at the request of the East Timorese Government, to help stabilise the situation. The Australian commitment (the core of the force was the ANZAC Infantry Company), ended with the last Service personnel leaving Timor in January 2013.

The Second Gulf War – 2003-2011

The Australian Government provided a more substantial commitment following the resumption of hostilities in Iraq in March 2003, when a US-led coalition force invaded Iraq to topple Saddam Hussein and support the establishment of a democratic State in Iraq. This war was also part of the greater 'War on Terror' launched as a result of the 11th September 2001 terrorist attack on the US. Australia staged a three-phase deployment: (1) Operation BASTILLE, comprising the movement and build-up phase, (2) Operation FALCONER, the period of conflict and (3) Operation CATALYST, the stabilisation and rebuilding phase. The Army's commitment prior to Operation CATALYST was limited to Special Forces, operating as Task Force 633.3. Once the brief but intense period of conventional war ended and the task of the coalition force turned to stabilisation and nation-building, the composition of the Australian Army commitment changed.

Coalition force levels had declined following the US President's victory claim in 2003; however, in response to a deteriorating security situation, a major reinforcement of troops occurred in 2005. The focus for the Australians became twofold: (1) an Overwatch function to ensure continued security in Al Muthanna and Dhi Qar Provinces, and (2) a renewed emphasis on training the new Iraqi Army. A number of battle groups rotated through the main base at Tallil, while a smaller contingent (the Security Detachment) provided security for Australian diplomatic personnel in Baghdad.

Many individual Service personnel were embedded within the coalition forces. At any one time, about 1,450 Australian personnel were in Iraq during this phase of operations. Operation CATALYST ended when the final 11 personnel embedded in coalition forces were withdrawn on 29th July 2009. The 35-strong Security Detachment (Operation KRUGER) came to an end in Baghdad in late-July 2011.

In 2014, due to the Islamic terrorists in Syria and Iraq, the Australian Government sent a detachment of Special Forces to boost security at the Australian Embassy in Baghdad and has committed other ADF resources to a 'humanitarian mission' in that region.

Afghanistan – 2001-2013

With the terrorist attack on the US on 11th September 2001, the Australian Government invoked the mutual defence clause of the ANZUS treaty to commit Australian combat forces to the International Coalition Against Terrorism (ICAT). Australia designated this involvement Operation SLIPPER. The perpetrators of the terrorist attacks, Al Qaeda, were operating from the Taliban-governed country of Afghanistan. The collapse of the communist Government of Afghanistan in 1992 was followed by several years of civil war between a number of different factions, including the Taliban (a fundamentalist Islamist group) and several warlords. Much of the fighting was based on tribal divisions. By 1996, the Taliban had gained control over much of Afghanistan.

Image courtesy of Department of Defence - 20050725cpa8267338_003. Bushmaster on Patrol – Afghanistan

Image courtesy of Department of Defence - 20100220adf8246638_234. Australian Patrol - Afghanistan

The US President, George W. Bush, initiated 'Operation ENDURING FREEDOM' on 7th October 2001 with the express intention of removing the Taliban Government and suppressing terrorist activity in the country. Occupation of the country was largely achieved within a few weeks and on 22nd December a new interim Government of Afghanistan was formed. On 2nd December 2001, the Australian and New Zealand Special Forces Task Group arrived to join coalition forces in the hunt for terrorist cells in the more remote and rugged parts of the country. After a year of intense operations, the Australian land commitment was reduced to small numbers of liaison and mine clearance personnel.

In 2005, following an upsurge in Taliban activity in Afghanistan, the Australian Government recommitted ground forces to the operation. In September, the first elements, the Special Forces component of the renewed Special Forces Task Group, arrived followed by a detachment of two helicopters.

In May 2006, additional troops were committed to support a new NATO-led International Security Assistance Force (ISAF) with a Reconstruction Task Force deployed to operate with Dutch troops in Uruzgan Province. The Australian commitment increased in number over subsequent years. In 2010 there were 1,550 ADF personnel serving in Afghanistan, plus another 800 Operation SLIPPER personnel elsewhere in the Middle East.

On 26th March 2013 the Australian Government announced the withdrawal of all combat troops from Afghanistan, with the exception of some specialist elements, by the end of that year.

Four 'Victoria Cross for Australia' (VC) were awarded to soldiers of RAR, the Special Air Service Regiment (SASR) and the 2nd Commando Regiment (2 Cdo Regt) during the Afghan engagement.

Army Titles[83]

It is easy to get confused by the various shortened forms used to describe the military organisations that have served the country during both peace and war. Both the full-time and part-time Army have had many different names. The following is a list of abbreviations, acronyms and initialisms used:

1901-1915:	**Commonwealth Military Forces (CMF)**
PMF	Permanent Military Forces
CF	Citizen Forces
SC	Senior Cadets
AIEF	Australian Imperial Expeditionary Force (later shortened to AIF and used until 1921)
1916-1929:	**Australian Military Forces (AMF)**
PMF	Permanent Military Forces
CF	Citizen Forces
CMF	Citizen Military Forces (formed 1921)
SC	Senior Cadets (discontinued in 1929)
AIF	Australian Imperial Force
1930-1939:	**Australian Military Forces (AMF)**
PMF	Permanent Military Forces
Militia	Also referred to unofficially as either the CMF or Australian Militia Forces (AMF)
1939-1942:	**Australian Military Forces (AMF)**
PMF	Permanent Military Forces
Militia	Also referred to unofficially as the Australian Militia Forces (AMF)
AIF	Australian Imperial Force
1943-1947:	**Australian Military Forces (AMF)**
PMF	Permanent Military Forces
CMF	Citizen Military Forces
AIF	Australian Imperial Force
ARA	Australian Regular Army (ARA)
1947-1985:	**Australian Military Forces (AMF)**
ARA - NS	Australian Regular Army (six-year initial enlistment) – National Service
ARA-S (O)	Australian Regular Army Supplement (three-year initial enlistment)
ACMF	Australian Citizen Military Forces
1985-1996:	**Australian Army**
ARA	Australian Regular Army
GRes/ARes	General Reserve or Army Reserve
RRes	Ready Reserve
1996-2010:	**Australian Army**
ARA	Australian Regular Army
GRes/ARes	General Reserve or Army Reserve

---

83 Australian War Memorial. https://www.awm.gov.au/atwar/structure/

Military Districts[84]

On Federation (1 January 1901), for various reasons, the States were permitted to maintain control of their local forces whilst the newly-appointed GOC (the Army), MAJGEN ETH Hutton, in concert with the new Parliament, drafted what was to become the *Defence Act 1903*. Initially each MD was responsible for the raising and training of local Militia units; these areas were simply known by the States' name.

The introduction of the Universal Training Scheme (UTS) in 1911[85] necessitated altering the existing MD boundaries in order to establish a more viable system of command and control, although the old State boundaries continued to be the basis for the newly-established MDs. The new MDs were given numerical designations from 1st to 6th (see Figure 1), the Northern Territory initially being administered by South Australia.

After WWI, and until WWII, the designation of the districts was changed to District Base (DB), for example, 2nd District Base (2DB – New South Wales) or 3rd District Base (3DB – Victoria).

This change was superficial and lasted only until the beginning of WWII when the old commands were reorganised into geographical commands, with 1MD becoming Northern Command, 2MD Eastern Command, 5MD Western Command and the three southern States combined under Southern Command. In 1939, the Northern Territory was designated 7MD whilst Papua New Guinea, a protectorate of Australia, had been designated 8MD (see Figure 2).

This new system lasted until 1942, after which Queensland, New South Wales, Victoria, South Australia and Tasmania were designated Lines of Communications Areas, Western Australia remained unchanged, 7MD became Northern Territory Force and 8 MD became New Guinea Force.

The geographical commands were re-established after the war (see Figure 3) with South Australia becoming Central Command and New Guinea Force reverting to Papua New Guinea Command.[86] These headquarters exercised command over all units, for example, field force training and support units within their area of control until Functional Commands were set up in 1972 (see Figure 4).

The three new Functional Commands, Field Force Command, Logistic Command and Training Command, took on the role of commanding all units allocated to their organisation, regardless of their geographical location. The functional arrangement created some command and control concerns with GOC Training Command having responsibility for approximately 57 direct-command units. This reduction in responsibilities reduced the MD HQs to a purely administrative organisation charged with commanding those units not allocated to one of the Functional Commands, such as training areas, rifle ranges, cadets, Army Reserve administration, local ceremonial commitments and providing liaison between the State Governments and the Army for Defence Aid to the Civil Community (DACC) and Defence Force Aid to the Civil Authorities (DFACA) tasks.

84 Dennis P, Grey J, Morris E, Prior R. *The Oxford Companion to Australian Military History*, South Melbourne, Oxford University Press: 2008, pp. 362-3

85 Wood J. *Chiefs of the Australian Army: Higher Command of the Australian Military Forces 1901-1914*. Bayswater, Victoria, Shannon Books: 2006.

86 Dennis P, Grey J, Morris E, Prior R. *The Oxford Companion to Australian Military History*, South Melbourne, Oxford University Press: 2008, p. 404

Military District Evolution

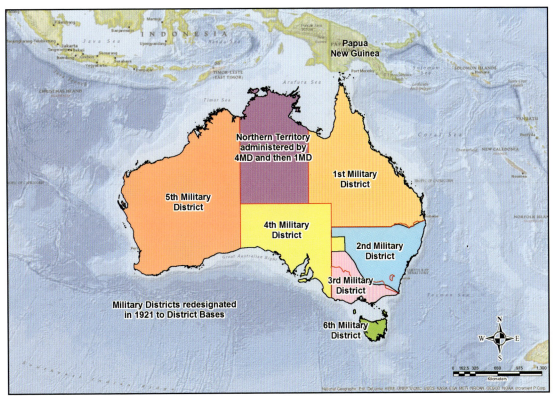

Figure 1 – about 1911 to 1938[87]

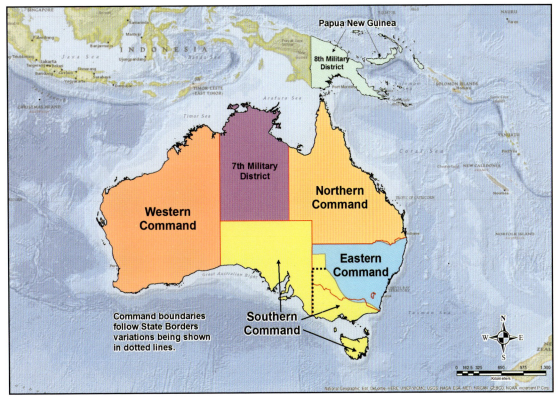

Figure 2 – about 1939 to 1950

---

87 Long G. *Australia in the War of 1939-1945, Series 1, Army, Volume I, To Benghazi.* Adelaide, The Advertiser Printing Office: 1961, p. 28 (The three maps showing 1911 to 1972 are based on the single map contained in the book)

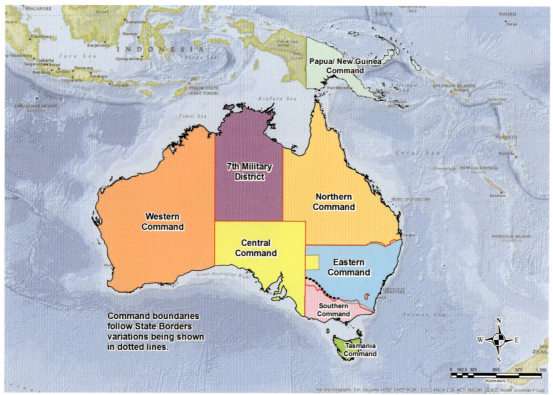

Figure 3 – about 1950 to 1972

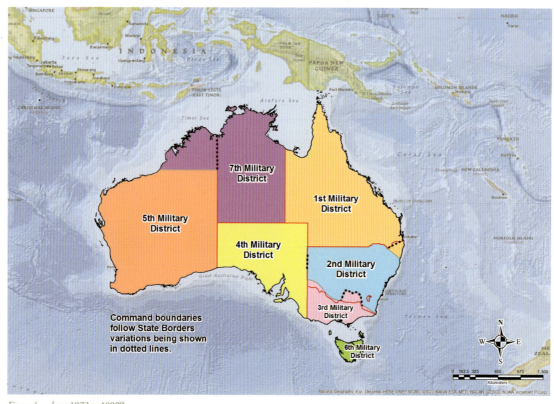

Figure 4 – about 1972 to 1990[88]
Mapas courtesy of Alex Taubert

---

88   Map adapted from 'The Soldiers Handbook' – 1969

Chapter Two

Military Ranks, Insignia and Flags

Badges of rank are used to indicate seniority within the Australian Army and provide a hierarchical structure where members may be superior, equal or subordinate in rank. The Australian Army rank structure is based on the British system and is divided into four distinct groups, being: Commissioned Officers, Warrant Officers, Non-Commissioned Officers and Other Ranks (OR). Ranks provide structure to the military organisation and gives authority to a commander, at whatever level, to exercise command over subordinate formations, units or individuals.

Army Command Structure

Understanding the Army command structure is an important step in being able to understand the hierarchy of ranks in the Army. Manning is flexible and subject to change according to Corps and operational needs. The basic building block of an army is the infantry (INF) section (SECT) usually consisting of nine men including their LCPL 2IC and CPL. Three SECTs make a platoon (PL), commanded by a LT. Three rifle PLs and a small headquarters (HQ) form a company (COY), generally with a MAJ as the Officer Commanding (OC). Three rifle COYs, a HQ and internal support elements such as specialist weapons PLs including mortars, snipers, reconnaissance and anti-tank, medical personnel and so on make up a battalion (BN), commanded by a LTCOL (the Commanding Officer or CO). This organisation is termed a unit; its component parts are called sub-units.

A brigade (BDE) consists of a HQ, three INF BNs, and a Royal Australian Corps of Signals (RASigs) squadron supplemented by other Arms and Services units such as The Royal Regiment of Australian Artillery (RAA), Armour (RAAC), Ordnance (RAAOC), Engineers (RAE) and Transport (RACT) totalling between 3000 and 5000 personnel and commanded by a BRIG. A division (DIV) (the smallest formation to be self-supporting) comprises three BDEs, includes additional supporting units and is commanded by a MAJGEN. A corps consists of two or three DIVs, and is a LTGEN's command, and is similar to a DIV in possessing additional Corps Troops held at the HQ level. A minimum of two Corps may be grouped to form an Army, commanded by a General along with an allocation of Army Troops. Finally two or more Armies would be commanded by a Field Marshall (the highest rank possible within the British system), equivalent to a 'General of the Army' within the United States Army (5 Star General).

The following shows the basic command hierarchy:

Rank	Element Commanded	Second-in-Command	Span of Command
Private (PTE)			
Lance Corporal (LCPL)			
Corporal (CPL)	Section (SECT)	Lance Corporal (LCPL)	9 soldiers
Sergeant (SGT)			
Warrant Officer Class Two (WO2)			
Warrant Officer Class One (WO1)			
Lieutenant (LT)	Platoon (PL)	Sergeant (SGT)	3 Sections (SECT)
Captain (CAPT)			
Major (MAJ)	Company (COY)	Captain (CAPT)	3 Platoons (PL) plus support – Task Element/Combat Team.
Lieutenant Colonel (LTCOL)	Battalion (BN)	Major (MAJ)	4 Companies (COY) plus support – Task Force/Battle Group
Colonel (COL)			
Brigadier (BRIG)	Brigade (BDE)	Colonel (COL)	3 Battalions (BN) plus support
Major General (MAJGEN)	Division (DIV)	Brigadier (BRIG)	3 Brigades (BDE) plus support
Lieutenant General (LTGEN)	Corps	Major General (MAJGEN)	3 Divisions (DIV) plus support
General (GEN)	Army	Lieutenant General (LTGEN)	3 Corps plus support
Field Marshal (FM)	Army Group (GP)	General (GEN)	More than 1 Army – an Army Group plus support

The size of a standard rifle SECT has varied over the years from 6 to 12 riflemen. Since the 2000s, depending on the battalion, it could be as low as eight or as high as 10 in a motorised or mechanised BN, whilst a Cdo SECT is usually a team of up to 12. Furthermore a rifle PL can vary from three to four SECTs and a BN from four to six COYs. The ranks without 'command elements' perform specific roles, generally operational and logistical planning, within the command structure.

Regiment or Battalion

The term 'regiment' has always enjoyed a precise organisational definition in the American and similar armies, which it lacks entirely in the British system. In the INF, a regiment may comprise three BNs, or nine as in RAR, or may be used to encompass the whole organisation such as in RAA. In the American system a 'regiment' is the equivalent of a BDE, or if designated a Regimental Combat Team as used in Korea and Vietnam, a BDE Group. There were numerous other variations to the Army organisation in the 20th century, including those involving machine gun BNs, mounted, armoured and army tank regiments, and the introduction and demise of the Task Force in the 1960s-1970s briefly resurrected for trial purposes in 1990.[89] The Australian regimental structure is also used in RAA, RAAC, RAE, RASigs and AAAvn.

---

89 Dennis P, Grey J, Morris E, Prior R. *The Oxford Companion to Australian Military History (Second Edition)*. Australia, Oxford University Press: 2008, p. XVII

Rank Terminology

The ranks used in today's Army can be traced to Cromwell's New Army[90] in which the ranks of the Officers were:

- Captain-General   Commander-in-Chief
- Lieutenant-General   Commanded the Cavalry
- Sergeant-Major-General   Commanded the Infantry
- Colonel   Commanded a Regiment
- Sergeant-Major   Staff Officer of the Regiment
- Lieutenant-Colonel   Second-in-Command to a Colonel
- Captain   Commander of a Company
- Lieutenant   Assistant to the Captain
- Ensign   Carried the Standard or Colour

Remove the word 'Captain' from Captain-General, the word 'Sergeant' from Sergeant-Major-General and the Sergeant Major rank and the seniority of our modern Army ranks remain almost unaltered. This highlights the fact that then as now the cavalry were considered senior to infantry troops and were therefore commanded by a person of higher rank. The rank of Sergeant-Major was originally a commissioned officer.

Soldier

Soldier is a generic term for any member of the Australian Army.

The term 'soldier' comes from ancient Rome, where soldiers were given a handful of salt each day which they could trade. The salt ration was subsequently replaced by a sum of money, which relieved the commissariat of the trouble of transporting salt. The money received was referred to as their 'salt money' (salarium in Latin). Eventually, the term would make its way into medieval France, where a soldier's payment was known as his solde (which is still in use today as the term for a soldier's or sailor's pay), and it was paid with a special coin called a sol; which came to refer, not only to a soldier's wage, but also to the soldier himself. The Old French word 'soudier' became the Middle English 'souder' from which we get the English word 'soldier'.

Private

The origin of the word Private is the Latin 'privatus' and derives from the French 'privies' meaning single. One train of thought has it that the rank of PTE is a corruption of the term Private Man or Gentleman; up to the end of the 17th century a soldier was described as a private sentinel: 1 of 100, which is approximately the strength of an army company. Whatever the truth may be, there is no doubt that modern terminology has the Private as the base rank and denotes a fully-trained soldier.

When enlisted into the military a soldier begins his career as a Recruit. Although legally a PTE soldier, he retains this title until he has completed his initial training and subsequent Corps specific training at which stage he is formally referred to as a PTE soldier or Corps-equivalent.

The following ranks are equivalent to a PTE but have different names within their respective organisations or Corps:

- Trooper (TPR) – Royal Australian Armoured Corps, Australian Army Aviation and Special Air Service Regiment
- Gunner (GNR) – Royal Australian Artillery
- Sapper (SPR) – Royal Australian Engineers
- Signaller (SIG) – Royal Australian Corps of Signals
- Craftsman (CFN) – Royal Corps of Australian Electrical and Mechanical Engineers
- Musician (MUSN) – Australian Army Band Corps.

In most modern armies the PTE is often referred to in slang terms; for instance the American 'GI' (General Issue) or 'Doughboy', or the British 'Tommy' or 'Squaddie', whilst the Australian soldier has since WWI been called 'Digger'. Although used prior to 1917, the common usage of the term 'digger' has been credited to Captain (CAPT) Sandy's greeting to his troops at Flanders.[91]

---

90   Gentles I. *The New Model Army – In England, Ireland and Scotland 1645-1653*. Oxford, Blackwell Press: 1994
91   Horne CD. *Salt*. Melbourne, Educational Publications, Army Headquarters: 24 April 1944

The rank of PTE (Proficient) written PTE (P) denotes recognition of proficiency with an accompanying pay increment and does not indicate seniority within the rank. This is equivalent to Able Seaman in the RAN and Leading Aircraftman/woman in the RAAF.

Some Corps have retained the rank of PTE; however, they use the member's qualification as a method of addressing them, for example:

- Patrolman (PTLN) – used locally by Regional Force Surveillance Units (RFSUs) in Northern Australia, and

- Medic.

Rank Insignia. The rank of PTE has no distinctive rank insignia.

Non-Commissioned Officers

Non-commissioned officers (NCO) hold ranks from LCPL through to Staff Sergeant (SSGT). Junior non-commissioned officers (JNCO) hold the rank of LCPL or CPL whereas senior non-commissioned officers (SNCO) hold the rank of SGT or SSGT. Rank and File (R&F), also known as Other Ranks (ORs), refers to the ranks of PTE through to CPL.

Lance Corporal

This is normally a PTE soldier's first promotion and is termed a JNCO. A LCPL is normally the 2IC of a SECT of soldiers in an INF unit. Originally, called Lancespesate[92], taken from the Italian meaning broken or spent lance. Various spellings of this rank may be found in English books dating back to the 1600s such as 'lantsprezado' and 'lanspesado'.[93] Regardless of the difference in the way the rank is spelt, the rank was always subordinate to that of CPL.

The Lancespesate (LCPL) is a gentleman of ancient standing in the militia as he draws his pedigree from the time of the wars between the kings of France, Francis I and his son Henry II. In a skirmish, battle or encounter the Lancespesate had broken his lance on the enemy and lost his horse in the scuffle, he was then entertained, under the name of 'broken lance', by a Captain of a foot company as his comrade until he was again mounted. Sometime after the Monsieur Lancespesate (as he later became known) was forced to descend from being the Captain's comrade, he became the CPL's companion, who assimilated him in the exercise of his charge, and therefore was sometime called by the French, 'aide caporal' (or the CPL's assistant) and for that, some extra allowance was paid.[94]

Lance Bombardier

This rank title, which is inherited from the British Army, is exclusive to RAA and is equivalent to the rank of LCPL. An original Bombardier (BDR) was the specialist who looked after the bombard (early cannon), howitzer or mortar. Their main responsibility was to cut the fuse of the mortar or howitzer shell to length so that it would explode just before or as it touched the ground after being fired. They also inserted the fuse into the shell.

The rank of BDR dates back to at least the 17th century. Originally, the Royal Artillery had CPLs (but not LCPLs, a bombardier held full non-commissioned rank and was not an acting appointment). The rank was equivalent to second corporal in the Royal Engineers and Army Ordnance Corps.

In 1920, CPLs were abolished in the Royal Artillery and BDR became the equivalent and acquired the normal two chevrons.

The rank of LBDR originated as acting BDR, an appointment similar to LCPL, which was also indicated by a single chevron. The appointment was renamed LBDR in February 1918 and became a full rank in the British Army, as did LCPL, in 1961.

Rank Insignia. LCPL/LBDR rank insignia is a single chevron.

There is no equivalent rank for LCPL or LBDR in the RAN or the RAAF.

Corporal

This word is a corruption of the Italian 'Caporale' (head of a section) and is also from the Spanish 'Cabo de esquarda' or 'Caporall'. This in turn is derived from the Latin Capo meaning a head or leader. The earliest use of this rank can be traced back to pre-1588 when it was used to describe the individual parts of a British company as 'Corporolates' commanded by CPLs or SGTs.[95] A variation of the rank of CPL was introduced into the British Army by Charles II in 1661, when he created The Life Guards Regiment.[96] It was logical therefore for Charles II to introduce that rank when he wanted some junior officers in the Body Guard. For many years in both the Life Guards and the Yeomen of the Guard the rank of CPL denoted the lowest commissioned rank, equivalent to that of LT in the rest of the British Army. The appointment of CPL in France was a commissioned rank roughly equivalent to Captain (which is how Napoleon Bonaparte later came to be known as 'le petit caporal', 'the little Corporal').

92 Gordon, LL. *Military Origins.* New York, A. S. Barnes: 1971, p. 217
93 Markham F. *Five Decades of Epistles of Warre.* Augustine Matthewes, England: 1622, p. 73
94 Grose F. *Military Antiquities Respecting a History of the English Army V2.* London, Kessinger Legacy: 1786, p. 312

95 Smythe J. *Certain Discourses.* London, Richard Johns: 1590, p. 7-C3
96 Paget J. *The Yeomen of the Guard, Five Hundred Years of Service 1485-1985.* Poole, Dorset, Blandford Press: 1984, p. 96

*Left: Colour Sergeant Rank
– Ceremonial White*

*Right: Colour Sergeant Rank
– Patrol Blues*

Bombardier

This rank is exclusive to RAA and is equivalent to the rank of CPL; see LBDR.

Rank Insignia. CPL/BDR rank insignia is two chevrons.

Sergeant

The rank of SGT dates back to the English feudal system where landowners used serfs to fight their battles. As a mark of respect, sons and personal servants of the great vassals were put in charge of groups of field serfs and others with a lesser station in life. After a few changes in nomenclature, these 'chosen ones' were merged together under the generic name of 'servientes' (from the Latin meaning 'serving'), and this term was finally corrupted into its present form of sergeants.

Rank Insignia. SGT rank insignia is three chevrons.

Staff Sergeant

Staff Sergeant (SSGT) was a product of a later day, when a SGT, often the eldest son of the most powerful of the greater vassals who owed allegiance to a particular baron, was selected to carry the coat-of-arms of that baron into battle.

The Banner bearing his heraldic device was raised on a pole or staff, and thus SSGT became an accepted term. In more modern times this Banner holder was designated 'Colour Sergeant' in the British Army. In the Australian Army the rank of SSGT is the highest of the 'non-commissioned'

ranks which often brings confusion with the rank of Warrant Officer. WOs have a Warrant and therefore are not Non-Commissioned by definition. The rank of SSGT is no longer a rank on the Army establishment and therefore does not appear in the rank structure of the Army; however, remaining members holding the rank do so until they are either promoted or separated from the Service.

Rank Insignia. SSGT rank insignia is the St Edward's Crown over three chevrons.

The ranks of SGT and SSGT are classified as Senior Non-Commissioned Officers (SNCO).

Colour Sergeant

This rank was first introduced by the British as a reward for distinguished service, by a General Order dated 6 July 1813.[97] There was one Colour Sergeant to each company with the position attracting an increase in pay. The rank of Colour Sergeant is nominally maintained within the Australian Army by the Royal Military College - Duntroon (RMC-D) who have one Colour Sergeant per company in the Corps of Staff Cadets (CSC).

Rank Insignia. The rank badge consists of three chevrons surmounted by a St Edward's Crown and crossed Australian National Flags highlighted with gold thread.

97   Edwards TJ. *Standards, Guidons and Colours of the Commonwealth Forces*. Aldershot, England, Gale & Polden:1953, p. 104

Australian Army
Warrant

To *Stephen Craig Taubert*

By authority *of the Defence Act 1903 and of the Regulations made thereunder, you have been appointed to be a Warrant Officer in the Australian Army on and from* 8TH SEPTEMBER 1986

You are, therefore, carefully and diligently to discharge your duty by doing all things thereunto belonging as required by military law and so to conduct yourself that you ensure respect for lawful authority and uphold the honourable tradition of the rank to which you have been appointed.

Dated this 27th *day of* NOVEMBER *in the year* 1986

Canberra

Major General
Chief of Personnel

Warrant Certificate – 1986

Warrant Officer / Sergeant Major

One of the earliest records found (1598) describes a Sergeant Major as an officer appointed from amongst the available Colonels to command a regiment of sundry companies and to be 'Superintendent of all the sergeants of the same'.[98] The rank was also used prior to this as a prefix to denote higher classes of rank within a given appointment, for instance Sergeant Major-Major and Sergeant Major-General.[99]

By the end of the 17th century, Sergeant Major (Major denoting senior) was the rank of the SNCO in the unit. In 1879, the Sergeant Majors were given Warrant rank, thus becoming Warrant Officers as we know them today. A Royal Warrant was traditionally given to officers on appointment for a specific time or event which on expiration ceased to have effect. When appointed to the rank of Warrant Officer, it signified the member being presented with such a Warrant; the Warrant is issued on behalf of Army by the Director General Personnel. In earlier times a new Warrant was given when promoted to Warrant Officer Class One but this was changed to today's custom of presenting only one Warrant; regardless of promotion to WO1, or following discharge and later re-enlistment in either the regular or reserve force the Warrant is said to be still in force. The Australian Army has two levels of Warrant Officer.

Warrant Officer Class Two

Warrant Officer Class Two (WO2) can hold the appointment of Company Sergeant Major (CSM), Squadron Sergeant Major (SSM), Battery Sergeant Major (BSM), Operations Warrant Officer (OPSWO), Training Warrant Officer (TRGWO), Sergeant Major Instructor Gunnery (SMIG), Regimental Quartermaster Sergeant (RQMS), Technical Quartermaster Sergeant (TQMS), Artificer Sergeant Major (ASM), Troop Sergeant Major (TSM) a position now held in Artillery Gun Regiments, Battalion Chief Clerk or a number of training and/or administrative positions. A member holding the rank of WO2 who is appointed as a CSM (equivalent) is addressed as Sergeant Major. Conversely, a WO2 who is employed in another appointment, other than CSM or equivalent, is addressed as Warrant Officer or by their particular appointment, such as OPSWO.

Rank Insignia. WO2 rank insignia is the St Edward's Crown. To avoid confusion with the worn rank of MAJ, the St Edwards Crown for DPCU worn by WO2 has a black square around it.

WO2 is technically equivalent to Chief Petty Officer in the RAN and Flight Sergeant in the RAAF; Chief Petty Officer and Flight Sergeant do not hold a Warrant and are by definition Non-Commissioned.

---

98 Barret R. The *Theorike and Practike of Moderne Warres*. London, William Ponsonby: 1598, p. 92
99 Smythe Sir J. *Certain Discourses*. London, Richard Johns: 1590, p. 10-D1

Warrant Officer Class One

The rank of WO1 was introduced in the British Army in 1915[100] and in the Australian Army in 1917. A WO1 can hold the position of RSM of a BN or equivalent-sized unit, or RSM of a BDE or larger formation. There are, in addition to this, trade positions held by the most senior WO1 of a unit such as Artificer Sergeant Major (ASM) and Regimental Quartermaster Sergeant (RQMS) or Quartermaster (QM), RAA Regimental Master Gunner (RAA Corps RSM).

In 1983 the position of Regimental Sergeant Major–Army (RSM-A) was established. RSM-A is the senior WO1 in Army. The first incumbent was WO1 Wally Thompson, OAM. The RSM-A is personally selected by the Chief of Army (CA), from a list of the most experienced and highest-performing RSMs provided by the Directorate of Soldier Career Management. To be eligible a soldier must have served in several RSM appointments including at the Division or Command level. In 1991, the honorary rank of Warrant Officer (WO) was established to set RSM-A apart from all other WO1. A unique badge of rank for RSM-A was also established at that time. In 1993 the practice of appointing a senior, or Service-level, WO was established by the RAN and the RAAF.[101]

Rank Insignia. The rank insignia for WO1 is the Australian coat of arms; and the rank insignia for the appointment of WO (RSM-A) is the Australian coat of arms surrounded by a wreath.

Warrant Officers should never be referred to as SNCOs; they are officers by 'Warrant' issued from the CA on promotion to WO2.

Specialist Warrant Officer Appointments

WO1 is the senior rank of most trades within the Army. Trade specialist WO1 are seldom posted into the position of RSM and hold such positions as Master Gunner and other Corps-specific appointments.

Conductors. Within RAAOC 'Conductors' appointments are held by selected WO1 and are considered the most senior appointment that can be held by a Warrant Officer in a particular trade group. The appointment of Conductors ceased in the Australian Army in the 1940s but was reintroduced in 2005.

Master of the Band. The rank of Master of the Band was sanctioned in 1807. Although the title Drum-Major appears in old records, as a true rank it was not introduced into the Infantry until 1810, and the circumstances of its recognition are most interesting. Previously, Drum-Majors had been held on establishments, and from the point of view of the Treasury, were paid as drummers. In practice however, they had long enjoyed the status and pay of sergeants, the necessary funds

Appointment to
Regimental Sergeant Major - Army

Conferred upon

8261329 Warrant Officer David Malcolm Ashley, OAM

You are appointed as the Regimental Sergeant Major of the Australian Army and granted the privileges and responsibilities that go with the position. This imposes unique obligations on you and requires dedication to the values and ethos of the Australian Army and the nation.

I charge you with ensuring these values are upheld by personal example and through commitment to developing pride in these values in all ranks of the Army. Consulting widely and be impartial and fearless in delivering your advice. Strive to maintain self-control and discipline at all times, and ensure your personal integrity is above reproach. Swiftly correct any harassment or prejudice that you see and then inform the chain of command. Engage, challenge and empower all our junior ranks. Foster strong leadership amongst the Non Commissioned Officers of the Army. Carry out your assigned duties with diligence and initiative.

The appointment as the Regimental Sergeant Major of the Army set you apart from all other members of the organisation. Understand your authority and influence and use it wisely.

D.L. MORRISON, AO
Lieutenant General
Chief of Army

4   October 2011

Certificate of Appointment – RSM-A

having been raised by the levying of a small amount of pay from the remainder of the unit's drummers. In 1810, Drum-Majors were granted the actual rank and pay of sergeant. At the same time, the establishment of drummers was reduced by one.[102]

Mode of Address. Warrant Officers in the Army are addressed by subordinates according to their gender as either 'Sir' or 'Ma'am'. They can be addressed by commissioned officers by their rank, for example, Warrant Officer Bloggs, or according to their appointment, for example, CSM (Company Sergeant Major), SSM (Squadron Sergeant Major), BSM (Battery Sergeant Major) or RSM (Regimental Sergeant Major).

100 British Army Order 70/1915 XIX. *Warrant Officers, Class II*: 1915
101 Correspondence: WO Dave Ashley (RSM-A)/Les Terrett 5 June 2014

102 Farmer HG. *The Rise & Development of Military Music*. London, WM Reeves: 1882, p. 25

Wearing of Non-Commissioned Rank

Subject to the uniform being worn, badges of rank may be positioned on the sleeves on the upper arm, on the chest of field dress on a single slide and with the introduction of the new Mess Dress insignia the rank is worn on the shoulder epaulettes.

Redundant Non-Commissioned Officer Ranks

Although passed into history, the following ranks provide colour and depth to our rank structure.

King's Corporal and Kitchener Sergeant

The history of King's Corporal and Kitchener Sergeant in the Australian Army is known to some, but is frequently the subject of argument. A writer to the Journal of Army Historical Research 1935[103] stated that the current tradition of the rank was instituted as a reward for gallantry during the South African War and existed during that campaign only. Private soldiers, it was said, once promoted to the rank of King's Corporal (supernumerary to the Unit's establishment) could never be reduced in rank except by the King himself.

In the same journal for 1936, a reprint from the Naval and Military Journal quoted the following on the subject of King's Corporal, which apparently was a 'mention':

> There was an official suggestion in 1901 to the effect that soldiers who had distinguished themselves in war-time, but were unsuited to be an NCO in peace-time, should be given some mark of distinction on the right arm, preferably an embroidered band, carrying with it a step in rank whilst actually on active service, with additional pay, a donation of £10.

Some members of the War Office Committee who sat to consider the proposal objected to the monetary grant, arguing that such was derogatory to the soldier, but one member pointed out that 'Lord Roberts had not hesitated to accept £100,000, so could not see why a soldier should object to receiving £10.' The idea, however, was not adopted, though some men, in addition to those promoted to King's Corporal, were specially promoted in the field in the latter stages of the Boer War, to a rank generally known as 'Kitchener Sergeant'.[104]

Many inquiries were made during WWII as to whether the rank of King's Corporal had ever really existed. On 22nd October 1944 a letter appeared in the London Times referring to a statement made by the Secretary of State for War in the British Parliament on 10th October that year. It had been asked on what authority Lord Kitchener had promoted a rifleman of the Rifle Brigade to the rank of King's Corporal

on 8th December 1901. The Times writer asked: 'Can any authority say what the award is intended to convey to the recipient if it is not recognised by the War Office?'

During the South African War, Australian contingents had King's Corporals and Kitchener Sergeants. It is recorded in official orders that two Corporals and a Lance Corporal were promoted to Sergeant and five Troopers, a Lance Corporal and a Private were promoted to Corporal by the Commander-in-Chief for gallantry in the field. These were termed 'King's Corporals' and 'Kitchener Sergeants' and the promotions were announced in orders under the heading of 'mentions', and were published in the London Gazette.

The order announcing the promotions stated that 'the General Commander-in-Chief had been pleased to sanction the following promotions of NCO and men for distinguished gallantry in the field (should they be desirous of accepting it). Such promotion to take effect in each case from the date mentioned on which the act was performed.' All promotions were recorded in a Commonwealth General Order or British General Order.

Lance Sergeant

The word 'Lance' in Lance Sergeant and Lance Corporal literally means 'lance' (see LCPL). Mounted men were considered (and endeavour to appear) superior to those on foot and when unhorsed in battle the lance which the ex-mounted man carried still indicated his superiority and gave him certain prestige over the foot soldier. A CPL permanently acting in the position of a SGT, but not qualified to be promoted, was given this rank. It was discontinued after the end of WWII (about 1946).

Honorary Rank - WWI

Honorary rank is not 'substantive' rank and should not be confused as such. Regulations under the Defence Act 1903-1917[105] approved the granting of 'honorary rank' as follows:

> Warrant Officers Class I, after five years' service in that Class, may be granted the honorary rank of Lieutenant.
>
> Warrant Officers Class II, after five years' service in that Class, may be granted the honorary rank of Warrant Officer Class I.
>
> Warrant Officers with less than five years' service in Class I or II may be permitted to retain their rank.
>
> Staff Sergeants and Sergeants, after five years' service in the rank of Staff Sergeant or Sergeant, may be granted the honorary rank of Warrant Officer Class II.
>
> It is not known when the practice was repealed or superseded.

103 Society for Army Historical Research. *Journal of the Society for Army Historical Research. London:* 1936, p. 245
104 Society for Army Historical Research. *Journal of the Society for Army Historical Research. London:* 1936, p. 62

105 Defence Act 1903 – 1917. *Statutory Rules 1918 N0. 2:* 10 Jan 1918

Officers in Training[106] - Officer Cadet and Staff Cadet

There are three methods of graduating as an Army Officer from the Royal Military College - Duntroon (RMC-D) termed as a 'General Service Officer' (GSO):

- Direct entry into RMC-D 18-months' training,

- Entry via the Australian Defence Force Academy (ADFA) and on graduation enter RMC-D for a further 12-months' training, and

- University Regiments (for Reserve members) which conduct officer training but are administered by RMC-D.

The rank of Officer Cadet (OCDT) is given to those who are studying at the ADFA. Their rank is then changed to Staff Cadet (SCDT) upon entry to the RMC-D where they become a member of the Corps of Staff Cadets (CSC).

Historically, the title of SCDT technically referred only to those selected candidates undertaking training at the Royal Military College of Australia (RMC-A) who, upon graduation, were appointed to the Australian Staff Corps. The CSC was originally raised as a subordinate, or feeder, Corps to the Australian Staff Corps. With the disbanding of the Australian Staff Corps in 1981, the CSC became the senior Corps of the Australian Army.

The title SCDT continues to apply only to those full-time GSO cadets appointed to the CSC undertaking training at RMC-D. The title does not apply to OCDTs undertaking training under the Army Reserve Part-Time First Appointment Course within the various university regiments.

OCDTs wear a 10mm wide white stripe, on a Disruptive Pattern Camouflage Uniform (DPCU) slide or hard shoulder board, as their rank insignia. Officer Trainees in University Regiments undergoing Army Reserve Officer Training have, since November 2009, been known as OCDTs. Prior to this they belonged administratively to RMC-D and were known as SCDTs. SCDTs wear the title 'RMC' on their rank slides in order to distinguish them from other training establishments.

On commissioning, OCDTs' Commissions are now backdated to their enlistment date or, for those previously enlisted as soldiers, the date they entered RMC/ADFA; not the date of graduation which was previously the case before the advent of the Defence Force Disciplinary Act (1982) on 3rd July 1985. Commissions are issued by the Governor-General of Australia and co-signed by the Minister for Defence.

Other forms of Commissioning

Other forms of Commissioning into the Army include:

- Direct Entry Officer (DEO)

- Regular Army Supplement (RAS)

- Undergraduate Entry

- Appointment of Former Officers

- Army Pilot Training

- Army Senior non-commissioned Officer and Warrant Officer Commissioning Scheme

- Specialist Service Officer Pilot (SSO(P)) Scheme

- In-Service Training Scheme for the Appointment of Chaplains

- Appointment of Officers from Other Armies (Lateral Appointments)

- Graduate Medical Scheme

- Other Ranks Engineering Commissioning Scheme - ADFA, and

- Long-term Schooling Commissioning Scheme - Other Ranks.

On appointment, ARA and ARes officers are categorised in one of two career divisions, GSO or Specialist Service Officer (SSO).

GSOs are those officers whose education, training and experience prepare them for employment in a wide range of Corps and non-Corps regimental, training and staff appointments. GSOs are eligible for selection for a wide range of developmental training and postings, including attendance at the Australian Defence College. GSOs may be promoted to the highest ranks.

SSOs are those officers whose education, training and experience normally limit their employment to appointments with the speciality and Corps for which they were appointed. The majority of SSOs are professionally-qualified personnel who are appointed as officers to practice their profession within the Army. Officers who are recruited and trained for a specific employment area, such as pilots, are normally appointed as SSO. SSO are categorised into two groups as follows:

- SSO Professional Qualification (SSO PQ) are professionally-qualified personnel who are appointed as officers to practise their profession within the Army, for example; doctors, dentists and nurses.

- SSO Service Commission (SSO SC) are officers appointed from the non-commissioned ranks.

---

106 DI(A) PERS 47-9 *Officer Appointments:* 19 December 2008

COMMISSION

HIS EXCELLENCY THE GOVERNOR- GENERAL OF THE
COMMONWEALTH OF AUSTRALIA
COMMANDER- IN- CHIEF OF THE DEFENCE FORCE

To: *Leslie Irvin Terrett*

WHEREAS *you have been appointed to be, on and from the first day of January 1995, an officer of the Australian Army:*

AND WHEREAS *all things have happened to render it desirable that a commission be issued to you:*

NOW THEREFORE I, *William George Hayden, Companion of the Order of Australia, Governor- General of the Commonwealth of Australia, acting with the advice of the Federal Executive Council, pursuant to section 10 of the* **Defence Act 1903**, *charge and command you faithfully to discharge your duty as an officer and to observe and execute all such orders and instructions as you may receive from your superior officers.*

Signed and sealed with the Great Seal of Australia on the twenty-ninth day of November 1995.

GOVERNOR- GENERAL

By His Excellency's Command

MINISTER FOR DEFENCE

Officer's Commission of Appointment –1995

Commissioned Officers

Australian Army officers receive a commission that is personally signed by the Governor-General of Australia, acting for the Monarch, Queen Elizabeth II of Australia. Commissioned Officers are the managers, problem solvers, key influencers and planners who lead soldiers in all situations, planning operations, and organising the internal and external affairs of the Army and are entrusted with the welfare, morale and professional development of the soldiers under their command.

Second Lieutenant and Lieutenant

LT is derived from the French and means 'one who holds an office, in subordination to a superior, for whom they act'. The rank of 2LT was introduced throughout the British Army in 1871 to replace the rank of Ensign (Cornet in the cavalry), although it had long been used in the Royal Artillery, Royal Engineers and Fusilier regiments. At first the rank bore no distinct insignia; however, in 1902 a single Star of the Order of the Bath (Military Division), now commonly referred to as a 'pip', was introduced.

The rank of 2LT is the most junior of the Australian Army commissioned ranks. Throughout its history, the Australian Army has normally commissioned its most junior officers at the rank of LT, bypassing 2LT. 2LT was widely used as a first appointment GSO commissioning rank from 1952 to 1985 for Officers graduating from the Officer Cadet School (OCS) Portsea (except where a Cadet had an undergraduate degree which resulted in their Commissioning at the rank of LT). 2LT was also the commissioning rank for the Officer Training Unit (OTU) Scheyville (1965-1973) and for graduates of the Women's Royal Australian Army Corps (WRAAC) OCS from 1978-1984. Prior to 1978, WRAAC OCS graduates were commissioned at the rank of LT to compensate for lower pay and fewer promotional opportunities. The Coldham Report, published in 1977, resulted in equal pay for female members of the ADF and a result of this determination was that WRAAC OCS graduates would be commissioned at the rank of 2LT[107].

The 2LT rank ceased to be used for GSO with the graduation of the last class from OCS Portsea in December 1985. This class was promoted to LT on 14th June 1986.[108] The rank continued to be employed for some DEO after this period until the early 2000s. Currently there is only one avenue for appointing an Officer to the rank of 2LT in the Australian Army[109] - for Royal Australian Army Educational Corps (RAAEC) Officers who are undergoing tertiary studies[110].

2LT and LT are addressed as 'Sir' or 'Ma'am' by subordinate ranks; however, male members may be addressed as 'Mister' rather than by their rank[111] by Warrant and commissioned officers.

The word subaltern refers to the ranks of 2LT and LT and is derived from the Latin 'subalternus' or 'sub' meaning under or below and 'alternus' meaning another.

Insignia. The insignia of a 2LT is one Star of the Order of the Bath. LT insignia is two Stars of the Order of the Bath.

Captain

CAPT has been used as a military rank for centuries and can be interpreted as 'Chief Leader'. CAPT is one rank above LT and one below MAJ. In the past, a CAPT commanded a company of soldiers, but now holds the position of 2IC or Operations Officer of a company-sized organisation. In a headquarters a CAPT is often termed a Staff Officer Grade Three (SO3).

The word Captain is derived from the Latin 'Caput' meaning the head. Historically a Captain was a nobleman who purchased the right to head a company from the previous holder of that right. He would in turn receive money from another nobleman to serve as his Lieutenant. The funding to provide for the troops came from the monarch or the Government. If the Captain had not been court-martialled he would be dismissed (cashiered) and the monarch would receive money from another nobleman to command the company. Otherwise, the only pension for the Captain was selling his rights to another nobleman when he was ready to retire.

Insignia. CAPT insignia is three Stars of the Order of the Bath.

The Army rank of Captain should not be confused with the Navy rank of Captain or with the Air Force rank of Group Captain, both of which are more senior, being equivalent to an Army Colonel (COL). To avoid confusion and to distinguish different national naval forces, a Captain in the Royal Australian Navy will use the post-nominal 'RAN' after their name, for example, CAPT R Bloggs, RAN.

---

107 Bomford J, *Soldiers of the Queen*, Oxford University Press, 2001, p. 104.
108 Major Geoffrey O. Lever; Graduated OCS Portsea December 1985, ATO 1987, OC Supply Coy, 8 BASB 1996-7, Manager Army Museum Duntroon 2014: born Sydney 30 August 1963

109 Defence Instruction (Army) Personnel 47-9, Officer Appointments: 19 December 2008.
110 RAAEC Manual of Army Employment, Volume 16 (RAAEC), p. 1 Para 4, e, (1)
111 Australia, Department of Defence. *A Guide to Customs of the Army Australian.* Canberra, Government Publishing Service: 1984, p. 4

Major

The word is from the Latin meaning greater or superior. The ranks of MAJ and LTCOL are termed 'Field Rank'; Field Rank was created to bridge the gap between the higher command comprising senior officers, COL and above, who planned military operations, and the troops in the field who were implementing and carrying out the plans and orders of high command. Junior officers must always address a MAJ as either 'Sir' or 'Ma'am'. A MAJ generally holds the position of OC of a company or squadron-sized unit or 2IC or Operations Officer of a battalion-sized unit. In a headquarters a MAJ is often termed a Staff Officer Grade Two (SO2).

Insignia. MAJ insignia is the St Edward's Crown.

Lieutenant Colonel

LTCOL is one rank above a MAJ and one below a COL and typically commands a Bn or a regiment. The rank of LTCOL is often verbally shortened to 'Colonel'. In a headquarters a LTCOL is termed a Staff Officer Grade One (SO1).

Insignia. LTCOL insignia is one Star of the Order of the Bath surmounted by the St Edward's Crown.

Colonel

The rank of COL is one of the oldest in existence, dating as far back as the Roman Empire.

The term Colonel derives from Latin 'columnella' – 'small column' – referring to the shape of a marching body of troops; however, it was never actually a Roman rank. As a rank the term arose in the late 16th century in Italy where it referred to the officer in charge of a column (Italian 'colonna', plural 'colonne') or field force. Prior to 1588, individual regiments could consist of 4,000 men under the command of Knights and Esquires with sub- units of between 400 and 600 men commanded by an Ensign. The Earl of Leicester, the commander of Queen Elizabeth I's forces at Tilbury, standardised the regiments of the Army by reducing the size of the companies of infantry to 150 commanded by a Captain and each regiment to approximately 1000 men under the command of a 'Coronell'.[112]

In Britain in the 16th century, the Colonel was commissioned to raise a regiment and essentially 'owned' it. As time progressed the Colonel tended to be a 'Royal' or a senior noble and did not take to the field, leaving this role to the Lieutenant Colonel in command.

By the late 19th century, COL was a professional military rank though still held typically by an officer in command of a regiment or equivalent unit. A regiment usually consists of three battalions (equivalent to a Brigade).

As European military influence expanded throughout the world, the rank of COL was adopted by nearly every nation under a variety of names.

A COL, as with BRIGs and General Officers in the Australian Army, wears gorget patches (see Chap 3) and only wears Corps embellishments when appointed to a position as a 'Head of Corps' or 'Head of Regiment'.

Insignia. COL insignia is two Stars of the Order of the Bath surmounted by the St Edward's Crown.

Brigadier[113]

The title BRIG is derived from the equivalent former British rank of Brigadier-General, which was used until 1922, and is still used in many countries. The title was already in use as a term for a commander of a BDE irrespective of the specific rank held. Australian BDEs were commanded by COLs until May 1915 when an order was promulgated promoting them all to Brigadier-General.[114] The rank title Brigadier-General was short-lived (ceased in 1922) as, by definition, they are not in 'general command' of troops.

From 1922 to 1928 the British rank title used was that of Colonel-Commandant, which, although reflecting its modern role in the British Army as a senior COL rather than a junior General, was not well-received and was replaced with BRIG after only six years. Colonel-Commandant was only ever used for officers commanding brigades, depots or training establishments. Officers holding equivalent rank in administrative appointments were known as 'Colonels on the Staff' and were replaced by BRIG in 1928. Colonel-Commandants and Colonels on the Staff wore the same rank badge later adopted by BRIGs.

In many countries, especially those formerly part of the former British Empire, a BRIG is either the highest field rank or the most junior GEN appointment. Although not always considered a General Officer rank, it is always considered equivalent to the Brigadier-General or Brigade-General of other countries and is the equivalent of '1 star rank' in the US and other armies.

Insignia. BRIG insignia is the St Edward's Crown above three Stars of the Order of the Bath, in a triangular formation. Prior to 1922, a Brigadier-General wore the crossed sword and baton of a General rank.

112 Smythe J. *Certain Discourses*. London, Richard Johns: 1590, p. 9

113 The Times. *New Army Rank of Brigadier*. London, News International: 23 December 1997

114 Chapman ID. Iven G. Mackay. *Citizen and Soldier*. Melbourne, Melway Publishing: 1975, p. 10

General Ranks

The origin of the different ranks of General dates back to the early 16th century where the British Army was commanded by a Captain General, the cavalry by a Lieutenant General and the Infantry by a Sergeant Major General. However over time the term 'Sergeant' has been dropped from the Major General, which is why a Lieutenant General is senior to a Major General. Lieutenant General was created as a direct equivalent of the British military rank. The rank traces its origins to the Middle Ages where the title of Lieutenant General was held by the 2IC on the battlefield, who was normally subordinate to a Captain General.

Major General

MAJGEN was created as a direct equivalent of the British military rank. A MAJGEN may command a DIV or equivalent formation.

MAJGEN is equivalent to '2 star rank' in the US and other armies.

Insignia. MAJGEN insignia is a Star of the Order of the Bath above a crossed sword and baton.

Lieutenant General

In many countries, the rank of Corps General has replaced the earlier rank of Lieutenant General (LTGEN), for example, in France and Italy, the ranks of Corps General and Lieutenant Colonel General are intended to solve the apparent LTGEN/MAJGEN anomaly.

The most senior rank currently held in the Australian Army is LTGEN, which is worn by the officer holding the appointment of CA. Other positions at this rank are available to Australian Army Officers within the ADF.

LTGEN is equivalent to '3 star rank' in the US and other armies.

Insignia. LTGEN insignia is the St Edward's Crown above a crossed sword and baton.

General

GEN was created as a direct equivalent of the British military rank.

Prior to 1958, GENs and Field Marshals (FM) were only appointed in exceptional circumstances because the Army was so small. In 1958 the position which is currently called CDF was created, and since 1966, the rank of GEN has been held when an Army officer is appointed to that position. The position of CDF is held by an officer from one of the three Services (Army, RAN or RAAF). A GEN is the equivalent of Admiral in the RAN and Air Chief Marshal in the RAAF.

GEN is equivalent to '4 star rank' in the US and other armies.

Insignia. GEN insignia is the St Edward's Crown above a Star of the Order of the Bath above a crossed sword and baton.

Field Marshal

The rank of FM came into being in the British Army in 1736 when it replaced the rank of Captain General. The title of Captain General was re-introduced in 1950 by His Majesty King George VI and Her Majesty Queen Elizabeth II is the Captain-General of the Royal Regiment of Australian Artillery.

FM is the highest rank of the Australian Army and was created as a direct equivalent of the British military rank.

FM is equivalent to a '5 star rank' in the US and other armies.

The origin of the rank of FM dates to the early Middle Ages, originally meaning the keeper of the king's horses (from old German Marh-scalc which equates to 'horse-servant' from the time of the early Frankish kings.

Upon promotion, FMs were traditionally awarded a decorative baton, which they carried as a symbol of their 'office'; the baton is studded with jewels and inlaid with precious metals. Once promoted, the Field Marshall (FM) retains the rank for life.

AWM Neg No. ART27646 Courtesy of the Australian War Memorial. Field Marshal Sir Thomas Blamey, 1951

AWM Neg No REL AWM 31423 and NAA Image No. A8139. FM Blamey's Baton with hat and shoulder rank badges

Current protocol for Appointment of a Field Marshal

Only the Governor-General of Australia, on the recommendation of the Prime Minister of Australia, can appoint officers to the rank of FM. Sir Thomas Blamey[115] was the first and only Australian-born citizen to attain that rank (note: FM Blamey appears in the List of British Field Marshals).

Currently, the only living FM of the Australian Army is HRH Prince Philip, Duke of Edinburgh, who was promoted to the rank of FM in the Australian Army on 1st April 1954. However, as consort of Queen Elizabeth II, the Duke's rank is purely ceremonial. He has no command or control role in the ADF and is not part of the ADF's operational structure. He has never paraded as a FM with any units or elements of the ADF.

FM Sir William Birdwood was a British Army officer who commanded the AIF in WWI. Despite his British origins, 'Birdie', as he was affectionately known to the Australian soldiers, was a popular and respected Commander of the AIF. When he was promoted to the rank of FM in the British Army in 1925, he was also given the honorary rank of FM in the Australian Army.

Field Marshal Batons

Both FM Blamey's and FM Birdwood's batons are currently on display in the Australian War Memorial; FM Blamey's baton is held in the 'final case' in the 'Second World War Gallery'. The batons are approximately 40 centimetres (16 inches) long and at the top have a golden mount depicting St George slaying a Dragon with two rings of roses. The bases of the batons are engraved with the FM's name and other details.

Unique Ranks and Appointments

There are many ranks or appointments used by the military. Most of these ranks have no command and control function within the Army but are used to perform ceremonial roles. These ranks are traditional in nature and have been adopted from the British system.

Insignia. FM insignia is crossed batons enclosed in a laurel wreath surmounted with the St Edward's Crown. The FM's baton has long been a symbol of that office. The origin of the baton is believed to date back to pastoral societies in western Europe and most are variations of the baton received by Consuls (officials appointed by government) as they represented overall command and supreme authority over both civilian and military personnel. The Australian baton is based on that of the Marshal of France, Marshal Jean-Baptiste Jourdan, captured by Wellington at the Battle of Vittoria.

115 Dennis, P, Grey J, Morris E, Prior R. *The Oxford Companion to Australian Military History (Second Edition).* Australia, Oxford University Press: 2008, pp. 100-103

State Governors and the Governor-General of Australia

State Governors and the Governor-General of Australia hold honorary or symbolic ranks within the ADF as the Queen's representative, but have no functional position within the military chain of command. The Governor-General of Australia holds the title and position of Commander-in-Chief of the ADF. A State Governor may hold this position only when filling the role of Governor-General.[116]

Colonel-in-Chief

A Colonel-in-Chief is a titular[117] head of a Corps or Regiment, and is usually a member of the British Royal Family.

Honorary Colonels and Colonels Commandant, Regimental Colonels, Chaplain Commandant and Honorary Corps Representatives[118]

Corps of the Australian Army are entitled to appoint Honorary Colonels/Colonels Commandant and in some instances, Regimental Colonels, a Chaplain Commandant or Honorary Corps Representatives to assist in an honorary capacity in the domestic matters of that Corps, its regiments and/or units.

Honorary Colonels/Colonels Commandant, Regimental Colonels, the Chaplain Commandant and Honorary Corps Representatives are to be accorded the highest precedence due to their appointment in accordance with the Commonwealth Table of Precedence contained within the Army Ceremonial Manual. Due to their position and standing within their Corps, it is normally considered inappropriate for them to act as host on some formal occasions; however, these positions have no power of command.

Appointments can be made as follows:

- **Honorary Colonels/Colonels Commandant.** Honorary Colonels/Colonels Commandant are appointed by the CA. There is no difference in their roles or responsibilities (discussed below).

- **Representative Honorary Colonels/Colonels Commandant.** When a Corps has more than one Honorary Colonel/Colonel Commandant, one will be appointed representative Honorary Colonel/Colonel Commandant by the CA to assist the Head of Corps (HOC)/Head of Regiment (HOR)/sponsor in the coordination of the duties of the Honorary Colonels/Colonels Commandant of their Corps.

Honorary appointments are usually filled by distinguished senior serving or retired members of the Corps or regiment concerned. The Colonel of a regiment speaks for the regiment or Corps on all matters affecting the regiment's interests. He/she is responsible for regimental benevolence, funds, property and regimental orders, usually as chairperson of a regimental council.

- **Director General Chaplaincy - Army (to be renamed Chaplain Commandant).** The Chaplain Commandant will keep this title as it conforms with the changeover to Colonel Commandant. The changeover will occur as the position comes up for reappointment. The CA may approve the non-denominational appointment of the Chaplain Commandant. The Chaplain Commandant's role is to assist the Principal Chaplain in maintaining the Chaplain Department's morale, 'esprit de corps' and traditions.

- **Honorary Corps Representatives.** The CA may approve the positions of honorary Corps representatives. Head of Corps (HOC)/Head of Regiment (HOR)/sponsors are allocated responsibility for the nomination and administration of honorary appointments.

Aides-de-Camp (ADC)

It has been customary to appoint aides-de-camp (ADC) to the Governor-General of Australia and State Governors as well as to GEN officers. This was originally incorporated in Defence legislation; however all such reference to such appointments has been removed but the positions have been retained as Tri-Service appointments. In the past, the Governor-General had four Personal Staff drawn from the ADF: a Military Secretary and Comptroller of the Household at LTCOL rank (but a Tri-Service position); and one ADC from each of the single Services at Captain equivalent rank. The ADCs were appointed for a period of approximately 12 months, with a change-over every four months to provide continuity. Senior ADF officers, generally at BRIG equivalent rank, are appointed as Honorary ADCs in each major Military District to represent the Governor-General as required.

Appointments of ADCs to State Governors and Territory Administrators are an honorary distinction. Permanent officers are not normally appointed to these positions. Up to two honorary ADCs from each Service of Captain (equivalent) to LTCOL (equivalent) rank may be appointed for part-time duty with State Governors and the Administrators. The normal tenure of office for an ADC to a State Governor or Administrator is three years, with the provision for an extension, if requested by the State Governor or Administrator.

---

116 s.68 of the Constitution of Australia

117 "titular" adjective – existing or being such in title only; nominal; having the title but none of the associated duties, powers, etc.: *the titular head of the company* (Macquarie University NSW. *The Macquarie Dictionary*. Milton Queensland, The Jacaranda Press: 1987)

118 Australian Army. *Defence Instruction (Army) PERS 99-1. Honorary Colonels:* 14 Mar 2002

Protocol and Ranks of the Chaplains Department[119]

There are two tiers of chaplains within the Royal Australian Army Chaplains Department (RAAChD) being Chaplain (CHAP) and Principal Chaplain (PRINCHAP). Chaplains are classified in five Divisions and wear rank insignia shown as follows:

Worn Rank	Insignia	Employment
Chaplain Division 1	CAPT	Unit Chaplain
Chaplain Division 2	MAJ	Unit, Coordinating or Staff Chaplain
Chaplain Division 3	LTCOL	Coordinating, Staff or Senior Chaplain
Chaplain Division 4	COL	Command/Senior Chaplain
Principal Chaplain Division 5	BRIG	Principal Chaplain

Chaplains indicate their rank as 'Chaplain' (CHAP) or when the appropriate Division is required; for example, 'Chaplain Division 1 (CHAP1)'. Where appropriate, rank can be indicated in brackets, for example, Chaplain Division 1 (CAPT) or CHAP 1 (CAPT). Chaplains are not referred to by the rank of their Military insignia, but are referred to as either 'Chaplain' or 'Principal Chaplain'. An Army chaplain is normally called 'Padre' in spoken situations.

Colour of Rank Badges

The colour of thread used in the manufacture of rank badges has varied over the years from white cotton to a blend of various shades of green and finally to plain black on field dress and from gold bullion to yellow cotton on ceremonial dress. The rank insignia used on field dress tends to be small and of a subdued appearance, whilst that used on ceremonial uniforms are much larger and more colourful.

There are two main colour rank badges used on ceremonial dress, matching that used by the commissioned ranks of the same Corps. The majority of Corps in the Army use gold or yellow threaded patterned chevrons whilst the Armoured, Aviation and Nursing Corps use silver or white. Warrant Officers, regardless of Corps, wear the same badges of rank; the only variation from this is the RSM-A who wears a unique rank badge specific to that appointment.

There are however, two units within the Army who do not conform to the standard mentioned above; they are the Sydney University Regiment (SUR) and the 51st Battalion, Far North Queensland Regiment (51 FNQR).

119 Australian Army. *Defence Instruction (Army) PERS 170-5.*
Organisation, Roles and Responsibilities of the Royal Australian Army
Chaplains Department: 14 September 2006

Sydney University Regiment

In 1927 SUR formed an alliance with the then British Army light infantry regiment, The King's Royal Rifle Corps.[120] Following WWII and the reforming of SUR in 1948, approval was granted for unit members to wear special and unique rank embellishments to reflect this affiliation. Although the original British Regiment has long since been disbanded the affiliation continues with the unit's successor 'The Rifles' (a light infantry regiment of the British Army).

Officers wear their rank insignia in black on a scarlet background, whilst Warrant Officer badges of rank and NCO chevrons are black with a scarlet background. This emulates the embellishments worn by British rifle (or light infantry) regiments. These items were first worn by members of SUR on post-war battledress and polyester uniforms, never on field dress. They are currently worn on ceremonial dress, service dress, mess dress and general duty polyester; they are not worn on field dress.

120 Lilley AB. *Sydney University Regiment.* 1974. Lyneham ACT, Military
Historical Society of Australia: Chap 7 p. 43

51st Battalion, The Far North Queensland Regiment

When 51 FNQR was re-raised in October 1985, permission was granted for officers of the unit to wear black badges of rank matching the regiment's black hat badge. The unit's claim for approval was based on being initially raised in 1916 and the badges and rank insignia used by the AIF were oxidised brass (black).

A subsequent application was made to permit all ranks of the Regiment to wear black rank badges; approval was given in 2006.[121] The justification for this deviation was based solely on the unit's history and employment as a RFSU and is not based on any link or association with an equivalent British Army unit.

Insignia of Rank – Non-Commissioned Officers and Warrant Officers

Rank insignia evolved from an attractive and confusing array of embroidery and braiding to a straightforward emblem used in different arrangements to denote differing degrees of seniority.

The first laid-down dress regulation appeared in the British Army in 1832; from which we are able to trace the evolution of the rank badges in use today.

These badges were to be worn on the right arm only. It was not until after WWII that WO/NCO badges of rank were worn on both the left and right sleeves. There have been periods when INF WO2s informally wore their rank in the field, in the form of a metal crown fixed to a leather wrist band.

Insignia of Non-Commissioned Officers

The use of Chevrons is not a unique feature of the British Army system of rank badges, for in varying forms, they denote non-commissioned rank in most countries.

Originally chevrons or bars were used in the British Army to indicate a soldier with long service as an NCO. It was not until 1803 that a formal system of rank marking was introduced in the British Army. Initially a Sergeant Major or Quartermaster Sergeant wore four chevrons, a SGT three and a CPL two, with some regiments wearing the point up and others down. In May 1803 further standardisation was attained when an order was given that the chevron points were to point down.[122]

As is the custom today chevrons were originally worn on the upper sleeve. However in 1869, the four chevrons of the Sergeant Major were moved to the lower sleeve with the point of the chevrons pointing up toward the elbow. The last four chevron badge of rank was abolished as late as 1962 when Drum-Major reverted to wearing three stripes and a small drum.

Dress regulations of 1906 saw the four chevrons of QMS worn below the elbow with the point upwards surmounted by a star.

Colour Sergeant

The badge varied in each unit from one stripe surmounted by a bugle, crossed sword and crown enclosed in a wreath, to three stripes surmounted by crossed colours and crown. Up to 1901, in Britain, the rank appeared as crossed swords surmounted by a copy of the actual colour surmounted by a crown.

Insignia of Warrant Officers

In 1881 the badge of a Sergeant Major was altered from 4 chevrons to a single crown worn below the elbow. Today the crown is worn on the upper sleeve.

The present day WO1 wears the Australian Coat of Arms, which was introduced into service in 1977. The badge was originally worn on the lower sleeve but is now worn on the upper sleeve.

121 Rosenthal C. *Correspondence* Major Chris Rosenthal, 2IC 51st Battalion Far North Queensland Regiment: Nov 2013

122 Carman WY. *A Dictionary of Military Uniforms: London, B.T. Batsford Limited*: 1977, p. 39

Rank Badges

Lance Corporal (LCPL)/
Lance Bombardier (LBDR)

Corporal (CPL)/
Bombardier (BDR)

Sergeant (SGT)

Staff Sergeant (SSGT)
This rank has been removed from the rank structure but
remains in service until the last member holding the rank
is either promoted or separated from Service

Warrant Officer Class Two (WO2)

Warrant Officer Class One (WO1)

Regimental Sergeant
Major of the Army – WO (RSM-A)

Distinctive Rank Badges

51st Bn FNQR, SUR, RAANC, RAAC and AAAvn

Lance Corporal (LCPL)
SUR

Corporal (CPL)
RAAC, RAANC, AAAvn

Sergeant (SGT)
RAAC, RAANC, AAAvn

Staff Sergeant (SSGT)
51st Bn FNQR

Warrant Officer Class Two (WO2)
51st Bn FNQR

Warrant Officer Class One (WO1)
SUR

Rank badges shown above are examples of those worn by non-commissioned ranks in the RAAC, AAAvn Corps, RAANC, the 51st Bn FNQR and SUR. On promotion to WO2 and WO1, RAAC, AAAvn and RAANC personnel all wear the standard issue (coloured on green) badges of rank.

Officers rank badges for these units and Corps are likewise coloured as per those used by the other ranks in the corresponding Corps or regiment. The red felt border used on the SUR rank is the same as that used as a backing for their hat badge and forms an integral part of the badge.

Lieutenant
SUR

Captain
RAAC, AAAvn and RAANC

Major
51st Bn FNQR

Insignia of Rank – Mess Dress

Shoulder board rank insignia for Mess Dress Army was introduced into the Army in 2012.

Rank Insignia Shoulder Board for Mess Dress
RSM-A

Insignia of Rank – Commissioned Ranks

The 'star' worn by the commissioned ranks is not merely a metal mould or a patch of simple embroidery, but is very definite in its design form, being representative of the star of a Knight Grand Cross of the military division of the 'Most Honourable Order of the Bath', Britain's fourth most senior Order of Chivalry. Its use was established in a regulation of August 1830, by which it replaced the star of the 'Most Noble Order of the Garter' as a badge of rank.

When the star was introduced for military use it was reduced to one inch (2.54cm) in size, and with a few exceptions, is a replica of the brilliant star worn by Knights of the Bath (Military Division) at official occasions on their mantles. Square in outline, it is composed of rays bearing a Cross-patée (a form of cross in which the arms expand towards the end and are flattened at the outer edges), centred with a wreath of laurel (in the original form red berries were interlaced with leaves), enclosing a circlet edged and inscribed 'Tria Juncta in Uno', meaning 'Three Joined in One' – England, Scotland and Ireland). The centrepiece is charged with the badge or ensign of the Order, represented by three Albert Crowns (which look like acorns).

The crown used from the 19th Century, the Tudor Crown used for George VI, was slightly different in design from that in use today. The crown used since the accession of Queen Elizabeth II is a representation of the regal crown in the form adopted by Edward VII (the St Edwards Crown) on his accession in 1901. One inch by one inch, the outstanding difference is that the arches of the Tudor Crown are elevated acutely instead of being depressed in the centre.

The red velvet that can be seen within the arches on an officer's crown represents the loose lining of velvet (crown cap of an actual crown), which forms a base for the jewelled circlet.

The velvet forming the crown cap of the regal crown is purple, although red is used in heraldic designation and similarly in military form. For further information on crowns (see Chapter 13).

Order of the Bath
GCB Breast Star (Military Division)

Australian Rank Version (Pip)

2nd Lieutenant
(2LT)

Lieutenant
(LT)

Captain
(CAPT)

Major
(MAJ)

Lieutenant Colonel
(LTCOL)

Colonel
(COL)

Brigadier
(BRIG)

Major General
(MAJGEN)
(left shoulder)

Lieutenant General
(LTGEN)
(left shoulder)

General
(GEN)
(left shoulder)

Field Marshal
FM
(left shoulder)

State Governor
SG

Governor-General
G-G

VIPs' and Senior Officers' Distinguishing Flags[123]

Many Royal, Vice-Regal and senior Defence persons have an entitlement to Army Standards and Flags. The Governor-General of Australia, State Governors and certain General Officers who hold particular appointments within the ADF are entitled to fly 'Personal Flags' whilst travelling or in residence within Australia. Flags and pennants are flown, and 'star plates' displayed to recognise presence of these persons. It is therefore a requirement for members of the military, in uniform, to salute a vehicle flying one of these flags or displaying 'star plates'.

The following flags are shown in order of seniority with shapes varying from the standard flag; for example, the fly being twice the length of the width, to the slightly squarer shape used by the Prime Minister, Minister of Defence and senior Army commanders. Comparisons can be made to the shapes used for Standards, Guidons and Colours which are replicated in the squarish shape and swallow-tailed flag used by the senior General Officers down to the triangular-shaped pennant used by Brigadiers and Colonels. Flags used by the Governor-General of Australia and State Governors are made as both full-sized flags and vehicle pennants, whilst those personal flags used by senior members of the Defence Force are usually only made as vehicle pennants.

Other than the Australian National Flag (ANF), the design of which dates back to 1908, the oldest flags authorised for use are those of the GOC of an Army and that of a Corps. These were first authorised for use in late 1917[124] in France during WWI.

In 1992, two significant changes were made to Army flags; firstly, the then Army emblem of a Kangaroo over crossed swords surmounted by the St Edward's Crown was changed to that of the Army General Service (Rising Sun) badge; and secondly, the Royal Crest (Sovereign's Crown surmounted by a statant guardant Lion crowned proper) was removed from all flags, other than that of the Governor-General of Australia, being replaced with the Army General Service badge.

123 Australian Army. *Ceremonial Manual – 2003 Volume 1.* Canberra, Defence Publishing Service: 2003, Chap 22
124 Taubert S. *Formation Signs and Vehicle Marking of the Australian Army 1903-1984.* Brisbane, Queensland, Comtrain Enterprises: 1996, p. 458

Standards and Flags

Governor-General of Australia

Governor of Queensland

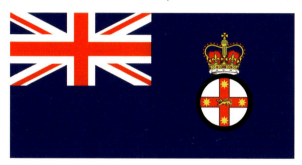

Governor of New South Wales

Governor of Victoria

Governor of South Australia

Governor of Western Australia

Governor of Tasmania

Prime Minister of Australia

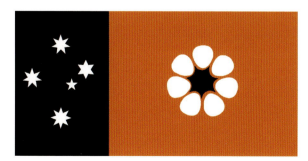

Chief Minister – Northern Territory

Chief Minister – Australian Capital Territory

Vehicle Pennants

Minister of Defence

Chief of the Defence Force

Vice Chief of the Defence Force

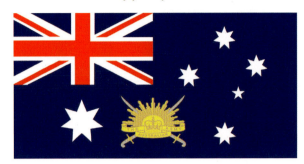

Chief of Army

Deputy Chief of Army

General Officer Commanding an Army

General Officer Commanding a Corps

Commander Forces Command

Commander of a Division (1st Division)
(Numeral indicates Division's number)

Commander Australian Theatre of Operations
or Joint Logistics Australia or Australian Defence College

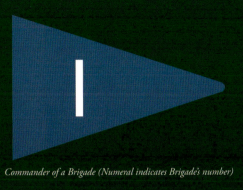

Commander of a Brigade (Numeral indicates Brigade's number)

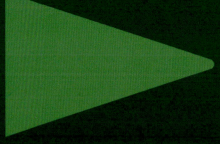

Commander of an Army Area

Commandant Royal Military College - Duntroon

Commandant – ADFA, Australian Command and Staff College, ADF Warfare Centre

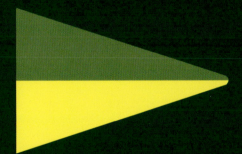

Commander of a Training Group

Commander of a Communications Zone or Logistic Support Force

Australian Military Attaché/Advisor

Chapter Three

Uniforms and Accoutrements

'Digger (to an irate Sergeant): I am standing to attention Sergeant; it's my uniform that's at ease'.[125]

Introduction

The Australian colonial Military Forces, and the early Federation Military Forces, closely followed the fashions of the British Army not only in uniforms but also in arms and equipment. It is therefore appropriate to show the development of the British uniform knowing that as changes and improvements were introduced these same changes were mirrored by colonial forces across the world.

Originally a soldier had a single uniform, which was worn on ceremonial parades, work parties and during the heat of battle. Usually the design of these garments was based on the fashion of the day and has therefore seen many changes over the years. However, the accoutrements worn indicating regiment, rank, trade and other qualifications have changed more slowly and often as a cost-saving measure; for instance, the change from gold thread to yellow cotton in the manufacture of rank chevrons.

It is to a large degree the uniform that sets soldiers apart from the community they serve, making them easily identifiable in all circumstances. The uniform can also be a symbol of their country often incorporating traditional dress or headwear.

Development of Military Uniforms

In 1337 a body of Welsh spearmen was raised for service abroad. Their appearance was so ragged that it shocked even the uncritical eye of King Edward III, who subsequently provided each man with a red tunic and mantle (cloak or shroud). This is the first known British military uniform.

In the days of King Charles II (r. 1660-1665), military dress was similar to civilian dress, except for the regimental uniformity of colour and facings. From 1870 military apparel began to diverge from civilian dress, and between the Peninsular (Spanish) War (1807-1814) and Crimean War (1853-1856), uniforms or 'regimentals' as they were called became extravagant, were changed frequently and lost all relationship to civilian dress. High collars and stocks almost strangled men on the march. After the Crimean War the tunic was introduced but uniforms as a whole remained impractical.

During the period 1870 to the end of the century there was, in the British Army, a constant battle between those who advocated adopting a more practical form of dress that allowed for ease of movement and those who preferred a tight-fitting uniform that looked smart on the parade ground. Finally, and at great cost, it was agreed to have two uniforms; one for working and fighting and the other for ceremonial and parades. Thus for the first time a service or battle-dress became distinct from a full 'dress' uniform. The current Army 'walking-out' uniform is titled 'Service Dress' which is a ceremonial uniform.

The khaki-coloured uniform was introduced in India about 1845 and was originally white drill cloth dyed with curry powder. It was worn in the Afghan War (1878-1879), but troops sent to Egypt in 1882 received special loose red serge jackets with roll collars. It was not until 1884 that an official khaki field service dress consisting of helmet, tunic, trousers and puttees was authorised for troops in India.[126]

Colonial units in Australia generally adopted the colour and design of uniforms of the various territorial forces in Britain. These colonial units were established as a reserve for the British Regular units, and the colonials modelled themselves on the British part-time soldier, which included wearing green and grey uniforms instead of the red of the British Regular Army.[127] However, the more traditional red coat of the British infantry was still used by various units throughout the Colonies.

---

125 Wannan B. *The Australia, Yarns Ballads Legends*. Melbourne, O'Neil Publishers: 1979, p. 80

126 Mollo J. *Military fashion: A Comparative History of the Uniforms of the Great Armies From the 17th Century to the First World War*. London, Barrie and Jenkins: 1972, p. 215

127 Dennis P, Grey J, Morris E, Prior R. *The Oxford Companion to Australian Military History (Second Edition)*. Australia, Oxford University Press: 2008, p. 538

In South Africa the increased range and accuracy of rifles demanded a degree of camouflage, so the troops were issued khaki-coloured uniforms.

In 1902 a universal service dress was introduced with the intention of being worn on all occasions other than those requiring full dress. This new dress consisted of a peaked cap, tunic and trousers, worn with a Sam Browne Belt (for officers). Mounted officers wore breeches and boots and the dismounted officers wore puttees. The various arms and service Corps were distinguished by the addition of coloured braid trimming on the shoulder straps. A wide-brimmed slouch hat with one side turned up was worn by those men on Foreign Service. This style of hat was very popular with colonial forces, having first appeared in Britain during the Jubilee celebrations of 1897. On that occasion an American observer described the uniforms of the Australian contingent as being:

> As a rule light brown or drab in colour, simply made, with little or no ornamentation. High boots, or leggings, were worn, and broad-brimmed soft hats of the same colour as the uniform, turned up on the side. In some cases feathers were fastened to the side of the hat, which was turned up. There was a dash of the Texan ranger or frontiersman about the uniform, which harmonised perfectly with the stalwart form and martial bearing of the men themselves.[128]

By 1904 the method of showing rank up to that of COL had changed to the now traditional star and crown worn on the shoulder.

Following Federation, it remained common for the Army to follow the British system. The standard uniform pattern adopted by the Commonwealth was:

> The Commonwealth Uniform will consist of a General Service Dress, which, will, by the addition of aiguillettes, breast-lines and girdles, be converted into Full Dress. By this means a single uniform coat will be provided which shall meet the requirements of a Fatigue or Service Jacket, and by the addition of lace attachments, &c., be readily converted into Ceremonial or Full Dress. Great economy … will be insured by this means.[129]

Only minor changes were made to the Australian uniform prior to WWI when the basic AIF uniform was introduced consisting of a loose-fitting, four-pocket, woollen service dress jacket, breeches, puttees, tan ankle boots and the now famous slouch hat. Almost all units of the AIF wore identical hat and collar badges. To distinguish the different formations, brigades and regiments, a system of colour patches was introduced.

After WWI until the 1930s the AIF pattern uniform was maintained. During the period prior to the outbreak of WWII, new and more attractive uniforms were issued to encourage enlistment in the Militia. Other than a few minor changes the 2nd AIF wore the same pattern uniform as their fathers. Later in the conflict, jungle warfare required a change in colour to that of jungle green, a colour that would remain in use after the war and through the conflicts in Malaya, Borneo, Korea and South Vietnam.

In the late 1980s the Army replaced its jungle green uniform with the disruptive pattern camouflage uniform (DPCU). This new pattern was designed in consultation with the Defence Science and Technology Organisation (DSTO) and was specifically designed for use on the Australian mainland. It therefore became necessary that with the large deployments to the arid regions of Iraq and Afghanistan to develop a new pattern. This led to the introduction of the Disruptive Pattern Desert Uniform (DPDU) and to the current Australian Multi-cam Camouflage Uniform (AMCU) or 'MultiCam'.

Accoutrements

Although the uniforms worn today have changed dramatically over the years, the accoutrements worn on the uniform have not. Some have a more recent history whilst others have a long and involved tradition of use. The following are items worn either on the uniform or as part of the equipment used by Australian soldiers since Federation.

Aiguillettes[130]

Aiguillettes are gilded cords ending in gold metal-tagged points or aglets worn by Senior Staff Officers and ADCs. Several accounts regarding their origin exist, one being that they denote the rope and pickets which were carried by the squires to tether their knights' horses. Another theory has it that they were 'aiguilles' or needles for clearing the touch hole of very old muskets and that the cords were originally lanyards, which fastened the needles to the soldiers' equipment. It is also suggested that they represent the Provost Marshall's rope with which he hung defaulters. A more plausible explanation is that they represent the pins used to secure a pauldron, or shoulder protector on the cuirass (chest armour) of a knight. These pins were permanently attached to the leather coat worn under the armour so that even when armour was not worn a knight could still be identified by the pins or aglets affixed to his coat.[131]

Governor-General Michael Jeffrey. Image courtesy of Department of Defence 20080705ran8100087_071

128 Mollo J. *Military fashion: A Comparative History of the Uniforms of the Great Armies From the 17th Century to the First World War.* London, Barrie and Jenkins: 1972, p. 217

129 Dennis P, Grey J, Morris E, Prior R. *The Oxford Companion to Australian Military History (Second Edition).* Australia, Oxford University Press: 2008, p. 538

130 Australian Army. *Army Standing Orders for Dress – 2000, Volume 1 and 2.* Canberra, Defence Publishing Service: 2003, *Vol 2* Pt 3

131 Carman WY. *A Dictionary of Military Uniforms:* London, B.T. Batsford Limited: 1977, p. 12

Image courtesy of Department of Defence. Army Generals in full dress uniform

Another theory has it that they represent the pencil, which every good Staff Officer had at hand, tied to his person by a piece of string. The aiguillette of the Japanese military is adapted for use as a pencil.

The type of aiguillette worn depends on the rank of the officer and/or the position or appointment they hold. The appointment also dictates on which shoulder the item is worn. Most senior officers wear the aiguillette on the right shoulder whilst Military Attachés wear it on the left; most ADCs, with the exception of officers on the Governor-General's Personal Staff, wear their aiguillette on the left shoulder.

There are two types of aiguillette in use by the Army:

- Type 1, which is made of 6mm gold wire cord with gold metal tags at the ends of the plaits; and

- Type 2, which is made of 6mm gold and red orris basket cord, with plait and cord loop in front and back, the plaits ending in plain cords with gold metal tags.

During the 1960s the Governors-General of the day wore a Platinum (silver) aiguillette. It is possible that these items of dress would have been supplied by the British Government via the Colonial Office and would have conformed to the standard dress requirements governing all such appointments across the Commonwealth.

After a succession of British-born Governors-General in the 1950s and 1960s, each with a military background, the appointment, in 1965, was again given to an Australian. This began an unbroken line of Australian ex-diplomats, politicians and judges who held the position until the appointment of MAJGEN the Honourable Michael Jeffery, AC, AO (Mil), CVO, MC (Retd) in 2003; he held the position until 2008.

Up until 1993 there was no allowance in the Army Dress Manual for a retired soldier to hold the appointment of Governor-General. It was at that time the Army Dress Manual was amended to include the position and authorised the wearing of the type 1 gold Aiguillette.

Army Individual Readiness Notice Badge

The Army is required to sustain military capability in order to perform any required task or mission. Increasingly the Army is required to provide personnel at short notice to perform a large variety of tasks on operations or other activities. To that end, personnel need to maintain a level of Individual Readiness which enables their deployment at short notice.

It is an individual's responsibility to ensure that they remain Army Individual Readiness Notice (AIRN) compliant at all times. Additionally, individuals are to ensure their chain of command is advised when they are not able to maintain AIRN-compliance.

The implementation of the Army's Force Generation Cycle affords both commanders and individuals the opportunity to effectively manage AIRN. AIRN requirements apply to all trade qualified full-time and part-time personnel, with the exception of those in the Standby Reserve.

Individual readiness comprises the following six components:

- Individual availability
- Employment proficiency
- Medical fitness
- Dental fitness
- Physical fitness
- Individual weapon proficiency.

The AIRN Badge is worn by compliant personnel above the right breast pocket, below emblems of unit citations and individual commendation badges or medallions. It is not worn on camouflage uniforms, maternity dress, mess dress, raincoats or any form of protective dress.

Hat Badges[132]

The size and shape of hat badges was largely influenced by the hat on which it was worn, but over the years they have been reduced in size as the type of headwear became smaller. With the introduction of the service cap it had been reduced considerably, and when the beret was adopted it was finally reduced to its modern size.

Although the Army uses the Rising Sun badge as its General Service badge, it has, since Federation, also used many different badges to identify its Corps and regiments. Many of these regimental badges disappeared with the introduction of State Regiments in the 1960s; however, there are numerous Corps badges which have remained virtually unchanged since Federation.

Collar Badges

Collar badges are in the main half-size versions of the hat badge and are used on both service and mess dress.

When a badge contains a single figure, be it human, animal or mythical creature, the collar badges are made in pairs so that when worn each can face inwards (affronted); for example, the dragons on the Royal Australian Army Dental Corps (RAADC) collar badges. Exceptions to this are the 2nd Cavalry Regiment[133] and the Pilbara Regiment who wear their collar badges with their eagles and emus respectively facing outward (or addorsed), to signify the courage and vigilance of their respective regiments in demonstrating their mottoes and in representing their preparedness. Royal Australian Army Ordnance Corps members ensure their 'cannons' are facing outwards. OCS cadets' collar badges were often checked to ensure their lions face inwards.

Chaplains wear collar badges (or patches) also on general duty dress to indicate their status as chaplains. Their badges/patches are relevant to their religion (for example, the Christian chaplains wear a Cross, Jewish chaplains a Star of David).

Parachutist Qualification Badges[134]

Trade qualification badges have been used by the military for many years, although many of those adopted are just as quickly set aside as trades become obsolescent or obsolete, for instance the 'Driver', or 'Blacksmith' badges used during WWI. Since being introduced during WWII, military-trained parachutists have worn cloth badges to show their qualification.

During WWII it was decided to develop a parachute operational capacity within the military. Because of its function it was only natural that the training of such an organisation would fall to a unit based on a RAAF unit. In late 1942, a Parachute Training Unit was raised, consisting of both RAAF and Army personnel, as Group 244 (Army) at Laverton in Victoria, and was tasked with developing a programme for the training of Paratroopers.

132 Wilkinson F. *Badges of the British Army 1820-1960: An Illustrated Reference Guide for Collectors.* London, Arms & Armour: 1972

133 Australia, Commonwealth of. *A History of the 2nd Cavalry Regiment.* Canberra, Department of Defence: 2005

134 O'Connor JM. *Australian Airborne: The History and Insignia of Australian Military Parachuting.* Kingsgrove NSW, John O'Connor: 2005

The first students of these courses were destined to become the nucleus of this new capability. After nearly 12 months training hundreds of soldiers, the 1st Australian Parachute Battalion was formed at Richmond NSW on 15 August 1943. The new unit adopted the dull cherry-coloured beret of the British Parachute Division although, for security reasons this beret was not worn whilst on leave.[135] The 1st Australian Parachute Battalion also adopted a new and distinctive shoulder badge. Throughout WWII many versions of this badge appeared on uniforms but the style and colour remained either a red or maroon backing with light blue stitching.

---

135 O'Connor JM. *Australian Airborne: The History and Insignia of Australian Military Parachuting.* Kingsgrove NSW, John O'Connor: 2005, p. 65

Army Parachutist Qualification Badges

At the time of the badges' introduction, several units were designated as parachute organisations. The following units' qualified members were entitled to wear an Australian parachute badge:

- 1st Australian Parachute Battalion
- 1st Australian Mountain Battery (Mechanised) RAA
- 1st Parachute Troop RAE
- Service Reconnaissance Department (Z Special Unit)
- 1st Australian Parachute Training Depot (Army Wing)

1st Australian Parachute Battalion – WWII
Photograph courtesy of Craig Lovejoy

SRD-Z Special Force
Photograph courtesy of Craig Lovejoy

Army Parachute Badge

3rd Battalion, The Royal Australian Regiment

Commando Regiments

Special Air Service Regiment

Regulations governing the wearing of these qualification badges required them to be worn on the right shoulder in line with the top of the tunic pocket. Members of the military who had completed at least one operational jump were permitted to wear the badge on the front of the uniform above the left pocket. The only personnel thus qualified were all members of the Service Reconnaissance Department (SRD), an organisation devoted to working behind enemy lines in either an information-gathering capacity or in offensive operations.

Another unique addition to the identification badges worn by this unit was the official unit colour patch which depicted an 'Eagle Alighting' on a maroon patch which was approved on 13th September 1943. This patch was not only worn on the puggaree of the slouch hat, but also on the upper left sleeve of the uniform.

After WWII the 1st Australian Parachute Battalion was posted to Singapore for a period of nearly 12 months[136], during which time permission was given for the qualification badge to be worn on the front of the shirt above the right breast pocket. It became common practice for the soldiers to attach the cloth badge to a metal backing plate fitted with pins so it could be transferred between shirts.

After the disbandment of the Australian Parachute Battalion in 1946, the Army remained without a parachute capacity until the formation of the SAS Company, Royal Australian Infantry, and Commando organisations in the 1950s. It was not until the formation of the 6 RAR Parachute Company Group in 1980 that RAR regained this important capability. Members of 6 RAR wore the standard Army parachute badge to identify parachute-qualified unit personnel. Although submissions were made for an official unit badge, this was not approved.

In 1983 3 RAR was tasked with developing a parachute capability that would ultimately develop into a Parachute Battalion Group (PBG), which included support elements such 'A' Field Battery, RAA. 3 RAR, wishing to foster a traditional link to the 1st Australian Parachute Battalion, applied for and was granted permission to wear the Australian Parachute badge. This Parachute badge is currently worn by all members posted to the PBG.

Within the Army there are currently four different parachute badges, although each badge has a primary qualification as the grounds for its award, three are regiment specific (3 RAR, Cdos and SASR) and are therefore only worn by members of those particular units.

Image courtesy of Department of Defence 20100906adf8439709_0743. Soldiers from 3 RAR parachute into the Shoalwater Bay Training Area

136 O'Connor JM. *Australian Airborne: The History and Insignia of Australian Military Parachuting.* Kingsgrove NSW, John O'Connor: 2005, p. 65

Bandoleers/Bandolier

The bandoleer (from the Spanish banda, or sash), of the 17th century was a leather belt which went over the shoulder and was used by a musketeer for carrying powder charges.[137] There was also a bullet bag at the lowest point under the right arm. The leather cartridge belt that was used to carry bullets in the 2nd Boer War was also given this name. After 1903 the Army was separated into mounted and dismounted troops. Mounted troops wore the five pocket bandolier unless they were Australian Light Horse (ALH), the ALH wore the nine pocket bandolier whereas dismounted troops wore the standard Pattern 08 infantry equipment.

The bandolier was used extensively by the ALH during its campaigns throughout the Middle East. Bandoliers were used as a means of carrying ammunition up until 1945; it is still used as a ceremonial accoutrement during parades by the armoured and light horse units.

The current design of the bandolier is based on the WWI Light Horse design, the nine pocket bandolier – five ammunition pouches to the front and four to the rear. Bandoliers worn for dismounted parades are made of black leather; bandoliers worn for mounted parades are made of brown leather. The buckles and fasteners of both black and brown bandoliers are chrome or silver. Bandoliers are worn on the left shoulder and fastened under the epaulette, with the adjustment buckle positioned to the lower right rear above the waist belt.

To perpetuate and symbolise the traditions of past light horse and cavalry units, which were traditionally linked to the 2nd Cavalry Regiment through the 4th/19th Prince of Wales's Light Horse, approval was sought and gained for selected members of the Regiment to carry lances and wear bandoliers on ceremonial occasions. Official approval was granted in February 1974 for WO2, SSGT and SGT to wear bandoliers and carry lances on ceremonial parades and guards.

---

137 Carman WY. *A Dictionary of Military Uniforms: London, B.T. Batsford Limited*: 1977, p. 23

Canes/Swagger Sticks

Canes have their origins in the original swagger stick. Swagger sticks were introduced as an item of commissioned rank equipment in the time of King Charles I (r. 1625-1649) but were used for a more serious purpose than they are today; in King Charles' time all junior officers were empowered to inflict punishment on the spot for minor offences. These original sticks were long heavy items.

The name is derived from the bamboo or rattan from which the cane was made during the early ninteeth century. The cane at that time, was carried by both soldiers and officers as part of their 'walking out dress'[138]; and the use of these items in the British Army was generally discontinued after WWII.

The current cane is an optional accoutrement that may be carried by members of the Australian Army of the rank of SGT and WO2, and may also be carried by CPLs, when ordered to do so, usually only within training establishments. The cane is not carried on ceremonial parades with troops.

Lances

Since ancient times the lance of the mounted soldier and the pike of the foot soldier gave the user an advantage in reach and were an important weapon. In medieval times the lance found favour with knights and it became a symbol of more chivalrous times. With the introduction onto the battlefield of the long bow, the lance and pike fell from favour as they no longer afforded the user a distinct advantage.

The lance of today is only carried on ceremonial parades by the RAAC. It is to be no more than 2.77m in length (measured from the bottom of the shoe to the tip of the head), and the weight is to be between 2.0 and 2.6kg. The stave of the lance can be made of black ash or bamboo and is tapered from a diameter of 3.7cm at the shoe to 2.7cm at the point where the stave is joined to the head.

The grip/sling of the lance is made of black leather and is positioned so that it is central to the balance point of the lance, which should be approximately 1.17m from the shoe. The grip/sling is to be no more than 33cm in length.

The unit pennant is attached to the stave of the lance immediately below the head. Lances are carried, when ordered, by WO, NCO and other ranks of the RAAC on ceremonial parades.

Image courtesy of Department of Defence 20110425adf8271092_ 118. Escorts of the 2nd/14th Light Horse Regiment (QMI) Guidon Party – Anzac Day 2011

138 Carman WY. *A Dictionary of Military Uniforms*: London, B.T. Batsford Limited: 1977, p. 15

Bayonets

Bayonets existed as a hunting weapon in the 16th century; they were reputedly first made in the 15th century and were later adopted as a military weapon in the French Army. The first general issue of bayonets to British Infantry and Dragoons occurred on 17th March 1662 with the purchase of 500 used 'plug' bayonets from Dunkirk for trials. The early designs resembled a dagger and were so called in early drill manuals, which date back to 1673. The origin of the name is a much-debated subject with no clear explanation being universally accepted. The bayonet was developed, initially, so that the early musket could still be used effectively as a weapon, in close combat, when reloading would be impossible; the 'plug' bayonet was inserted into the muzzle of the musket, therefore allowing the musket to be used as a pike.

Bayonets are not currently used by the Army on the Austeyr F88 on ceremonial occasions except for colour parties/guards. The Australian Federation Guard (AFG) on ceremonial occasions uses the previous standard issue rifle, the 7.62mm L1A1, with a chromed bayonet and magazine.

Standards and guidons of the RAAC are carried by SSMs with an escort of two SNCOs, the Queen's and regimental Colours of infantry battalions are carried by commissioned officers of the battalion and Corps banners are carried by commissioned officers escorted by SNCO. The Colour Party bayonets are chromed and usually have a small metal cap fitted to the tip to ensure that the Colours are not accidently ripped or damaged by the bayonets.

Above: Image courtesy of Department of Defence – 20110603adf8270845_063. A member of the AFG holding a 7.62mm L1A1 in the Reversed Arms Position

Left: Image courtesy of Department of Defence – 20080827adf809924_569. Australian Federation Guard parading with 7.62mm Self Loading Rifle

Right: Image courtesy of Department of Defence – 20101209adf8262658_343. Lieutenant General David Hurley, presents the Chief of the Defence Force Sword of Honour to Officer Cadet James McKew, 2013

Rifles

The 7.62mm L1A1 (Self Loading Rifle) and current service standard issue assault rifle (Austeyr F88) are both used for ceremonial purposes. The 7.62mm L1A1 is now only used by the AFG. The 7.62mm L1A1's continued use by the AFG is because most ceremonial drill movements, especially funeral drill, originally developed for the .303 inch Lee Enfield rifle, require a full-length weapon. The original .303 was 1.1 meters in length, the 7.62mm L1A1 was 1.09 meters, whilst the Austeyr F88 is only 790mm in length. Although it is possible to complete some modified versions of such movements as 'Rest on Arms' with the Austeyr, it is not possible to carry out the more formal drill used on such occasions as memorial services.

The two most important of these movements are 'Reverse Arms' and 'Rest on Arms Reversed'. There are still images and cinematic footage from WWI showing these drill movements being executed at military funerals during this period; the AWM holds footage of Australian troops carrying out these same drill movements for the funeral of the Red Baron, Manfred von Richthofen, after he was shot down by members of the Australian 24th Machine Gun Company in April 1918.[139]

Swords[140, 141]

Today's swords are facsimiles of the workmanlike weapons of the past and are essentially a ceremonial weapon. The pattern date referred to in the description of a sword should not be confused with the date of manufacture. There are six distinct types of swords carried in the Australian Army:

- Sword - General Officer 'Mameluke'
- Sword - Cavalry Officer Pattern 1912
- Sword - Cavalry (Trooper) Pattern 1908 Mark I
- Sword - Artillery Officer Pattern 1822 British
- Sword - Infantry Officer Pattern 1897 British
- Sword - Scottish Claymore or Broadsword.

139 Miller G. *The Death of Manfred von Richthofen: Who fired the fatal shot? Sabretache: Journal and Proceedings of the Military History Society of Australia*: 1998, vol. XXXIX, no. 2

140 Robson B. *Swords of the British Army: The Regulation Patterns, 1788-1914*. London, Arms and Armour Press: 1975

141 Bezdek RH. *Swords and Sword Markers of England and Scotland*. Colorado, USA, Paladin Press: 2004

Sword General Officer 'Mameluke' and
Scabbard. Photograph courtesy of Major
General Mick Slater DSC, AM, CSC

Sword – General Officer 'Mameluke' (Sword Mameluke)

Mameluke swords are a cross-hilted, curved, scimitar-like sword historically used by Mamluk warriors from whom the sword derives its name. During the French Egyptian campaigns (1798-1801), the French army adopted this new style of sword, which at the time was used by the Mamluk slave troops of the Ottoman Empire. Napoleon Bonaparte was so impressed by the bravery and discipline of these troops that he purchased the services of 2,000 troops from Syrian merchants. These Mamluk warriors eventually served as part of his Imperial Guard[142] with one individual, Mamluk Roustam Raza, chosen to be his personal bodyguard.[143]

The Mameluke sword is related to the shamshir, which had its origins in Persia from where the style migrated to India, Egypt and North Africa. It was adopted in the 19th century by several Western military forces, including the French Army, British Army and the United States Marine Corps.

Mameluke swords were carried as dress swords by officers of most light cavalry and hussar regiments, and some heavy cavalry regiments in the British Army at various times during the 19th century (after the Battle of Waterloo). The current regulation sword for Generals is the British 1831 Pattern General Officers' Dress Sword. It is a Mameluke-style sword, and is carried on ceremonial occasions, and unlike other regulation swords, must be supported by the bearer since a Sam Browne Belt is not worn.

Sword – Cavalry Officer Pattern 1912 (The Cavalry Sword)

The Cavalry Sword – British Pattern 1912 Cavalry Officer's Sword, the hilt has a nickel plated steel bowl guard decorated on the outside with a scroll design and has a sword knot slot near the pommel. The straight blade has a single fuller to each side to within eight inches of the sword point and is decorated with an engraved floral design.

Sword Cavalry Officer Pattern 1912 and Scabbard

142 Carman WY. *A Dictionary of Military Uniforms*: London, B.T. Batsford Limited: 1977, p. 88

143 Withers H. *The Illustrated Encyclopedia of Swords and Sabres*. North Melbourne, Alto Books: 2008, p. 57

Sword – Cavalry (Trooper) Pattern 1908 Mark I (The Sword Cavalry 1908)

The Sword Cavalry Pattern 1908 was used extensively by the light horse. Distinctive features of this sword include the pommel and ferrule at the bottom of the grip, which are of malleable cast iron, the grip is dermatine or similar light brown plastic with a large depression for the thumb with the guard of a sheet steel bowl with a beaded edge. The blade is straight-tapered with a single fuller on each side to within 8 inches of the spear point and double-edged for the last 6 inches.

Although a general issue sword in use before WWI, like the cavalry to which it belonged it saw little active service. It was finally issued to ALH units of the Desert Mounted Corps, although it arrived too late to be used in what is popularly, but erroneously, believed to be one of the last great cavalry charges in history, the mounted charge of the 4th Light Horse Brigade at Beersheba.[144]

Sword – Artillery Officer Pattern 1822 (The Artillery Sword)

The Artillery Sword – British Pattern 1822 Artillery Officer's Sword has a steel three bar hilt and back strap with a wire bound sharkskin grip. The sword knot is able to hang so that the strap could be wrapped around the wrist when mounted. The slightly curved blade (based on the cavalry sword) has a single fuller to each side to within 11 inches of the sword point.

144 Withers H. *The Illustrated Encyclopaedia of Swords and Sabres.* North Melbourne, Alto Books: 2008, p. 76

Sword Cavalry (Trooper) Pattern 1908 Mark I and Scabbard

Sword Artillery Officer Pattern 1822
British and Scabbard

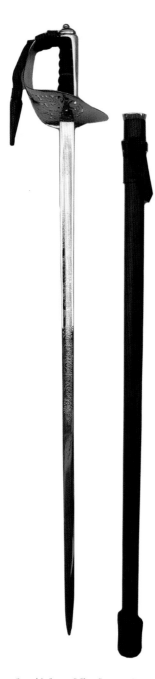

Sword Infantry Officer Pattern 1897 British and Scabbard

Sword – Infantry Officer Pattern 1897 British (The Sword Infantry)

The Infantry Sword – the British Pattern 1897 Infantry Officer's Sword and Scabbard. The hilt has a nickel-plated three-quarter 'scroll' pattern, pierced sheet steel guard currently with the 'EIIR' Royal Cypher, with a leather sword knot attached to the slot near the pommel. The grip is wire-bound black sharkskin. The straight blade is etched half-way on both sides with a foliage design having the Royal Cypher of Elizabeth II in the centre. There is a single fuller on each side. The brown leather scabbard is wood lined with a leather shoe. This model sword was an improved version of the 1895 Pattern, which combined a more robust blade with a thrusting point to the blade.[145]

The hand guard was also turned down on the inner edge to prevent the fraying of the uniform. On ceremonial occasions such as 'Trooping the Colours', the Ensign's brown scabbard may be replaced by a chrome scabbard.

All regulation swords include a leather or gilt cord that historically served the purpose of ensuring the user did not lose control of the sword in battle.

Sword – The Claymore or Broadsword (Scottish Units)

There are in fact three distinct types of Claymore sword; the original 'claidheamh mor' was a large two handed sword used in the late Medieval to early modern times; the claidheamh da laimh, also a two handed heavy broad sword; and the more commonly recognised type of 'lowland sword' or basket hilt sword which is in fact not of Scottish origin, although it is always associated with the Highland warrior. The original enclosed handle design was introduced to protect the hand during combat. Within the military the basket-hilted Claymore is still carried by officers in Scottish Regiments as part of their ceremonial dress.[146]

---

145 Withers H. *The Illustrated Encyclopedia of Swords and Sabres.* North Melbourne, Alto Books: 2008, p. 199

146 Withers H. *The Illustrated Encyclopedia of Swords and Sabres.* North Melbourne, Alto Books: 2008, pp. 50-53

Claymore or Broadsword and Scabbard
Photograph Courtesy of WKC Swords, Germany

The Dirk (Scottish Units)

The history of the Dirk can be traced back to 1050 in an early form known as a Scottish Ballock knife. By the 17th century the blade had increased in length and had become commonly known as a 'Durk'. The current spelling of the word is apparently the result of an incorrect spelling entry in a dictionary written by Dr Johnson in 1755.[147] The failure of the Jacobite Rebellions in 1715 and 1745 lead to several Disarming Acts which outlawed both the carrying and possession of weapons by Scottish Highlanders. In later years, these items found favour with the newly raised Scottish Regiments, and are now carried as part of military ceremonial dress by members of Scottish units.

The Dirk and Scabbard

147 Levine B, Weland G. *Knives, Swords, Daggers.* London, Quintet Publishing: 2004, p. 110

Image courtesy Department of Defence – 20110126ran8100087_025. Gunners conduct the Australia Day 21 Gun Salute   Darwin 2012

Artillery Pieces

Within RAA their 'Regimental Colours' are the guns and as with all Colours serve as rallying points in battle. The guns, as their Colours, are used on ceremonial occasions by artillery, and are always given suitable respect by troops.

Berets

Berets originated in the Basque Region of France. The first British unit to adopt this form of head dress was the Royal Tank Regiment in 1925. The reason for this seems to be the close fitting characteristic of the beret which allowed it to be worn in the confined spaces of an armoured vehicle. The iconic beret has been worn by Australian troops on battlefields across the world. The colour of an armoured regiment's beret was black, due to the impracticality of keeping any other colour clean.

During WWII, berets of various colours were adopted by special units, and Australia has adopted this same principle for its units and Corps. There are at present 11 different coloured berets used within the Australian Army:[148]

- Dark Blue – General Service beret used by the majority of Corps

- Black – RAAC

- Rifle Green – RAR (and AATTV Association)

- Light or Sky Blue – AAAvn

- Sherwood Green – Cdo. The British Commando Green Beret was originally introduced into service in late 1942[149]; this same beret was subsequently adopted by the Australian Cdos in 1955

- Scarlet – RACMP

- Dull Cherry – Airborne including RAAOC Parachute Riggers and RACT 176 Air Dispatch parachute-qualified members

- Slate Grey – RAANC

- Terracotta – Multinational Force Observer, and

- Light Blue – UN peacekeepers

- Fawn (Sand or Tan) – SASR.  The sand-coloured beret of the SAS is officially designated the beige beret, since it is made from material of that colour. When the British SAS was re-raised in 1947 an attempt was made to match the original WWII sand-coloured cloth beret from those still in the possession of veterans. This was not possible, given the choice of official approved cloth colour; as a compromise the nearest shade colour was selected and approved by an all-ranks committee of the SAS Regimental Association

In August 2010, the CA, in line with the 'sun smart' policy, ordered soldiers to wear, as dress of the day, their 'slouch hat'. Berets are only to be worn on ceremonial and special occasions. There are exceptions, for example the SASR. In 2013 the CA approved the wearing of the beret by the wider Army as an option for dress of the day head dress.

148 Australian Army, *Army Standing Orders for Dress – 2000, Volume 1 and 2*. Canberra, Defence Publishing Service: 2003, Vol 2 Pt 3 Chap 1 para 1.11

149 Collins P. Strike Swiftly: *The Australian Commando Story*. Sydney, Watermark Press: 2005, p. 6

Bush Hat (Hat Utility)

The bush hat or giggle hat as it is affectionately known is a soft-brimmed cloth hat made of the same coloured material as the uniform with which it is worn (jungle green or camouflaged). The term 'Giggle Hat' dates back to 1939, when soldiers of the 2nd AIF, in training at Ingleburn NSW, named their fatigue uniform 'Giggle Suits and Hats' because of their resemblance to the clothing worn by the inmates of a local lunatic asylum.[150]

Cloth and Metal Shoulder Titles

Metal shoulder titles have been used to identify a soldier's unit since colonial times. However it has only been since the introduction of Corps badges in the late 1940s that embroidered Shoulder Title Branch of Service (flashes) have been used. The embroidered shoulder flash was worn on the sleeve top of the Battle Dress jacket whilst the metal Unit or Corps Title is worn on the epaulette of the summer dress shirt. Metal Unit and Corps Titles are not worn outside of Australia.

A metal title 'AUSTRALIA' was issued to all troops for wear outside Australia and its Territories. Metal titles worn by the AIF were originally black; however in recent times two colours have been used; silver for RAAC, AAAvn and RAANC and gold for other Corps. The title was introduced during WWI and has been worn by Australian soldiers when serving overseas ever since. An embroidered title is also authorised for use on winter forms of dress such as the Winter Service Dress and Mess Kit. Titles are no longer worn on field dress; the cloth 'Rising Sun' is used in preference.

Colour Patches[151]

Colours were first used as identification badges by Australians during the latter stages of the 2nd Boer War in South Africa (1899-1902), when members of the contingents operating with MAJGEN Rimington's[152] column wore red ribbons fluttering from their left shoulder-straps.

Colour Patches were not introduced into the Army until March 1915, some six months after the formation of the AIF. Initially, the headquarters of the formation, units, accommodation areas and transport lines were identified by the use of small coloured square flags. These flags used a two colour system of identification; the flag was divided horizontally with the bottom colour representing the parent brigade and the upper the battalion according to its numerical seniority within that brigade.

When MAJGEN WT Bridges first approved the use of colour patches to be worn on the uniform, he was in command of a single division consisting of three brigades with a fourth brigade raised from the excess volunteers who rushed to join the force at the outbreak of the war. The patches were worn on the jacket on both sleeves 1 inch from the top of the sleeve. So as to present exactly the same in appearance when viewed from the front, all patches were made in pairs.

The colour coding selected appeared to satisfy his intention of allowing easy identification of soldiers and units. One anomaly was caused by the 13th Battalion whose colours were to be black over dark blue however this combination made it difficult for it to be easily distinguished from that of its own brigade headquarters. It was therefore decided to change its unit identifying colour to light blue. The reason for selecting light blue over dark blue was that at the time they were, and still are, the New South Wales Sport colour, and as the 13th was raised in NSW it seemed appropriate.

Originally the second battalion in each brigade was to use yellow as its identifying colour thus ensuring that no battalion would use a colour that was allocated to a brigade. When it became know that this was to occur, LTCOL Richard Courtney the CO of the 14th Battalion, immediately sent to Cairo for enough yellow cloth to not only satisfy the needs of his men's uniforms, but also for flags for the unit lines. A shortage of cloth at the time meant that the other units were forced to use purple, thus it was the other brigades which differed from the 4th and not the 4th from them.[153]

After its arrival in the Middle East the 4th Brigade was moved from under the command of the 1st Division and placed with the newly formed New Zealand and Australian Division. As this formation did not use colour patches, the Brigade was permitted to continue using its 1st Division-styled patch for the duration of the Gallipoli campaign.

150 Charlton P. *The Thirty-Niners*. South Melbourne, Macmillan: 1981

151 Glyde K. *Distinguishing Colour Patches of the Australian Military Forces 1915-1951: A Reference Guide*. Claremont Tasmania, DW Thorpe: 1999
(with colour matching information from the work of Dr Andrew Richardson, Australian Army History Unit)

152 Lieutenant General Sir Michael Frederic Rimington, KCB, CVO; commanded Rimington's Guides, 6th (Inniskilling) Dragoons, 3rd Cavalry Brigade, 1st Indian Cavalry Division, Indian Cavalry Corps appointed a commander of the legion d'honneur, and twice mentioned in despatches: born Penrith England 23 May 1858 – died 19 December 1928.

153 White TA. *The History of the Thirteenth Battalion, AIF.* Sydney, Tyrells Ltd: 1924, p. 24

AWM Neg No B 00101 - A member of the 7th Australian Light Horse Regiment (7ALH) sewing new colour patches on his uniform, circa 1918

The AIF continued to grow slowly with the addition of a second division and numerous mounted units. By early 1916, the majority of the AIF was concentrated in Egypt awaiting movement to France and the battlefields of Flanders. With the additional manpower available to the AIF it was decided to increase the structure of the force to a total of five divisions.

Each new division was allocated a distinctive colour patch shape which would form the basis of patches used by that division. The first major deviation from the system occurred at this time when the 4th Brigade was permitted to continue wearing their old 1st Division shape colour patch after it was allocated to the newly raised 4th Division.

When the 2nd AIF was formed (1939), colour patches were again utilised for the purpose of identification. The principle governing the allotment of the patches was the unit should wear the same patch as worn by the corresponding unit of the AIF, but with a grey background to distinguish these new units from similarly numbered units of the militia which still wore the colour patches applicable to the AIF. Patches were to be worn on the jacket as for the AIF; however they were also worn on the right side of the hat puggaree when summer field dress was worn, and also on the beret by armoured units.

The colour patch system was highly successful as a means of unit identification during WWI but became hopelessly confused during WWII due to:

- After the formation of the 6th and 7th Divisions the reduction in infantry battalions from four to three per brigade meant that two of the battalions reallocated to other divisions wore patches indicating their higher formation as their original division.

- The original system was never observed by Militia formations that were allocated to brigades according to military districts. It was possible to find in one Militia brigade three different shaped patches and five colours.

- The return to Australia of the 6th and 7th Divisions in 1942, added to the confusion because of the resultant duplication of colour patches that occurred when these formations began serving alongside the militia units many of which by this time had been granted the grey border of the 2nd AIF.

- The 25th Brigade which was formed in England chose its own colour patches which went against the principal intention of uniformity. A result of this was that the 24th and 25th Brigade headquarters wore identical patches for a period of two years.

- In 1942, MAJGEN Leslie Morshead gained approval for the 9th Division to change the shape of their colour patch to a "T" shape to commemorate that division's service at Tobruk.

- The colour patch system was designed to allow identification of units within a basic infantry division. By the conclusion of WWII the Australian Army structure had expanded to three corps or a total of 12 infantry divisions and four armoured/cavalry divisions. It also included all the normal support units, training organisations and heavy arms units found in corps or army-sized organisations.

The confusion associated with colour patches in WWII, highlighted the need for a more simplified system and consequently a new system (copying the British Army formation sign system) was adopted. The use of colour patches was discontinued in 1949.

Reintroduction of Colour Patches[154]

Colour patches were reintroduced on 3rd August 1987 for ceremonial use only; whereas the Series II colour patch was introduced for general use in 1995. The colour patch of an AIF unit is permitted to be worn on the slouch hat of a current unit that can trace its origin back to that original unit. This lineage is not just numeric, the requesting unit must be able to prove that the current organisation seeking approval:

- Is the same Corps as the original unit such as Infantry, Medical.

- Performs the same function as the original unit, such as Transport, Artillery.

- Is the same type of unit within the Army structure, such as a BDE, DIV or a Corps.

The wearing of the 1915-1949 colour patches was reintroduced primarily on the basis of fostering the Army's heritage, through unit lineage and similarity of roles to units of 1915-1949 which had approved colour patches. Those patches authorised since 1987 are, with the exception of some divisional troop units, specifically 'unit' colour patches, being unique to each authorised unit.

Introduction of New Patches

The nature of the structure of the Army in the early 1990s was such that only about 25 per cent of units, regular and reserve, had lineage and similarity of role to 1915-1949 units to be able to claim those patches. At the same time only a relatively small number of units had unique unit badges by which to be identified.

Because of these circumstances, the number of units unsuccessfully seeking approval for colour patches and the apparent need for a system of unit identification particularly in case of expansion, a second 'series' of colour patches was designed. These complemented the 1915-1949 series and provided every unit in the Army with its own unit colour patch. The Chief of the General Staff Advisory Committee approved the concept in 1994 and introduction was effected in 1995.

Two Series of Unit Colour Patches

Two series of Unit Colour Patches (UCP) are approved for the Australian Army:

- Series I are the patches for units of the AIF and the whole Army from 1921 to 1949. These are worn by units which have established their lineage and similarity of role to earlier units. A small number of these patches have been used as a basis for Series II patches for organisational reasons, others as a basis for completing pattern gaps to provide continuing heritage; these are referred to as Series I (Extended).

- Series II patches, introduced in 1995, are based largely on the colour combinations of Series I, which indicated headquarters, Corps and some functions. These are arranged as square base patches identifying Headquarters ADF. Smaller overlayed shapes in various colours identify uniquely non-Corps units under command of those headquarters, and Corps units respectively. These patches are worn by units which have not established lineage and similarity of role for a Series I patch.

---

154 Australian Army, *Army Standing Orders for Dress – 2000, Volume 1 and 2*. Canberra, Defence Publishing Service: 2003, Vol 2 Pt 6 Chap 1

AIF – Infantry Division Colour Patches

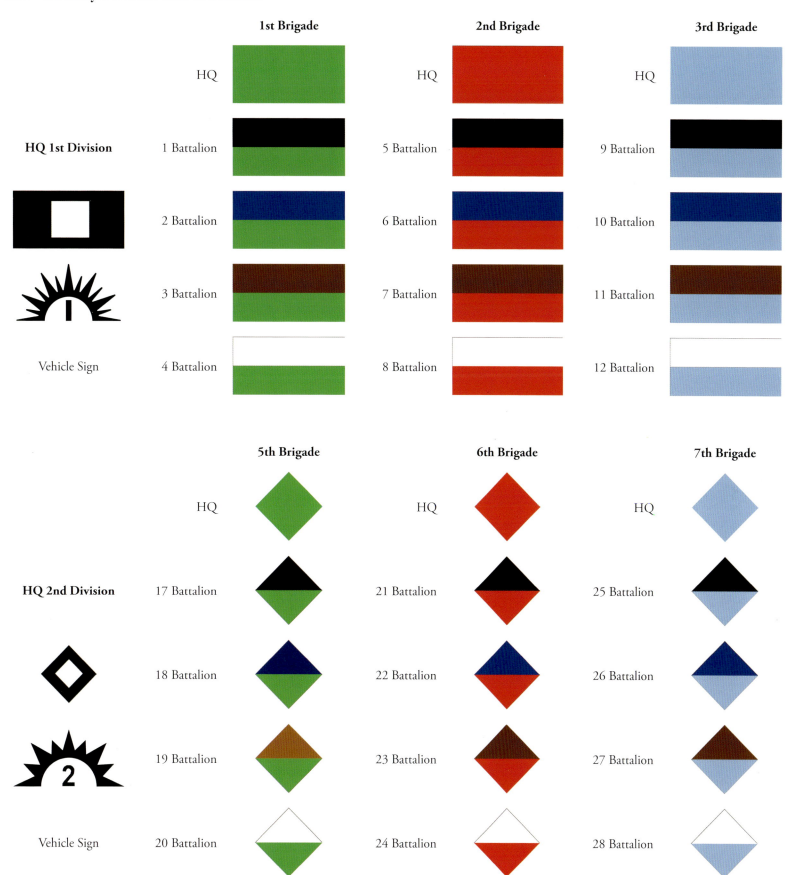

1st Brigade

HQ

HQ 1st Division

1 Battalion

2 Battalion

3 Battalion

Vehicle Sign | 4 Battalion

2nd Brigade

HQ

5 Battalion

6 Battalion

7 Battalion

8 Battalion

3rd Brigade

HQ

9 Battalion

10 Battalion

11 Battalion

12 Battalion

5th Brigade

HQ

HQ 2nd Division

17 Battalion

18 Battalion

19 Battalion

Vehicle Sign | 20 Battalion

6th Brigade

HQ

21 Battalion

22 Battalion

23 Battalion

24 Battalion

7th Brigade

HQ

25 Battalion

26 Battalion

27 Battalion

28 Battalion

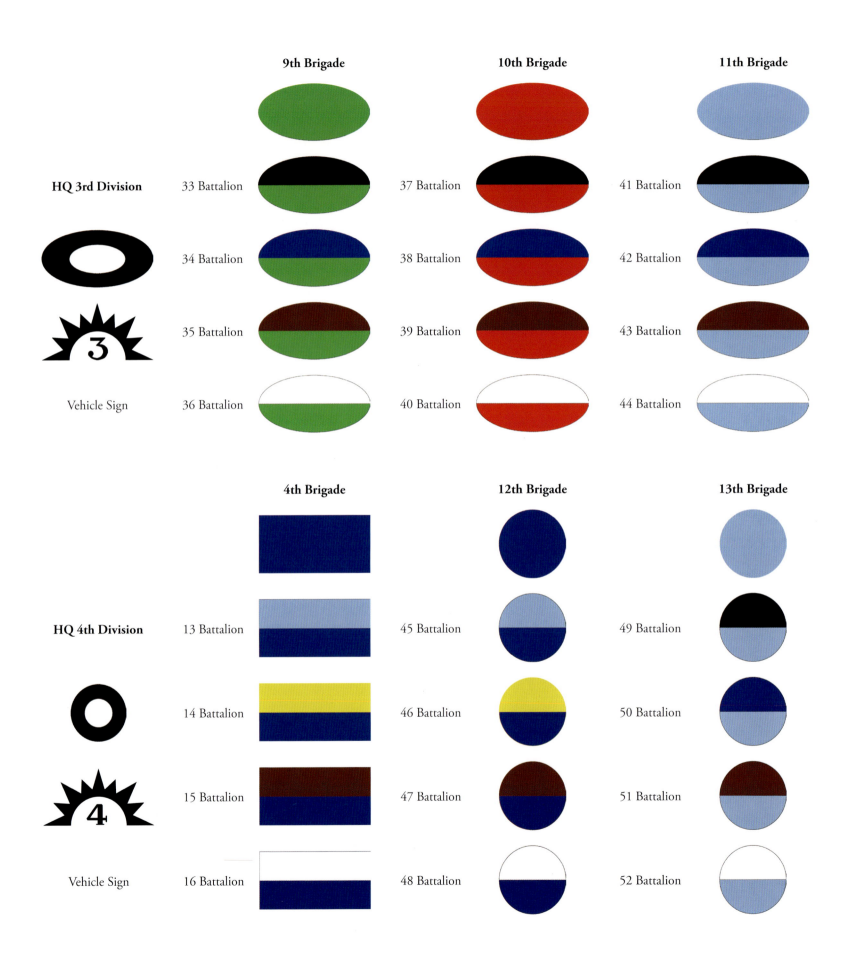

9th Brigade

10th Brigade

11th Brigade

HQ 3rd Division

33 Battalion

34 Battalion

35 Battalion

Vehicle Sign

36 Battalion

37 Battalion

38 Battalion

39 Battalion

40 Battalion

41 Battalion

42 Battalion

43 Battalion

44 Battalion

4th Brigade

12th Brigade

13th Brigade

HQ 4th Division

13 Battalion

14 Battalion

15 Battalion

Vehicle Sign

16 Battalion

45 Battalion

46 Battalion

47 Battalion

48 Battalion

49 Battalion

50 Battalion

51 Battalion

52 Battalion

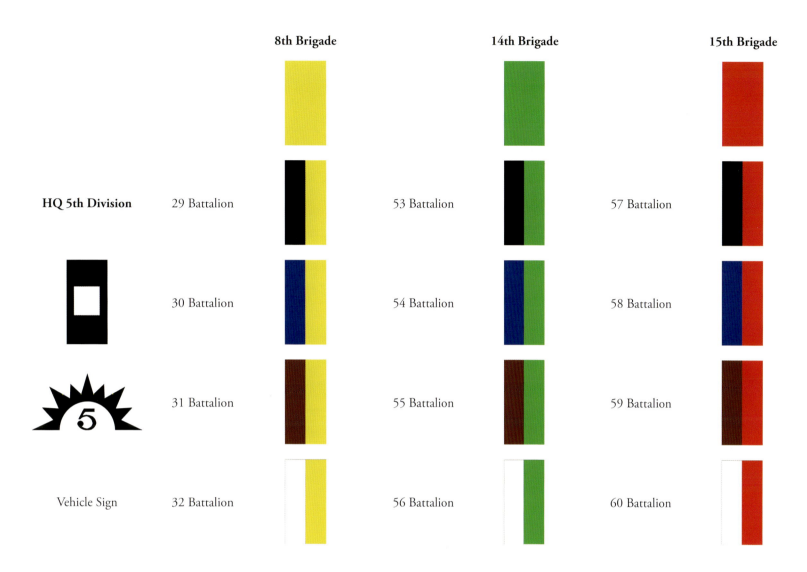

	8th Brigade		14th Brigade		15th Brigade
HQ 5th Division	29 Battalion		53 Battalion		57 Battalion
	30 Battalion		54 Battalion		58 Battalion
	31 Battalion		55 Battalion		59 Battalion
Vehicle Sign	32 Battalion		56 Battalion		60 Battalion

AIF – Light Horse Colour Patches

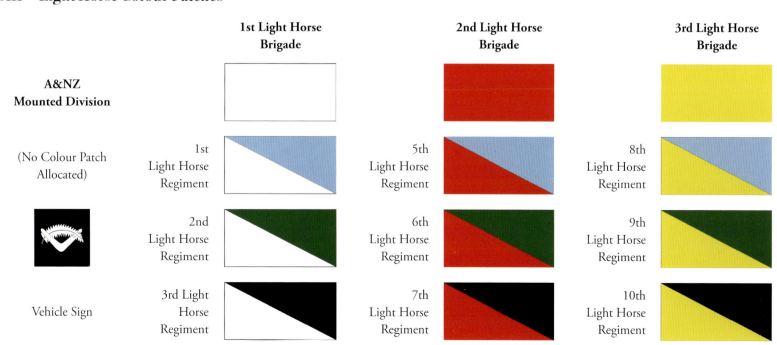

	1st Light Horse Brigade	2nd Light Horse Brigade	3rd Light Horse Brigade
A&NZ Mounted Division			
(No Colour Patch Allocated)	1st Light Horse Regiment	5th Light Horse Regiment	8th Light Horse Regiment
	2nd Light Horse Regiment	6th Light Horse Regiment	9th Light Horse Regiment
Vehicle Sign	3rd Light Horse Regiment	7th Light Horse Regiment	10th Light Horse Regiment

4th Light Horse Brigade

5th Light Horse Brigade

Australian Mounted Division

(No Colour Patch Allocated)

Vehicle Sign

4th Light Horse Regiment

11th Light Horse Regiment

12th Light Horse Regiment

14th Light Horse Regiment

15th Light Horse Regiment

French Mounted Unit

(No Colour Patch Allocated)

1st ANZAC Corps

13th Light Horse Regiment

(Redesignated 1st ANZAC Mounted Regiment – 1916)

Vehicle Sign

Original 2nd Australian Imperial Force (2nd AIF) – Colour Patches

		16th Brigade		**17th Brigade**		**19th Brigade**
HQ 6th Division	Headquarters		Headquarters		Headquarters	
	2/1 Battalion		2/5 Battalion		2/4 Battalion	
	2/2 Battalion		2/6 Battalion		2/8 Battalion	
Vehicle Sign	2/3 Battalion		2/7 Battalion		2/11 Battalion	

		18th Brigade		**21st Brigade**		**25th Brigade**
HQ 7th Division	Headquarters		Headquarters		Headquarters	
	2/9 Battalion		2/14 Battalion		2/25 Battalion	
	2/10 Battalion		2/16 Battalion		2/31 Battalion	
Vehicle Sign	2/12 Battalion		2/27 Battalion		2/33 Battalion	

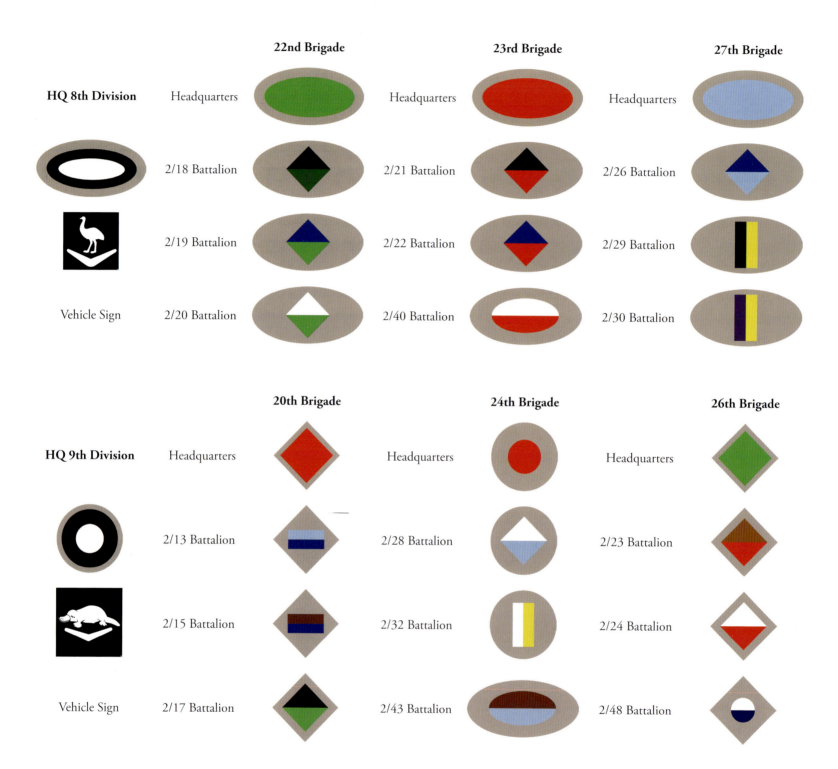

22nd Brigade

23rd Brigade

27th Brigade

HQ 8th Division

Headquarters

Headquarters

Headquarters

2/18 Battalion

2/21 Battalion

2/26 Battalion

2/19 Battalion

2/22 Battalion

2/29 Battalion

Vehicle Sign

2/20 Battalion

2/40 Battalion

2/30 Battalion

20th Brigade

24th Brigade

26th Brigade

HQ 9th Division

Headquarters

Headquarters

Headquarters

2/13 Battalion

2/28 Battalion

2/23 Battalion

2/15 Battalion

2/32 Battalion

2/24 Battalion

Vehicle Sign

2/17 Battalion

2/43 Battalion

2/48 Battalion

Divisional Supporting Arms and Service Units

	6th Division	7th Division	8th Division	9th Division
Cavalry				
Artillery				
Engineers				
Signals				
A.A.S.C.				
Medical				
Provost Coy				

Patches shown are 'Left Hand' about 1940-1942

Principles Governing Colour Patch Allocation

- **Unit identity.** With the exception of units authorised, Series I patches worn originally by divisional troops, each colour patch is to be unique to a unit.

- **Identification of units for Series I patches.** The priority in selecting a colour patch for a unit on raising is an appropriate Series I patch, subject to relevance of lineage and similarity of role, before allocation of a Series II patch.

- **Heritage within Series I patches.** In the selection of a Series I patch for authorisation, with a choice between, for example a WWI and WWII patch for the same infantry battalion, the older patch is selected because of its heritage value. In some cases, however, the first unit of a particular type may have been raised only for WWII service and be authorised a 2nd AIF patch.

- **Changes in Series II patches - Corps units.** Units are to retain the originally-approved patch regardless of change in role or seniority within the Corps.

- **Changes in Series II patches - non-Corps units.** Changes from one role to another role represented by a different superimposed colour will necessitate a change in colour patch to conform to the new role. The colour patch from the previous role is to be reserved for allocation to the next unit raised with that role regardless of the initial basis of allocation, such as seniority.

- **Change of Corps and non-Corps status.** Units allocated to another Corps, or from Corps to non-Corps, or non-Corps to Corps status are to be authorised the appropriate change in Series I or II colour patch.

- **Linking and unlinking of units.** Following the precedent established in WWI, units on linking are to wear the colour patch of the unit first-named in the linking. The colour patch of the second-named unit is to be reserved for re-authorisation on unlinking of those units.

- **Amalgamation.** On amalgamation, the identity to be established by unit colour patch is that of the newly-named unit. The principles addressed in the linking or unlinking of units should be followed in seeking colour patch authorisation.

- **Disbanding.** On disbanding, a unit's colour patch is normally reserved in case of its re-raising, in order to retain the lineage and enhance the heritage value. This principle applies equally to Series I and Series II patches; with Series II patches developing heritage value when worn by the one unit over a period of years.

Colour of Uniform Cloth

The term khaki is derived from the Persian 'Yak' (or khaki) and there are two versions as to its origin. The first being that in 1845 COL Lumsden[155] of the Indian Guides discarded the scarlet, dark blue and dark green uniform of the British Army as too conspicuous and hard to clean. The adopted uniforms were then called khaki (dust coloured[156]) and were only worn by the Punjab Frontier Force until the Afghan War of 1878-1881 when it came into general use within the British Army and gradually spread to other European armies.

The second version of its origin was that in 1857-1858 during the Indian Mutiny, the Buckinghamshire Light Infantry who normally wore white uniforms (a form of hot weather dress) opted to dye their uniforms a more natural colour. These uniforms were stained with brown mud, although one authority quotes curry powder as being used for staining purposes. Khaki was first adopted in Australia in 1890, but the official adoption as British Service Dress dates from the 2nd Boer War (South African War 1899-1902).

Cummerbunds

The name comes from the Persian for a waist restraint (*kamar* = middle or waist) and was adopted into English around 1616. The cummerbund or cumberbund is a broad waist sash, usually pleated, which is often worn with single-breasted dinner jackets. The cummerbund was first adopted by British military officers in colonial India as a cooler alternative to wearing a waistcoat. The cummerbund is worn with Mess Dress White Jacket. It is made of silk and is generally the same colour as the colour prescribed for the formal Mess Waistcoat worn by commissioned officers with the following exceptions:

- A member of RAA or RACT is to wear a blue-black cummerbund.

- A member of RAE is to wear a scarlet cummerbund.

- Regimental Sergeant Major – Army (RSM-A) and Tier C RSMs are to wear a black cummerbund.

- A member of RMC-D is to wear a scarlet cummerbund.

- Cummerbunds are also worn by members of the Australian Army Band Corps (AABC) when in prescribed forms of ceremonial dress.

- A grey cummerbund by stewards[157] of the Australian Army Catering Corps (AACC) when working on formal occasions.

---

155 Lieutenant General Sir Harry Burnett Lumsden, KCSI, CB; 59th Bengal Native Infantry 1838, Corps of Guides 1847, Lieutenant General in 1875: born India 21 November 1821 – died Scotland 12 August 1896.

156 Carman WY. *A Dictionary of Military Uniforms*: London, B.T. Batsford Limited: 1977, p. 78

157 The Steward trade was disestablished from the Army on the 30 June 2014

Emu Plumes

The Diggers of WWI pulled many British legs with their tall stories (kangaroo and bunyip farms, and treacle mines), but one of the best was convincing the 'Poms' that the emu plumes on their hats were actually kangaroo feathers.

The credit for the introduction of emu plumes is given to GEN Sir Harry Chauvel[158] during the great shearer's strike in Queensland. In 1891, the Queensland Mounted Infantry were called out, as soldiers to aid the Civil Power. During quiet time, the soldiers would ride their horses alongside the emus and pluck the breast feathers as a form of 'sporting' activity and then place the feathers on their hat. The Gympie Squadron were the first to wear the feathers, a fashion soon followed by the regiment. The Queensland Government permitted the Regiment to adopt the plume as part of their uniform in recognition of their service. The then Minister for Defence Sir GF Pearce[159], ruled in September 1914, that the whole of the Queensland light horse might wear the plume[160]; this privilege was extended in 1915 to all ALH regiments by Prime Minister Fisher.[161]

Emu tufts of approved design and dimensions are now worn by all members of the RAAC as an item of dress. All RAAC personnel were given authority to wear emu plumes in the slouch hat, brim up or down in 1996; this was extended to all personnel serving in an RAAC Regiment in 2000.

The tuft is worn as a backing to the regimental badge on the beret. The plume is worn on the Slouch Hat (Hat Khaki Fur Felt) with both ceremonial and general duty orders of dress; it is fixed centrally on the left side, behind the puggaree.

First Lady: 'That's one of them Australian soldiers'
Second Lady: 'How do you know?'
First Lady: 'Why, can't you see the Kangaroo feathers in his hat?'

Punch, February 1916

Drum-Major's Staff

The Drum-Major's staff has its origin back to at least the 18th Century where Napoleon's Drum-Majors were renowned for their spectacular displays of tossing and whirling the staff into the air; however, there is a far more practical purpose for the staff whereby the Drum-Major can direct the band by signals as the loud music makes it impossible to give verbal orders to direct the band when they are playing.

Uniform Facings and Lace

The military coats in the 18th century were faced or lined with material different from the basic colour of the coat. Thus, when the sleeves were turned back to make a cuff, and lapels were introduced, the different colour made a strong contrast. Each regiment could therefore be recognised at a distance by the colour of its facings and the different coloured lace that was used as an edging to the material. Many British Regiments maintain these colours as part of the heritage and use them as backing for their hat badges or the colours of their regimental formal dress, for example, facings on Winter Mess Dress Jackets. SUR is the only unit within the Army to have adopted a coloured backing for its badges and rank based on its alliance with a British unit.

158 General Sir Harry Chauvel, GCMG, KCB; Comd Desert Mtd Corps 1917-1919, Inspector General AMF 1919-1920, CGS 1922-1930, Inspector-in-Chief Volunteer Defence Corps 1940: born Tabulam Clarence River NSW 16 April 1865 – died 4 March 1945.

159 Sir George Foster Pearce KCVO; French Légion d'honneur, Minister for Defence 1914-1921, Minister for Home and Territories 1923-1926 and 1934-1937, Minister for Defence 1932-1934, Minister for External Affairs 1934-1937: born Mount Barker South Australia 14 January 1870 – died Melbourne 24 June 1952.

160 Dennis P, Grey J, Morris E, Prior R. *The Oxford Companion to Australian Military History (Second Edition).* Australia, Oxford University Press: 2008

161 Bou J. *Light Horse: A History of Australia's Mounted Arm.* Port Melbourne, Cambridge University Press: 2010

AWM Negative No. REL 15747
Courtesy of the Australian War
Memorial. Identity Discs - Sister V
Bullwinkel, AANS about 1945

Identity Discs (Dog Tags)[162]

It was not until the 2nd Boer War (1899-1902) that British soldiers started wearing regulation methods of personal identity and these were in the form of strips of tape.

The strips were supposedly carried in tunic pockets; however, it seemed that soldiers being soldiers, the strips could end up being placed anywhere and more often than not, a detailed search had to be conducted of the seriously wounded and dead to locate them.

In 1906, each soldier was issued with a tin disc and given specific orders that it was to be worn around the neck.

With the raising of the AIF in 1914, MAJGEN Bridges ordered that, 'Each officer and man will carry on a string round his neck an identity disc showing his name, number if any, unit and religion.'[163] In 1916 the British Army Council directed that the single metal disc was to be replaced by two discs, one round (red) and one octagonal (green), manufactured from compressed fibre.[164] The upper, octagonal, disc was to be known as 'Disc, Identity, No.1, Green' and was to be worn around the neck. The second, 'Disc, Identity, No. 2, Red' was then suspended from the first. The intent was that in the event of the death of a soldier the round red disc would be removed from the body and attached to a sandbag or similar, containing the man's personal effects; the octagonal green disc was to be left with the remains to enable identification to be made.

A widely-accepted myth connected with the 1916 discs is that the red disc was the colour of blood and thus was to be taken away, while green was the colour of grass and was to left with the man when he was committed to the earth.

Although the intent was that the metal disc was to be withdrawn at the time of the issue of the fibre discs, extensive photographic evidence exists to confirm that at least some members of the AIF retained their original metal disc. After extensive wear the compressed fibre used in the manufacture of the 1916 discs took on the appearance of leather and discs where often mistaken for this material. Unfortunately, the material used for the 1916 discs was subject to deterioration due to local climatic and earth conditions, with the result that many remains could not and still cannot be identified when disinterred.

Fibre discs were originally issued during WWII; however, there was the continuing problem of deterioration. It was found that the remains of men killed and hurriedly buried in Papua in 1942, when disinterred in 1943 as the Australian Forces advanced, could not be identified. As a result an order was issued in 1944 that fibre identity discs were to be replaced with stainless steel discs. Metal discs have been used by the Australian Army since that time.

Today, the Australian Army's Personal Identification Tags are referred to as Number 1 Tag (the octagonal shaped disc) and Number 2 Tag (the circular disc). They are embossed with the title AUST, the soldier's number (regimental/PMKeyS), initials and name, religion and blood group.

Formation Signs[165]

The practice of using Formation Signs began in the Australian Army during WWI. It was during 1916 that the Allied Command, fearful of spies operating behind the Allied lines, decided to dispense with the practice of marking equipment with the unit's full title. The system adopted was to be simple, easily understood and able to be applied rapidly and inexpensively to all equipment. Australia wished to retain national identity by using the basic design of the Australian General Service Badge worn by all Australian soldiers during that period. Unlike the British, the Australian Formation Sign was not used as a dress embellishment; rather, colour patches were used for unit personnel identification.

Formation signs were again used during WWII, but only as markings for divisional vehicles and equipment, the colour patch being retained for identification of personnel.

The use of formation badges on uniforms and as vehicle markings was approved on 10th May 1950. Unlike the formation signs used during the two world wars, the new system was also used to identify personnel and equipment belonging to organisations as small as brigade-sized formations.

The cloth badge was approximately 2¼ inch (5.71cm) square and was sewn onto the jacket sleeve below the embroidered shoulder titles (if worn). Again some were made in pairs so as to present the observer facing the soldier the same design on either side. A departure from this was personnel serving with the Far East Land Force (FARELF), who wore the unit formation sign on the right sleeve and the AMF Rising Sun cloth-badge on the left. There were several other instances where British Commonwealth and ANZUK Forces serving overseas had their own distinctive formation signs. A small selection of designs is shown below:

162 Gordon LL. *Military Origins.* New York, A. S. Barnes: 1971, p. 213
163 AIF Orders, Order No.2 (vi), dated 26 August 1914
164 British Army Order (AO) No.287 1916, of April 1916, published
    under authority of Military Order (MO) No.507 of 1916

165 Taubert S. *Formation Signs and Vehicle Marking of the Australian Army*
    1903-1984. Brisbane, Queensland, Comtrain Enterprises: 1996

Formation Signs Circa 1949 to 1960s

1st Armoured Brigade

2nd Armoured Brigade

1st Infantry Brigade - ARA

2nd Division

3rd Division

7th Infantry Brigade

11th Infantry Brigade

13th Infantry Brigade

28th ANZUK Brigade

1st Commonwealth Division - Korea

*1st Army Group
Royal Artillery*

ANZUK Force

Army Headquarters

BCOF

HQ FARELF

Singapore Command

The wearing of formation signs on uniforms was discontinued in Australia in 1960; however personnel posted to British Commonwealth and ANZUK units overseas continued to wear these badges into the mid-1970s. Vehicles continue to use formation signs, but have returned to the accepted practice of only identifying formations not smaller than Divisional or Functional Command-sized organisations or their equivalent.

Gorget Patches

The red tabs (gorget patches) on the collar of the coats or shirts of General Officers, Brigadiers and Colonels have a long ancestry reaching back at least to the 14th century, first appearing on French and Italian made suits of plate armour. Originally the gorget was a piece of armour which protected the throat or gorge.[166] Improvements in musketry brought about the gradual demise of protective armour, and by the beginning of the 18th century any pieces that remained had no practical value, being in the nature of ornamental or ceremonial equipment. The gorget, as one of the distinguishing marks of an officer's uniform remained well into the 19th century.

Under the clothing warrant of 19th December 1768, it was directed that the 'King's Arms' be engraved on the gorget and also the number of the regiment. They were to be gilt or silver, according to the colour of the buttons on the uniform. They were usually hung around the neck from ribbons and rested upon the upper part of the breast.

During the 2nd Boer War (1899-1902), a type of khaki uniform was introduced, and to distinguish General Officers, red cloth patches, the 'Gorget Patches' were introduced, thus symbolising the original metal Gorgets.[167]

There are two types of gorget[168]; they are both are worn on the collar, identical in shape and colour, but with different design features. That worn by COLs and BRIGs have a central line of silk gimp, (the term refers to a thread with a cord or wire in the centre), the same colour as the gorget patch. The only exception to this is the RAANC who wear a silver silk gimp. MAJGEN and above have an oak-leaf embroidery on the full-size patch and a strip of gold braid on the small-size patch.

When worn with a peak cap, a coloured band is worn around the cap the same colour as the Gorget Patch. Although the standard colour of the Gorget is scarlet, some selected Corps have unique colours:

- Purple – RAAChD
- Dull Cherry – RAAMC
- Burnt Orange – RAADC

OCDTs attending either the now-disbanded OCS or an OTU wore a white gorget. After the closure of these units the tradition of OCDTs wearing Gorgets was continued for a short time at the ADFA, however was discontinued in 1999. Members of the CSC at RMC-D have never worn gorget patches.

---

166 Carman WY. *A Dictionary of Military Uniforms*: London, B.T. Batsford Limited: 1977, p. 66
167 Edwards TJ. *Military Customs*. Aldershot, England, Gale and Polden: 1954, p. 93
168 Australian Army. *Army Standing Orders for Dress – 2000, Volume 1 and 2*. Canberra, Defence Publishing Service: 2003

Senior Officers' Gorget Patches
Service Dress (Full Size)

Colonel and Brigadier

Major General and above

Summer General Duty Dress (Small)

Lanyards

Virtually nothing is written in authoritative texts that mention a dress lanyard or details its early development except in the period immediately after WWII. What little is known can be classified as modern myth. Stories have it that the lanyard was developed for the cavalry to bundle fodder for animals and later used by the artillery to hold various implements, when in fact nothing can be found to support these contentions.

The word 'lanyard' describes 'a short rope to hold something', and can therefore be used to describe various items in use by the military. For instance a lanyard can be used to hold a knife or can opener and can even be part of the trigger mechanism of an artillery piece, but these items are not the forerunner of the modern day Lanyard.

Lanyards of the type worn today were first mentioned in the British Army's Dress Regulation of 1900, which states 'all Officers of a unit should carry a whistle that must be attached to a silk lanyard the same colour as the coat or jacket except for the Light Infantry which will wear a lanyard of dark green'.[169] This first mention gives a clear glimpse of the possible development of the lanyard, given that it was to be made of silk and for one select organisation coloured. The use of silk meant that it was to be worn on dress uniforms and not just work dress, giving the lanyard a special status and given that one elite group was given special favour to colourise the item; it was only natural that other variations of colour and style would develop over time.

The first mention of a lanyard in an Australian manual[170] only describes it as an item issued with a military clasp knife to enable it to be secured to the uniform so as to prevent loss; this was particularly the case for 'field' use. This type of lanyard was a simple piece of twine looped in the same fashion as a modern lanyard but coloured (sometimes by dirt) a natural brown or khaki. Lanyards were worn by the artillery and cavalry and were used for holding a knife for cutting horse head and heel ropes and for digging out stones from horse's hooves; gunners also carried a fuse key on their lanyard. The lanyard was a length of cord made of cotton and generally matched the buff coloured canvas webbing that was in general service for many years. These lanyards were still issued to soldiers until the 1980s, and are not the forerunner of the lanyard used on the dress uniforms in more recent times.

Although not mentioned in the various dress manuals covering the period from Federation to the post war period, it is clear from photographic evidence that some units of the Artillery wore a dress lanyard as part of their formal uniform.

The lanyard was generally worn looped around the left shoulder with the loose end in the breast pocket. In 1920 the position was changed to the right side to simplify retrieval of the loose end from the pocket when a bandolier was worn.

Today, lanyards of various colours are worn on the right shoulder by all members of the Army; the exception to this being members of the Infantry Corps serving with an infantry battalion or regiment, 'A' Field Battery RAA, and soldiers serving with the Australian Federation Guard, who all wear the lanyard on the left shoulder.[171]

With the creation of the Regular Army in September 1947 many changes were introduced into the new permanent force, which were determined to put aside many of the traditions established by the AIF and militia. These changes included adopting new uniforms, Corps badges and other accoutrements styled on the sister organisations within the British Army. During the early 1950s whistles were introduced as an item of general issue to all ranks of the Corps of Staff Cadets and to personnel of the rank of sergeant and above. These whistles were attached to a coloured lanyard and worn round the right shoulder with the whistle placed in the top pocket. With their formal introduction in 1952[172], there were seven different coloured lanyards, covering the nine Corps of the day, with two being used by RMC-D. By 1955 the number of Corps and regiments doubled, with many more colours being introduced. At this time lanyards were not worn by the junior ranks of the Army, however, within a short period of time they were on general issue to all ranks.[173]

By 1963 the Dress Manual directed that the wearer may at his own discretion attach a whistle to the end of the lanyard that was again to be held in the top pocket.[174] This is a clear link with the origins of the current dress lanyard to the first silk lanyard used for this purpose by the British Army.

Image courtesy of Department of Defence – 20060304adf8185016_0024

169 Her Majesty's Stationary Office, London. *Dress Regulations for the Officers of the Army (Including the Militia) – War Office, 1900.* London, Harrison and Sons: 1900, Para. 31

170 Australian Military Forces. *Standing Orders for Clothing, Part 1 Permanent Forces.* Melbourne, Military Board: 1935, p. 7

171 Jobson C. *Royal Regiment of Australian Artillery: Customs and Traditions.* Manly, NSW, Directorate of Artillery: 1997, p. 42

172 Australian Military Forces. *Military Board Instructions, Standing Orders for Dress (Provisional) MBI No 86.* Military Board, Army Headquarters: 1952, p. 7

173 Australian Military Forces. *Military Board Instructions, Standing Orders for Dress (Provisional) MBI No 90.* Military Board, Army Headquarters: 1958, para. 35

174 Australian Army. *Dress Manual – 1963.* Canberra, Australian Government Printing Service: 1963, Para 312

Given the available evidence there can be little doubt that the humble dress lanyard started out its military service as a simple cord to neatly secure a whistle to the uniform.

Today's lanyards are worn with some forms of work and ceremonial dress but not all. Lanyards are not worn with field dress except by members of the Australian Army Cadets.

The Origin of the Artillery White Lanyard

There have always been assumptions made about the reason why the Artillery wear a white lanyard, whilst other Corps wear a wide array of colours in varying types and styles from single colours to twisted and plaited versions with two colours.

As with any piece of uniform that was worn for both daily and ceremonial use, the lanyard would become soiled and stained. Belts and other accoutrements minus the actual packs would also be worn on ceremonial parades and to improve their appearance it was the custom to paint the webbing with a product called 'Blanco'. This liquid paste, white in colour, was applied to the webbing material to give it an even and uniform appearance. The lanyard originally worn by the Artillery, as a piece of work dress, was just another piece of equipment to which Blanco was applied.

It is therefore an extension of this basic beginning that gave us the white lanyard, the Artillery being the first organisation to use this piece of dress merely maintained the original colour whilst other regiments and Corps chose to move away from the standard colour to individualise the item.

Colour patches had for many years allowed regiments and units within the Army to be identified. These had been removed in the post war period; the use of lanyards was therefore seen as a way of retaining individual identification by allowing members of units the ability to identify different battalions/Corps within the same regiment/organisation by the use of different coloured lanyards.

The Black Lanyard

The 2 RAR's band received its drums on the same day as the death of King George VI. As an enduring mark of respect the drums were coloured black as was the battalion lanyard.

Lanyards of the Army[175]

Corps and Regiments are identified by lanyards of various colours:

Corps/Regiment (in order of seniority)	Shoulder on which worn	Acronym of Corps Title	Lanyard Colour
Corps of Staff Cadets (excluding the Sovereign's Company who wear a scarlet red lanyard)	Right	CSC	Khaki Scarlet Red
Royal Australian Armoured Corps	Right	RAAC	Yellow
Royal Australian Artillery	Right	RAA	White
Royal Australian Engineers	Right	RAE	Blue/Black
Royal Australian Corps of Signals	Right	RASigs	Royal Blue
Royal Australian Infantry Corps	Right	RAInf	Scarlet
Australian Army Aviation	Right	AAAvn	Light Blue
Australian Intelligence Corps	Right	AustInt	Bottle Mid Green
Royal Australian Army Chaplains Department	Right	RAAChD	Purple
Royal Australian Corps of Transport	Right	RACT	Dark Royal Blue/Scarlet – twisted*
Royal Australian Army Medical Corps	Right	RAAMC	Dull Cherry
Royal Australian Army Dental Corps	Right	RAADC	Burnt Orange
Royal Australian Army Ordnance Corps	Right	RAAOC	Scarlet
Royal Corps of Australian Electrical and Mechanical Engineers	Right	RAEME	Dark Blue
Royal Australian Army Educational Corps	Right	RAAEC	Pale Blue
Australian Army Public Relations Service	Right	PR	Bottle Green/Gold
Australian Army Catering Corps	Right	AACC	Slate Grey
Royal Australian Army Pay Corps	Right	RAAPC	Gold
Australian Army Legal Corps	Right	AALC	Maroon

175 Australian Army. *Ceremonial Manual – 2003 Volume 2.* Canberra, Defence Publishing Service: 2003, Chap 1 Annex A

Corps/Regiment (in order of seniority)	Shoulder on which worn	Acronym of Corps Title	Lanyard Colour
Royal Australian Corps of Military Police	Right	RACMP	Scarlet/Black
Australian Army Psychology Corps	Right	AAPsych	Maroon
Australian Army Band Corps	Right	AABC	Scarlet/Rifle Green
Royal Australian Army Nursing Corps	Right	RAANC	Scarlet/Slate Grey

Corps/Regiment (in order of seniority)	Shoulder on which worn	Lanyard Colour
General Reserve Officer Cadet Training Unit (junior class)	Right	Scarlet
General Reserve Officer Cadet Training Unit (senior class)	Right	Khaki
'A' Field Battery, Royal Australian Artillery	Left	White
1st Battalion, The Royal Australian Regiment	Left	Garter Blue
2nd Battalion, The Royal Australian Regiment	Left	Black
3rd Battalion, The Royal Australian Regiment	Left	Rifle Green
5th Battalion, The Royal Australian Regiment	Left	Gold
6th Battalion, The Royal Australian Regiment	Left	Khaki
7th Battalion, The Royal Australian Regiment	Left	Maroon
8th/9th Battalion, The Royal Australian Regiment	Left	Slate Grey/Brown*
Special Air Service Regiment	Left	Garter Blue
1st Commando Regiment	Left	Garter Blue
2nd Commando Regiment	Left	Garter Blue
9th Battalion, The Royal Queensland Regiment	Left	Garter Blue
25th/49th Battalion, The Royal Queensland Regiment	Left	Scarlet/Khaki*
31st/42nd Battalion, The Royal Queensland Regiment	Left	Black/Gold*
51st Far North Queensland Regiment	Left	Rifle Green
2nd/17th Battalion, The Royal New South Wales Regiment	Left	Black/Gold*
4th/3rd Battalion, The Royal New South Wales Regiment	Left	Scarlet/Rifle Green*
1st/19th Battalion, The Royal New South Wales Regiment	Left	Garter Blue/Slate*
41st Battalion, The Royal New South Wales Regiment	Left	Khaki
5th/6th Battalion, The Royal Victoria Regiment	Left	Gold/Khaki*
8th/7th Battalion, The Royal Victoria Regiment	Left	Brown/White*
10th/27th Battalion, The Royal South Australia Regiment	Left	Garter Blue/Black*
11th/28th Battalion, The Royal Western Australian Regiment	Left	Garter Blue/Rifle Green*
16th Battalion, Royal Western Australian Regiment	Left	Black
12th/40th Battalion, The Royal Tasmanian Regiment	Left	Garter Blue/Black*
North West Mobile Force	Left	Bottle Green/Spectrum Orange*
Pilbara Regiment	Left	Burnt Orange
Queensland University Regiment	Left	Slate Grey
Sydney University Regiment	Left	Black
University of New South Wales	Left	Maroon
Melbourne University Regiment	Left	Rifle Green
Deakin University Company	Left	Yellow/Garter Blue*
Adelaide Universities Regiment	Left	Khaki
Western Australian University Regiment	Left	Scarlet
Australian Federation Guard	Left	Green/Gold*

* All multi-coloured lanyards are braided unless stated otherwise.

Pace Stick

RAA lays claim to being the originator of the pace stick. It was used by its field gun teams to ensure correct distances between the guns. The original pace stick was more like a walking stick with a silver or ivory knob. It could not be manipulated like the modern pace stick as it opened just like a pair of callipers. It is suggested that the infantry developed the pace stick to its present configuration as an aid to drill.

Pace Stick and Stand

The RSM-A carries the first pace stick brought to Australia as a symbol of office. The Regimental Master Gunner and the Master Gunner 6th Brigade carry replicas of the 'Gunner's Stick' as their symbol of office.[176] RSMs carry a pace stick as a symbol of their appointment. The pace stick is used to measure the correct length of pace. Rhythm and uniformity in marching is achieved by using the pace stick as well as the drum, metronome and pace ladder. Correct pace length is necessary not only for ceremonial purposes, but also to reduce fatigue on long marches and to set the standard of accuracy required of soldiers.

As with other accoutrements such as the Sam Browne Belt, the pace stick comes in two colours, brown (natural stained timber) and black lacquer. The black version is used by RSMs of the RAAC, AAAvn and RAANC; all other Corps use the natural timber version; the RSM RAE's pace stick has a 'field service level' fitted into it.

Puggaree

From the Hindi 'pagri', it is a cloth wound around the head or headdress (kullah, pag or helmet) in India.[177] In the British Army it was worn around the hat sometimes falling down behind the neck to protect from the sun. In the Australian military forces the puggaree was originally of a flat folded type, but Victorians and Tasmanians had a three-pleated puggaree. During WWI a plain khaki cloth band was worn, and this practice continued until compulsory training was suspended in 1929. With the introduction of Voluntary Training in 1930 new puggarees were issued to the CMF with different coloured folds denoting Arm or Service. During WWII a flat type of band was issued, but troops in the Middle East introduced a folded puggaree as a distinguishing mark of active service. The Army eventually reverted to various types of plain bands, green

dyed puggarees for example, for jungle warfare. However the official puggaree at the conclusion of WWII was still the flat band. The current puggaree has seven folds, one for each State and one for the Australian Territories and is made from a light khaki-coloured cotton material, and it is worn on the slouch hat with a colour patch sown on the right side. 1 RAR wear a distinctive dark green puggaree, while members of the CSC at RMC-D wear an olive drab puggaree with eight pleats instead of the normal seven - the eight pleats represent the Australian States and Territories, plus New Zealand.

Rising Sun Badge[178]

The Rising Sun Badge (the Australian Army General Service Badge) remains one of the most recognised and respected emblems in Australia, yet its lineage has long been in dispute. The rising sun symbol had been used on a variety of colonial military insignia for forty years before Federation. Badges from the Queensland Scottish Regiment (about 1885), Victorian Cadet Regiment (about 1890s) and 6th New South Wales Infantry Regiment (1896-1903) all featured stylised versions of a rising sun motif on them, and all pre-date the first Army Rising Sun badge.

In 1902, a badge was urgently sought for the Australian contingents raised after Federation for service in South Africa during the 2nd Boer War. MAJGEN Sir Edward Hutton, the newly appointed Commander-in-Chief of the Australian Forces, desired a distinctive emblem that the Australian contingents could wear to distinguish them from British forces.

Probably the most widely accepted version of the origin of this badge is that which attributes the selection of its design to MAJGEN Hutton, after earlier receiving as a gift from BRIG General Joseph Gordon[179] a Trophy of Arms comprising mounted Naval bayonet shield with alternating triangular

176 Australian Army. *Land Warfare Procedures – General LWP-G 7-7-5 Drill 2005.* Puckapunyal, Land Warfare Development Centre: 2005, Chap 9 Annex A

177 Carman WY. *A Dictionary of Military Uniforms*: London, B.T. Batsford Limited: 1977, p. 106

178 Cossum JK. *Australian Army Badges: The Rising Sun Badge.* Sunbury, Victoria, J.K. Cossum: 1986

179 Major General Joseph Maria Gordon, CB; GOC CMF (Victoria), GOC CMF (NSW), CGS AMF 1912-1914: born Spain 18 March 1856 – died Surry England 6 September 1929.

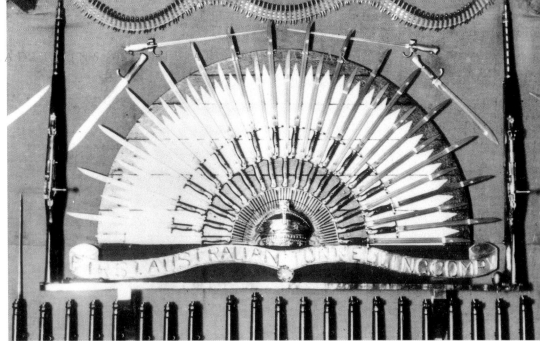

Martini Henri bayonets arranged in a semi-circle around a brass crown. To Hutton the shield was symbolic of the coordination of the Naval and Military Forces of the Commonwealth. A refurbished replica of Hutton's original shield is on display in the main foyer within AHQ Canberra (Figure 1).[180]

One account for the design argues that it was taken from the badge of the 'Australian Rifles' designed by CAPT (later COL) Cox Taylor[181]. A further account cites the influence of the logo of commercial jam producers Hoadleys, whose labels and jars sported a rising sun logo not dissimilar to the designs that were eventually adopted. This version may account for the widespread adoption of the nickname for the Commonwealth Horse as 'Hoadleys Horse'[182]. Yet another account attributes the design to Mr CF Gaunt (of JR Gaunt & Son, British badge, button and medal manufacturers), who was asked to submit drawings for a badge. He actually submitted three pencil drawings of which one is believed to have been accepted; the first-known badge consisted of seven rays or star points of triangular shapes above the word 'Australia' and the crown on a wreath base.

The original design, created in 1902 (first pattern - Figure 2) was subsequently amended and produced in haste for issue to the contingent departing for South Africa (second pattern). It has also been suggested that the badge was produced for the Australian Coronation Corps which proceeded to England to represent Australia at the coronation celebrations of King Edward VII. The design was further modified to incorporate the words AUSTRALIAN COMMONWEALTH HORSE.

In 1904, the third pattern badge was approved (Figure 3), introducing the basic design concept that survives to this day. This badge was worn during both World Wars and bore the inscription on the scroll: 'Australian Commonwealth Military Forces.' Taken into general issue in 1911, the third

---

180 Photograph Courtesy of Defence Publishing Service Audio Visual – Duntroon.
181 Colonel Herbert James Cox-Taylor, DSO: born 1873 – died Campbelltown Tasmania 5 February 1936.
182 Cossum, JK. *Australian Army Badges: The Rising Sun Badge.* Sunbury, Victoria, J.K. Cossum: 1986

pattern Rising Sun Badge was worn only by some; the Militia regiments took advantage of the permission granted them to retain their own distinctive regimental badges if they preferred.

The fourth pattern badge appeared in 1949 (Figure 5) following the raising of the Regular Army, where the scroll wording was changed to 'Australian Military Forces.' This badge was worn by Australian soldiers in Korea. The fifth pattern was approved in 1954 (Figure 6) but not issued until 1966, and the main change was the replacement of the Imperial State Crown with the St Edward's Crown. The sixth pattern badge was approved in 1969 (Figure 7), although it was never fully issued throughout Army. There were substantial revisions to the design, as the central scroll wording was changed to 'Australia', a single star was added to each side scroll, and the smaller St Edward's Crown was backed with the Commonwealth Star's seven points to represent the six states and one point for the territories. The seventh (current) pattern badge was approved in 1991 (Figure 8). The scroll wording was again changed to 'The Australian Army', and the Commonwealth and other stars were removed.

The distinctive shape, worn on the upturned brim of a slouch hat, is readily identified with the Australian soldier and the spirit of the ANZAC.

During WWI, many locally-produced versions appeared, one in particular worn by the Australian Camel Corps (Figure 4), which although unofficial, was in common use.

After WWI the AIF was disbanded and the Militia was reorganised into a divisional structure based on the old AIF. The Australian Instructional Corps (AIC) was formed on 14th April 1921 to carry out training of all Corps in the AMF. The AIC replaced the Administrative and Instructional (A&I) Staff who had been the Army's instructors since Federation. It was at this change-over that the officers of the old A&I Staff were transferred to form the Australian Staff Corps whilst the Warrant Officers and NCOs were transferred to the AIC. A new distinctive Rising Sun Badge was authorised for this organisation based on the original design but having a scroll highlighted with blue enamel and showing the name of the new Corps in gold lettering.

The 'Rising Sun' as devised by Sapper J. Vawden - October 1917

Figure 1 – Original concept

Figure 2 – 1902

Figure 3 – 1904-1949

Figure 4 – Camel Corps WWI (unofficial)

Figure 5 – 1949-1954

Figure 6 – 1954-1969

Figure 7 – 1969-1991

Figure 8 – from 1991

Administrative and Instructional Staff

Australian Instructional Corps[183]

This Corps remained an active organisation until it was formally disbanded on 19th May 1955.[184]

Rising Sun Cloth Badge

The Rising Sun cloth-badge was introduced during the mid-1950s to identify Australian troops serving overseas. This introduction ensured that the emblem of the Army has been worn by Australian soldiers during every military campaign since its introduction. When first introduced, the cloth-badge was only worn by soldiers whilst on overseas service. In 1994, after a major change to the Army Dress Manual, the wearing of this most important symbol was approved for all forms of dress, positioned on the left upper arm.

Vietnam War Era badge for Jungle Greens

Modern Camouflage badge

183 Photograph by Hagen Amtsberg from the Grey Collection, Courtesy of the Army Museum of South Australia.
184 Dennis P, Grey J, Morris E, Prior R. *The Oxford Companion to Australian Military History (Second Edition). Australia,* Oxford University Press: 2008, p. 65

Sam Browne Belt[185]

One of the most familiar pieces of military equipment is the Sam Browne Belt, yet little is known about the inventor of this belt, Sir Samuel James Browne, VC.[186] More is recorded of his military service, than of his development of the belt which bears his name.

LT SJ Browne began his service in India in April 1849 as 2IC of the newly-raised 2nd Regiment of Punjab Cavalry, the unit which also later took his name (22nd Sam Browne's Cavalry). His career followed the normal course within this unit, until the Indian Mutiny. Lord Roberts recorded a story of Browne at this time:

> During the Mutiny an officer of the Punjab Cavalry had told Sam Browne that he had taken to wearing a chain on his shoulders as a means of warding off sword cuts, and he had strongly advised Browne to do the same. He gave Browne two curb chains, which he insisted be sewn on his coat. Sometime after the officer was killed, Sam Browne and his friends were talking together, and the man said that at the sale of the officer's effects he had bought some saddlery which had belonged to the dead officer, and he said that it was a curious thing that neither of the bridles he had bought had curb chains on them. 'I know where they are' said Browne, and went to his tent and returned with the two curb chains and gave them to the purchaser of the bridles.

A short time afterwards, on 31st August 1858, at Seerporah, Browne silenced a field gun, single handed, which blocked the advance, but during the fighting he received two sword cuts, one on the knee, and the other on the left shoulder (now unprotected by chain) which cut off his arm. For this action, Browne was awarded the Victoria Cross (VC) and his citation at this time gives his rank as LTCOL, and his unit as the 46th Punjabis. Browne had previously been made a Companion of the Order of the Bath (CB).

The dress regulations for British Officers of the 2nd Punjabis after the mutiny required them to wear their waist belts under their tunics. Browne found this ungainly with his left arm missing, and devised an external belt, supported on the left-hand (sword) side by a shoulder strap. The belt had two shoulder pieces when a pistol was added. The Sam Browne Belt was not worn universally in the British Army until 1897 when units began adopting more practical field uniforms, to replace the traditional dress uniforms, which had previously been worn in battle.

Top: Sam Browne Belt about 1899

Below: Sam Browne Belt – Current Version

The British Dress Regulations of 1911 stated that there should be two braces (straps) but that the second one was only for use when wearing a revolver. The belt was later adopted by other countries, and is now an almost universal piece of equipment. Slight variations on the original pattern exist and in the British Commonwealth forces, it is worn by commissioned officers and Warrant Officers Class One.

Sam Browne, as a LTGEN, commanded the Peshawar Field Force at the capture of Ali Masjid during the Afghan War. He was knighted, and was promoted to GEN in 1888.

There are two colour types of belt worn within the Army, brown and black. The black Sam Browne is worn by those Corps and regiments who wear silver dress embellishments (RAAC, AAAvn and RAANC)[187] and brown is worn by all other Corps. Because the Sam Browne Belt's historical association with weaponry, Australian Army Chaplains may opt not to wear it.

History of the Sash

In the British Army, the sash was worn around the waist by Sergeants and Sergeant Majors of infantry and all ranks of cavalry, staff and artillery, across the right shoulder by line officers of infantry, and across the left shoulder by officers in highland dress, so as not to be covered by the tartan worn over the right shoulder. Wearing the sash over the right shoulder seems to be a result of the Cardwell reforms of 1881, when an attempt was made to regulate regimental facings, badges and customs of dress; the wearing of a sash developed into an insignia of rank.

It is only in the English language where texts suggest the original purpose of the sash was for the carrying a wounded officer off the field[188], to which end they were usually made of silk being strong as well as light and full enough to enclose the human form.

In General Order No. 90 (1st April 1882) it was directed the sash be worn around the waist. In 1912, however, all officers wore their sashes around the waist knotted on the left side, whilst Warrant Officers and Sergeants wore their sash over the left shoulder, falling to the right (the reverse of the general method).

185 Barnes RM. *A History of the Regiments and Uniforms of the British Army*. London, Sphere: 1972, p. 191

186 General Sir Samuel James Browne, VC, GCB, KCSI; Commanding Officer 2nd Punjab Irregular Cavalry: born India 3 October 1824 – died Isle of Wight 14 March 1901.

187 Australian Army. *Army Standing Orders for Dress – 2000*. Canberra, Defence Publishing Service: 2003 *Vol 2* Pt 3 Chap 1

188 Edwards TJ. *Military Customs*. Aldershot England, Gale and Polden: 1954, Chap 6 p. 85

Ceremonial Waist Sash

The gold and crimson or crimson ceremonial waist sash is worn by senior officers and those officers holding special appointments. A rifle green waist sash is worn by AABC Officers and Warrant Officers in charge of bands. The ceremonial waist sash is worn with the Patrol Blue or White Jacket and AABC ceremonial uniforms. The sash is worn with the tassels on the left side.

Shoulder Sash Scarlet

When ordered, a scarlet shoulder sash is to be worn on ceremonial parades, barrack guard duties and at regimental, mess or unit functions by:

- WO2, SSGTs and SGTs of the RAInf, and

- An authorised member of the CSC.

The sash is worn diagonally over the right shoulder under the epaulette with the tassels hanging from the left side. The front of the sash is worn under the belt and the rear of the sash is worn over the belt.

The sash is worn outside the coat with Patrol Blue or White Jacket and Service Dress. With Mess Dress White Jacket, it is worn under the jacket. The front of the sash is worn under the cummerbund in Mess Dress White Jacket and Mess Dress White Shirt.

Slouch Hat (Hat Khaki Fur Felt)

Lord Gort accompanied by his ADC arrived at the Somme battle front one day to carry out a tour of inspection. At the time the Somme front was an ocean of mud and Lord Gort had to negotiate a long line of duck boards. Presently he spied a slouch hat in the mud, and asked his aide to retrieve it. After a bit of straining he recovered the slouch hat by a few inches when an Aussie voice came from underneath – 'Go easy mate! I still have the hat chin strap underneath my chin!' Hearing this, Lord Gort and ADC hurried to rescue the Digger. After about 10 minutes of straining the voice spoke again; 'Ah-h! It's no bloody good. I have still got me flamin' feet in the stirrups!' [189]

The Army refers to the slouch hat by its official designation, the Hat Khaki Fur Felt; to everyone else it is a 'Slouch Hat'. The word slouch refers to the sloping brim. It is made from rabbit fur felt or wool felt and is always worn with a puggaree.

History has it that the origins of the Slouch Hat began with the Victorian Mounted Rifles. A hat of similar design had been worn in South Africa by the Cape Mounted Rifles for many years before 1885. The design of the Victorian Mounted Rifle hat originated from headgear of native police in Burma where LTCOL Tom Price[190] had recognised its value.

The Victorian hat was an ordinary bush felt hat turned up on the right side so that it would not be caught during the drill movement of 'shoulder arms' from 'order arms'. By 1890, State military commandants had agreed that all Australian forces, except the artillery, should wear a looped-up hat of uniform pattern that was turned up on the right side in Victoria and Tasmania, and on the left side in all other States to allow for different drill movements.[191] The Slouch Hat became standard issue head dress in 1903 and its brim position was mostly standardised. The slouch hat became a famous symbol of the Australian fighting man during WWI although it seems to have been worn in different ways; for example GEN Monash's 4th Infantry Brigade wore it at Gallipoli with the brim turned down at all times. In the campaigns waged by the light horse throughout Palestine, it is believed that the Turkish soldiers came to identify the Australian by his 'Big Hat' and after the charge of the Light Horse at Beersheba in 31st October 1917; it is reputed that the enemy would at times refuse to stand their ground when seeing them approach.

The hat's continued use through both World Wars and its use since that time have made it a national symbol.

MAJGEN Bridges, the first commander of the AIF, was wearing his slouch hat with the chinstrap buckle on the right side of the face and the brim down when he was fatally wounded at Gallipoli. He was actually wearing his hat back-to-front. When the slouch hat is worn at the RMC-D, it has become traditional that the chinstrap buckle is worn on the right side of the face and the brim down in remembrance of MAJGEN Bridges. This tradition was started at RMC-D in 1932. When the slouch hat is worn ceremonially, for example, on Anzac Days, it is worn in accordance with the wider Army custom, that is, brim up and chin strap on the left hand side. In recent times it has become general practice to wear the slouch hat with the brim down when not on ceremonial occasions to give soldiers additional protection from the sun. It is for this reason that the peaked cap traditionally worn by officers and warrant officers has ceased to be worn except with Dress Whites, and by Drill Instructors and cadets at RMC-D and ADFA.

---

189 Modified from the: *Australasian Post*. Melbourne, Southdown Press: 26 April 1956

190 Colonel Thomas Caradoc Rose Price, CB; Commanding Officer Victoria Rangers 1888-1889: born Hobart 21 October 1842 – died Warrnambool 3 July 1911.

191 Hall RJG. *The Australian Light Horse*. Blackburn, Victoria, WD Joynt: 1968, p. 49

Image courtesy of Department of Defence – 20110627dps8434824_ s096_003. Graduation Parade – Duntroon 2013, LTGEN Ken Gillespie, AC DSC, CSM (Retd).

Shoulder Cords

The shoulder cord is a decorative item of ceremonial dress. One of the earliest mentions of their use is in the Royal Engineer's Dress Regulations of 1857, in which it is described that 'Corresponding with the grades the sergeants and staff sergeants have finer cloth and wear royal gold cord on those parts (shoulders) where the rank and file display yellow worsted cord'. Over the past one and a half centuries the rank badges of officers have moved from the collar to the shoulder and in some Corps to the lower sleeve. In 1880 the badges of rank for officers were moved from the collar to the epaulet[192] where they remain on ceremonial forms of dress.

Shoulder cords are worn with Patrol Blue or White Jacket orders of ceremonial dress by entitled officers. Although all General Officers wear broad gold shoulder cords, junior officers only wear them when holding a specific appointment; for instance the ADC to the Governor-General. Entitled officers of the RAAC, AAAvn or RAANC wear silver shoulder cords. All other entitled officers wear gold shoulder cords. Backings of shoulder cords are scarlet, except RAANC backings, which are grey.[193]

General officer shoulder cords are of plaited gold wire basket cord 5mm in diameter, with small gold gimp down the centre. The strap of the cord is 57mm wide, terminating in a 95mm wing. Other shoulder cords are 40mm wide and are made of twisted gold or silver basket cord 5mm in diameter.

Shoulder cords are worn in pairs, badges of rank are worn on shoulder cords, gold insignia are worn on silver cords and silver insignia are worn on gold cords.[194] Rank badges made specifically for cords have longer prongs than normal badges due to the excessive thickness of the cord. The following illustrations show a selection of both gold and silver shoulder cords. Silver cords are not used by the rank of COL or above unless the officer is serving in the capacity of a Corps appointment such as the HOC or similar.

---

192 Carman WY. *A Dictionary of Military Uniforms*: London, B.T. Batsford Limited: 1977, p. 119
193 Australian Army, Army *Standing Orders for Dress, 2000*. Canberra, Defence Publishing Service: 2003, *Vol. 2 Pt 3*
194 Australian Army, Army *Standing Orders for Dress, 2000*. Canberra, Defence Publishing Service: 2003, *Vol. 2*

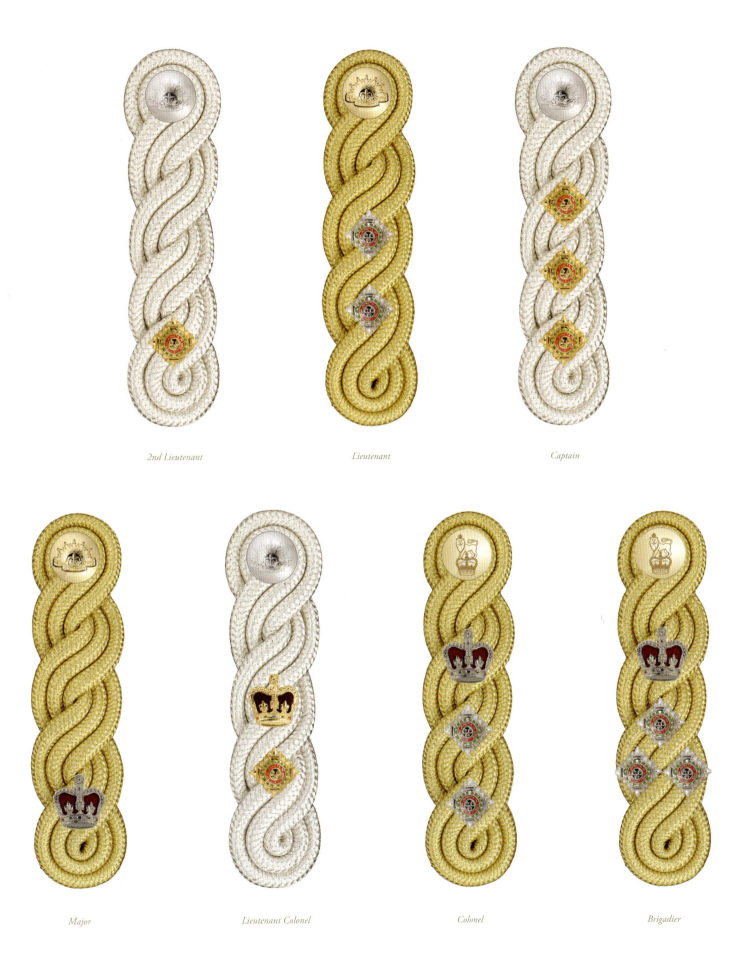

2nd Lieutenant   *Lieutenant*   *Captain*

Major   *Lieutenant Colonel*   *Colonel*   *Brigadier*

Major General
(left shoulder)

Lieutenant General
(left shoulder)

General
(left shoulder)

Field Marshal
(left shoulder)

State Governor

Governor-General of Australia

Chapter Four

Corps, Regiment and Unit Traditions

Introduction

Over the years many units and training establishments have developed unique traditions and some of these traditions are recognised throughout the Army. The only difference between Army, regimental and unit traditions is the scope of their acceptance and observance.

Customs observed within the wider military community, and also at unit-level, with explanations about their origin and development are included below. Some organisations with a long history have developed more detailed customs than those units that have existed for a relatively short time. There is also some contention as to what constitutes an Australian tradition as many of our current customs and traditions are taken either directly or indirectly from the British Army. These Army traditions do not include sporting trophies, which tend to enjoy only a temporary or intermittent status.

Seniority of Services

The ADF takes its 'Seniority of Service' from the British, being:

- **Navy.** The history of the Royal Navy may be said to have begun with the long ships of King Alfred the Great; however, the 'Senior Service', as a standing force, originated in the early 16th Century during the reign of Henry VIII. The RAN was formed from the Commonwealth Naval Forces (old colonial navies) on 10th July 1911; this is the birthday of the RAN.

- **Army.** The British Regular Army dates from the Restoration period of the 1660s, before which date armies were raised in a haphazard manner as and when required; the Australian Army was established in 1901 by an amalgamation of the forces of the six colonies.

- **Air Force.** The RAAF was established in 31st March 1921. Its predecessor, the Australian Flying Corps (AFC), was established in March 1912 as part of the Army.

Seniority of Army Corps and Regiments[195]

The following is the order of Corps and Regiment seniority. There are other factors that can influence this sequence such as Royal and Vice-Regal patronage; however it is usually maintained on ceremonial occasions.

The precedence of Corps, are laid down in *Army Military Regulation* (AMR) No. 68:

- The Corps of Staff Cadets
- The Royal Australian Armoured Corps
- The Royal Regiment of Australian Artillery
- The Royal Australian Engineers
- The Royal Australian Corps of Signals
- The Royal Australian Infantry Corps
- Australian Army Aviation
- Australian Intelligence Corps
- The Royal Australian Army Chaplains Department
- The Royal Australian Corps of Transport
- The Royal Australian Army Medical Corps
- The Royal Australian Army Dental Corps
- The Royal Australian Army Ordnance Corps

195 Australian Army. *Ceremonial Manual – 2003 Volume 2.* Canberra, Defence Publishing Service: 2003, Chap 1 Annex A

- The Royal Corps of Australian Electrical and Mechanical Engineers
- The Royal Australian Army Educational Corps
- The Australian Army Public Relations Service
- The Australian Army Catering Corps
- The Royal Australian Army Pay Corps
- The Australian Army Legal Corps
- The Royal Australian Corps of Military Police
- The Australian Army Psychology Corps
- The Australian Army Band Corps
- The Royal Australian Army Nursing Corps

Units of the same arm or service take precedence within that arm or service according to the order of their numerical succession, or, if not included in a numerical succession, according to the order in which the Commands to which they belong are specified in the instrument appointing Commands. A unit of the Permanent or Regular Forces takes precedence over a unit of the same arm or service of the Army Reserve.

Within the RAAC the following is the accepted order of precedence of regiments and independent squadrons:

- 1st Armoured Regiment
- 2nd Cavalry Regiment
- 1st/15th Royal New South Wales Lancers
- 2nd/14th Light Horse Regiment (Queensland Mounted Infantry)
- 4th/19th Prince of Wales's Light Horse Regiment
- 12th/16th Hunter River Lancers
- 'B' Squadron 3rd/4th Cavalry Regiment
- 'A' Squadron 3rd/9th Light Horse Regiment (South Australian Mounted Rifles)
- 'A' Squadron 10th Light Horse Regiment

Within the RAA, 'A' Battery, when on the Order of Battle (ORBAT) as an independent Battery, is to take the position of precedence within the Regiment, thereafter units according to the order of their numerical succession.

Within the RAInf the following is the accepted order of precedence of regiments:

- The Royal Australian Regiment
- 51st Battalion, The Far North Queensland Regiment
- The Royal Queensland Regiment
- The Royal New South Wales Regiment
- The Royal Victoria Regiment
- The Royal South Australia Regiment
- The Royal Western Australia Regiment
- The Royal Tasmania Regiment

- Special Air Service Regiment
- North West Mobile Force
- The Pilbara Regiment
- The Commando Regiments

The accepted order of precedence of University Regiments is:

- Sydney University Regiment
- Melbourne University Regiment
- Adelaide Universities Regiment
- Queensland University Regiment
- Western Australia University Regiment
- University of New South Wales Regiment

Royal Military College - Duntroon[196]

Duntroon opened in 1911 as Australia's own military education and training facility for officers. It has developed many interesting and unique traditions. Some of these traditions have not stood the test of time with some being put aside due to changes in uniform, social pressure or injury.

- **Banner Parade.** The Banner Parade is held in the week prior to the June and December Graduations each year to transfer The Queen Elizabeth II Banner formally to the succeeding Champion Company. On receipt of the Banner, the Sovereign's Company Troop the Banner through the remainder of the CSC and assume their position on the right flank of the inspection line.

  When the CSC parades, the position of each Company on the inspection line is determined by their relative position in the Lee Shield Competition.[197] This competition determines the Sovereign's Company and Company seniority generally. The senior Company is called The Sovereign's Company and is always on the right of the line.

- **Chinstrap and Brim of the Slouch Hat.** MAJGEN Bridges, the original commander of the AIF, was supposedly wearing his hat with the brim down and the chinstrap buckle on the right side when he was shot by a sniper at Gallipoli. Being the first Commandant of RMC, cadets have worn their slouch hats in this manner as a mark of respect since 1932; the only usual exception being Anzac Day ceremonies, when the hat is worn in the normal manner with the left-hand side brim up.

- **Company Names.** Prior to 1954, CSC Companies were named in the same manner as those of an infantry battalion; A, B, C Company and so on. In 1954, with cadet

---

196 Royal Military College Archives. *Traditions and Customs of the Royal Military College, 1998.* Canberra, RMC-D: 2002

197 The Lee Shield was presented to the College in December 1928 by MAJ JE Lee who was the CO of the CSC (the first graduate (1914) to hold this position); from 1929 the "Lee Shield" became the prize in the inter-company competition.

numbers in excess of 210, the CSC was re-organised into four companies renamed Gallipoli, Kokoda, Alamein and Bardia. By 1957, with cadet numbers raising to 260, an additional company was added and some of the existing companies renamed; they were then called Gallipoli, Romani, Alamein, Kokoda and Kapyong. By 1958 the numbers had dropped and the last-placed company in the annual Lee Shield competition, Kokoda, was disbanded. Given the greater historical significance of Kokoda, Romani was renamed Kokoda the following year. Long Tan Company was raised in 1974, with Romani being re-raised in 1976.[198] In 1986 the Corps was again reduced to four companies. As at 2014, RMC-D comprised Alamein, Gallipoli, Kokoda, Kapyong and Romani as full-time CSC Companies, with Romani used for Reserve officer cadets completing their training each six months, and a rehabilitation and administration Company called Bridges.

- **Casey.** Years ago at Duntroon, SCDT Casey, a member of 4th Class, was skylarking prior to departure of the Corps on Christmas leave and was inadvertently locked in a broom closet. He was not missed from the leave draft and remained in the cupboard until the Corps returned to RMC the following year. Casey's skeleton was found but his ghost still haunts the corridors and cavities of RMC. As he will never graduate, to appease his spirit, he is present at each Graduation Ball. The horse he rides is called 'Invader'.

- **Days to Go Board.** Initially presented by the Graduating Class of 1937, the board is displayed at the end of the CSC Mess Dining Room. It was upgraded by the Class of 1988. Previously the Board was updated by the junior cadet, listed alphabetically, of the 4th Class, or sometimes by the largest entry number (for example, the last member to enlist). It is now updated by the youngest cadet from 3rd Class at the evening meal at 1830hr daily. The Days to Go Board is changed to zero on midnight at the annual Graduation Ball.

- **Graduation Day.** Records indicate that Graduation has always occurred on the second Tuesday of December. Initially, the Training Programme probably finished on that day. In modern times, the Training Management Plan works back from that day to determine the start date of the course. With the advent of two intakes, there is now a mid-year graduation for GSO cadets.

- **Hats and Weapons in the CSC Mess.** The tradition of not wearing hats or carrying weapons into the Mess is Army-wide. However, unlike other Messes, belt buckles are not broken (undone) within the CSC Mess. This is seen as a sign of trust that a cadet would never use a weapon against a fellow cadet.

- **National Flag.** The RMC flagpole has been officially designated a Flag Station since 1913. Every Sunday since 1946, the New Zealand and Australian flags have flown side-by-side on the yard-arms. Whilst no written authority exists for this, it appears to have been adopted to symbolise the close association between the two countries at RMC; there have always been New Zealand cadets at RMC.

- **Puggaree on Slouch Hat.** The puggaree worn at RMC is darker in colour than the standard issue to the rest of the Army, except for 1 RAR who also wear a unique puggaree. In addition, the RMC puggaree has eight folds rather than the normal seven. It is believed that the folds represent the seven States and Territories of Australia and the eighth for New Zealand; who have always placed cadets at RMC and in fact had 10 students in the first intake of 41.

- **Saluting the Memorial Tablets.** MAJGEN Parnell initiated plans in 1920 to erect a memorial to commemorate the service of the college graduates. In 1922, a stone of Russian ebony granite was set into the walls of the College Square bearing the names of those graduates killed during WWI. A WWII Memorial tablet was erected in 1953 from monies raised by graduates and a Korean Tablet added in 1958. The 'Vietnam and Other Actions' Tablet was erected in 1972. In March 1995, the Commandant ordered that, henceforth, as a mark of respect, all staff and cadets would salute the Tablets when passing. Originally this memorial was located outside the Commandant's house, but in 2004 was moved to its present location in Starkey Park along with the OCS Memorial, opposite the College Military Instruction Block, where the cadets have most of their lessons during their time in barracks.

- **Colours to the Corps - Sovereign's Company Banner.** When Her Majesty Queen Elizabeth II, visited RMC in 1954, she presented new Colours to the Corps, and granted approval for the champion cadet company to be given the added title of 'The Sovereign's Company'. She also granted the privilege of that company to carry The Sovereign's Banner on ceremonial parades. The Sovereign's Company is the winner of the combined Inter-Company sporting, shooting academic performance and drill competitions collectively called the Lee Shield.

- **Staff Cadet.** The term only applies to a Regular Army GSO cadet under training at RMC-D; all other officer trainees are called OCDTs. This term was initially used as cadets of the College graduated as members of the Australian Staff Corps, hence the term. Although the Australian Staff Corps no longer exists the term has endured.

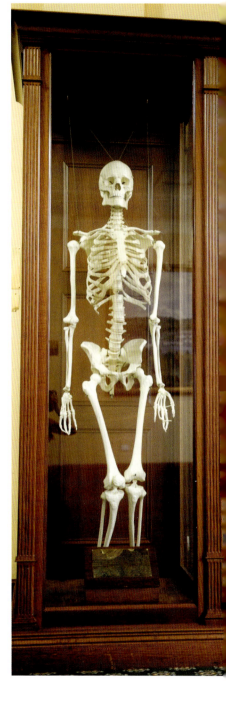

---

198 Coulthard-Clark C. *Duntroon – The Royal Military College of Australia, 1911-1986*. Sydney, Allen & Unwin: 1986, p. 235

- **Sword of Honour.** The first Swords of Honour were awarded retrospectively in 1919 to the Senior Cadets from 1914 onwards. The first recipient was AM Forbes[199], by then a MAJ, who had been awarded the MC during WWI. The Sword of Honour is awarded for exemplary conduct and performance of duties, and is normally presented to the Cadet appointed as the Corps Battalion Sergeant Major (BSM). The winner of the Sword of Honour receives a personal sword, previously funded by the Department of Defence, but now donated by Pooley Swords Ltd, London.

- **RSM Sword Drill.** The only time the RSM, RMC-D, draws his sword on a parade is during the 'Trooping the Colour' ceremony. From receiving the Colour from the Colour Bearer and passing it to the Ensign, the RSM has his sword drawn; he returns the sword to its scabbard at the completion of the Trooping. This custom dates back to Waterloo, when if the Ensign fell the RSM would draw his sword, then retrieve and protect the Colour, until he could hand it over to a replacement Ensign.

- **The Tiger Jacket.** The original RMC blazer was introduced in 1912. The jacket was dark blue with red binding on the edges of the jacket and pockets, and around the sleeves above the wrists. The Tiger Jacket was introduced in the period 1929-1932, with a thin black stripe woven into the red stripe, said to represent the memory of those killed in WWI. The Tiger Jacket was replaced in 1954 with a double-breasted navy yachting jacket, which became single-breasted as fashion changed. The Tiger Jacket was re-introduced in 1977 following a survey of cadets who voted overwhelmingly in its favour.

- **MV Duntroon Bell.** The bell of the MV Duntroon is located next to the flagpole. The MV Duntroon was a 10,000 ton passenger ship built at Newcastle-on-Tyne in 1935 for the Melbourne Shipping Company. At the outbreak of WWII, the MV Duntroon was requisitioned by the Australian Government for war service, during which she carried 180,000 Australian and allied troops. The bell was presented to the College on 9 March 1978 by the widow of BRIG BC Forward (a graduate of the College in 1948). The bell is tolled in accordance with CSC Standing Orders as part of the College routine.

- **Pinning-on of Pips.** The tradition of a graduating cadet having their 'pips' pinned on Mess Kit, by his mother and or girl/boyfriend at the Graduation Ball on the stroke of midnight began in 1937.

- **Queen's Medal.** First awarded in 1919 to the cadet graduating top of his Class, and then known as the King's Medal. When the College was a tertiary institution, the Medal was awarded for outstanding academic performance. Singaporean cadets performed particularly well by winning the medal in 1975, 1978, 1979, 1980 and 1982. The Queen's Medal is now awarded to the cadet with the highest aggregate marks for all assessed subjects in 1st and 2nd Class.

- **The Gun Gates.** The Gun Gates provide access to Duntroon from Fairbairn Avenue. This was once the main entrance to Duntroon. The gates are guarded by two German WWI artillery pieces captured by Australian troops in 1918.

- **Patterson Hall.** Patterson Hall is the building that houses Headquarters RMC-D. The Hall was named after LT Penistan James Patterson, who graduated from RMC in 1914, and was killed in action 25th April 1915 on the Gallipoli Peninsula.

Royal Australian Armoured Corps

In July 1944, LTCOL TE Williams proposed that Australian Armoured Corps personnel be issued Black Berets instead of the khaki colour which had been worn since the Corps was first formed in 1941. This was approved by the Chief of General Staff, LTGEN J Northcott[200] on 3rd August 1944; however, photographic evidence held at the AWM clearly show that the black beret was in general use both in Australia and by the AIF serving overseas as early as 1940 and had been worn by the Australian Tank Corps from about 1931.[201] The Black Beret has been worn by RAAC troops, on parade and on ceremonial duties, in barracks, out bush and on operations, since that time and continues to be worn to this day.

In 1989, a military contingent was formed to attend the 75th Anniversary celebrations at Gallipoli. Prior to the contingent's departure, RAAC personnel were reminded that the official ceremonial headdress for the Army was and has always been the Slouch Hat and they were forbidden to wear berets whilst outside Australia. When the new Army Standing Orders for Dress were introduced in the 1990s there was a greater emphasis placed on the wearing of the slouch hat on all ceremonial occasions in the Army.

Some Light Horse units of the Corps had, by tradition, worn emu plumes in their slouch hats on ceremonial occasions; for example, 10th Light Horse. With the new requirement for all RAAC units to wear slouch hats it was

---

199 Brigadier Alexander Moore Forbes, MVO, MC; Class of 1914: born 1892 – died 1961. He was the first Sergeant Major and recipient of the first Sword of Honour at RMC. In 1961 his son, the Right Honourable Doctor Alexander James Forbes, CMG, MC (graduate of RMC (1942) and Minister for the Army (1963-1966) presented his father's Sword of Honour to RMC and since that time this Sword has been carried by the BSM on all ceremonial occasions.

200 Lieutenant General Sir John Northcott, KCMG, KCVO, CB; DCGS AMF 1939-1940, GOC 1st Armd Div 1941-1942, CGS AMF 1942-1945, C in C BCOF 1945-1946, Governor NSW 1946-1957: born Creswick Victoria 24 March 1890 – died Wahroonga NSW 4 August 1966.

201 Hopkins RNL. *Australian Armour: a History of the Royal Australian Armoured Corps, 1927-1972.* Canberra, Australian War Memorial and Australian Government Printing Service: 1978, pp 15-16

seen as an opportunity to establish links to the original ALH, from which all RAAC units claim heritage.

In 1996 all RAAC personnel were given authority to wear emu plumes on their slouch hat brim up (ceremonial) and brim down (general use). This was extended to all personnel serving in an RAAC Regiment in 2000. The black beret is retained for Regimental use and some other ceremonial occasions.

Royal Regiment of Australian Artillery

Artillery is the oldest Corps in the Australian Permanent Force and has existed continuously since Federation (originally raised in 1871 as 'A' Battery, New South Wales Artillery) and therefore is the oldest single unit in the Army, having first fought in the 2nd Boer War. 'A' Battery, RAA is the only non-infantry unit in the Army to wear its lanyard on the left shoulder; this custom is said to date back to the 1920s when a change in dress saw the Army change to the present standard of wearing the lanyard on the right side; 'A' Battery, RAA maintained the original order of dress.[202]

Artillery Colours

Centuries ago the largest or first gun in an artillery train carried the equivalent of today's Queen's Colour and was thus known as the Colour or Flag Gun. The custom of carrying such flags was discontinued in the 18th century and since that time the guns themselves have become the Regiment's Colours.

As an Arms Corps, the RAA is entitled to carry Colours but through tradition, they maintain their guns as their Colours with the Motto 'Ubique', meaning 'Everywhere', as their only 'Battle Honour'.

The Royal Cypher is embossed on the barrel of guns of British origin or barrels proofed to British standards. Australian made-guns have the Australian Coat of Arms on the barrel. This mark was originally placed on the barrel to indicate that the item had passed all testing requirements of the Board of Ordnance and was therefore safe to use. The mark has nothing to do with the tradition that the guns of the regiment are their Colours.

Although the RAA have a Banner, when paraded together, the Guns of the Regiment have precedence. It is for this reason that you will never see a gunner leaning or resting on a gun, as to do so would be the ultimate insult to the Regiment.

Artillery Guns at Duntroon

An ongoing point of discussion has been the issue of the 25 Pounder Artillery Guns on the parade ground at RMC-D that face inwards rather than outwards, the traditional way of indicating 'holding ground'. Holding ground is by definition

"Troops Keeping the Ground".[203] On selected unit ceremonial occasions troops are positioned in the corners of a parade ground to 'Hold Ground'; these troops being equipped with weapons which range from lances to mortars or guns. The symbolism is to afford protection to the unit parading in order to permit it to carry out its ceremonial duties safely.

The tradition stems from the British 'Hollow Square' when a square was formed to defend against a pending cavalry charge, in order to enable troops to rest in place, pickets were posted at sufficient distance from the square to give early warning of attack. This warning system provided the unit time to 'stand to' and fight off the enemy.

There is no explanation for the inward-placement of the guns at Duntroon; the best reason given is that the guns have been placed that way for aesthetics (rather than facing a wall and building); further to this, as both guns are out of service pieces and unmanned, they are not therefore considered to be 'holding ground'.

102nd (Coral) Field Battery, RAA

The Honour Title 'Coral' was presented to the 102nd Field Battery, RAA by the Governor-General of Australia in May 2008.[204] This was a first for an artillery unit in Australia and follows a British Army tradition which dates back to 1925.[205] The title recognises the Battery's involvement in the Battle of Coral[206] in South Vietnam between 12th May and 6th June 1968.

102nd (Coral) Field Battery, RAA – Official Badge

202 Australian Army. *The Royal Regiment of Australian Artillery – Standing Orders*: 2008

203 Infantry Centre. *Military Traditions and Customs*. Singleton, Infantry Centre: 7 April 1977, Chap 4, p. 4-14 and para 96

204 Royal Australian Artillery Association NSW. *Gunfire Newsletter of the Royal Australian Artillery Assoc (NSW) Inc Issue 2*. Sydney NSW: June 2008

205 Edwards TJ. *Military Customs*. Aldershot, England, Gale and Polden: 1954, p. 103

206 McAulay L. *The Battle of Coral*. Hawthorn, Victoria, Hutchinson Australia: 1988

Above: Image courtesy Department of Defence – 20081209DPS8434824-123-196. Parade Ground RMC – Duntroon

Right: AWM Neg No. MELJ0702 Courtesy of the Australian War Memorial. Lieutenant Colonel GB Combes, CO 1 RAR, carries out rifle exercises, in the now traditional 'Shovel Ceremony' – Sergeants' Mess, Korea, February 1955

1st Battalion, The Royal Australian Regiment[207]

The 1st Battalion is one of the oldest within RAR, having been formed in 1948. The following traditions have been adopted by the Battalion over the years:

- **Dark Green Puggaree.** There are many stories about the introduction of the unique puggaree worn by 1 RAR. The dark green puggaree was first worn during the Malayan Emergency in 1959-1960. The battalion at the time was unable to get puggarees from Australia, and as they were needed for an official parade, the task of producing them was given to the Battalion tailor, Mr Mohavved Beseek. He used 'bush shirts' to make the puggarees as he was unable to obtain the khaki material needed, either locally or from Australia. The green 'bush shirt' was the common issue British field uniform used at the time. As far as can be determined the Commanding Officer of the time, LTCOL W Morrow,[208] made the decision that the green puggaree would be the puggaree worn by 1 RAR in Malaya. After the battalion's return to Australia the dark green puggaree was adopted for permanent use by the unit. Because this puggaree is so distinctive, 1 RAR does not wear a colour patch as do the other battalions of the Regiment.

- **Shovel Drill – Commanding Officer 1 RAR.** In March 1953, at Camp Casey in Korea, at a farewell to troops returning to Australia, the CO of the Battalion, LTCOL Maurice Austin, DSO,[209] commented on how sloppy he considered the rifle drill was. He then proceeded to demonstrate to the acting RSM, WO2 LE Brennen, how the movements were supposed to be performed. The CO used a shovel for the demonstration. There was certain disagreement between the two on how the drill should be performed, so the two adjourned to the Sergeants' Mess where the CO was drilled by the acting RSM before the Mess members in a variety of drill movements. On the completion of his drill, LTCOL Austin decreed that the shovel should be packed and returned to Australia to be held in the Battalion's Sergeants' Mess. The shovel was to be used upon the first visit to the Sergeants' Mess by the incoming CO. The actual drilling of the CO is carried out by the junior CSM, and on completion the CO's name is inscribed on the handle of the shovel.

207 Department of Defence. *1 RAR Official Unit History*: 2007
208 Lieutenant Colonel William John Morrow, OBE; CO 1 RAR 1958-1960: born Glenn Innes, 1 June 1921.
209 Brigadier Maurice Austin, DSO, OBE; CO 2 RAR 1952, CO 1 RAR 1952-1953, COMDT JTC Canungra 1957-1958, ADC (Hon) GG of Aust. 1961-1964; editor 1st edition, The Australian Army – A Brief History: born Geelong Victoria 15 December 1916 – died 13 October 1985.

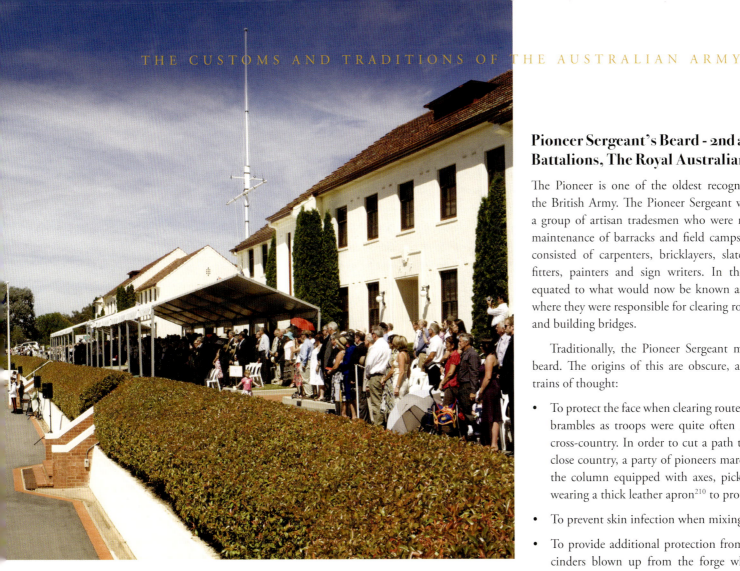

Pioneer Sergeant's Beard - 2nd and 4th Battalions, The Royal Australian Regiment

The Pioneer is one of the oldest recognised trades within the British Army. The Pioneer Sergeant was responsible for a group of artisan tradesmen who were responsible for the maintenance of barracks and field camps. These tradesmen consisted of carpenters, bricklayers, slaters, plumbers, gas fitters, painters and sign writers. In the field, their task equated to what would now be known as Assault Pioneers, where they were responsible for clearing routes and obstacles, and building bridges.

Traditionally, the Pioneer Sergeant may wear a full-set beard. The origins of this are obscure, and there are three trains of thought:

- To protect the face when clearing routes through trees and brambles as troops were quite often required to march cross-country. In order to cut a path through rough and close country, a party of pioneers marched in advance of the column equipped with axes, picks and shovels and wearing a thick leather apron[210] to protect their uniform;

- To prevent skin infection when mixing explosives; or

- To provide additional protection from the heat and hot cinders blown up from the forge whilst working as a blacksmith, repairing equipment and shoeing horses.

In 1965, the then Governor-General of Australia, William Philip Sidney, 1st Viscount de L'Isle, VC, KG, GCMG, GCVO, KStJ, PC, presented 4 RAR with its new Colours. During his time with the unit he remarked that the Battalion's Pioneer Sergeant should wear a beard and carry an axe as is the custom in many British Army Regiments. The battalion adopted this suggestion and was the only unit in the Australian Army, until 2007, with a soldier who was officially authorised to wear a beard. When on ceremonial parades, the Pioneer Sergeant carries a chrome axe and wears a white leather apron; he also carries a tomahawk on parade in lieu of a bayonet. It has become tradition that outgoing pioneer sergeants have their beard removed in front of the entire Battalion, by the CO.

From 1973 to 1995 4 RAR was linked with 2 RAR, and the tradition of the Battalion Pioneer Sergeant wearing a beard continued within the linked Battalion, 2/4 RAR.

In the early years of the 21st century 4 RAR became a commando unit. As the manning of a commando unit does not have a Pioneer Platoon, the position of Pioneer Sergeant was removed from its establishment, but the relevant Standing Orders allow for the Battalion to reinstate the position at a later date. In 2007 it was formally established that 2 RAR

210 Carman WY. *A Dictionary of Military Uniforms*: London, B.T. Batsford Limited: 1977, p. 15

could also have the bearded Pioneer Sergeant, making the 2nd and 4th Battalions the only units within the Australian Army officially authorised to have bearded members.

The 4 RAR tradition is now held in abeyance due to the Battalion being disbanded in 2009.

Kapyong Day - 3rd Battalion, The Royal Australian Regiment

Kapyong Day is celebrated annually on 24th April to commemorate the Battle of Kapyong (Korea 1951). Although not rigidly adhered to, training and operational requirements taking precedence, a parade and other unit activities are held to mark the date of the battle.

Long Tan Day - 6th Battalion, The Royal Australian Regiment

Long Tan Day is celebrated annually on 18th August to commemorate the Battle of Long Tan (Vietnam 1966). Training and operational requirements take precedence but a parade and other unit activities are normally held to mark the date of the Battle. To maintain links to D Company, which fought the Battle of Long Tan, 6 RAR's three Rifle Companies are maintained as 'A', 'B' and 'D', with 'C' Company not established.

Beige-Coloured Beret - Special Air Service Regiment (SASR)

Based on the British organisation of the same name, the 1st Special Air Service Company was formed at Swanbourne, Western Australia in July 1957. During WWII, the authorised headwear worn by parachute-qualified troops was the maroon beret which had been adopted by the airborne forces of Britain. Because all members of the Company were parachute-qualified, the Company also wore a maroon beret with the hat badge of the RAInf Corps.[211] In November 1960, the company was transferred to The RAR and therefore all members commenced to wear the RAR badge. This was changed again in September 1964, when the Australian Special Air Service Regiment (SASR) was formed.[212] However, it was not until the following year that the new regiment adopted the beige or sandy-coloured beret, 'flaming sword' badge[213] with dark blue felt crusader's shield backing, the motto 'Who Dares Wins' and the parachute wings as worn by the British SAS.

211 Kuring I. *Red Coats to Cams: A History of Australian Infantry 1788 to 2001.* Loftus NSW, Australian Military History Publications: 2004 p. 260

212 Horner DM. *Duty First: The Royal Australian Regiment in War and Peace.* Sydney, Allen & Unwin: 1990: 1990, p. 138

213 Stevens G. *The Originals – The Secret History of the Birth of the SAS in Their Own Words.* London, Random House: 2006, p. 57

Image courtesy Mr Mick Toal.
Pioneer Sergeant

The unique hat badge worn by unit members is not only a Regimental insignia but also a qualification badge that can only be worn by members of SASR who have qualified as an SASR trooper.

The British SAS badge is woven onto the dark blue felt backing; when introduced to SASR, their badge was produced as a removable metal badge, which is pinned onto the uniform without a backing. The reason for this may stem from the fact that in the Australian Army, only officers above LTCOL are permitted to wear cloth-badges on berets. Therefore when wearing a ceremonial slouch hat, the SASR soldier would normally wear the badge without its backing. The British have always considered the insignia and backing to be a single badge and it has only been in recent times that this oversight has been rectified, with approval given for members of SASR to wear the cloth crusader's shield backing on their ceremonial slouch hat.

In addition, they also wear special SAS pattern parachutist-qualified wings, the original designed by a British officer, LT Jock Lewes[214], based on the stylised sacred Ibis wings of Isis of Egyptian mythology.[215]

Toast to Fallen Comrades - 1st/19th Battalion, The Royal New South Wales Regiment[216]

The 1st/19th RNSWR observes the tradition of the Toast to Fallen Comrades, which is conducted by the Officers' and Sergeants' Mess at formal dinners. Among the Battalion's Mess silver are many silver and pewter tankards, each inscribed with the name of one of the Battalion's Fallen Comrades, who was a member of one of the ancestral Battalions whose Battle Honours are emblazoned on the unit's Queen's and Regimental Colours.

The Toast is conducted with the tankard of a fallen member positioned in front of a Mess or former Mess member. These are then filled and the member who is appointed to propose the toast rises, raises his tankard, and says, 'Tonight I drink with … and reads the rank, name, appointment and date and place of death inscribed on the tankard'. He then drinks with his Fallen Comrade, and remains standing. The member to his left then rises, and does the same. This continues around the room, until it finishes back with the member who led the Toast, who says, 'Lest we forget', and all reply, 'Lest we forget'. All then sit, and that is the end of the Toast.

Fairbairn-Sykes Fighting Knife - Commando Regiments

Australian Commando units trace their origins back to WWII when, in line with a like introduction by the British Army, it was determined that there was a need to develop an ability to conduct long-range raids against the enemy. The techniques to be employed by the commando were to use small independent units of highly-trained and motivated men that could strike quickly at an enemy, creating maximum damage and withdrawing before superior forces could be brought into battle against them.

214 Lieutenant John (Jock) Steel Lewis has been credited with the invention of the Lewes Bomb, a highly successful explosive projectile combining an incendiary and explosive charge used throughout WWII: born 21 December 1913 – died 31 December 1931.

215 Davis BL. *British Army Uniforms and Insignia of World War Two.* London, Arms and Armour Press: 1983 p. 67

216 Morrissey P. Unit History 1st/19th RNSWR: 2009

Australia employed what were then termed 'Independent Companies' to undertake the same training as the commando units in the British service; these companies were later renamed Commando Squadrons (Cdo SQNs). In 1949, military commanders did not consider it necessary to include these specialist type units in the 'New Army'. However, by 1955, in line with developments in the British Army, it was decided to raise two commando companies as Army Reserve units, to be based in Sydney and Melbourne respectively.

The true icon of the commando has always been the Fairbairn-Sykes fighting knife, not only because of its unique shape but because of its special slim carbon steel blade, designed specifically for hand-to-hand fighting. Although the original knife had a cross-hatched patterned handle, it was the Mark 3 version used in the later part of WWII that was ultimately selected as the shape to be depicted on the Commando Regiment's hat badges. Unlike the British Commandos who do not have a specific Commando Regimental Badge, the Australian Army decided, in 1956, to adopt a regimental badge even though the actual strength of the unit was only two companies.

Sergeants' Mess Bell - The Royal Australian Infantry Corps

From June 1965 to February 1972, HMAS SYDNEY was involved in transporting troops and equipment to and from South Vietnam. During the Vietnam conflict the vessel made 24 voyages in support of Australian forces fighting in Vietnam, earning her the nickname the 'Vung Tau Ferry'. All members of the Australian Army were shown great courtesy on the voyages both to and from Australia. The Army members appreciated this show of respect and comradeship, and after the decommissioning of HMAS SYDNEY in 1973 and her final sale in 1975, members of the Royal Australian Infantry Corps Sergeants' Mess at Singleton, wishing to obtain a memento commemorating the friendly ties between the RAN and the Army, issued a request to the Navy. The Flag Officer Commanding Eastern Australia Area (FOCEA) responded to this request and released the ship's bell, considered to be the most significant item from a ship, as a symbol of the bond of friendship that still exists today. The bell was inscribed for presentation as follows:

- **Front:** 'Presented to the Infantry Centre SINGLETON on behalf of the RAN by Commodore JLW Merson, RAN, who served on board HMAS SYDNEY during her first commission and was her Captain in 1972-73', and

- **Back:** 'To commemorate the close association between RAR and HMAS SYDNEY during the hostilities in Vietnam this bell has been released by the Navy to the care of the Regiment on permanent loan'.

Adelaide Universities Regiment

As recognition of the affiliation between the Royal Irish Regiment and the Adelaide Universities Regiment (AUR), they have adopted a green felt backing to their hat badge. The headdress of the Royal Irish Regiment includes a Caubeen[217] with silver regimental badge and green hackle.[218] The dark green felt used by AUR represents the traditional green hackle worn by the Royal Irish Regiment since its introduction in the 1940s.

Regimental Mascots[219]

Animals have always been used by soldiers in war whether it was a horse, an elephant, dog and even geese whose loud noise when startled could warn of an impending attack as happened in ancient Rome. Animal mascots however serve no purpose in war other than to allow the soldier an opportunity to remind himself of his own humanity.

The ADF, like many military forces, has maintained strong links with the tradition of having both official and unofficial mascots. Military mascots are meant to bring luck, to boost morale and provide companionship. They are also kept for ceremonial purposes and as a symbol of a particular unit's identity. Many military units, especially during WWI and WWII, acquired unofficial mascots through various means. Dogs were perhaps the most common; however, records also show photographs of kangaroos and koalas in Egypt during WWI. Although some animals went to war with their owners, most mascots were strays that were picked up along the way. Many were only temporary companions, but some served through entire campaigns. A few combined their mascot roles with other duties; dogs were especially useful for helping stretcher-bearers find wounded soldiers in 'no man's land' at night during WWI.

217 The Caubeen is an Irish beret, formerly worn by peasants. It has been adopted as the headdress of Irish regiments of the British and Commonwealth armies.

218 The hackle is a colored clipped feather plume that is attached to a military headdress

219 Australian Army. *Army Ceremonial and Protocol Manual – 2014*. Canberra, Defence Publishing Service: 2014, Chap 28

*Above: WO2 Courage II
2 CAV REGT*

*Left: Quintus-Septimus-Sabre
5 RAR*

The continuing popularity of mascots during WWII was revealed in a 1945 article in the Army magazine 'Salt', which reported attempts by Australian servicemen to bring home, 'at least 10 goats, 220 dogs, 170 cats, 150 birds and 50 assorted monkeys and squirrels' from the start of the Pacific War through to its conclusion.

Animals continue to play an important role as mascots as they have both a psychological and a practical means of defining a unit's identity. The Army is keen to preserve the distinction between pets kept by soldiers (unofficial) and official mascots.

An animal's characteristics should be taken into consideration as follows:

- **Legality.** The animal or bird is protected under Commonwealth or State law or if the animal or bird has been declared to be noxious under any law.

- **Disposition.** The animal or bird's nature permits it to be safely handled on unit ceremonial parades.

- **Size.** The animal or bird is large enough to be seen.

- **Feeding.** The animal or bird requires special foods.

- **Climatic tolerance.** The animal or bird is adversely affected by extremes of weather.

- **Aesthetic qualities.** The animal or bird possess habits that are likely to cause derision or embarrassment in public places.

- **Housing or kennelling.** The animal or bird has special housing or kennelling requirements.

- **Movement.** The animal or bird is able to travel safely over distances.

In the case of units holding an official mascot, recognition must be given by the Director General Personnel – Army (DGPERS-A) in order to gain official status, assume a proper rank, have prospects for promotion and to get its fair share of Army rations. Mascots no longer receive a Regimental/Mascot Number. There are rules and guidelines that must be satisfied and set prior to getting official mascot status. First, the unit must ensure that the mascot is properly fed and housed. Second, the unit's CO or OC must give approval before the case goes to DGPERS-A. Third, DGPERS-A will consider whether the mascot is 'appropriate', and therefore is capable of taking an active role in Army life, which includes participation in ceremonial occasions, demonstrating a symbolic and historic connection with the unit wishing to take on the mascot. Ceremonial Cell – Army is responsible for the enlistment of the mascot and for subsequent reportable occurrences. Currently there are only 18 animals recognised as 'official' regimental mascots by the Army; it is a privilege jealously guarded by those who have it.

Service Mascots – Current as at 1st July 2014

Rank	Name	Type of Animal	Unit
CPL	Albert Lane II	Sulphur Crested Cockatoo	3 CSR
SPR	Crikey	Goanna	1 CER
WO2	Courage II	Wedge Tailed Eagle	2 CAV REGT
SGT	Crock-Soult-Water	Johnson River Crocodile	102 FD WKSP
CPL	Falco Peregrinus Alert	Peregrine Falcon	1 AVN REGT
SPR	Foghorn Leghorn	Rhode Island Red Rooster	21 CONST SQN
SIG	Mac Mercury	Lion	17 SIG REGT
PTE	Macarthur (John VI) (aka Stan)	Merino Ram	8/9 RAR
CPL	Mr Yathody Ila Al Asharg (aka Vernon)	Camel	9 FSB (26 TPT SQN)
PTE	Mrs Yathody Ila Al Asharg (aka Penny)	Camel	9 FSB (26 TPT SQN)
CFN	Pat Gecko	Marbled Velvet Gecko	JLU(N)
PTE	Porton	Blue Winged Kookaburra	51 FNQR
CPL	Quintus-Septimus-Sabre	Tiger	5 RAR
PTE	Ridgeliegh Blue III	Cattle Dog	6 RAR
CPL	Rocky	Belmont Red Bull	31/42 RQR
PTE	Septimus Quintus	Shetland Pony	1 RAR
TPR	Sabot Resolute	Doberman Dog	B SQN 3/4 CAV
SPR	Wooleston Boorooma (aka Wooley)	Dingo	3 CER

Naming of Soldiers' Clubs

The naming of Soldiers' Clubs provides a unique opportunity to establish historical links and provide recognition to notable persons and add character and emphasis to the unique nature of the Club. As a rule, the following guidance applies to the naming of both Army Services and unit-operated soldiers' clubs:

- Clubs should be named after Victoria Cross (VC) and George Cross (GC) recipients.

- The name should be selected from Other Rank (OR)[220] recipients of the awards, preferably from those who had an association with a local unit or with the district. Should there be more than one name with a suitable association, preference will be accorded to recipients who were awarded the VC posthumously, or who were subsequently killed in action.

- When a suitable VC or GC recipient is not available, clubs may be named after persons identifiable with the unit and who have had a distinguished Service career or after the unit, installation or locality in which their unit is situated.

Permission for such naming rights is usually obtained not only from the relevant command hierarchy, but also from the VC recipient or his family. Once dedicated, the club and its participants typically take great pride in the deeds of the VC recipient with whom their club is associated. Existing clubs include:

- Henry Dalziel VC Club – Gallipoli Barracks, Enoggera

- John Edmondson VC Club – Army Recruit Training Centre (ARTC) Kapooka, NSW

- William Matthew Currey VC – Singleton, NSW

- Clarence Smith Jeffries VC – Singleton, NSW

- William Dunstan VC Club – Puckapunyal, Victoria

- Robert Mactier VC Club – Simpson Barracks, Macleod, Victoria

- John Hamilton VC Club – Robertson Barracks, Darwin

- Reginald Rattey VC Club – Larrakeyah Barracks, Darwin

- Arthur Hall VC Club – Victoria Barracks, Sydney

- Keith Payne VC Club – Lavarack Barracks, Townsville

- Albert Lowerson VC Club – North Bandiana.

---

220 Other Ranks comprise PTE, LCPL and CPL.

Naming of Army Installations and Facilities[221]

The naming of Army installations and facilities provides an opportunity to show historical links and add character and emphasis to the unique nature of the installation or facility. As a rule, historical links of significance are to be retained; barracks are to be named after:

- Campaigns and major battles, example: Gallipoli Barracks, Brisbane.

- Notable military personnel, example: Taylor Barracks, Karratha.

- The locality in which they are situated, example: Gaza Ridge Barracks, Bandiana.

- Lines are usually to be named after minor battles, example: Coral Lines, Holsworthy.

- Training depots are usually named after suburbs, towns, localities or streets in which they are located.

- Airfields and airstrips are to be named after the nearest city, town or recognised locality. If under Army control, the word 'Army' may be used after the place name, example: 'Bindoon Army Airstrip'.

Facilities within a barracks or unit are to take the name of the barracks or unit as appropriate, unless application is made for another name.

The naming of roads, streets and other thoroughfares within Army installations may be approved by the senior military officer or the Army Area Representative of the military area in question.

Naming of Armoured Vehicles

Since WWI it has been the practice of many armies to name tanks or other significant armoured vehicles. One such example is 'Mephisto'[222], a German tank captured by Australian troops during WWI. One of only 21 built, it is the last surviving example of the first German military tank, the A7V *Sturmpanzerwagen*, and is displayed at the Queensland Museum. The name Mephisto is painted on the end facing of the box-shaped tank. The tank was captured at the Second Battle of Villers-Bretonneux on 24 April 1918 by a battalion of Australian troops, drawn mostly from Queensland.

The first official Australian document sanctioning the use of vehicle names appeared in 1940 when Headquarters Australian Military Force (AMF)[223] released an instruction permitting the naming of Armoured Fighting Vehicles provided they did not disclose the identity of the unit or interfered with other official markings.

It would appear that since that time the marking of vehicles has remained a unit prerogative with the individual CO being the approving authority for all such markings.

The currently accepted procedure for all such naming within the RAAC is based on the following:

- All names selected must not contain profanity and be generally acceptable for use on an Anzac Day parade.

- Names should start with the first letter of the squadron to which the vehicle belongs, with Regimental Headquarters' vehicles beginning with the letter 'R'.

16016

---

221 Australian Army. *Defence Instruction (Army) ADMIN 26-1 Naming of Army Installations*: 18 Nov 1999

222 *Mephisto* or Mephistopheles is one of the seven princes of Hell originally appearing in literature as the name of the demon in the Faust legend.

223 Taubert S. *Formation Signs and Vehicle Marking of the Australian Army 1903-1984*. Brisbane, Queensland, Comtrain Enterprises: 1996, p. 99

Image courtesy Department of Defence – 20060625adf8271007_016. Christening Ceremony – Regional Force Water Craft

Naming of Watercraft[224]

Naming of watercraft within the Army has a long tradition promoting historical links within the Army and between the Army and the community. The naming protocols are designed to be recognisable as Australian. Small craft, such as assault boats, inflatable boats other than rigid-hulled inflatable boats (RHIB) and dinghies, are not named.

The following principles apply to the selection of names for Army watercraft:

- Landing craft are to be named after harbours, rivers, bays, islands or areas of operation.

- Special Forces craft are named to reflect heritage and to promote 'esprit de corps'.

- RFSU craft will normally be named after Australian Army vessels that have served on operations or in conflict.

- Amphibious craft are to be named to recognise individuals.

- Support and RAE vessels are to be named so as to reflect heritage and promote 'esprit de corps'.

Army watercraft are not to be named after cities, towns, or districts as this is reserved for vessels operated by the RAN. When naming watercraft after a campaign, battle or notable person, the proposal must state the nature of the association or the reason for such naming.

Alliances and Bonds of Friendship

Alliances and unofficial bonds of friendship with the RAN and RAAF have occurred between units, regiments and Corps. Such bonds also occur between units, regiments and Corps of other countries. The aim of these alliances is to foster friendship and goodwill and, ideally, an alliance should be based on operational, traditional or historical contexts, but may also be based on similar regimental titles, regimental numbers or dress and similar roles.

The Army has specific policies on these friendships and alliances that create a link; alliances must have the assent of the Prime Minister. An unofficial bond of friendship creates an informal link, by mutual consent, between a unit, regiment or Corps of the Australian Army and a unit, regiment or Corps of another country. In the case of the RAA, unofficial bonds of friendship are also arranged on a battery to battery basis. Further to this, there are inter-Service affiliations which establish formal associations between ships, units and sub-units of the Services; which are at the discretion of unit COs.

Regiments of the RAAC and RAInf may enter into alliances with the armies of other Commonwealth countries; however, alliances are normally based on a regimental foundation; are limited to one per regiment from each Commonwealth country other than the UK; and usually no two Australian regiments are to be allied with the same regiment of any Commonwealth country. Exceptions are the alliance with the Princess of Wales's Royal Regiment, The Royal Green Jackets and the Adjutant General's Corps.

Alliances, bonds of friendship and inter-Service affiliations have been a long-term tradition supported by the Army as they assist in providing a strong bond of mutual interest, friendship and goodwill.

Approved alliances are as follows:[225, 226]

---

224 Australian Army, *Defence Instruction (General) ADMIN* 12-1 Australian Defence Force Ensign: 10 Jul 2008

---

225 Australian Army, *Ceremonial Manual Ceremonial Manual – 2003 Volume 2*. Defence Publishing Service, Canberra: 2003, Chap1 Annex A

226 Note: Due to the constant re-organisation within the Australian Army and those Units within Commonwealth Alliances, it is not possible to guarantee currency of information.

Australian Army	Current approved Commonwealth alliances
The Royal Australian Armoured Corps	Royal Armoured Corps
	Royal New Zealand Armoured Corps
1st Armoured Regiment	The Royal Tank Regiment
1st/15th Royal New South Wales Lancers	The Light Dragoons (15th/19th The King's Royal Hussars)
2nd/14th Light Horse (Queensland Mounted Infantry)	The Queen's Royal Hussars
	The King's Royal Hussars
3rd/9th South Australian Mounted Rifles	The Royal Dragoon Guards
	The Queen's Royal Hussars
4th/19th Prince of Wales's Light Horse	The Royal Dragoon Guards
	The Queen's Royal Hussars
	The King's Royal Hussars
10th Light Horse	The King's Royal Hussars
12th/16th Hunter River Lancers	The Royal Scots Dragoon Guards
	The Queen's Royal Lancers
The Royal Regiment of Australian Artillery	Royal Regiment of Artillery
The Royal Australian Engineers	Corps of Royal Engineers
	The Royal New Zealand Engineers
The Royal Australian Corps of Signals	Royal Corps of Signals
The Royal Australian Regiment	The Brigade of Gurkhas
	The Royal New Zealand Infantry Regiment
	The Royal Malay Regiment
	Princess Patricia's Canadian Light Infantry
1st Battalion, The Royal Australian Regiment	Grenadier Guards
2nd Battalion, The Royal Australian Regiment	Coldstream Guards
3rd Battalion, The Royal Australian Regiment	Scots Guards
	The Queen's Royal Hussars
4th Battalion, The Royal Australian Regiment	Irish Guards
5th/7th Battalion, The Royal Australian Regiment (now de-linked)	The Welsh Guards
	The Highlanders, 4th Battalion, Royal Regiment of Scotland (The Highlanders)
The Special Air Service Regiment	Special Air Service
The Royal Queensland Regiment	The King's Own Royal Border Regiment (The Duke of Lancaster's Regiment)
	1st Battalion Royal Regiment of Scotland (The King's Own Scottish Borderers)
	The Black Watch, 3rd Battalion The Royal Regiment of Scotland (The Black Watch, Royal Highland Regiment)
	The Lincoln and Welland Regiment (Canada)
The Royal New South Wales Regiment	Royal Marines
	The Princess of Wales's Royal Regiment - The Queen's Regiment
	The Black Watch, 3rd Battalion The Royal Regiment of Scotland (The Black Watch)
	The Highlanders, 4th Battalion, Royal Regiment of Scotland (The Argyll and Sutherland Highlanders)

Australian Army	Current approved Commonwealth alliances
The Royal Victoria Regiment	The Royal Regiment of Fusiliers
	Mercian Regiment (The Staffordshire Regiment)
	The Highlanders, 4th Battalion, Royal Regiment of Scotland (The Gordon Highlanders)
	The Royal Regiment of Canada
5th/6th Battalion, The Royal Victoria Regiment	The Highlanders, 4th Battalion, Royal Regiment of Scotland (The Highlanders)
The Royal South Australia Regiment	The Duke of Lancaster's Regiment - The King's Regiment
	The Highlanders, 4th Battalion, Royal Regiment of Scotland (The Highlanders)
	2/4th Battalion, Otago and Southland (RNZIR)
The Royal Western Australia Regiment	The Rifles - The Gloucestershire Regiment
	The Princess of Wales's Royal Regiment - The Queen's Regiment
	The Highlanders, 4th Battalion, Royal Regiment of Scotland (The Highlanders)
11th/28th Battalion, The Royal Western Australia Regiment	The Rifles - The Royal Gloucestershire, Berkshire and Wiltshire Regiment
The Royal Tasmania Regiment	Royal Anglian Regiment
	The Duke of Lancaster's Regiment - The Queen's Lancashire Regiment
2nd Commando Company	45 Commando, Royal Marines
Australian Army Aviation	Army Air Corps - British Army
Australian Intelligence Corps	Intelligence Corps - British Army
The Royal Australian Army Chaplains Department	Royal Army Chaplains Department
The Royal Australian Corps of Transport	Royal Logistic Corps
The Royal Australian Army Medical Corps	Royal Army Medical Corps
	Malaysian Medical and Dental Corps
The Royal Australian Army Ordnance Corps	Royal Logistic Corps
The Royal Corps of Australian Electrical and Mechanical Engineers	Corps of Royal Electrical and Mechanical Engineers
	Royal New Zealand Electrical and Mechanical Engineers
The Royal Australian Army Educational Corps	Adjutant General's Corps
The Australian Army Catering Corps	Royal Logistic Corps
The Australian Army Legal Corps	Adjutant General's Corps
The Royal Australian Corps of Military Police	Adjutant General's Corps
The Royal Australian Army Nursing Corps	Queen Alexandra's Royal Army Nursing Corps
Sydney University Regiment	The Rifles - The Royal Green Jackets
Melbourne University Regiment	The Rifles - The Royal Green Jackets
	Otago University Medical Company (NZ)
Adelaide Universities Regiment	The Royal Irish Regiment
Western Australian University Regiment	The Rifles - The Royal Green Jackets
University of New South Wales Regiment	The Princess of Wales's Royal Regiment - The Queen's Regiment
	5/7 Battalion (RNZIR)
Monash University Regiment	The Rifles - The Light Infantry

Changes in unit names/designations have occurred over the years, in these cases the current unit alliance is shown with the original allied unit name also shown.

Patron Saints of the Military

Whilst there is no existing formally-accepted policy in regards to patron saints in the Australian Army, there are some Army Corps that claim a patron saint. This does not reflect any endorsed religious policy within the Army. While the tradition of having patron saints is a practice in the life of Roman Catholic Christianity, it is not a tradition or practice usually endorsed or followed by the other Christian denominations or other religious groups represented within the ADF.

Over the centuries many saints have been adopted and accepted by military organisations that include many non-Roman Catholics. There are several exhaustive publications detailing lists of Catholic patron saints that number in the thousands, representing every conceivable trade or calling; many being rebadged pagan gods and goddesses. The following specifically aligned with soldiering:

- **Artillery.** Saint Barbara[227] is considered to be the patron saint of artillery. She was a Christian martyr living in the 3rd century and was delivered up by her own father, a fanatic heathen, who, after she had been tortured, he himself beheaded her and was immediately struck by lightning. Hence to this day Saint Barbara is prayed to by sailors in a storm and is the image frequently used on arsenals and powder magazines. Ammunition Technicians within the RAAOC also consider Saint Barbara to be their patron saint.

- **Catering Corps.** The Patron Saint of the Australian Army Catering Corps is the martyr, Saint Lawrence.[228] In 257 ADE Emperor Valerian published his edicts (a decree issued by a sovereign or other authority) against Christians and Pope Saint Sixtus the Second was arrested and put to death. The Pope's Deacon, Saint Lawrence, followed him to martyrdom three days later. Tradition holds that Saint Lawrence anticipated the martyrdom predicted for him by the Pope and gave all the money in his care to the poor; he assembled church supporters who rallied against Emperor Valerian. It has been said that Saint Lawrence is the most venerated of martyrs of the Roman church since the Fourth Century and the Basilica of Saint Lawrence is named after him.

- **Cavalry.** The patron saint of cavalry is Saint George.[229] He became an equestrian soldier at the age of 16 and was, according to tradition, a young and handsome centurion of Lydda. He is said to have slain an immense and powerful dragon, thus saving the King's daughter from death. He stands out as the ideal of the cavalry spirit and how horse and sword can tackle any difficulty, no matter how ugly or dangerous, in the fair cause of right.

- **Educational Corps.** The Patron Saint of the RAAEC is St. John Bosco (referred to within the Corps as Bosker Jack), who was adopted by the Corps because of his lifetime commitment to education, his devotion to the poor and dispossessed and his dependence for his good work on the charity of others.

- **Engineers.** St. Barbara accounts for the symbol of the 'Thunderbolt', a twisted bar inflamed at the ends with wings and having four forked and barbed darts issuing from the centre, usually displayed in Engineers' and kindred badges.

- **Infantry.** According to one authority the patron saint of the infantry is Saint Michael[230], an archangel and one of the principal 50 angels in Christian and Islamic tradition. He is viewed as the field commander of the Army of God. His name was said to have been the battle cry of the angels in the war in heaven against Satan and his followers. In the British honours system, a chivalric order founded in 1818 is named for him and the patron saint of cavalry, the Order of St Michael and St George. St Michael is considered in many Christian circles as the patron saint of the warrior and soldiers.

- Another authority quotes Saint Maurice[231] as the patron saint of foot soldiers. He lived in the 3rd century and was an officer of the Theban Legion[232] composed almost entirely of Christian soldiers. These Christian soldiers refused to attend a sacrifice to the Gods of Rome and were consequently massacred.

- **Military Chaplains.** Saint John of Capistrano[233] is the patron saint of judges, jurists and military chaplains. St John was most noted for leading a Christian army of 70,000 soldiers against the Muslim Turks. He won the Battle of Belgrade in the summer of 1456. He died a few months later, but his army had, by then, delivered Europe from the invading Muslims.

227 Kirsch JP. *The Catholic Encyclopaedia Volume 2*. New York, Robert Appleton Coy: 1907
228 http://www.catholic.org/saints/patron.php?letter=C
229 Thurston H. '*St. George*' In *The Catholic Encyclopaedia*. New York, Robert Appleton Company: 1909
230 Holweck F. *St. Michael the Archangel. In The Catholic Encyclopaedia*. New York, Robert Appleton Company: 1911
231 Mershman F. '*St. Maurice*' In *The Catholic Encyclopaedia*. New York, Robert Appleton Company: 1911
232 The Theban Legion was a Christian legion of soldiers during the reign of Emperor Diocletian (284-305).
233 Benedictine Monks of St Augustine's Abbey. *The book of saints: a dictionary of servants of God canonized by the Catholic Church*. London, A. & C. Black: 1921

- **Royal Corps of Australian Electrical and Mechanical Engineers.** Saint Eligius[234] is the patron saint of goldsmiths and other metalworkers. Appointed the Bishop of Noyon-Tournai three years after the death of Dagobert I, Merovingian king of France in 642, Eligius worked for 20 years to convert the pagan population of Flanders to Christianity.

- **Paratroopers.** Paratroopers also regard Saint Michael as their patron. Paratroopers claim that, as a winged soldier of God, St Michael brings death from above to the followers of Satan; a task they both perform.

- **Quartermasters.** Saint Martin of Tours (316-397)[235] is the patron saint of military Quartermasters as well as providing support against alcoholism and poverty. In Saint Martin's early years, when his father, a military tribune, was transferred to Pavia in Italy, he accompanied his father, and when he reached adolescence was, in accordance with the recruiting laws of the time, enlisted in the Roman Army. He was baptised into the Christian Church at age 18. Trying to live his faith, he refused to let his servant wait on him. Once, while on horseback in Amiens in Gaul (modern France), he encountered a beggar. Having nothing to give but the clothes on his back, Martin cut his heavy officer's cloak in two, and gave half to the beggar. Later he had a vision of Christ wearing the cloak.

- **Retired Soldiers.** Saint Adrian[236] is protector against the plague and patron of old soldiers, arms dealers, butchers and communications phenomena. He was the chief military saint of Northern Europe for many years, second only to St George, and is much revered in Flanders, Germany and the north of France. He is usually represented armed, with an anvil in his hands or at his feet.

Australian Scottish Regiments

The first Australian Scottish Battalion was formed in New South Wales in 1868, named the Duke of Edinburgh's Highlanders; they wore a kilt of Black Watch tartan. Although the unit only existed for ten years it established a tradition of highland regiments that continues to this day.

Scottish Battalions were raised in all mainland States of Australia from Colonial times and as recently as the 1960s. Originally these battalions consisted in large part of either native Scotsman, or men of direct Scottish descent or heritage. As the years went by the continuation of these units became more about tradition than any real link with Scotland.

In recent years some Army Reserve units have been selected to carry on Highland traditions; these units have been reduced in size, from battalion to company-sized organisations.

Although not all of these battalions can trace their lineage directly to an original Australian Scottish colonial unit they all help to maintain the traditions established by those early regiments. Currently there are five Scottish companies located in New South Wales, Victoria, South Australia and Western Australia. Each is affiliated with a different Scottish Regiment in Britain and therefore wear distinctive tartans. They are:

- 2nd/17th Battalion RNSWR – Black Watch Tartan,

- 41st Battalion RNSWR – Black Watch Tartan with Argyll sett,

- 5th/6th Battalion RVR – Gordon Tartan,

- 10th/27th Battalion RSAR – Mackenzie Seaforth Tartan, and

- 16th Battalion RWAR – Cameron Tartan.

The wearing of Scottish orders of dress has never been restricted exclusively to these units or their bands as they are also worn by the pipes and drums of the Royal Australian Regiment and other Corps' pipes and drums such as the RACT.

Right: Image courtesy Department of Defence – 20090621adf8262658_143. Honour Guard 'A' Company 2nd/17th Battalion RNSWR

---

234 Van der Essen L. *'St. Eligius.' The Catholic Encyclopaedia. Vol. 5.* New York, Robert Appleton Company: 1909

235 Clugnet L. *'St. Martin of Tours' In The Catholic Encyclopaedia.* New York, Robert Appleton Company: 1910

236 Benedictine Monks of St Augustine's Abbey. The Book of Saints: a Dictionary of Servants of God Canonised by the Catholic Church. London, A. & C. Black: 1921

Chapter Five

Standards, Guidons, Colours and Banners[237]

Introduction

Colours are the symbol of the spirit of a regiment, for on them are borne the battle honours and badges granted to the unit in commemoration of gallant deeds performed by members of the unit from the time their unit was raised.

There are four distinctive forms of Honourable Insignia currently in use by the Australian Army[238]; in order of seniority they are:

• Standards

• Guidons

• Colours

• Banners.

A 'Battle Honour' is the public recognition and commemoration of an outstanding achievement on the battlefield by a unit or formation of the Australian Army. Customarily, the honour links the unit's performance to a specific geographical location, hence the name of that specific geographical location being emblazoned on the Colour.

Colours and their Significance

Originally the Colour was the rallying point in the noise and confusion of battle; it was the focal point of the regiment. Even if the commander was killed, hope was always present whilst the Colours remained intact. On the verge of ultimate defeat the troops would rally around the Colours which would become the scene of their final defence. Records of epic gallantry and acts of heroic self-sacrifice have been associated with reverence for and protection of the Colours.

This association of Colours with heroic deeds has caused the Colours to be regarded with veneration, in a sense, they are the essence or embodiment of the history of the regiment. The full history of a regiment is contained within written records, but as these are not portable in a convenient form, the Colours, emblazoned with battle honours for long and distinctive service, are something in the nature of a silken history, the sight of which creates a feeling of pride in soldiers and ex-soldiers alike.[239]

History and Development of Colours

The origins of Ensigns, Banners and Standards reach back through the centuries to Biblical times. There are numerous references in the Bible to each of the tribes of Israel having a standard for identification purposes; Numbers 1:52, 'And the children of Israel shall pitch their tents every man by his own camp, and every man by his own standard, throughout their hosts'.[240] These standards were used both as a general means of identifying members of a particular tribe as well as serving as a rallying point on the battlefield. Although such standards were the precursors, they were not the true equivalent of the Colours that would come in later years.

The Romans divided their armies into units which, when compared to the modern armies of today, have recognisable equivalents. The smallest unit in the Australian Army is a section of soldiers consisting of nine men commanded by a Corporal, whilst the smallest organised unit of soldiers in the Roman Army was a Contubernia composed of eight legionaries led by a non-commissioned officer (NCO) called a decanus. Ten Contubernia formed a centuria. A centuria or century consisted of 80-100 men under the command of a centurion and his optio (2IC).[241]

---

237 Taubert SC. Standards, Guidons, Colours and Banners of the Australian Army (Draft)

238 Australian Army, *Ceremonial Manual – 2003*, Canberra. Defence Publishing Service, 2003

239 Edwards TJ. *Standards, Guidons and Colours of the Commonwealth Forces*. Aldershot, England, Gale & Polden: 1953, p. 48

240 Bible, King James edition 1611, Numbers 1:52

241 Goldsworthy A. *The Complete Roman Army*. London, Thames and Hudson Ltd: 2011, p. 51

Within the post-Marian Roman Army (107 BCE) six centuria formed a cohort (Latin: cohor) which consisted of 480 men. The most senior centurion of the six centuria commanded the entire cohort. A legion was composed of ten cohorts, with the legion's overall command vested in the 'Legatus Legionis'[242], assisted by the Praefectus Castrorum and other senior officers.

There were two Standards carried into battle by units of the Roman army: the Aquila; and the Signum.

The Aquilifer carried the Aquila which was a silver eagle with up-raised wings surrounded by a laurel wreath on a narrow trapezoidal base mounted on top of a pole, sometimes a small banner (vexillum, placed directly below the eagle) on which was embroidered the legion number.[243] The eagle Standard was the most important possession of a Legion and its loss resulted in total disgrace, in fact, the legion's existence depended on its safekeeping.[244]

The Signifer carried the Signum for a cohort or centuria. Each centuria had a Signum, which comprised a number of philerae (disks, badges, emblems or medallions) with a number of other elements mounted on a pole.[245] The pole could be topped with a leaf-shaped spear head or a manus (open human hand) image thought to denote the oath of loyalty taken by the soldiers on enlistment. It sometimes included a representation of a wreath, which may have been used to signify an honour or award given to the unit.

The task of carrying the Signum in battle was dangerous as the Signifer had to stand in the first rank and could carry only a small shield for personal protection. It was this Banner that the men from each individual century would rally around. The word 'ensign' is derived from the Latin word 'Insignia', which, in turn, is the word used to denote a mark or badge.

Unlike the flags, standards, banners and pennants of countries, King's and members of the aristocracy, these early standards identified the soldiers unit and not an individual leader. There can be little doubt that the early Signum of a Roman Cohort was the equivalent of the modern regimental Colours of today, whilst the Aquila would have equalled the King's or Queen's Colour.

First British Colours

The use of the term, 'Colours', to describe a military flag carried by a regiment of infantry, can be traced back to the year 1588.

In the years leading up to 1588, the Spanish had controlled the lowland area of Flanders in what is today Belgium and Holland, known then as the Spanish Netherlands. While England had unofficially encouraged the Dutch revolt against the Spanish for years, Elizabeth I had not openly supported them because she was afraid it might lead to open conflict with Spain.

However, in 1584, the Catholics of France signed a treaty with Spain in order to destroy the French Protestants. Afraid that France would fall under the control of the Spanish Habsburgs, Elizabeth I decided to act. In 1585, under the Treaty of Nonsuch, the Queen sent the Earl of Leicester along with 5,000 to 6,000 troops, including 1,000 cavalry, to assist her Dutch allies against the Spanish. Philip II of Spain took the treaty as a declaration of war against him by Elizabeth I and three years later launched the Spanish Armada in an attempt to invade and conquer England.

By this time the Earl of Leicester was back in England and, having been appointed 'Lieutenant General of the Queen's Armies and Companies',[246] he gathered together an army at Tilbury to face the threatened invasion. The British Army at this time was composed mainly of volunteers, regiments of which consisted of 4,000 foot soldiers, with Knights and their Squires being appointed to command bands of men which varied in size from 400 to 600. The Earl decided to reorganise the army, along similar lines to the great European armies of the day, by standardising the size of the companies and regiments.

Photo Courtesy Ermine Street Guard, UK. Roman Legion re-enactment group carrying Aquila and Signum

242 Goldsworthy A. *The Complete Roman Army.* London, Thames and Hudson Ltd: 2011, p. 60

243 Harkness A. *The Military System of The Romans.* New York, D Appleton & Company: 1887, p. LVII

244 McNab C. *The Roman Army: The Greatest War Machine of the Ancient World.* Oxford, England, Osprey Publishing Ltd: 2012, p. 96

245 Goldsworthy A. *The Complete Roman Army.* London, Thames and Hudson Ltd: 2011, p. 54

246 Smythe J. *Certain Discourses.* London, Richard Johnes: 1590, p. 6

Sir John Smythe (1534-1607), a knight of the period, chronicled these changes in great detail noting:

> … whole regiment should bee reduced into bands of 150 Soldiers to an Ensigne, or into 200. At the most, and therewithal that all those small bands should bee committed to the charge of our trained Low Countrie Captaines (as they call them).

These Low Country Captains were company commanders who had, until recently, been fighting the Spanish in the Netherlands.

Prior to 1588, flags were named in accordance with the personage to whom the flag belonged; for example, the Queen had a Royal Standard whilst members of the aristocracy used banners and pennants according to their rank. The banners or pennants of a Knight were ornate and varied in size, often being embroidered with the Knight's Coat of Arms. Even in this early time it was becoming obvious that drawing attention to yourself on a battlefield, which included an enemy with long-range weapons, was not wise. This new attitude was highlighted in Francis Markham's work[247] when he wrote about the introduction of Colours and the need to ensure they were plain in detail:

> First, hee that in his Colours shall carry Coat-armour, doth indiscreetly, for he puts that honour to hazard, which he may with more honour keepe in safetie, and inticeth his enemy by such ostentation to dare beyond his owne nature.

Sir John Smyth records the introduction of new words and terminology into the English military, in which he could see no value, such as the adoption of the Dutch word 'lagar' being commonly used by soldiers instead of the word 'camp'. When referring to company flags, he wrote:

> Their Ensigns also they will not call by that name, but by the name Colours, which term is by them so fondly and ignorantly given.[248]

The importance of his writings lay in the fact that the word was only newly-adopted, and therefore fixes a time for its introduction into the military to around 1588, most likely at Tilbury.

At this time each flag bore the name as the officer responsible for its carriage. In his book, 'The Theorike and Practike of Moderne Warres', Robert Barret detailed the manning of a company of horse troops and stated:

> Unto every Companie of these doth belong, one Trumpet, one Ensigne, one Guidon, and one Cornet: the Ensigne over the Men at Armes, the Cornet over the Lancers, and the Guidon over the shot on horseback.[249]

Both the Ensign and Cornet continued as a rank through the centuries, whilst the name Guidon as a rank designation disappeared within a few years. This gives us a clear understanding to what Sir John Smythe was referring when he said: '*which term is by them so fondly and ignorantly given*', he is merely saying that the Ensigns should have called the flags they carried Ensigns not Colours!

Over the next few decades various military authors wrote of these times, each making special reference to the use of the new term, Colours. For instance, Robert Barret's work confirmed the adoption of this new terminology when he stated:

> We English men do call them of late Colours, by reason of the variety of colours they be made of; whereby they bee the better noted and knowne to the companie.[250]

The only writer of the time to detail reasons for the change to a new system of identification on the battlefield, as well as give descriptions of the Colours themselves, was Francis Markham (1565-1627), a Captain of infantry who had served through the period in question, and who, like Sir John Smythe, had documented events within his own lifetime providing eyewitness accounts.

To understand the development and design of these new flags, an understanding of basic heraldic principles (Coats of Arms) is needed. It is not necessary to discuss the various designs that can be used to make a Coat of Arms but only to have an understanding of the basic tinctures.

Shields formed the background of the Coat of Arms and were coloured with one of two main tinctures (metals or colours). Each of the tinctures indicates a virtue of the bearer's nobility or strength of purpose:

- Metals
  - Gold or Yellow (Or) signifies honour or height of spirit showing virtue in all things
  - Silver or White (Argent) is innocence or purity of conscience, truth and integrity without blemish.

- Colours
  - Black (Sable) indicates wisdom and sobriety
  - Blue (Azure) signifies faith, strength, loyalty, truth and chastity
  - Red (Gules) shows justice or nobility and justifiable anger in defence of religion or in defence of the oppressed
  - Green (Vert) signifies good hope, or the accomplishment of holy or honourable actions
  - Purple (Purpure) signifies fortitude with discretion
  - Tawny – Orange (Tenne) shows merit, and is the enemy of ingratitude

247 Markham F. *Five Decades of Epistles of Warre.* London, Augustine Matthewes: 1622

248 Smythe J. *Certain Discourses.* London, Richard Johns: 1590, p. 3

249 Barret R. *The Theorike and Practike of Moderne Warres.* London, William Ponsonby: 1598, p. 141

250 Barret R. *The Theorike and Practike of Moderne Warres.* London, William Ponsonby: 1598, p. 20

- Blood Red (Sanguine) signified fortitude or victorious.

- Ermine
  - Ermine is not a true colour, but a fur which signifies holiness.

The use of Coats of Arms on the battlefield was not encouraged because of the unnecessary and excessive danger the Ensign was subjected to from the enemy. This, coupled with the need for the new Low Country Captains to have their own Ensigns, required a new system of flags. The new flags consisted of two tinctures evenly divided. The records of the period do not specify how this was done and it was most likely a mixture of horizontal, vertical or diagonal. The Colours used by Captains were in strict accordance with heraldic principles, being a mixture of both metals and colours (metal on metal, or colour on colour was not acceptable). Captains who had an entitlement to a Coat of Arms were required to use the two main colours of their heraldic shield; whereas those with no such entitlement were able to select their own combination of tinctures.

There were only four ranks entitled to carry Ensigns at this time and their Colours were described as follows: [251]

- Captain – two tinctures equally mixed with a Cross of St George in the upper canton near the staff. The cross was plain red on a white background and stated to be one-sixth the size (assumed to be the length along the pike) of the Colour.

- Colonel – the same as that of a Captain but was of only one colour or metal.

- Colonel General or other superior officer – the same as that of a Colonel, but the Cross of St George was reduced in size to one-eighth of the size (assumed to be the length along the pike) of the Colour.

- General in charge of the force – a single colour or metal with no other markings whatsoever.

In 'A History of the British Army', John Fortescue discussed the events of 1585:

Before the end of the century the term infantry had also passed into the language, while the flags of the infantry, from their diversity of hues, had gained the name of Colours'. [252]

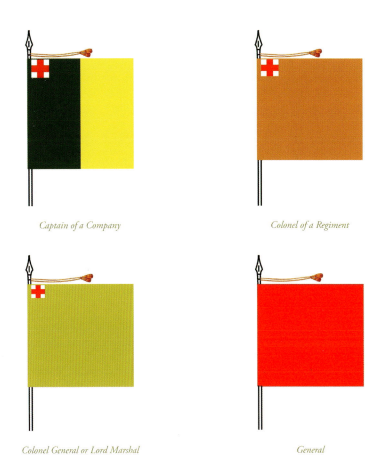

Captain of a Company

Colonel of a Regiment

Colonel General or Lord Marshal

General

Original Colours of the English Forces of Queen Elizabeth I – about 1588

From this work it would be easy to misunderstand the comment, '*from their diversity of hues*', to mean that each Colour had a large variety of different colours sown onto each individual Ensign. What was really meant was that when observing an entire army arrayed upon a field with hundreds of these Ensigns held aloft, the multitude of flags displayed a diversity of colours.

These basic Ensigns, introduced in 1588, were developed and changed over the years and by the time of the English Civil War (1642-1651) the Colours had been modified to reflect the different manning levels of Cromwell's[253] New Model Army.

251 Markham F. *Five Decades of Epistles of Warre.* London, Augustine Matthewes: 1622, p. 74

252 Fortescue JW. *A History of the British Army Volume 1.* London, Macmillan: 1910, p. 136

253 Oliver Cromwell; Member of British Parliament, Captain to Lieutenant General in three years (1642-1645), Army Commander (1649-1651), Lord Protector England, Wales, Scotland and Ireland (1653-1658): born Huntingdon 25 April 1599 – died London 3 September 1658.

No 'King's Colour' or its equivalent was carried at that time; the Colonel's Colour was the senior Colour in the regiment and had a plain field with no distinctions. The Lieutenant Colonel's Colour was 'differenced', usually by adding a cross of St George in the upper left canton. The Sergeant-Major's Colour was differenced by having a small device such as a 'pile or paly wavy' (this is an heraldic term referring to the addition of segmented wavy lines drawn down and across the top of the flag) coming down from the canton; while the Captains' Colours could have different devices (small discs, stars or crosses) to show their seniority within the regiment. Thus the 4th Captain's Colour of the White Regiment, New Model Army had a white field, a St George's cross and four rose-red diamonds set on the field.[254]

R Symonds as quoted by TJ Edwards ('*Enseignes of the Regiments in London in 1643*'), shows the Colours of the Red Regiment of Cromwell's Parliamentary Forces attending the last General Muster held on 26 September 1643.[255] These Ensigns had one thing in common with those of the Royalist Forces of Charles I; they both used the Cross of St George[256] in the canton, a symbol which had long been the accepted Ensign of England.

New Standing Army

Following the restoration of the monarchy and the coronation of King Charles II[257] in 1660, the Army of the Commonwealth was disbanded and replaced, in 1661, by what would become the first Standing Army. A Royal Warrant approved at the time describes in detail the first Colours of the period:

CHARLES R.

Our will and pleasure is, and we do hereby require you forthwith to cause to be made and provided, 12 Colours or Ensigns for our Regiment of Foot Guards of white and red taffeta, of the usual largeness, with stands, heads and tassels, each of which to have distinctions of some of Our Royal Badges, painted in oil, as our trusty and well-beloved servant Sir Edward Walker, Knight, Garter Principal King-of-Arms, shall direct, and for so doing this shall be your warrant.

Given under our Sign Manual at Our Court at Whitehall, this 13th day of February, 1661.

To our right trusty and right well-beloved cousin and Councillor Edward Earl of Sandwich, Master of our Great Wardrobe, or his Deputy.

By His Majesty's Command
Edward Nicholas[258]

The Royal Badges referred to in the Warrant were painted on the material rather than being embroidered, which became the normal method in later years. In the years that followed, more regiments were raised which were not connected with the Royal Household and therefore did not have Royal badges on their Colours. The accepted system, which was carried on from the Civil War period, was for the armorial devices of the regiment's Colonel to be born on the unit Colours.[259] This meant that every time the regiment gained a new Colonel, its Colours would change. This was the beginning of a long tradition where a retiring Colonel would take the Regiment's Colours with him when leaving the unit.

By 1707, many changes had been made in design and the materials used in manufacturing Colours, as well as a reduction in the total number carried by a single battalion, the number had been reduced to three. The first regulation issued detailing the requirements and restrictions relating to the use of Regimental Colours were issued in 1747. This regulation was the first of three such Regulations and Royal Warrants issued over the next 20 years which finally standardised the size and design of Colours.

The most important changes instituted during these years were:

- The practice of the Colonel placing his personal arms, crests or other devices on to the Regiment's Colours was ceased.

- No regiment could change their Colours without Royal approval.

- Two Colours were approved for each battalion. The King's or First Colour of every Regiment was to be the Great Union flag. The second Colour which soon became known as the Regimental Colour was to be the colour of the 'Facing' of the Regiment with the Great Union in the upper canton –the Facing was the colour of the material on the jacket collar, lapels and cuffs.

- Each Colour had the number of the regiment centrally placed within a wreath, except those approved to have Royal Badges. The wreath consisted of Roses and Thistles on a single branch, and, in 1801, the Shamrock of Ireland was added.

254 Gush, G. *Renaissance Armies 1480-1650*. Cambridge, Stephens: 1975, p. 120
255 Edwards TJ. *Standards, Guidons and Colours of the Commonwealth Forces*. Aldershot, England, Gale & Polden: 1953, p. 15
256 Lawson, CCP. *History of the Uniforms of the British Army*. London, Peter Davies: 1940, p. 127
257 Charles II; King of England, Scotland and Ireland, whose restoration to the throne in 1660 marked the end of republican rule in England: born 29 May 1630 – died 6 February 1685.
258 *Royal Warrant for Colours of the present Standing Army*: 13 February 1661
259 Edwards TJ. *Standards, Guidons and Colours of the Commonwealth Forces*. Aldershot, England, Gale & Polden: 1953, p. 21

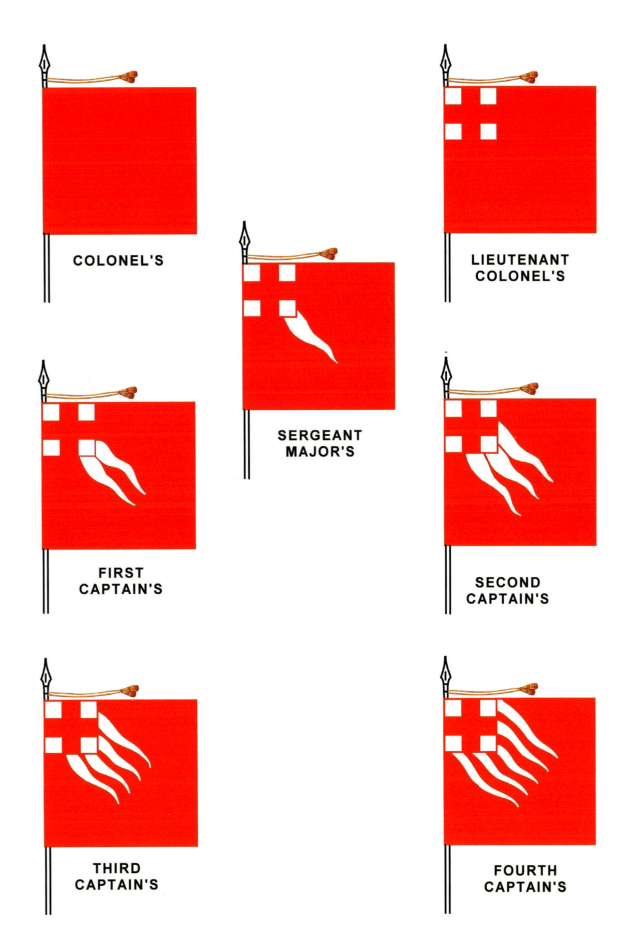

Colours of the Red Regiment, Parliament Forces, 1643

- Units were permitted to have their Motto emblazoned on the Colour, however the 15th King's Light Dragoons had been given permission to have the word 'Emsdorff' shown on their Colour instead. The Battle of Emsdorff was fought on 16th July 1760, and is the earliest instance of a battle honour being granted in the form of the name of the action.

- Regulations for Cavalry Standards and Guidon were introduced, which included a general description of the size and shape of both Standards and Guidons.

The next regulations to be issued relating to Colours were during the reign of Queen Victoria, in 1844. These orders reiterated most of what had been in use for many years, but clarified some points and amended the name of the King's Colour to The Royal or First Colour and became gender-specific; the Colours became known as either the King's Colour or the Queen's Colour dependent upon who presented the Colours.

One of the more interesting points included in the new regulations was the official name change of the Second Colour, when it was described as '*The Regimental or Second Colour*'. Prior to these regulations, devices, distinctions and battle honours in general had been placed on all Standards, Guidons and Colours, but the use of these were then restricted to the Regimental Colour.

To remove the confusion between the shapes of Standards and Guidons of the time, the fly corners of all Standards were ordered to be square. Whilst the shape of the Guidon was standardised by the same regulation, the upper and lower corners to be rounded off at 12 inches (30.48cm) distance from the end of the flag.

Size and Shapes of Colours

The size and shape of Standards, Guidons and Colours have varied considerably. The first Royal Warrant of 1661, when referring to the Foot Guards, stated that the Colours were to be '*of the usual largeness*'. By the time of the Coronation of James II in 1685, the Colours of the Foot Guards were recorded as being 8 feet 3 inches (251.46cm) on the fly and 7 feet 6 inches (228.6cm) on the staff.[260] The 1751 Warrant makes the same vague reference to sizes and mentions Cavalry Standards which were: '*to be the same as those of the Horse and Horse Grenadier Guards*'.

By 1747 the size of Colours had been reduced to 6 feet 6 inches (198.12cm) on the fly and 6 feet 2 inches (187.96cm) on the staff. This remained the standard size for over 100 years. By 1858 it was realised that, as the Ensigns responsible for carrying these Colours were boys aged between 14 to 17 years, the overall size of the Ensigns needed to be reduced for the boys to satisfactorily carry the Colours. The size was subsequently reduced to 3 feet 9 inches (114.3cm) on the fly and 3 feet 6 inches (106.68cm) on the staff.

Although Standards and Guidons always had fringes of gold or silver, this extra adornment was not added to Colours until 1858; the reason is revealed in a letter from the Horse Guards dated 5 July 1859:

Sir,

The new pattern Colours for the Infantry having, from their reduced size, a poor effect on Parade, I am directed by the General Commanding in Chief to intimate to you that Her Majesty has been pleased to sanction the addition of a silk and gold fringe of the pattern sent herewith.

The Border for the Queen's Colour is to be of Crimson silk and gold, and that for the Regimental Colour of the Facings of the Corps and Gold.

I have the honour to be, Sir,

Your obedient servant,
(Sgd.)   T. Troubridge, D.A.G.

The 1873 Queen's Regulations set the size of the fringe to be two inches (5.08cm) wide; the measurement that is still in use today.

Although many British Army Colours show a great deal of variation between the different regiments this is due to their individual histories; for example, the date the unit was raised and the fashion of Colours at the time. However the basic layout of a standard set of Colours was, by the early 1900s, almost identical to that in use today.

Colonial Colours

Prior to Federation, some units of the Australia colonies were presented with Colours. The Colours were of varied designs and not always in accordance with British Army Regulations. There is evidence that 18 units in the six colonies received Colours, the first being the Royal Victoria Yeomanry Cavalry in 1858 and the last the Perth Company of the Western Australian Rifle Volunteers in 1896.

Colours of the Militia

The first militia unit to receive Colours after Federation was the Adelaide Rifles, in December 1901.[261] The Adelaide Rifles changed its name in 1903 to become the 10th Australian Infantry Regiment (Adelaide Rifles)[262]; it was also on this date that the new Commonwealth Army (the Australian Army) officially came into being.

---

260 Edwards TJ. *Standards, Guidons and Colours of the Commonwealth Forces*. Aldershot, England, Gale & Polden: 1953, p. 34

261 The Register. Adelaide South Australia: 2 December 1901, p. 7
262 Military Order, GO 296/1903: 1903

The new Commonwealth Army's first unit to receive Colours was the 1st Australian Infantry Regiment (Militia).[263] These Colours were a gift from the Women's Branch of the British Empire League and were presented by Lady Northcote, wife of the then Governor-General of Australia, in the Sydney Domain on 24th May 1906.

From that period, until 1921, very few units were presented Colours, which prompted the Army to seek The Sovereign's approval for Australian units to carry Colours. Approval was given for those units of the Australian Army, equivalent to those of the United Kingdom who had approval to carry Colours or Guidons, to be so presented.

King's Colour

Regimental Colour

Initially the Army did not produce its own instructions for standardising Colours, instead used the King's Regulations dealing with the matter and reproducing it as *Military Order 524/1913*. Part of that original document included scale drawings of the approved pattern Colours to be used, which was the British pattern showing the Colours of the '4th Battalion

The Norfolk Regiment'. The order also stipulated that the badge and territorial name on the Regimental Colour was to be '*within the Union-wreath of roses, thistles and shamrocks*'.

In 1913, the 58th Battalion (The Essendon Rifles) was formed and by May 1914 the unit had raised the funds to purchase a set of Colours. The local shire council had been instrumental in aiding the Battalion to achieve this aim. One of the Council members, Councillor Goldsworthy, had been asked to both design and have a set of Colours manufactured for the Battalion.[264] That design submitted to the Military Board by the Battalion Commanding Officer, LTCOL HE Elliott[265], for the regimental colour was later adopted by the Board and reproduced in *Military Order No. 184/1914*, as the standard design to be used by all infantry battalions of the Commonwealth.

264 http://trove.nla.gov.au/ndp/del/article/74492953
265 Major General Harold Edward "Pompey" Elliott, CB, CMG, DS0, DCM, V.D; Commanded 58th Bn 1913/14, 7th Bn 1914/16, 15th Inf. Bde 1916/19, 3rd Division 1927, Solicitor City of Melbourne 1919, Member of Australian Senate 1919-1931: born Charlton Victoria 19 June 1878 – died 23 March 1931.

Below: Design drawing shown in MO 184/1914

263 Military Order GO 296/1903: 1903

This order also detailed the new specifications aimed at fixing those issues associated with the design of the regimental colour detailed in the previous Military Order. The main changes were:

- All regimental Colours were to be dark green

- The complete and exact regimental badge of the unit was to be shown within the circle containing the gazetted unit territorial title

- The wreath of roses, thistles and shamrocks was changed to that of Australian wattle, and

- The number of the unit was to be standard Arabic numerals and not Roman as detailed on the British Colour.

The reorganisation of Infantry battalions in 1921, and the reallocation and changes of unit designation and titles, necessitated changes in the design of the King's and Regimental Colours. All battalions possessed a King's Colour (issued in 1920) but few had a Regimental Colour. The changes consisted of substituting the Territorial Title of the unit with the gazetted numeric title and replacing the unit Regimental badge with the WWI unit colour patch.

Colours of the Australian Imperial Force (AIF)

The Defence Department adopted the policy that units raised exclusively for war service were not entitled to be presented Colours; all units of both the South African contingent and the AIF were included in this category.

Notwithstanding this policy, a number of units were presented with Colours by various community organisations; usually with the approval of the relevant authority.

The citizens of St Kilda submitted a request to present a set of Colours to the newly-formed local AIF unit, the 14th Battalion; and although initially rejected by the Minister of Defence, the request was eventually approved; the Minister citing 'special circumstances' as the reason for this decision. The Colours were presented by the Governor-General of Australia, Sir Ronald Munro Ferguson at St Kilda on 13th December 1914.

The 38th Battalion, a unit raised in Ballarat, was also given approval to receive a set of Colours, which were presented on 14th June 1916 by the Governor-General at Campbellfield[266], a suburb of Melbourne, just six days before the unit sailed for England.

Regimental Colour
14th Battalion – AIF

Regimental Colour
3rd Pioneer Battalion – AIF

The only other AIF unit to receive Colours was the 3rd Pioneer Battalion which were presented by the wife of the State Governor, Lady Stanley, on 28th May 1916 at the Melbourne Cricket Ground; uniquely it was the only non-infantry battalion[267] to be so honoured. Approval was only granted on the proviso that the Colours be laid up on the same day as their presentation. Therefore, immediately after the ceremony, the unit marched with the Colours to St Paul's Cathedral, Melbourne, where the Battalion's Commanding Officer, LTCOL Robert Law, handed them over to the Archbishop and Dean of the Cathedral.

---

266 Fairey E. *The Story and Official History of the 38th Battalion AIF.* Bendigo, 38th Battalion History Committee: 1920, p. 2

267 Note: Although Pioneer Battalions have been awarded Battle Honours in the past (WWII) they have never been officially presented with Colours; they are not considered Infantry.

Regimental Colour
49th Battalion – Australian Military Forces
Laid Up 1958

Colours – 1920 to 1959

In 1920, silk Union Flags,[268] which were to receive all honours and compliments paid to Colours, were presented to each of the 60 Battalions of Infantry, the five Pioneer Battalions and the 13th Light Horse Regiment that had fought as Infantry in the AIF. Most of the flags that were presented to the infantry battalions were later converted to King's Colours by having a crimson circle and crown added to them. The Colours presented to the Light Horse Regiment were not permitted to be carried on parade after the introduction of Guidons in 1927; however, they were retained by the regiment as 'Honourable Insignia' for services rendered.

After WWI, the existing Militia units were redesignated by adopting the numbering of and battle honours of the AIF units. It was hoped that this move would perpetuate the history and distinctions earned by the AIF and foster a close bond between the two. This move was only partially successful, as, over the years, many units were disbanded or linked with other battalions, thereby creating new units and traditions.

There are no units recorded as having been presented Colours during WWII. Following the cessation of hostilities in 1945 the Government decided to establish a regular standing army and reorganise and rationalise the existing CMF.

Initially the Army comprised 11 armoured units, a multi-battalion regular infantry regiment, 22 reserve battalions and five university regiments, all of which were entitled to Guidons or Colours.

The Army assumed the financial responsibility for the supply and maintenance of all Colours, including a decision to manufacture all Colours in Australia, but it was not until 12th April 1954 that the first order was placed with the Commonwealth Government Clothing Factory in Melbourne.

There were three major changes affecting Colours during this period of time. The first followed Australia's involvement in the Korean War, when the President of the United States of America awarded the Distinguished Unit Citation to 3 RAR for their action at Kapyong in April 1951.[269] The following year, Her Majesty the Queen gave approval for the Battalion to display, on the pike of the Regimental Colour, the streamer of the emblem of the citation.[270]

The next major change followed the final selection of WWII battle honours in 1959. In Britain the honours from the Great War had been emblazoned onto the King's Colour and consequently the honours from WWII were to be emblazoned on the Regimental Colour. However, in Australia, as the Army had previously placed their WWI honours on the Regimental Colour, it was decided to emblazon WWII honours on the Queen's Colour.[271]

The detail shown in the centrepiece, which had since the 1920s included the regimental colour patch, was uniformly replaced with the unit badge or emblem. This badge or emblem did not show the whole regimental badge but rather the badge's central theme, minus the royal crown and any floral embellishments and scroll work.

Regimental Colour – 41st Battalion,
The Byron Scottish Regiment
about 1956-1969

---

268 Society for Army Historical Research. *Journal of the Society for Army Historical Research – ACI 444.* London: 21 July 1919, p. 50

269 Renamed the Presidential Unit Citation in November 1966.
270 Australian Army Order 54/1952: 1952
271 Australian Army Order 97/1960: 1960

Image courtesy Department of Defence. HM Queen Elizabeth II, presenting new Colours to the Royal Military College - Duntroon on 27th April 1970

Colours – 1960 to Present

During the first half of the 1960s the Army trialled the Pentropic establishment which reduced the existing CMF battalions by half, creating large State regiments. When this trial ended in 1965, the old CMF battalions were not re-raised; rather multi-battalion State regiments were formed along the same lines as the existing RAR. These units were soon renumbered to mirror the former militia battalions, thus re-establishing historical links to the battalions of the AIF; however the traditional territorial titles were not restored.

In 1962 it was first proposed[272] to replace the existing Union Jack with the Australian National Flag as the Queen's Colour. Although this proposal was accepted, it took many years of bureaucracy, culminating with the Queen's approval on 29th September 1969.

The last unit to receive the old style Colours was the OCS, Portsea on 1st June 1968 when they were presented by His Royal Highness, Prince Phillip, The Duke of Edinburgh.

The first unit to receive the new design was the RMC-D on 27th April 1970, when it received its replacement Colours from Her Majesty Queen Elizabeth II.

Restriction on Units Carrying Colours

Those regiments whose duty it was to skirmish ahead of the main body, where speed and concealment were essential to the execution of this duty, did not carry Colours. These were termed Rifle Regiments, in the case of the infantry (including light infantry), and Lancers and Hussars, in the case of the cavalry, which is the reason why these units do not carry Colours; they do however emblazon their Colours/Battle Honours on their Regimental Drums.

The term 'Rifle Regiments' is sometimes confusing, when it is assumed that soldiers of any infantry battalion that carry rifles are equivalent. To understand the difference, one must consider not only the term 'rifle' but also the role played on the battlefield by these rifle regiments.

In earlier times, line infantry regiments were armed with muskets which had a smooth-bore and were not accurate. The introduction of rifling in the barrels increased accuracy and also increased cost of manufacture. It was therefore the practice to arm only selected regiments with the new more expensive weapons and change their role on the battlefield to one that maximised their increased efficiency.[273] This tradition has been adopted by the Australian equivalent of those original infantry regiments, such as Commandos and the Special Air Service Regiment (SASR), which likewise do not carry Colours.

---

272 Festberg AN. *Australian Army Guidons and Colours.* Melbourne, Allara Publishing: 1972, p. 123

273 Talbot-Booth EC. *The British Army, Its History, Customs, Traditions and Uniforms.* London, Sampson Low, Marston Company: 1937, p. 290

On 10th May 2013, the 2nd Special Air Service Squadron of the SASR and 2 Commando Regiment were jointly awarded the first Army Battle Honour since the end of the Vietnam War. The Battle Honour 'Eastern Shah Wali Kot' was awarded to both units for outstanding performance during the Shah Wali Kot offensive in Afghanistan (May-June 2010). As neither unit carries Colours, the award was made in the framed presentation shown below.

All Australian cavalry units carry Guidons including those units with 'Lancers' in their name (for instance, 1st/15th Royal New South Wales Lancers or the Hunter River Lancers). This tradition exists because Light Horse units are considered equivalent to the Dragoon Regiments of the British Army.[274]

Carrying Colours into Battle

The Colours were carried into battle in the centre front rank where they could be easily seen and recognised and to act as a guide and rallying point. There is no doubt that their presence in the battle had a positive effect on morale.

Originally when the Colours were carried in companies they were borne (accepted) by the youngest officer of the company, who was known as 'The Ensign'. The company officers in those days consisted of a Captain, a Lieutenant and a number of Ensigns. When the two Colours of the Regiment were carried,

the duty of bearing them was divided among the Ensigns of the regiment. As the number of guns captured generally gauged the importance of a victory so too did the number of Colours that were captured. This meant that the Colour Party became an obvious target and their location was often the scene of the most intense hand-to-hand fighting. This resulted in a very high rate of mortality amongst Ensigns because as one fell another would pick up the Colours and carry on. With a view to giving the Ensigns some local protection, the rank of Colour Sergeant was introduced in 1875.

The sergeants forming the escort to the Colour was formed by five Colour Sergeants, armed with halberds[275] and were chosen from the senior and bravest sergeants as they had to stand in the most exposed places on the field of battle.

The Colour Party was expected to fight to the death to defend the Colours. For the same symbolic reason the Colours are paraded in the centre of the Regiment when on the march and not at its head.

A different custom existed in the cavalry as their battles were not fought around a fixed spot marked by the Colours; their Standard or Guidon is carried by a Sergeant Major and no fighting escort is provided.

---

274 Note: The word 'dragoon' original meant 'mounted infantry'; however, usage altered over time and during the 18th century dragoons evolved into conventional light cavalry units. The title has been retained in modern times by a number of armoured and ceremonial mounted regiments, for this historic reason Australian cavalry units carry Guidons not Standards.

275 "Halberd" – a long-handled weapon with a head combining both axe blade and spear point (Macquarie University NSW. *The Macquarie Dictionary*. Milton Queensland, The Jacaranda Press: 1987)

Consecration, Blessing and Dedication of Colours

After Federation in 1901 it took a further two years for the Federal Government to pass into law the *Defence Act 1903*. This new act was mainly an enabling act both appointing and giving power to the new Commander-in-Chief[276], the Governor-General[277], and allowing him in turn to appoint a Military Board to administer the newly-established defence force.

To ensure a smooth transition from colonial administration to federal, imperial administrative orders and regulations were kept in use; these included such general instructions as *King's Regulations*.[278] Over the years these orders and regulations were slowly superseded or rescinded, being replaced by instructions and laws issued by the Military Board, initially using the *Commonwealth of Australia Gazette*[279] and later through the introduction of *Military*

276 Original term as per the *Official year book of the Commonwealth of Australia 1908* currently written as Commander-in-Chief.
277 Commonwealth Bureau of Census and Statistics (Australia). *Official year book of the Commonwealth of Australia:* 1908, p. 895
278 Great Britain. War Office. *The King's regulations and orders for the Army, 1908* H.M.S.O London 1908
279 Commonwealth Bureau of Census and Statistics (Australia). *Official year book of the Commonwealth of Australia:* 1908, p. 896

Image courtesy Department of Defence – 20080704ran8100087_091. Guidon of the 1st Aviation Regiment prepared for consecration

Board Instructions and *Military Orders*. However, it was not until the introduction of *Australian Military Regulations 1927* that the last of the *King's Regulations* were finally rescinded.

Although the ceremony occasioning the presentation of Colours was not considered imperative and was officially regarded as a private arrangement between the unit and the individual invited to make the presentation[280], the act of consecration was an integral part of that presentation process.

King's Regulations had specifically stated the full requirements for the consecration of King's and Regimental Colours.[281] It had also restricted the autonomy of the officiating chaplain by allowing him to only use one of two officially authorised '*Forms of Prayer*'. These prayers covered the two major religious denominations within Great Britain and Ireland at the time, Anglican and Roman Catholic. Ministers of other denominations could perform the consecrations of Colours; however special approval had to be obtained from the General Officer Commanding in Chief before this could occur.

The two forms of prayer used differed only in the use of specific wording, whilst the Anglican Church would '*bless and consecrate*' the Colours, the Roman Catholic Church chose to '*dedicate*' them. Put simply, this meant that in the eyes of the Anglicans the Colours became sacred or were made holy, whilst the Roman Catholics would only dedicate them to '*be a sign of our duty toward our King and Country*'.[282]

The British Army had long accepted and incorporated religious differences into its regulations; thus any issue of a religious nature was to a large degree easier than in the Australian military. Britain's Army was a permanent force and therefore not able to withhold their attendance for duty on any grounds, let alone religious differences. However, the Australian Militia was in the majority a voluntary force and as such, at times required delicate negotiations by all involved to ensure they remained effective. When confronted with questions of compulsory attendance at consecration services the Military Board avoided the problem by stating in 1925 that '*as a portion of the ceremony is of a religious nature, compulsory parades are not to be held*'.

In 1926, preparations began for a royal visit by HRH Prince Albert, The Duke of York (later King George VI) and his wife Elizabeth. The planned visit was to include the official opening of the new Parliament House in Canberra, on 9th May 1927. To ensure the event was as spectacular as possible all battalions and regiments within the Army were invited to send their King's and Regimental Colours for what was envisaged as a mass parade highlighting our military heritage.

280 Despatch 092/1170 (QMG 7) War Office, 1913 Defence 1874/3/67
281 Great Britain War Office. *The King's regulations and orders for the Army, 1908*. London, H.M.S.O: 1908
282 Program of Presentation, 23 August 1908, *Consecration* (as Reproduced in Festberg AN. Australian Army Guidons and Colours. Melbourne, Allara Publishing: 1972 p. 34)

Unfortunately, other than the original converted banners, now King's Colours, presented in 1904, few units had bothered to acquire regimental Colours or guidons, the cost of which could be as high as £70.0.0[283] each, an enormous sum well beyond the financial capabilities of the average battalion or regiment. Regardless of this limitation and with no financial help available from the Army[284], units across the country began fund-raising drives with the aim to acquire these important regimental symbols.

Around this time the Secretary of the Australian Catholic Federation wrote to the Minister for Defence, advising that, 'where a religious ceremony was to be performed by a non-Catholic Minister', it would be in direct violation of paragraph 123B of the *Defence Act 1903-1915*. From evidence cited[285] it would appear that the catalyst for this complaint was the blessing of the Colours by a Methodist Minister officiating at the presentation of Colours to the 59th Battalion (The Coburg-Brunswick Regiment) on 24th April 1927.[286] This complaint highlighted the absence of the necessary regulations within the Army to deal with basic administrative matters caused in part by the removal of *King's Regulations*.

In 1927 *Australian Military Regulations* were introduced; however they not only failed to address the issues of presentation and the consecration of Colours, they avoided them entirely. Thus, without clear direction, there was confusion about the correct procedures or standardised prayers for the consecration of Colours. Many units avoided this quandary by accepting their newly-acquired Colours or Guidons into service without pomp and ceremony either during annual camps or at regimental balls held to celebrate the occasion.

Although few Colours or Guidons were presented in the period after 1927 and before the 1950s, there is no evidence that the issue of consecration had been solved. From 1952 until 1956 a religious war of words erupted between the Chaplain-General (RC), Archbishop Daniel Mannix, and the Prime Minister, Robert Menzies, over Catholic claims that attendance at Colours presentation ceremonies, where the religious part of the ceremony was conducted by non-Catholic clergy, was in violation of Canon Law. The Australian Defence Force had, by this time, become a permanent force and the threat of the non-attendance of personnel at military parades could have dire repercussions not only for the Service but for the members involved.

Image courtesy Department of Defence – 20060818adf8161479_225. Consecration of Colours at a presentation Ceremony

Finally after much debate a conference was called by the Adjutant General of the Army, MAJGEN Mervyn Brogan, of the Chaplains-General Committee in Canberra to find a solution. At the conference it was agreed that at all future Colours presentation ceremonies each major denomination would be represented; the Colours would be 'consecrated' by the Anglican Chaplain-General or his representative, 'blessed' by the Roman Catholic Chaplain-General or his representative, and 'dedicated to God and the country' by the Other Protestant Denominations Chaplain-General or his representative. This arrangement finally solved the problem created by the Military Board's original reluctance to tackle the issue when it first arose in 1927.

The first unit to receive its Colours under the new religious arrangements was the 2nd Battalion (City of Newcastle Regiment) on 15th April 1956.[287]

From the time that the Religious Advisory Committee to the Services (RACS) replaced uniformed Chaplains-General, the tradition and practice has been that the three denominational Army Principal Chaplains (Anglican, Roman Catholic and Protestant) perform these services as delegates of their respective RACS members and denominations.

283 Equivalent to approximately $21,700 in 2014 calculated by comparing the Average Weekly Earnings in 1926 and 2014 as the baseline.

284 Military Order 524 of 1923 and MBI A.120 of 1926

285 Festberg AN. *Australian Army Guidons and Colours.* Melbourne, Allara Publishing: 1972 page 53

286 The Argus (Melbourne, Victoria: 1848-1957), Thursday 7 April 1927, p. 14

287 Festberg AN. *Australian Army Guidons and Colours.* Melbourne, Allara Publishing: 1972, p. 94

Parading of Standards, Guidons, Colours and Banners[288]

Standards, Guidons, Colours and Banners may be carried on all ceremonial parades. The drill for Standards and Guidons is as far as practicable the same as for Colours.

Standards and Guidons of the Armoured Corps are to be carried by Squadron Sergeant Majors (SSM) Warrant Officers Class Two with an escort of two Senior Non-Commissioned Officers (SNCOs). The Queen's and Regimental Colours of infantry battalions are carried by commissioned officers and each is escorted by two SNCOs of the Battalion. Where multiple Colours are paraded together, the Colour Party also has a Senior Escort along with the two escorts.

The Australian Army Aviation (AAAvn) Guidons are carried in the same fashion as that of an infantry battalion, by an AAAvn subaltern escorted by two SNCOs. However, the subaltern is to be a qualified military pilot whilst the escorts may be selected from any Corps. All members of the Guidon Party are to be posted to the Regiment parading the Guidon.

Origins of Trooping the Colour

As early as the 16th century the Colour of the company was always placed in safe-keeping in the Ensign's quarters, or elsewhere, at the conclusion of a day's parade or when on active service, after a day's fighting. The Colour was lodged in quarters in the same way that members of the company were lodged, similar circumstances which gave the ceremony the name of 'Lodging the Colour'. Originally it was a simple ceremony, but gradually grew in complexity and dignity until 1755 when it was incorporated into the regular guard mounting parade of the Foot Guards to lend interest to the occasion. The origin of 'Trooping the Colour' has been erroneously attributed to guard mounting.

The music played during the 'Lodging' was called a 'Troop', and gradually the words 'Trooping the Colour', already two centuries old, was tacked onto guard mounting.

Replacement of Colours/Banners

All Standards, Guidons and Colours are embroidered with the reigning monarch's cypher and/or crown whilst Banners bear the emblems of the Royal or Vice-Royal person whose banner it is. Generally speaking it could be assumed that on the death of the Monarch or other personage that a Colour/Banner would be laid up and replaced; this is not normally the case.

Due to the high cost of manufacture, Colours are only replaced at the end of their serviceable life. As a general rule a set of Colours is expected to last up to 30 years. Some Colours that had been laid up for periods of time, have been subsequently brought back into service due to a unit being brought back onto the Order of Battle (ORBAT).

Laying Up of Colours

After service, Colours are laid up in sacred or public buildings in order to maintain an atmosphere of veneration. Colours are not disposed of or destroyed when their appearance has deteriorated beyond recognition, they are meant to be left to turn to dust as do the bodies of the fallen soldiers who served them. Some museums and State authorities such as the Australian War Memorial ignore this custom and spend large sums of money conserving the material, preventing its natural decay. Although well-meaning, this interference is not consistent with the treatment traditionally afforded to sacred objects.

The fact that Colours have, from the early ages, been consecrated, this would give them an aspect of sacredness, which could not be wholly ignored when consideration was given to their disposal. In view of the reverence paid them whilst they are in service, it is not surprising that care has been taken to ensure that they ultimately repose in sacred edifices or other public buildings, where their preservation is ensured, with due regard to their symbolic significance and historic association.

The custom in the Australian Army is that Guidons or Colours will be laid up in a place selected by the Commanding Officer in the case of an existing unit, or by the last CO or Unit Association in the case of a unit not now on the ORBAT. The laying up place will be selected from one of the following:

- The Australian War Memorial in Canberra

- A State war memorial

- A cathedral, church or military chapel

- A military Corps regimental or unit museum

- A civic building.[289]

It was formerly the practice that 'laid up' Colours could not be removed from their resting-place and taken back into service. This policy however has now been amended and the laid up Colours of disbanded or amalgamated units may be retaken into service, by those units should they be brought back onto the ORBAT, provided the Colours are deemed serviceable.

The 'laying up of Colours' is not to be confused with the practice of depositing Colours for safe custody, on occasions such as mobilisation during war.

288 Edwards TJ. *Standards, Guidons and Colours of the Commonwealth Forces*. Aldershot, England, Gale & Polden: 1953, p. 104

289 Australian Army. *Ceremonial Manual – 2003 Volume 2*. Canberra, Defence Publishing Service: 2003, Chap 10

Precedence of Flags and Colours

The ANF has precedence over all other flags, including State Flags, Service Ensigns, Standards, Guidons, Colours and Banners. When on parade together the following precedence applies: Army Banner; Standards; Guidons; Colours; and Banners. At all times the position of seniority is from the right of the parade to the left in descending order. In all cases The Sovereign's Colour is senior to a Regimental Colour.

The order of precedence for Banners is:

- The Army Banner
- The Banners of Queen Elizabeth II (by order of seniority of Corps)
- The Banners of the Duke of Edinburgh (Prince Philip)
- The Banner of the Princess Anne
- The Banner of the Princess Royal
- The Banners of The Governor-General of Australia (by order of Service, Corps and within units, by date of presentation).

When the Army Banner is paraded with existing Unit/Corps Standards, Guidons, Colours and Banners, the Army Banner is to be paraded in the centre.

When the Colours, including the guns of RAA and Banners of a Corps, appear together on the same parade, the Banners are to be marched on and off, (or driven on and off in the case of a mounted parade), by seniority of Banner.

Within the RAAC the seniority of Standards and Guidons is by the order of units in seniority of Army Corps and Regiments.

The seniority of Colours is:

- Corps of Staff Cadets
- RAInf (within the Corps the order of seniority is by regiments, as listed in Seniority of Army Corps and Regiments, and within the regiments by battalions in numerical order)
- University regiments, by order of seniority as listed in the Seniority of Army Corps and Regiments.

General Description of Flags and Colours

The descriptions of the ANF and the various types of military Colours are:

- **ANF.** The ANF, when carried, is made of lustrous nylon. The dimensions are 68cm on the pike and 137cm on the fly, exclusive of the pike pocket. The ANF does not have a fringe.

- **Standard.** A Standard is made of crimson silk damask (Exeter pattern). The dimensions are 65cm on the pike and 74cm on the fly, exclusive of the 5cm gold fringe and the pike pocket.

- **Guidon.** A Guidon is made of crimson silk damask (Exeter pattern) and is swallow-tailed in shape. The dimensions are 68cm on the pike and 103cm on the fly to the end of the swallow tail which is rounded off 30cm from the ends. The point of the slit is 78cm from the pike. The dimensions are exclusive of the 4cm gold fringe and the pike pocket.

- **Colours.** Colours are made of silk. A Queen's Colour is in the basic design and colours of the ANF. A Regimental Colour of regiments or units with the title Royal is dark blue. Other Regimental Colours are dark green. The dimensions are 90cm on the pike and 113cm on the fly, exclusive of the 5cm gold fringe and the pike pocket.

- **Banners.** The Army Banner is manufactured from Red English Silk. A Sovereign's Banner or a Banner of a Corps which has Her Majesty The Queen as its Colonel-in-Chief is made of dark blue silk. Other Banners are of crimson silk. The usual dimensions are 68cm on the pike and 88cm on the fly, exclusive of the 5cm gold fringe. An exception is the Banner of the Australian Army Cadets which is 55cm on the pike and 68cm on the fly, exclusive of the fringe. Eligibility to Banners is:

  - **Sovereign's Banner.** Any Corps or unit including those who hold Standards, Guidons or Colours, may receive a Sovereign's Banner.

  - **Banner.** All Corps, other than armour and infantry, may receive a Banner from a member of the Royal Family or the Governor-General of Australia. Training establishments which do not have an entitlement to Colours may receive a Governor-General's Banner.

- **Other Honourable Insignia.** Occasionally, other Honourable Insignia may be privately presented to Corps or units. These have no status and compliments are not paid to them.

Standards

From available evidence, the word 'Standard' was used to describe several different shapes of flags, from the extremely long to the more square style in use today. The following diagram is an engraving produced in 1670, showing Sir Jeremy Smith carrying the ducal Standard during the funeral procession of George Monck, 1st Duke of Albemarle.

The Standard carried by the Cavalry since these times was smaller and always nearly square; the earliest records show the size as 2 feet 5 inches wide by 2 feet 3 inches on the lance, not including the fringe.[290] The overall size of both Cavalry Standards and Guidons was always much smaller than the Infantry Colours. This was primarily because of the difficulty in controlling a large flag on horseback whilst galloping into battle.

---

290 Edwards TJ. *Standards, Guidons and Colours of the Commonwealth Forces.* Aldershot, England, Gale & Polden: 1953, p. 35

The Standard.

Tho: Segar Esq.
Blewmantle Pursivant
at Armes.

Sr Stephen
Fox Kt.

Sr Jeremie
Smith Kt.

Richard Mason
Esq. his Maties
Avenor.

Standard – 1st Armoured Regiment

Standards were made from double silk damask with fringes made from silver, gold and coloured silk or combinations thereof. Damask silk is a type of silk weave which has a pattern clearly visible within the material. It is not recorded which pattern was used by the various cavalry units; however, within the Australian Army all damask silk has the Exeter Pattern. The badge of the regiment or its commander was embroidered on both sides of the Ensign which is carried on the head of a lance. Since Victorian times all standards and guidons have been made from red damask silk.

Cavalry Standards were called cornets, as were the officers who carried them.[291] Dragoons originally used the title Guidon for the officer carrying their Guidon, but later changed it to Cornet.[292]

When Colours were first introduced into the infantry, Standards and Guidons had already been in use for some time. In 1598, Barratt discussed at length the various ranks that made a cavalry unit including the Standard and Guidon bearer, but made no comment regarding their names or their rank. Therefore it can be safely assumed that Standards and Guidons predate Colours; however, it is not possible to establish exactly when these Ensigns began to resemble the Standards and Guidons in use today.

In the British Army, cavalry units carry either the Queen's Regimental Standard in the case of heavy cavalry regiments or the Queen's Regimental Guidon in the case of light cavalry regiments. These are equivalent to infantry Colours.

291 Lawson CCP. *History of the Uniforms of the British Army.* London, Peter Davies: 1940, p. 149
292 Barret R. *The Theorike and Practike of Moderne Warres.* London, William Ponsonby: 1598, p. 141

George Monck 1st Duke of Albemarle

2nd Troop of Life Guards

Colonel Royal Regiment of Dragoons

HRH Prince Charles presented a Standard to the 1st Armoured Regiment in April 1981, making it the only unit within the Australian Army to be so honoured. This is because the 1st Armoured Regiment is classed as a heavy cavalry unit being equivalent to a British Regiment of Dragoon Guards, rather than light dragoons or hussars that would normally carry a Guidon.

Guidons

Guidons, from the Italian 'guida' (a guide), correctly pronounced 'Guy-don' but in the Australian Army commonly pronounced 'Gee–on', are the counterpart of Infantry Colours and are carried by both the RAAC and AAAvn.

Like the Standard, Guidons have varied in shape and size since their introduction into the military. The earliest drawings available are from the late 1600s and show that Guidons have not always been swallow-tailed; in fact, they only differed from a Standard in that the ends were rounded and had a slit in the end.[293]

Both Standards and Guidons are heavily embroidered and this naturally necessitated their being made of double silk damask; they also have a fringe made from silver, gold and coloured silk or combinations thereof.

The task of carrying the Guidon into battle was given to a junior officer until this was changed by the King in 1822.[294] The following order was issued from Army Headquarters on 30th November 1822:

> His Majesty has been pleased to command that standards in the Cavalry regiments shall be carried in the future by troop Serjeant-Majors, and the Commander-in-Chief desires the same may be observed accordingly.
>
> H. Torrens, Adjt. Genl

In 1926, approval was granted for the Light Horse Regiments of the Australian Army to possess and carry Guidons similar in design to those sanctioned for the Light Dragoon or Lancer Regiments of the British Army. This was later amended to entitle armoured units, which were converted from Light Horse and Cavalry units, to carry a Guidon.

Above: Guidons about 1670-1685

Guidon – 10th Light Horse

Australian Army Aviation Guidons[295]

The evolution of the AAAvn has its lineage from the WWI Australian Flying Corps (AFC), also an Army unit. Although the RAAF claim this honour as well there is little doubt that both organisations share a passion for flight that encompasses similar roles. As a Combat Arm, Aviation Regiments are entitled to carry Guidons displaying Battle Honours; however due to the original size of the Corps (a few independent reconnaissance squadrons) there was never an entitlement.

293 Lawson CCP. *History of the Uniforms of the British Army.* London, Peter Davies: 1940, p. 150
294 Edwards TJ. *Standards, Guidons and Colours of the Commonwealth Forces.* Aldershot, England, Gale & Polden: 1953, p. 104
295 Australian Army. *Australian Army Aviation Corps, Corps Procedures 2008: 2008* (incorporating amendment 4)

During 2004, Aviation was given a more active role on the battlefield when it was made responsible for the armed reconnaissance helicopter role. The CA approved the issue of Guidons to both the 1st and 5th Aviation Regiments in recognition of their status as fighting units and their increased offensive role within the ADF.

Designs for the new Guidons were submitted and approved by AHQ in 2007. Both Guidons were completed with the 5th Aviation Regiment being presented their Guidon by the Governor-General at a ceremony in Townsville on 20th November 2007. The 1st Aviation Regiment Guidon was presented by the Governor-General on 4th July 2008 at Robertson Barracks, Darwin. The 6th Aviation Regiment received its Guidon in 2009.

Guidon – 5th Aviation Regiment

Death before Dishonour

Both Standards and Guidons were carried on the head of a lance, which originally was made exactly like the old tilting lance of the Middle Ages.[296] This differed from the Colours of the infantry in that unlike the staff that held the Colour, the lance was an offensive weapon used in combat. This difference was also reflected in the attitude adopted by each Cornet or Ensign in the preservation of his flag.

The earliest writings detail how infantry Ensigns were expected to prevent their Colours being lost in battle at the cost of their own lives. One such example quoted by Robert Ward was when Ensign Epps, at the Battle of Flanders, wrapped his body in his Colours and leapt into the 'merciless waters where he perished', in order that they not fall into enemy hands. He goes onto say how the reputation of both his Captain and the soldiers of the company depend on the

welfare of the Colours and how there is no greater dishonour than to lose them.[297]

This attitude is contrary to that of the Cavalry where the Cornet will not retrieve his Standard from the field of battle as long as it is lost through the breaking of his lance upon the enemy.[298] He was also instructed that it is forbidden to recover his Standard during the battle especially not to alight from his horse in order to retrieve it.[299]

These two attitudes do not reflect a lack of respect for their individual charges; rather it is a practical approach to the visual importance of the items to the soldiers under their respective commands. The infantry used their Colours as a rallying point taking direction from the Ensign in both the attack and defence whilst the cavalry because of their vantage point above the battle field did not have the same needs.

Sacred Symbols

Special reverence has always been accorded Colours, but the following examples show how they were revered beyond that of normal man-made objects and almost given the status of a holy relic, able to cleanse the spirit and impart divine forgiveness. This may have been in part due to the fact that Colours were consecrated by the church, or it could also have been that as the King's Colour it embodied the same virtues as did the King who governed by divine right.

Some military units[300] sent to Quebec in 1763 mutinied over a pay dispute which required them to pay for their own rations; which in essence meant that each soldier's pay of six pence per day would be reduced to two pence. The Governor of the Province of Quebec, COL James Murray, directly interceded to bring the matter to a successful conclusion. An eye witness to the events of the day wrote:

> Murray went to the head of the 15th Foot's grenadier company, and promised to kill the first man who refused to obey his orders. The governor's firm stance proved effective. The grenadiers were ordered to march between two Royal Colours, in token of submission, which they did and 'returned with cheerfulness, to their duty.

This example was followed by the rest of the men. The crisis now past, Murray declared that the garrison had 'recovered their character as good soldiers, and restored the battalions to their Colours'.[301]

---

296 Lawson CCP. *History of the Uniforms of the British Army.* London, Peter Davies: 1940, p. 149

297 Ward R, Marshall W. *Anima'dversions of Warre.* London, John Dawson: 1639, p.197

298 Ward R, Marshall W. *Anima'dversions of Warre.* London, John Dawson: 1639, p. 282

299 Cruso J. *Militarie Instructions for the Cavallrie.* England, University of Cambridge:1632, p. 12

300 The main units in Quebec at the time included the 15th, 27th, 47th and 60th Regiments of Foot.

301 Brumwell S. *Redcoats: The British Soldier and War in the Americas 1755-1763.* New York, Cambridge University Press: 2007 p. 134

The next example is taken from the writings of PTE William Wheeler, who served with the 51st of Foot from 1809 to 1829. PTE Wheeler wrote of an incident that occurred on the 4th June 1810 when the regiment's COL Mainwaring:

> began a lecture that lasted some time, he was in one of his best of good humours – an act of grace was to be performed, the prison doors were to be opened and the prisoners set free, but there was one unfortunate man whose crime was so great, that it required something extraordinary to be done before he could be purged from his guilt. It was Serjeant Harrison, he had been on Command and had lost or spent the public money entrusted to him, about £2 – and deserted. He had been brought back on the 2nd inst. The Colonel lectured poor Harrison a long time, was afraid if he released him without thoroughly wiping away all his guilt, it would be of little or no benefit to him or to the service. After a little consideration, he shouted out, 'is there none can advise me in this important affair?' All was silent, no one tendered their advice. 'What' he cried 'will no one put their shoulders to the wheel. Then I must lift the wagon myself, spread the Colours.' The Colours were brought to the middle of the square, the tops put together, thus forming a kind of arch. 'Now Harrison' said the Colonel 'pass uncovered under those honourable Colours.' This done, he shouts out, 'He's half clean, he must pass under them again, let the Colours touch him this time, now his crime he's blotted out for ever he is regenerated, the new born babe is not more innocent, and woe to the first man who ever mentions the affair to him.' No one had been appointed in his place, he was therefore ordered to join his Company and retain his rank. He was not disliked, so everyone was pleased to see him restored to his former situation again.[302]

It is interesting to note that COL Mainwaring lost his command the following year for prematurely burning that same set of Colours when it appeared they would be lost to the French at the Battle of Fuentes de Oñoro in Portugal in May 1811.[303]

Australian Army Royal Regiments

Infantry Colours are made of silk with Royal Blue being reserved for units which have been granted the title 'Royal', whilst a dark green is used by non-Royal regiments. Prior to 1960, only one battalion had the prefix 'Royal', that being the 6th Infantry Battalion, The Royal Melbourne Regiment. Now that all reserve battalions are part of royal regiments, they are entitled to carry blue regimental Colours. University regiments continue to carry Colours of dark green silk.

Prior to 1960, RAR was the only multi-battalion regiment in the Army. In that year, a complete reorganisation of the CMF's 31 infantry battalions saw them combined into six regiments, reducing the total number of battalions to 20. Each new regiment was granted the title 'Royal' and was based entirely upon the State in which it was located.

The Royal Queensland Regiment (RQR) comprised five battalions:

- 9th Battalion
- 25th Battalion
- 31st Battalion
- 42nd Battalion
- 51st Battalion.

The Royal New South Wales Regiment (RNSWR) comprised six battalions:

- 1st Battalion
- 2nd Battalion
- 3rd Battalion
- 4th Battalion
- 17th Battalion
- 41st Battalion.

The Royal Victoria Regiment (RVR) comprised four battalions:

- 1st Battalion
- 2nd Battalion
- 5th Battalion
- 6th Battalion.

The Royal South Australia Regiment (RSAR) comprised two battalions:

- 1st Battalion (later redesignated 10th Battalion)
- 27th Battalion.

The Royal Western Australia Regiment (RWAR) comprised two Battalions:

- 1st Battalion (later redesignated 16th Battalion)
- 11th Battalion.

The Royal Tasmania Regiment (RTR) comprised one battalion.

- 1st Battalion (later split and redesignated 12th and 40th Battalions).

Since that time the Reserve battalions of the various States have undergone many reductions in size, role changes or lost to history in line with Government policy. Many of these reductions have resulted in the battalions being linked to preserve traditional links with the original units of the AIF.

---

302 Wheeler W, Liddell Hart BH (editor). *The letters of Private Wheeler, 1809-1828* London, Michael Joseph Ltd: 1951, p. 41
303 Wheeler W, Liddell Hart BH (editor). *The letters of Private Wheeler, 1809-1828.* London, Michael Joseph Ltd: 1951, p. 66

Queen's and Regimental Colours

Two Colours; the Queen's and Regimental, are carried by all Australian Infantry Regiments, including battalions of the reserve, by parachute battalions and by certain training establishments such as the CSC and University Regiments as their structure is based on an Infantry Battalion.

The Original Queen's Colour

The Queen's Colour of every battalion was the Great Union (also known as the Union Jack – the colour of the United Kingdom of Great Britain and Ireland), in which the Cross of St George is conjoined with the Crosses of St Andrew and St Patrick, on a blue field, as approved by Queen Victoria in 1844. Although the Great Union Flag came into being in 1801 it was not until 1844 that the first official regulation was signed detailing its use as a Queen's Colour.

The Queen's Colour bears, in the centre, a crimson circle surmounted by the Sovereign's Crown (of the time), and upon the circle is inscribed in gold the unit's gazetted title and in addition if desired, the territorial title of the battalion.

Changes to the Queen's Colour

In 1969, Queen Elizabeth II approved the new design of the Queen's Colour, based on the Australian National Flag. The first unit to receive this new design was RMC-D on the 27th April 1970. The Colour was presented by Her Majesty the Queen during her Australian tour. All future Queen's Colours are to be of this design.

Left: King's Colour 46th Infantry Battalion - AMF

Right: Queen's Colour Royal Military College - Duntroon

The Regimental Colour

The base colour for Royal Regiments is dark blue, and for all other, non-Royal Regiments, dark green. The Colour bears a device, centrally placed comprising:

- The regimental badge embroidered in gold or silver as appropriate on a crimson background. The badge is modified by the omission of the gazetted or Territorial title of the regiment, the regimental motto and any wreath or crown incorporated in the design. As shown in the following illustrations:

- A crimson circle surrounds the badge, and upon the circle is inscribed in gold the gazetted title (and in addition, if desired, the territorial title) of the battalion. The centre device is encompassed within a wreath of wattle, tied with a gold knot at the bottom centre, the whole surmounted by an Imperial Crown. Only once has this tradition been varied in recent times and that was when the Papua New Guinea Volunteer Rifles opted to display 'Flora of the Forest Flowers' as a wreath.

The number of the battalion, embroidered in gold, is placed in the top corner near the pike. Arabic numerals are used for single battalion regiments and Roman numerals for multi-battalion regiments, for instance I, II, III for individual battalions of RAR and State Regiments.

Queen's Colour Royal Military College - Duntroon

1st Armoured Regiment

Regimental Badge

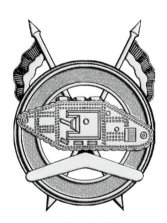

Badge on Standard

Royal New South Wales Regiment

Regimental Badge

Badge on Colour

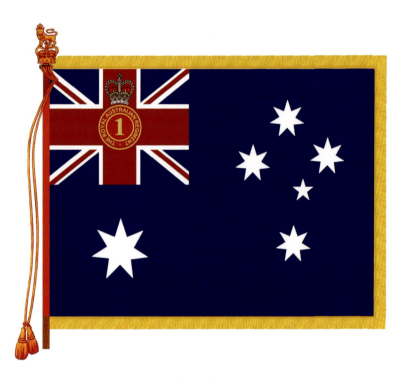

Queen's Colour
1st Battalion, The Royal Australian Regiment

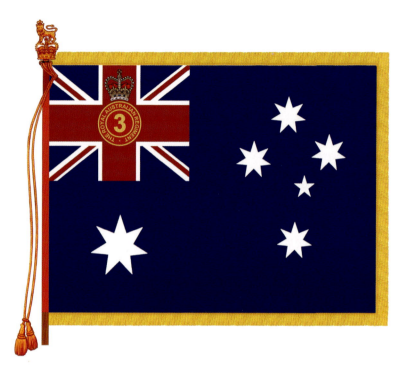

Queen's Colour
3rd Battalion, The Royal Australian Regiment – Post 1970s

Regimental Colour
1st Battalion, The Royal Australian Regiment
US Army Meritorious Unit Citation Streamer

Regimental Colour
3rd Battalion, The Royal Australian Regiment
Post 1970s with US Presidential Unit Citation Streamer

Queen's Colour
19th Battalion, The Royal New South Wales Regiment

Queen's Colour
9th Battalion, The Royal Queensland Regiment

Regimental Colour
19th Battalion, The Royal New South Wales Regiment

Regimental Colour
9th Battalion, The Royal Queensland Regiment

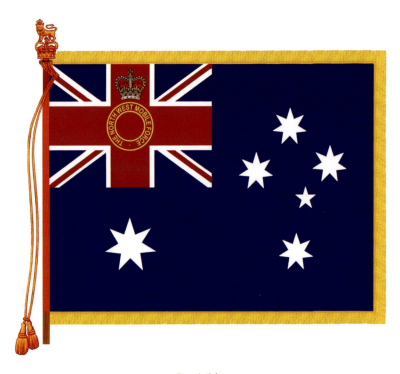

Queen's Colour
The North West Mobile Force (NORFORCE)

Queen's Colour
Adelaide Universities Regiment

Regimental Colour
The North West Mobile Force (NORFORCE)

Regimental Colour
Adelaide Universities Regiment
(Unit name changed from Adelaide University Regiment
to Adelaide Universities Regiment in 1992)

Guidons and Colours of Linked Units

In the British Army the original ordinance covering the use of Colours specifically ordered that a unit shall only carry one Queen's Colour and one Regimental Colour regardless of a unit's title. However, the general practice in Australia by a linked unit, if in possession of the Standards, Guidons or Colours of parent units, is to parade them together. They are only paraded separately at activities specific to one of the former units, for example anniversaries and memorial days.[304]

When deciding this question it was argued that, except for the 10th Light Horse, all Reserve Armoured Corps units were linked, comprising two or three regiments within a single regiment. It was further successfully argued that, in the case of expansion, these units would be constituted as separate regiments. These armoured regiments therefore retained their identity and are entitled to carry a maximum of two Guidons.

This decision to allow each regiment to maintain their respective Guidons did not allow for the two triple-linked units (see below). These maintained the link with the third unit of the regiment by the inclusion of its title within the linked units' title. These units only carry two Guidons.

Regiment Title	Parent Unit Title
1st/15th Royal New South Wales Lancers	1st Royal New South Wales Lancers 15th Northern River Lancers
2nd/14th Light Horse (QMI)	2nd Light Horse Moreton Regiment (QMI) 14th Light Horse West Moreton Regiment (QMI)
3rd/9th South Australian Mounted Rifles	3rd South Australian Mounted Rifles 9th Flinders Light Horse
4th/19th Prince of Wales Light Horse	4th Corangamite Light Horse 17th Prince of Wales Light Horse 19th Yarowee Light Horse
8th/13th Victorian Mounted Rifles	8th Indi Light Horse 13th Gippsland Light Horse 20th Victorian Mounted Rifles
12th/16th Hunter River Lancers	12th New England Light Horse 16th Hunter River Lancers

Theatre Honours, Battle Honours, Honour Titles and Honour Distinctions [305][306]

For administrative purposes, in the process leading to the issue of campaign medals and the determination of conditions of service, the terms 'warlike' and 'non-warlike' are used. These are Ministerial decisions, usually made before deployment. Similar terms may be used in determining Honours but such consideration can only occur at the end of an action, engagement, battle or deployment.

There are five steps to the issue of an Honour:

- CA, either on advice from the Battle Honours Committee (BHC), or on receipt of a compelling submission, will direct the BHC to initiate an investigation into the appropriateness of awarding Honours for a recent or current operation or deployment.

- The BHC prepares a brief for the CA that recommends the category of Honour, identifies its title, defines its geographical and time limits and provides a list of units and sub-units that may be eligible for the award of the subject Honour.

- CA endorses, amends or rejects recommendations in the brief.

- If endorsed by CA, the BHC drafts a Ministerial Submission (MINSUB) from CA to be passed through the CDF to the Parliamentary Secretary responsible for Defence Honours and Awards. The MINSUB includes two draft letters: the first to the Prime Minister from the Parliamentary Secretary, requesting that vice-regal approval for the honour be sought; and the second from the PM to the Governor-General requesting approval.

- On receipt of the Governor-General's approval, the Deputy Chief of Army (DCA) authorises the BHC to undertake the actions required to implement the award of the Honour.

For the purposes of the award of an Honour, a unit is defined as an organisation normally commanded by a LTCOL and is the equivalent of a Task Force/Battle Group. A sub-unit is an organisation normally commanded by a MAJ and is the equivalent of a Task Element/Combat Team. Normally, Honours will not be awarded below sub-unit level.

304 Australian Army. *Ceremonial Manual – 2003*. Canberra, Defence Publishing Service, 2003: *Vol 1* Chap 5 Para 5.12

305 Australian Army. *Ceremonial Manual – 2003*. Canberra, Defence Publishing Service, 2003: Vol 2 Chap 2

306 DI(A) ADMIN 38-3 Administration of Australian Battle Honours, Theatre Honours, Honour Titles and Honour Distinctions: 1 February 2013

The definitions of action, engagement and battle are relevant in terms of defining Theatre Honours, Battle Honours and Honour Titles. The term deployment, which has not been used in previous Honours' Instructions, is used to cover a number of warlike and non-warlike commitments that include peacekeeping and peace enforcement operations and other security and humanitarian activities:

- **Theatre Honours.** A theatre of operations is a designated geographic area in which a campaign or series of operations is conducted and for which an operational level joint or combined commander is appointed. A theatre may contain one or more joint force areas of operations. The award of a Theatre Honour is for creditable performance of an allocated task in a theatre of operations where a unit or sub-unit of any Corps is deployed under warlike conditions. A unit or sub-unit deployed to a theatre of operations may receive a Theatre Honour even though it has not taken part in a battle, action or engagement. It must, however, have creditably performed an allotted task. A unit or sub-unit qualifying for a Battle Honour will automatically qualify for a Theatre Honour. Examples of Theatre Honours are Gallipoli 1915, France and Flanders 1916-1918, Middle East 1941-1944, South West Pacific 1942-1945, Korea 1950-1953 and Vietnam 1965-1972.

- **Battle Honours.** A battle is an operational action conducted under warlike conditions. Factors that are considered include the size of the deployed and opposing forces, intensity of fighting, duration and casualties, strategic and operational importance and public perception. A Battle Honour is defined as the title of a battle or a series of battles fought as a campaign, an action or an engagement and is awarded to close combat elements consisting of the RAAC, RAA, RAInf, SASR, Cdo or AAAvn, as a public commemoration of their outstanding achievement in battles, action or engagement. The term is also used in a generic sense to denote both battle and theatre honours where appropriate. A unit may receive a Battle Honour provided at least one sub-unit is committed to a battle, action or engagement. Where a sub-unit of a Battle Group or an independent sub-unit is committed to a battle, action or engagement, the parent unit may be awarded the Battle Honour. Examples of Battle Honours are:

  – Landing at ANZAC
  – Hamel
  – Tobruk
  – Kokoda Track
  – Kapyong
  – Coral-Balmoral.

A Battle Honour has not been awarded without the appropriate Theatre Honour also being awarded.

- **Honour Title.** An Honour Title is awarded to any non-combat unit or sub-unit that is not entitled to a Battle Honour but which satisfies the same requirements for the award of a Battle Honour. An example of the award of an Honour Title is the title Coral, awarded to 102nd Field Battery for its outstanding achievement during the Battle of Coral in South Vietnam.

- **Honour Distinctions.** An Honour Distinction is defined as a public commemoration of creditable performance in an operation which, by the nature of the operation, does not attract a Theatre Honour, a Battle Honour or an Honour Title. Honour Distinctions are intended to recognise service under operational conditions in security-related, peacekeeping and peace enforcement and similar operations. Honour Distinctions are not intended to recognise domestic aid operations. Honour Distinctions may be awarded to units or sub-units. The criteria for Honour Distinctions, as were awarded for participation in the Sudan and South Africa, did not demand distinction in battle. Conversely an Honour Distinction did not preclude participation in battle as occurred in South Africa, a conflict in which many significant actions occurred. The distinctions for South Africa are qualified by dates (years) of involvement of the recipient regiments.

- **Campaign Honours.** The term Campaign Honours is not used in Australian Battle Honours, Theatre Honours, Honour Titles and Honour Distinctions and, although not an official definition of an Honour, is in general academic use and may be encountered from time to time. Campaign Honours are generally considered to be actions which occurred in a particular theatre that may have comprised more than one battle. These were subsequently grouped as a campaign. The Honour 'Liberation of Australian New Guinea' could reasonably be described as a Campaign Honour since it involved many battles over a protracted period.

- **Conflict Honours.** The Conflict Honour terminology was originally introduced specifically for the 'Army Banner' and is not used in Australian Battle Honours, Theatre Honours, Honour Titles and Honour Distinctions and is not an official definition of an Honour. The correct term as detailed in the Army Ceremonial and Protocol Manual for Honours emblazoned on the Army Banner is Theatre Honours.

Unit Citations/Commendation Streamers

Prior to the introduction of the Australian Honours System, units serving on warlike operations were at times honoured for exceptional group bravery by being awarded citations by either the country in which they were serving or by Allied Forces serving alongside them, in particular the USA.

The Unit Citation for Gallantry (UCG) and the Meritorious Unit Citation (MUC) were introduced into the Australian Honours System in 1991.[307] Unlike awards for individuals, recognition of group endeavour has limited history in honours systems around the world. The relatively recent tradition of unit citations has promoted broader recognition for collective endeavour. Prior to the introduction of the Victoria Cross for Australia (VC) there was provision under warrants issued in connection with the Victoria Cross number 13 which allowed for a ballot of troops that displayed outstanding gallantry. The Warrant reads:

Thirteenthly. It is ordained that in the event of a gallant and daring act having been performed by a squadron, ship's company, or detached body of seamen and marines not under fifty in number, or by a brigade, regiment, troop or company in which the admiral, general, or other officer commanding such forces may deem that all are equally brave and distinguished, and that no special selection can be made by them, then in such case the admiral, general, or other officer commanding, may direct that for any such body of seamen or marines, or for every troop or company of soldiers, one officer shall be selected by the officers engaged for the Decoration, and in like manner one petty officer or non-commissioned officer shall be selected by the petty officers and non-commissioned officers engaged, and two seamen or private soldiers or marines shall be selected by the seamen, or private soldiers, or marines engaged, respectively for the Decoration, and the names of those selected shall be transmitted by the senior officers in command of the Naval force, brigade, regiment, troop, or company, to the admiral or general officer commanding, who shall in due manner confer the Decoration as if the acts were done under his own eye.[308]

In 2004 the CDF authorised the practice, under single-Service arrangements, of issuing a streamer to units awarded a unit citation (UCG/MUC). Streamers are not a part of the official award within the Australian Honours System. When issued, the streamer is also embroidered with either the name of the battle or the location in which the unit was serving at the time, for example, 'AFGHANISTAN' or 'LONG TAN', and it can also include date qualification as shown on Battle Honour scrolls.

Where a unit has been recognised or is to be recognised with a Unit Citation that includes a Streamer, that particular Streamer may be fitted to the Army Banner by those units that do not have a Guidon, Regimental Colour or Banner.

Guidon of the 4th/19th Prince of Wales's Light Horse with Streamer United States of America Meritorious Unit Commendation (Army)

Since the end of WWII, there have been only five foreign unit citations awarded to regiments and battalions and one unit commendation to the Australian Army; all having been approved for use by Her Majesty, Queen Elizabeth II. Unit citations are worn on the uniform[309] and are attached as a streamer to the regimental Colour/Guidon.[310] Foreign nation citations have been awarded to the following units:

Serial	Unit	Citation
1.	4th/19th Prince of Wales's Light Horse	United States of America Meritorious Unit Commendation (Army), for active service with the 173 Airborne Brigade in South Vietnam 1965-1966.
2.	1st Battalion, The Royal Australian Regiment Battle Group[(a)]	United States of America Meritorious Unit Commendation (Army), for active service with the 173 Airborne Brigade in South Vietnam 1965-1966.
3.	3rd Battalion, The Royal Australian Regiment	United States of America Presidential Unit Citation for the Battle of Kapyong.
4.	'D' Company 6th Battalion, The Royal Australian Regiment	United States of America Presidential Unit Citation (Army), for the Battle of Long Tan.
5.	8th Battalion, The Royal Australian Regiment	Republic of Vietnam Cross of Gallantry with Palm Unit Citation (for operations in the Minh Dam Special Zone).
Other – Unit Commendation		
6.	Australian Army Training Team – Vietnam (AATTV)	United States of America Meritorious Unit Commendation (Army) – Republic of Vietnam Cross of Gallantry with Palm Unit Citation.

(a) The Battle Group originally consisted of the following units: 1 RAR, 1 APC TP, 105 FD BTY, 3 FD TP (RAE), 161 Recce Flight and 1 LOG SPT COY.

307 Australian Commonwealth Government. http://www.itsanhonour.gov.au

308 Warrants Issued in Connection With the Victoria Cross, War Department, 5 February 1856

309 Australian Army. *Army Standing Orders for Dress – 2000, Vol 1 and 2.* Canberra, Defence Publishing Service: 2003, Vol 2 Pt 4 Chap 9 Annex A

310 Australian Army. *Ceremonial Manual – 2003.* Defence Publishing Service, Canberra: 2003, Vol 1

The authorisation of Battle Honours did not start generally until after the Peninsular War (Spain 1807-1814), this being officially confirmed in 1811. However Royal Warrants had authorised the bearing, on the Regimental Colour, of 'Egypt' as a Battle Honour to those regiments that took part in the Egyptian Campaign of 1801.

Guidon

Queen's Colour

As Battle Honours were gradually introduced, they were not placed solely on the Colours but on clothing, hats and other accruements such as drums and the like.

The current policy in respect of the emblazonment of Battle Honours on Australian Queen's and Regimental Colours is that Battle Honours awarded during colonial times and the post-federation era may be added to the Regimental Colour along with WWI and WWII honours (to a maximum of 10) and Battle and Theatre Honours awarded during WWI

and WWII (to a maximum of 10)[311] are emblazoned on the Queen's Colour. Guidons are not restricted by the same requirements as infantry Colours as both pre-federation, WWI and WWII honours appear on the one Guidon.

The sequence to which the Honour is added to the Guidon or Colour[312] is not entirely dependent upon the date of the action but is taken from the date on which the Honour is approved by the reigning monarch. The preceding diagrams illustrate the layout and placement of Honours on a Guidon and the current-style Queen's Colour.

Banners

In ancient times a Banneret was a knight privileged to display, in the field, a square Banner (as distinct from the tapering pennant of a simple knight). In 13th century England, any commander of a troop of 10 or more lancers who was not an Earl was usually a Banneret. Later, in both England and France, the style became a title of honour, conferred for distinguished military service. A Banner was carried by a 'knight banneret' and bore their coat of arms. It was also used as a company flag (for example, the crosses of Saint George carried by English companies of archers), was rectangular (originally the staff greater than the fly, though gradually they became more square) and was carried by middle nobility or those commanding a company of troops.

The custom of presenting Banners to Australian Army units started on 14th November 1904 when Banners were presented to the eighteen Light Horse Regiments, the RAA and the Australian Army Medical Corps (AAMC) to commemorate the service in South Africa of those Regiments and Corps. A further 23 Banners were presented to infantry units in 1911. It was stipulated that the Banners presented to the non-infantry units were not 'King's Colours', but honourable insignia presented by the King as a special mark of favour in recognition of valuable services rendered to the Empire during the 2nd Boer War (1899-1902) and that Honourable Distinctions (Battle Honours) were not to be borne on the Banners.

By March 1956, these Banners, with the exception of the RAA Queen's Banner, had been 'laid up'. The RAA Queen's Banner was replaced on 1st August 1971 during their centenary year celebrations.

When more than one Banner is 'on parade', Corps seniority generally governs which Banner is carried in the senior position (on the right). However, when the RAAOC's Queen's Banner, is paraded with that of the RACT, which possesses the Princess Anne's Banner, RAAOC, even as the junior Corps, would carry their Banner on the right.

311 Australian Army. *Ceremonial Manual – 2003 Volume 2.* Defence
  Publishing Service, Canberra: 2003: *Chap 2*
312 Australian Army Order (AAO) 91-9/3/1927. *Battle Honours*: 1927

Although Ordnance is junior to Transport, it assumes the position of seniority because their Banner is that of Her Majesty The Queen.

Generally speaking as Banners are replaced due to old age, they are replaced with a Governor-General of Australia Banner, not a Banner from a member of the British Royal Family.

With the introduction of the 'Army Banner', it now assumes the position of seniority regardless of any other Standard, Guidon, Colour or Banners that are paraded at the same time.

General Description of Banners

Banners generally conform to a similar style containing three basic components or a combination of these design features. The following are designs which are common to most Banners:

- The year the Banner was presented or approved for presentation,

- Royal Cypher typically consisting of the initials of the monarch's name and title, often surmounted by a crown – the cypher design represents the personage who presented the Banner, and

- The Australian Coat of Arms, Corps or unit badge (Proper).[313]

Department of Defence No. 20130618dps8513881s055_300. The Army Banner on parade - Duntroon

Examples of a cross-section depicting the different types and styles of Banners in current use within the Australian Army are shown below. Note should be made of the Royal Blue used for Sovereign's Banners, which also include Her Royal Cypher. The other examples show how the personal cyphers of members of the Royal family are incorporated into the design of their Banners.

The 1st Recruit Training Battalion's Banner is the only Banner in current use that depicts a unit badge that has never been an approved hat badge.

Obverse or Reverse (Banners)

The Rules governing how to identify what is termed the obverse or front of the Banner and the reverse or back are usually quite straightforward. The accepted principle is that if the Banner depicts a Royal Cypher, regardless of the personage, that side is considered the Obverse. A Royal personage includes all members of the British Royal family including The Sovereign's Australian representative, the Governor-General of Australia.

The Australian Coat of Arms is used as the next most senior icon. As with all rules there are always some authorised variations that do not follow the accepted standard. For instance, the obverse of the RAE Banner shows The Sovereign's Cypher with the Coat of Arms; whilst on the

RAEME Banner, the Corps badge is shown with the Cypher of Prince Phillip on the obverse, with the Australian Coat of Arms being relegated to the reverse.

A common feature of all Banners is the inclusion of the year that the Banner was presented. The year of presentation or 100 years of service, which is usually shown on the obverse of the Banner, may be depicted; however, on the Banner of the RAAMC, these dates were shown on the reverse.

The Army Banner

The Army Banner is a 'Gift from the Nation' to commemorate the Centenary of the Australian Army. The banner was consecrated, blessed and dedicated at St Christopher's Cathedral, Manuka, Australian Capital Territory (ACT) on the Army Birthday (1st March 2001).

The Banner was officially presented as part of the Army Centenary Parade on 10th March 2001. The then Prime Minister, Mr John Howard[314], invited the Governor-General of Australia, Sir William Deane[315], to present the Banner on behalf of the people of Australia. The Banner was presented to the Regimental Sergeant Major – Army (RSM-A), Warrant Officer Peter Rosemond, who accepted the Banner on behalf of the Australian Army.

---

313 The term 'Proper' denotes something that is truly what it is said or regarded to be, genuine.

314 John Winston Howard, OM, AC; solicitor, politician; Minister for Business and Consumer Affairs 1977-1983, Treasurer 1977-1983, Prime Minister 1996-2007: born Sydney 26 July 1939.

315 Sir William Patrick Deane, AC, KBE, KStJ, QC; Justice High Court Australia 1982-1995, Governor-General of Australia 1996-2001: born Sunbury 4 January 1931.

Corps Banners

Three of the Army's Corps classified as combat or combat support Corps do not carry standards, guidons or Colours. They are RAA, RAE and RASigs. These Corps have banners as do most of the other Corps that support the combat elements of the Army.

The following have been presented banners (shown in order of presentation, not banner seniority):

Serial	Corps / Unit / Organisation	Banner	Year Presented
1	Corps of Staff Cadets	The Sovereign's Banner	1954
2	Army Apprentice School	Governor-General of Australia	1969
3	Australian Army Cadets	Duke of Edinburgh's Banner, Prince Philip	1970*
4	Royal Regiment of Australian Artillery	The Banner of Queen Elizabeth II	1971
5	Royal Australian Army Medical Corps	The Queen Mother's Banner	1974*
6	Royal Australian Army Ordnance Corps	Sovereign's Banner to the Royal Australian Army Ordnance Corps	1981
7	Army Recruit Training Centre – Kapooka	Governor-General of Australia	1982*
8	Royal Australian Corps of Transport	HRH Princess Alice, Duchess of Gloucester	1983*
9	Royal Corps of Australian Electrical and Mechanical Engineers	The Prince Philip Banner	1986
10	Royal Australian Corps of Signals	Her Royal Highness The Princess Royal (Princess Anne)	1986
11	Royal Australian Engineers	Royal Australian Engineers Corps Sovereign's Banner	1992
12	Army	Army Banner	2001
13	Royal Australian Corps of Military Police	Governor-General of Australia	2001
14	Australian Army Catering Corps	Governor-General of Australia	2003
15	Australian Army Intelligence Corps	Governor-General of Australia	2004
16	Australian Army Cadets	Duke of Edinburgh's Banner, Prince Philip	2005
17	Royal Australian Army Medical Corps	Governor-General of Australia	2011
18	Royal Australian Corps of Transport	Banner of the Princess Royal	2013
19	Army Recruit Training Centre – Kapooka	Governor-General of Australia	2014

* Denotes that the Banners have been laid up and the relative Corps has been presented with a new Banner

Army Banner – Obverse

Army Banner – Reverse

The Banner of Queen Elizabeth the Second
Royal Australian Artillery – Obverse

The Banner of Queen Elizabeth the Second
Royal Australian Artillery – Reverse

Sovereign's Banner Corps of the Royal Australian Engineers – Obverse

Sovereign's Banner Corps of the Royal Australian Engineers – Reverse

Royal Australian Corps of Transport
Princess Alice's Banner – Obverse

Royal Australian Corps of Transport
Princess Alice's Banner – Reverse

Note: This banner was replaced in 2013 but is shown in its original format
as it was the only Banner within the Army to be presented by a Royal
Personage other than the Queen and her immediate family.

The Queen Mother's Banner
Royal Australian Army Medical Corps – Obverse

The Queen Mother's Banner
Royal Australian Army Medical Corps – Reverse

Note: This banner was replaced in 2008 by a Governor General's Banner,
but is shown in its original format to highlight the difference between the
new style of Banner and older styles.

The Prince Philip Banner
Royal Corps of Australian Electrical and Mechanical Engineers – Obverse

The Prince Philip Banner
Royal Corps of Australian Electrical and Mechanical Engineers – Reverse

Governor-General's Banner
1st Recruit Training Battalion – Obverse

Governor-General's Banner
1st Recruit Training Battalion – Reverse

Replaced August 2014

Honour Title – Royal Regiment of Australian Artillery

RAA does not carry regimental Colours. Therefore the awarding of campaign and other battle honours as granted to Cavalry and Infantry units does not apply. Since RAA takes part in every significant military campaign to some degree, the list of honorary distinctions that it would bear on Colours (if they had them) would be unmanageable.

As a way of recognising the significant contribution individual artillery batteries have made to the outcome of particular battles, a system of granting Honour Titles was instituted within the British Army in 1925.[316] The Honour Title would consist of either names of battles, names of famous battery commanders, or the badge that had been granted for the campaign. The Honour Title would then be incorporated into the battery's name, for example, 32nd (Minden) Coast Battery Royal Artillery, thus indicating the unit's part in the defeat of the French forces at the Battle of Minden (1st August 1759).

Although used in the British Army for many years this custom was first approved for use by RAA in 2008. The 102nd Field Battery, RAA, was the first unit to be so honoured recognising its part in the Battle of Coral in South Vietnam between 12th May and 6th June 1968[317] (further details of this award are contained in Chapter Four).

Honour Scroll of the 102nd (Coral) Field Battery, RAA

---

316 Edwards TJ. *Military Customs.* Aldershot, England, Gale and Polden: 1954, p. 103
317 Gunfire. *Newsletter of the Royal Australian Artillery Association.* NSW: June 2008

Honour Scroll of the 102nd
(Coral) Field Battery, RAA

102nd
(CORAL) Field Battery
Royal Regiment of Australian Artillery

The Honour Title 'CORAL' is awarded to 102nd Field Battery, Royal Regiment of Australian Artillery, in recognition of its conduct during the Battle of Coral in South Vietnam between 12th May and 6th June 1968.

During Operation Toan Thang 102nd Field Battery deployed to Fire Support Patrol Base Coral in support of 1st Battalion, Royal Australian Regiment. Early morning on 13th May an intense enemy barrage of rocket propelled grenades and small arms fire was directed into Coral. This barrage was the prelude to an assault by 2nd Battalion, 141st Regiment, 7th North Vietnamese Army Division, against the Battery and the 1st Battalion's Mortar Platoon (minus). The Battery engaged the assault waves with small arms and Delta Gun firing anti-personnel rounds over open-sights. The enemy overran Foxtrot Gun and the Mortar Platoon; Bravo Gun was hit by a rocket propelled grenade; and Alpha Gun's ammunition bay caught fire. At the request of the Mortar Platoon's Second-In-Command, the Battery engaged the mortar position with anti-personnel rounds. Throughout the assault Echo Gun was laid onto Foxtrot Gun with orders to destroy the equipment if the enemy attempted to move or fire it. The Battalion Fire Support Centre coordinated and controlled close air and artillery support during the attack. At dawn two Gunner patrols cleared the position, recaptured Foxtrot Gun and gave assistance to the Mortar Platoon. The enemy left 52 dead and evidence of a significantly higher number of casualties.

The gun position defence was a close quarter infantry-style battle fought by Gunners and Mortarmen to defeat a conventional North Vietnam Army battalion (plus) assault. Whilst fighting against a sustained ground attack, three Battery guns remained in support of the 1st Battalion's companies deployed in ambush positions away from Coral. On at least three occasions the Battery responded to calls for fire from the Battery's forward observers.

On 16th May another major enemy assault was launched against Coral. Whilst the brunt of the attack was directed at 1st Battalion's Alpha and Bravo Companies, a heavy mortar and rocket barrage was directed at the Battery and 'A' Battery 2nd/35th United States Artillery. The Companies repulsed the attack supported by fire support from the Battery and other gun batteries, mortars and close air support. Throughout the attack the Battalion Fire Support Centre coordinated close fire support from field, medium and heavy artillery, and close air support which was controlled by the Battery's forward observers.

Although Fire Support Patrol Base Coral was never seriously threatened after the second attack, the Battery continued to support the 1st Australian Task Force until 6th June 1968 when it redeployed to Phuoc Tuy Province. These operations encountered heavy resistance and required Battery fire support of the highest calibre.

There were many acts of bravery accompanying the exceptional set of circumstances that the Gunners of 102nd Field Battery confronted. The Battery displayed professionalism, dedication and courage under extremely dangerous and confusing conditions at Coral.

The Honour Title 'CORAL' recognises these attributes and the outstanding contribution 102nd Field Battery made in supporting 1st Battalion, Royal Australian Regiment, on operations in South Vietnam.

His Excellency Major General P.M. Jeffery AC, CVO, MC

Governor-General
May 2008

Honour Distinction

In 2012 the Army BHC amended the Battle and Theatre Honours system to provide for the recognition of outstanding service in operations outside declared theatres of war. These approvals lead to the recommendation for the awarding of a new type of decoration. The Honour Distinction for 'Namibia 1989-1990' to 17 Construction Squadron was the first of its type awarded.

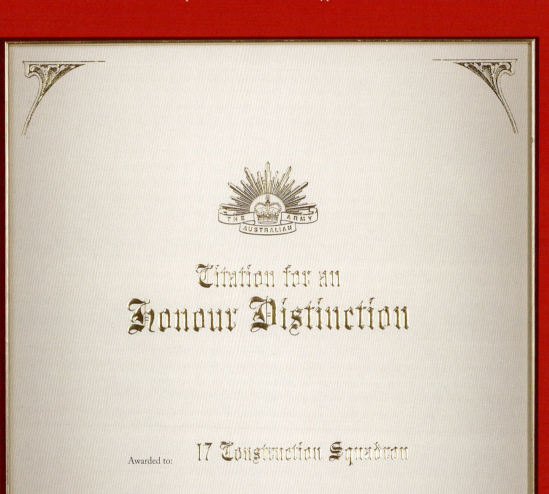

Titation for an

Honour Distinction

Awarded to: **17 Construction Squadron**

17 Construction Squadron is awarded the Honour Distinction, *Namibia 1989-1990*, in recognition of its creditable performance in support of the United Nations Transition Assistance Group operation managing the transition of Namibia to independence in 1990. Despite being deployed to provide engineering support, when the ceasefire broke down at the start of the mission, members of the Squadron helped establish Assembly Points, which enabled the mission to continue. This activity was conducted in the face of hostility from elements of the former colonial power and personal danger. Later, 17 Construction Squadron became involved in the election process itself, providing security, transport and logistic support to election officials, monitors, other UN personnel, voters and polling stations. Members of 17 Construction Squadron ensured that, as much as possible, the election was able to proceed without interruption or interference and ensured that all parties were free from intimidation or duress. With the selfless support of individuals from other units of the Australian Defence Force, 17 Construction Squadron played a key role in the smooth and effective transition of Namibia from colonial rule to independence. The Squadron performed a role well beyond what was expected and brought great credit on itself, the Australian Army and Australia.

11th May 2013
Date

Ms Quentin Bryce AC CVO
Governor-General

Chapter Six

Flags and Unit Logos

Introduction

The origins of flags are very similar to those of standards, guidons and Colours, with the most important difference being the symbolism and religious significance given to one over the other. Flags are not Colours and are therefore not entitled to any of the compliments or ceremony given to 'honourable insignia'.

Evolution of the British Flag

The Union Flag of Great Britain (sometimes known as the Union Jack – although more correctly a 'jack' is a small squarish flag flown from the jackstaff of a ship); carries its country's history upon its face. The word 'Union' commemorates the union of the three Parliaments of England, Scotland and Ireland in 1801.

The Union Flag is a combination of three flags:

- The English flag of St George

- The Scottish flag of St Andrew

- The Irish flag of St Patrick.

    Most British possessions used the Union Flag emblazoned with their own badge for official purposes.

- In addition to the Union Flag, there are three British Ensigns:

- Red Ensign – a national emblem worn by all British merchant ships

- White Ensign – used at sea by ships of the Royal Navy and some privileged Yacht Clubs

- Blue Ensign – used by ships of the Royal Naval Reserve and Yacht Clubs.

The Australian National Flag

The Australian Army has no separate Ensign as has the RAN and RAAF but has the ceremonial role of protector of the ANF.

    The ANF is a modified version of the British Blue Ensign and consists of:

- The Union Flag in the upper canton to depict Australia's link with the United Kingdom,

- The constellation of the Southern Cross in the fly – symbolic of the great southern land, and

- A seven-pointed star in the third quarter representing the six States of Federation and the Commonwealth Territories.

    The following diagram shows the detailed parts of the ANF, their correct names, scaled sizes and relative positions on the flag.

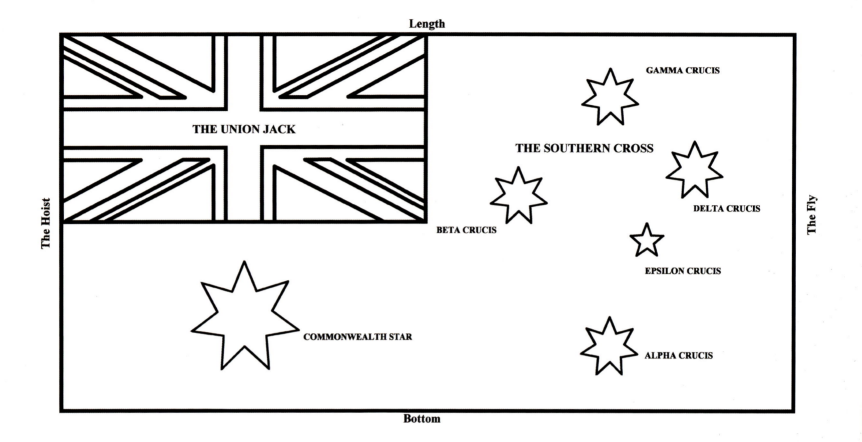

Above: ANF

Ensigns

Although there are other flags flown by various government departments there are only four official ensigns in use within Australia:

- The Australian Defence Force Ensign (ADFE) which represents the three Services of the ADF: The Dark Blue stripe represents the RAN; the Red the Army; and the Light Blue the RAAF. The Defence Force emblem in the centre of the flag also represents the three Services: the anchor the Navy; the crossed swords the Army; and the Wedge-tailed Eagle the Air Force. The Federation Star and Boomerang represent Australia.

- The RAN adopted the Australian White Ensign (AWE) in 1967. Prior to this the White Ensign of the Royal Navy was used.

- His Majesty King George VI approved the blue RAAF Ensign in 1948. The light blue background symbolises the sky. The British roundel in the bottom fly corner of the ensign was changed to include a red kangaroo in 1982.

- Her Majesty Queen Elizabeth II has a special ensign that is only flown whilst she is visiting Australia, which acknowledges her role as Queen of Australia. Her Majesty approved the flag's design on 20th September 1962 and it was first used during her 1963 Royal visit.

The Red Ensign – Australia's Forgotten Flag or 'Red Duster'

The Australian Red Ensign (Maritime) is a red version of the ANF and is a reserved civil ensign. From 1901 to 1954 the flag was used as a civil flag, to be flown by private citizens on land while the government used the Blue Ensign reflecting British practice. The Blue Ensign was reserved for use by the Commonwealth Government, the Australian Olympic team and the military as a saluting flag at all reviews and ceremonial parades.[318]

Under the *Navigation and Shipping Act 1912* and the *Shipping Registration Act 1981* the Red Ensign remains the only flag permitted for use by merchant ships registered in Australia. Pleasure craft may use either the Red Ensign or the ANF, but not both at the same time.

---

318 Australian Army Military Order 58/08 Australian Ensign: 1908 (Statutory Rule 27/08 published in MO 58/08) states: 'The Australian Ensign will accordingly be flown at all flag stations throughout the Commonwealth' and Australian Army Military Order 135 [1911] Saluting Flag, directed that in future the Australian Flag is to be used as the saluting flag at all reviews and ceremonial parades).

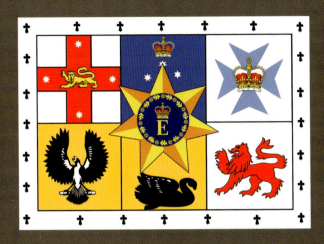

HRH Queen Elizabeth II
Queen of Australia's Personal Flag

Governor-General of Australia

Australian National Flag – Original

Australian Nation Flag – Current

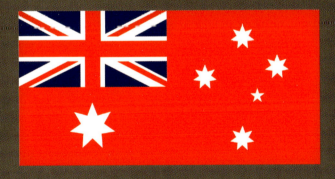

Australian Nation Flag (The Red Ensign) Maritime – Current

Australian Defence Force Ensign

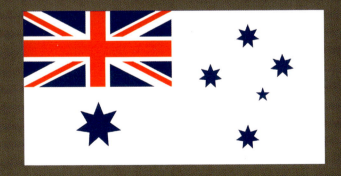

Royal Australian Navy Ensign

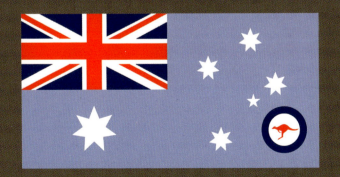

Royal Australian Air Force Ensign

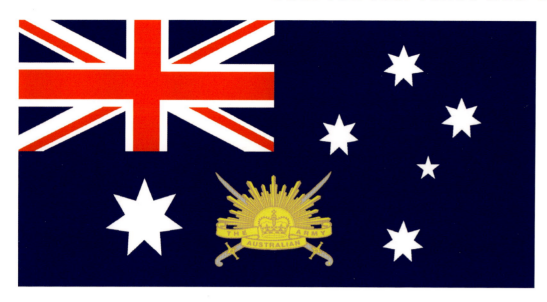

CA's Personal Flag

Army Flags

Flags authorised for use within the Army fall into five categories:

- CA's personal flag

- Corps flags

- Regimental flags

- Unit flags

- Sub-unit flags.

The design of these flags may contain the Corps or unit badge and/or the Corps or territorial title of the unit. These flags may be flown with, but not in line with or higher than, the ANF or the ADFE. Corps flags take precedence over regimental/unit or sub-unit flags.

Chief of Army's Personal Flag[319]

There are set protocols for flying the CA's personal flag. The flag is flown when the CA is present as a reviewing officer in accordance with the customs and regulations of the Service concerned, when visiting major headquarters or installations, and as a car flag on official occasions. The CA may also direct its use for other purposes not detailed above.

The flag dimension is 900mm by 1800mm and the car flag dimension is 150mm by 230mm.

Precedence

The other Chiefs of Defence Services (RAN and RAAF) are likewise entitled to fly personal flags, as are the CDF, VCDF and Chief of Joint Operations (CJOPS). At Russell Offices, Headquarters Joint Operations Command Canberra, joint service units or joint establishments, the usual practice is for only one personal flag to be flown at any one time which is that of the senior member present. The exception to this is where the reviewing officer of a parade is not the senior officer, in which case the flag of the reviewing officer will be flown.

Corps Flags

Corps flags are based on the approved Corps colours with the Corps badge displayed centrally on the flag. The only exceptions to this are the flags of the RAE and RAAMC which do not display their Corps badge. All Corps are entitled to a flag, but not all have approved flags, mainly because of their size and the fact that single units of sufficient size do not exist to allow them to be flown; the Australian Army Public Relations Service (AAPRS) and the RAAChD being examples.

Regimental and Unit Flags

Regimental and unit flags are not confined to the same colour restrictions as those applied to Corps flags. However, their design must undergo the same approval process as that of Corps flags. Although most of these designs are relatively new, some are based on unit colour patches from WWI, whilst others are based on the standard colour system used within individual regiments. Examples of this are the flags of RAR whose basic colour is the same as the lanyard worn by members of each separate battalion (examples of each original battalion flag are shown later in this chapter).

Sub-Unit Flags

Sub-unit flags are usually but not always the same pattern and colour as that of their parent Corps or unit. They normally have the Corps or unit badge in the upper canton. These flags are of plain design and are not permitted to have elaborate cords, tassels or fringes.

Sub-units of Combat Services Support Battalions (CSSB) are also entitled to fly small flags; however these are of a single plain colour with the sub-unit number or identifier centrally placed in black or white lettering.

Training Unit Flags[320]

Training units of the Army are permitted to fly certain flag types in accordance with their designation or type and level of training conducted within the establishment. The backing colour of Army school flags is green and yellow whilst joint schools fly the ADFE. Officer training establishments, which include RMC-D and the State university regiments, have individual regimental flags.

319 Australian Army *Defence Instruction (General) ADMIN 12-1 Australian Defence Force Ensign*: 10 July 2008

320 Australian Army. *Ceremonial Manual – 2003 Volume 1.* Defence Publishing Service, Canberra: 2003, Chap 22 Annex D

Army Maritime Flags

The RAN by tradition is tasked with the security of the oceans and trade lanes of Australia whilst the Army is responsible for land warfare. Although these tasks can sometimes become blurred, during wartime the delineation between their separate tasks is clear. The Army is specifically responsible for the operation of sea ports or terminals and in addition the security of inland waterways which are likewise used as supply routes.

To achieve this function the Army operates a fleet of small boats and landing craft of various designs. During WWII, this function was first carried out by a specially-established Transportation Corps which soon became the Transportation Service, a part of the RAE (Terminal). In line with the British Army Terminal groups, the Australian Transportation Service watercraft likewise had the distinction of flying their own ensign on-board all vessels operated by them. This tradition has been inherited by the current maritime service units of the Army.

The RACT was formed on 1st June 1973[321], when the road transport, air dispatch (AD) and postal functions of the Royal Australian Army Service Corps (RAASC) were amalgamated with the water transport, terminal and movement functions of the RAE Terminal (RAE Tn) squadrons. The RACT is responsible for the movement of the Army, its equipment and personnel, using all modes of available transport, in Australia and overseas, during peace and in war. This organisation is now the only Army Corps to own and operate small cargo watercraft and as such is entitled to fly its Corps flag from vessels operated by its units.[322]

For many years it was the custom for a commander of a military district or a formation to fly a distinctive flag whilst aboard a military vessel, the design of which included the Royal Cypher within a laurel on a Union Jack. The rationale for the design is unknown.

Australian Army Transportation Corps[323]

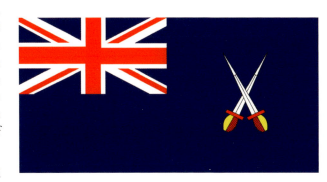

Transportation Service RAE[324]

Commander of a MD

Royal Australian Corps of Transport 'Current'[325]

321 Lindsay N. *Equal to the task.* Kenmore Queensland, Historia Productions: 1992, p. 65

322 Australian Army. Ceremonial Manual – 2003 Volume 1. Canberra, Defence Publishing Service: 2003, Chap 22 para 74

323 Australian Military Forces. Standing Orders for Vehicle Operation and Servicing (Australia). Melbourne, Military Board: 1961, Section 21 para 141

324 Askey MW. "By the mark five", A Definitive History of the Participation of Australian Water Transport Units in World War II. Turramurra NSW, Murray David: 1998, Appendix 10

325 Australian Army. Ceremonial Manual – 2003 Volume 1. Canberra, Defence Publishing Service: 2003, Chap 22 para 74

Examples of Army Flags

Examples of flags used by the various Corps, regiments, units, sub-units, training schools and army maritime organisations of the Army over the years are depicted below. Included are the flags of RAR. Although some of these battalions have been linked, the original flags illustrate the distinctive colours used by each of the battalions.

Corps Flags

Corps of Staff Cadets

Royal Australian Armoured Corps

The Royal Regiment of Australian Artillery

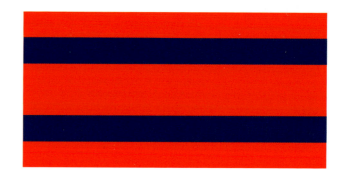

Royal Australian Engineers

Royal Australian Corps of Signals

Royal Australian Infantry Corps

Australian Army Aviation

Australian Intelligence Corps

Royal Australian Corps of Transport

Royal Australian Army Medical Corps

Royal Australian Army Dental Corps

Royal Australian Army Ordnance Corps

Royal Corps of Australian Electrical and Mechanical Engineers

Royal Australian Army Educational Corps

Australian Army Catering Corps

Royal Australian Army Pay Corps

Royal Australian Corps of Military Police

Australian Army Band Corps

Royal Australian Army Nursing Corps

Regimental and Units Flags

1st Armoured Regiment Royal Australian Armoured Corps

'A' Squadron 10th Light Horse Regiment

2nd/14th Light Horse Regiment (Queensland Mounted Infantry)

6th Aviation Regiment

1st/15th Royal New South Wales Lancers

1st Commando Regiment

7th Brigade

Special Air Service Regiment

1st Health Support Battalion

2nd Commando Regiment

Forces Command

11th Combat Service Support Battalion

2nd Force Support Battalion

8th/9th Battalion, The Royal Australian Regiment

The Pilbara Regiment

3rd Calvary Regiment
(Unit amalgamated – now 'B' Squadron, 3rd/4th Calvary Regiment)

Sub-unit Flags

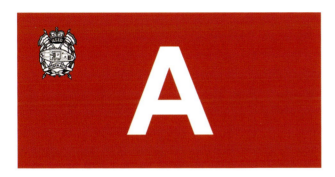

'A' Squadron 1st Armoured Regiment

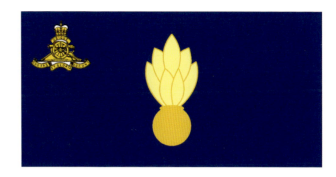

'A' Battery Royal Australian Artillery

Artillery Battery Royal Australian Artillery

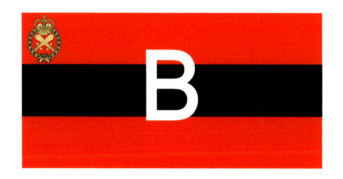

Company Flag Royal Australian Corps of Military Police

3rd Detachment Royal Australian Army Pay Corps

Squadron Flag Royal Australian Corps of Signals

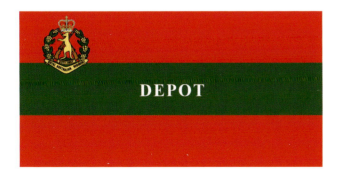

Depot Company (now Rifleman Wing) Royal Australian Regiment

Squadron Australian Army Aviation
(Number of unit shown in white)

Training Unit Flags (current and obsolete)

Land Warfare Centre – Canungra

Joint Service Training School

2nd Training Group (Training Groups)

School of Military Police (Corps School)

Parachute Training School (Army School)

Command and Staff College

Sydney University Regiment

Adelaide Universities Regiment

Original Flags of The Royal Australian Regiment

Royal Australian Regiment

1st Battalion – Garter Blue

2nd Battalion – Black

3rd Battalion – Rifle Green

4th Battalion – Scarlet

5th Battalion – Gold

6th Battalion – Khaki

7th Battalion – Maroon

8th Battalion – Slate Grey

9th Battalion – Brown

Top: Standard of the 1st Regiment, RAA

Bottom: tandard of the 2nd Divisional Artillery, RAA (Disbanded)

Royal Regiment of Australian Artillery – Standards

All artillery regiments and independent batteries of the RAA are entitled to fly the RAA Standard.[326] The standard was granted by Royal Warrant of King George VI in 1947[327], and was adopted by the RAA in 1952. Like all Corps and Unit flags it is not paid compliments, as would a Guidon or Colour, as it is a standard in name only.

Normally the unit's numeric identifier is shown in the centre of the standard; however the command or formation insignia may also be emblazoned as shown in the examples on the right.

This flag is used in three sizes according to the height of the flagpole from which it is to be flown:

- 3 Metre Pole – 91cm by 34cm

- 4.9 Metre Pole – 1.22m by 46cm

- 10.7 Metre Pole – 2.44m by 91cm[328]

326 Army. *The Royal Regiment of Australian Artillery – Standing Orders*: 2008, Chap 7
327 Edwards TJ. *Standards, Guidons and Colours of the Commonwealth Forces.* Aldershot, England, Gale & Polden: 1953, p. 43
328 Festberg AN. *Australian Army Guidons and Colours.* Melbourne, Allara Publishing: 1972, pp. 133-134

Unit Logos and Motifs

Unit or formation badges are used throughout the Army. They are usually made into plaques or worn as printed logos on sports shirts and even at times used as motifs on flags. These badges are not Corps, cap or collar badges. A register of these badges is maintained by AHQ. Formal approval is required prior to either adopting or changing a unit badge.

The following are examples of some official badges with no consistent theme other than the appearance of a boomerang in some.

Australian Defence Force Emblem

Special Operations Command

Australian Command and Staff College

1st Recruit Training Battalion – Kapooka

WO and NCO Academy

Special Forces Training Centre

Australian Defence Force Investigative Service

3rd Brigade

Land Warfare Centre

Forces Command – Australia

Infantry Centre – Singleton

2nd Combat Engineer Regiment

Parachute Training School

Defence Force School of Music

16th Aviation Brigade

1st Regiment RAA

17th Signal Regiment

Joint Logistics Group

Australian Army History Unit

Land Warfare Development Centre

Rotary Wing Aircraft Maintenance School

Chapter Seven

Ceremonial Drill and Salutes

Introduction

A military parade is a formal gathering of troops to conduct a specific event; a morning administrative parade through to the celebration of a special day, a unit's birthday, opening of Parliament or the birthday of the Head of State. These parades will vary significantly in pomp and ceremony but they all place troops on show for inspection or display. This form of ceremony provides the occasion for a series of manoeuvres to be performed according to ritual procedure and according to tradition. All modern-day military drill movements can be traced back to a logical beginning and purpose. The occasion will dictate the ceremony; for instance, the morning administrative parade will normally be conducted by a junior member to confirm attendance and would occur with the calling of the 'Roll' whereas major parades have large bodies of troops, and can take significant time with both detailed procedures and complex drill movements.

In the simplest or most common form of ceremony, saluting is an important aspect of military protocol and as with many drill movements its origin is steeped in as much legend as fact. Simply stated a salute is a greeting, the nature of which can vary from a personal exchange between troops to a formal salute accompanied by military music[329], and involving anything from a simple hand salute to a rifle salute through to the use of artillery fire.

The following examples of drill procedures and salutes are part of the more formal aspects of ceremonial military drill and are included with explanations on their origin and history. Often, various aspects of ceremonial drill and salutes are combined together into a single event. It is not the intention of this book to explain every variation and theme that may be used to celebrate an event but rather to show the separate parts of these actions with their origins which have been accepted as part of customs and traditions within the Australian Army.

Turn Out the Guard

To understand why a 'guard' is turned out on various occasions it is necessary to understand that, in medieval times (5th to 15th century), a guard on the gates of the city would turn out on the approach of any armed party as a precaution against a surprise attack. Also in these times troops stood to arms, 'Stand-to' or 'Stand-to-Arms', at dawn and dusk, as these were considered to be the times of the day when an enemy was most likely to attack. In more recent times guards are 'turned out' to salute dignitaries entering or leaving a unit area or base; these salutes may include an inspection of the guard by the dignitary.

Guard Salute

If a detachment was commanded by an officer, the guard 'Presented Arms', the drummer beat, and the pipes played a march, provided the party which intended to enter the town also beat a march.

In those days this was not done by way of respect to those who were about to enter, but for the security of the town, lest an enemy, having forged papers sent a party to seize the gate while his main body lay concealed at some little distance.

On the occasion of a fire, it has been the custom since the Middle Ages for the guard to turn out, as it was natural that everybody ran to that part of the city which was burning. At such times, particularly in frontier garrisons, it was essential that the guard remain under arms to prevent an enemy taking advantage of the disturbance.

---

329 Makepeace-Warne A. *Brassey's Companion to the British Army*. London, Brassey's: 1995, p. 316

Reveille – Rouse – Retreat

Dawn and dusk have always been the most likely times for attack and therefore it was the practice for the guard to 'turn out' at Reveille and Retreat. A bugle is used to signal Reveille, Rouse and Retreat. The first verifiable formal use of a brass bugle as a military signalling device was the Halbmondbläser (or half-moon bugle), used in Hanover in 1758.

Reveille originated to wake military personnel at sunrise. The name comes from réveillé (réveilléz or réveil), the French word for 'wake up'. 'Rouse' was the signal for the soldier to arise. In modern times, Rouse is the call commonly used in conjunction with the 'Last Post' at funerals and services of dedication and remembrance; to the layman it is often incorrectly called Reveille or the 'Short Reveille'. Reveille is only played at dawn for remembrance services and in barracks.

The bugle call played after the 'One Minute Silence' or 'Two Minute Silence' during the Anzac Day Dawn Service ceremonies is 'Reveille' as it calls the soldier's spirit to rise.

In the Australian Army, Reveille is pronounced as, 're-valley', not 'rev-velly'.

Drummers' Call

In days past there were no complete bands in the line with the Foot Regiments, only drummers and buglers. The 'Drummers' Call' was used to assemble all the drummers of the regiment prior to Trooping the Colours through the ranks. Drummers were also used to set a steady marching pace and in some armies they assisted in combat by keeping cadence for the firing and loading drills with muzzle-loading guns.

The Advance in Review Order

In 1780 a manual was produced[330] which laid down in detail 18 manoeuvres to be carried out by all Infantry units. These manoeuvres were designed to combat, in the most effective manner possible, the tactical moves of an enemy both in attack and in defence.

It is the last of these 18 manoeuvres that nowadays forms the great parade tradition known as the 'Advance in Review Order'. The Advance was usually the last movement of tactical manoeuvring, with the Colours being brought to the centre and the front, out of the ranks where the commander controlled the whole attack before the final phase. Therefore, even now, dressing is by the centre, the troops maintain their alignment in order that an enemy, trying to drive a wedge in the line, would have to cope with at least two men, one on either side of him, as opposed to one if the dressing were lost. It was done in two or more ranks so that any gaps in front caused by casualties could be sealed immediately and the line preserved.

Ranks were in 'open order' so that, when the volleys were fired, the leading rank could lie down, the second rank kneel, and the third, if there was one, stand. The extent of the advance was controlled from the centre and broadcast to the line by the drums beating, thus accomplishing three major tasks: firstly, the start and finish; secondly, the rate of the advance, in order that the long line might not waver; and thirdly, keeping the centre and the battle under control, for in the swirl and dust of battle, the Colours might not easily be seen. Any change in tempo of the drums would immediately strike the senses, with the result that all would know that the centre was threatened and be prepared for counter-measures.

Point of War

If an enemy could attack the nerve centre successfully, the battle would often be lost; it was often the enemy's intention to strike at and seize the Colours, in order to destroy the regiment's rallying symbol, and thereby cause alarm and loss of confidence.

Every unit took into battle its drummers, buglers (although these were not introduced until late in the 18th century), fifers (who in the 16th century were known by the expressive word 'whiffers', which is the old form of the word 'whistlers'), and any other musician who might make up the band.

Upon an attack developing, the CO would order the various instruments to be beaten or blown as hard as their players could manage. Thus the attention of the unit was drawn to the fact that danger threatened the centre of operations and countermeasures were to be employed.

One can imagine a CO, in the days of peace following battles won, having the Colours marched on parade and ordering the musicians to beat or blow their hardest to remind his men of their greatest achievements. After the parade the men would talk, as their descendants do today at their reunions, of stirring moments in battle. Thus regimental tradition was born and fostered. So it occurs today in most regiments, the musical salute to the Colours, 'Point of War' is played when the Colours are in position after having marched on, or before the Colours are marched off the parade and during a Royal or General salute. The tune has no military rhythm but strikes the ear most forcibly.

Changing the Guard

Even the most trivial feature of Army tradition has its origin from occurrences of great interest and often of great antiquity. The ceremony of 'Changing the Guard' takes place outside Buckingham Palace each day[331] and any casual spectator will see that, while the sentries are being posted and the main bodies of the 'New' and 'Old' Guards are standing facing each other, their respective officers pair off and march to and fro in the space between. When the change of sentries has been completed, they part company and take post again with their guards.

330 General Sir David Dundas, 1st Baronet, GCB; British General, Commander-in-Chief of the Forces 1809-1811: born 7 December 1749 – died 10 January 1826.

331 Paget J. *Discovering London Ceremonial and Traditions (2nd edition)*. Princes Risborough, Shire Publications: 2003, p. 32

These movements originated in 1709, when Queen Anne, for some inexplicable reason, suggested that a little added interest and animation might be provided by having the officers of the 'Old' and 'New' Guards occupy the interval during the reposting of the sentries by dancing the stately paces of the minuet. The Royal request was carried into effect, and astonished onlookers were regaled with the sight of the officers in their handsome, full-skirted jackets, silk breeches, hose and white wigs, advance towards each other, and after a ceremonious bow, hand their canes to a waiting orderly, and then proceed to dance a minuet to the music of violin, flageolet and cello.

It would seem however, that this innovation found no favour with the great warrior, The Duke of Marlborough.[332] Soon after his return from the Spanish Netherlands campaign, the Duke attended the Guard Changing at St James's Palace, the Royal residence at the time. Striding into the centre of the courtyard, he harshly suggested that, as it was not customary for one man to dance with another, one of each pair of officers might enhance the spectacle by donning a skirt for the occasion or, better still, pay greater attention to the conduct of their men, several of whom had left the ranks and were gathered under the balcony drinking mugs of ale.

The Duke, having expressed his views even more forcibly at the War Office, the terpsichorean[333] portion of the ceremony was immediately changed to a simple walk.

Feu De Joie – 'Fire of Joy' or 'Joy Sound'[334]

The ceremony of *Feu-de-Joie*, a feature of military ceremonial seldom seen these days, originated in a demonstration of a new weapon before Queen Elizabeth I (r. 1558-1603). The new wheellock musket had just been adopted as a more reliable and handy weapon than the cumbersome matchlock. Her Majesty was invited to a demonstration of the effectiveness of the new firearm at Tilbury. The musketeers, having completed the procedure of loading and getting the forked rests in position, an operation which took some time, tensely awaited the order to fire a volley. When the order came, the primitive mechanism produced only a ragged series of bangs one after the other up and down the lines. The Queen took a very dim view of the performance and expressed her opinion as such.

However, it is a woman's privilege to change her mind, and presently the Queen had an idea – why not use the one after the other firing business as a planned feature of military ceremony.

The only trouble was the inability to ensure an unbroken ripple of fire right along the line. This problem was solved by forming the men in three ranks, the second file letting go if

his front rank man failed to 'make fire'. If both failed the third rank file came into action. This procedure prevailed until the introduction of the flintlock, a weapon which was sufficiently reliable to ensure an unbroken chain of fire right along the line.

The new ceremony was endowed with the name '*Joy Sounde*'. The French Army also adopted this novel form of musketry for festive occasions, and gave it the name of 'Feu-de-Joie'. Under this latter name the ceremony has passed down through the centuries as one of Britain's favourite military displays, and now a tradition within the Australian Army. Of interest, the Royal Navy's system of gunfire salutes was copied from the Army's '*Feu-de-Joie*' in 1730.

United Drumhead Service

Outdoor religious services were conducted for fighting men long before armies were coordinated under the crown and long before the advent of bands into military units. The most primitive recorded use of the drum indicates that its prime purpose was to banish evil and undesirable spirits. At a later stage it was realised that the deep resonant note provided an ideal means of communication between tribal groups over considerable distances. In time, the drum was found to be useful for attracting attention and for maintaining a regular rhythmic beat. Despite its modern usage the drum has never entirely lost its reputation as a pagan instrument; hence during the Christian era drums have never been widely associated with religious music.

6th Battalion, The Royal Australian Regiment's Colours and Drums piled for the United Drumhead Service – 18th August 2006. Image courtesy of Department of Defence 20060818adf8161479_212

---

332 John Churchill, 1st Duke of Marlborough, Prince of Mindelheim, KG, PC: born Devon 26 May 1650 – died London 16 June 1722.

333 Paget J. *Discovering London Ceremonial and Traditions (2nd edition)*. Princes Risborough, Shire Publications: 2003, p. 32

334 "Feu-de-Joie" – fire of joy "French" (Macquarie University NSW. *The Macquarie Dictionary*. Milton Queensland, The Jacaranda Press: 1987)

Drum Head Service

The piling of drums during a religious service dates back to the 17th century and was apparently a means of ensuring that the drums were not beaten during the service, whilst also creating an altar around which the ceremony took place.

With military ceremony, the piling of the drums is completed as part of the parade and with all due solemnity. First the side drums are placed in a circle then the bass drum or drums are placed centrally on top. Finally, and only if paraded, the unit Colours are placed over the drums with the Queen's Colour on top. After this final act the parade is handed over to the clergy who conduct the religious service which is the 'centre-piece' of the parade.

A United Drumhead Service is only held on special occasions such as the formation of a new unit, a unit birthday or a memorial service. It is always an essential part of the consecration of new Colours, Guidons or Banners prior to their being handed to a Corps, regiment, battalion or unit.

Inspections

Many of the ceremonies and customs that play an important part in Army life have an origin which would hardly be suspected from the manner in which they are performed today. The familiar ceremony of 'Inspection of the Guard of Honour' begins when the inspecting officer arrives and passes along the ranks, stopping occasionally to chat to an individual soldier. Actually, the ceremony originated in circumstances that compelled the inspecting officer not only to make a close scrutiny of every man's face, but also to be ready for an attempt on his life as he passed along the ranks.

When King Charles II returned to England (1660) to claim the throne, one of Cromwell's cavalry regiments decided to switch its allegiance to the King. The regiment was encamped at Reading, and on hearing that His Majesty had landed, the commanding officer dispatched one of his squadrons to meet the King and beg leave to serve under the Crown.

Above: Image courtesy Department of Defence 20101209adf8262658_146. Parade Inspection by the then VCDF at the Australian Defence Force Academy

Right: Image courtesy Department of Defence – 20110530adf8178707_0028. Chief of the Defence Force and other Officers Saluting at a Ramp Ceremony

In a desolate, uninhabited stretch of country, one of the royal courtiers, riding alongside the coach, observed a body of strange troops approaching and at once told the King. As he was not yet sure of the reception he would receive from the populace, he was naturally alarmed, and instructed a number of his entourage to ride forward and ascertain the intentions of the column.

When contact was made, the squadron commander explained the purpose of his mission. The King was a little suspicious, but lack of courage was not one of his faults. Leaving his coach and accompanied by only one attendant he strode forward to the squadron drawn up on the side of the road. Charles passed slowly along the ranks, keenly scrutinising each man's face to determine his attitude from his facial expression. Satisfied with his inspection, Charles accepted the squadron commander's offer of allegiance and ordered him to act as his escort on the journey to London.

A little later, another unit of ex-Cromwellian troops, COL Monks' Coldstream Regiment, begged permission to enter the King's service. On Blackheath Common, Charles subjected them to the same close scrutiny, before accepting them as members of the Royalist Army.

In making these inspections, King Charles II could not have known that he was establishing a custom that was to be handed down through the centuries. The custom of inspecting troops continues to be performed by dignitaries and inspecting officers on ceremonial parades, while it still performs its original purpose of confirming the readiness of units and the state of discipline in a unit. The Inspecting Officer also inspects the band, albeit rather more cursorily, to show his appreciation of their music.

Saluting

Saluting and the paying of compliments may be said to be no more than good manners; however, they encourage a proper pride in the uniform and effectively combine discipline with the respect due to superiors. The paying of compliments elevates the soldier in his own eyes by reminding him of all that is implied by the Profession of Arms and its traditions of chivalry and courtesy.

Compliments and salutes are reciprocated at the highest levels up to and including Heads of State and therefore should never be construed as acts of servility, but rather indicative of a feeling of mutual trust and respect.

One popular misconception has long been that it is the 'member' holding the commission who is being saluted. This is wrong, the salute is in recognition of The Sovereign's Commission, not the member.

There are a number of theories regarding the origin of the hand salute. The earliest suggestion of a military salute is to be found on Stone Age rock paintings. Stones were usually thrown by the right hand whilst the left bore the spear. To show

peaceful intent when approaching a stranger it was apparently the custom to raise the open right hand above the head and trail the spear, point to the rear. There is also some evidence to suggest that the armies of ancient Babylon and Egypt raised their open right hand as a form of soldierly greeting.

A less plausible theory is that in medieval times the victors at tournaments would shade their eyes with the hand on approaching the Queen of Beauty to accept their prizes, or risk being blinded by her dazzling loveliness.

The most probable origin of the modern salute is one based on the mutual trust and respect, as already mentioned, exercised by the nobility in the days of chivalry. Knights on meeting each other placed themselves in an attitude of defencelessness by uncovering their heads or raising their visors. Headdress, whether iron casque, shako, bearskins or cloth helmet, have not always been easy to remove and so the preliminary movement of raising the hand to the head became accepted as the earnest intention of completing the whole movement.

At the beginning of the 19th century the salute with the hand, palm to the front, was firmly established. This practice has been maintained by both the Army and Air Force. The Navy salute is palm down and shortest way up – shortest way down; it is believed this practice is due to saluting in confined spaces on ships and to avoid ladies being offended by calluses on the sailors' hands when coming on board.

Image courtesy Department of Defence 20090621adf8262658_072. Honour Guard 'A' Company 2nd/17th Battalion, The Royal New South Wales Regiment

It is interesting to note that for many years saluting was performed with the hand farthest from the officer. This involved saluting with the left hand when passing an officer on the right hand side. For many Indian troops, saluting with the left hand was an insult and the present practice of only using the right was instituted in 1918.

Theories aside, practical experience has demonstrated the relationship between saluting and good discipline, both on and off the battlefield.

The Sword Salute

Until recently the salute with the sword was reminiscent of crusader times when the knight kissed the hilt before entering a conflict. The hilt represented the Christian cross and the motions of the salute roughly described a cross. In the present salute some of the motions have been omitted. The drill sword movement 'Recover' is symbolic of kissing the cross.

The Rifle Salute (Present Arms)

The rifle salute performed on parade, known as 'Present Arms', has the weapon held in such a way as to be entirely harmless. As one of the movements to reload muskets, it suggested the weapons were not loaded and were presented as a token of submission. The convention of holding the weapon so that it cannot be used is universal and very ancient. The Arab grasps his spear and trails it with the point on the ground. The Crusader offered his sword, hilt foremost, to be touched by his Sovereign before going to war.

The 'Present Arms' has a more interesting origin; when King Charles II accepted the allegiance of the Coldstream Regiment, the unit was drawn up in two ranks. The command 'Present your weapons for service under His Majesty' was given, whereupon every man, in accordance with a rehearsed exercise, held forward at arm's length and at the 'high port' position his musket or pike. The order, 'Ground your weapons', was then given followed by 'In His Majesty's Cause, recover your weapons'.

The King was so pleased with this ceremony of surrendering weapons into his service that he ordered the 'Present Arms' to be a feature of all future inspections as a mark of respect. It was not until 1817, that the position of the musket was changed from the 'high port' to the present position in 'Present Arms'. Even tanks, our modern engines of war, elevate their guns during a drive past and lower them when passing the saluting dais.

The Australian Army salutes officers of Field rank (MAJ and above) on ceremonial occasions by 'Presenting Arms'.

The Rifle Butt Salute

Military members holding a weapon whilst not on parade are incapable of saluting in the traditional manner; to overcome this, the member brings the left forearm across the body at waist height with the hand crossing the weapon, palm facing inward.

Turning the Head and Eyes in Salute

In medieval times the population was rigidly divided; there were freemen and bondmen or serfs. The freemen were trained archers and their freedom signified that they were always available for war, whilst bondmen were not permitted to bear arms. It was customary for a freeman to look a knight in the face as he passed but the bondman was obliged to bow his head and look at the ground to ensure his eyes did not meet his betters as equals. The drill movement of 'Eyes-Right' and 'Eyes-Left' to look the Reviewing Officer in the eyes symbolises equality in the service to the Crown of members of the Profession of Arms.

Lowering (or Veiling) Colours in Salute of Route

The lowering, or veiling as it was formerly called, of Regimental Colours as part of a salute is a custom of ancient origin, and is regarded as the salute according the highest honours.

This custom of lowering Colours in salute was officially recognised in the earliest form of *King's Regulations*, the *'General Regulations and Orders of His Majesty's Forces'* dated 12th April 1786.

In the 16th and 17th centuries, when Colours were veiled, they actually touched the ground even in wet weather, but in order to prevent Colours from becoming soiled they are now only lowered to the horizontal and not allowed to touch the ground in wet conditions.

Gun Salute

The custom of firing a number of guns, to salute both Royalty and officers of high rank, dates from the time when considerable time and effort was required to reload a gun. The old muzzle-loaders used shot charges which were difficult to mix and required much skill on the part of the gunner. It was therefore a sign of trust when the charges were fired away as part of a salute, as the ship or battery was then rendered defenceless by effectively disarming themselves for a period of time and in the power of the individual so honoured.

Above: Image courtesy Mr Mick Toal No. MT2_0471. Colours of The Royal Australian Regiment

Below: Image courtesy Department of Defence 20080705ran8100087_034. Eyes Right – Marching Past in Column

Origin of the 21 Gun Salute[335]

Queen's *Regulations* lay down 21 guns as the number of shots to be fired for a Royal Salute except at Hyde Park in London where the number is 41, and at the Tower of London where the number is as laid down in *Regulations for the Tower*.

There are, in addition, special occasions such as the 56 minute guns fired for the Late King or Royal Jubilees, for which The Sovereign may order a special number of guns to be fired. As with other customs sanctified by ancient usage before being codified in writing, the precise reasons for these numbers are now not known.

By 1810 it was recognised that a Royal Salute consisted of the discharge of 21 pieces of ordnance; but from a list of salutes authorised on 2nd May 1827[336] to be fired on the King's Birthday, it appears that great diversity existed in the number of guns fired. Some places fired 9, some 7, and some 21; at St James's Park '41 chambers', and at the Tower '21 guns and 41 chambers' were fired. An enquiry made in 1830 as to the reason why such diversity existed agreed to a fixed number of 21 guns as 'the established rule of the service in respect to Royal Salutes'. It was stated:

'In respect of the Royal Salutes fired from the chambers at the Tower of London and St James's Park, the number of rounds has been 41, in addition to which 41 guns have been fired at The Tower on the anniversary of the King's accession, the King's

Birthday, and the King's Coronation, and as these salutes are at the seat of Government, we do not think it would be advisable to propose any alteration.'

It appears that 41 was the number of guns in the old Royal Salute, as it was observed that on the accession of George IV, William IV and Queen Victoria, orders were issued for 'a Royal Salute of 41 guns to be fired at all stations at home and abroad, and at the Coronation of The Sovereign, 41 rounds were fired when the crown was placed on The Sovereign's head.'

The basis of the present regulations is the 'Order in Council' of 1st February 1838, which, after the enquiries mentioned above, fired a Royal Salute of 21 guns except at the Tower and St James's Park where Salutes remained 41 guns. This was embodied in *Queen's Regulations* in 1844 and although the exact wording of the regulations was altered in 1874, 1892 and 1902, the number of guns fired for a Royal Salute remained as 21.

In 1902 it was noted that the salute of 41 guns at St James's Park was 'of very old standing'. The only change since that date has been the move of the saluting station from St James's Park to Hyde Park as notified for the first time in *King's Regulations* of 1923.

Various theories have been advanced in respect to the origin of the particular numbers of 21 and 41. But plausible as some of the explanations may appear, they are based only on speculation, and in the course of enquiries in 1899, these explanations were discussed as 'fable' and 'popular superstition'. It now seems that the question cannot be settled.

---

335 Copied from an original document held by the British War Office.
336 Note: It is considered that the word 'fired' is intended to mean 'ordained' (ordinated [ecclesiastical] – the ceremony of consecration)

Left: Image courtesy Department of Defence 20110126ran8100087_013

Above: Image courtesy Department of Defence 20080717adf8239716_013. Artillery Salute - Sydney Harbour 2008

Australian Artillery Gun Salutes[337]

Artillery gun salutes are fired on special occasions usually involving Royal or Vice-Regal personages. They may also be provided for funerals and State occasions. Specific saluting stations are used for salutes to vessels carrying members of the Royal Family and to foreign warships only. Special saluting localities are to be used for all other salutes. Other suitable locations such as cemeteries may be used for the firing of minute guns at funerals.

A 'Minute Gun', of the appropriate number of rounds, is to be fired at the place of service for the funeral (for instance, cathedral, church or chapel) during the period the coffin is being borne from the church to either the place of burial, entombment, or cremation. The rounds are fired from one gun; however, a second gun is to be in location in case of a misfire. The interval between rounds is one minute; hence the name.

Royal Gun Salutes

A 21-gun salute is to be fired as a Royal salute in honour of the following personages on their arrival at and departure from Canberra and on other occasions when ordered by AHQ:

- The Sovereign

- A Member of the Royal Family who has the title of HRH

- A foreign crowned head or sovereign prince/princess or consort

- The Governor-General of Australia

- A prince who is a member of a reigning foreign Imperial or Royal Family

- The president of a republic or head of State.

When a personage for whom a salute is to be fired is travelling by air, the salute is to be fired on arrival at and on departure from the appropriate airport or RAAF Base.

337 Australian Army. *Army Ceremonial and Protocol Manual – 2014.* Canberra, Defence Publishing Service: 2014, Chap 10

Salutes on Fixed Anniversaries

The fixed dates on which Artillery gun salutes are to be fired in each capital city of every State and Territory are as follows:

- Australia Day – 26th January

- The Sovereign's official birthday in all States and Territories is on the second weekend of June and the salute is to be fired on the Saturday of the June holiday long weekend, except in Western Australia

- The Sovereign's official birthday in Western Australia is normally the last weekend of September and the salute is to be fired on the last Saturday of September.

These salutes are to be fired, with a ten-second interval, beginning at noon on the day nominated.

Salutes for Parliament

A 19-gun salute may be fired at the opening, proroguing or dissolving of Federal, State and Territory Parliaments, and the time of firing the salute is to be arranged with a representative of the parliament concerned. If The Sovereign is opening parliament, a 21-gun salute is to be fired for that particular ceremony. A Royal (or full) guard of honour is also normally mounted by a tri-Service contingent at the opening, proroguing or dissolving of Federal, State and Territory Parliaments.

Salutes in Honour of Vice Regal Personages

Artillery gun salutes may be fired in honour of the following personages:

- The Governor-General of Australia – a 21-gun salute

- The Administrator of the Commonwealth of Australia – a 21-gun salute

- The Governor of a State – a 19-gun salute

- The Lieutenant-Governor or commissioner, if administering a government – a 15-gun salute.

- The occasions on which salutes may be fired for the personages listed above are:

- When the personage is first arriving in the Commonwealth of Australia

- At the conclusion of the reading of the proclamation of the assumption of office

- When the personage is departing from the Commonwealth of Australia or State of jurisdiction on a leave of absence exceeding three months

- When the personage is returning to the Commonwealth of Australia or State of jurisdiction from a leave of absence exceeding three months

- When the personage is quitting office

- For official visits to places within the personage's jurisdiction.

Salutes for Senior Officers

With the exception of a retiring Army officer in the position of CDF, gun salutes for Army officers are only to be fired at their funerals if still serving at the time of death. Retired Generals are not entitled to gun salutes at their funeral.

An additional salute, of the appropriate number of guns, is to be fired at either the place of burial, entombment or cremation, after the coffin is lowered into the grave, placed in a tomb, or as the coffin is withdrawn at a crematorium. The rounds are fired from four guns, with an interval between guns of 10 seconds.

A 17-gun salute may be fired on the retirement from office of the CDF. The salute is to be fired once only and at a time and location selected by CDF.

Salutes for Diplomatic Personages

As well as salutes for the funerals of military personnel, gun salutes may also be fired at the funerals, within Australia, of diplomatic personages accredited to the Australian Government, whether they be of British or foreign nationality.

Freedom of Entry

The terms 'Freedom of the City' (FOC) and 'Freedom of Entry' (FOE) are quite often used to describe the same event; however they originate from two different honours bestowed for entirely different reasons.

In London during the Middle Ages, FOC was granted to individuals encompassing the right to trade, and enabling members of a Guild or Livery to carry out their trade or craft within the city. A fee could be charged for such freedom and in return the Livery Companies would ensure that the goods and services provided would be of the highest standards. In 1835, the FOC was widened to incorporate not just members of Livery Companies but also people living or working in the City[338].

The term 'Freedom of Entry' however refers to a martial honour that bestows no legal right or privilege on the recipient body but it is accepted that such conferment is the most honourable distinction that a city, town or shire can bestow on a military body. The privilege is usually extended only to a unit which has had a long and close association with the city.

FOE into a city by military units is a long-standing tradition that can trace its history back to ancient Rome. During the time of the Republic it was against the law for any of the legions of the Roman Army to enter the city of Rome. This was in part due to the fear held by the Senate that some rogue General might, given the opportunity, invade and take control of the city.

---

338 https://www.cityoflondon.gov.uk/about-the-city/history-and-heritage/Pages/freedom-of-the-city.aspx: retrieved 13 January 2014

The one exception to this was during the *vir triumphalis* (man of triumph) or Triumph Ceremonies[339] held to celebrate great victories against the enemies of Rome. Although these celebrations were to honour the victorious general, the parade procession always included his army (without its weapons). An integral part of the ceremony was the lustrating[340] or purification of the soldiers who had taken part in the battle.[341]

In medieval times similar laws were passed by other European cities, as a reward for faithful, heroic and loyal service generally in times of great peril. Armies whose trustworthiness was beyond doubt would be allowed to enter the city without breaking ranks. As a sign of trust, the soldiers so honoured would not have to disarm before the city gates were opened to them.

The British tradition of granting FOC[342] dates back to the City of London in 1237, which granted such freedom to certain of its citizens who would purchase these rights. It was not until shortly after King Charles II was crowned in 1660 that the Aldermen of the City of London, basing their claims on 'ancient right', restricted bodies of armed troops from marching through the city, with bayonets fixed, Colours flying and music playing; this provided the setting for today's tradition.

Today, the military's FOE remains an entirely ceremonial honour, and is the oldest and one of the highest civic honours bestowed by the citizens of a city, town or regional area on a military unit within the Commonwealth of Nations.

Although a long-held tradition in England it was not until 1958 that this ceremony was introduced into Australia. During a visit to Britain, the mayor of Shepparton, Councillor Lloyd Trevaskis, JP, learned of the ceremony and other requirements of granting Freedom of Entry to a military unit. On his return to Australia Councillor Trevaskis proposed the idea, at a council meeting held on 11th November 1957 that such a grant should be given to the local reserve infantry battalion.

The Council voted unanimously in favour of the proposal and consequently the 59th Battalion (The Hume Regiment) was offered the distinction of being the first unit in the Australian Army to be so honoured.

At this time there was no formal military procedure covering a ceremony of this type, in fact, it was not until 1977 that the *Army Ceremonial Manual* was amended to include a standardised ceremony for a parade of this type. The procedure used in that first parade is still largely in use today, although some modifications have been made.

LTGEN H Edgar, CBE, (GOC Southern Command) with COL E Hill, MM, ED, and Councillor L Trevaskis, JP, with the first Freedom of Entry Scroll

The outline of the FOE parade is based on the general description of the activity in the parade brochure produced on 23rd March 1958:

The presentation was made at Deakin Reserve, Shepparton. The battalion then marched past the dais where the salute was taken by Councillor Trevaskis, the GOC Southern Command, LTGEN HG Edgar CBE and the Honorary Colonel of the Hume Regiment and former CO of the 59th Battalion, COL E Hill MM, ED. The battalion marched off the reserve and was challenged by the local Police superintendent mounted on a horse, before entering the streets of Shepparton. After the challenge the battalion marched through the town and on to its barracks.[343]

When originally approved, this honour could only be accepted by a unit, regiment or Corps.[344] However, in 2014 the acceptance was extended to include formation-sized units such as BDEs. The catalyst for this change was the granting of FOE to the 3rd Brigade by the citizens of Townsville to recognise the long association the formation has had with the city and its people. The acceptance of the honour was timed to coincide with the centenary celebrations of the 3rd Brigade.

339 Versnel HS (editor). *Triumphus; An Inquiry Into the Origin, Development and Meaning of the Roman Triumph.* Leiden Netherlands, Brill: 1970, p. 1

340 'lustrating' - purify by expiatory sacrifice, ceremonial washing, or some other ritual action (Pearsall J (editor). *The Concise Oxford Dictionary (10th edition).* Oxford, Oxford University Press: 1999, p. 847)

341 http://classics.mit.edu/Plutarch/marcellu.html: retrieved 12 Jan 2014

342 Edwards TJ. *Military Customs.* Aldershot, England, Gale and Polden: 1954, p. 49

343 Leckie N. *Country Victoria's Own.* Loftus NSW, AMH Publications: 2008, p. 299

344 Australian Army. *Ceremonial Manual – 1977.* Brunswick Victoria, Defence Printing Establishment: 1977, Chap 17 para 1701

Description of the Scroll

On many of the scrolls awarded to military units the title 'Freedom of the City' is used instead of 'Entry'; in today's society this title or salutation is a generic one with no intended historic difference. The actual wording within the document stipulates the exact nature of the honour, after the normal preamble, naming the unit in question. The text goes on to read '*the right of entry on ceremonial occasions*', and then describes the exact rights and limitations placed on the unit receiving the honour.

Although modern 'FOE' scrolls may differ according to the City, Council or Shire bestowing the honour and the battalion or regiment receiving it, there are certain words common in all such scrolls. These words, drawn from history, go on to describe in detail the ceremonial aspects of the right of entry: '*in full panoply345 with swords drawn, bayonets fixed, drums beating, bands playing and Colours (guidons) flying*'.

The scroll, usually drawn or printed on vellum[346] or other high quality material, would also contain the Corps or unit badge and the City, Council or Shire's Coat of Arms and Seal and any other such devices authorised by the local authority.

Restrictions on Approval

The military restricts the acceptance of this high honour to units of a particular size, or type such as a Corps, formation, regiment/battalion or independent sub-unit. A sub-unit or unit of the Australian Army Cadets (AAC) is not eligible to be either offered or accept the granting of FOE.

Originally, State-based regional infantry battalions and artillery regiments, scattered throughout regional cities, were common place; however over time these units have been reduced in size to company or battery-sized organisations. This often means that sub-units such as these are commanded by a headquarters that can at times be hundreds of kilometres away. This separation often causes problems especially on occasions such as when the local shire council is desirous of making an award to its local military unit.

The eight examples shown highlight not only the various formats used but the types of organisations that can be honoured by cities, towns or shires throughout Australia. Although not limited to these types of units, the following are shown because:

- The scroll presented to the 59th Battalion is of historical importance as the first example in the Australian Army; it clearly shows the title as 'Freedom of Entry'.

- The second is much more ornate showing both the city crest and the battalion badge with battle honours in full colour. Noting that the City of Maryborough is 244 kilometres from Brisbane where the battalion headquarters is located, this is an example of a city wishing to honour its own citizens who have served their country and the local area, but as the recipient is not an independent sub-unit it cannot accept the honour in its own title.

- This scroll is presented to a non-Arms unit by the City of Canberra; however the document is signed on behalf of the Australian Capital Territory, a high honour indeed and the only example of such a privilege being bestowed on a military unit to date.

- This rather understated scroll is almost entirely black and white on an equally plain piece of card-like paper. The scroll is addressed to the OC and not the CO.

- This fine example of a scroll was presented to the 2nd/14th Light Horse Queensland Mounted Infantry, and is in full colour except for the unit badge which is in black and white outline.

- This example was presented to an entire Corps rather than a single unit. To date this is only the second of its kind, the other being to the RAAMC on 14th March 1981.

- This example is the first such honour to be afforded to a formation (3rd Brigade), granted by the City of Townsville in 2014.

- Army Reserve sub-units of company, battery or platoon size have long been isolated from their commanding headquarters. This separation often causes problems especially on occasions such as when the local shire council wishes to bestow an award to its local military unit. It is common for most country units to be of company-size or smaller so when such an honour is given, it is to the battalion as a whole that the 'Freedom' is normally bestowed and not to the sub-unit. This rare certificate was presented to the 5/11 Field Regiment RAA, which at the time of presentation was located at Southport, south of Brisbane approximately 124 kilometres from the Shire of Pine Rivers. The 13th Field Battery is a local reserve unit in the Pine Rivers Shire and is named on the certificate as representing its parent unit. It is very unusual for the sub-unit to be named on the certificate.

Right: The Hume Regiment. Freedom of Entry to the City of Shepparton, Victoria – Scroll

---

345 'Panoply' – A complete suit of armour or covering translates to mean the equivalent of full ceremonial dress.
346 'Vellum' – Sheet of calfskin prepared as fine parchment for writing or bookbinding (Macquarie University NSW. *The Macquarie Dictionary*. Milton Queensland, The Jacaranda Press: 1987)

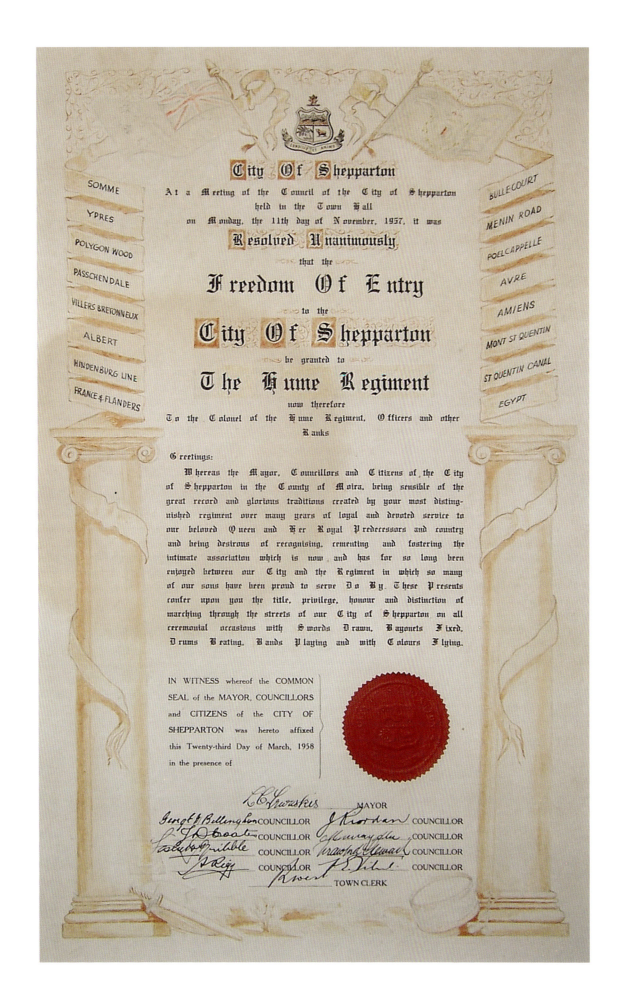

THE CITY OF MARYBOROUGH Qld

On the 15th day of July 1997, we extend to The Commanding Officer and Men of the...

9th BATTALION

THE ROYAL QUEENSLAND REGIMENT

GREETINGS

Whereas many of our Citizens have served with pride and distinction in your Gallant Battalion and its Predecessors which, by their great achievements in times of peace and of war, have established glorious traditions in the Profession of Arms; the Mayor and Councillors of the City of Maryborough meeting in Council on the 15th day of July, 1997, have resolved in appreciation of your loyal services to Our Sovereign, Our Country. and Our City to confer upon such Battalion, by this Deed and in perpetuity, the privilege, honour and distinction of

THE FREEDOM OF THE CITY

with the right of entry on Ceremonial Occasions in full panoply with swords drawn, bayonets fixed, drums beating, bands playing and Colours flying, and that the Common Seal of the Council be affixed to such Deed.

In Witness whereof the Common Seal of the Council was hereto affixed on the 15th day of July, 1997, in the presence of

Mayor

Chief Executive Officer

FIDES ROBUR ET FORTITUDO
MARYBOROUGH CITY COUNCIL
QUEENSLAND
PRO ARIS ET FOCIS
SOUTH AFRICA 1899-1902
POZIERES
BULLECOURT
YPRES 1917
MENIN ROAD
POLYGON WOOD
PASSCHENDALE
AMIENS
ANCRE 1918
HINDENBURG LINE
LANDING AT ANZAC
BALIKPAPAN
TSIMBA RIDGE
DEFENCE OF TOBRUK
SYRIA 1941
MERJAYUN
KOKODA TRAIL
CAPE ENDAIADERE SINEMI CREEK
MILNE BAY
LIBERATION OF AUSTRALIAN NEW GUINEA
BORNEO
LYNCH

Left: 9th Battalion, The Royal Queensland Regiment. Freedom of the City of Maryborough, Queensland – Scroll

Right: Band of the Royal Military College - Duntroon. Freedom of Entry to the City of Canberra, Australian Capital Territory – Scroll

Freedom of Entry
to the City of Canberra

Be it known that

FREEDOM OF ENTRY TO THE CITY OF CANBERRA HAS BEEN GRANTED TO THE OFFICER COMMANDING AND MEMBERS OF THE

Band of the Royal Military College Duntroon

This honour is conferred in recognition of the close association between the City and the Band of the Royal Military College-Duntroon. It recognizes that many of our Citizens have served with pride in your distinguished Band which, by its great achievements in times of peace and war, has built up and fostered the close association enjoyed between the City and the Band of the Royal Military College-Duntroon. We are proud to acknowledge your great services to our Sovereign, our Country and our City.

We confer upon the Band of the Royal Military College-Duntroon the privilege, honour and distinction of the right of entry on Ceremonial Occasions to march through the streets of the City of Canberra in full panoply with swords drawn, bayonets fixed, drums beating, band playing and banner flying.

GIVEN UNDER MY HAND ON BEHALF OF THE CITIZENS OF CANBERRA ON THIS FOURTEENTH DAY OF MAY 2004

JON STANHOPE MLA
CHIEF MINISTER OF THE AUSTRALIAN CAPITAL TERRITORY

Left: 5th Field Engineer Regiment Royal Australian Engineers. Freedom of the City of Ipswich, Queensland – Scroll

Right: 2nd/14th Light Horse Regiment (Queensland Mounted Infantry). Freedom of the City of Brisbane, Queensland – Scroll

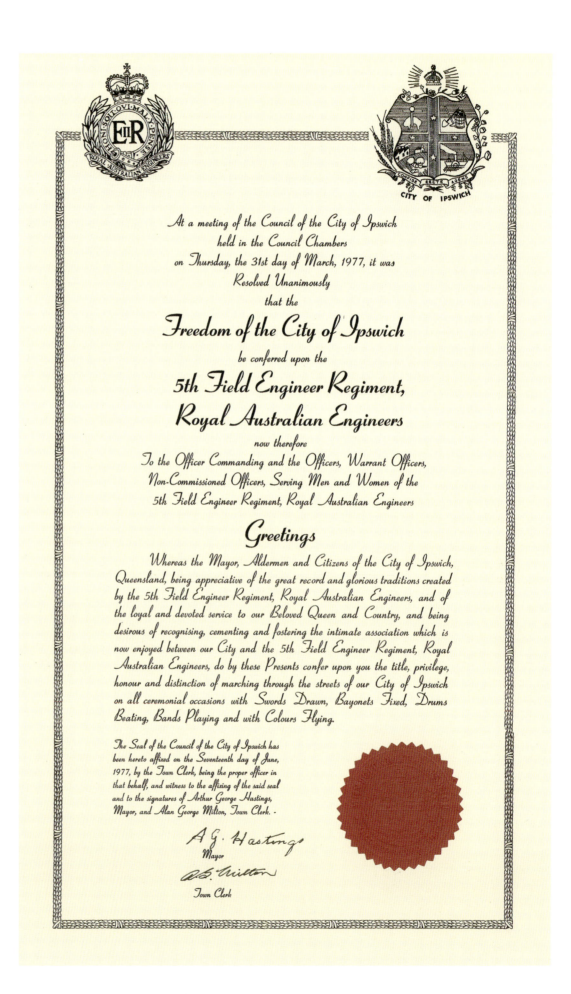

At a meeting of the Council of the City of Ipswich
held in the Council Chambers
on Thursday, the 31st day of March, 1977, it was
Resolved Unanimously
that the

Freedom of the City of Ipswich

be conferred upon the

5th Field Engineer Regiment, Royal Australian Engineers

now therefore
To the Officer Commanding and the Officers, Warrant Officers,
Non-Commissioned Officers, Serving Men and Women of the
5th Field Engineer Regiment, Royal Australian Engineers

Greetings

Whereas the Mayor, Aldermen and Citizens of the City of Ipswich,
Queensland, being appreciative of the great record and glorious traditions created
by the 5th Field Engineer Regiment, Royal Australian Engineers, and of
the loyal and devoted service to our Beloved Queen and Country, and being
desirous of recognising, cementing and fostering the intimate association which is
now enjoyed between our City and the 5th Field Engineer Regiment, Royal
Australian Engineers, do by these Presents confer upon you the title, privilege,
honour and distinction of marching through the streets of our City of Ipswich
on all ceremonial occasions with Swords Drawn, Bayonets Fixed, Drums
Beating, Bands Playing and with Colours Flying.

The Seal of the Council of the City of Ipswich has
been hereto affixed on the Seventeenth day of June,
1977, by the Town Clerk, being the proper officer in
that behalf, and witness to the affixing of the said seal
and to the signatures of Arthur George Hastings,
Mayor, and Alan George Milton, Town Clerk. -

A.G. Hastings
Mayor

A.G. Milton
Town Clerk

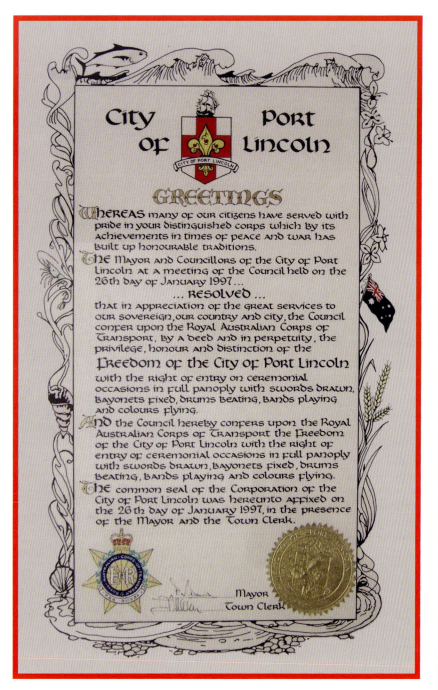

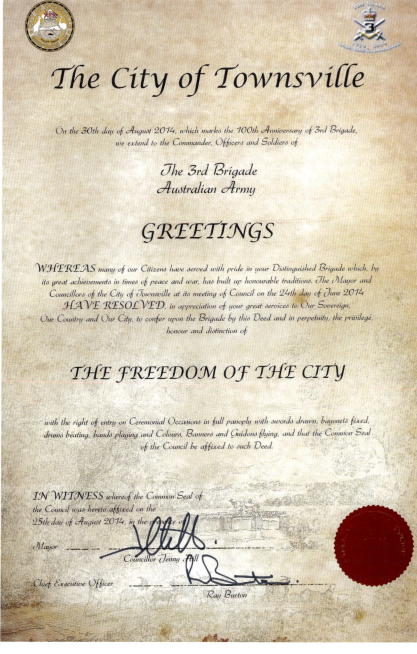

Left: Royal Australian Corps of Transport. Freedom of the City of Port Lincoln, South Australia – Scroll

Right: 3rd Brigade. Freedom of the City of Townsville, Queensland – Scroll

Opposite: 5/11 Field Regiment RAA – represented by 13th Field Battery. Freedom of the Shire of Pine Rivers, Queensland – Scroll

The Shire of Pine Rivers

We extend to the Commanding Officer and Men of the
5/11 Field Regiment, Royal Regiment of Australian Artillery

Greetings

Whereas many of our Citizens have served with pride in your Distinguished Service which, by its great achievements in times of peace and war, has built up honourable traditions. The Chairman and Councillors of the Shire of Pine Rivers meeting in Council on the Second day of November, 1987. Have resolved in appreciation of your services to Our Sovereign, Our Country and Our Shire to confer upon the

5/11 Field Regiment

Royal Regiment of Australian Artillery

represented by 13 FIELD BATTERY

by this Deed and in perpetuity, the privilege, honour and distinction of

Freedom of the Shire

with the right of entry on Ceremonial Occasions in full panoply with swords drawn, bayonets fixed, drums beating, bands playing, and guns in tow, and that the Common Seal of the Council be affixed to such Deed

In Witness whereof the Common Seal of the Council was hereto affixed on the 22nd day of April, 1989 in the presence of

Chairman   Shire Clerk

Freedom of Entry – Cities/Towns and Shires

The freedom of entry list is for current operational, disestablished or disbanded units, regiments, formations and Corps in date granted order.[347]

Ser.	Unit	Date Granted	City or Town	State
1	59th Battalion, The Hume Regiment[a]	23 Mar 58	Shepparton	VIC
2	31st Battalion, The Kennedy Regiment	25 Jul 58	Townsville	QLD
3	38th Battalion, Northern Victoria Regiment[b]	24 Aug 58	Bendigo	VIC
4	34th Battalion, The Illawarra Regiment	08 Mar 59	Wollongong	NSW
5	Capricornia Regiment	27 Apr 59	Mackay	QLD
6	42nd Infantry Battalion	29 Aug 59	Rockhampton	QLD
7	The Royal Australian Engineers	05 Sep 59	Liverpool	NSW
8	1st Battalion (Commando), City of Sydney's Own Regiment	10 Oct 59	Sydney	NSW
9	1st/15th Royal New South Wales Lancers	18 Oct 59	Parramatta	NSW
10	6th Battalion, The Royal Melbourne Regiment	14 Mar 60	Melbourne	VIC
11	6th Field Regiment, RAA	20 Apr 60	Melbourne	VIC
12	10th Battalion, The Adelaide Rifles	23 Apr 60	Adelaide	SA
13	1st Battalion, The Royal Western Australia Regiment	02 Oct 60	Perth	WA
14	12th/16th Hunter River Lancers	23 Oct 60	Tamworth	NSW
15	11th Base Ordnance Depot (RAAOC)	22 Apr 61	Prahran	VIC
16	2nd Signal Regiment	19 Aug 62	Heidelberg	VIC
17	Kapooka Military Area	17 Nov 62	Wagga Wagga	NSW
18	5th Field Regiment, RAA	16 May 64	Ipswich	QLD
19	3rd Division Royal Australian Engineers	27 Mar 65	Ringwood	VIC
20	Singleton Military Area	22 Jun 66	Singleton	NSW
21	9th Battalion, The Royal Queensland Regiment	06 Jun 67	Brisbane	QLD
22	41st Battery, 11th Field Regiment, RAA	03 Dec 67	Gold Coast	QLD
23	15th Field Regiment, RAA	17 Mar 68	Dandenong	VIC
24	2nd Battalion, The Royal New South Wales Regiment	10 May 68	Newcastle	NSW
25	1st Signal Regiment	10 Nov 68	Campbelltown	NSW
26	17th Battalion, The Royal New South Wales Regiment	18 Aug 69	Bathurst	NSW
27	Army Apprentices School	23 Aug 69	Mornington	VIC
28	25th Battalion, The Royal Queensland Regiment	27 Sep 69	Toowoomba	QLD
29	1st Battalion, The Royal Victoria Regiment	06 Oct 69	Essendon	VIC
30	31st Supply Battalion, RAAOC	30 May 70	Wodonga	VIC
31	Army Survey Regiment	14 Jun 70	Bendigo	VIC
32	42nd Battalion, The Royal Queensland Regiment	05 Sep 70	Rockhampton	QLD
33	10th Medium Regiment, RAA	28 Nov 70	Geelong	VIC
34	4th/19th Prince of Wales Light Horse	29 Nov 70	Traralgon	VIC
35	'A' Field Battery RAA	26 Jan 71	Sydney	NSW
36	6th Engineer Support Group	12 May 71	Penrith	NSW
37	6th Battalion, The Royal Australian Regiment	04 Jun 71	Townsville	QLD
38	42nd Battalion ,The Royal Queensland Regiment	04 Sep 71	Mackay	QLD
39	2nd Battalion, The Royal Australian Regiment	18 Oct 71	Townsville	QLD
40	1st Battalion, Pacific Island Regiment	Mar 73	Port Moresby	PNG
41	3rd/9th South Australian Mounted Rifles	01 Apr 73	Unley	SA
42	35th Field Squadron, RAE	11 Aug 73	Mount Isa	QLD

---

347 Australian Army. Ceremonial and Protocol Manual – 2013. Canberra, Defence Publishing Service: 2013

Ser.	Unit	Date Granted	City or Town	State
43	7th Transport Company	03 Sep 73	Coburg	VIC
44	41st Battalion, The Royal New South Wales Regiment	14 Oct 73	Lismore	NSW
45	51st Battalion, The Royal Queensland Regiment	28 Oct 73	Cairns	QLD
46	41st Battalion, The Royal New South Wales Regiment	04 Nov 73	Grafton	NSW
47	130th Signal Squadron	08 Dec 73	Port Stephens	NSW
48	23rd Field Regiment, RAA	06 Apr 74	Burwood	NSW
49	4th Signal Regiment	24 Jun 74	Brisbane	QLD
50	5th/7th Battalion, The Royal Australian Regiment	31 Aug 74	Liverpool	NSW
51	1st Battalion, The Royal Australian Regiment	12 Oct 74	Normanton	QLD
52	2nd/14th Queensland Mounted Infantry, RAAC	02 Nov 74	Brisbane	QLD
53	School of Army Health	10 Nov 74	Healesville	VIC
54	7th Signal Regiment	29 Aug 75	Toowoomba	QLD
55	12th Field Squadron, RAE	16 Feb 76	Glenorchy	TAS
56	4th/19th Prince of Wales Light Horse	04 Sep 76	Kyneton	VIC
57	5th/11th Company RAAOC	18 Sep 76	Northam	WA
58	16th Air Defence Regiment Light, RAA	04 Dec 76	Lobethal	SA
59	4th/19th Prince of Wales Light Horse	14 Mar 77	Melbourne	VIC
60	5th Field Engineer Regiment, RAE	17 Jun 77	Ipswich	QLD
61	1st Battalion, The Royal Australian Regiment	23 Jun 77	Charters Towers	QLD
62	3rd Ordnance Service Unit	04 Aug 78	Caulfield	VIC
63	17th Battalion, The Royal New South Wales Regiment	17 Sep 78	Ku-ring-gai	NSW
64	RAEME Training Centre	21 Oct 78	Wodonga	VIC
65	25th Battalion, The Royal Queensland Regiment	28 Oct 78	Warwick	QLD
66	10th Medium Regiment, RAA	02 Dec 78	Colac	VIC
67	1st Special Air Service Regiment	30 Mar 79	Perth	WA
68	Proof and Experimental Establishment, Port Wakefield	31 Mar 79	Port Wakefield	SA
69	A Squadron, 10th Light Horse	28 Apr 79	Northam	WA
70	133rd Signal Squadron	15 Jun 79	Penrith	NSW
71	7th Independent Rifle Company	07 Jul 79	Darwin	NT
72	40th Independent Rifle Company	03 Nov 79	Hobart	TAS
73	2nd Commando Company	01 Mar 80	Williamtown	NSW
74	41st Battalion, The Royal New South Wales Regiment	29 Mar 80	Casino	NSW
75	41st Battalion, The Royal New South Wales Regiment	25 Jun 80	Coffs Harbour	NSW
76	126th Signal Squadron	01 Jul 80	Box Hill	VIC
77	4th Battalion, The Royal New South Wales Regiment	27 Aug 80	Wollongong	NSW
78	2nd Battalion, The Royal Victoria Regiment	30 Aug 80	Maryborough	VIC
79	11th Independent Rifle Company, The Royal Western Australian Regiment	11 Oct 80	Bunbury	WA
80	176th Air Despatch Squadron, RACT	08 Nov 80	Gosford	NSW
81	3rd Battalion, The Royal New South Wales Regiment	14 Mar 81	Canberra	ACT
82	The Royal Australian Medical Corps	14 Mar 81	Marion	SA
83	9th Battalion, The Royal Queensland Regiment	23 Mar 81	Hervey Bay	QLD
84	7th Field Engineer Regiment, RAE	11 Jul 81	Ringwood	VIC
85	25th Battalion, The Royal Queensland Regiment	06 Mar 82	Stanthorpe	QLD
86	4th/19th Prince of Wales's Light Horse	03 Apr 82	Sale	VIC
87	North West Mobile Force	03 Jul 82	Darwin	NT

Ser.	Unit	Date Granted	City or Town	State
88	41st Battalion, The Royal New South Wales Regiment	03 Jul 82	Kempsey	NSW
89	1st Armoured Regiment	26 Sep 82	Seymour	VIC
90	7th Field Ambulance	06 Nov 82	Fremantle	WA
91	101st Field Workshops	27 Nov 82	Campbelltown	NSW
92	North West Mobile Force	09 Jul 83	Derby	WA
93	2nd Field Supply Battalion	16 Jul 83	Charters Towers	QLD
94	3rd Ordnance Services Unit	23 Jul 83	Sandringham	VIC
95	Army Aviation Training Centre	03 Sep 83	Shire of Jondaryan	QLD
96	27th Battalion, The Royal South Australia Regiment	03 Sep 83	Mount Gambier	SA
97	10th Battalion, The Royal South Australia Regiment	10 Sep 83	Broken Hill	NSW
98	2nd Battalion, The Royal Victoria Regiment	26 Nov 83	Ballarat	VIC
99	44th Transport Squadron	27 Mar 84	Devonport	TAS
100	42nd Battalion, The Royal Queensland Regiment	04 Aug 84	Gladstone	QLD
101	North West Mobile Force	25 Aug 84	Alice Springs	NT
102	21st Construction Squadron	24 Nov 84	Kilmore	VIC
103	1st/15th Royal New South Wales Lancers	02 Mar 85	Sydney	NSW
104	School of Signals	16 Mar 85	Shire of Diamond Valley	VIC
105	7th Field Engineer Regiment RAE	24 Mar 85	Moe	VIC
106	Officer Cadet School	18 May 85	Shire of Flinders	VIC
107	27th Battalion, The Royal South Australia Regiment	29 Jun 85	Unley	SA
108	2nd EME Services Unit, RAEME	14 Sep 85	Strathfield	NSW
109	18th Transport Squadron	21 Oct 85	Coonabarabran	NSW
110	School of Artillery	02 Nov 85	Manly	NSW
111	72nd Signal Squadron	30 Nov 85	Shire of Crows Nest	QLD
112	12th/16th Hunter River Lancers	23 Mar 86	Armidale	NSW
113	3rd Field Squadron, RAE	24 Mar 86	Marion	SA
114	4th Field Engineer Regiment, RAE	05 Apr 86	Municipalities of Ryde and Hunters Hill	NSW
115	25th Battalion, The Royal Queensland Regiment	10 Apr 86	Kingaroy	QLD
116	North West Mobile Force	28 Apr 86	Katherine	NT
117	North West Mobile Force	10 Jun 86	Wyndham	WA
118	North West Mobile Force	20 Jun 86	Broome	WA
119	Queensland University Regiment	12 Jul 86	Brisbane	QLD
120	12th Independent Rifle Company	25 Aug 86	Launceston	TAS
121	3rd RAAPC Unit	08 Nov 86	Northcote	VIC
122	Land Warfare Centre	22 Nov 86	Beaudesert	QLD
123	15th Transport Squadron	06 Dec 86	Horsham	VIC
124	Armoured Centre	05 Mar 87	Broadford Shire	VIC
125	Canungra Transport Unit	11 Apr 87	Beaudesert	QLD
126	108th Signal Squadron	04 Jul 87	South Melbourne	VIC
127	11th/28th Battalion, The Royal Western Australia Regiment	22 Sep 87	Albany	WA
128	Army Aviation Training Centre	28 Aug 87	Toowoomba	QLD
129	4th Field Regiment, RAA	14 Oct 87	Thuringowa	QLD
130	11th Supply Company	22 Oct 87	Shire of Caboolture	QLD
131	144th Signal Squadron	07 Nov 87	The Corporation of the City of Burnside	SA
132	8th Transport Squadron	14 Nov 87	Port Lincoln	SA
133	3rd Transport Squadron	26 Jan 88	Municipality of Ashfield	NSW

Ser.	Unit	Date Granted	City or Town	State
134	12th/16th Hunter River Lancers	21 Feb 88	Merriwa Shire	NSW
135	Monash University Regiment	24 Apr 88	City of Oakleigh	VIC
136	1st Military District Band	14 May 88	Brisbane	QLD
137	7th Field Engineer Regiment, RAE	20 Jun 88	Croydon	VIC
138	42nd Battalion, The Royal Queensland Regiment	13 Jul 88	Shire of Sarina	QLD
139	The Pilbara Regiment	11 Aug 88	Port Hedland	WA
140	16th Battalion, The Royal Western Australia Regiment	10 Sep 88	Geraldton	WA
141	8th/7th Battalion, The Royal Victoria Regiment	17 Sep 88	Swan Hill	VIC
142	41st Battalion, The Royal New South Wales Regiment	21 Sep 88	The Shire of Tweed	NSW
143	25th Battalion, The Royal Queensland Regiment	08 Oct 88	Dalby	QLD
144	25th Battalion, The Royal Queensland Regiment	12 Nov 88	Wondai	QLD
145	Monash University Regiment	04 Mar 89	City of Waverley	VIC
146	49th Battalion, The Royal Queensland Regiment	06 Mar 89	Brisbane	QLD
147	5/11 Field Regiment, RAA - 13 Field Battery	22 Apr 89	Pine Rivers Shire	QLD
148	12th/16th Hunter River Lancers	23 Apr 89	Gunnedah	QLD
149	Queensland Agricultural College	31 Aug 89	Laidley	QLD
150	1st Signals Regiment	31 Aug 89	Gympie	QLD
151	1st Military District Band	07 Sep 89	Gold Coast	QLD
152	1st Military District Band	26 Sep 89	Shire of Redland	QLD
153	Army School of Transport	19 Oct 89	Seymour	VIC
154	8th/7th Battalion, The Royal Victoria Regiment	21 Oct 89	Echuca	VIC
155	41st Battalion, The Royal New South Wales Regiment	18 Nov 89	Taree	NSW
156	1st Commando Regiment	29 Apr 90	Mosman	NSW
157	6th Battalion, The Royal Australian Regiment	06 Jun 90	Brisbane	QLD
158	NORFORCE	16 Jun 90	Kununurra	NT
159	7th Field Regiment, RAA	29 Jul 90	Willoughby	NSW
160	8th/7th Battalion, The Royal Victoria Regiment	27 Oct 90	Hamilton	VIC
161	3rd Military District Band	07 Dec 90	Melbourne	VIC
162	Puckapunyal Logistic Battalion	20 Mar 91	Shire of Goulburn	VIC
163	141st Signal Squadron	18 Apr 91	Livingstone	NSW
164	12th/16th Hunter River Lancers	28 Apr 91	Muswellbrook	NSW
165	23rd Field Regiment, RAA	14 Jul 91	Rockdale	VIC
166	5th/6th Battalion, The Royal Victoria Regiment	12 Sep 91	Sunshine	VIC
167	University of New South Wales Regiment	14 Mar 92	Randwick	NSW
168	7th Field Regiment, RAA	07 Jun 92	Newcastle	NSW
169	The Pilbara Regiment	08 Aug 92	Shire of Ashburton	WA
170	8th/9th Battalion, The Royal Australian Regiment	08 Aug 92	Brisbane	QLD
171	Australian Army Band - Perth	13 Aug 92	Perth	WA
172	Australian Army Band - Melbourne	29 Aug 92	Traralgon	VIC
173	School of Survey	07 Dec 92	Shire of Hume	VIC
174	16th Battalion, The Royal Western Australia Regiment	22 Apr 93	Kalgoorlie	WA
175	10th Terminal Regiment	07 Aug 93	Mosman	NSW
176	Joint Services Telecommunications School	11 Nov 93	Nanango	QLD
177	9th Field Supply Company	02 Nov 93	Glenelg	SA
178	Army College of TAFE	13 Nov 93	Deniliquin	VIC
179	5th Aviation Regiment	20 Nov 93	Thuringowa	QLD

Ser.	Unit	Date Granted	City or Town	State
180	Australian Army Band - Sydney	19 Mar 94	Sydney	NSW
181	10th/27th Battalion, The Royal South Australia Regiment	23 Apr 94	Kadina	SA
182	The Pilbara Regiment	30 Jul 94	Shire of Roebourne	WA
183	North West Mobile Force	03 Sep 94	Tennant Creek	NT
184	Royal Regiment Australian Artillery, RAA	04 Nov 94	Adelaide	SA
185	1st Signal Regiment	25 Nov 95	Pine Rivers Shire	QLD
186	1st Battalion, The Royal Australian Regiment	26 May 96	Adelaide	SA
187	16 Air Defence Regt, RAA	01 Jun 96	Woodside	SA
188	1/19th Battalion, The Royal New South Wales Regiment	07 Dec 96	Orange	NSW
189	Royal Australian Corps of Transport	26 Jan 97	Port Lincoln	SA
190	9th Battalion, The Royal Queensland Regiment	15 Jul 97	Maryborough	QLD
191	Monash University Regiment	28 Feb 98	Monash	VIC
192	Northern Command	25 Jul 98	Darwin	NT
193	10th Force Support Battalion	13 Mar 99	Charters Towers	QLD
194	9th Brigade Administrative Support Battalion	08 Apr 00	Marion	SA
195	Army Logistic Training Centre	03 Mar 01	Albury	NSW
196	Army Logistic Training Centre	03 Mar 01	Wodonga	VIC
197	4th/3rd Battalion, The Royal New South Wales Regiment	24 Mar 01	Wollongong	NSW
198	Army Combat Arms Training Centre	28 Apr 01	Seymour	VIC
199	Royal Military College	09 Jun 01	Canberra	ACT
200	13th Combat Service Support Battalion	21 Oct 01	Fremantle	WA
201	22nd Construction Regiment	10 Aug 02	City of Monash	VIC
202	3rd/9th Light Horse (SAMR)	01 Nov 02	Gawler	SA
203	11th/28th Royal Western Australian Regiment	02 Mar 03	Bunbury	WA
204	Australian Army Band - Darwin	13 Sep 03	Darwin	NT
205	5 Combat Service Support Battalion	20 Sep 03	Botany Bay	NSW
206	2 Force Support Battalion	28 Nov 03	Glenorchy	TAS
207	Royal Military College - Duntroon Band	14 May 04	Canberra	ACT
208	7th Field Regiment, RAA	06 Nov 04	Warringah	NSW
209	25th/49th Battalion, The Royal Queensland Regiment	15 Oct 05	Roma	QLD
210	41st Battalion, The Royal New South Wales Regiment	16 Jul 05	Hastings	NSW
211	School of Artillery	15 Oct 05	Kilmore	VIC
212	16 Air Defence Regiment, RAA	03 Jun 06	Adelaide	SA
213	8th/7th Battalion, The Royal Victoria Regiment	11 Nov 06	Bendigo	VIC
214	9 Combat Service Support Battalion	09 Jun 09	Marion	SA
215	Australian Army Band - Kapooka	01 Aug 09	Wagga Wagga	NSW
216	1st/19th Battalion, The Royal New South Wales Regiment	26 Sep 09	Bathurst	NSW
217	Melbourne University Regiment	14 Mar 10	Melbourne	VIC
218	4th Field Regiment, RAA	01 May 10	Townsville	QLD
219	9th Force Support Battalion	31 Jun 10	Ipswich	QLD
220	17th Signal Regiment	20 Nov 10	Campbelltown	NSW
221	3rd Brigade	30 Aug 14	Townsville	QLD

(a) Leckie N. Country Victoria's Own. Loftus NSW, AMH Publications: 2008, p. 299
(b) Leckie N. Country Victoria's Own. Loftus NSW, AMH Publications: 2008, p. 300

Note: Units that have assumed command of independent unit(s) which have previously been granted Freedom of Entry are not entitled to exercise that right.

Chapter Eight

Military Bands and Music

*The idea of a band playing troops into battle would
now be considered impracticable, to say the least,
though it may contain a valuable element of surprise.*[348]

Introduction

Since Federation, military bands of the Australian Army continued to follow the British customs and traditions and only recently have developed their own uniquely Australian style.

The Army School of Music was established in 1953 at Balcombe, Victoria, marking the development of the modern Army bands as we know them today. The original battalion bands were converted from brass to military instrumentation during the period 1964 and 1974 and the Australian Army Band Corps (AABC) was created in 1968, culminating with the transfer of musicians from the various battalions to the AABC. Many battalions, wishing to maintain their tradition, created new bands (mostly pipes and drums) from within their own ranks.

Army bands provide military commanders with an important and effective means of stimulating and maintaining esprit de corps and morale among troops; and bands are a powerful public relations medium for the civilian community. Bands contribute directly to the well-being of the Army and the community through participation in military ceremonies and parades, Regal, Vice-Regal, Federal, State and Territory Government ceremonial functions, music education programs, concerts and community activities.[349]

348 Sydney Morning Herald, around 1940, author unknown
349 Australian Army. *Defence Instruction (G) Pers 31-1 Australian Awards for Long Service*: 27 Feb 2007

The term 'Military Band' to the uninitiated means any band in the armed forces, when in fact the term is used to express a combination of woodwind, brass and percussion instruments with good resonance for outdoors and reasonable portability for transport. In Australia, we did not refer to bands as 'military bands' until 1965.

Music has been an integral part of military life for hundreds of years and, besides entertaining the troops, it was employed for the practical purposes of conveying messages. Sun Tzu in his book '*The Art of War*' wrote of the use of military bands 'for the better regulation of the stepping together of troops'. We are left with a relic of this with the familiar 'quick march' and the four-bar drum solo that acts as a prelude to most military marches.

Military Music – Historic Development[350]

Military music had its origins with the humble drum that was used by ancient man to create fear and dismay in his enemies. Later the horn was developed, the blast of which could be heard over great distances.

The 20th century has seen wonderful advances in the military band, both as a medium of artistic expression and as a distinct Army organisation. The advances in wind instrument techniques, and the unique quality of band tone, as distinct from the string orchestra, has excited the imagination of composers the world over, and led them to use the band as a medium for original composition.

Up to the present, marches and arrangements of operatic potpourri had been the mainstay of the repertoire of military bands. Many noted composers such as Sousa, Stravinsky, Hindemith, Rimsky-Korsakoff, Roussel and Schmitt have written marches, symphonies, concertos and other types of music for military bands.

The work done by military bands to this time is proof of their usefulness during two world wars as a morale booster. War and music have had an unusual partnership, and in the future there is no reason to expect the dissolution of this partnership.

Military Music – Scottish Influence

The Scottish influence in colonial Army units is self-evident with such units as the Victorian Scottish Regiment, NSW Scottish Regiment and the South Australian Scottish Infantry Regiment to name just a few. With these regiments the bagpipes were introduced into common use within the Australian military.

It has often been said, in jest, that the noise made by the bagpipes alone make them a true weapon of war. This statement is closer to the truth than many people realise,

as hundreds of years ago during a Scottish rebellion the Scots refused to go into battle without their pipes being played. The English therefore declared them a weapon of war and subsequently banned their use throughout Scotland.[351]

Little has been written on the subject of the development of pipes and drums in Australia since colonial times, but available photographic evidence shows that they have been used in every State colonial force, alongside the more traditional brass band.

Since the 1960s each Australian Scottish Battalion raised included a pipes and drums band.

Unlike a military brass band that requires numerous types of wind, string, and percussion instruments, a basic pipes and drums band can be made up of only a few members. It would not be practical or desirable for a brass band to play music during a battle; but pipers have played music as they accompanied their units into battle. A pipes and drums band is by the very nature of its instruments restricted in its musical repertoire. A pipe band is unable to play the Australian or British national anthem accurately as pipes do not have the full range of musical notes that are available to military bands. Instead the melody of the anthem is changed to accommodate the pipers thus allowing them to play a version that is only just recognisable. Although not capable of accurately playing the British national anthem, pipe bands often play Scotland the Brave as a Royal Salute in lieu as it is immediately recognisable.

As early as the Korean War the original battalions of RAR boasted large brass bands at times also incorporating pipes and drums. The members of these bands also filled the role of stretcher bearers during times of conflict. By 1968, the Regiment was fully committed to the war in South Vietnam, when it was decided to establish the AABC. To man this new organisation these musicians were removed from their units and posted to the newly-raised MD Bands. Unfortunately this left the battalions without their bands and more importantly their stretcher bearers, although the battalions were permitted to retain the pipes and drums elements of their bands. Since that time reductions in manpower have seen a further decline in the number of small independent unit bands.

Drum Major

The traditional office of Drum Major dates back to the later years of King Charles I (r. 1625-1649), when it had been adopted throughout the British Army. By 1661 the importance of drummers in all regiments was recognised as their duties included not only the setting of pace on the march but also the setting of the watch, beating retreat and the 'Tap Toe' (Tattoo). The Drum Major was directly responsible to

---

350 Farmer HG. *The Rise & Development of Military Music.* London, WM Reeves: 1912

351 Cassin-Scott J, Fabb J. *Military Bands and their Uniforms.* Poole Dorset, Blandford Press: 1978 p. 111

Image courtesy Department of Defence – 20090621adf8262658_158. AABC Drum Major

the Major of the Regiment for these daily routine matters as well as recruiting and the administration of punishment (this included the actual whipping of offenders), as well as the training of young drummers.[352]

Drum Majors were granted a more distinctive uniform and carried a cane or walking stick. These uniforms were not normally supplied by the Government, but rather by the officers of the regiment, hence the wealthier the officers the more flamboyant the uniform of the band. This tradition can be seen in the dress of modern military bands, where the members' uniforms are always more decorative than that of the common soldiers. The cane or walking stick that was used in the British Army developed into the mace which is carried by Drum Major. As the Drum Major's duties no longer involved drumming, his two drumsticks were secured on or under his sash, thus leaving his hands free, although they could be retrieved if the need arose. Ornamental facsimiles of these drumsticks are sometimes included on the sash as a reminder of the origins of the Drum Major's trade.[353]

The Drum Major is now usually a Warrant Officer who is responsible for the conduct of the military members, and with the guidance of the Bandmaster, the musical standards of the band. The Drum Major is responsible for the drill of both the regimental band and the drums. The Drum Major takes precedence over the Bandmaster on ceremonial occasions when both parade together.

Martial Music – Music in Battle

There are no known cases where Australian soldiers have sung their way into battle. The one instance of a battalion using martial music during a battle occurred in Korea on 2nd July 1952 when 'A' Coy 1 RAR was attacking Hill 227[354], and the Officer Commanding, MAJ DS Thomson[355], MC, had his company piper, PTE Jock Burgess, pipe the Company into and through the attack.

352 Makepeace-Warne A. *Brassey's Companion to the British Army*. London, Brassey's: 1995 p. 111

353 Makepeace-Warne A. *Brassey's Companion to the British Army*. London, Brassey's: 1995 p. 111

354 http://www.awm.gov.au/cms_images/AWM85/2/AWM85-2-12.pdf

355 Brigadier David Scott Thomson, MC; OC A Company 1 RAR 1951-1952, CO 4 RAR 1964-1966, Comd 3 Task Force 1970-1972, MHR, Leichhardt, 1975-1983: born Sale Victoria 21 November 1924.

Image courtesy Department of Defence – 20110425adf8181999_105

Bugle Calls

It cannot be clearly established whether the following words, written by WG Bentley,[356] to accompany the bugle calls, was an original work or an old soldier recording traditional lyrics passed-down over the years. It is, however, a fact that his book, first published in 1916, was reproduced almost without correction (minus the lyrics) by the British Army in 1927.

Rouse

Get up at once, get up at once, the bugle's sounding,
the day is here and never fear, old Sol is shining.
The Orderly Officer's on his rounds,

Quarter Call

Here's Quarter Call, time to hurry up.

Markers

Markers are out, quick now, the Adjutant is there.

356 Bentley WG. *Trumpet and Bugle Calls for the Australian Army: Including Instructions for Trumpeters and Buglers.* Sydney, Angus and Robertson: 1916

Fall In

Fall in All, Fall in All, answer to the Bugle call,
Short and tall, great and small, Stand up straight then in you fall.

Mess Call 1

Oh, come to the cook house door boys,
Come to the cook house door.

Mess Call 2

Oh, pick 'em up, pick 'em hot po-ta-toes,
Hot po-ta-toes,
Pick 'em up, pick 'em up, hot po-ta-toes all.

Officers' Mess

The Officers' wives have puddings and pie
But soldiers' wives have skilly,
But officers' all deserve what they get,
For those
Who lead in battle you bet, are not
Too blooming silly.

The Last Post

Come home! Come home!

The last post is sounding for you to hear.

All good soldiers know very well there is nothing to fear while they do what is right, and forget all the worries they have met in their duties through the year. A soldier cannot always be great, but he can be a gentleman and he can be a right good pal to his comrades in his squad.

So all you soldiers listen to this – Deal fair by all and you'll never be amiss.

Be Brave! Be Just! Be Honest and True Men

Retreat

Close the day, wend your way grave or gay, to your rest, comes the moon, goes the sun that is setting in the west. Drill is done, leave begun, now for fun with a zest; for soldiers are free of all the little fun spots in town, of the canteen and billiard room too; but defaulters must answer their names until Tat-Too.

Do a drill with a pack on their back around the track so keep out of this squad. Then you will have no pack-drill to do.

Reveille

Rev-eil-lee! Rev-eil-lee is sounding

The bugle calls you from your sleep; it is the break of day You've got to do your duty or you will get no pay Come, wake yourself, rouse yourself out of your sleep And throw off the blankets and take a good peek at all The bright signs of the break of day, so get up and do not delay.

Get Up!

Or-der-ly officer is on his round!

And if you're still a-bed he will send you to the guard And then you'll get a drill and that will be a bitter pill So be up when he comes, be up when he comes, Like a soldier at his post, a soldier at his post, all ser-ene.

Salute for Guard

Here comes the guard, boys, the smart swagger guard. Give 'em all they ought to get, and don't blow too hard.

Lights Out

Lights out, All Out.

Sick Call

All the sick, all the lame, come here

And get cured of all

Your aches, sickness and pain.

First Post

The first post is sounding, the canteen is shut and you'd Better be gone to your barrack or hut. All Defaulters Answer your name for the last time tonight, But no

More of your games, the bugles and pipes Will be spitting

Out their lives with a rub-a-dub-a-dub, and Ord-ly corp'rals call out the roll, and those who Are not on leave will have a mark placed Against their names if they are 'e ab-sent From call. Get to your cots and just answer The roll. Good night, good night, good night, Pleasant

Dreams, Sleep!

Reveille

Reveille (from the French word 'réveilléz' meaning to 'wake-up'), was originally played as a drum beat just prior to daybreak and has always been the soldiers' 'alarm clock' and as such has never really been accepted as a cheerful call. Its traditional purpose was to wake up the sleeping soldiers and let the sentries know that they could cease challenging. It was also a signal to open the town gates and let out the horse guard, allowing them to do a reconnaissance of the immediate area beyond the walls.

As the first call of the soldiers' daily routine it is employed symbolically and ceremonially to:

- Indicate the rising of the warriors' spirit in the next world (as used at military funerals)

- Indicate triumph over 'material' aspects (as used in commemorative services).

Tattoo

Military Tattoos have evolved into shows including theatrics, musical performances, national dances, military competitions and the display of armed force capabilities in general.

It is believed the term 'Tattoo' dates from the 'Thirty Years' War' (1618-1648), in the Low Countries (generally the area now comprising Belgium and the Netherlands). The Dutch fortresses were garrisoned with mercenary troops; at that time the Dutch Federal Army consisted mostly of Scottish, English, German and Swiss mercenaries, commanded by a Dutch officer corps. Drummers from the garrison were sent out into the towns at 9.30pm each evening to inform the soldiers that it was time for them to return to their barracks. The process was then known as the Old Dutch 'Doe den Tap toe' meaning 'Turn off the Taps';[357] an instruction for the innkeepers to stop serving beer. The drummers continued to play their drums until the curfew at 10pm.

The best known tattoo is the 'The Royal Edinburgh Military Tattoo' in which Australian Army bands and soldiers have often participated. In 1988, Australia's Bicentennial Year, the Australian Army conducted a touring tattoo which travelled extensively throughout the nation.

At the beginning of the 19th century it became customary to use the 'First Post' and 'Last Post' which are still in use today:

- **First Post** – which embraces what was originally the 'first' and 'second' posts, usually sounded at 9.30pm (2130h) when all soldiers were required to be present beside their beds and the Orderly Sergeant checked the barrack rooms for absentees

357 Edwards TJ. *Military Customs*. Aldershot, England, Gale and Polden: 1954, p. 5

- **Last Post** – which embraces what was originally the 'third' and 'fourth' posts usually sounded at 10.00pm (2200h) when soldiers were expected to be in bed and the Orderly Sergeants paraded at the Guard Room to make their reports. Thus the original significance of the word 'Post' was lost.

The practice was to check barrack rooms at Last Post and this is still known as the Tattoo Roll Call. 15 minutes after Last Post the Lights Out was sounded, this period presumably being allowed for the soldiers to compose themselves for the night's slumber. The Infantry 'Last Post' has been generally accepted as an accompaniment to a soldier's obsequies (from the Latin exsequiae - 'funeral rites' influenced by obsequium 'dutiful service') where the closing bars wail out their sad farewell to the departing warrior – a similar analogy has been applied in many other countries in the world.

Retreat

The Retreat was definitely separated from the Tattoo about the middle of the 18th century.

It is generally believed that gun firing at Retreat was a medium introduced to communicate when the troops were so far spread as to be unable to hear the drums. A further possibility is that it was a means of indicating the end of the day's work when weather conditions were such that the precise time of sunset could not be otherwise indicated.

For several centuries it has been the custom to change the daily duties at Retreat, and we know that 'Watch Setting' effectively meant mounting of the guard.

The special ceremonial, known today as 'Beating Retreat', incorporates a number of ancient customs:

- Parading and Mounting the Guard – for example, 'Watch Setting'

- Drums beating Retreat – ancient usage

- The Musical Troop – a relic from the daily Trooping of the Colour before it was lodged

- Gun Fire – from ancient usage – usually fired as volleys

- Rifle Volleys – sometimes fired by the Watch to 'put flight to the evil spirits of departed soldiers'

- Sacred Music – many of the old regiments had a custom of 'reciting prayers for their fallen comrades' – this was often followed by the singing of a hymn

- The lowering of the ANF – a procedure which now replaces the daily Trooping the Colour.

Present-day ceremonial may include all or any of the above procedures with the Retreat call, sometimes with a musical background, combined with the lowering of the ANF terminating the ceremony.

Corps and Regimental March Music

The table of musical tunes shown in this Chapter contains a list of the regimental march music and bugle calls of the current Corps and Regiments of the Army[358] and some disbanded units.[359] Also mentioned are some miscellaneous Airs authorised for use on certain ceremonial parades.

The tradition of adopting particular tunes for a regimental march has been part of British military tradition for many years and naturally has been passed onto the Australian Army. Many tunes currently played have been taken from traditional tunes used by affiliated sister Corps and Regiments of the British Army.

Only two regimental march tunes and one bugle call in current use have been adopted from foreign countries in which soldiers had served. They are the traditional Afrikaans song, 'Sari Marais' or 'Sarie Marais' from South Africa; the 'Apple Picking' song 'Ringo' from Japan; and the bugle call, 'D445', from Vietnam.

Sarie Marais – (also known as 'My Sarie Marais') is a traditional Afrikaans folk song, written during the Boer War. The tune was taken from a song called Ellie Rhee, dating from the American Civil War, with the lyrics modified and translated into Afrikaans. This tune was adopted by the 1st Infantry Battalion, The City of Sydney's Own Regiment which claims direct lineage to the contingent of troops sent from New South Wales to the 2nd Boer War (1899-1902).

Ringo – 2 RAR was without an official regimental march in 1954. The then RSM suggested that as the British Army had adopted 'Lili Marlene' from the Germans, it seemed appropriate that the Battalion adopt the 'Apple Picking' song, 'Ringo' from the Japanese.[360]

D445 – The bugle call 'D445' was named after the Provincial Mobile Battalion 'D445' of the Liberation Army of South Vietnam. This unit operated in many areas of South Vietnam including the Nui Dat/Long Tan area during the war. 6 RAR first encountered D445 during Operation HOBART in July 1966 and it was this battalion, along with the North Vietnamese regular army 275th Regiment (NVA), which fought against D Company 6 RAR at the Battle of Long Tan.

During the first encounter with the enemy it is recorded that, at various times throughout the engagement, bugle calls were heard coming from the enemy position, being used for both command and control of men and mortar teams.[361]

The official history of the Battle of Long Tan[362] and other books on the subject[363] do not indicate any bugle calls coming from the position occupied by D445; the available evidence indicates all bugle calls came from the area occupied by 275th Regiment. At no time is there mention of a withdrawal bugle call being heard at the end of either contact.

The original calls would have been played on the French instrument in use by the North Vietnamese, and as such would have been in the key of C. The Australian Army-issue bugle is a B flat instrument and the music has been transposed to fit. The tune comprises two sections – the 'Attack'; and the 'Withdrawal'; and was said to be recalled by a battalion soldier to a member of the battalion band.

The Army Hymn – Soldiers of Australia[364]

Tune: Waltzing Matilda, Words: J. Deorrado/J. Cosgrove

Soldiers of Australia gathered now to worship God,
Under the badge of the Rising Sun;
Giving thanks for our country, our families, our freedom,
Let hearts and voices arise as one!

Chorus:

God of salvation, guide of our Nation
You give us strength to follow your ways;
With the cross raised so high shining bright across our southern sky,
We'll serve Australia through all our days.

Soldiers of Australia ready to be called to serve,
Training together we strive for peace;
When at home or away through the darkest night and longest day,
We trust God's guidance will never cease.

Chorus:

Soldiers of Australia gathered as God's family,
Brothers and sisters stand side by side;
Through our God we are one as we do the work that must be done,
Courage and friendship will be our pride.

Chorus:

Soldiers of Australia have bought our freedom with their lives,
They grow not old as we grow old;
At the setting of the sun and also in the morning,
We shall remember their deeds so bold.

Chorus:

358 Australian Army. *Ceremonial Manual – 2003 Volume 1.* Canberra, Defence Publishing Service: 2003, Chap 27 plus additions.

359 Australian Army Order (AAO) 91/1953. *Regimental Marches – Australian Military Forces*: 1953

360 The Royal Australian Regiment Association. *The Battalions*: undated, Chap 6 p.1

361 McNeill IG. *To Long Tan: The Australian Army and the Vietnam War 1950-1966.* St Leonards NSW, Allen & Unwin: 1993, p. 280

362 McNeill IG. *To Long Tan: The Australian Army and the Vietnam War 1950-1966.* St Leonards NSW, Allen & Unwin: 1993, p. 328

363 Grandin R. *The Battle of Long Tan: As Told by the Commanders to Bob Grandin.* Crows Nest NSW, Allen & Unwin: 2004, pp. 128-198

364 Note: Although sung on occasion in some Army services and commemorations, this hymn/song has never been formally adopted as 'The Army Hymn'.

Regimental Marches and Bugle Calls of the Australian Army

At the rear of this book is a CD containing Regimental and other music with short histories (where available). By using the 'Start' icon, the CD can be played on any computer/mobile device with a modern 'web' browser (such as Google Chrome), the CD can also be cross loaded onto and played on computer/mobile devices that do not have a disc drive - the CD also contains a number of 'hyperlinks' to the requested histories; the CD cannot be played on a traditional 'CD Player'.

Serial		Quick March	Slow March	Bugle Call	Remarks
1	Australian Army	'The Australian Army March'			Special arrangement of 'Brown Slouch Hat/ Waltzing Matilda'
2	The Corps of Staff Cadets	'The Staff Cadet'	'General Bridges'	'The College Regimental Call' (RMC Order No. 15 of 1919)	
3	The Company of Officer Cadets	'Portsea'	'By Land and Sea'		
4	The Royal Australian Armoured Corps	'Radetsky'			
5	The Royal Regiment of Australian Artillery	'Royal Artillery (Quick March)' 'The Keel Row (Drive Past)'	'Royal Artillery (Slow March)'		Regimental Quick March also used by 'A' Field Battery, RAA
6	The Royal Australian Engineers	'Wings'			
7	The Royal Australian Corps of Signals	Combination of 'Be Gone Dull Care' and 'Click Goes the Shears'	'Her Royal Highness, The Princess Royal'		
8	The Royal Australian Infantry Corps	'Our Director'			
9	Australian Army Aviation	'Those Magnificent Men In Their Flying Machines'			
10	Australian Army Intelligence Corps	'The Rose and Laurel'	'Trumpet Tune and Ayre' (Purcell)		
11	The Royal Australian Army Chaplains Department	'Trumpet Voluntary'			
12	The Royal Australian Corps of Transport	'Wait for the Wagon'	'Par Oneri'		
13	The Royal Australian Army Medical Corps	'Here's a Health Unto His Majesty'			
14	The Royal Australian Army Dental Corps	'Puff the Magic Dragon'			Written by Leonard Lipton and Peter Yarrow
15	The Royal Australian Army Ordnance Corps	Combination of 'The Wild Colonial Boy' and 'The Quartermaster's Store'	Combination of 'To the Warrior His Arms' and 'The Village Blacksmith'		
16	The Royal Corps of Australian Electrical and Mechanical Engineers	Combination of 'Lilliburlero' and 'The Boys in the Back Room'	'The Harmonious Blacksmith'	RAEME Call	
17	The Royal Australian Army Educational Corps	Combination of 'Gaudeamus Igitur' and 'The Good Comrade'			
18	The Australian Army Catering Corps	Combination of 'Roast Beef of Old England' and 'Tavern in the Town' ('Beef and Burgundy')			
19	The Royal Australian Army Pay Corps	'March Militaire' (Schubert)			
20	The Australian Army Legal Corps	'March of the Peers'			
21	The Royal Australian Corps of Military Police	'The Gendarmes Duet'			
22	The Australian Army Psychology Corps	'The Campbells are Coming'			
23	The Australian Army Band Corps	'The Minstrel Boy'	'The Corps'	Band Call	

Serial		Quick March	Slow March	Bugle Call	Remarks
24	The Royal Australian Army Nursing Corps	Combination of 'The Girls in Grey' and 'Second to None'			
ARMOURED CORPS UNITS					
25	1st Armoured Regiment	'Radetsky'	'Grand March from Aida'		
26	2nd Cavalry Regiment	Combination of 'Garry Owen' and 'The Girl I Left Behind Me'	'Song of Joy' from Beethoven's Ninth Symphony		
27	3rd/4th Cavalry Regiment	Combination of 'Old Comrades' and 'Light Cavalry'			
28	1st/15th Royal New South Wales Lancers	'El Abanico'			
29	2nd/14th Light Horse Regiment (QMI)	'Soldiers of the Queen'	'Duke of York'		
30	3rd/9th Light Horse (SAMR)	'Fare Thee Well, Inniskilling'			
31	4th/19th Prince of Wales's Light Horse	'Australian Light Horse'			
32	10th Light Horse	'Marching through Georgia'			
33	12th/16th Hunter River Lancers	'Our Director'			
THE ROYAL AUSTRALIAN REGIMENT					
34	The Royal Australian Regiment	1. 'El Alamein' 2. Black Bear	'Infantry Song'		1. Military Brass 2. Pipes and Drums
35	1st Battalion	'Waltzing Matilda'			
36	2nd Battalion	1. 'Ringo' 2. 'Back in Black'			1. Military Brass 2. Pipes and Drums
37	3rd Battalion	1. 'Our Director' 2. 'Kapyong'			'Kapyong' Reserved for Kapyong Day only
38	4th Battalion	'Inverbrackie'			Combination of 'Ringo' and 'Inverbrackie'
39	5th Battalion	'Dominique'			
40	6th Battalion	1. 'Spirit of Youth' 2. 'The Crusaders'		D445	1. Military/Brass Bands 2. Pipes and Drums
41	7th Battalion	1. 'Australaise' 2. 'Cock O' the North'			1. Military/Brass Bands 2. Pipes and Drums
42	8th Battalion	'Let's Go'			
43	9th Battalion	'Pass Me By'			
44	2nd/4th Battalion	1. 'Ringobrackie' 2. 'Second Fourth Battalion'	2. 'Sons of ANZAC's'	Call to Arms	1. Combination of 'Ringo' and 'Inverbrackie' 2. Pipes and Drums
45	5th/7th Battalion	'Dominaise'			Combination of 'Dominique' and 'Australaise'
46	8th/9th Battalion	'The Brown and Grey Lanyard'			Written by Cpl A. Gorrie (6 RAR)
THE ROYAL QUEENSLAND REGIMENT					
47	The Royal Queensland Regiment	'Southern Cross'			
48	9th Battalion	1. 'El Abanico' 2. 'Frog Hollow Rangers'			1. Military/Brass 2. Pipes and Drums
49	25th Battalion	'Sussex by the Sea'			
50	31st Battalion	'John Peel'			
51	42nd Battalion	'Blue Bonnets Over the Border'			

Serial		Quick March	Slow March	Bugle Call	Remarks
52	49th Battalion	'Colonel Bogey'			
53	25th/49th Battalion	'Southern Cross'			
54	31st/42nd Battalion	1. 'John Peel' 2. 'Blue Bonnets Over the Border' and 'Cock O' the North'			1. Military/Brass 2. Pipes and Drums
THE ROYAL NEW SOUTH WALES REGIMENT					
55	1st/19th Battalion	1. 'Sari Marais' 2. 'Colonel Bogey'			1. 1st Battalion 2. 19th Battalion
56	2nd/17th Battalion	1. 'Breganza' 2. 'Boys of the Old Brigade'			1. 2nd Battalion 2. 17th Battalion
57	4th/3rd Battalion	Combination of 'New Colonial' and 'My Regiment (Blankenburg)'			1. 3rd Battalion New Colonial 2. 4th Battalion 'My Regiment'
58	41st Battalion	'Cock O' the North'			
THE ROYAL VICTORIA REGIMENT					
59	5th Battalion	'Cock O' the North'			
60	6th Battalion	'Waltzing Matilda'			10 August 1992
61	5th/6th Battalion	'Our Director'			
62	8th/7th Battalion	'I'm Ninety Five'	'Men of Harlech'		
63	22nd Battalion	'Our Director'			
THE ROYAL SOUTH AUSTRALIA REGIMENT					
64	1st Battalion (Pentropic)	'Song of Australia'			
65	10th Battalion	'Song of Australia'			
66	27th Battalion	'Scotland the Brave'			
67	43rd Battalion	'Waltzing Matilda'			
68	10th/27th Battalion	Combination of 'Song of Australia' and 'Scotland the Brave'			
THE ROYAL WESTERN AUSTRALIA REGIMENT					
69	The Royal Western Australia Regiment	'Pride of Youth'			
70	16th Battalion	'March of the Cameron Men'			
71	11th/28th Battalion	Combination of 'Sussex by the Sea' and 'Colonel Bogey'			
THE ROYAL TASMANIA REGIMENT					
72	12th Battalion	'Captain Oldfield'			
73	40th Battalion	'Invercargill'			
74	12th/40th Battalion	'Captain Oldfield'/'Invercargill'/ Alternate: 'Lions of Menin Gate'			A note in Regimental documentation lists 'The Royal Tasmanian Regiment- The Southlanders' as the Regimental tune but no copy of the music or tune is known to exist.
AVIATION UNITS					
75	1st Aviation Regiment	'Eagle Squadron'			
76	5th Aviation Regiment	'Pegasus'			
77	6th Aviation Regiment	'Light Cavalry'	'Winged Trojan'		

Serial		Quick March	Slow March	Bugle Call	Remarks
RACT UNITS					
78	1st Air Transport Support Regiment	'Farewell to the Creeks'			
79	9th Transport Regiment	'The Brown Haired Maiden'			
80	10th Terminal Regiment	'Meeting of the Waters'			
HEADQUARTER UNITS					
81	Forces Command	'Cloak and Dagger'			Approved 12 Jun 2013
82	HQ Training Command – Army	'Georges Heights'			
83	2nd Division	'March of the 2nd Division'			'Pozieres'
84	HQ NT Command	'Under the Double Eagle'			AAO 91/1953
INFANTRY OTHER UNITS					
85	The Special Air Service Regiment	'Happy Wanderer'	'Lilli Marlene'		
86	10th Independent Rifle Company	'Men of Harlech'			
87	1st Commando Regiment,	'Strike Swiftly'			
88	1st Commando Company	'Sari Marais'			
89	2nd Commando Company	'Cockleshell Heroes'			
90	2nd Commando Regiment	'Without Warning'			
91	NORFORCE	'The Vedette'	'The Never-Never'		16 May 1986
92	51st Battalion, FNQR	1. The Far North Queensland Regiment'			1. Military/Brass
		2. 'The Black Kookaburra'	2. 'Soldiers of the North'		2. Pipes and Drums
93	School of Infantry	'Goodbye Dolly Grey'	'Infantry Song'		
94	The Pilbara Regiment	'Always Alert'			
95	PNGVR	'Imperial Echoes'			
UNIVERSITY REGIMENTS AND TRAINING UNITS					
96	The Queensland University Regiment	'Pour Bacchus'			
97	The Sydney University Regiment	'Men of Harlech'			
98	The University of New South Wales Regiment	'Blue Blood'			
99	The Melbourne University Regiment	'The Thin Red Line'			
100	The Monash University Regiment	'Imperial Echoes'			
101	The Adelaide Universities Regiment	'Highland Laddie'	'Morag of Dunvegan'		
102	The Western Australia University Regiment	'Sons of the Brave'			
103	The Army Logistic Training Centre	1. 'Servare-Discemus'	'Balcombe'		1. Military/Brass
		2. 'Bonegilla'			2. Pipes and Drums
104	1st Recruit Training Battalion	'Rose Gloria'			
CORPORATE SERVICE AND INFASTRUCTURE CENTRES					
105	HQ CSIC Qld Region	'Queen of the North'			
106	HQ CSIC Eastern Region	'St Kilda'			
107	HQ CSIC Southern Region	'March of the Heralds'			
108	HQ CSIC SA	'The Wizard of Oz'			
109	HQ CSIC WA	'Westralia'			Westralian – AAO 91/1953
110	HQ CSIC Tasmania	'Old Tower'			

Serial		Quick March	Slow March	Bugle Call	Remarks
LIGHT HORSE UNITS – AMF					
111	8th/13th Victorian Mounted Rifles	'The Victorian Rifles'			
112	6th New South Wales Mounted Rifles	'The Kynegad Slashers'			Alliance: The Queen's Own Hussars
113	7th/21st Aust. Horse	'Light of Foot'			
INFANTRY UNITS – AMF					
114	1st Battalion	'Sari Marais'			
115	2nd Battalion	'Braganza'			
116	3rd Battalion	'The Repasz Band'			
117	4th Battalion	'Men of Harlech'			
118	5th Battalion	'Cock O' the North'			
119	6th Battalion	'Waltzing Matilda'			
120	8th/7th Battalion	'I'm Ninety Five'			
121	9th Battalion	'El Abanico'			
122	10th Battalion	'The Manchester'			
123	11th/44th Battalion	'Sussex by the Sea'			
124	12th Battalion	'Captain Oldfield'			
125	13th Battalion	'The Standard of St George'			
126	16th Battalion	'March of the Cameron Men'			
127	17th/18th Battalion	'Boys of the Old Brigade'			
128	25th Infantry Battalion	'Sussex by the Sea'			
129	27th Infantry Battalion	'The Campbells are Coming'			
130	28th Infantry Battalion	'Colonel Bogey'			
131	30th Infantry Battalion	'Highland Laddie'			
132	31st Infantry Battalion	'John Peel'			
133	34th Infantry Battalion	'Blaze Away'			
134	38th Infantry Battalion	'Sussex by the Sea'			
135	40th Infantry Battalion	'Invercargill'			
136	41st Infantry Battalion	'Cock O' the North'			
137	42nd Infantry Battalion	'Blue Bonnets over the Border'			
138	43rd/48th Infantry Battalion	'Nachtlager in Granada'			
139	45th Infantry Battalion	'Men of Harlech'			
140	47th Infantry Battalion	'Pibroch O'Donuil Dhu'			
141	51st Infantry Battalion	'Madelon'			
142	56th Reconnaissance Battalion	'Steadfast and True'			
143	58th/32nd Infantry Battalion	'The Northamptonshire'			
144	59th Infantry Battalion	'Marine Artillery' 'Moray Firth'			
MISCELLANEOUS MUSIC					
145	'Soldiers of Australia'	'Soldiers of Australia' (Instrumental) 'Soldiers of Australia' (Vocal)			
146	The Women's Royal Australian Army Corps	'Soldiers of the Queen'			
147	The Royal Australian Survey Corps	'Wandering the King's Highway'			
148	Officer Cadet Training Unit – Scheyville	'Along the Road to Gundagai'	'Never Never'/'Michael Rowed the Boat Ashore'		

Serial		Quick March	Slow March	Bugle Call	Remarks
149	1 RQR (Pentropic)	'Royal Queensland' *Note			
150	16 Army Lt AC Sqn	'Recce Flight'			AAO 93/1961
151	Commemorative Tune – Sunset	'Sunset' (with Bugle Call)			
152	Played during the 'Sobriety Test Handover Procedure'	'The Dashing White Sergeant'			Ceremonial Manual Chap 7 Appendix 3 to Annex A
153	Graduations and Farewell Ceremonies, Marching Off Old Colours	'Auld Lang Syne'			Ceremonial Manual Chap 8 Annex C
154	Salutes – Point of War	'Point of War'			
155	Played during a 'Freedom of Entry' Ceremony – arrival and departure of a City Mayor	'Duke of York'			Ceremonial Manual Chap 17 Annex A
156	Salutes – Advance Australia Fair	'Advance Australia Fair'			
157	Salutes –Advance in Review Order	'British Grenadiers'			
158	Salutes – Used for Chief of Defence Force	'The Field of the Cloth of Gold'			
159	Salutes – General Salute	'Scipio'			
160	Salutes – Foreign Chiefs of Army	'Cavalry Brigade'			
161	Salutes – for the Prime Minister	'Waltzing Matilda'			
162	4th Battalion AIF 2nd/4th Battalion 2nd AIF	'There must be little cupids in the briny'			Selected in 1917 by the battalion CO[a] Lt Col Iven Mackay[b]

(a) Chapman ID, Mackay IG. Citizen and Soldier. Melbourne, Melway Publishing: 1975, p. 87 & 241
(b) Lieutenant General Sir Iven Mackay, KBE, CMG, DSO and Bar, VD, Croix De Guerre (France); AIF: Commanding Officer 4 Bn 1916-1917, 1 MG Bn 1918, Comd 1 Inf Bde 1918-1919, 2nd AIF GOC 6 Div 1940-1941, Home Forces 1941-1942, NGF 1943-1944. High Commissioner for Australia in India 1944-1948; born Grafton NSW 7 Apr 1882 – died Sydney 30 Sep 1966.

Note: Although 'Royal Queensland' is confirmed by AAO 93/1961 as the authorised regimental tune to be used by 1 RQR, there is no evidence to show that this tune was ever written nor was it used by the unit during its existence; however, the air 'El Abanico' was used by the Battalion and later adopted by 9 RQR when it was raised in its stead.[365]

Copyright:

Every effort has been made to trace and acknowledge Copyright. Where the attempt has been unsuccessful, the Producer/ Project Manager would be pleased to hear from the Copyright Owner so any omission or error can be rectified.

A Special Note of Thanks

The authors wish to sincerely thank the members of the Australian Army Band Sydney and AAB-S sound engineers, production crew and arrangers for undertaking such a significant recording project. Notable appreciation is given to the arrangers who transcribed and arranged many compositions specifically for this project. Appreciation is also extended to all Australian Army Band Corps musicians and Members of the Pipes and Drums of the Royal Australian Army Regiment past and present for use of previously recorded tracks. Without the significant dedication, time and input of CAPT Rod Mason, OAM, and the support of MAJ Peter O'Connor, LTCOL Gordon Lambie, CSM, and LTCOL Ian McLean, AM, CSC (Retd), this project would not have been possible. Sincere thanks go to Richard NL Terrett for his work on software design and layout of the Regimental Music CD.

---

365 Newland P, Taubert S. *Interview with MAJ Peter Newland RFD ex-1 RQR 1960, Brisbane*: interviewer – Stephen Taubert: September 2012.

Chapter Nine

Honours and Awards

Introduction

From colonial times, Australia subscribed to the British or Imperial system of orders, decorations, awards and medals to recognise gallantry, bravery, outstanding achievement meritorious and long service. The Australian system of honours and awards was instituted on 14th February 1975 with the establishment of the Order of Australia, the Australian Bravery Decorations and the National Medal. Both new and old systems operated in parallel until 1992 when it was agreed between Australia and the United Kingdom that no further nominations for Imperial awards would be recommended to The Sovereign for conferral on Australians.

It should be noted that The Sovereign can still confer honours upon Australians in exercise of the Royal Prerogative, for example, appointments within the Order of Garter, the Order of the Thistle, the Order of Merit and the Royal Victorian Order; however, since 5th October 1992 other imperial honours and awards to Australian citizens are considered foreign awards and approval from the Governor-General of Australia is required to wear them; and they come after all Australian Honours, Awards and medals in precedence of wearing.

With few exceptions, medals are worn on the left breast. This regulation aims at uniformity and trimness of dress. This military tradition is observed by the armies of every nation in the world, and points to a common origin. Practical considerations also influenced the choice of position, the left arm carried the fighter's shield which thus guarded the heart and allowed the right arm to be free to wield a weapon. To protect the badge of honour, this was placed behind the shield on the left side of the shoulder over the heart.

The British System

The evolution in Britain of Orders of Chivalry over many centuries was the foundation of the system of honours and awards that exist today. Excluding awards restricted to the Royal Family, there have been fourteen Imperial orders established since the first was introduced in 1348.[366] Of the nine surviving orders of chivalry Australians have received recognition in all of them.

Medals as decorations for bravery were first instituted by King Charles I (r. 1625-1649) who, in 1643, ordered medals for gallantry to be distributed to certain soldiers who had demonstrated 'merited valour and loyal service'.[367] One such award was given to CAPT John Smith (of Lord Grandison's Regiment of Horse), who at the *Battle of Edge Hill*, the year before this proclamation, had rescued the King's Standard that had been lost during the battle. The King being so pleased with the efforts of CAPT Smith, after the battle knighted him[368], therefore making him the last Knight Banneret created in England.[369]

Later medals were also issued to officers and men who were victorious against the Dutch fleet in 1653 and again after Lord Howe's victory in 1794 a naval medal was instituted. The first medal to be issued to both officers and men of the British Army was the Waterloo Medal, minted and issued in 1816.

---

366 Maton M. *Imperial Honours and Awards to Australians 1901-1992.* St Ives, NSW: 1996, p. 29
367 Gordon LL. *British Battles and Medals (7th edition).* Gale Aldershot, Naval and Military Press: 1962 p.2
368 Carlton C. *Going to the Wars: The Experience of the British Civil Wars, 1638-1651.* e-Library, Taylor & Francis: 2003, p. 193
369 Sidney L. *Dictionary of National Biography Volume LIII Smith-Stanger.* London, Smith Elder & Co: 1898, p. 74

Imperial Orders and the Order of St John

*Knight of the Order of St Michael
and St George – KCMG*

*Companion of the Order of St Michael
and St George – CMG*

*Knight of Justice of the Venerable Order
of St John of Jerusalem – KStJ[12]*

*Knight Commander of the Order
of the Bath – KCB*

*Commander of the Order
of the Bath – CB*

*Commander of the Order
of the British Empire - Military Division – CBE*

*Officer of the Order of the
British Empire - Military Division – OBE*

*Member of the British Empire
- Military Division – MBE*

*British Empire Medal
- Civil Division – BEM*

Awards for Bravery

As there were no permanent awards instituted for bravery for other ranks, awards such as the Meritorious Service Medal (1845), a type of long service and good conduct award was often used instead. It was not until the Crimean War that it was decided to award common soldiers medals in recognition for acts of gallantry. In 1854, the Distinguished Conduct Medal (DCM) was introduced to give recognition to acts of gallantry by other ranks.[370] Two years later Queen Victoria approved a second award for extreme gallantry, to be given to any member of a force regardless of rank. Indeed it was also to be awarded to civilians who qualified under the same conditions, and was named, in honour of Her Majesty, the 'Victoria Cross'.

As successive conflicts became longer and bloodier than those before, it was found that there was a requirement to recognise distinguished service and gallantry in varying degrees. Awards were also introduced that were rank-specific such as the Military Cross (1914), which was only available to officers and warrant officers. In fact this two-tiered system of awards extended throughout the military and included such awards as long service decorations for which part-time officers (officers of the permanent forces were not entitled to long service awards) were entitled to post-nominal letters, signifying an award, whereas other ranks were not entitled to use post-nominal letters for the equivalent other rank award, which was generally awarded for the same length of service. This rank-biased system was abolished following a major review of the Imperial system in 1992 and all gallantry awards are made on merit, not rank.

Early Development of Campaign Medals and Clasps

The man who can be credited with making military awards universal was Napoleon Bonaparte who, in 1802, established the *Legion d'Honneur* (Legion of Honour), a decoration for both bravery and merit, which could be bestowed on anybody, from a Marshal of France to the newest-joined recruit. Bonaparte was quoted as saying '*Donnez-moi assez ruban et je vais encercler le globe*' ('Give me enough ribbon and I shall encircle the globe'), and '*C'est avec ces babioles que les hommes sont conduits*' ('It is with such baubles that men are led').

While Bonaparte was the first to establish a universal decoration, available to every man and woman, the Empire never established any type of campaign medal, let alone a medal for all ranks. The credit for this must go to the British and, specifically, the much maligned Prince Regent (later King George IV), who decreed that a medal be struck to commemorate the Battle of Waterloo (18th June 1815) and that it should be presented to all ranks, not just officers.

Although titled 'The Waterloo Medal', and named after the Battle of the same name, it was also issued to those who took part in the earlier battles at 'Ligny' and 'Quatre Bras', both of which occurred on 6th June 1815. It was also the first time that any medal had been officially named with the recipient's regimental details.[371] In later times medals would take many years to be approved and issued with most being unnamed.

The next development in campaign medals took over 20 years to occur. The British Honourable East India Company (HEIC) was for a time at the forefront of this progress. Although a privately-run trading company (established 1757), it had developed a large military force primarily used to enforce the Company's will on the local population. Some of the first campaign medals were produced to give official recognition by the Honourable Company to both local and British Imperial troops engaged in what became known as the First Afghan War (1839-1842). The area encompassing Afghanistan and modern-day Pakistan became a regular battleground for the British armies based in India over the next 80 years.

The first medals were used to commemorate specific battles in the same manner that battle honours were presented to regiments for outstanding conduct during a particular battle or siege. The Ghuznee Medal was presented to all those who took part in the taking of the Fortress of the same name. The Ruler of Afghanistan at the time rewarded all those involved by presenting the Order of the Dooanee Empire to all officers of field rank and above and having a medal struck using the same ribbon of the Order for all others involved.

370 Litherland AR, Simpkin BT. *Spink's Standard Catalogue of British and Associated Orders, Decorations and Medals, With Valuations.* London, Spink: 1990, p. 57

371 Litherland AR, Simpkin BT. *Spink's Standard Catalogue of British and Associated Orders, Decorations and Medals, With Valuations.* London, Spink: 1990, p. 87

Decorations and Awards

Victoria Cross

Albert Medal

George Cross

Distinguished Service Order

Military Cross

Distinguished Flying Cross

Distinguished Conduct Medal 1854

George Medal

*Military Medal
(Reverse)*

The next campaign in the war to pacify the region occurred between October 1841 and October 1842 and involved the securing of three major towns within the area of operations, namely Candahar (Kandahar), Ghuznee and Cabul (Kabul). The method used to give recognition for this campaign was somewhat unusual in that there were four medals produced; each had the same obverse, the diademed head of Queen Victoria, and the same rainbow-patterned ribbon common to all HEIC medals of the period. However, the reverse of the medal, although similar in design, having a laurel wreath surmounted by a crown, differed in the centre wording, which was changed depending on which parts of the Campaign the individual took part. The four different inscriptions emboldened on the reverse: Ghuznee-Cabul, Candahar, Candahar-Ghuznee-Cabul, and Cabul. Two of these medals had very limited strikes with the Ghuznee-Cabul (360 issued) and the Candahar Medal (130 issued).[372] Each Medal had the date 1842 below the name of the battle.

There were two further battles that took place in 1842; Jellalabad and the Defence of Kelat–I–Ghilzie, both of which were recognised by the issue of medals with the distinctive ribbon of the HEIC.

Following the end of the First Afghan War and the withdrawal of British and Indian troops, the Amirs of Scinde (in modern-day Pakistan) opened hostilities against the British forces. The first task of the new force assembled, under MAJGEN Sir Charles Napier, to negate this threat, was the destruction of the fort of Emaum Gur, situated in the desert. During the siege, MAJGEN Napier began naming, in his official despatches, NCOs and men who had distinguished themselves during the conflict.

Imperial Campaign Medals

Although Mentioning in Despatches as a form of military recognition had been in use since at least the 17th century, up until the Scinde Campaign only officers were mentioned. MAJGEN Napier's innovation was to extend this recognition to ranks other than officers. This manner of recognition was to develop into what became known as Mentioned in Despatches (MID),[373] an additional method of award fully developed during WWI.

The Scinde Campaign which followed had a total of two major engagements over the period 6th January to 24th March 1843. They were at the town of Meeance on the Indus River and Dubba (then known as Dubbo and the likely reason for the naming of modern-day Dubbo in New South Wales first settled six years after the battle) on the outskirts

of Hyderabad.[374] Both of these victories were commemorated with the issue of a medal. There were three versions, each having the same obverse and ribbon (HEIC-pattern) and, as with the medals issued for the First Afghan War, they varied on the reverse by having the names of the battles (Meeance, Hyderabad, and Meeance-Hyderabad), each above the date 1843 and again surrounded by a laurel wreath surmounted by the royal crown.

The final medal issued by the HEIC was for the Gwalior Campaign, touted as the shortest campaign in history, lasting a total of one day. On 29th December 1843, two separate columns engaged the enemy on the same day when they crossed the border at Maharajpoor and the other near the town of Punniar. Two near identical medals were struck to commemorate this victory, both in the shape of a star showing on the obverse the date '29th Dec' and around the date the name of the action for which it was awarded, either Maharajpoor or Punniar. Naturally as the actions occurred on the same day no one person could be awarded both.

The first medal to be awarded with bars or clasps to both officers and men, (indicating the awardee's presence at multiple actions), was for the Sutlej Campaign that took place three years later in 1846. However, like those issued before, this medal continued to be made as an individual award. Each medal was made with the name of the first action minted on the reverse with extra awards being shown by additional clasps. The campaign resulted in four actions for which the award could be made (Moodkee, Ferozeshuhur, Aliwal and Sobraon). This new style of striking still required the production of four different medals for the one campaign, a cost which the British Government would in time review.

In 1847 the British Government introduced two new medals that would standardise the system of awards and reduce costs. The new awards were the Naval General Service Medal 1793-1840 and the Military General Service Medal 1793-1814.

It would seem that the dates selected for the naming convention of the Military Medal (1793-1814), were chosen to align it with those of the Naval Medal and not to recognise any particular military action of that period. In fact the first clasp issued for the medal was for 'Egypt 1801'. A total of 29 clasps were approved for this medal, which was not issued without at least one clasp; 21 of the clasps were directly associated with the Peninsular War 1808-1814. The design of the medal showed the diademed head of Queen Victoria with the words 'VICTORIA REGINA' and the date the medal was struck, 1848. The reverse depicts Queen Victoria standing on a dais about to place a laurel wreath on the head of a kneeling Duke of Wellington.

372 Joslin EC, Litherland AR, Simpkin BT, Gordon LL. *British Battles & Medals.* London, Spink: 1988, p. 160

373 Litherland AR, Simpkin BT. *Spink's Standard Catalogue of British and Associated Orders, Decorations and Medals, With Valuations.* London, Spink: 1990, p. 91

374 Joslin EC, Litherland AR, Simpkin BT, Gordon LL. *British Battles & Medals.* London, Spink: 1988, p.167

Imperial Campaign Medals

Waterloo Medal 1815 (reverse)

Ghuznee Medal 1839

Candahar Medal 1842 (reverse)

Gwalior Campaign Maharajpoor Star 1843

Sutlej Medal 1845

Military General Service 1793-1814

Crimea 1854

Kabul to Kandahar Star 1880

Queen's South Africa Medal 1899-1902

Imperial Long Service Medals

Long Service and Good Conduct Medal (permanent forces)

Volunteer Officers' Decoration 1892

Colonial Auxiliary Forces Officers' Decoration 1899

Volunteer Long Service Medal – 1894

Efficiency Decoration Officers – 1930

Efficiency Medal – 1930

Efficiency Decoration Officers – 1953

Efficiency Medal – 1953

Long Service and Good Conduct Medal – Military

Pre-Federation System of Awards

Prior to 1901, each Australian colony was responsible directly to the Colonial Office of the British Government, each having direct access to the Imperial system of awards and would nominate their citizens as required each year for recognition in the Monarch's birthday honours list.

The number of awards available to the different colonies for either civil or military achievement varied in accordance with a quota system. This system required that all colonies within the Empire were given an allocation dependant on their population. This meant that the small colonies of Australia seldom received a mention.

The only awards available for distinguished service within the military were either an appointment to the military division of the Order of the Bath (1725), the Distinguished Service Order (DSO) (1886-1923), or the Order of St Michael and St George (KCMG/DCMG/CMG) (1818). These orders could only be conferred on an officer holding the minimum rank of MAJ and it was therefore rare for such awards to be made.

During the conflicts involving Australian troops in the pre-Federation period only four appointments to Imperial orders were made. They were a Companion of the Order of the Bath (CB); a Companion of the Order of St Michael and St George (CMG) for the Sudan campaign in 1885; and two CMGs for the China War of 1900.

The VC was awarded to three soldiers in the months leading up to Federation; these were: CAPT NR Howse (July 1900), TPR JH Bisdee and LT GG Wylly (September 1900).

Post-Federation System of Awards

Little changed in the awards system after Federation; the States still maintained their right of direct access to the Colonial Office; State rights of any kind were jealously guarded and only given up under special circumstances. Even though the Commonwealth Government was seen as an additional entity within Australia, the Colonial Office would not increase the number of awards available. Therefore the same allocation based on the country's population had to be shared differently, and at times to the detriment of the Commonwealth.

All honours at this time were notified first in the *London Gazette* (LG) and then secondly in the applicable State gazette. After Federation all honours were promulgated in the *Commonwealth of Australia Gazette* (CAG), including military long service and good conduct awards. In the 1990s, due to a staff shortage at Government House, a decision was made to exclude military long service awards from this publication, although non-military long service awards are still recorded.

Honours were announced once a year on The Sovereign's birthday (the date of which varied in accordance with the wishes of the Monarch). During the reign of King Edward VII, the date selected was '30th June for Home Stations and 30th November for Other Stations'. In 1911, a new List was added to the existing Birthday List, the 'New Year's Honours List' to allow for greater recognition to be given, which eventually evolved into the Australia Day Honours List first announced on 26th January 1990.

Australian Honours and Awards

Creation of a separate Australian Honours system took many years to introduce, starting as early as 1918 when the Labor Party adopted a policy of not recommending Australian citizens for Imperial Honours.

Through the intervening years attempts were made to replace the British system, but it was not until the Whitlam[375] Government took office in 1972 that the Australian Government was able to introduce a wholly-Australian system.

The Canadian Government had introduced its own system, commencing with the Order of Canada in 1967, and as this was the only Commonwealth country to have its own system, Australia modelled its system along similar lines.

---

375 Edward Gough Whitlam, AC, QC; barrister, politician, Prime Minister 1972-1975: born Melbourne 11 July 1916 – died Sydney 21 October 2014.

Top: Knight/Dame of the Order of Australia

Far Right: Companion of the Order of Australia

Bottom Right: Officer of the Order of Australia

The New System

Maintaining the age-old custom of the Monarch being the fount of all honours, Queen Elizabeth II established the Order of Australia on 14th February 1975.[376] The new Order consisted of a Civil (later named General) Division and a Military Division, the general division taking precedence, with each division having the same four levels and each level carrying a post-nominal entitlement. The Governor-General of Australia was appointed Chancellor of the Order and Principal Companion of the Civil Division.

The Order initially comprised three levels in each division: a Companion (AC), an Officer (AO) and a Member (AM). With the return of the Liberal Government in 1975, two awards were added – that of Knight and Dame of the Order (AK/AD). This new order ranked above the AC and was restricted to two appointments per year, making it an extremely rare award. This new level (Knight and Dame) was removed from the 'Order' in January 1986; and the Medal of the Order of Australia (OAM) was added, ranking below the Member of the Order (AM). As the OAM was a medal, a recipient was originally not actually appointed to the Order of Australia. This was amended in 1993 to formally admit

the OAM to the Order. In 2014 Her Majesty The Queen approved the reinstatement of the appointment of Knights and Dames of the Order of Australia. These additions may only be awarded within the General Division and in addition to the statutory appointment of the current Governor-General, are restricted to a maximum of four Knights or Dames annually.

When introduced, the new system also included the National Medal and a group of Bravery Medals. The National Medal was introduced to recognise diligent and long service in the various uniformed services including the Navy, Army, Air Force, Police, Fire Services and Ambulance Services. This award did not prove popular with the ADF as it was felt that the ADF's unique conditions of service justified a separate award. In 1982, new long service awards were introduced for the Defence Force, recognising three different levels, namely the Permanent Force and two separate awards for the Reserve Force mirroring the old Efficiency Decoration and Medal.

Bravery Medals in the Australian Honours System are the Cross of Valour (CV), the Star of Courage (SC), the Bravery Medal (BM) and the Commendation for Brave Conduct.

Rather than replace the British system, the new Order of Australia and bravery medals were integrated with the existing system entitling Australians to continue to be nominated for British awards, including those carrying titles.

In 1986, the Government again introduced changes to the system by adding new awards for the ADF designed specifically to replace the many British awards for gallantry, distinguished service, campaign service and other categories. The Australian Conspicuous Service Decorations were established in 1989 to recognise outstanding performance, meritorious achievement and devotion to duty. The VC however was retained and instituted by Letters Patent as an Australian Award in 1991.

In February 1990, the Queen's Private Secretary, Sir William Heseltine (a Western Australian), wrote to the Governor-General of Australia, stating that the Queen: 'feels . . . that it is more appropriate at this stage in Australia's development that Australian citizens should be recognised exclusively by an Australian system of honours, of which she herself is proud to be The Sovereign'.[377] The Prime Minister, in 1992, announced that no further recommendations would be made for British honours.

376 Australia, Commonwealth of. *Australian Government Gazette Special 28.* Canberra: 17 February 1975

377 Petre C. *Review of Australian Honours and Awards: A matter of honour.* Canberra, Australian Government Publishing Service: 1995, p. 21

Order of Australia

There are two divisions within the Order; general and military (the general division takes precedence over the military division). Each division has the same four levels and each level carries a post-nominal entitlement.

The symbol of the Order is represented by a single Acacia pycnantha (Golden Wattle) flower which is Australia's national floral emblem. The flowers of the tree, which bloom in late winter and spring, produce a mass of fragrant, fluffy, golden blooms.

Knight/Dame of the Order of Australia (AK/AD) is bestowed upon persons for extraordinary and pre-eminent achievement and merit in service to Australia or to humanity at large. The neck badge of a Knight and the shoulder badge of a Dame consist of the emblem of the Order, approximately 60mm in diameter, of gold, inlayed with scattered citrines[378] quartz and having in the centre of its convex surface, within a circle of gold, a representation of the arms of the Commonwealth of Australia in full colour on a background of blue with two branches of mimosa, the whole ensigned with the crown of St Edward, proper (in full colour).

On recommendation of the Prime Minister, Anthony Abbott MP, on 25th March 2014, Her Majesty the Queen again amended the Letters Patent for the Order of Australia re-instituting the level of Knight and Dame.

Only two Knights of the Order with military backgrounds have been appointed since its inception, they are, Sir Roden Cutler VC AK KCMG KCVO CBE (appointed on 7th April 1981) and Sir Peter Cosgrove AK, AC (Mil), MC, on appointment as Governor-General on 28th March 2014.

Companion of the Order of Australia (AC) bestowed upon persons for eminent achievement and merit of the highest degree in service to Australia or humanity at large in the general division, and for eminent service in duties of great responsibility in the military division. The insignia of a Companion of the Order is a badge consisting of the emblem of the Order, approximately 60mm in diameter, of gold, inlayed with scattered citrines quartz, surmounted by the crown of St Edward, proper (in full colour) and having in the centre of its convex surface a circlet of blue enamel edged in gold, inscribed with the word 'AUSTRALIA' in gold and containing two sprigs of mimosa in gold.

Officer of the Order of Australia (AO) bestowed upon persons for distinguished service to a high degree to Australia or to humanity at large in the general division and for distinguished service in a responsible position in the military division. The insignia of an Officer of the Order is a badge consisting of the emblem of the Order, approximately 55mm in diameter, of silver gilt, with the adornment of the crown of St Edward, proper (in full colour) and having in the centre of its convex surface a circlet of blue enamel edged in gold, inscribed with the word 'AUSTRALIA' in gold and containing two sprigs of mimosa in gold.

---

378 'Citrine' is a variety of quartz whose color ranges from a pale yellow to brown. Natural citrines are rare; most commercial citrines are heat-treated amethyst. Citrine contains traces of Fe^{3+} and is rarely found naturally. The name is derived from Latin citrina which means 'yellow'.

Member of the Order of Australia (AM) bestowed upon persons for service in a particular locality or field of activity, or to a particular group in the general division, and for exceptional service or performance of duty in the military division. The insignia of a Member of the Order is a badge consisting of the emblem of the Order, approximately 45mm in diameter, of silver gilt, with the adornment of the crown of St Edward, proper (in full colour) and having in the centre of its convex surface a circlet of the same material as the emblem containing the word 'AUSTRALIA' and containing two sprigs of mimosa.

Medal of the Order of Australia (OAM) bestowed upon persons for service worthy of particular recognition in the general division, and for meritorious service or performance of duty in the military division. The Medal of the Order shall consist of the emblem of the Order, approximately 40mm in diameter, of silver gilt, with the adornment of the crown of St Edward in silver gilt and having in the centre of its convex surface a circlet of the same material as the emblem containing the word 'AUSTRALIA' and containing two sprigs of mimosa. The Medal of the Order, when worn on uniform shall be worn on the left breast suspended from a bar attached to a riband 32mm wide and of the same pattern as the riband of the Order.

Top: Member of the Order of Australia

Left: Medal of the Order of Australia

The Riband of the Order of Australia

The riband of the Order of Australia in the general division is a ribbon of moiré[379] Royal blue silk, between 36 to 38mm wide, depending on the level of the Order, with a central band 12mm wide featuring scattered golden mimosa blossoms of various sizes. The mimosa design is repeated every 6.3cm and is described as a 'non-reversible repetitive pattern'. The riband of the Order in the military division is a ribbon as described for the general division with the addition of a gold band 1.5mm wide on each edge of the riband.

The Victoria Cross

The VC was instituted by Queen Victoria on 29th January 1856 and was made retrospective from 1st August 1854, so as to encompass the beginning of the Crimean War. Prior to the Crimean War (1854-1856), there was no recognised gallantry medal available to all ranks of the British Army. The Instituting Royal Warrant established the rules and ordinances governing its bestowal stating that it:

> Shall only be awarded for the most conspicuous bravery or some daring or pre-eminent act of valour or self-sacrifice or extreme devotion to duty in the presence of the enemy.

Regardless of this requirement since its introduction, six VCs have been awarded for valour not in the face of the enemy. Civilians are also eligible to be awarded the VC, if serving with one of the armed forces. Four civilians have received the award since it was instituted.

After the Gwalior Campaign in India had ended in 1843 some of the enemy guns captured during the fighting were used to produce a medal to commemorate the two major battles fought at both Maharajpoor and Punniar. The Gwalior Star[380] as it became known was the first recorded time that part of the enemy's arsenal was used to produce a medal. Likewise the VC is made from the Russian cannons captured at Sebastopol (September 1854), during the Crimean War.

The VC design is in the form of a Maltese cross featuring the Royal Cypher, a lion guardant upon the Royal Crown, surmounted on a scroll containing the words 'For Valour'. The suspension bar is decorated with laurel leaves and incorporates a 'V', (for Queen Victoria), from which the cross is attached by a metal ring. The medal is suspended from a riband of crimson silk 38mm wide (most medal ribands are 32mm wide). The original Warrant (Clause 2-1856) specification for the award stated that the ribbon should be red for Army

recipients and blue for naval recipients. However the dark blue ribbon was abolished soon after the formation of the Royal Air Force on 1st April 1918. On 22nd May 1920 King George V signed a Warrant that stated all recipients would now receive a red ribbon, and the living recipients of the naval version were required to exchange their ribbons for the new colour. Although the Army Warrants state the colour as being red it is defined by most as being crimson or 'wine-red'.

The reverse of the VC is inscribed with more detail than other medals; however due to its size, the recipient's service number, rank, name and unit are shown on the suspension bar whilst the date of the action is engraved on the reverse centre of the medal.

It is tradition that whenever possible the reigning Monarch presents the award at an official investiture ceremony.

The medal was valued in 1904 at 4½ pence (approximately 4 cents in today's currency), and although critics have said it is of poor design, it remains the most highly-prized decoration that a British or Commonwealth soldier can be awarded.

The question of which awards qualify as an Australian VC is difficult to explain. For instance, the first Australian VC recipient has always been attributed to CAPT Neville

Military Division Riband

Ribbon Bar

Left: Layout of engraving conventions used on the reverse of the Victoria Cross

---

379 The term 'moiré' originates from moire, or *moiré* in its French form, a type of textile, traditionally of silk but can also be of cotton or synthetic fibre, with a rippled or 'watered' appearance.

380 Litherland AR, Simpkin BT. *Spink's Standard Catalogue of British and Associated Orders, Decorations and Medals, With Valuations.* London, Spink: 1990, p. 91

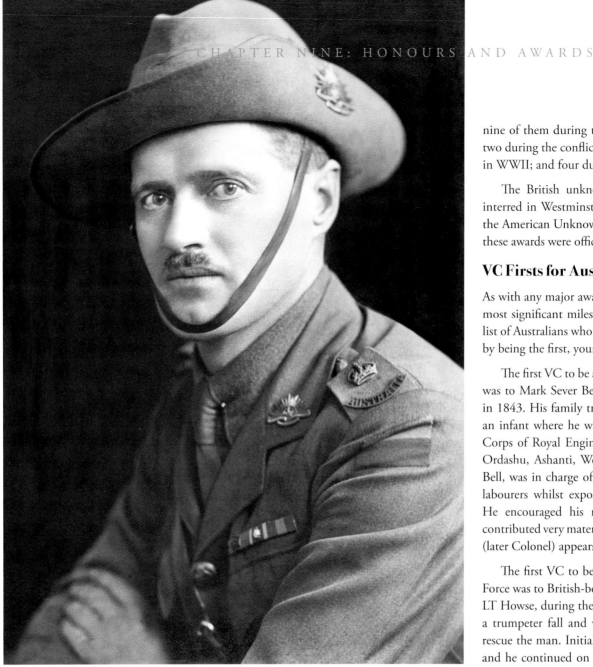

AWM Neg No. PO2939.053
Lt Col H.W. Murray

nine of them during the Gallipoli Campaign with a further two during the conflict in Russia after the war; 20 for actions in WWII; and four during the Vietnam War.

The British unknown warrior of the 1914-1918 War, interred in Westminster Abbey was awarded the VC as was the American Unknown Warrior of the same war. Neither of these awards were officially gazetted.[381]

VC Firsts for Australians

As with any major award it is interesting to note some of the most significant milestones in its history. The following is a list of Australians who have achieved a special place in history by being the first, youngest, oldest and most decorated.

The first VC to be awarded to a soldier of Australian-birth was to Mark Sever Bell who was born in New South Wales in 1843. His family travelled to England whilst LT Bell was an infant where he was educated and eventually joined the Corps of Royal Engineers. As a Lieutenant at the Battle of Ordashu, Ashanti, West Africa, on 4th February 1874, LT Bell, was in charge of an unarmed working party of Fantee labourers whilst exposed to both enemy and friendly fire. He encouraged his men to continue working and thus contributed very materially to the success of the battle. LT Bell (later Colonel) appears on the list of British VC recipients.

The first VC to be awarded to a soldier of an Australian Force was to British-born Neville Howse, on 24th July 1900. LT Howse, during the action at Vredefort, South Africa, saw a trumpeter fall and went through very heavy cross-fire to rescue the man. Initially his horse was shot from under him and he continued on foot, reached the casualty, dressed his wound and then carried him to safety.

The first VCs awarded to Australian-born soldiers, serving in an Australian Colonial Contingent, were also in the 2nd Boer War and were earned by TPR Bisdee and LT Wylly on the 1st September 1900 during the same action. Both were members of the Colonial Force, the Tasmanian Bushmen. The action occurred near Warm Baths, Transvaal, South Africa; LT Wylly and TPR Bisdee were in the advance scouting party, passing through a narrow gorge, when the enemy suddenly opened fire at close range. Six out of the party of eight were wounded, including LT Wylly who, seeing that one of his men was badly wounded in the leg and that his horse had been shot, went back to aid him. He made the wounded man take his horse while he opened fire from behind a rock to cover the retreat of the others, at the imminent risk of being cut off. Meanwhile the horse of the other wounded officer bolted and TPR Bisdee dismounted, put him on his own horse and took him out of range of very heavy fire.

Howse who served as a doctor in the Boer War. When it is considered that CAPT Howse was born and educated in England, arriving in Australia after his 26th birthday, only months before he enlisted for service, it can hardly be claimed that he was an Australian. One method of assessing a claim to a VC as Australian is that the person in question must either be a member of a colonial State contingent, Australian Commonwealth military unit or an Australian-born citizen serving with a British Commonwealth military force. Strangely enough, these requirements do not include Australian citizens enlisting with British units as is shown by the case of COL Mark Sever Bell, VC, who, although born in Australia, after immigrating to England, enlisted in the British regular army and therefore his VC is counted amongst those of Britain.

A total of 96 Imperial Victoria Crosses have been awarded with 91 received for actions whilst serving with Australian forces and another five for actions whilst serving with South African and British forces. Of the total, six were awarded for actions in the 2nd Boer War; 64 were for actions in WWI,

381 http://www.nationalarchives.gov.uk/documentsonline/victoriacross.asp:
2 Aug 132 Aug 13

Frederick William Bell was the first 'colonial' to be awarded a VC. LT Bell was born on 3 April 1875 in Perth, Western Australia. He was 26 years old, and a Lieutenant in the 1st West Australian (Mounted Infantry) Contingent, during the 2nd Boer War. On 16th May 1901, at Brakpan, Transvaal, South Africa, while under heavy fire, LT Bell noticed a dismounted man. He immediately returned and took the man up on the rear of his horse, but the horse not being equal to the weight fell. The Lieutenant then remained behind, covering the man's retreat until he was out of danger.

The most highly-decorated Australian was LTCOL HW (Mad Harry) Murray, VC, CMG, DSO and Bar, DCM, *Croix de Guerre* (France). Murray rose from the rank of PTE to LTCOL in three-and-a-half years of war. He is often described as the highest decorated infantry soldier of the British Empire during WWI1.

The youngest Australian to be awarded the VC was PTE JWA Jackson, VC, of the 17th Battalion during WWI; he was 18 years 9 months. The oldest recipient was 44 years 11 months of age and was also the highest ranking, LTCOL CGW Anderson, VC, MC, of the 2/19th Battalion.

In every conflict that Australians have fought in since the 2nd Boer War to WWII, the vast numbers of soldiers enlisted were drawn from either the Militia or the civil community. Because there was only a very small permanent force, the number of permanent soldiers transferring to these volunteer forces was very small in comparison to the total force raised. Prior to the establishment of the Australian Regular Army (ARA) in September 1947, there had been at least two VC awarded to members of the Permanent Military Forces, being: CAPT James Newland, VC, and SGT John Whittle, VC, DCM. At the time of the award both men were members of the 12th Battalion, AIF. Both men had transferred from the PMF to serve with the AIF and after the war returned to continue to serve as full-time soldiers.

Victoria Cross for Australia

On 15th January 1991, the Queen instituted the Victoria Cross for Australia (VC) as the highest Australian award in the Australian Honours and Awards System. The decoration can be awarded to members of the ADF or other persons determined by the Minister for Defence. The VC may also be awarded posthumously and recipients are entitled to use the post-nominal letters VC. It is awarded to a person who, in the presence of the enemy, performs an act or acts of the most conspicuous gallantry, or daring or pre-eminent acts of valour or self-sacrifice, or display extreme devotion to duty. Bars may be awarded for further similar acts of bravery.

Other Commonwealth countries have followed Australia's lead with Canada adopting a new Canadian Victoria Cross in 1993 and New Zealand the Victoria Cross for New Zealand in 1999. These awards are separate from and not part of the original VC and therefore recipients of these awards do not appear on the official British list of recipients of the VC.[382]

The first person to be awarded the VC for Australia was TPR Mark Donaldson, for extreme heroism under fire whilst serving in Afghanistan. All four VC for Australia have been presented by the Governor-General of Australia, CPL Baird's being awarded posthumously to his parents.

The Australian Award is still hand-made by the original manufacturers, Hancocks Jewellers of London, and is still produced from the captured Sebastopol Guns from the Crimean War (there has been some conjecture that Chinese guns have also been used in the manufacture of the Medal but this is incorrect).

Saluting of Victoria Cross Recipients

It has become a recent practice at investiture ceremonies that VC recipients receive their award before any others, including those receiving a knighthood. An erroneous myth has grown that it is mandatory for all ranks to salute a recipient of a VC; there is no requirement for this stated in the original Warrant of the VC, nor is it mentioned in Queen's Regulations and Orders or within Army Regulations.

Image courtesy Department of Defence – 20110123adf8262658_520. Victoria Cross for Australia Recipients Mark Donaldson, VC, Benjamin Roberts-Smith, VC, MG, with Mr Keith Payne, VC

---

382 http://www.nationalarchives.gov.uk/documentsonline/victoriacross.asp

Australian Recipients of the Victoria Cross

BOER WAR
BELL FW
BISDEE JH
HOWSE NR
MAYGAR LC
ROGERS SJ
WYLLY GG

WORLD WAR I
AXFORD TL
BEATHAM RM
BIRKS F
BLACKBURN S
BORELLA A
BROWN WE
BUCKLEY AH
BUCKLEY MV
BUGDEN PJ
BURTON AS
CARROL J
CARTWRIGHT G
CASTLETON CC
CHERRY PH
COOKE T
CURREY WM
DALZIEL H
DARTNELL WT
DAVEY P
DUNSTAN W
DWYER JJ
GABY AE
GORDON BS
GRIEVE RC
HALL AC
HAMILTON JP
HOWELL GJ
INGRAM GM
INWOOD RR

JACKA A
JACKSON JWA
JEFFRIES CS
JENSEN JC
JOYNT WD
KENNY TJB
KEYSOR LM
LEAK J
LOWERSON AD
MACTIER R
MAXWELL J
McCARTHY LD
McDOUGALL SR
McGEE L
McNAMARA FH
MOON RV
MURRAY HW
NEWLAND JE
O'MEARA M
PEELER W
POPE C
RUTHVEN W
RYAN J
SADLIER CWK
SEXTON G (aka
BUCKLEY MV)
SHOUT AJ
STATTON PC
STORKEY PV
SYMONS WJ
THROSSELL HVH
TOWNER ET
TUBB FH
WARK BA
WEATHERS LC
WHITTLE JW
WOODS JP

RUSSIA
PEARSE SG
SULLIVAN AP

WORLD WAR II
ANDERSON GW
CHOWNE A
CUTLER AR
DERRICK TC
EDMONDSON JH
EDWARDS HI
FRENCH JA
GORDON JH
GRATWICK PE
GURNEY AS
KELLIHER R
KENNA E
KIBBY WH
KINGSBURY BS
MACKEY JB
MIDDLETON RH
NEWTON WE
PARTRIDGE FJ
RATTEY RR
STARCEVICH LT

VIETNAM
BADCOE P
PAYNE K
SIMPSON RS
WHEATLEY KA

**Victoria Cross
for Australia:**

AFGHANISTAN
DONALDSON M
ROBERTS-SMITH B
KEIGHRAN DA
BAIRD CS

Left: Star of Gallantry

Middle: Medal for Gallantry

Right: Commendation for Gallantry

Gallantry Awards

The Gallantry Awards were established on 15th January 1991 to accord recognition to members of the Defence Force, and certain other persons, for outstanding heroism or gallantry in action. There are three levels of the award; the Star of Gallantry (SG), the Medal for Gallantry (MG), and the Commendation for Gallantry. The Star and Medal carry the post-nominal entitlements SG and MG respectively. These decorations may be awarded posthumously.

Star of Gallantry (SG) is a gold-plated silver Federation Star surmounted with the crown of St Edward in gold-plated silver. The obverse has a superimposed central device of a smaller Federation Star surrounded and partly overlapped by stylised flames representing action under fire. The reverse bears a central horizontal panel on a stepped background for the name of the recipient. The Star is suspended from a bar which is an integral part of the Star and is slotted to take the riband. The suspender bar has the words 'FOR GALLANTRY' embossed upon it. The riband is 32mm wide and has chevrons of deep orange alternating with chevrons of light orange, angled at 60 degrees as a stylised 'A' (for Australia).

Medal for Gallantry (MG) is a circular gold-plated silver medal 38mm in diameter surmounted by the crown of St Edward. The obverse bears a central device of a Federation Star surrounded by stylised flames representing action under fire. The medal is suspended from a bar which is an integral part of the Star and is slotted to take the riband. The suspender bar has the words 'FOR GALLANTRY' embossed upon it. The riband is 32mm wide and has chevrons of deep orange alternating with chevrons of light orange, angled at 60 degrees as a stylised 'A' (for Australia).

Commendation for Gallantry is an emblem consisting of a Federation Star superimposed centrally on a row of flames. The commendation is attached to a plain orange riband 32mm wide and 90mm in length. The commendation is placed centrally and 19mm from the bottom of the riband.

Above: Cross of Valour

Left: Star of Courage

Middle: Bravery Medal

Right: Commendation for Brave Conduct

Bravery Awards

The Australian Bravery Decorations originally consisted of the Cross of Valour (CV), the Star of Courage (SC), the Bravery Medal (BM) and the Commendation for Brave Conduct. In 1990, a Group Bravery Citation was added. These awards recognised brave conduct in other than warlike situations and although mainly a civil award, they can also be awarded to members of the military. The Cross, Star and Medal carry the post-nominal entitlements of CV, SV and BM respectively. These decorations may be awarded posthumously.

Cross of Valour (CV) is a gold, straight-armed cross pattée (triangular arms, narrow at the centre and broadening to squared ends) 42mm across with diminishing rays between the arms, and surmounted with the Crown of St Edward. The obverse has the Coat of Arms of Australia, minus supporters, placed centrally within the cross. The cross is suspended from a bar which is an integral part of the cross and is slotted to take the riband. The suspender bar has the words 'FOR VALOUR' embossed upon it. The magenta-coloured riband is 38mm wide and has a central blood-red band 16mm wide.

Star of Courage (SC) is a silver seven-pointed ribbed star 50mm across surmounted with the Crown of St Edward. The obverse has the Coat of Arms of Australia, minus supporters, placed centrally within the Star. The Star is suspended from a bar which is an integral part of the Star and is slotted to take the

riband. The suspender bar has the words 'FOR COURAGE' embossed upon it. The blood-red-coloured riband is 32mm wide and has a central magenta band 14mm wide.

Bravery Medal (BM) is a circular bronze medal, 38mm in diameter surmounted with the Crown of St Edward. The obverse has the Coat of Arms of Australia, minus supporters, placed centrally within a circular zigzag border. The reverse has a similar design minus the Coat of Arms. The Medal is suspended from a bar which is an integral part of the Medal and is slotted to take the riband. The suspender bar has the words 'FOR BRAVERY' embossed upon it. The riband is 32mm wide and has 15 alternating stripes of blood-red and magenta.

Commendation for Brave Conduct is an emblem consisting of a silver gilt sprig of mimosa 30mm long mounted on a blood-red riband 32mm wide and 90mm long. The centre of the sprig is 19mm from the bottom and placed centrally on the riband at an angle of 45 degrees with the stem of the sprig pointing to the bottom left of the riband. When worn with other orders, decorations or medals the bottom of the riband is level with the bottom edge of the other medals so that the sprig is approximately level with the centre of the other medals. This award has no post-nominal.

Group Bravery Citation was introduced on 5th March 1990 and is a Warrant awarded for a collective act of bravery by a group of people in extraordinary circumstances. The insignia of the award consists of a bronze gilt sprig of wattle, Australia's floral emblem, positioned in the centre of a silver rectangle.

Distinguished Service Awards

The Distinguished Service Awards were established 15th January 1991, to recognise distinguished command and leadership in action, or distinguished performance of duty in warlike operations by members of the Defence Force and certain other persons. There are three levels of the award: the Distinguished Service Cross (DSC); the Distinguished Service Medal (DSM); and the Commendation for Distinguished Service (no post-nominal). These decorations may be awarded posthumously:

Distinguished Service Cross (DSC) is a modified Maltese cross of nickel-silver surmounted by the Crown of St Edward. The obverse shows a Federation Star superimposed on a circle of flames centrally placed on the cross. The reverse bears a raised horizontal panel for the recipient's details. The cross is suspended from a riband, 32mm wide, having a vertical stripe 16mm wide of ochre-red flanked by two silver-blue stripes each 8mm wide.

Distinguished Service Medal (DSM) is a 38mm diameter nickel-silver circular medal surmounted by the Crown of St Edward. The obverse bears the Federation Star superimposed on a circle of flames. The reverse bears a raised horizontal panel for the recipient's details; this panel is superimposed over a design of fluted rays of varying lengths.

Commendation for Distinguished Service is a 22mm long bar with a central 7mm high Federation Star on a nickel-silver row of flames. The Commendation for Distinguished Service insignia is mounted on a plain ochre-red riband.

Left: Distinguished Service Cross

Middle: Distinguished Service Medal

Right: Commendation for Distinguished Service

Left: Conspicuous Service Cross

Middle: Conspicuous Service Medal

Right: Nursing Service Cross

Conspicuous Service Awards

The Conspicuous Service Awards were established 18th October 1989 to recognise outstanding or meritorious achievement or devotion to duty in non-warlike situations by members of the Defence Force and certain other persons. There are two levels of the award, both of which carry post-nominal entitlements, being the Conspicuous Service Cross (CSC) and the Conspicuous Service Medal (CSM). Both awards may be awarded posthumously.

Conspicuous Service Cross (CSC)

The Award is a nickel-silver modified Maltese cross surmounted by the Crown of St Edward, with the arms of the cross interspersed with fluted rays. The obverse bears a central device of the Southern Cross surrounded by a laurel wreath. The reverse has a horizontal panel on to which is inscribed the recipient's details. The cross is suspended from a bar which is an integral part of the cross and is slotted to take the riband. The riband is 32mm wide and has alternating diagonal stripes of brush green and sandy-gold 6mm wide.

Conspicuous Service Medal (CSM)

The Award is a circular nickel-silver medal 38mm in diameter surmounted by the Crown of St Edward. The obverse has a central design of the Southern Cross surrounded by a laurel wreath. The reverse has a horizontal panel superimposed over a design of fluted rays. The Medal is suspended from a bar which is an integral part of the medal and is slotted to take the riband. The riband is 32mm wide and has alternating diagonal stripes of brush green and sandy-gold 3mm wide.

Nursing Service Cross

The Nursing Service Cross (NSC) was established 18th October 1989 to recognise outstanding performance of nursing duties in both operational and non-operational situations by members of the Defence Force, and certain other persons. The award carries the post-nominal entitlement of NSC. The design incorporates a four-stepped sterling silver, straight-armed cross surmounted by the Crown of St Edward. The obverse bears a transparent red enamel cross overlayed on a flecked pattern radiating from the centre of the Cross. The reverse has a horizontal panel superimposed on a design of fluted rays of varying lengths. The riband is 32mm wide with a central red vertical band 12mm wide flanked by two white 8mm bands, the riband is edged on both sides by a 2mm gold stripe. Second and subsequent awards are shown by a sterling silver bar with a 6mm red enamelled cross centrally superimposed on the bar which is attached to the riband of the award. The award may be awarded posthumously.

In October 2007, the VCDF announced the establishment of a review into Defence Honours, Awards and Commendations policies. This review was conducted with a focus to ensure the current system of recognition supported the men and women of the ADF from that time and into the future.

One of the recommendations of the review was that the Nursing Service Cross be retired. It was determined that the existing system provided ample opportunities for nurses to be recognised and concluded that the retention of an award to recognise the nursing service separately was anachronistic and should not be continued.

While the recommendation to retire the award was put forward to Government by Defence, Government did not want to retire the award; it was agreed that the award would be retained within the honour system; however that it would no longer be used; the CDF published a determination to this effect in March 2010.

Campaign Medals

Following the end of WWII Australian personnel continued to be entitled to Imperial war and campaign medals. These campaigns included the Korean War, the Malayan Emergency, Indonesian Confrontation and the Vietnam War. The Australian system of honours and awards introduced in 1975 includes campaign medals for warlike and non-warlike operational service after that date. The decision that there should be uniquely Australian medals awarded for service in the campaigns during the period 1945-1975 resulted in the introduction of the following:

- Australian Active Service Medal 1945-1975 (AASM 45-75)

- Korea Medal

- United Nations Service Medal for Korea

- General Service Medal 1918-1962

- General Service Medal 1962

- Vietnam Medal

- Vietnam Logistic and Support Medal

- Australian Service Medal 1945-1975 (ASM 45-75)

- Australian General Service Medal Korea.

There have been several campaign medals issued to Australians since 1975. Most of them have been introduced as part of the Australian system of honours and include medals to recognise service on warlike and non-warlike operational service after 1975. These campaign medals are:

- Australian Operational Service Medal (OSM)

- Australian Active Service Medal (AASM)

- International Force East Timor Medal

- Afghanistan Medal

- Iraq Medal

- Australian Service Medal (ASM)

- Rhodesia Medal

The AASM, Humanitarian Overseas Service Medal (HOSM), and ASM are issued with a clasp showing the name of the campaign for which the medal was awarded. The OSM is issued with a unique riband to denote the campaign for which it is issued; additional devices for each additional period of service in that campaign are attached to the riband.

Gallipoli Star

The Gallipoli Star[383] and its riband and ribbon were designed in 1917 by Mr RK Peacock, and approved by King George V in 1918. The medal was specifically for Australians and New Zealanders who had served at Gallipoli, but not British or other Empire soldiers involved in the campaign. Some ANZAC veterans are known to have been issued with lengths of ribbon during the war in anticipation of the medal's production. The medal was abandoned, when complaints were made in England that it could not be conferred on British troops. In 1990 Mr Ross Smith, a former Australian Army Warrant Officer and Vietnam veteran, arranged, at his own expense, for 'dies' from the original design to be manufactured, and for AJ Parkes & Co Pty Ltd of Brisbane, to strike 1000 examples of the medal. 200 of these stars were presented to surviving Australian and New Zealand Gallipoli veterans to mark the 75th anniversary of the campaign. The remainder were sold to the public. A further 1,000 were later struck for sale to collectors. The design features an eight-pointed star, representing the States and Territories of Australia (seven points) and New Zealand. The colours of the ribbon are blue, representing the Aegean Sea, gold, representing Australian Wattle, silver-grey, representing New Zealand fern, and red for the colour of Australian gum blossom and the New Zealand Rata flower.

---

383 The Age Newspaper. *The ANZAC Star That Never Shone.* Melbourne, Fairfax Media: 24 April 1990, p. 18

Campaign Medals

Australian Active Service Medal 1945-1975

Australian Service Medal 1945-1975

General Service Medal 1918-1962

Korea Medal (reverse)

Australian General Service Medal for Korea

Campaign Service Medal 1962

Vietnam Medal (reverse)

Vietnam Logistic and Support Medal

Australian Active Service Medal

Australian Service Medal

International Force East Timor Medal

Rhodesia Medal

Afghanistan Medal (reverse)

Iraq Medal (reverse)

Humanitarian Overseas Service Medal

National Emergency Medal

Australian Operational Service Medal (Border Protection)

Gallipoli Star (Unofficial)

Long Service Awards

The National Medal introduced in 1975 to recognise long service did not prove popular within the ADF community as there was a strong feeling that military service should be recognised separately from civil service organisations such as the fire and police service. Although the National Medal was retained for use by Federal and State uniformed service organisations, in 1982 new long service awards for the Australian Defence Force were established:

- The Defence Force Service Medal (DFSM) (for all permanent members of the Royal Australian Navy, Army and Royal Australian Air Force)

- The Reserve Force Decoration (RFD) (for Reserve service officers only)

- The Reserve Force Medal (for other ranks of the Reserve Forces).

Note: The RFD (1982-1998) replaced the imperial Efficiency Decoration (ED) which had likewise entitled the recipient to post-nominals. With its removal from the awards system the last link with Imperial rank distinctions for recognition of service was severed.

The Defence Long Service Medal (DLSM) was established 26th May 1998 by Letters Patent. The Medal replaced the existing three military long service awards. Service that previously would have gone unrecognised when individuals moved between Regular and Reserve Forces is now acknowledged by the Defence Long Service Medal. It does not discriminate between ranks or between Regular and Reserve service

Unclassified Medals

The medals in this section cannot be classified as either long service awards or campaign medals but are significant in that they have been issued to recognise commitment by a wide cross-section of Defence personnel.

Australian Defence Medal

The Australian Defence Medal was introduced to recognise the contribution of those who have served in the Australian Defence Force since the end of WWII and fulfilled their initial enlistment commitment, or served for four years, whichever is the lesser.

Champion Shots Medal

The Champion Shots Medal was established on 13th September 1988 to replace the Imperial King's/Queen's Medal for shooting. Each of the three Services may conduct target shooting competitions with standard issue weapons annually. Three medals, one for each force, are awarded to the individual winners.

Anniversary of National Service Medal

The Anniversary of National Service 1951-1972 Medal commemorates the 50th anniversary of the two NS schemes that operated in Australia during that period. This is one of three commemorative medals issued under the current Australian system of honours and awards.

Foreign Awards

Imperial Honours not awarded by Royal Prerogative since 5th October 1992 are considered foreign awards. Prior to a member of the ADF accepting or officially wearing an award presented by a foreign government or organisation, permission must be given by the Governor-General of Australia. Over the years many Australians have received individual recognition for their efforts by foreign governments. Recently such recognition has included that given by organisations such as the United Nations and NATO. The following foreign awards are examples of those group awards, either campaign or commemorative, earned by soldiers.

Republic of Vietnam Campaign Medal

The Republic of Vietnam Campaign Medal was issued to Australian members by the Government of the Republic of Vietnam for service in Vietnam during the period 31st July 1962 to 27th January 1973.

Papua New Guinea Independence Medal

The Independence Medal was established and issued in 1976 to personnel (civilian and emergency forces) and members of the ADF who served in Papua New Guinea (PNG) between 1st December 1973 and 16th September 1975. The medal is cupro-nickel (copper that contains nickel and strengthening elements) with the PNG colours on the riband (rust-red with narrow stripes of white and yellow with black edges).

Pingat Jasa Malaysia

In 2004, the Australian Government accepted the offer of the Malaysian Government for the Pingat Jasa Malaysia Medal to commemorate those ADF members who served to uphold the sovereignty of Malaysia during the Malayan Emergency and the Indonesian Confrontation (31st August 1957 to 31st December 1966).

East Timor Solidarity Medal

In November 2008 the Australian Government formally accepted an offer from the East Timor President José Ramos-Horta for ADF members to accept and wear the East Timor Solidarity Medal in relation to service in stability and peace keeping operations in East Timor (1st May 2006 to 31st December 2012).

Long Service and Unclassified Medals

Defence Long Service Medal

Defence Force Service Medal

Reserve Force Decoration (RFD)

Reserve Force Medal

National Medal

Australian Defence Medal

Champion Shots Medal

Anniversary of National Service (1951-1972)

Foreign Awards

South Vietnamese National Order of Vietnam, Fifth Class (Knight)

Republic of Vietnam Campaign Medal

Papua New Guinea Independence Medal

Pingat Jasa Malaysia

East Timor Solidarity Medal

United Nations (UN) Medal with Clasp 'KOREA'

UNTAG Medal

UNAMET/UNTAET Medal

North Atlantic Treaty Organization (NATO) Medal with Clasp 'ISAF'

United Nations Medals

- **United Nations Transition Assistance Group** (UNTAG) was established to ensure the early independence of Namibia through free and fair elections under the supervision and control of the United Nations. The Mission was established in April 1989 with a mandate for one year and closed in March 1990; the UNTAG Medal was awarded for 90 days service with the Mission.

- **United Nations Assistance Mission in East Timor/ United Nations Transitional Administration in East Timor (UNAMET/UNTAET)** medals were established on 9th December 1999. The Mission was established on 25th October 1999 by the adoption of the UN Security Council Resolution 1272. The main goals of the Mission were to provide security and maintain law and order throughout the territory of East Timor, to establish an effective administration, to assist in the development of civil and social service and to support capacity-building for self-government. Qualifying time of service for the UNAMET/UNTAET medal was 90 days.

NATO Medals

- **North Atlantic Treaty Organization (NATO) Medal with Clasp 'ISAF'**. On 2nd November 2007 the CDF announced that the NATO Medal with clasp 'ISAF' had been formally accepted for wear by ADF members for their service in Afghanistan in support of the International Security Assistance Force (ISAF). Defence civilians working with ISAF are also eligible for the award.

Medals and their Terminology

The term medal includes the badges of the lower classes of orders worn as medals rather than as neck badges or breast stars and medals associated with decorations. Medals are divided into the following groups:

- Medals for gallantry in war or for bravery in peacetime

- Medals for meritorious service and special service or achievement

- Medals for war service and non-warlike service

- Medals for long service

- Coronation, Jubilee or other commemorative medals.

There are many terms used in connection with orders, decorations and medals:[384]

- **Bar to Awards.** A bar is a full-width metal device worn on the riband which is awarded to the holder of certain Australian awards, indicating that recipient has performed an additional yet similar act of gallantry, bravery or distinguished service. If a second award of a particular decoration is made, only one medal is worn with a 'bar' on the medal, hence the term, for instance, DSC and Bar.

- **Clasps.** A clasp is a full-width metal device worn on the riband of medals to indicate one of the following:

  - The geographical area of a campaign

  - An additional period of qualifying long service

  - The date of an award, (for example, the Champion Shots Medal).

- **Cypher.** Each reigning monarch has a monogram which is a design combining or interweaving both letters and numbers showing a unique individual design. This design is sometimes used on medals to show which monarch authorised a particular medal; for example the campaign medals of WWII all have the Royal Cypher of George VI on the obverse.

- **Decorations.** A decoration is an award for gallantry, bravery, or distinguished or conspicuous service. These awards take the form of either a star or cross, for example, VC or SG. Decorations may have an associated medal which is lower on the order of precedence, for example, MG or CSM.

- **Effigy.** The likeness of the monarch who authorised the medal is usually shown on the obverse. The monarch's effigy may be shown in various styles for example in uniform, with or without crown as a bust or coinage head.

- **Emblems.** The term emblem denotes surcharges affixed to ribbons, such as the miniature crosses on the VC and Cross of Valour (CV) ribbons and the rosettes worn on long service ribbons to denote additional periods of service. Emblems also include the various Commendations awarded.

- **Emblems of Unit Citations.** Emblems of unit citations are worn on the opposite side to medals generally centralised over the breast pocket.

- **Foreign Awards.** Foreign awards are those official awards presented by the Government of a foreign nation in recognition of service by Australians. Foreign awards can only be worn when officially sanctioned by the Governor-General of Australia.

---

384 Australian Army, *Army Standing Orders for Dress – 2000*. Canberra, Defence Publishing Service: 2003, Vol 2 Pt 5 Chap 1

- **Honours and Awards.** Collective term for orders, decorations, medals, commendations and citations awarded to individuals or units. This is a non-financial symbol of achievement bestowed on an individual or unit at the behest of the Government on behalf of the people of Australia.

- **Obverse.** The front face of a medal; under the Imperial System, usually shows the effigy of the reigning monarch.

- **Official Awards.** An official award is one which is instituted by Letters Patent authorised by The Sovereign. Official awards are worn in accordance with the Order of Wearing Australian Honours and Awards. Except for neck badges, official awards are worn above the left breast.

- **Order.** An Order is a group of awards with varying degrees of precedence under a single title. Whilst the British have many Orders in their system that has been developed over hundreds of years, the only order in the Australian system is the Order of Australia. The term is applied to those insignia or badges which are worn as neck badges or breast stars. The lower classes of the order are medals.

- **Order of Wearing.** Honours and awards are worn in accordance with the Order of Wearing Australian Honours and Awards. This list is approved by The Sovereign and Gazetted in accordance with Government protocol.

- **Posthumous.** An individual who dies prior to or as a result of an incident in which he or she is awarded a medal for bravery or gallantry is said to have been awarded the honour posthumously. Only decorations for bravery or gallantry can be awarded posthumously.

- **Post-nominal.** Some awards entitle the recipient the use of post-nominals after their names. The full list is shown in this Chapter.

- **Reverse.** The back of a medal usually showing a design unique to the award, sometimes if left blank, it can contain the recipient's name and date of the award.

- **Riband.** The term riband is used to denote the silk ribbon from which an order, decoration or medal is suspended or the ribbon-like device which may be incorporated in the actual badge of an order.

- **Ribbon.** The term applies to the silk ribbon of an order, decoration or medal when it is sewn or affixed via a ribbon bar onto uniforms.

- **Ribbon Bar Emblem.** A miniature of an award which is worn on a ribbon bar (for example, the Victoria Cross).

- **Rim.** The thin outer edge of a circular coin style medal on which the recipient's name is often engraved or impressed.

- **Unofficial Awards.** Unofficial awards are those medals issued by private organisations. These medals are not permitted to be worn whilst a member of the Defence force is in uniform unless sanctioned by the Army.

- **Warrant.** A warrant is presented with many Australian awards and includes the citation for the award.

Medal Riband/Ribbon Colours

The riband colours for honours and awards are generally selected to show a theme with like colours being used within a group denoting the various levels of the honour. For instance, the ribands of the two Conspicuous Service Awards (Cross and Medal) both use the same colours; however, the different thickness of the stripes denote the difference between the Cross and the Medal. The ribands of the Distinguished Service Cross and Medal use a similar method to show the two different award levels.

The campaign riband colours are generally chosen to reflect the country or region and the forces that took part in the campaign. Examples are:

- The Africa Star (WWII) which used the colours of the three Services involved in the campaign on a desert-coloured ribbon

- United Nations Medal for Korea used the colours of the United Nations (blue and white), with a bar with the inscription 'KOREA'

- The Vietnam Medal ribbon has three central pinstripes of red on a yellow background to represent the RVN flag. Beside this are stripes of red, dark blue and light blue representing the Army, RAN and RAAF

- The Afghanistan Medal ribbon is khaki representing the dominant ground colour, edged with light blue and white stripes representing the sky and the snow with central stripes of purple and red representing the ADF and active service.

Miniature Medals[385]

The earliest miniature medals were made in 1817, when officers who had received the Waterloo Medal had small replicas made for their wives to wear. The date when miniature medals were authorised by regulation is not known, but it is said that Queen Victoria favoured their use at dinners due to the loud clinking full-sized medals made.

Miniature medals (half normal size) are generally worn on evening wear or Mess Dress, at formal dinners and occasions.[386] Originally miniature medals were purchased privately by the recipient but are now provided as part of the award.

385 Taprell Dorling H. *Ribbons and Medals*. London, George Philip and Son Limited: 1963
386 Grebert R. *The Significance of Ribbon Colours on Medals Worn Since 1815 by Australians*. Dural NSW, Landers Publishing: 2007

Medal Ribbon Bars

Originally medals were worn on the uniform at all times; however, over a period of time, this could cause damage to both the medals and the uniform. Therefore when not on ceremonial duty it became general practice for the wearer to cut a small slot in his tunic beneath the medal through which the medal could be pushed and thereby prevent it being damaged. This of course left a small piece of riband showing and eventually led to the adoption of ribbon bars being worn on military dress for other than ceremonial occasions.[387]

Clasps, Emblems and Devices Worn on Ribands and Ribbons

Definitions from the *Defence Honours and Awards Manual* confuse meaning by the level of duplication in both the definition and the usage of terms; as a result the terms clasps, devices etc. have become blurred. For example, 'device' has a heraldic application but is also used to describe items worn on ribands and ribbon bars. Clasp and bar have always been confused and definitions do appear to be skewed towards the Imperial system rather than the Australian system.

A Clasp is:

- A metal strip that is attached to a medal riband to signify service in a theatre of operations in the case of service medals, the completion of additional qualifying periods in the case of long service awards, or date of awards of the skill at arms medal.

Worn on ribands of medals to denote further periods of qualifying service for long service awards (DLSM, DFSM, RFD, RFM and ACFSM). Clasps are worn on AASM, ASM, AASM 1945-1975, ASM 1945-1975, HOSM, NEM and OSM (Civilian) to denote areas of qualifying operational service. Date clasps are worn on the Champion Shots Medal.

An Emblem is:

- A small metal insignia awarded for specific acts of gallantry or bravery worn on the ribbon of the most appropriate medal or directly on the jacket breast if no medals are held. For example, Mentioned in Despatches after 1920 is signified by an emblem in the form of a bronze oak leaf (see 'Rosette').

A Bar is:

- A second or subsequent award of a decoration denoted by a metal bar attached to the riband or ribbon. A bar should not be confused with a 'clasp' (see 'Clasp').

A Device is:

- A symbolic element forming part of a design (see 'Emblem').

  - Devices worn on medal ribbon bars for the VC, CV, SC, and BM, are the miniature emblem of the award; additional emblems are worn for subsequent awards. For example, a person awarded the BM and two bars will wear three emblems.

  - The SG, MG, DSC, DSM, CSC, CSM, NSC, do not have a ribbon bar emblem for the original award. A miniature emblem of the award is worn for first and subsequent bars to the award. For example, a person awarded the SG with two bars will wear two ribbon bar emblems.

  - For the DLSM, DFSM, and ACFSM, a cupro-nickel round rosette is worn on medal ribbon bar for each clasp awarded. For fifth clasp a silver Federation Star device is worn. The sixth and subsequent clasps are denoted by additional Federation Stars.

  - For the RFD/RFM, the same principles apply as for the DLSM, DFSM and ACFM, but the first four clasps are denoted by an oval cupro-nickel rosette.

  - The National Medal has a plain round bronze device worn on medal ribbon bar for each clasp awarded.

  - The Champion Shots Medal has a bronze wreath device added to the riband/ribbon for the second and each subsequent award.

  - The OSM miniature accumulates service device (numeral) which is worn on the medal ribbon bar.

  - No ribbon bar emblems are worn for clasps to AASM and other related awards.

  - Commendations for Gallantry, Distinguished Service and Brave Conduct recipients wear a single miniature emblem worn on the medal ribbon bar, irrespective of the number of awards held.

A Rosette is:

- A second or subsequent award of a medal is sometimes denoted by a metal rosette sewn to the medal ribbon. In the Imperial system this emblem was in the form of a rose but the term is now used to refer to other designs including the ribbon emblems used to signify the award of clasps to long service medals (see 'Bar' and 'Clasp').

In the Australian Honours System, there have been no devices worn on the ribands of medals with the exception of the OSM which has provision for an accumulated service device (numeral).

Commendations for gallantry, distinguished service and brave conduct have the relevant insignia (full-size) worn on a full length of ribbon worn with other full-size medals. Additional insignia are worn for subsequent awards (this also applies to miniature medals).

---

387 Grebert R. *The Significance of Ribbon Colours on Medals Worn Since 1815 by Australians.* Dural NSW, Landers Publishing: 2007

Victory Medal – WWI and MID

Commendation for Gallantry

Vietnam Medal and MID

Commendation for Brave Conduct

Commendation for Distinguished Service

Commendations

In the Australian Honours System, commendations are used as the lower order of three different grades of awards. The use of this type of recognition can be traced back to WWI. A commendation emblem signifies that the recipient had performed a noteworthy action that did not result in the awarding of a medal.

The first type of commendation used was the MID which referred to the physical recording of an individual's conduct in action, originally printed in the *London Gazette*[388], a practice that dated back to the 17th century. During the 2nd Boer War period, the fact of being mentioned in formal despatches sometimes formed the basis for justifying the awarding of a decoration such as the DSO and the DCM.

In 1919 King George V ordered that a special certificate be given to all persons 'Mentioned In Despatches' during WWI and later in 1920 it was decided to issue an oak leaf emblem to be worn on the Victory Medal. Later the oak leaf was worn on the applicable service medal riband awarded for the particular war or period in question. While the MID does not have a recognised post-nominal, for administrative reasons it is common to use the initialism 'MID'.

Until 1977 only the VC, GC and the MID could be awarded posthumously for acts of valour or courage performed in the face of the enemy. The MID was more often used in these cases, to recognise acts of extreme gallantry that did not meet the standard required for the award of a VC.[389]

Since the formal introduction of the MID there have been two variants of the oak leaf. For noteworthy action during WWI the emblem was a cluster of bronze oak leaves which was changed in 1920 to a single oak leaf. This symbol was used in the Australian Army until the introduction of the Australian Honours and Awards System in 1991. The MID was replaced in the Australian Honours and Awards System with three separate commendations for:

- Gallantry

- Bravery

- Distinguished Service.[390]

As these new awards are not associated with a particular war or campaign they are worn with an award-specific ribbon.

Miniature emblems of the Commendation for Gallantry, Commendation for Brave Conduct and Commendation for Distinguished Service are worn on a ribbon of the authorised colour of the specific conflict.

388 Gordon LL. *Military Origins.* New York, A. S. Barnes: 1971, p. 225
389 Dennis P, Grey J, Morris E, Prior R. *The Oxford Companion to Australian Military History (Second Edition). Australia,* Oxford University Press: 2008, p. 356

390 Dennis P, Grey J, Morris E, Prior R. *The Oxford Companion to Australian Military History (Second Edition). Australia,* Oxford University Press: 2008, p. 356

Infantry Combat Badge

The Infantry Combat Badge (ICB) was instituted in 1970 to recognise infantrymen who are 'force assigned' on the Operational Manning Document (OMD) to an operation and employed in infantry roles of a combat team/battle group on warlike operations. The qualifying period for the ICB is for 'operational service' since 16th June 1948.

The ICB is a metal badge with a bronze antique finish with a bayonet, styled from a 7.62mm L1A1 bayonet, surrounded by an oval-shaped laurel wreath. It is worn centrally over the left breast above any medals or ribbon bars. The award recognises the unique role and the particular training, skills and hardships attendant upon service as an infantryman. This badge is awarded to a serving member who has given 90 days qualifying service either continuous or aggregated as an infantry soldier in warlike operations. In exceptional circumstances, the ICB may be awarded to members of other Corps.

The Chief of the General Staff (LTGEN Sir Thomas Daly KBE, DSO) added that, whilst he appreciated the views expressed, it was to be borne in mind that the proposed badge was meant to be a visible distinction for the infantryman and was not a general combat badge. He said the other Corps had their responsibilities and neither their worth, nor performance, were in question. However he could not accept that an infantry award should be granted to members of other Corps unless they qualified for it as infantrymen.[391]

Army Combat Badge

The purpose of the Army Combat Badge (ACB) is to recognise any ADF member who was 'force assigned' to an infantry, armour, artillery, aviation or combat engineer-based combat team/battle group, or similar unit/sub-unit, and who has served for 90 days continuous or aggregated on warlike operations. The purpose of the ACB is not to recognise combat duties, but to recognise service with a combat element through formal force assignment. The ACB does not replace the ICB; therefore, infantrymen cannot be issued an ACB if an entitlement exists for the ICB.

Top: Infantry Combat Badge

Bottom: Army Combat Badge

---

391 Australian Defence Force. *Minute No. 7/1970 of the Military Board:* 23 January 1970

Active Service Badges

During WWI patriotic feelings supporting the war ran high even though a referendum to introduce compulsory service had been defeated twice. Men at home were subjected to many forms of harassment for not volunteering for active service. As a method of improving the morale of those forced to remain in Australia the Government introduced a range of official badges that were to be worn on civilian attire. These badges included:

- Reserved Occupation Badge, Volunteered

- Unfit for Service Badge, Volunteered

- Returned from Active Service Badge (RASB).

The Discharged Returned Soldiers Badge was authorised by *Military Order No. 279 of 1916* (MO279/1916) for issue to officers, warrant officers, non-commissioned officers and soldiers who returned to Australia from active service and who were discharged in honourable circumstances. Issue of the badge to members of the Australian Army Nursing Service (AANS) who had been returned to Australia and discharged under the same condition as male members of the AIF was authorised in MO314/1916. During WWII a new badge, referred to as the RASB, was issued to members of the RAN, 2nd AIF (including the AANS, RAAF, Voluntary Aid Detachments, approved representatives of philanthropic bodies, and Official Press Correspondents and Official Photographers), upon return from service abroad.

Currently the RASB is issued to members of the ADF who have rendered warlike service. As the award of the RASB is not governed by statute, it has been the practice of successive Australian Governments to determine conditions of eligibility for each conflict in accordance with the circumstances existing at the time. Since 1945, with the award of the AASM 1945-1975 and the current AASM, the RASB badge has been awarded automatically with those medals.

The current bronze RASB was introduced in 1953, and is identical to the earlier post-WWII RASB, apart from the replacement of the Tudor crown with the St Edward's crown. The RASB is a personal issue and is not issued to relatives of deceased ex-members. The badge enables individuals to display their involvement in warlike service while wearing civilian attire. It is worn on civilian dress when the wearing of service medals is not appropriate or possible.

Before the establishment of the Operational Service Medal (OSM) in 2013, those who received the AASM were also issued with the RASB. The OSM recognises all declared operational service in which a member has been involved; and a Bar for each individual conflict. The RASB will continue to be issued with the AASM for current warlike operations. In contrast to the RASB, the Operational Service Badge (OSB) may also be issued to the next-of-kin of deceased members to complement the award of the OSM.

Unit Citations

The UCG and the MUC were introduced into the Australian Honours System in 1991.[392] Recognition of group endeavour can trace its history back over the centuries to Roman times, in particular during the 1st and 2nd Centuries. During those times, service to the State was rewarded with citizenship, but only after completion of 25 years' service. One Legion raised by Tiberius, in 21 CE, twice distinguished itself in battle and as a result each member of the unit serving at the time was granted citizenship as a reward.[393]

The Australian UCG is a gilt gold-plated frame with a design of flames emanating from the edge to the centre. The frame surrounds a ribbon bar of deep green, which displays a gilt sterling-silver Federation Star at its centre.

The Australian MUC is a gilt sterling-silver frame, with a design of flames emanating from the edge to the centre. The frame surrounds a ribbon bar of old gold, which displays a sterling-silver Federation Star at its centre.

An Australian unit member present during the action cited is entitled to wear the emblem with Federation Star in perpetuity, whilst members who join an Australian unit after the citation is awarded may be entitled to wear the insignia without the Federation Star only whilst posted to the unit. The citation is worn centrally over the right-hand breast pocket; if awarded more than once they are worn in order of approval.

The US Presidential Unit Citation[394] is awarded to units of the United States Armed Forces and Allied nations for extraordinary heroism in action against an armed enemy occurring on or after 7 December 1941.

The US Army Meritorious Unit Commendation[395] is awarded to units for exceptionally meritorious conduct in performance of outstanding services for a period of at least six continuous months during a period of military operations against an armed enemy occurring on or after 1 January 1944.

392 Australian Commonwealth Government. http://www.itsanhonour.gov.au

393 McNab C. *The Roman Army: The Greatest War Machine of the Ancient World.* Oxford England, Osprey Publishing Ltd: 2012, p. 166

394 Strandberg J, Bender RJ. *The Call of Duty.* San Jose California, R. James Bender Publishing: 1994, p. 254

395 Strandberg J, Bender RJ. *The Call of Duty.* San Jose California, R. James Bender Publishing: 1994, p. 256

The Vietnam Gallantry Cross (awarded by the Republic of Vietnam) was also issued as a unit award and is an entirely separate decoration from the full-sized medal. Known as the 'Vietnam Gallantry Cross Unit Citation with Palm'[396], the unit citation was issued as the Gallantry Cross ribbon, with a metal palm device, enclosed within a gold frame. The unit citation was issued in the name of South Vietnam to many Australian Military Units which had distinguished service to the same level as would be required for the issue of an award to an individual. 6 RAR was an exception to this in being refused approval to accept the award; however, in 2008 the Commonwealth Government of Australia overturned one of the original reviewing recommendations and authorised 'D' Company, 6 RAR to wear the South Vietnamese Cross of Gallantry Unit Citation with Palm, awarded originally to them in 1967 following Long Tan. Regulations for the Vietnam Gallantry Cross permit the wearing of both the individual and unit award simultaneously, since they are considered separate decorations.

The Defence Commendation Scheme[397]

Within the Department of Defence a system has been developed to allow awards outside of the Australian Honours and Awards System to formally recognise outstanding and/or exceptional achievement, specific acts of bravery or, dedication to duty. This policy exists because awards from the Australian Honours System were either not an appropriate medium of recognition, or, due to an awards quota, were not available.

The only other recognition available for many years was the Australia Day Medallion, which is an important symbol, but it is not easily associated with achievement within the Defence Organisation.

The Defence Commendation Scheme, introduced on 1st September 2012, is a recognition system which applies to all Defence personnel, including members of the ADF and foreign exchange personnel serving with the ADF, Defence Australian Public Service (APS), Defence contractors and consultants and any other person deemed, by an awarding authority, to be providing a service to Defence. The circumstances attracting the award of a Commendation may relate to an isolated instance or to a series of instances over a period of time. Defence Commendations are a part of the Defence system of recognition and are of a lower precedence than awards within the Australian Honours System.

396 http://www.tioh.hqda.pentagon.mil/Awards/VIETNAM%20
GALLANTRY%20CROSS1.html

397 Interim Policy. DEFGRAM 4/2010: 26 Aug 2010

*Australian
Unit Citation for
Gallantry – Individual*

*Australian Meritorious
Unit Citation – Individual*

*Australian
Unit Citation for
Gallantry*

*Australian
Meritorious Unit Citation*

*US Army
Presidential Unit Citation*

*US Army
Meritorious Unit Citation*

*RVN Gallantry Cross
Unit Citation with Palm*

The scheme is hierarchically-based and allows for Commendations to be awarded based on the merit of the service or act. All individual Commendations, except the Joint Secretary for Defence and CDF Commendation, the Secretary Commendation and CDF Commendation, are awarded at three levels, being: Gold, Silver and Bronze.

The Secretary for Defence and the CDF may award Commendations, either separately or jointly, to recognise performance or achievement that is considered worthy of a level of recognition above the Gold commendation. The Secretary for Defence and CDF may agree to award a joint Commendation, in those cases where the recognition is for service that is considered to have been of benefit to both the ADF and the Department of Defence. The Secretary for Defence, CDF, and Principal Awarding Authorities being the single-Service Chiefs, CJOPS, Defence Group Heads and CEO Defence Materiel Organisation (DMO) may also award Group Commendations which are recognised by the issue of a single one-level Certificate, although members of the group or team so awarded may be given a copy.

The emblem on the Commendation badge and the accompanying certificate is that of the appointment making the award.

Soldier's Medallion

The Soldier's Medallion[398] was introduced into the Army to recognise outstanding service by soldiers who would not normally gain recognition in the Australian Honours System. The Medallion is intended as an Army award to be conferred by COs and OCs of independent sub-units. The Medallion is bronze, approximately 10cm in diameter, and the obverse design is based on the two central figures of the Army Memorial on Anzac Parade in Canberra. The reverse is engraved with the recipient's regimental number, rank, initials and surname. The Medallion is contained in a presentation case and is accompanied by a badge and certificate.

The Badge is bronze, approximately 22mm in diameter. It is worn on the uniform in accordance with the *Army Dress Manual*.[399]

Eligibility criteria for the Soldier's Medallion are the recipient is to be of the rank of CPL or below and has given exemplary service well above that expected of soldiers in the performance of their duties, and whose service has not been recognised by another award. While recruits and trainees are not excluded from consideration for the medallion, it is expected that it will normally be awarded to trained soldiers. A maximum of 350 medallions are available for presentation in each calendar year.

398 Australian Army. *Defence Instruction (Army) PERS 97-4 The Soldier's Medallion:* 6 Dec 2010
399 Australian Army. *Army Dress Manual – 2013.* Canberra, Defence Publishing Service: 2013

Joint Secretary/CDF Award

Secretary Award

CDF Award

CA Award - Gold

CA Award - Silver

CA Award - Bronze

Left: Soldier's Medallion

Obverse

Reverse

Left: Australia Day Medallion

Obverse

Reverse

Australia Day Medallion[400]

Each year the National Australia Day Council invites the Department of Defence to participate in celebrating Australia Day through awarding Australia Day Medallions to employees of the Department. The Australia Day Medallion is not an extension of the Australian Honours and Awards System but like the Soldier's Medallion, it is intended to provide recognition of achievement which does not qualify for and has not been recognised through any other award. Current serving ADF personnel and civilian employees of the Department of Defence are eligible for nomination. Eligible members may be nominated for outstanding achievement in the last 12 months or over a number of years.

400 Australian Army *Defence Instruction (General) PERS 31-7 Australia Day Medallion*: 23 Oct 2001

I'm an Australian Soldier Medallion

The Army's 'I'm an Australian Soldier' Medallion is issued to all serving Army members; and is part of the awareness campaign to promote a wider understanding of the initiative of Australian soldiers as well as reinforcing a feeling of pride in service in the Army.

The Medallion was endorsed by the CA's Senior Advisory Committee (CASAC) in 2006. The Medallion is silver in colour and is issued in a polished timber presentation and display case. The front of the Medallion features the Australian Rising Sun badge dating from 1902 and was worn with pride during both World Wars and in all subsequent ADF deployments; it is inscribed with the member's name; and also features the Army's core values of Courage, Initiative and Teamwork.

The reverse of the medallion features four common themes from answers given by soldiers to the question: 'What makes you proud of being in the Australian Army?' The first two themes relate to the role of soldiers as custodians of both the ANZAC legend and the heritage of service, mateship and sacrifice of previous generations; Army holds these in trust for the Australian nation. The other themes relate to service in securing Australia's future and in helping the people of other nations.

110 Years Medallion

On 1st March 2011 the Australian Army celebrated the 110th anniversary of its formation. To commemorate this event, the Army released a medallion designed by PTE Joel Shaddock which reinforces the core values of Courage, Initiative and Teamwork. The medallion was made available to all serving members at that time.

Australian Honours and Awards [401][402]

Order of Precedence (Modified)

All Imperial British awards made to Australian citizens after 5th October 1992 are deemed to be foreign awards and should be worn accordingly. Those honours and awards listed in the Schedule in grey print are either old or superseded Imperial awards.

VICTORIA CROSS FOR AUSTRALIA	**VC**	(1)
George Cross	GC	
Cross of Valour	**CV**	
Knight/Lady of the Garter	**KG/LG**	
Knight/Lady of the Thistle	**KT/LT**	
Knight/Dame Grand Cross of the Order of the Bath	GCB	
Order of Merit	OM	
Knight/Dame of the Order of Australia	**AK/AD**	(2)
Knight/Dame Grand Cross of the Order of St Michael and St George	GCMG	
Knight/Dame Grand Cross of the Royal Victorian Order	**GCVO**	
Knight/Dame Grand Cross of the Order of the British Empire	GBE	
Companion of the Order of Australia	**AC**	
Companion of Honour	CH	
Knight/Dame Commander of the Order of the Bath	KCB/DCB	
Knight/Dame Commander of the Order of St Michael and St George	KCMG/DCMG	
Knight/Dame Commander of the Royal Victorian Order	**KCVO/DCVO**	
Knight/Dame Commander of the Order of the British Empire	KBE/DBE	
Knight Bachelor (NB: Confers title of 'Sir' – no post-nominal)		
Officer of the Order of Australia	**AO**	
Companion of the Order of the Bath	CB	
Companion of the Order of St Michael and St George	CMG	
Commander of the Royal Victorian Order	**CVO**	
Commander of the Order of the British Empire	CBE	
Star of Gallantry	**SG**	
Star of Courage	**SC**	
Companion of the Distinguished Service Order	DSO	
Distinguished Service Cross	**DSC**	
Member of the Order of Australia	**AM**	
Lieutenant of the Royal Victorian Order	**LVO**	
Officer of the Order of the British Empire	OBE	
Companion of the Imperial Service Order	ISO	
Member of the Royal Victorian Order	**MVO**	
Member of the Order of the British Empire	MBE	
Conspicuous Service Cross	**CSC**	
Nursing Service Cross	**NSC**	
Royal Red Cross (1st Class)	RRC	
Distinguished Service Cross	DSC	
Military Cross	MC	
Distinguished Flying Cross	DFC	
Air Force Cross	AFC	
Royal Red Cross (2nd Class)	ARRC	
Medal for Gallantry	**MG**	
Bravery Medal	**BM**	
Distinguished Service Medal	**DSM**	
Public Service Medal	**PSM**	

---

401 Government House. *Commonwealth Government Gazette. The Australian Order of Precedence of Honours and Awards: 15 Jan 1993*, S17
402 The Sovereign can still confer honours upon Australian citizens in exercise of the Royal Prerogative, for example KG, KT and OM.

Australian Police Medal		**APM**	
Australian Fire Service Medal		**AFSM**	
Ambulance Service Medal		**ASM**	
Emergency Services Medal		**ESM**	
Medal of the Order of Australia		**OAM**	
Order of St John	GC, K/D, C/Ch, O, SB/SS or Esq	**StJ**	(3)
Distinguished Conduct Medal		DCM	
Conspicuous Gallantry Medal		CGM	
Conspicuous Gallantry Medal (Flying)		CGM	
George Medal		GM	
Conspicuous Service Medal		**CSM**	
Australian Antarctic Medal		**AAM**	(4)
Queen's Police Medal for Gallantry		QPM	
Queen's Fire Service Medal for Gallantry		QFSM	
Distinguished Service Medal		DSM	
Military Medal		MM	
Distinguished Flying Medal		DFM	
Air Force Medal		AFM	
Sea Gallantry Medal		SGM	
Queen's Gallantry Medal		QGM	
Royal Victorian Medal		**RVM**	
British Empire Medal		BEM	
Queen's Police Medal for Distinguished Service		QPM	
Queen's Fire Service Medal for Distinguished Service		QFSM	

Commendation for Gallantry

Commendation for Brave Conduct

Mentioned in Despatches, Queen's Commendation for Bravery, Queen's
Commendation for Bravery in the Air

Commendation for Distinguished Service

War medals, campaign medals, active service medals and service medals

Colonial Wars:

New Zealand Medal
Egypt Medal
Khedive's Star
China War Medal

South African War:

Queen's South African Medal
King's South African Medal

World War One:

1914 Star	
1914-1915 Star	(5)
British War Medal	
Mercantile Marine War Medal	
Victory medal	
Naval General Service Medal 1915-1962	(6, 7)
General Service Medal 1918-1962	(6, 7)

World War Two:

The 1939-1945 Star	(8)
The Africa Star	(8)
The Air Crew Europe Star	(8)
The Arctic Star	(8)
The Atlantic Star	(8)
The Burma Star	(8)
The France and Germany Star	(8)
The Italy Star	(8)
The Pacific Star	(8)
Defence Medal	
War Medal 1939-1945	
Australian Service Medal 1939-1945	

Post-World War Two:

Australian Active Service Medal 1945-1975	(7)
Korean Medal	
United Nations Service Medal for Korea	(9)
General Service Medal 1962	(7)
Vietnam Medal	
Vietnam Logistic and Support Medal	(10)
Australian Active Service Medal	(7)
International Force East Timor Medal	
Afghanistan Medal	
Iraq Medal	
Australian Service Medal 1945-1975	(7)
Australian General Service Medal for Korea	
Australian Service Medal	(7)
Rhodesia Medal	
Operational Service Medal	

Police Overseas Service Medal	(7)
Humanitarian Overseas Service Medal	(7)
National Emergency Medal	(7)
Civilian Service Medal 1939-1945	
National Police Service Medal	
Polar Medal	
Imperial Service Medal	

Coronation, Jubilee, Remembrance and Commemorative medals (in order of date of receipt):

King Edward VII Coronation Medal	
King George V Coronation Medal	
King George V Silver Jubilee Medal	
King George VI Coronation Medal	
Queen Elizabeth II Coronation Medal	
Queen Elizabeth II Silver Jubilee Medal	
Queen Elizabeth II Golden Jubilee Medal	
Queen Elizabeth II Diamond Jubilee Medal	(11)
80th Anniversary Armistice Remembrance Medal	
Australian Sports Medal	
Centenary Medal	

Australian Long Service Awards:

Defence Force Service Medal	
Reserve Force Decoration	**RFD**
Reserve Force Medal	
Defence Long Service Medal	
National Medal	
Australian Defence Medal	(12)
Australian Cadet Forces Service Medal	
Champion Shots Medal	
Long Service Medals (Imperial)	(13)

Independence and Anniversary Medals (in order of date of receipt:

Anniversary of National Service 1951-1972 Medal

Foreign Awards (in order of date of authorisation of their acceptance and wearing)

Honours and Awards listed in the Schedule above shown in BOLD print include:

• Those within the Australian honours and awards system

• Those conferred by The Sovereign in exercise of the Royal Prerogative

• Those within the Order of St John

• Foreign awards, the acceptance and wearing of which have been authorised by the Governor-General of Australia.

Notes:
1. Refers to the Imperial Victoria Cross and the Victoria Cross for Australia.
2. Provision for further awards at this level within the Order of Australia was removed by Her Majesty The Queen on 3rd March 1986 on the advice of the Prime Minister. Reinstituted 25th March 2014.
3. Listed to indicate where any awards within the Order of St John should be worn; however, the Service Medal of the Order of St John should be worn as a Long Service Medal after all other Imperial Long Service awards. Post-nominals within the Order of St John are not recognised as notified in the Governor-General of Australia's media release of 14th August 1982 (the Life Saving Medal is worn on the right side).
   When the ribbon of the Order of St John of Jerusalem is worn, either on uniform or on civilian clothes, a small silver Maltese Cross is worn on the ribbon.
4. The Australian Antarctic Medal was known as the Antarctic Medal until 18th December 1997.
5. Recipients of the 1914 Star were not eligible for the award of the 1914-1915 Star.
6. The order of wearing of the Naval General Service Medal 1915-1962 and General Service Medal 1918-1962 (Army and Air Force) will vary from person to person depending on when the person was awarded the first clasp. If the first clasp relates to service between WWI and WWII, the medals should be worn immediately after WWI medals. If the first clasp relates to service after 2nd September 1945, the medal should be worn immediately after the United Nations Service Medal for Korea if awarded.
7. Clasps to these medals should be worn on the ribbon in order of date of receipt.
8. See Additional Notes on WWII Campaign Stars.
9. Uniquely, although a foreign award, the United Nations Service Medal for Korea is worn immediately after the Korea Medal. All other foreign awards for which official permission has been given to accept and wear are worn as foreign awards.
10. A person who has been awarded the Vietnam Medal is not eligible for the award of the Vietnam Logistic and Support Medal.
11. Only one of these awards is known to have been made to a current serving military member, that being Benjamin Roberts-Smith VC MG.
12. This award is not a long service award.
13. Refers to Imperial efficiency and long service awards.

Additional Notes on WWII Campaign Stars

There are nine different stars which are almost identical in design; all have six-pointed stars with the crowned cypher of King George V1 in the centre. The central cypher is surrounded by the name of the medal, which reads either, the 1939-1945 Star, the Atlantic Star, the Air Crew Europe Star, the Africa Star, the Pacific Star, the Burma Star, the Italy Star, the France and Germany Star and the Arctic Star.

The stars are made of a copper and zinc alloy (to inhibit corrosion) and each has a unique ribbon denoting the particular campaign they represent.

It was decided that the maximum number of stars that could be earned by any one individual was five, being made up from the 1939-1945 Star and one campaign star from each of the four Operational Theatres.

Those who qualified for multiple awards in the same theatre wore the first medal received plus a clasp on the riband of that star indicating the additional award. There are a total of ten different clasps available including the newly introduced 'Bomber Command'; only one clasp can be worn regardless of extra entitlement.

When ribbons only are worn, the possession of a bar was represented by a silver rosette; with the 'Battle of Britain' bar represented by a gilt rosette.

War/Theatre	Campaign Star	Clasps
WWII	1939-1945 Star	*Battle of Britain*
		Bomber Command
Europe	Atlantic Star	*Air Crew Europe or France and Germany*
	Air Crew Europe Star	*Atlantic or France and Germany*
	France and Germany Star	*Atlantic*
	Arctic Star	*N/A*
North Africa	Africa Star	*1st Army*
		8th Army
		North Africa 1942-1943
Mediterranean	Italy Star	*N/A*
Asia	Burma Star	*Pacific*
	Pacific Star	*Burma*

World War II – Campaign Stars and Clasps

1939-1945 Star

Air Crew Europe Star

Atlantic Star

France and Germany Star

Italy Star

Africa Star

Pacific Star

Burma Star

Arctic Star

Chapter Ten

Officers' and Sergeants' Messes Customs and Etiquette

Origin of the Mess[403]

The likely root of the term 'mess' is the old word 'mes' which is a portion of food, drawn from the Latin verb 'mittere', meaning 'to send' or 'to put', the original sense of the word being 'a course of a meal put on the table' or from the Latin 'Mensa' (Messum) for table. This sense of the word 'mess' appeared in English in the 13th century when it was often used for cooked or liquid dishes, such as in a 'mess of pottage' (porridge or soup). By the 15th century, a group of people who ate together was also known as a 'mess', and it is this sense of the word that persists in the 'mess halls' of the Other Ranks, the Sergeants' Mess and the Officers Mess' of the modern Australian Army.

Army Messes embody the customs of the Service and are based on traditions handed down from generation to generation. They are unique organisations that have no exact counterpart outside British Commonwealth Armies.

The earliest record of officers joining together to dine at a common table was in 1740, mainly in Militia Messes. Regular units first introduced Officers' Messes around 1770. A Military Guide for Young Officers (1772)[404] appears to be the first authoritative document to mention any form of Officers' Mess, which states:

> By this scheme each field officer and Captain is to contribute six guineas and each subaltern and staff officer one day's pay each, towards the purchasing of a dining tent, kitchen tent and also to enable a sutler[405] to buy a cart and two horses, table linen, kitchen furniture.[406] Wine, punch, ale, cider etc. being distinct articles must be paid for by those only who choose to call them; and for each stranger's dinner sent from the mess.

The development of the Mess within the Military can be traced back over many years. For a full and proper appreciation, it is as well to understand the system by which regiments were raised in the early days, the method of granting commissions, and the evolution of the Officers' Mess.

In the 16th and 17th century, regiments were raised by means of an indenture (a formal legal agreement, contract, or document) or commission issued by the King to a nobleman or gentleman who became the Colonel and who, in return undertook to raise a body of troops to serve The Sovereign. Thus the regiment was virtually the property of the Colonel, who was responsible for clothing and equipping it. Similarly, each Company within the regiment was the responsibility of its Captain.

At a later date, to provide additional funds for The Sovereign, a Colonel was required to pay a fee for his commission. The scale of fees was increased over the years and as a natural outcome, to recoup the heavy outlay, the Regimental Commander required in turn payment from subordinates. Thus the origin of the custom of buying and selling commissions; a strange custom by today's standards, continued to be practised until abolished by law in 1870.

The current term 'Mess', generally refers to the buildings and surrounding areas belonging to the Mess (car park, outdoor drinking facilities, barbecue area, gardens, swimming pool, tennis court, and any detached accommodation buildings).

---

403 Department of Defence. *Army Protocol Manual*. Canberra, Defence Publishing Service: 2001
404 Simes T. *The Military Guide for Young Officers*. London, J. Millan: 1772
405 "Sutler" – noun (formerly) a person who followed an army or maintained a store on an army post to sell provisions to the soldiers (Macquarie University NSW. *The Macquarie Dictionary*. Milton Queensland, The Jacaranda Press: 1987)
406 Dickson RJ. *Enlivened Anecdotes of Mess Times remembered from a host of one time mess members and the progress of Charles Oswald Littlewart from 2nd Lieutenant to Major General*. Tunbridge Wells, Midis Books: 1973, p. 1

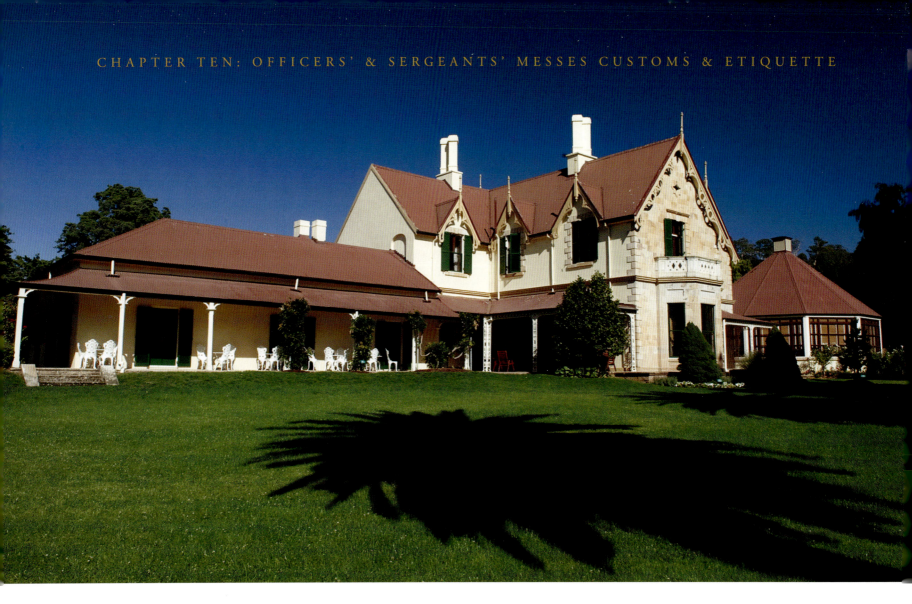

Duntroon House is the Mess for Officers posted to Duntroon. Built from 1863, it is the oldest building in Canberra and, along with its gardens, is listed by the National Trust and is on the Register of the National Estate

The Function of the Mess[407]

In recent years, with changing social standards, Defence funding and expectations placed on members' social life, the Mess is not as central to the Officers, Warrant Officers and SNCOs as it once was. That said, the Mess and the conduct of members still follow a pattern based on traditional customs and procedures. The Mess played and still plays an important part in the life of a Corps, Regiment or unit, albeit the late 20th and early 21st Centuries have seen unit messes decline, to be replaced by formation or area messes. Although the Mess provides a gathering place for all authorised members, particularly during duty hours, it is more particularly the home of the living-in members.

Mess Rules

The conduct of each Mess is contained in the individual Mess constitution and rules. These rules are not unnecessarily restrictive, but ensure the smooth operation of a Mess for the benefit of all members and their guests. A Mess will also have 'Local Mess Rules' pertaining to dress, dining, bar timings and the like.

Dress in the Mess

Uniforms and civilian attire may be worn in the Mess, but a mix of the two is not acceptable. Members and their guests are expected to maintain agreed standards of dress. Local Mess Rules should stipulate the standard of dress that applies. Generally, the minimum acceptable standard of dress is 'neat casual'. Dress standards may be relaxed at special Mess functions such as 'fancy-dress' parties.

In deciding dress rules, consideration is given to the needs of living-in members, other members and the functions of the Mess. An appropriate balance should be struck so that a Mess is not too restrictive where this would be to the detriment of those members to whom the Mess is a home. Generally, it is expected that all officers maintain a full range of uniforms, plus a suit, jacket and slacks.

The tradition of not wearing hats or carrying weapons (except when escorting Colours) into any Mess is Army-wide. There is no requirement to remove or break belts prior to entering the Mess. If the Mess Committee wish to maintain a local custom it must be addressed in 'Local Mess Rules'.

---

407 Department of Defence. Army Protocol Manual. Canberra, Defence Publishing Service: 2001, pp. 3-8

The tradition of 'breaking the belt' is a continuing tradition at RMC-D, whereby the duty staff, whilst wearing a Sam Browne Belt, unbuckle (unlatch) the shoulder strap indicating they are in the Mess to relax and not in an 'On Duty' capacity. However, a specific tradition within the CSC Mess at Duntroon is not to break the belt; this is seen as a sign of trust between cadets.

Visiting Another Mess

On visiting another Mess, visitors should always wait until invited to enter. Immediately on entry, visitors should place their name in the Visitors' Book and seek out the President of the Mess Committee (PMC) or senior member. The normal courtesies are paid on arrival and departure. Care should be taken to ensure observance of the local rules and customs of the Mess.

Officers Visiting the Sergeants' Mess

The Sergeants' Mess is the home of the Warrant Officers and SNCOs and may only be visited by officers from the Officers' Mess when invited by the PMC of the Sergeants' Mess, and with the permission of:

- The PMC of the Officers' Mess, and

- The Commanding Officer (CO) of the Sergeants' Mess.

When officers have been invited to the Sergeants' Mess, their hosts expect behaviour of the same standard that officers expect from their guests. Courtesies should be paid on arrival and departure to the PMC of the Sergeants' Mess. Members of the Sergeants' Mess should be treated with friendly courtesy.

The CO, or senior officer present, may be expected to give the lead when it is time to depart and other officers must conform so that they do not overstay their welcome.

Warrant Officers and SNCOs are not to be invited to the Officers' Mess except during the visit, conventionally before Christmas leave, by all members of the Sergeants' Mess to the Officers' Mess. Many units practise this custom each year between the two respective Messes, or on a turn and turn-about basis every second year.

Entry to the Mess

A Visitors' Book is normally kept in every Mess, for visitors to sign. Officers should sign this book on arrival at, and when leaving a 'station' adding in the remarks column, 'on joining station', 'on leaving station'. On entering a Mess for the first time, the new member should seek out the PMC who will introduce him or her to the Mess.

Compliments

There are two ways to pay compliments in a Mess: rising from a chair, or coming to attention; each is appropriate, and what is correct at the time should be apparent.

Within a Mess, compliments are paid to:

- Senior Officers: General Officers, Commanders, Commandants and their equivalents

- The Mess CO

- The PMC

- To civilian women always, as a matter of courtesy.

- Additionally, in a Sergeants' Mess, compliments are paid to:

- All officers during a formal visit to the Sergeants' Mess

- All functional command and formation RSMs

- The senior RSM, or equivalent.

Courtesy to General Officers, Commanders, Commandants and the PMC. When these persons enter the Mess, those who are present rise. If a member enters the Mess after these people, good manners dictate that their respects should be paid when possible. Similarly, when leaving the Mess, members and their guests should bid their farewell to these persons.

Methods/Mode of Address. Mess life is a blend of formality founded on military custom, and informality arising from comradeship. Officers, Warrant Officers and SNCOs treat their seniors with the courtesy due to their rank and commensurate experience, and should conform to the customs of their unit when addressing superiors. As a guideline, within a Mess:

- Persons of equal rank address each other by their first names; juniors normally address their seniors by their rank and name, or as 'Sir' or 'Ma'am'

- In the Sergeants' Mess the PMC and RSM is addressed as 'Sir' or 'Ma'am'

- In the Officers' Mess the Adjutant is always addressed as 'Sir', or 'Ma'am' by Lieutenants[408]

- An officer may invite another officer who is junior in rank to use first names when not on duty; this is the custom in British Messes, perhaps surprisingly, but is still not common in the Australian Army

- When addressing persons by rank or name, ranks are always used in full except that:

  - MAJGENs and LTGENs are addressed as 'General', and

  - LTCOLs are addressed as 'Colonel'.

When a person introduces a non-Service guest to a senior member, the use of the senior person's rank would be the most natural and acceptable mode of address by the guest, unless otherwise advised.

---

408 'Subaltern' – this refers to commissioned ranks with the Army below the rank of Captain.

Hospitality

A Mess is often judged by the way its members treat their guests. If a visitor is unaccompanied, a member should, without hesitation greet and entertain the visitor until the visitor's host arrives. The visitor's host should be notified of the guest's arrival when practicable.

Guests should be asked to write their name in the Visitors' Book. Guests are then introduced to the PMC and the CO, if present, and to other members.

Official guests are normally received by the PMC, but in his or her absence the senior member present should act for the PMC. If no members are present in the Mess, the staff should notify the PMC or Secretary, or any member as quickly as practical.

Civilian guests may be invited into the Mess at the CO's discretion. Local Mess Rules should define the Mess attitude to this aspect of Mess life.

Conversation

All conversation in the Mess should contribute to a free and relaxed atmosphere. Personalities should never be discussed. Members should not use obscene or indecent language. Prohibiting the discussion of 'shop' in the Mess is unrealistic, but such discussion should remain within bounds and should not be allowed to degenerate into a dissection of the daily routine. In particular, 'shop' of the kind in which a visitor is unable to join should be avoided.

Mess members should not be reprimanded or rebuked in the Mess, especially in the presence of peers or subordinates.

Dining in the Mess

Formal Meals and Dining-In Nights. Formal meals are under the control of a Dining President and should follow the general procedure for a Formal Mess Dinner. Formal meals are usually attended by resident members only. Members move into the dining room with the Dining President and remain standing until the Dining President sits. The meal is served by courses and members should not leave until the Dining President gives the lead. Members arriving late for a formal meal tender their apologies to the Dining President and request permission to take their seats. Late arrivals are not allowed at Dining-In Nights.

Informal Meals. At informal meals, members may enter or leave the dining room within the hours laid down by the Mess Committee.

Special Dietary Requirements. Special dietary requirements can usually be met by the Mess, for example for vegetarian or observance of faith reasons.

Letters or Notes

Letters or notes are not written or read at the table during formal meals. On informal occasions letters or notes are not written or read without the sanction of other members.

Newspapers and Magazines

Newspapers are normally read in the ante-room or another room set aside for that purpose. Newspapers and magazines may be read at the breakfast table with the sanction of other members.

Smoking

In line with current health regulations, smoking is not permitted in the enclosed areas of Messes. The practice of smoking at the table after the Loyal Toast is no longer appropriate and is not permitted. Those wishing to smoke do so in designated areas.

Alcohol

There is no custom or tradition that requires a Mess member to accept an invitation to drink with fellow members or to drink alcoholic beverages at all. On the contrary, excessive indulgence is not to be tolerated and is a sign of a lack of self-discipline. No embarrassment should be caused to those who decline to have alcoholic drinks. Each member is only required to pay for their own drinks, or for personal guests. Members are not under any obligation to join a 'shout'. Where the Mess invites Mess guests, members share costs as determined by the Mess Committee.

Any ceremony or activity that requires, or encourages, the excessive consumption of alcohol is not permitted.

Only in exceptional circumstances, such as entertaining Official Guests, should alcohol be consumed during normal working hours. In such cases members are advised not to return to their work.

Fines

The imposition of 'fines' within a Mess, as a disciplinary measure for breaches of mess etiquette, either actual or supposed, is illegal.

Mess Staff

Mess staff should be treated with courtesy and consideration, without encouraging familiarity. All Mess staff should be addressed by their rank and/or title. Civilian or contractor's employees should be referred to as Mr, Mrs or Ms (surname) as appropriate. The Mess staff should not be employed on personal errands.

Formal Mess Dinner - The Royal Welsh Fusiliers

Mess Functions

A Mess normally holds various types of functions including social events and formal occasions, which enable members to give and return hospitality. These functions are arranged by the Mess Committee and may take many forms, such as a cocktail party, BBQs, theme night, fancy dress, a dance, garden party or dinner, depending on circumstances. When a member is unable to attend a dining-in night because of duty or other pressing reasons, permission to be excused is sought from the PMC. As a matter of courtesy, members should indicate as required by the Mess Committee whether they will be attending other Mess functions. Functions should be neither so lavish nor so frequent, that they become a financial or social burden on any member.

Guests

The number of guests to be invited to any Mess function will depend on the occasion. Personal guests should be entertained by their hosts and the host remains responsible for their guests, ensuring the guest is familiar with Mess customs and procedures to avoid embarrassment. A Mess member should be appointed to host each Mess guest and a spouse who is not a member of the Mess is to be treated as a guest at all times.

Members should mix freely with their guests and each host should attend to their guest's needs and well-being.

Guests should be introduced to the CO and the PMC by their host, on arrival or shortly after. A host should also arrange for guests, before departing, to speak again with the CO and the PMC.

A Mess member whose spouse is a Service member whose rank does not entitle them to Mess membership may, with the approval of the CO and/or PMC, be accompanied by their spouse on those occasions when mixed functions are held provided uniform is not worn and normal courtesy is observed to superior officers.

The Dining-In Night/Formal Mess Dinner[409]

The Dining-In Night/Formal Mess Dinner is a traditional social gathering within the Mess. Simple procedures have become established to heighten the enjoyment of the meal, and impart graciousness to the occasion not often found elsewhere. Such dinners are a regular feature of Mess life.

Formal Mess Dinners differ from informal and formal meals, in that both non-resident and resident members are expected to attend and guests may be invited. A member should only be excused from a Formal Mess Dinner with the permission of the PMC.

Procedure

In all Messes a similar procedure is followed and minor variations for their own sake, or those that suggest pretentiousness, should be avoided. On the other hand, customs that have some truly traditional basis are encouraged except where they may contravene Army policy or military/civil law.

409 Department of Defence. *Army Protocol Manual.* Canberra, Defence Publishing Service: 2001, pp. 8-12

Dining President

Every Formal Mess Dinner is under the control of a Dining President. This member is appointed by the PMC for a particular occasion or for a period and may be any member of the Mess; the PMC or CO may choose to act as Dining President.

The Dining President is responsible for the service of the meal, the beverages and the observance of customs and traditions.

Dining Vice-President

The Dining Vice-President is normally the most junior member of the Mess and is appointed by the PMC to assist the Dining President.

The Dining Vice-President may be referred to as 'Dining Vice-President'; however:

- 'Mr Vice' may be used for a male member

- 'Madam Vice' for a female member.

Assembly

Members should assemble in the Ante-Room before the first guests arrive, for example, members assemble before 7.30pm if the function is to commence at 8.00pm. Here the members and their guests, if there are any, will expect to move into the dining room at 8.00pm.

Reception of Guests

All the guests are greeted by the Dining President assisted by the Dining Vice-President. Guests should then be introduced to the PMC and the CO, provided with refreshment and introduced to the other members present. This is the task of the host member and should be carried out naturally and without haste. If there are many guests, or the time is short, an introduction after dinner is preferable to an enforced bout of hand-shaking for guests who have only recently arrived.

Seating Plans

Formal Meals with Guests and Formal Mess Dinners. When guests are invited, or when the dinner is a Formal Mess Dinner, a seating plan should be prepared and placed in a convenient position. Each member conforms to the plan and ensures that their guests know where they are to be seated before moving into the dining room.

Formal Meals, without Guests. For formal meals when no guests are invited a seating plan is not needed. Seats are reserved for the Dining President, Dining Vice-President and the CO only. The remaining seats should be filled beginning with those nearest the Dining President.

Table Layout. In preparing the seating plan, consideration must be given to the layout of the tables and the positions occupied by dining appointments, CO and principal guests. Seating plans will vary due to the number of diners and the requirement for single, 'U' shaped or a multi wing table layout.

Seating Arrangements

When male and/or female guests are present the following guides for seating should be observed:

- As far as possible men and women should be seated alternately

- Spouses/partners should normally be seated opposite or diagonally opposite

- At a single table when the host and hostess are seated centrally opposite each other, the senior official guest and his/her spouse are seated on the host/hostess' right

- At a 'U' shaped table, the senior official guest is seated on the host's/hostess' right and the spouse of the senior official guest is seated on the host/hostess' left

- Prior to moving into a mixed dinner, gentlemen should check the seating plan and if a lady is seated on their right be prepared to escort her to the table, joining her in the Ante-Room, not later than five minutes before moving in.

Moving into Dinner

The Dining Vice-President quietly warns members and their guests that dinner will be announced in five minutes. In large Messes, or when there are many guests attending, more warning time should be given. If there is a bugler or trumpeter available, the 'Warning for Dinner' call should be played.

When satisfied that all guests are ready, the Dining President should advise the CO or PMC. With the approval of the CO or PMC, the Mess Supervisor will announce 'Gentlemen, (or Gentlemen and Ladies), Dinner is served'. The dinner announcement may be replaced by the playing of the appropriate 'Mess Call'.

The Dining President will then lead the way into the dining-room. If a band or piper is present, the 'Army March', or the Corps or Regimental march as appropriate, is played. The piper would lead the party into the dining room continuing to play while members and guests take their places at the table.

When moving into dinner, at a mixed dinner, the male officer offers his right arm to any woman who may be seated on his right. The piper marches out when everyone has taken their seat.

The Dining Vice-President, who must ensure that everyone moves in quickly, should be last to enter.

In the dining room, members and guests go to their assigned places as shown on the seating plan and stand behind his/her chair.

The Dining President will remain standing behind his/her chair until the Dining Vice-President is in position. The Dining President will then call upon the Chaplain, if present, or another Mess member, to say Grace. At the conclusion of Grace, the Dining President will take his/her seat. No one should sit until the Dining President does so.

Vacant Places

The table is usually set for the exact number expected. If, for some reason there are more places than necessary, the spare table settings and chairs are removed by the Mess stewards before dinner is served. Mess staff may assume that no one will enter the dining room after the Dining Vice-President.

Chair for Fallen Comrades

A Chair for Fallen Comrades is an old custom within a few Messes where it is customary have a chair positioned at the dining table draped with the National Flag. The program for an Anzac Day dinner in Durban, South Africa held by the Memorable Order of Tin Hats (MOTHs) in 1929 notes:

The toast of 'Fallen Comrades' will be taken in silence, during which the room will be placed in darkness and a 'Light of Remembrance' is lit by the Commander. The MOTH be placed in darkness and a 'Light of Remembrance' anthem 'Old Soldiers Never Die' will be sung, after which the light in the room will be restored.

If seating spaces allow, this chair is placed at the end of the arm of the 'U' opposite the Dining Vice President. If not, the chair is placed in the centre of, and level with, the ends of both arms of the 'U'. Other items such as the Service Ensigns and the ANF on Pikes, Identity Tags (wording may say 'To Fallen Comrades, Lest We Forget'), a Service Hat or Cap or a Service Jacket can also be added to the chair to embellish the tribute to the Fallen.

The Dinner

Dinner is always served clockwise and sufficient Mess stewards should be available to do this expeditiously. Service will commence at station points agreed between the Dining President and the Mess Supervisor. No station should be more than 10 places, if plated service is provided; and not more than six places, if 'silver service' is provided.

Plates and food should be served and removed from the left. Drink service should always take place on the right of the diner.

Beverages are also served clockwise. Diners should be offered a choice of wines and non-alcoholic beverages. Non-alcoholic drinks are to be served concurrently with wine.

Throughout the dinner the stewards are supervised and controlled by the Mess Supervisor who must be attentive to the Dining President and Dining Vice-President for any instructions.

Occasionally the Dining Vice-President may be called upon by the Dining President to do some duty. If this occurs, a junior member close to the Dining Vice-President should act as Dining Vice-President during his/her absence.

Dining with Colours

If the ANF, a Standard, Guidon, Queen's Colours, Regimental Colours or Banner are to be displayed during the dinner, they are marched in by a Colour Party when the Mess has assembled in the dining room, prior to those dining taking their seats. The Dining President gives the command 'March in the Colour/s', the Colour Party then with all due ceremony brings the Colours in and positions them. The Colour party, after falling out, take their places. The Dining Vice President then states to the Dining President, 'the Mess is assembled'.

Music During Dinner

If a band is present, unobtrusive music may be played during dinner.

Breaks During Dinner

Normally, a dinner is not interrupted. However, if, for some reason a diner has to leave the room, it should be done quietly and without any comment or fuss. If the diner is a guest, the escort, or the member seated on the left should escort the guest to and from the dining room.

Port

After the last course, the table is cleared except for the port glasses, centre piece trophies, candles and floral arrangements, if any. Decanters of port are then placed on the table in front of the Dining President and Dining Vice-President, though if the gathering is large, additional decanters may be needed.

Following the Dining President, those with decanters in front of them remove the stoppers, place them on the table and pour a little port into their glass. The decanter is then passed to the next person on the left who fills their glass and passes the decanter. When a decanter reaches each original member they complete the filling of their glass and place the decanter on the table in front. There is no special mystique about passing the decanter though many flourishes have been introduced. Any practical and courteous method, which reduces the time for passing, and ensures that no decanter is left unnoticed during conversation, may be used. Some Corps Messes use miniature, silver, wheeled gun-carriages and the like, for passing the Port.

As the decanters are passed around the table, stewards follow to replace emptied decanters or to serve non-alcoholic beverages, usually water, to those who do not wish to drink port. Up until the 1980s it was customary for members of the Australian Army Intelligence Corps to be offered whisky as an alternative to port or water.[410] When all have been served, the Mess staff must then leave the dining room but, at the discretion of the Dining President, the Mess Supervisor may remain.

If there are to be several toasts, there may be a requirement to circulate the decanters more than once.

---

410 Discussions, Lieutenant Colonel Neil James (Executive Director ADA)/Les Terrett, 22 February 2014

Example of one method of Regimental Colours displayed for a Dining-In Night. Note: The actual Colour hangs free with the poles supported by a stand to achieve the angled effect.

Toasts

Sequence of Toasts and Speeches. Where honoured guests are either at or represented at a formal dinner, the sequence of toasts and speeches is:

- The Loyal Toast (always occurs)
- Commonwealth Heads of State, in alphabetical sequence
- Other Heads of State, in alphabetical sequence
- The Colonel-in-Chief
- The Army
- The Corps or Regiment
- Other toasts, if appropriate
- Any speeches, if appropriate.

The Loyal Toast.[411] When all glasses are charged, the Loyal Toast is given. The Dining President, remaining seated, calls the table to order, usually by tapping a gavel and then saying 'Dining Vice-President' (may call 'Mister Vice'/'Madam Vice'). No other words are necessary or customary.

The Dining Vice-President, now in charge of proceedings, will rise and say 'Gentlemen', or 'Gentlemen and Ladies'. This shows that all should now rise. Glasses should remain on the table.

When all members have risen and are silent, the band, if present, plays the first four and last four bars of the National Anthem. After the playing of the National Anthem the Dining Vice-President then proposes the Loyal Toast 'The Queen'. However, if there is no band, when all have risen and everybody is silent the Dining Vice-President proposes the Loyal Toast.

In response to the Dining Vice-President all repeat 'The Queen' raise their glasses from the table, drink the toast and resume their seats. The Australian Army does not embellish the Loyal Toast in any way before or after drinking the Toast.

---

411 'Toast' – An act or instance of raising glasses at a gathering and drinking together in honour of a person or thing. In the Army the toast is customarily accompanied with a gesture towards The Sovereign's portrait.

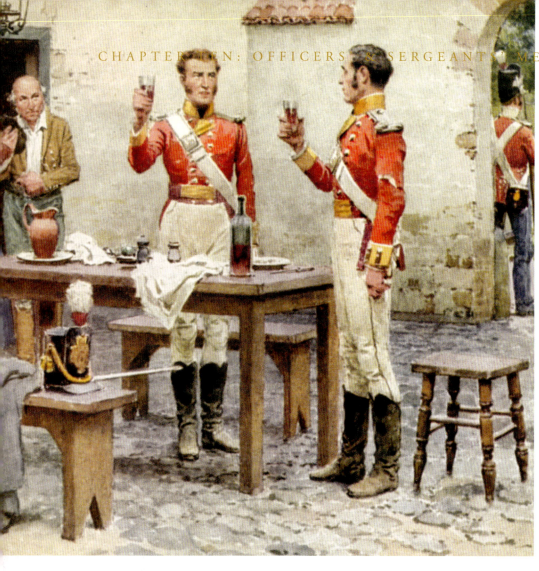

The Loyal Toast – 28th Foot in the Peninsula War 1811

Colonel-In-Chief. Those Corps and regiments which have a member of the Royal Family as their Colonel-in-Chief may include a toast to their Colonel-in-Chief. For example, a regiment of the RAAC could propose and drink a toast to 'Our Colonel-in-Chief, The Prince of Wales'. This toast may be proposed by a member previously nominated by the Dining President.

The Army, Corps or Regiment. On certain appropriate occasions a toast to the Army and a Corps or regiment could be proposed, for example, a toast could be proposed to 'The Army'. This toast should be proposed by a member previously nominated by the Dining President. The band if present plays a short phrase of not more than 32 bars, of the Army, Corps or Regimental March.

Other Toasts and Speeches. Toasts, other than these, are not normally proposed, nor are speeches made, except on special occasions, such as a Corps or regimental birthday, or when a member is being dined out at the end of his/her service.

After the Toasts

If a band has been present, it is normally dismissed after the Toasts. The Dining President may invite the senior band member, or piper, as applicable, to the 'top table'. The Mess Supervisor is to place a chair between the Dining President (or the CO) and the senior official guest. Normally a band member is offered port or water; it is customary to offer whisky to a piper. After no more than two drinks, the band member or piper withdraws and the chair is removed.

The port is normally circulated again, unless the President replaces the stopper in the decanter, in which case no more port is poured.

In the past, cigars and cigarettes were passed around after the toasts. This practice is no longer appropriate as smoking is not permitted in the enclosed areas of Messes.

On occasion coffee and cheese may be served at the table but it is usually served in the Ante-Room after leaving the table.

Leaving the Table

The Dining President should be sensitive to the wishes of the guests, and when ready to leave the table, call the Mess to 'attention' by using the gavel and then rise. All present rise and the Dining President invites the guests to join them in the Ante-Room for coffee and cheese.

The Dining Vice-President automatically assumes the place and duties of the Dining President. Within the Officers' Mess, Mr Vice/Madam Vice may then convene a 'subaltern's court', to arraign selected senior officers or guests prior to re-joining the Dining President and the guests in the Ante-Room.

A similar custom known as a 'kangaroo court' occurs within the Sergeants' Mess. No member should leave the Formal Dinner without the express permission of the PMC and the Dining President.

Foreign Heads of State. When a foreign person or guest is present, a toast may be proposed to their Head of State.[412] The officer or guest concerned should always be consulted beforehand to gain agreement. If two or more foreign persons or guests are present it is permissible to toast all Heads of State.

The Heads of State of Commonwealth countries are toasted before others. The sequence for both is alphabetical order, by country. If there are any doubts about the sequence, or the slightest suspicion that offence might be taken by one or more of the guests, the idea of toasting foreign Heads of State should be abandoned.

The toast is proposed as follows: 'The President of the United States of America'. Like the Loyal Toast, a toast to a foreign Head of State should not be embellished in any way.

If several foreign persons are present the toast proposed may be to 'The Heads of State of the countries represented'.

If a band is present the authorised version of the National Anthem is played. Foreign National Anthems need not be played if two or more foreign persons are present, because of the time involved.

---

412 Note: The toast is to the Head of State and not the Head of Government, as the two are not always the same.

Chapter Eleven

The Australian Character and the ANZAC Tradition

Anzac originates from the 'Australian and New Zealand Army Corps' title that was used by the clerks of GEN Birdwood's staff in his headquarters at Shepheard's Hotel in Cairo, Egypt. The acronym ANZAC was approved by GEN Birdwood as the code for the Corps, when the word was proposed by a MAJ CM Wagstaff. It is thought the suggestion came from a LT AT White of the Royal Army Service Corps. It is recorded in the official history that 'it was some time before the code word came into general use, and at the Gallipoli landing many men in the divisions had not heard of it'. After the landing, GEN Birdwood gained permission to use the name for the area occupied by the Australian and New Zealand Forces.[413]

The Australian soldiers who stormed Gallipoli and served with equal distinction on the other battlefronts were receivers of the characteristics of a perceived legacy of manhood given to them by former generations of bushmen, drovers, miners, shearers, selectors, and workers from urbanised areas in Australia. The courage of the soldiers, their comradeship, their laughter and lack of pretentiousness, their mockery towards undeserved authority, were all traits of their fathers and forefathers. Dr CEW Bean had stressed the team spirit, the very real need for the Australian character of mateship, which existed among the Australian soldiers.

In his pre-WWI book '*Life in the Australian Backblocks*'[414] Edward Sorenson summed up the essentials of the 'digger' spirit of the Anzacs in the following passage:

> Like all high-spirited animals, the bushman frets under restraint, and of authority he has a hatred that is liable at any moment to blaze into fierce rebellion. If he is ordered or commanded instead of asked respectfully to do things by his employer, the position becomes intolerable. Though he may not have a second shirt to his back at the time, he is likely to inform the boss to do it himself, or sarcastically inquire, 'are you talking to me or to the dog?' Neither can he tolerate the word 'master'. As I heard one say to the squatter: You are my employer, not my master. If you think otherwise, take your coat off and prove it. For this reason he makes an unsatisfactory sailor. He won't go sailoring. In war he combines all the essentials of a fine soldier, a superb fighter, but he must be led by a fighter and a shrewd, solid thinking man, not by a gilded Johnny. Used to thinking and acting for himself in all manner of emergencies, and to doing things according to his own ideas and inclinations, he is not inclined to obey unquestioningly the command of one in authority, but will judge for himself and argue the point if the step appears unnecessary or unwise.

The Australian soldier is motivated by mateship, team-spirit and patriotism and has always been seen as a highly-disciplined team member; the words of Edward Sorenson were not intended to be derogatory but were written as an endearment and characterisation of the forming Australian personality.

So, why do we commemorate Anzac Day, that date that has become our national day of commemoration, where we respect those who served and sacrificed their lives in WWI in the hope that it would be the war to end all wars? Anzac Day was first celebrated in 1916 at Serapeum in the Suez Canal Defence Zone. Anzac Day now serves to remember all who served and those who made the ultimate sacrifice in all conflicts that Australians have participated up to the present time.

---

413 Bean CEW. *Official History of Australia in the War of 1914-1918 Volume 1*, Sydney, Angus & Robertson: 1941, Chap XXIV page 546
414 Sorenson ES. *Life in the Australian Back-blocks*. Melbourne, Whitcombe & Tombs Ltd: 1911

History of the Dawn Service[415]

'WE DARE NOT FORGET, though there would be much we would rather forget … we dare not forget the spirit of the Anzac Tradition', the words of the New Zealand Chaplain Commandant Peter Savage in his opening prayer to commemorate Anzac Day in Wellington in 2012.

The Dawn Service on Anzac Day has become a solemn Australian and New Zealand tradition. The first anniversary of the landing was observed in Australia, New Zealand, England and by troops in Egypt and was officially named 'Anzac Day' in Australia by the then Acting Prime Minister, George Pearce. By the mid-1930s, all the rituals we now associate with the day; dawn vigils, marches, memorial services, reunions and two-up games were firmly established as part of the Anzac Day culture.

The Dawn Service symbolises the half-light of dawn at the Gallipoli landing. Dawn has always been one of the most favoured times for an attack as sleeping soldiers are very vulnerable. It was important for soldiers in defensive positions to be alert, and manning their weapons, this is still known as 'stand-to'.

Returned soldiers sought the comradeship they had felt in those quiet, peaceful moments before dawn. A dawn vigil, recalling the wartime front-line practice of the dawn 'stand-to', became the basis of a form of commemoration in several places both during and after the War.

During the 1920s, the form of Anzac Day services and commemorations was developing with a strong religious focus, albeit Christian; although not strongly one church over the others, particularly from the Anzac Day Commemoration Committee which was formed in Brisbane in January 1916.[416]

Within Australia, the Dawn Service is not an Army-specific ceremony. It is a public ceremony normally conducted on behalf of the community by the Returned and Services League of Australia (RSL) with involvement across all three Services of the ADF. As the origin of the Dawn Service is not clear, being subject to many differing views, there is ongoing research into this area by a number of historians that may assist in clarifying this issue.

There are a number of theories about the origins of the Dawn Service:

- A day-time service held on the Western Front by the 14th Infantry Brigade on 25th April 1916

- A service held at Toowoomba Queensland in 1919[417]

- A dawn stand-to or dawn ceremony during the 1920s in New Zealand on Anzac Day as a remembrance

- A service held at the newly-build Cenotaph at Martin Place, Sydney in 1927

- A service conducted in Albany, Western Australia in 1930.[418]

The advent of the Dawn Service (as indicated above) is subject to conjecture but two strong contenders for the first Dawn Service, and the one that appears and is noted by the AWM to be the first 'Official' Dawn Service, is the one held at the Cenotaph in Martin Place, Sydney's CBD; the other is the story of Reverend Arthur Ernest White.

1. **Martin Place, Sydney.** In 1927, the Cenotaph was still under construction and was a building site. As the story goes, five men, 'winding their way home after an Anzac Eve function in the early hours of Anzac Day 1927', came across an elderly woman laying some flowers on the building site that was the still to be completed Cenotaph. The men joined the woman and bowed their heads and resolved to arrange a Dawn Service for the next year's Anzac Day. In 1928 about 150 people attended the Cenotaph for a Dawn Service where flowers were laid and two minutes silence was observed. Dawn Services attracted more and more attention and by 1935, 10,000 people were attending the service at the Cenotaph.

2. **Reverend Arthur Ernest White.**[419,420,421] His story is buried in a small cemetery carved out of the bush some kilometres outside the northern Queensland town of Herberton. Almost ironically, one grave stands out by its simplicity; it is covered by a protective white-washed concrete slab with a plain cement cross at its head. No epitaph recalls even

415 A Parade is primarily a military ceremony while the Service is Church (Religious) that is led exclusively by a Padre, and may consist centrally of prayers and hymns while it might also be a Requiem Mass or Eucharist, depending on the Padre's 'churchmanship'.

416 Moses JA, Davis GF. *Anzac Day Origins*. Canberra, Barton Books: 2013, Chap 4, p. 79

417 Darling Downs Gazette: 24 April 1919, p. 6 - 'ANZAC DAY. OBSERVANCE IN TOOWOOMBA. The Fourth Anniversary of Anzac Day will be commemorated in Toowoomba on Friday. Services will be held in all churches in the morning. In the Roman Catholic Churches, will commence at 7 am and in the other churches at 11 am' (Note: Dawn actually occurred at 6.13 am)

418 Note: On Anzac Day 1930, it is recorded in the Church Service Register that Reverend White celebrated a Dawn Service Eucharist which is documented in his own hand writing. The handwritten notation beside the Service entry reads: "procession to memorial, wreaths laid, collection for distressed soldiers fund and first Dawn Service in Australia". While Reverend White believed that he conducted the first Dawn Service, research shows that there had been other Dawn Services, but Arthur White did contribute to a tradition of celebrating the Dawn Service in a memorable and moving way.

419 Discussions with St Mark's National Theological Centre, Barton, ACT: 27th July 2014.

420 Captain (Chaplain) Arthur Ernest White, BA University of Leeds; enlisted 17 Mar 1916, Chaplain 44 Bn, embarked ex-Fremantle 31 May 1916, appointment terminated 26 Feb 1918: born England 27 August 1883 – died Herberton Queensland 26 September 1954.

421 Emails and discussions, Terrett/John Moses (priest), Professorial Associate, St Mark's National Theological Centre, Barton, ACT: 25 July 2014

the name of the deceased, the inscription on the cross a mere two words – 'A Priest'. Nobody could identify the grave as that of a dedicated clergyman who is purported to have assisted in the creation of the Dawn Service, without the simple marker placed in recent times next to the grave. It reads:

> Adjacent to, and on the right of this marker, lies the grave of the late Reverend Arthur Ernest White, a Church of England clergyman and padre, 44th Battalion, 1st Australian Imperial Force. On 25th April 1923[422] at Albany in Western Australia, the Reverend White led a party of friends in what was the first ever observance of a dawn parade on Anzac Day, thus establishing a tradition which has endured, Australia-wide ever since.

Arthur Edward White was a Londoner who had trained for Holy Orders in England and migrated to Western Australia to serve as a priest in the Brotherhood of St Boniface. As a Church of England clergyman he belonged to the Anglo-Catholic wing of the Church. Reverend White was serving as one of the civilian padres of the earliest AIF troop movements to leave Australia in November 1914. The convoy assembled at Princess Royal Harbour and King George Sound in Albany, Western Australia. Before embarkation, at four in the morning, he conducted a service for all the men of the battalion. The people of Albany then climbed to the peak of Mt Clarence, overlooking the Sound, to farewell the convoy as it sailed away. Soon after the Gallipoli campaign, Reverend White applied to his Bishop for release from the brotherhood in order to serve overseas as a Chaplain. This took place and Reverend White began service on the Western Front in France where he reputedly celebrated the Eucharist in the trenches. His portable altar and some sacred vessels are preserved in a vitrine in the sanctuary of his old church in Albany and the chalice is held by the Forbes (NSW) RSL. When Reverend White returned to Australia in 1919, he served for some time in Victorian and NSW parishes and, after Forbes, he was appointed in 1929 as relieving Rector of St John's Church in Albany.

It was a coincidence that the starting point of the AIF convoys should now become his parish. It is thought the memory of his first Dawn Service for the departing soldiers many years earlier and his experiences overseas, combined with the overwhelming cost of lives and injuries inspired him to honour permanently the valiant men, both the living and the dead, who had joined the fight for the Allied cause. He was quoted as having said:

Albany was the last sight of land these ANZAC troops saw after leaving Australian shores and some of them never returned. We should hold a service (here) at the first light of dawn each Anzac Day to commemorate them.

It has been reported that on Anzac Day he came to hold the first Commemorative Dawn Service. As the sun was rising, a man in a small dinghy cast a wreath into King George Sound while Reverend White, with a band of about 20 men gathered round him on the summit of nearby Mount Clarence and silently watched the wreath floating out to sea. He then quietly recited the words:

'As the sun rises and goeth down, we will remember them'.

All present were deeply moved and news of the Ceremony soon spread throughout Australia; and the various Returned Service communities came to emulate the Ceremony.

The Dawn Service Window, Forbes NSW

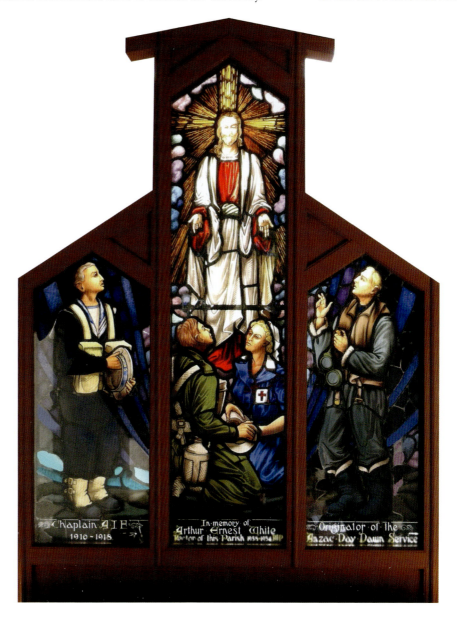

---

422 Note: There is no evidence to show Reverend White in Albany, WA in 1923; research appears to indicate that he did not return to Albany until 1929. Albany Advertiser (WA). Welcome Social, Large Gathering in St John Hall: 28 September 1929, p.3

Eventually, Reverend White was transferred from Albany to serve other congregations, first in South Australia, then Broken Hill where he built a church, then later at Forbes NSW. In his retirement from parish life, he moved to Herberton where he became Chaplain of an Anglican convent. Soon after his arrival in Herberton, he died on 26th September 1954 and was buried modestly and anonymously as 'A Priest'.

Reverend White's memory is honoured by a stained glass, which was fitted in the All Soul's Church at Wirrinya, a small farming community near Forbes. Members of the parish built the church and fitted the windows which are referred to as the 'The Dawn Service Window', as their tribute to Reverend White's service to Australia. Although the church no longer exists, the windows were removed and are now installed in the cloister at St John's the Evangelist Anglican Church, Forbes. Reverend White's memory is further honoured by a tradition that he began on ANZAC Day 1930 when he conducted a Dawn Service which ended with a wreath being laid on the War Memorial next to the St John's Anglican Church; and on ANZAC Day 1931 he instigated the twin traditions of casting a wreath into King George Sound (Albany's Harbour) and, with members of his congregation, climbed to the top of Mt Clarence as had occurred in 1914. He kept these traditions passionately for the rest of his incumbency – this

tradition has continued. Herberton RSL place a wreath on Reverend White's grave each ANZAC Day.

By 1933 Dawn Services were held in every State capital memorial and also in many suburbs and towns.[423]

Rosemary and Anzac Day

Since ancient times this aromatic herb has been believed to have properties to improve memory. Perhaps because of this, rosemary became an emblem of both fidelity and remembrance in literature and folklore and is an emblem for occasions such as funerals and weddings. Shakespeare makes reference to rosemary in Hamlet (Act IV Scene 5) where Ophelia, decked with flowers, says to Laertes:

'There's rosemary, that's for remembrance'.

Rosemary has particular significance for Australians, as it is found growing wild on the Gallipoli Peninsula. Traditionally, sprigs of rosemary are worn on Anzac Day and sometimes on Remembrance Day, usually handed out by Legacy and the RSL. It is thought the tradition arose at Gallipoli as there was no other green foliage available save rosemary to decorate the graves of the fallen soldiers.

423 Inglis KS. *Sacred Places, War Memorials in the Australian Landscape, 3rd Edition*. Melbourne, Melbourne University Press: 2008, Chap 7, pp. 313-314

Catafalque party on ANZAC Day

On each ANZAC Day, a symbolic vigil is provided by a catafalque party consisting of four armed members who are placed facing outwards approximately one metre from the altar or memorial. It could be said that the altar or memorial is a symbolic coffin or grave of those who have fallen.

Remembrance Day Tradition

A brief silence, usually one or two minutes, characterises remembrance ceremonies throughout the British Commonwealth and our other allies.

At 11am on 11th November 1918 the guns of the Western Front fell silent after more than four years of continuous warfare. The Allied armies had driven the German invaders back, having inflicted heavy losses over the preceding four months. In November the Germans called for an armistice in order to secure a peace settlement. They accepted the Allied terms of unconditional surrender.

That day, Armistice Day (the moment when hostilities ceased on the Western Front), attained a special significance in the post-war years, becoming universally associated with the remembrance of those who had died. This first modern world conflict had brought about the mobilisation of over

70 million people and left between 9 and 13 million dead; perhaps as many as one-third of them with no known grave. The Allied nations chose this day and time for the commemoration of their war-dead.

For many years, a South African politician, Sir Percy Fitzpatrick[424], had been credited with the concept of 'a remembrance silence', but, in 1962, a group of Melbourne citizens formed a committee to conclude that the solemn ceremony of silence now observed was originated by Australian journalist Edward George Honey[425],[426] (1885-1922), and that he was the man 'who taught the world to remember'. The Melbourne committee noted:

> The idea of silence as a token of respect to the dead was not new; there was silence on the death of King Edward VII, there was silence in South Africa when WWI was going badly for the allies, and there was silence in Australia for miners killed during the reign of Queen Victoria.

424 Sir Percy Fitzpatrick, KCMG; author, politician, mining financier: born Cape Colony 24 July 1862 – died South Africa 24 January 1931.
425 http://en.wikipedia.org/wiki/Edward_George_Honey: accessed 2 August 2013
426 Edward George Honey; educated Caulfield Grammar School, Melbourne, Journalist WWI: born St Kilda 1885 – died London 1922.

Left: AWM Negative No P01102.01. Sydney, NSW, 8th November 1918. Crowds in Martin Place waiting with upturned faces for the flag to be hoisted and bells to be rung to mark the German agreement to terms for an armistice to end the war

Above: AWM Negative No. H12241. Cambrai, France. 11th November 1918. FM Sir Douglas Haig, Centre front, with British Army Commanders on Armistice Day

FOR FREEDOM

A Victory Souvenir

THE GREAT WAR

War declared With Germany Aug 4 1914 Armistice Signed Nov. 11. 1918

Honey had published a letter in the *London Evening News* on 8th May 1919 under the pen-name of Warren Foster, in which he appealed for a five-minute silence amid the joy-making planned to celebrate the first anniversary of the end of WWI:

Five little minutes only. Five silent minutes of national remembrance. A very sacred intercession. Communion with the Glorious Dead who won us peace, and from the communion new strength, hope and faith in the morrow. Church services, too, if you will, but in the street, the home, the theatre, anywhere, indeed, where Englishmen and their women chance to be, surely in this five minutes of bitter-sweet silence there will be service enough.

No official action was taken on the idea until more than five months later, when on 27th October 1919 Lord Milner forwarded a letter from his friend Sir Percy Fitzpatrick, to the King's private secretary Lord Stamfordham, proposing a period of silence on Armistice Day, in all countries of the British Empire.

Sir Percy Fitzpatrick wrote:

When we are gone it may help bring home to those who will come after us, the meaning, the nobility and the unselfishness of the great sacrifice by which their freedom was assured.

King George V was evidently very moved, and issued a proclamation on 6th November 1919 asking 'that at the hour when the Armistice came into force, the 11th hour of the 11th day of the 11th month, there may be for the brief space of two minutes a complete suspension of all our normal activities … so that in perfect stillness, the thoughts of everyone may be concentrated on reverent remembrance of the glorious dead'.

There is no record that Sir Percy Fitzpatrick was prompted by Honey's letter in the London Evening News, but that both Honey and Sir Percy attended a rehearsal with the King for a five-minute silence involving the Grenadier Guards at Buckingham Palace gives this supposition credence. Five minutes proved too long and the two minute interval was agreed, and it was instituted as part of the main commemorative ceremony at the new Cenotaph in London on 11th November 1919.

On the second anniversary of the Armistice, in London and Paris, the commemoration was given added significance when it became a funeral, with the return of the remains of an Unknown Soldier from the battlefields of the Western Front. Unknown soldiers were interred with full military honours in Westminster Abbey in London and the Arc de Triomphe in Paris. The entombment in London attracted over one million people within a week to pay their respects at the Tomb of the Unknown Soldier. Many other Allied nations adopted the tradition of entombing unknown soldiers over the following decade.

In Australia, on 11th November 1993, the 75th anniversary of the Armistice, the Remembrance Day ceremonies became a funeral, when the remains of an unknown Australian soldier, exhumed from a military cemetery in France was entombed in the AWM. Ceremonies were conducted simultaneously in towns and cities all over the country, culminating at the moment of burial at 11am and coinciding with the traditional two minutes silence. This ceremony, which touched a chord across the Australian nation, re-established Remembrance Day as a significant day of commemoration.

Four years later in November 1997, the Governor-General of Australia, Sir William Deane, issued a proclamation formally declaring 11th November 'Remembrance Day', and urging all Australians to observe one minute's silence at 11am on that day each year, to remember those who died or suffered for Australia's cause in all wars and armed conflicts. The reason that one rather than two minute silence was decided on is not known.

On the 80th Anniversary, an Armistice Remembrance Medal was announced by Prime Minister John Howard. It was designed by sculptor Peter Corlett and specially produced for the 70 surviving Australian veterans. Alec William Campbell, born Launceston, Tasmania, February 1899, the last surviving Australian veteran of the Gallipoli campaign died on 16th May 2002 in Hobart.

AWM Negative No. 137060. Melbourne, 11th November 1942 – Armistice Day 'Two Minutes Silence'

293

Tomb of the Unknown Australian Soldier in the Hall of Memory, AWM

Left: AWM Negative No. PAIU1993/288.16

Right: AWM Negative No. PAIU2006/057.02

Two Minute Silence within the RSL

At every RSL function, no matter how small, members stand in silence for a brief interval to remember departed comrades.

At League clubs around Australia the remembrance silence has become part of the now nightly six o'clock (previously nine o'clock) ritual, when any light other than a memorial flame is dimmed, members stand in silence, and then recite the Ode:

> They shall grow not old, as we that are left grow old
> Age shall not weary them, nor the years condemn
> At the going down of the sun and in the morning
> We will remember them

> Lest we forget

How the remembrance silence was adapted by the League to become an essential feature of League functions, and particularly the nine o'clock ceremony, is not documented. Some members have tried to explain the League's nine o'clock ritual in terms of the nightly nine o'clock ceremony at Menin Gate, France. An extract from a 1980 edition of the 'Thirty-niner', published in the Highgate sub-branch newsletter in 1981, sought an explanation concerning the chiming of the bells of Big Ben in London at 9pm. According to this report, the practice of silencing BBC radio transmissions while Big Ben chimed 'nine'

began in November 1940 'as a propaganda symbol to free men in the captive nations of the world'. Moreover, this account has it that the then chairman of the Big Ben Council, which introduced the practice, had been influenced by a fellow officer who, in a premonition of his own death, had asked on behalf of the dead, 'We will help you spiritually … Lend us a moment of your time each day and by your silence give us our opportunity, the power of silence is greater than you know'.

Some League members take a more practical view and, in the absence of written records, say the most likely reason for the timing of the 9pm service was when meetings would have to finish, to give members time to catch the tram home in those early days, and that the men would have chosen to close their meetings with the remembrance silence. This view holds that a simple coincidence of practicality and the wish to remember dead mates gave rise to the Australian ritual.

The League's national president, Gilbert Dyett, had introduced the practice of beginning RSL Federal executive meetings with a minute's silence in memory of departed comrades in July 1930.

The RSL members in South Australia had developed a nine o'clock service before WWII, and at the League's 21st Annual Congress in Adelaide in 1936, the National Congress resolved '… that it be a suggestion to State branches that at all meetings of ex-servicemen a simple ceremony for departed comrades be carried out at 9 o'clock similar to that observed in South Australia'.

The time change from 9pm (2100h) to 6pm (1800h) for the nightly ritual would seem to have come about in recent years as a direct result of a 'family-friendly focus' as many members would leave prior to the nine o'clock ritual. The time change gave members and their families the opportunity to participate whilst meeting other family commitments.

The Ode

The Ode comes from 'For the Fallen', a poem by the English poet and writer Laurence Binyon, published in London in 'The Winnowing Fan: Poems of the Great War (1914)'. The verse, which became the League Ode, was already used in association with commemoration services in Australia in 1921:

For the Fallen

With proud thanksgiving, a mother for her children,
England mourns for her dead across the sea.
Flesh of her flesh they were, spirit of her spirit,
Fallen in the cause of the free.

Solemn the drums thrill: Death august and royal
Sings sorrow up into immortal spheres.
There is music in the midst of desolation
And a glory that shines upon our tears.

They went with songs to the battle, they were young,
Straight of limb, true of eye, steady and aglow.
They were staunch to the end against odds uncounted,
They fell with their faces to the foe.

They shall grow not old, as we that are left grow old;
Age shall not weary them, nor the years condemn.
At the going down of the sun and in the morning
We will remember them.

They mingle not with their laughing comrades again;
They sit no more at familiar tables at home;
They have no lot in our labour of the day-time;
They sleep beyond England's foam.

But where our desires are and our hopes profound,
Felt as a well-spring that is hidden from sight,
To the innermost heart of their own land they are known
As the stars are known to the night;

As the stars that shall be bright when we are dust,
Moving in marches upon the heavenly plain,
As the stars that are starry in the time of our darkness,
To the end, to the end, they remain.

Laurence Binyon (1869-1943)

Each year, after Anzac Day and Remembrance Day, debate arises over the word 'condemn' (express complete disapproval, denounce, rebuke, censure or criticise)[427] or 'contemn' (to treat or regard with contempt, despise, scorn or look down on).[428] The Ode used is the fourth stanza of the poem 'For the Fallen' by Laurence Binyon and was written in the early days of WWI. By mid-September 1914, less than seven weeks after the outbreak of war, the British Expeditionary Force in France had already suffered severe casualties. Long lists of the dead and wounded appeared in British newspapers. It was against this background that Binyon wrote 'For the Fallen'. The poem was first published in The Times on 21st September 1914 using the word 'condemn'. Some people have suggested that the use of 'condemn' in The Times was a typographical error. However, The Winnowing Fan, published a month or two later and for which Binyon would have had galley proofs on which to mark amendments, 'condemn' was again used.

Binyon was a highly-educated man and very precise in his use of words. There is no doubt that had he intended 'contemn', it would have been used.

Dr John Hatcher, who in 1955 published a biography of Binyon, does not refer to any doubt over condemn/contemn, despite devoting a solid chapter to 'For the Fallen'.

The British Society of Authors, executors of the Binyon estate, says the word is definitely 'condemn', while the British Museum, where Binyon worked, says its memorial stone also shows 'condemn'. Both expressed surprise when told there had been some debate about the matter in Australia. The condemn/contemn issue seems to be a distinctly Australian phenomenon. Inquiries with the British, Canadian and American Legions revealed that none had heard of the debate.

'Contemn' is not used in Binyon's published anthologies and the two-volume set of Collected Poems, regarded as the definitive version of Binyon's poems, uses 'condemn'. The RSL handbook shows 'condemn' and a representative of the Australian War Memorial said it always used 'condemn' in its ceremonies.

---

427 Pearsall J (editor). *The Concise Oxford Dictionary (10th edition)*. Oxford, Oxford University Press: 1999, p. 297
428 Pearsall J (editor). *The Concise Oxford Dictionary (10th edition)*. Oxford, Oxford University Press: 1999, p. 306

The Red Poppy[429]

In the lead-up to 11th November each year, the RSL sells millions of red cloth poppies for Australians to pin to their lapels, with the proceeds going to the RSL welfare work. Why a red poppy?

John McCrae (later Lieutenant Colonel), who was Professor of Medicine at McGill University in Canada (joining the McGill faculty in 1900 after graduating from the University of Toronto), first described the red poppy, the Flanders' poppy, as 'the flower of remembrance'.

He had served in the Boer War as a gunner and went to France as a medical officer with the first Canadian contingent.

It was impossible to get used to the suffering, the screams, and the blood, and MAJ McCrae had seen and heard enough in his dressing station to last him a lifetime. As a surgeon attached to the 1st Field Artillery Brigade, MAJ McCrae had spent 17 days treating injured men; Canadians, British,

Indians, French, and Germans in the Ypres salient, an ordeal that he had hardly thought possible. He later wrote:

> I wish I could embody on paper some of the varied sensations of that 17 days … 17 days of Hades! At the end of the first day if anyone had told us we had to spend 17 days there, we would have folded our hands and said it could not have been done.[430]

One death particularly affected MAJ McCrae; a young friend and former student, LT Alexis Helmer of Ottawa, who was killed by a shell burst on 2nd May 1915. LT Helmer was buried later that day in the little cemetery outside McCrae's dressing station, and McCrae performed the funeral ceremony in the absence of the chaplain.

The next day, sitting on the back of an ambulance parked near the dressing station, just a few hundred metres north of Ypres, he could see the wild poppies that sprang up in the ditches in the nearby cemetery. McCrae vented his anguish by scribbling for 20 minutes in pencil in his dispatch book the 15 line poem that has come to be known as 'In Flanders'

Roll of Honour – Australian War Memorial

429 Dancocks DG. *Welcome to Flanders' Fields – The Great Canadian Battle of the Great War: Ypres, 1915.* Toronto, Canada, McClelland and Stewart: 1988, pp. 250-251

430 Bassett J. *The Canadians: John McCrae.* Markham, Ontario, Fitzhenry & Whiteside: 1984, p. 44

Fields' which described the poppies that marked the graves of dead soldiers. He was no stranger to writing, having authored several medical texts and dabbled in poetry.

22 year-old Sergeant Major Cyril Allinson watched MAJ McCrae write the poem. MAJ McCrae looked up as he approached, then went on writing while Allinson stood there quietly. Allinson recalled: 'His face was very tired but calm as he wrote, he looked around from time to time, his eyes straying to Helmer's grave'. When McCrae finished five minutes later, he took his mail from Allinson, and without saying a word, handed his pad to him. Allinson was moved by what he read, 'The poem was an exact description of the scene in front of us both. The word blow was not used in the first line though it was used later when the poem appeared in the magazine Punch. But it was used in the second last line. He used the word blow in that line because the poppies actually were being blown that morning by a gentle east wind. It never occurred to me at that time that it would ever be published. It seemed to me just a description of the scene.'[431]

In fact, it was very nearly not published. Dissatisfied with it, McCrae tossed the poem away, but a fellow officer (either LTCOL Edward Morrison, the former Ottawa newspaper editor who commanded the 1st Brigade of Artillery[432], or LTCOL JM Elder[433], depending on which source is consulted) retrieved it and convinced McCrae to publish it. 'The Spectator' in London rejected it, but 'Punch' published it on 8th December 1915.

McCrae's 'In Flanders' Fields' remains to this day one of the most memorable war poems ever written. It is a lasting legacy of the terrible battle in Ypres in the spring of 1915.

In Flanders' Fields

In Flanders' Fields the poppies blow
Between the crosses, row on row,
That mark our place; and in the sky
The larks, still bravely singing, fly
Scarce heard amid the guns below.
We are the dead. Short days ago
We lived, felt dawn, saw sunset glow,
Loved, and were loved, and now we lie
In Flanders' Fields.

Take up our quarrel with the foe:
To you from failing hands we throw
The torch; be yours to hold it high.
If ye break faith with us who die
We shall not sleep, though poppies grow
In Flanders' Fields.

LTCOL McCrae fell ill and was taken to the coast of France for hospitalisation, where on the third evening he was wheeled to the balcony of his room to look over the sea towards the cliffs of Dover. The verses were obviously in his mind, for he said to the doctor, 'Tell them, if ye break faith with us who die we shall not sleep'. On 28th January 1918 after an illness of five days, he died of pneumonia and meningitis. The day he fell ill, he learned he had been appointed consulting physician to the 1st British Army, the first Canadian so honoured. In Australia in 1921 the League announced:

The Returned Sailors and Soldiers Imperial League of Australia and other Returned Soldiers Organisations throughout the British Empire and Allied Countries have passed resolutions at their international conventions to recognise the poppy of Flanders' Fields as the international memorial flower to be worn on the anniversary of Armistice Day. In adopting the Poppy of Flanders Fields as the Memorial Flower to be worn by all Returned Soldiers on the above mentioned day, we recognise that no emblem so well typifies the Fields whereon was fought the greatest war in the history of the world nor sanctifies so truly the last resting place of our brave dead who remain in France. The Returned Sailors and Soldiers of Australia join their comrades of the British Empire and Allied Countries in asking people of Australia to wear the poppy; firstly in memory of our sacred dead who rest in Flanders' Fields; secondly to keep alive the memories of the sacred cause for which they laid down their lives; and thirdly as a bond of esteem and affection between the soldiers of all Allied nations and in respect for France, our common battle ground.

The League brought one million poppies from France to sell on 11th November 1921 at one shilling (12 pence/10 cents) each. Five pence per poppy was to go back to France towards a fund for the children of the devastated areas of France, with sixpence per poppy retained by each State branch and one penny going to the League's National Office. The RSL has kept up this tradition of selling poppies to mark the 11th of November, even when the poppies were no longer obtained from France. The little silk poppies worn on Armistice Day are an exact replica in size and colour of the Poppies that bloom in Flanders' Fields.

Poppies adorn the panels of the Australian War Memorial's Roll of Honour, placed beside names as a personal tribute to the memory of a particular serviceman; this practice began at the interment of the Unknown Australian Soldier on the 11th November 1993.

431 Mathieson WD. *My Grandfather's War.* Toronto, Macmillan: 1981, p. 264
432 Hickmore G. *Origin of In Flanders' Fields.* Ottawa Canada, Public Archives: MG30 EI33, Vol 4
433 Canadian Daily Record: 5/3/1919

ANZAC

'ANZAC' with or without full stops is an acronym, standing for the 'Australian and New Zealand Army Corps'. 'Anzac' on the other hand, is an accepted Australian English word, which came into regular use as early as May 1915. The fact that 'Anzac' is a proper word is confirmed by the '*Protection of the Word Anzac Regulation*', made under the *War Precautions Act Repeal Act 1920*; this Act and Regulation are still in force:

> No person shall, without the authority of the Governor-General of Australia or of a Minister of State, proof whereof shall lie upon the person accused, assume or use the word Anzac, or any word resembling the word Anzac, in connection with any trade, business, calling or profession, or in connection with any entertainment or any lottery or art union, or as the name or part of the name for any private residence, boat, vehicle, or charitable or other institution, or any building in connection there with. Penalty £100 or imprisonment for six months, or both.[434]

The Anzac Biscuit – also known as The Soldiers' Biscuit

Some believe the recipe for the Anzac Biscuit pre-dates the Gallipoli landings as the Scots had a similar biscuit known as Scottish Oatcakes. The biscuit became known as the Soldiers' Biscuit; the current name, 'Anzac (Biscuit)' being part of the diet at Gallipoli. The Anzac biscuit is one of the few commodities that is able to be legally marketed in Australia using the word Anzac, which is protected by Federal Legislation.

During WWI, the friends and families of soldiers and community groups sent food to the fighting men but, due to the time delays in getting food items to the front-lines, had to send food that would not spoil but remain edible without refrigeration for long periods of time. To ensure that the biscuits remained crisp, they were packed in used tins such as Billy Tea tins. Anzac Biscuits continue to be sent to Australian troops serving overseas.

Although there are variations, the basic ingredients for the biscuits are:

- 1 cup of rolled oats
- 1 cup of sugar
- 1 cup of plain flour
- ½ cup of coconut
- 125g of butter
- 2 tablespoons of golden syrup
- ½ teaspoon of bi-carbonate of soda
- 1 tablespoon of water.

The Gum Leaf

During wars and otherwise posted abroad, Australian soldiers have used gum leaves to remind them of home. During WWI and WWII, gum leaves and golden wattle were enclosed with letters to the soldiers as reminders of things they loved. Often soldiers would gather their leaves together to burn them for the nostalgic effect the aroma of the burning leaves would give.

It was rumoured that on one such occasion, the smell of burning gum leaves stirred some men from the bush so much that one discharged his rifle in glee. Unfortunately the Germans were not to know that and replied with rifle fire, which induced machine guns to join in, and so it spread until artillery of both sides was engaged.

THREE GUM LEAVES IN TOBRUK

Have you ever in the bushland felt the strength of this great land
Smelt a burning gum leaf or held it in your hand
Then you'll know the scent of freedom of courage and of home
These things you will remember no matter where you roam

On a far and distant battlefield in a cruel and senseless war
The soldiers are Australian like the slouch hats that they wore
Their youthful faces taunted with a grey and shattered look
They've been to hell and back again these soldiers of Tobruk

Amongst them was a soldier with a letter in his hand
A letter from down under it's a letter from a dad
As he lifts the page to read it the leaves fall in his hand
Three gum leaves from Australia to remind him of this land

With trembling hands he burns a leaf and blows smoke in the air
To share the scent of Australia with those young men fighting there
As it drifts through the trenches each soldier sighs with joy
As it brings back pleasant memories of their homeland as a boy
Round a campfire at twilight or a horseman on his throne
Each soldier has a memory that takes him to his home

So now with spirits lifted came the haunting bugle sound
And each man went with courage to do Australia proud
In the heat and dust of battle as they watched their comrades fall
With the scent of burning gum leaves these brave men gave their all

On a still and silent battlefield a letter found next day
With a half burnt gum leaf on the ground there where it lay
As the Captain read the letter a letter from a dad
His eyes filled with tears as this is what he read

Son, have you ever in the bushland felt the strength of this great land
Smelt a burning gum leaf or held it in your hand
Then you'll know the scent of freedom of courage and of home
I hope these leaves will help you son until you're safely home

Dianne Lindsay and Peter Simpson 2007

---

[434] War Precautions Act (Act has been repealed but this clause is still in effect): 1920

Legacy

On returning to Australia, some Servicemen felt their colleagues were failing to assist other returned men adequately. In 1923, MAJGEN Sir John Gellibrand[435] founded the Remembrance Club in Hobart. Its aim was to encourage returned Servicemen in business to care for the dependants of deceased Australian Servicemen and women, including any death which was deemed Service-related. LTGEN Stanley Savige[436], who had also served with Gellibrand, visited Hobart in August 1923 where Gellibrand urged him to set up a similar club in Melbourne.

On Savige's return to Melbourne, he brought the idea to the fore using Gellibrand's Remembrance Club as his model. After several informal meetings, the Melbourne club's inaugural meeting was held at Anzac House in Melbourne. For the next 26 years, due to Savige's commitment, energy and enthusiasm, his name became inseparable from both the club and the movement. In 1925 it was suggested that Legacy look at caring for the children of deceased Servicemen. This proposal was accepted and Legacy found its soul. This legacy of care continues to this day.

Volunteer members (usually ex-Service members) are called 'Legatees' because they accept the 'legacy of care' for their comrades' families. Legacy's assistance depends on the individual situation of the person being supported. With the help of Legatees, who stay in touch with all families, Legacy ensures families receive their entitlements and access to Government benefits. As well as financial support, Legacy provides companionship for ex-personnel and their families and assistance with the education of children and maintenance of War Widows' residences.

---

435 Major General Sir John Gellibrand, KCB, DS0, psc; Commanded 3rd Aust Div 1918, Chief Commissioner of Police Victoria 1920-1922: born 'Lleintwardeine' Ouse Tasmania 5 Dec 1872 – died Murrindindi Victoria 3 June 1945.
436 Lieutenant General Sir Stanley Savige, KBE, CB, DSO, MC, ED; AIF: 24 Bn 1914-1917; Comd Urmia Force, Persia 1918, 2nd AIF Comd 17 Bde 1939-1941, GOC 3 Div 1942-1944, I Corps and NG Force 1944, II Corps 1944-1945. Manufacturers' agent and company director: born Morwell Victoria 26 June 1890 – died 15 May 1954.

Chapter Twelve

Military Funerals and Remembrance

Military Funerals

At the time of King Henry VIII (r. 1509-1547), military bands were not formally included in military units, but every body of fighting men boasted a party of drummers and trumpeters, to set and maintain the marching pace, provide signalling in battle, and to break the monotony during long marches by blowing an occasional fanfare. Henry VIII directed that these instruments should be employed in the funeral ceremonies of high-ranking officers.

The coffin would be carried to the place of burial on a wagon, normally that used to move the heavy cannons of the period. The wagons were huge, cumbersome vehicles drawn by a team of draught horses at a speed scarcely above a crawl. Behind the wagon marched a party of drummers playing what was then called the 'Dede Sounde' at a pace in keeping with the extremely slow rate of progress of the wagon. In 1723 the term 'Dede Sounde' was changed to 'Dead March'; thus was born the 'Dead March' or 'Slow March' of the present time. Although speedier vehicles have been introduced, the original slow step has been retained, being seen as more befitting the dignity of a military funeral.

The procedure followed at the graveside was also inaugurated in Tudor times (1485-1603). After the coffin had been lowered into the grave, musketeers posted on either side fired three volleys. The firearms of the period, being either 'matchlock' or 'wheellock', some six feet long and about 15lbs (6.8kg) in weight, required support in the shape of a forked rest which was stuck in the ground under the muzzle. In order to elevate the weapons, firing parties were formed in a kneeling position opposite each other. After the volleys, 'Last Post' and 'Reveille' were played. At that time, 'Last Post' took the form of 'Taps' (or 'Tap Toe').

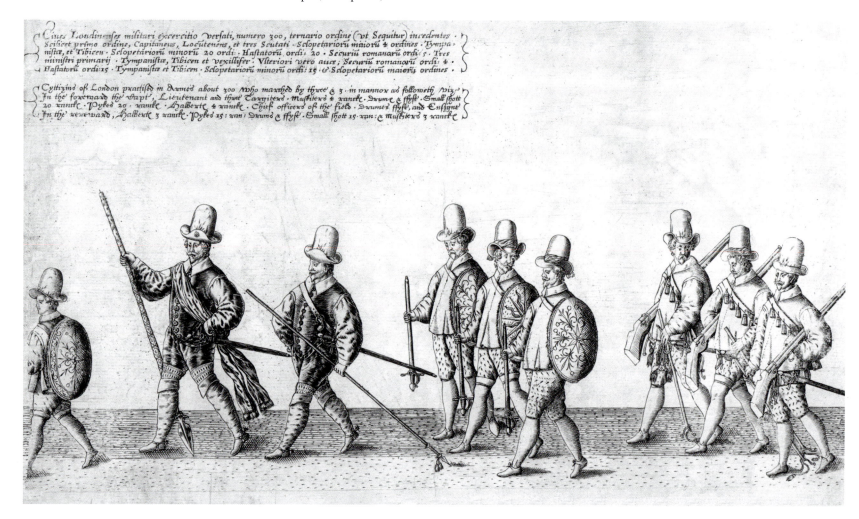

Above: AWM Neg No AWM E05067. AIF Soldiers marching with Arms Reversed

Left: Sir Philip Sidney's Funeral Procession, 1586 (Printed 1587)

Symbolism at Funerals

There are some remarkable symbols still used at Military funerals. The following are examples:

Insignia. The personal servants of nobles would follow the coffin of their deceased masters, carrying the honours and regalia of the various Orders to which the nobles belonged. This custom is perpetuated today by the carrying of the deceased member's decorations and medals, behind the coffin and pinned to a scarlet silk or velvet cushion, which is then placed on a table positioned near the coffin in sight of the congregation

The ANF on the Coffin. The ANF is draped over the coffin with the Union Jack positioned above the deceased's left shoulder. The ANF is used as a token indicating that the person died in the service of the State and that the State accepts the responsibility for his fate. The ANF is the appropriate flag for covering coffins of all Service personnel who die on operations and is also used at funerals conducted by the RSL for returned Servicemen and Servicewomen.

Reverse Arms. The origin of reversing arms for funerals can be traced back over many centuries. Prior to the introduction of firearms, it was common practice for lances, pikes and halberds to be dragged along the ground by those in funeral processions. The Standard or Guidon of the deceased would also be trailed along the ground in the same manner.

Muskets had been in use in Europe since about 1400, but it was not until the 1500s that they were introduced into the English militia. From copper plate engravings of the funeral procession of Sir Philip Sidney[437], engraved in 1587, the method of carrying weapons can be seen; lances or pikes dragging along the ground, swords held by the blade and muskets carried under the arm.

The tradition that gave birth to the drill movement 'reverse arms' is not known; however, it is known the 'reverse arms' was used by a Commonwealth soldier at the execution of Charles I in 1649; the soldier was, however, duly punished for his symbolic gesture of support for the King. It was later recorded that at the funeral of John Churchill, 1st Duke of Marlborough, the troops carried out a formal 'reverse arms' drill, especially invented for the service, as a unique sign of respect for the great soldier.[438]

As with all drill movements, this most solemn gesture from one soldier to another has been modified from time to time according to the type of weapon on current issue to the Army. The Australian Army was armed with the Martini Henry, the Short Magazine Lee Enfield .303 and then later with the 7.62mm L1A1, both rifles of approximately the same length. Because of this, the drill movements for funerals remained almost unchanged until the introduction of the much shorter Austeyr F88 assault rifle in 1989.

437 Sir Phillip Sidney; MP Kent 1581, soldier: born Kent 30 Nov 1554 – died Netherlands 17 Oct 1586.
438 Australian Army. *Ceremonial Manual – 2003 Volume 1.* Canberra, Defence Publishing Service: 2003, Chap 18

Above: AWM Neg No AWM 087280.
Reversing Boots in Saddle Stirrups

Centre: AWM Neg No AWM 050015.
Firing Party – WWII

Right: AWM Neg No 147997.
Kure, Japan – 1952. Catafalque Party
from 1st Reinforcement Holding Unit
stand in the 'Rest on Arms Reverse'
position in the Garrison Chapel

Reversing Boots in Saddle Stirrups. The tradition of reversing the boots of a deceased mounted soldier seems to stem from about the same time (pre-1650s), as that of Reverse Arms. It was normal for all British officers to be mounted even in the infantry, and their horse was added to the funeral possession riderless with boots reversed as a symbol of respect, being led by a groomsman behind the hearse.

The Three Volleys. The firing of volleys at military funerals first appeared in Orders of 1573 where it was stated that matchlocks would be fired over graves. An old superstition has it, that during times of grief, the door to a man's heart stands ajar and volleys are fired into the air thus recreating the noise of war to represent the essence of the soldier's life. There was also the belief that it was to ward off devils.

Belief in the Holy Trinity is responsible for the actual number of volleys being fired. As a child is baptised in the name of the Father, Son and the Holy Ghost, so now, at the soldier's death, he was blessed by the symbol of the Trinity, this time expressed not in words but by their military equivalent, the firing of three volleys. The firing takes place after the solemn words, 'Earth to earth, ashes to ashes and dust to dust'.

Firing Party. A firing party in the Australian Army consists of one Sergeant, one Corporal and 10 other ranks.

Gun Salutes. Refer to Chapter 7.

Accoutrements Placed on the Coffin. The following items are placed on the coffin after it has been placed inside the church prior to the service:

- **Headdress.** The appropriate headdress is placed on top of and at the head end of the coffin. The headdress is that normally worn by the deceased member's Corps, regiment, or unit.

- **Arms.** The only weapon to be placed on the coffin of a commissioned officer or WOI is a sword. A serving or ex-serving RSM may have a pace stick placed on the coffin in lieu of the sword. A bayonet in a scabbard is used for soldiers of the rank of WO2 and below. The scabbard is placed centrally on top of the coffin, with the point facing towards the feet. In the case of a Chaplain, no sword is used as Chaplains do not normally carry weapons; a suitably appropriate device is obtained from the Chaplains Department for placing on the coffin.

- **Wreath.** A wreath may be supplied by the next of kin or the deceased's unit and is placed on top at the foot of the coffin.

- **Baton.** For the funeral of a Field Marshal, the Marshal's personal baton is placed on top of the coffin in a position as if it was resting on the deceased's left thigh.

- **The Last Post.** This is the 'Nunc Dimittis'[439] of the dead soldier. The Nunc Dimittis is a canticle that uses text taken directly from the *Bible*. The significance of the high ascending note with which it ends is one of hope and expectancy. It is the last bugle call, but it gives promise of Reveille, which ultimately the Archangel Gabriel will blow. Following is one translation of the original text by St Luke (2: 29-32):

> Lord, now you let your servant go in peace;
> Your word has been fulfilled.
> My eyes have seen the salvation
> You have prepared in the sight of every people,
> A light to reveal you to the nations and the
> glory of your people, Israel.

Rifle and Helmet Markers

The 'modern act' of sticking rifles muzzle-down into the ground as a temporary memorial to a fallen soldier (with a helmet or a hat over the butt) is believed to have originated with the introduction of tanks. When a soldier fell during an advance, his comrade would pick up the fallen soldier's rifle and stick it into the ground with the bayonet fixed, as a marker to indicate to tanks that a wounded or dead soldier lay there; and in this way the armoured vehicle would not accidentally run over the injured or dead soldier.

439 'Nunc Dimittis': A prayer offered to God attesting to the fact that a soldier has kept his faith and departs this life with hope.

Composition of a Catafalque Party and the Vigil

A catafalque party consists of four members who are placed facing outwards approximately one metre from the coffin or catafalque. A catafalque is a raised structure supporting a stand upon which a coffin is placed for display before burial. People can then file past and pay their last respects to the deceased person.

If a catafalque party is required to be mounted for an extended period during a 'lying-in-state', the party is divided into 'watches' each six hours in duration. A watch is made up of four vigils, with each vigil mounting for a period of half an hour (followed by a break of one and one-half hours). Vigils are not changed during a religious service.

Historically a vigil was mounted around the coffin to ensure that the body was not interfered with whilst laying-in-state. Today, vigils, and catafalque parties, are mounted as a sign of respect around the coffins of deceased personages as they lie-in-state awaiting burial, and also around cenotaphs on Anzac and Remembrance Day.

The Gun Carriage

There appears to be little symbolism attached to the use of a gun carriage to carry the coffin in a funeral procession, this may have been adopted as a dignified military method of carrying a coffin. In the mid-1800s, the Queen's Regulations were amended to permit the use of a gun carriage and horses to carry a coffin to a burial ground, but only when it was over a mile away. Since those days, a motorised gun carriage has become an accepted part of military and State funerals.

War Cemeteries

Until 1982 all British and Australian Serviceman and civilians killed by enemy action were buried and commemorated as close to the place of death as possible. This tradition developed from the impracticality of returning to Britain and Australia large numbers of war-dead from the far-flung reaches of the World. The Commonwealth War Graves Commission, formed by the British Government on 21st May 1917, was charged with the management of these graves. Since 1982 the Office of Australian War Graves has fulfilled this role on behalf of the Australian Government.

Over the years there have been some exceptions to this rule. The most significant was the first commander of the AIF, MAJGEN WT Bridges, who was mortally wounded by a sniper's bullet at Gallipoli on 15th May 1915. He was the only Australian killed in WWI to have his remains returned to Australia. He is buried at Duntroon where years earlier he had served as the College's first commandant. His horse, Sandy, was the only one of the 136,000 walers[440] shipped to the Great War that was repatriated, being put down in 1923. One of Sandy's preserved hooves was turned into an ink-well used in Duntroon House for many years; his head and neck were mounted and became part of the AWM's collection. Sandy was displayed for many years, although is currently not on exhibition owing to deterioration through age.

Australian policy for the repatriation of fallen Servicemen changed much earlier than that of the British, due mainly to pressure from the families of National Servicemen.

Due to the operational nature of the conflict in Vietnam there was little or no opportunity for ceremony prior to the repatriation of deceased soldiers. Wounded soldiers were usually evacuated directly to the US 36 Casevac Hospital and 1st ALSG (8 Field Ambulance RAAMC). When a soldier died from his wounds, his remains were normally repatriated to Australia by C130 Hercules from the Area of Operations.[441] This system did not allow the member's friends and comrades, still fighting in the forward areas, the opportunity to

---

440 The Waler is an Australian breed of riding horse that developed from the horses brought to the colonies in the 19th century. The name comes from their early breeding origins in New South Wales; they were originally known as New South Walers.

441 Terrett LI. *Interview with Gary Cole ex-SGT/WO2 176 AD Coy (RAASC). 1966/67 and 1969:* 27 July 2014

Left: The grave of Major General Sir William Throsby Bridges, in a bushland setting at Mount Pleasant, Duntroon

Right: Department of Defence – Army 20080425adf8234827_003. Anzac Day, Australia Island (Camp Victory), Baghdad

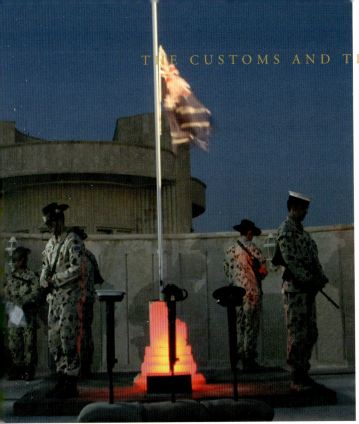

Flying Flags at Half Mast

The tradition of flying flags or sails at half-mast had its beginnings in the Royal Navy and can be traced back to the 17th century. In March 1952[444], Buckingham Palace asked the Board of Admiralty for information on the origin of the custom of half-masting flags to signify a death. Mr Peter Kemp, the Archivist at that time, replied:

> The earliest record we have of the lowering of a flag to signify a death was an occasion in 1612, when the Master of the 'Hearts Ease', William Hall, was murdered by Eskimos while taking part in an expedition in search of the North West Passage. On re-joining her consort, the vessel's flag was flown trailing over the stern as a mark of mourning. On her return to London, the 'Hearts Ease' again flew her flag over the stern and it was recognised as an appropriate gesture of mourning.

> It was the habit, after the restoration of the Monarchy in 1660, for ships of the Royal Navy to fly their flags at half-mast on the anniversary of the execution of King Charles I (30th January 1649); and it is from this custom that, so far as we can determine, the present practice of announcing a death by the flying of a flag at half-mast has evolved.

In a subsequent minute on the subject Mr Kemp added:

> We know that the hoisting of black sails was a sign of mourning from the very earliest times. The black sail was superseded by the black flag, probably because it was a nuisance to have to carry black sails for use only on rare occasions. It was probably the position, rather than the colour, that caught the attention, particularly at a distance.

The position of a flag at half-mast will depend on the size of the flag and the length of the flagpole. It is essential that the flag be set in a position that is easily recognisable as being at half-mast. As a guide, the top of the flag should be down one-third from the top of the pole. When flown on a flagpole with a yardarm, the top of the flag is in line with the yardarm. No other flags should be flown when the ANF is at half-mast on a flagpole without a yardarm. If the ANF is flown on a flagpole with a yardarm, other flags may be flown as long as the top of the ANF, at half-mast, is still above the other flags.

When hoisting a flag that is to be displayed at half-mast, it should be hoisted to the mast-head for an instant, and then lowered to half-mast. Likewise when it is lowered at the end of the day, it is to be hoisted back to the Mast-head for an instant, and then lowered in the normal manner.

farewell their companion in arms. It was standard procedure for bodies to be shipped in lead-lined coffins to funeral homes in Australia.[442] The Australian population's growing disaffection with the war in Vietnam may have contributed to this seemingly informal procedure for the reception of the soldiers' remains. This was the first time in history that our war-dead were returned to Australia for burial and the sight of coffins arriving from Vietnam draped in an Australian Flag might have caused further antagonistic reactions from the civilian population. It was only after the member's body had been handed over to civilian undertakers that arrangements were made for either a private or formal military funeral (at the request of the member's family); the actual burial place was selected by the soldier's next of kin.

All 521 Servicemen who lost their life during the Vietnam War have now been returned to Australia for burial.

In recent times, the Office of Australian War Graves has created ten 'Gardens of Remembrance'[443] memorials to commemorate officially those eligible Servicemen and Servicewomen whose deaths have been attributed to war service. These Gardens of Remembrance are an almost exclusively Australian form of official commemoration where veterans are remembered in the company of those with whom they served. The Gardens are landscaped and contain a series of walls upon which memorial plaques are placed. Generally, veterans are commemorated in the State in which they resided. The Gardens are situated adjacent to or within existing cemeteries throughout Australia. The Office of Australian War Graves also financially assists War Graves Walls within public cemeteries throughout Australia.

442 Taubert SC. Interview with David Taubert ex-driver 392 Transport Platoon, Brisbane 1971-1973: August 20104

443 http://www.dva.gov.au/commems_oawg/OAWG/post_war_ commemorations/gardens_remembrance/Pages/locations.aspx: accessed 2 August 2014

444 Kent B. *Signal! A History of Signalling in the Royal Navy.* Clanfield United Kingdom, Hyden House: 1993, p. 336

Department of Defence – Army No. 20100824adf8115142_563. Ramp Ceremony, Afghanistan

The ANF is flown at half-mast on the following occasions:

- The death of The Sovereign – from the time of announcement of the death up to and including sunset on the day of the funeral.

- The death of a member of the Royal family but only on the day of the funeral.

- The death of the Governor-General of Australia or a former Governor-General of Australia from the time of the announcement of the death up to and including sunset on the day of the funeral.

- The death of the Head of State of another country, with which Australia has diplomatic relations, on the day of the funeral.

- The death of a distinguished Australian citizen. Flags in any locality may be flown at half-mast on the death of a notable local citizen, or on the day, or part of the day of their funeral.

- On Anzac Day the flag is flown at half-mast until noon.

- Remembrance Day flags are flown at peak till 10:30am, at half-mast from 10:30am to 11:01am or 11:02am (subject to a one-minute or two-minute silence), and then re-raised to the peak for the remainder of the day.

- Other occasions as directed by the Department of Defence upon orders from the Governor-General of Australia.

Ramp Ceremony

The Ramp Ceremony is a recent observance developed in part to give the comrades of the deceased member the opportunity to pay respect to their fallen friends and comrades in the Area of Operations.

A Ramp Ceremony occurs when the body of a dead soldier is carried on and off an aircraft. The Ceremony entails a vigil mounted by members of the unit, and a memorial service followed by the grouping of all off-duty non-essential personnel forming a guard of honour lining the route to the aircraft. The coffin is carried on or in a unit combat vehicle. Unit members act as the mourners and the pall-bearer party follows the coffin to the waiting military aircraft. The coffin is then removed from the vehicle and placed, with all due ceremony, in the waiting aircraft. The deceased is then returned to Australia where a formal 'returning home', sometimes termed 'repatriation', ramp ceremony is conducted. This ceremony is a military occasion that allows the Service to welcome home the fallen soldier formally and acknowledge their service and sacrifice. The deceased's next of kin are invited to attend the 'repatriation' ramp ceremony. The arrangements for the funeral are at the discretion of the next of kin who have the option of a full military funeral or a private ceremony, either of which is paid for by the Commonwealth.

Chapter Thirteen

Titles, Mottoes and Badges

Regimental Territorial Titles

In line with the British system, '*Territorial Titles*' were in use since colonial times and were noted in *Military Order 427* of 1914 and Military Order 1/1916; it is likely that these titles were in common use prior to that time. Territorial Titles received official sanction in 1927 in *Australian Army Order* (AAO) 132/1927 as tabled below.[445] Although closely associated with mottoes, the Territorial Title indicated a unit's recruiting area and although these areas were at times increased or decreased, as the situation required, their regional title remained unchanged. Some regions were not easily defined and boundaries were also changed from time to time to permit the establishment of new units.

The following table shows AMF units and their Territorial Title along with the State of origin, and if known, the region which made up its recruiting base. Many city-based battalions used the names of suburbs in their titles, and therefore their recruiting area is self-explanatory.

Unit	Territorial Title	Location
Light Horse Regiments		
1st Light Horse	Royal New South Wales Lancers	New South Wales
2nd Light Horse	Queensland Mounted Infantry	Queensland
3rd Light Horse	South Australia Mounted Rifles	South Australia
4th Light Horse	Corangamite Light Horse	Western District of Victoria
5th Light Horse	Wide Bay and Burnett (QMI)	Bundaberg Region, Queensland
6th Light Horse	NSW Mounted Rifles	New South Wales
7th Light Horse	Australian Horse	New South Wales
8th Light Horse	Indi Light Horse (Indi is an Aboriginal name for the Murray River)	Federal Electoral Region of Indi, Country Victoria
9th Light Horse	Flinders Light Horse	South Australia
10th Light Horse	Western Australian Mounted Infantry	Western Australia
11th Light Horse	Darling Downs Light Horse (QMI)	Queensland
12th Light Horse	New England Light Horse	New South Wales
13th Light Horse	Gippsland Light Horse	Victoria
14th Light Horse	West Morton Light Horse (QMI)	Queensland
15th Light Horse	Northern Rivers Lancers	New South Wales
16th Light Horse	Hunter River Lancers	New South Wales
17th Light Horse	Prince of Wales's Light Horse	Victoria
18th Light Horse	Adelaide Lancers	Adelaide, South Australia
19th Light Horse	Yarrowee Light Horse	Victoria
20th Light Horse	Victorian Mounted Rifles	Victoria
21st Light Horse	Riverina Horse	New South Wales
22nd Light Horse	Tasmanian Mounted Infantry	Tasmania
23rd Light Horse	Barossa Light Horse	Barossa Valley, North of Adelaide
24th Light Horse	The Gwydir Light Horse	Gwydir District, New South Wales
25th Light Horse (MG)	None Selected	Southern Districts, Western Australia

445 Australian Army Order (AAO) 132/1927. *Territorial Titles and Mottoes – Regiments and Battalions, AMF*: 1927

Unit	Territorial Title	Location
AMF Infantry Battalions		
1st Infantry Battalion	City of Sydney's Own Regiment	New South Wales
2nd Infantry Battalion	The City of Newcastle Regiment	New South Wales
3rd Infantry Battalion	The Werriwa Regiment	New South Wales
4th Infantry Battalion	The Australian Rifles	New South Wales
5th Infantry Battalion	The Victorian Scottish Regiment	Victoria
6th Infantry Battalion	The Royal Melbourne Regiment	Victoria
7th Infantry Battalion	The North West Murray Borderers	Victoria
8th Infantry Battalion	The City of Ballarat Regiment	Ballarat, Victoria
9th Infantry Battalion	The Moreton Regiment	Brisbane, Queensland
10th Infantry Battalion	The Adelaide Rifles	South Australia
11th Infantry Battalion	The City of Perth Regiment	Western Australia
12th Infantry Battalion	The Launceston Regiment	Tasmania
13th Infantry Battalion	The Macquarie Regiment	New South Wales
14th Infantry Battalion	The Prahran Regiment	Victoria
15th Infantry Battalion	The Oxley Regiment	Queensland
16th Infantry Battalion	The Cameron Highlanders of Western Australia	Western Australia
17th Infantry Battalion	The North Sydney Regiment	New South Wales
18th Infantry Battalion	The Kuring-Gai Regiment	New South Wales
19th Infantry Battalion	The South Sydney Regiment	New South Wales
20th Infantry Battalion	The Parramatta and Blue Mountains Regiment	New South Wales
21st Infantry Battalion	The Victorian Rangers	Victoria
22nd Infantry Battalion	The Richmond Regiment	Victoria
23rd Infantry Battalion	The City of Geelong Regiment	Victoria
24th Infantry Battalion	The Kooyong Regiment	Victoria
25th Infantry Battalion	The Darling Downs Regiment	Toowoomba, Queensland
26th Infantry Battalion	The Logan and Albert Regiment	Logan, Beenleigh, Redland Bay Area, Queensland
27th Infantry Battalion	The South Australian Scottish Regiment	South Australia
28th Infantry Battalion	The Swan Regiment	Western Australia
29th Infantry Battalion	The East Melbourne Regiment	Victoria
30th Infantry Battalion	The NSW Scottish Regiment	New South Wales
31st Infantry Battalion	The Kennedy Regiment	Queensland
32nd Infantry Battalion	The Footscray Regiment	Victoria
33rd Infantry Battalion	The New England Regiment	New South Wales
34th Infantry Battalion	The Illawarra Regiment	New South Wales
35th Infantry Battalion	Newcastle's Own Regiment	New South Wales
36th Infantry Battalion	St George English Rifles Regiment	New South Wales
37th Infantry Battalion	The Henty Regiment	Victoria
38th Infantry Battalion	The Northern Victorian Regiment	Victoria
39th Infantry Battalion	The Hawthorn-Kew Regiment	Victoria
40th Infantry Battalion	The Derwent Regiment	Tasmania
41st Infantry Battalion	The Byron Scottish Regiment	New South Wales

Unit	Territorial Title	Location
42nd Infantry Battalion	The Capricornia Regiment	Queensland
43rd Infantry Battalion	The Hindmarsh Regiment	South Australia
44th Infantry Battalion	The Western Australian Rifles	Western Australia
45th Infantry Battalion	The St George Regiment	New South Wales
46th Infantry Battalion	The Brighton Rifles	Victoria
47th Infantry Battalion	The Wide Bay Regiment	Queensland
48th Infantry Battalion	The Torrens Regiment	South Australia
49th Infantry Battalion	The Stanley Regiment	Queensland
50th Infantry Battalion	The Tasmanian Rangers	Tasmania
51st Infantry Battalion	The Far North Queensland Regiment	Queensland
52nd Infantry Battalion	The Gippsland Regiment	Victoria
53rd Infantry Battalion	The West Sydney Regiment	New South Wales
54th Infantry Battalion	The Lachlan-Macquarie Regiment	New South Wales
55th Infantry Battalion	The NSW Rifles Regiment	New South Wales
56th Infantry Battalion	The Riverina Regiment	New South Wales
57th Infantry Battalion	The Merri Regiment	Victoria
58th Infantry Battalion	The Essendon-Coburg-Brunswick Regiment	Victoria
59th Infantry Battalion	The Hume Regiment	Victoria
60th Infantry Battalion	The Heidelberg Regiment	Victoria

Note: 5/6 RVR has the unofficial title of 'Melbourne's Own'. This is to recognise its lineage to the original 6th Battalion, 'The Royal Melbourne Regiment', the oldest Royal Regiment in the Australian Army.

Regimental Mottoes

Regimental mottoes are a brief statement used to express a principle, goal or ideal of the appropriate character for a unit or organisation. Corps, regimental and some miscellaneous mottoes have been used by units of the Army since Federation; many are in Latin, Welsh, French and German, with a small number in plain English.

Although mottoes were in use well before Federation, it was not until 1927 that formal approval for their adoption occurred with the issue of Australian Army Order (AAO) 132/1927. Approval to have the unit's regimental motto incorporated onto the Regimental Colour was approved in the same year, although initially units had to pay for the work to be completed at their own expense.[446]

Mottoes were not specifically allocated to units because of their numerical identifier; usually a unit that existed within an area or territory passed its motto onto a newly-raised unit when it was disbanded. Therefore it was common that a unit's territorial title would be associated with a particular motto, for example: 'The Gwydir Light Horse – Deo Regi Patraie' was used by both the 12th and 24th Light Horse Regiments at different times. It was also frequently the practice for units wishing to maintain some linkage to their original parent units such as when the 4th Light Horse joined the 19th Light Horse; they adopted the hat badge from one unit and incorporated the motto from the other.

Since these mottoes were first created, some of the translations have been varied to facilitate understanding of their meanings. When an original meaning was available it has been included. The translation of Latin to English does not always follow grammatically and at times translations were rudimentary at best. It goes without saying that not all approving authorities, or originators of mottoes, were Latin scholars!

---

446 Australian A*rmy Order (AAO) 548/1927. Regimental Colours and Mottoes – Battalions, A.M.F.* 1927

Indigenous Unit Motto[447]

There is only one Australian Army unit that has a Regimental motto based on an Australian aboriginal language, that being the Pilbara Regiment. Their motto 'Mintu Wanta' loosely translates as 'always alert'. The motto is taken from one of the Western Desert dialects. The Pilbara Regiment is one of the three Regional Force Surveillance Units (RFSU) based in the north of Australia.

The Regiment's badge depicts an emu on crossed Short Magazine Lee Enfield .303 Mk 1 rifles, within a wreath of Sturt's desert pea in flower.

The emu was selected as the central theme as:

- It is common throughout the Pilbara
- It has a wary yet inquisitive nature
- It has an ability to blend with the environment
- It has an ability to move swiftly over vast distances
- It has an ability to survive harsh conditions.

The Sturt's Desert Pea was selected for the wreath because of its local profusion. When Pilbara Regiment members wear mess dress, their collar badges are worn so that the emus face outward (addorsed). Members who have served with The Pilbara Regiment for 20 years have their commitment and contribution recognised by being authorised to wear a burnt orange felt-backing behind the regimental badge on their slouch hat.

447 Information taken from the unpublished RFSU's official unit history.

Regimental Mottoes and Translations[448]

Unit	Motto	Translation
Army	Serving the Nation	Serving the Nation
Light Horse Regiments		
1st Light Horse	Tenax in Fide	Steadfast in Faith
2nd Light Horse	Forward	Forward
3rd Light Horse	Nec Aspera Terrent	1. Not Even Hardship Deters Us 2. Neither Do Difficulties Deter Us
4th Light Horse	Prest D'Accomplir	1. Quick to Act 2. Ready to Act
5th Light Horse	Forward	Forward
6th Light Horse	Toujour Pret	Always Ready
7th Light Horse	For Hearths and Homes	For Hearths and Homes
8th Light Horse	More Majorum Indi	More, greater every day
9th Light Horse	Pro Gloria Et Honore	For Glory and Honour
10th Light Horse	Percute Et Percute Velociter	Strike and Strike Swiftly
11th Light Horse	Forward	Forward
12th Light Horse	Virtutis Fortuna Comes	Fortune Favours the Brave
13th Light Horse	Loyal Till Death	Loyal Till Death
14th Light Horse	Forward	Forward
15th Light Horse	Nomina Desertis Inscripsimus	We Have Written Our Names in the Desert

448 This incomplete list of Mottoes was extracted from many sources including: Army Order (AAO) 175/1937 and *Territorial Titles and Mottoes – Australian Military Forces*: 1937. The translations are from: Urdang L, Robbins C. *Mottoes*. Indiana, Gale Research Company: 1986 and the Australian War Memorial Research Department to whom we give thanks.

Unit	Motto	Translation
16th Light Horse	Tenax Et Fidelis	Steadfast and Faithful
17th Light Horse	1. Ich Dien 2. Loyalty	1. I Serve 2. Loyalty
18th Light Horse	For God King and Country	For God King and Country
19th Light Horse	Pro Gloria	For Glory
20th Light Horse	Pro Rege Pro Patria	For King, For Country
21st Light Horse	Virtus in Arduis	Virtue in Adversity
22nd Light Horse	Pro Rege Pro Patria	For King, For Country
23rd Light Horse	Swift and Sure	Swift and Sure
24th Light Horse	Deo Regi Patriae	God, King, Country
25th Light Horse	None Selected	
1st Armoured Car	Celere Exploratu	Explore Swiftly
6th New South Wales Mounted Rifles	Toujours Pret	Always Ready
2nd Armoured Car Regiment	Speed and Vigilance	Speed and Vigilance
AMF Infantry Battalions		
1st Infantry Battalion	Nominis Memento[13] Primus Agat Primus	Remember This Name 1. First Always First 2. Let the First be Foremost
2nd Infantry Battalion	Nulli Secundus	Second to None
3rd Infantry Battalion	Verity Frondescit Honore	Its Ancient Honour Flourishes
4th Infantry Battalion	For Home and Country	For Home and Country
5th Infantry Battalion	Mori Quam Foedari	I Prefer to Die than to be Dishonoured
5th Battalion Scottish	Nemo Me Impune Lacessit	Provoke Me Not with Impunity
6th Infantry Battalion	Semper Paratus	Always Ready
7th Infantry Battalion	Cede Nullis	Yield to None
8th Infantry Battalion	Celer Et Audux	Swift and Bold/Brave
9th Infantry Battalion	1. For King and Country 2. Proud to Serve	1. For King and Country 2. Proud to Serve
10th Infantry Battalion	Pro Patria	For Country
11th Infantry Battalion	Vigilans	Vigilant
11th/16th Infantry Battalion	Vigilans Et Vincens	Be Vigilant and Conquer
12th Infantry Battalion	Ducit Amor Patriae	Love of Country Leads Us
13th Infantry Battalion	Vigor in Arduis	Strength in Adversity
14th Infantry Battalion	Stand Fast	Stand Fast
15th Infantry Battalion	Caveant Hostes	Let the Enemy Beware
16th Infantry Battalion	Vigilans Et Vincens	Be Vigilant and Conquer
17th Infantry Battalion	Facta Probant	1. Deeds are the Proof 2. Deeds Prove
17th/18th Infantry Battalion	Legionis Lampada Tradamus	We Hand on the Legion's Lamp
18th Infantry Battalion	Legionis Lampada Tradamus	We Hand on the Legion's Lamp
19th Infantry Battalion	Fortiter Est Fideliter	1. Strongly and Faithfully 2. Bravely and Faithfully 3. Boldly and Faithfully
20th Infantry Battalion	Pro Patria	For Country
21st Infantry Battalion	Pro Deo Et Patria	For God and Country

Unit	Motto	Translation
22nd Infantry Battalion	Famam Extender Factis	1. We Extend our Fame by Deeds
		2. To Increase our Renown Through Deeds
23rd Infantry Battalion	Nulli Secundus	Second to None
24th Infantry Battalion	I Hold Fast	I Hold Fast
25th Infantry Battalion	Vestigia Nulla Retrorsum	No Step Backwards
26th Infantry Battalion	Nunquam Non Paratus	At No Time Not Ready
27th Infantry Battalion	Primus Inter Pares	First to Make Ready
28th Infantry Battalion	Urgens	Urgent
29th Infantry Battalion	Nulli Secundus	Second to None
30th Infantry Battalion	Ommi Modo Fidelis	In Always Faithful
31st Infantry Battalion	Semper Paratus Defendere	Always Ready to Defend
32nd Infantry Battalion	Audax Pro Patria	Courageous for Country
33rd Infantry Battalion	Strenue Percute	Strike Hard
34th Infantry Battalion	Malo Mori Quam Foedari	I Prefer to Die than to be Disgraced
35th Infantry Battalion	Fidelis Et Paratus	Faithful and Ready
36th Infantry Battalion	St George for Merrie England	St George for Merrie England
37th Infantry Battalion	Indivisible	Indivisible
38th Infantry Battalion	Honorem Custodite	Guard your Honour
39th Infantry Battalion	Factis Non Verbis	By Deeds Not Words
40th Infantry Battalion	Pro Aris Et Focis	For Altars and Hearths
41st Infantry Battalion	Mors Ante Pudorem	1. Death without Shame
		2. Death before Dishonour
42nd Infantry Battalion	Cede Nullis	1. Yield to None
		2. Never Surrender
43rd Infantry Battalion	Nil Desperandum	Do Not Despair
44th Infantry Battalion	In Hoc Signo Vinces	In This Sign You Will Conquer
45th Infantry Battalion	Quo Fata Vocant	Wither Destinies Summon
46th Infantry Battalion	Prorsum Simulque	Forward at Once
46th Infantry Battalion	Delectat Amor Patria	For Love of Country
47th Infantry Battalion	Defendere Non Provocare	To Defend Not Provoke
48th Infantry Battalion	Nunquam Victis	Never Conquered
49th Infantry Battalion	Semper Fidelis	Always Faithful
50th Infantry Battalion	Quo Fas Et Gloria	Where Duty and Glory Lead
51st Infantry Battalion	Ducit Amor Patriae	Love of Country Leads Us
52nd Infantry Battalion	Always Ready	Always Ready
53rd Infantry Battalion	1. Be Prepared	1. Be Prepared
	2. Usque Ad Finemm	2. Until the End
54th Infantry Battalion	Deo Patriae Tibi	1. For God My Country and Thee
		2. For God My Country and My Native Land
55th Infantry Battalion	Faugh-A-Ballagh (Irish Origin)	Clear the Way
55th Infantry Battalion	Animo Et Fide	Courageously and Faithfully
56th Infantry Battalion	Trutina Probatus	Proved in the Balance
57th Infantry Battalion	Strike Hard	Strike Hard
58th Infantry Battalion	Nulli Cedere	Yield to None

Unit	Motto	Translation
59th Infantry Battalion	Fidelis Et Audax	Faithful and Bold
60th Infantry Battalion	Celer Et Audax	Swift and Bold
University Regiments		
Queensland University Regiment	Scientia Ac Labore	1. Through Knowledge and Hard Work 2. Knowledge and Hard Work
Sydney University Regiment (Sydney University Scouts)	Sidere Mens Eadem Mutato	1. Unchanging in Resolve 2. The Stars Change, [but] the Mind [remains] the Same 3. Though the constellations change, the mind is universal
University of New South Wales Regiment	1. Honi Soit Qui Mal Y Pense 2. Scientia	1. Evil to He who Evil Thinks 2. Knowledge
Melbourne University Regiment	Postera Crescam Laude	1. May I Grow Famous to Posterity 2. We Grow in the Esteem of Future Generations
Monash University Regiment	Ancora Imparo	I Am Still Learning
Adelaide Universities Regiment	Sapientia Omnia Vincit	Wisdom Conquers All
Western Australia University Regiment	Seek Wisdom	Seek Wisdom
Queensland Agriculture College Queensland Regional University Regiment	Science with Practice	Science with Practice
Deakin University Company	Aut Pace Aut Bello	Either by Peace or by War
State Infantry Regiments		
Royal Queensland Regiment	Pro Aris Et Focis	1. For Hearth and Home 2. For Altars and Hearths
Royal New South Wales Regiment 1/19 RNSWR 2/17 RNSWR 4/3 RNSWR 41 RNSWR	Primus in Terra Australis	First in Australia 1. Strongly and Faithfully 2. Bravely and Faithfully 3. Boldly and Faithfully
Royal Victoria Regiment 5 RVR 6 RVR 7 RVR 8 RVR	Melbourne's Own Nemo Me Impune Lacessit Semper Paratus Bold, Steady, Faithful Cede Nullis Celer et Audax	Melbourne's Own Provoke Me Not with Impunity Always Ready Bold, Steady, Faithful Yield to None Swift and Bold/Brave
The Victorian Rangers	Pro Deo et Patria	For God and Country
Richmond Volunteer Rifle Corps	Famam extendere factis	To Increase Our Renown Through Deeds
Royal South Australia Regiment	Pro Patria	For Country
Royal Western Australia Regiment	Vigilant	Vigilant
Royal Tasmania Regiment	Pro Aris Et Focis	1. For Hearth and Home 2. For Altars and Hearths
Other Battalions and Regiments		
Royal Australian Regiment	Duty First	Duty First
Special Air Service	Who Dares Wins	Who Dares Wins
51st Battalion, The Far North Queensland Regiment	Ducit Amor Patriae	Love of Country Leads Us
NORFORCE	Ever Vigilant	Ever Vigilant

Unit	Motto	Translation
Pilbara Regiment	Mintu Wanta	Always Alert
1st Commando Regiment	Strike Swiftly	Strike Swiftly
2nd Commando Regiment	Foras Admonitio	Without Warning
2/2nd Commando Squadron	Nearest to Tokyo	Nearest to Tokyo
Papua New Guinea Volunteer Rifles	Per Augusta Ad Augusta	Through Glory to Glory
Pacific Islands Regiment	To Find a Path	To Find a Path
2/6th Battalion	Nothing Over Us	Nothing Over Us
2/9th Battalion	Will Not be Late	Will Not be Late
2/18th Battalion	Legionis Lampada Tradamus	Hand On the Torch of the Legion
2/72nd Light Aid Detachment	Celerus Quam Luce	Faster Than Light
161 Recce Squadron	Paragon	Model of excellence
2nd Recruit Training Battalion	Nulli Secundus	Second to None
3rd Training Battalion	Duty and Knowledge	Duty and Knowledge
Australian Army Training Team Vietnam	Persevere	Persevere
Armoured Regiments		
1st Armoured Regiment	Paratus	Ready
2nd Cavalry Regiment	Courage	Courage
3rd Cavalry Regiment	Resolute	Resolute
4th Cavalry Regiment	Tenacious	Tenacious
3rd/4th Cavalry Regiment	Resolute/Tenacious	Resolute/Tenacious
1st/15th Royal NSW Lancers	Tenax in Fide	Steadfast in Faith
2nd/14th Light Horse Regiment (Queensland Mounted Infantry)	Forward	Forward
3rd/9th Light Horse, South Australian Mounted Rifles	Nes Aspera Terrent	Not Even Hardships Deter Us
4th/19th Prince of Wales's Light Horse	Ich Dien	I Serve
1st/15th Royal NSW Lancers	Nomina Desertis Inscripsimus	In the Deserts We Have Written Our Names
8th/13th Victorian Mounted Rifles	Pro Rege Et Patria	For King and Country
12th/16th Hunter River Lancers	Virtutis Fortuna Comes	1. Fortune Favours the Brave 2. Fortune is the Companion of Valour
A Sqn 10th Light Horse	Persecute et Persecute Velociter	Strike and Strike Swiftly
8th/12th Victorian Mounted Rifles	Pro Rege et Patria	For My King and Country
7th/21st Australian Horse	Virtus in Arduis	Courage In Difficulties
4th Australian Light Horse (HRL)	Prest D'Accomplir Tenax et Fidelis	Ready to Accomplish Steadfast and Faithful
6th Australian Light Horse	Virtutis Fortuna Comes	Fortune is the Companion of Valour
Aviation Regiments		
1st Aviation Regiment	Alert	Alert
5th Aviation Regiment	On Time – Intact Bold	On Time – Intact Bold
6th Aviation Regiment	Valour	Valour
Training Schools		
Officer Cadet School	Loyalty and Service	Loyalty and Service
Australian Command and Staff College	Wisdom is Strength	Wisdom is Strength

Unit	Motto	Translation
Command and Staff College	Tam Marte Quam Minerva	1. As Much by War as by Wisdom 2. By Arts and Science as well as by War
Combat Arms Training Centre	Professional Mastery. Fighting Spirit	Professional Mastery. Fighting Spirit
Army Logistic Training Centre	Excel with Honour	Excel with Honour
Army Recruit Training Centre	Home of the Soldier	Home of the Soldier
Miscellaneous Units		
131 Divisional Locating Battery	Eyes of the Task Force	Eyes of the Task Force
Special Operations Command	Acies Acuta	The Cutting Edge
Headquarters Special Forces	Festina Lente	Hasten Slowly
HQ 6 Engineer Support Regiment	Accuratio Viribusque	Strength and Precision
1st Combat Support Regiment	Scire Est Potestatem Habere	Information is Power
1st Intelligence Battalion	Periculum aliis arcete	Keep others from danger
39th Personnel Support Battalion	Factis non verbis	Deeds not Words
9th Field Support Battalion	Ubiquitous	Everywhere
10th Field Support Battalion	Unity, Strength and Commitment	Unity, Strength and Commitment
4th Combat Support Services Battalion	Support by Service	Support by Service
1st Military Police Battalion	In Good Company	In Good Company
Tropical Trials Establishment	Diligenter Probamus	Diligently Honest
Australian Army History Unit	Tam Exercitus defendere hereditatem quam historiam adjuvare	Protecting Army Heritage, Promoting Army History
1st Health Support Battalion	Omnis Ad Unus Finis	All to One Purpose
Australian Comforts Fund	Keep the Fit Man Fit	Keep the Fit Man Fit
Australian Defence Force Academy	To lead, to Excel	To Lead, to Excel
14th Battalion, AIF	Ora Et Labora	Pray and Work
Corps Mottoes		
Corps of Staff Cadets	Doctrina Vim Promovet	1. Knowledge Increases Power 2. Learning Promotes Strength
Royal Australian Artillery	Consensu Stabilus	By Public Opinion Unwavering
	Ubique	Everywhere
	Quo Fas et Gloria Ducunt	1. Where Right and Glory Lead 2. Whither Right and Glory Lead
'A' Field Battery, RAA	Semper Paratus	Always Ready
Royal Australian Infantry	Duty and Honour	Duty and Honour
Royal Australian Engineers	1. Ubique 2. Honi Soit Qui Mal Y Pense 3. Facimus Et Frangimus	1. Everywhere 2. Evil to Him, Who Thinks Of It 3. We Make and We Break
Royal Australian Survey Corps	Videre Parare Est	To See is to Prepare
Royal Australian Army Dental Corps	Honour the Work	Honour the Work
Royal Australian Corps of Signals	Certa Cito	1. Swift and Sure 2. I summon (up) with Certainty
Australian Army Aviation	Vigilance	Vigilance
Australian Army Intelligence Corps	Forewarned, Forearmed	Forewarned, Forearmed
Royal Australian Army Chaplains Department	In Hoc Signo Vinces	In This Sign Conquer

Unit	Motto	Translation
Australian Army Service Corps/Royal Australian Army Service Corps/Royal Australian Corps of Transport	Par Oneri	Equal to the Task (Burden)
Royal Australian Army Medical Corps	Paulatim	Little by Little
Royal Australian Army Ordnance Corps	1. Sua Tela Tonanti 2. Honi Soit Qui Mal Y Pense	1. To the Thunderer, His Bolts 2. Evil to Him, Who Thinks Of It
The Royal Corps of Australian Electrical and Mechanical Engineers	Arte Et Marte	With Skill and Fighting
Royal Australian Army Educational Corps	Through Awareness Strength	Through Awareness Strength
Australian Army Catering Corps	We Sustain	We Sustain
Royal Australian Corps of Military Police	For the Troops and with the Troops	For the Troops and with the Troops
Australian Army Public Relations Corps	Stilus Potentior Est Gladio	The Pen is Mightier than the Sword
Royal Australian Army Pay Corps	Integrity	Integrity
Australian Army Legal Corps	Justitia in Armis	Justice in Arms
Royal Australian Army Nursing Corps	Pro Humanitate	For Humanity
Australian Volunteer Automobile Corps	Sicut Aquilae Pennis	Upon Wings of Eagles

9th Battalion, The Royal Queensland Regiment

The 9th Battalion, The Royal Queensland Regiment (9RQR) claims the additional motto 'First Ashore' as a unit tradition. Whilst first landing at Gallipoli there were two companies of each of the 9th, 10th and 11th Battalions of the Australian 3rd Brigade; the 9th Battalion claims that men of their unit were the first ashore.

Badge Colours and Unique Badges

Traditionally Corps and regimental badges are made of brass or silver. It was common practice at the Army Apprentices School (1967-1969) for brass to be gold-plated so that badges and belt fittings only required a quick wipe-over. In modern times the use of the more expensive metals has given way to cheaper metals and coating that do not require polishing.

Over the years there have been many examples of differences between the badges of officers and other ranks. Not only have officers' badges been made of superior metals but quite often were also enamelled. The RAASC officers' badge was one of the few that differed from the rest of the Corps, consisting as it did of two metals (white metal and brass and two enamels, blue and red). This badge was worn by all RAASC officers and WO1s.

RAA still has a unique hat badge for officers and WO1s where the 'wheel' on the front of their badge rotates freely, whereas the hat badge for the rest of the Corps does not.

Standardisation of colours has only been a recent innovation with the use of enamel being restricted to only a few Corps and one Regiment, although some regiments use a bi-metal badge to improve its appearance. The accepted colour standard currently used is gold for infantry regiments and most other Corps, with silver used by the Armoured, Aviation, Legal and the Nursing Corps.

As with all standards there are exceptions: The Pilbara Regiment, North West Mobile Force (NORFORCE) and the Australian Army Cadet Corps use a badge with an antique burnished bronze finish; and two regiments wear a black badge, SUR and the 51st Battalion, Far North Queensland Regiment (51FNQR).

51FNQR was formed on 1st October 1936 in Cairns, North Queensland, and retains the original unit motto 'Ducit Amor Patriae' (Love of Country Leads Us). The Battalion was granted a distinctive black badge described as 'within a belt bearing the motto, a kookaburra perched on a branch, holding in its beak a snake, within a wreath of bay issuant from behind a rose, the whole surmounted by a crown'. The choice of badge colour seems to be taken from the original 51st Battalion; whereas SUR links with the King's Royal Rifle Corps.

Hat Badges

Corps or regimental hat badges are worn by nearly all members of the Army below the rank of Colonel. The embroidered hat badges worn by senior officers are not technically badges of rank as they are worn by several different rank levels, except for a Field Marshal who wears a unique badge. Senior officers do not wear the Corps-related accoutrements worn by other members of the military and do not wear lanyards or Corps shoulder titles unless they are appointed as Head of a Corps.

Unlike hat badges worn by senior officers which indicate a specific senior rank, there are two hat badges worn by selected Warrant Officers which show both a rank and an appointment:

- The Functional Command RSM who is appointed to the position of the most senior warrant officer within a particular Command, for example Forces Command

- The RSM-A.

Colonels and Brigadiers

Major General
Lieutenant General
General

Field Marshal

Functional Command RSM

RSM-A

Corps and Regimental Badges

The following Corps and regimental badges are shown in colours authorised for use on unit flags and associated items. The reason the authors have used this approach rather than photographs of the badges, is to ensure that these authorised colours are recorded for future generations. All colours shown are the nearest shade possible given the difficulty of reproducing colours from cloth to the printed medium.

It should be noted that all Corps badges are surmounted by the St Edward's Crown. The use of any Imperial honours within the design of badges is restricted to RAE and RAAOC; both of which use the 'Order of the Garter' Belt and Motto incorporated into the design of their badges. These honours were bestowed on the original British parent Corps from which the Australian badges were copied; and was not an indication of the grant of special favour to these Corps.

Corps and Regimental Badges[449]

Corps of Staff Cadets

Royal Australian Armoured Corps

Royal Australian Artillery

Royal Australian Engineers

Royal Australian Corps of Signals

Royal Australian Infantry Corps

449 Note: Graphical images of badges are coloured in line with the original intended badge colourings used on Corps and Regimental Flags, which may vary from that manufactured. As multiple versions of each badge may have been manufactured over the years, only one version has been depicted to represent each badge – the prime difference for many badges was the change from the Tudor Crown to the St Edward's Crown.

Australian Army Aviation

Australian Intelligence Corps

Royal Australian Army Chaplains Department (Christian)

Royal Australian Army Chaplains Department (Jewish)

Royal Australian Corps of Transport

Royal Australian Army Medical Corps

Royal Australian Army Dental Corps

Royal Australian Army Ordnance Corps

Royal Corps of Australian Electrical and Mechanical Engineers

Royal Australian Army Educational Corps

Australian Army Public Relations Corps

Australian Army Catering Corps

Royal Australian Army Pay Corps

Australian Army Legal Corps

Royal Australian Corps of Military Police

Australian Army Psychology Corps

Australian Army Band Corps

Royal Australian Army Nursing Corps

1st Armoured Regiment

2nd Cavalry Regiment

3rd Cavalry Regiment

1st/15th Royal New South Wales Lancers

2nd/14th Light Horse Regiment (QMI)

3rd/9th South Australian Mounted Rifles

4th/19th Prince of Wales's Light Horse

10th Light Horse Regiment

12th/16th Hunter River Lancers

Royal Australian Regiment

Special Air Service

51st Battalion, The Far North Queensland Regiment

Royal Queensland Regiment

Royal New South Wales Regiment

Royal Victoria Regiment

Royal South Australia Regiment

Royal Western Australia Regiment

Royal Tasmania Regiment

North West Mobile Force

The Pilbara Regiment

1st Commando Regiment

2nd Commando Regiment

1st Aviation Regiment

5th Aviation Regiment

6th Aviation Regiment

Queensland University Regiment

Sydney University Regiment

University of New South Wales Regiment

Melbourne University Regiment

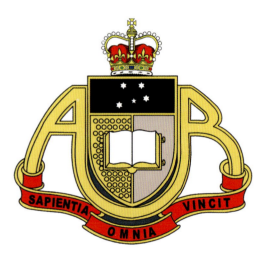

Adelaide Universities Regiment

Western Australia University Regiment

Royal Australian Regiment Badge

In 1949, the then Director of Infantry, BRIG IR Campbell, CBE, DSO, wrote to the battalion commanders of the Regiment asking for suggestions for the design of a new regimental badge. The final design was a combination of many suggestions incorporating a kangaroo standing alert in front of crossed .303 Lee Enfield rifles above a boomerang on which is inscribed the name 'Royal Australian Regiment' held within a wreath of Wattle surmounted by the Royal Crown. The kangaroo was selected because it is uniquely Australian and universally accepted as an Australian symbol. The .303 Lee Enfield rifle was included as it was and had been the personal weapon of the Australian Infantryman. To embellish and finish the badge it was decided to include a wreath, using sprigs of Golden Wattle, the national floral emblem.

The badge is emblazoned with the simple yet highly appropriate motto, 'Duty First'. MAJ KB Thomas, MC, who was at the time serving with 1 RAR, first suggested the motto. It was deemed appropriate as it was: original; short; in English; and reflected *the unhesitating and unquestioning performance of the infantryman as duty is the fundamental requirement of a soldier'*. The motto was developed for inclusion with the new RAR Badge and was approved in 1949.[450]

Although used on stationary and Christmas Cards, the Regimental badge was not issued until early 1954 when 2 RAR, whilst serving in Korea, received their new hat badges, which the Regiment has worn ever since.

In June 1950, 3 RAR, serving in Japan as part of the British Commonwealth Occupation Force (BCOF), had members of their Assault Pioneer Platoon cast four large badges from spent brass shell cases. Each of the (three) battalions and 1st Infantry Brigade Headquarters received a badge. When the 1st Infantry Brigade Headquarters was disbanded at Holsworthy in 1960 to form Headquarters 1st Division at Moore Park, their badge was handed over to 2 RAR for safe-keeping. On formation of 4 RAR, as a regular battalion at Woodside in 1964, this badge was transferred to that unit.

With further expansion of the Regiment in 1965, newly-raised battalions investigated the possibility of having similar badges cast. At this early date it was not financially practical and the new battalions temporarily displayed a smaller version of the Regimental badge with a dull finish. The remaining battalions of the Regiment have since acquired large badges as follows:

- 5 RAR's badge was presented by the 2nd/5th Infantry Battalion Association in November 1967

- 7 RAR's badge was donated and presented by the 2nd/7th Infantry Battalion Association on 3rd September 1966

- 5/7 RAR displayed two badges until de-linking in 2006.

The badge displayed by 6 RAR was cast, in part, using spent artillery and small arms cases fired during the Battle of Long Tan (18th August 1966). It was cast in 1968 at the Stuart Copper Refinery, Townsville.

The 8 RAR badge was presented by 4 RAR on the occasion of 8 RAR's first birthday on 8th August 1967. This badge was cast from spent shell cases fired by 'V' Battery Royal Artillery and 'Dragon' Battery Royal Artillery in support of 4 RAR operations in Sarawak (April to September 1966). The badge of 9 RAR was cast by the Naval Dockyard Foundry, Sembawang, Singapore in 1970 using the 1 RAR badge, less the crown, as a diecast. The crown was replaced with

the Queen's Crown.[451] Both of these are currently displayed within the 8/9 RAR area at Gallipoli Barracks, Enoggera.

With the de-linking of 5/7 RAR in 2006, each unit retained its original badge and they are now displayed at their respective new locations. 4 RAR was suspended from the Order of Battle (ORBAT) in 2009 when it was reformed as a commando regiment, 4 RAR (Cdo); its badge was sent to the School of Infantry at Singleton, NSW for safe-keeping and is currently displayed outside the Regimental Headquarters.

One additional badge was manufactured in 2007, for display outside Depot Company at the School of Infantry, Singleton. This wing is responsible for the training of new infantry soldiers for the Royal Australian Regiment. Rifleman Wing was renamed Depot Company on 21st November 2014. Not all new soldiers pass through Depot Company, as in times of rapid expansion soldiers are sometimes sent directly to their battalion for their Initial Employment Training (IET).

The brass for this new badge was obtained from fired small arms casings collected by members of the Australian Rifle Company Butterworth, Malaysia. The badge was cast from a mould of the 4 RAR badge and was manufactured in Malaysia.

450 Horner DM. *Duty First: The Royal Australian Regiment in War and Peace.* Sydney, Allen & Unwin: 1990, p. 44

451 Jones RW. *Australian Infantry Magazine:* January-June 1981, pp. 28-29

1st Commando Regiment Badge

The original hat badge of the 1st Cdo Regt was designed by unit members and consisted of a silver Australian commando dagger passing through a golden boomerang on which was embossed the regimental motto 'Strike Swiftly'. This badge was redesigned in 2009, not only to show the dagger's proper design, but also to correct what was seen as an original manufacturing limitation that prevented a true replica of the dagger being mass-produced on the original badge. The new badge has a silver dagger with the pronounced shape of the original Fairbairn-Sykes fighting knife passing through a golden boomerang on which the Regiment's motto appears recessed into the metal. The Fairbairn-Sykes knife was designed and used exclusively by British commando units during WWII.

2nd Commando Regiment Badge

When 2 Cdo Regt was raised in 2009, it was decided to introduce a 'Double Diamond' shape to be incorporated into the design of the new unit's badge. This shape represents the colour patches of the original WWII Australian Commando Squadrons and establishes a clear lineage with those units. The badge also incorporates the Fairbairn-Sykes fighting knife in the centre of the badge, with a scroll on which the regimental motto 'Foras admonitio' – 'Without Warning' is inscribed.

Original Design

Modified Post-2009

Obsolete Badges – Various

Officer Cadet School
Portsea

Officer Cadet Training Unit
(CMF/Ares)

Officer Training Unit
Scheyville

Deakin University Company

Queensland Agricultural College Training Unit

Regional Universities of Queensland Regiment

Royal Australian Army
Service Corps – Officer/Warrant Officer Class 1 Badge

Royal Australian Army
Service Corps – Other Ranks' Badge

Australian Army
Educational Corps

Australian Army Veterinary Corps

Army College of TAFE

Australian Army Chaplains Department (Christians)

Royal Australian Survey Corps

Women's Royal Australian Army Corps

Royal Australian Infantry Corps

University of New South Wales Regiment

Australian Army Training Team – Vietnam

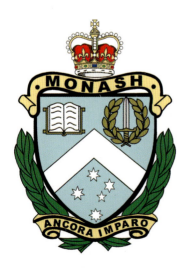

Monash University Regiment

Obsolete Armoured and Light Horse Badges

1st Armoured Car Regiment

2nd Armoured Car Regiment

4th Cavalry Regiment

7th/21st Australian Horse

*8th/13th Victorian
Mounted Rifles*

*1st Light Horse Royal
NSW Lancers*

*2nd Light Horse Regiment
Queensland Mounted Infantry*

*3rd Light Horse
South Australia Mounted Rifles*

*4th Light Horse Regiment
Corangamite Light Horse*

5th Australian Light Horse
Wide Bay and Burnett QMI

6th Light Horse Regiment
NSW Mounted Rifles

7th Light Horse Regiment
Australian Horse

8th Light Horse Regiment
Indi Light Horse

9th Light Horse Regiment
Flinders Light Horse

10th Light Horse Regiment
Western Australian Mounted Infantry

11th Light Horse
Darling Downs Light Horse QMI

12th Light Horse Regiment
New England Light Horse

13th Light Horse Regiment
Gippsland Light Horse

14th Light Horse Regiment
West Moreton Light Horse QMI

15th Light Horse Regiment
Northern Rivers Lancers

16th Light Horse Regiment
Hunter River Lancers

17th Light Horse Regiment
Prince of Wales's Light Horse

18th Light Horse Regiment
Adelaide Lancers

19th Light Horse Regiment
Yarrowee Light Horse[a]

20th Light Horse Regiment
Victorian Mounted Rifles

21st Light Horse Regiment
Riverina Horse

22nd Light Horse Regiment
Tasmanian Mounted Infantry

(a) This badge is similar in design to that of the 4th Light Horse with whom this unit was linked in 1937; the badge of one unit was maintained with the inclusion of the motto and name of the other.

23rd Light Horse Regiment
Barossa Light Horse

24th Light Horse Regiment
Gwydir Regiment

25th Light Horse Regiment
(Machine Gun)

Obsolete Infantry Badges

1st Infantry Battalion
The City of Sydney's Own Regiment

2nd Infantry Battalion
The City of Newcastle Regiment

3rd Infantry Battalion
The Werriwa Regiment

4th Infantry Battalion
The Australian Rifles

5th Infantry Battalion
The Victorian Scottish Regiment

6th Infantry Battalion
The Royal Melbourne Regiment

7th Infantry Battalion
The North West Murray Borderers

8th Infantry Battalion
The City of Ballarat Regiment

9th Infantry Battalion
The Moreton Regiment

10th Infantry Battalion
The Adelaide Rifles

11th Battalion
The City of Perth Regiment

12th Infantry Battalion
The Launceston Regiment

13th Infantry Battalion
The Macquarie Regiment

14th Battalion
The Prahran Regiment

15th Battalion
The Oxley Regiment

16th Infantry Battalion
The Cameron Highlanders of Western Australia

17th Battalion
The North Sydney Regiment

18th Battalion
The Kuring-Gai Regiment

19th Battalion
The South Sydney Regiment

20th Battalion
The Parramatta and Blue Mountains Regiment

21st Battalion
The Victorian Rangers

22nd Battalion
The Richmond Regiment

23rd Battalion
The City of Geelong Regiment

24th Battalion
The Kooyong Regiment

25th Infantry Battalion
The Darling Downs Regiment

26th Battalion
The Logan and Albert Regiment

27th Infantry Battalion
The South Australian Scottish Regiment

28th Infantry Battalion
The Swan Regiment

29th Battalion
The East Melbourne Regiment

30th Infantry Battalion
The NSW Scottish Regiment

31st Infantry Battalion
The Kennedy Regiment

32nd Battalion
The Footscray Regiment

33rd Battalion
The New England Regiment

34th Infantry Battalion
The Illawarra Regiment

35th Battalion
Newcastle's Own Regiment

36th Battalion
St George English Rifles Regiment

37th Battalion
The Henty Regiment

38th Infantry Battalion
The Northern Victorian Regiment

39th Battalion
The Hawthorn-Kew Regiment

40th Infantry Battalion
The Derwent Regiment

41st Infantry Battalion
The Byron Scottish Regiment

42nd Infantry Battalion
The Capricornia Regiment

43rd Battalion
The Hindmarsh Regiment

44th Battalion
The West Australian Rifles

45th Infantry Battalion
The St George Regiment

46th Battalion
The Brighton Rifles

47th Infantry Battalion
The Wide Bay Regiment

48th Battalion
The Torrens Regiment

49th Battalion
The Stanley Regiment

50th Infantry Battalion[b]
The Tasmanian Rangers

51st Infantry Battalion
The Far North Queensland Regiment

(b) This badge may have been worn by the 50th Battalion St Kilda Regiment which was disbanded in 1918. No records of its motto exist; however, the Tasmanian Rangers used the motto Quo Fas Et Gloria in the 1930s. The original badges of both Officer and Other Ranks are held in the Grey Collection of the South Australian Military Museum, Keswick Barracks.

52nd Battalion

The Gippsland Regiment

53rd Battalion

The West Sydney Regiment

54th Battalion

The Lachlan-Macquarie Regiment

55th Battalion

The NSW Rifle Regiment

56th Battalion

The Riverina Regiment

57th Battalion

The Merri Regiment

58th Battalion

The Essendon – Coburg – Brunswick Regiment

59th Infantry Battalion

The Hume Regiment

60th Battalion

The Heidelberg Regiment

61st Infantry Battalion
The Queensland Cameron Highlanders

Pacific Islands Regiment

Papua New Guinea
Volunteer Rifles

8th/7th Infantry Battalion
The North Western Victorian Regiment

11th/44th Infantry Battalion
City of Perth Regiment

12th/40th Infantry Battalion
Tasmania Regiment

16th/28th Infantry Battalion
Cameron Highlanders of Western Australia

58th/32nd Battalion
The Melbourne Rifles

43rd/48th Infantry Battalion
The Hindmarsh Regiment

Introduction

The Australian Army, like all military forces, has customs and traditions that do not fit in to any particular subject heading. However, they are important in their own right.

The Army's Birthday[152]

The separate States of Australia were federated into the Commonwealth of Australia on 1st January 1901. The legal instrument for this change, the *Commonwealth of Australia Constitution Act*, was a statute of the British Parliament, assented to by Queen Victoria in September 1900. Although this Act formally joined the independent colonial forces, it was to be some time before a formal command structure was created. On 20th February 1901, the Governor-General of Australia made a proclamation under section 69 of the *Constitution*, which transferred control of the existing Colonial Forces to the Commonwealth Defence Minister, effective as at 1st March 1901. The former Colonial Forces were administered under separate State legislations until the first Commonwealth *Defence Act 1903* came into force on 1st March 1904. The Army therefore celebrates its official birthday on the 1st of March each year.

Mateship

'Mateship' is a concept that can be traced back to early colonial times where the harsh environment in which convicts and new settlers found themselves meant that men and women closely relied on each other for help. In Australia, a 'mate' is more than just a friend; the endearment implies a sense of shared experience that created a bond, mutual respect, social equality, the larrikin spirit and unconditional assistance. It is a part of the national lexicon found nowhere else in the world.

Mateship is a term more commonly used among men. The popular notion of mateship came to the fore during WWI and was defined through the common experience of trench warfare, concentration camps, hunger, injury, forced labour, boredom, suffering and the terror of war. During this period the word 'mate' became interchangeable with the word 'digger', which had its roots in the gold fields of the 1850s.

The History of Women in the Australian Army[153]

Throughout Australia's history, women have made valuable contributions to enhance Defence's capability.

Among the many challenges faced by the Australian Government in 1941 was the shortage of men to support the economy and to fight in the Armed Forces. Australia had a population of approximately 7.1 million with an available workforce of about 2 million. It was estimated that by mid-1943 Australia would require a combined Armed Force of 500,000, supported by 250,000 working in the munitions, shipbuilding and aircraft industry and another 50,000 directly supporting other war related industries. Relying on men to fulfil these roles was unsustainable and the employment of women became a necessity.

During 1941, proposals were developed to create a women's element in the Royal Australian Navy, the Army and the Royal Australian Air Force. The RAAF and the RAN commenced enlistment of women in February and March 1941. Their early success created pressure for a 'women's service' in the Army.

Army planners were eager for women to assume responsibility for a variety of tasks which would release men to undertake combat related roles. On 13th August 1941, the War Cabinet led by Prime Minister Mr (later Sir) Robert Menzies, approved the formation of the Australian Army Women's Service. This name was changed by December 1941 to the Australian Women's Army Service (AWAS).

452 Woods J. Chiefs of the Australian Army. Loftus NSW, Australian Military History Publications: 2006
453 http://www.army.gov.au/Our-history/History-in-Focus/Womens-historical-contribution-recognised-on-Anzac-Day (Author Major GO Lever)

It was decided that no women were to be sent overseas without the approval of the War Cabinet. Although as a contingency, it was also decided that in the event this did occur, only single women without dependents would be eligible for overseas service. Women's pay and allowances were also set at approximately 68 per cent of those paid to men in the Army.

On 29th September 1941, Miss Sybil Irving, MBE, was appointed as Controller of the new service (AWAS) with the rank of Lieutenant Colonel. She commenced duties in early October with the aim to establish the service and initially recruit women to undertake a three week course for commissioning as officers. Twenty nine women were selected from an outstanding group of volunteers, each of whom had already proved themselves as leaders in their own professions and in the community. These Officers formed the core of the AWAS for the period 1941-1947 and built the service into an organisation that contributed significantly to Australia's war effort.

The women of the AWAS served throughout Australia in many roles including clerks, typists, drivers, cooks, signallers, stewards, intelligence analysts, butchers, mechanics, provost, searchlight operators, and canteen staff. In addition, 3,618 women served with the Royal Australian Regiment of Artillery manning fixed gun emplacements from Hobart to Cairns and in Perth.

In early 1945 the War Cabinet gave approval for up to 500 members of the AWAS to serve in Papua New Guinea in positions within Headquarters 1st Australian Army, and in May 1945, 350 members of the AWAS sailed on the MV Duntroon for New Guinea. Unofficially, some members of the AWAS had served overseas prior to this. The AWAS was the only non-medical service to send female personnel overseas during WWII.

A total of 24,082 women served in the AWAS and at their peak, represented approximately five per cent of the total Army strength. During the war, 41 members of the AWAS died on active service, no deaths were due to enemy action.

The end of hostilities in August 1945 brought a rapid reduction in the size of the Army and this included the AWAS. Post war planners determined that there was no need for a women's service in the Army and all AWAS members were demobilised by 30th June 1947.

In recognition of the valuable service provided by women in the Army during the war, five members of the AWAS were selected for inclusion in the 10th June 1946 Victory March contingent that marched in London.

The reputation and high esteem held by senior members of the military and Government for the dedication and service provided by the AWAS led to Cabinet's decision

Right: PTE (Recruit) Vikki I Sinclair – WRAAC School. Georges Heights – November 1980

on 15th July 1950 to reintroduce women in the Army. The Australian Women's Army Corps was renamed in April 1951, the Women's Australian Army Corps; and in June 1951, was granted the 'Royal' prefix in recognition of the wartime contribution of the women's Services, to become the Women's Royal Australian Army Corps (WRAAC). Her Majesty Queen Elizabeth appointed Her Royal Highness The Princess Margaret, as Colonel-in-Chief of the WRAAC, in 1953 until the disbandment of the Corps in 1985. It was recorded in Parliament that female members were never to be referred to as 'WRAACs'. The early leaders of the WRAAC were veterans of the AWAS and this influence lasted for many years.

From 1980 individual members were allocated directly to those previously all-male Corps to which they were posted; and in 1983 WRAAC uniform buttons and badges were replaced with their new Corps insignia. The WRAAC Corps was disbanded on 31st January 1985 and female officer cadets, who had previously been commissioned through WRAAC School, were posted to OCS Portsea.

The Army has made significant progress to expand the opportunities available to women by moving from the 1977 recommendations of the Coldham Report permitting women to serve on active service, but not in combat-related roles, to the 2013 removal of gender restrictions for combat-related employment.

The Army has always acknowledged the efforts of its Servicewomen, who have shown enormous dedication, professionalism and sacrifice.

*Far right: AWM PA1U2002.023.18
Courtesy Australian War Memorial
PTE Albert Du Frayer*

*Right: AWM A04542 Courtesy
Australian War Memorial
'The Queen Victoria Scarf'*

The Queen Victoria Scarf

An unusual award, in the form of a long scarf crocheted by Queen Victoria, was made to selected British and Empire servicemen during the South African (2nd Boer) War. It was worn over the shoulder, passing under the shoulder strap, across the chest and buckled on the hip. Description of the scarf is; 'crocheted in Khaki-coloured Berlin wool, approximately nine inches (22.8cm) wide and five feet long (152cm), including a four inch (10cm) fringe at each end, and bears the Royal Cypher V.R.I. (Victoria Regina Et Imperatrix)'. A total of eight were awarded; one to the Australian soldier, PTE Alfred Du Frayer, of the NSW Mounted Rifles on 29th May 1901. The official notification for the award was announced in *Commonwealth General Order* 155/1902.

Under the heading '*Honours and Mentions gained by N.S.W. Contingents*'[454] are the names of officers and men mentioned in each despatch and give the date of the despatch. Du Frayer's name does not appear until '*Lord Roberts Final Despatch 1 March 1902 – Pte. Du Frayer, Mounted Rifles got one of the four scarves worked by her late Majesty for distribution among men of Colonial Contingents.*'

There has been much speculation as to the exact degree of honour that the award of the scarf carried. It was at one time believed to be equivalent to the Victoria Cross, but this is not the case. During 1902 the New Zealand Government requested that the title 'Queen's Scarf' be used in the *Army List* and other official documents but, in a reply dated 4th June 1902, the Secretary of State refused to grant permission. The

question of precedence has continued over the years and, even as late as 1956, it was raised by a descendant of one of the holders, requesting permission to attend the VC Centenary Celebrations. The official reply stated:

> … while the Queen's Scarf is regarded as a unique and most distinguished award, relatives of those who received it are not being included in the present ceremony as it does not carry equal status with the Victoria Cross.

The solitary official instance of the initials '*QS*' appearing after the name Du Frayer is found in *The NSW Army and Navy List of 1901*, where the initials appear in one of three insertions against Du Frayer's name. They are, however, erased from the next edition of the same List and from any subsequent List, but a footnote added denoting '*Awarded Queen's Scarf for service in South Africa*'.

The Queen's Scarf awarded to PTE Alfred Du Frayer is currently held in the AWM.

---

454 Stirling JF. *The Colonials in South Africa, 1899-1902: Their Record, Based on the Despatches.* Edinburgh, W. Blackwood and Sons: 1907, p 441

The History of Two-up

'Two-up', or 'Swy', was originally brought to Australia by the convicts in the 18th Century, becoming part of the Australian Army's and national folklore and tradition. As early as 1798, Judge Advocate David Collins noted that gambling was rife amongst convicts and some had been known to lose everything on the toss of a coin.

This early tradition continued through both World Wars in the AIF and the 2nd AIF. The Australian War Memorial has the two-up set used by NX203594 PTE Milton George Heuston of the 2/12th Commando Squadron, throughout his WWII service. Nowadays two-up is a popular pastime for serving and ex-serving veterans on Anzac Day when traditionally the law turns a blind eye on this generally illegal form of gambling.

The History of the Australian Army Training Team Vietnam Unit Badge[455]

In 1962 Australia sent the first contingent of the AATTV to join the United States Army in assisting with the training of the Army of the Republic of Vietnam who were engaged in a civil war against the communist North. The Australians, all Regular Army officers and warrant officers, were posted to both South Vietnamese and American units spread throughout the Republic of South Vietnam. Design work for a 'Unit Badge' was put forward by WO2 Laurie Nicholson which in essence was accepted and authorised by the AHQ Dress Committee in July 1971. Despite being recognised, the Dress Committee ruled that members of the AATTV were to wear a 'rifle green' beret and the 'badge' only whilst in Vietnam and the badge was to be purchased from 'their own resources. This decision was overruled and deleted in the meeting minutes by the AHQ Dress Committee Secretary, thus ostensibly authorising the beret and badge to be worn by team members in Australia while they were still a member of the AATTV. At the end of the Vietnam War AATTV ceased to exist.

On 20th September 2012, the CA, LTGEN David Morrison, AO, officially recognised the 'Badge' which allowed the Team's identity to be maintained into the future[456]; and more importantly, has permanently protected the design from misuse by anyone duplicating the badge for resale.

455 Information provided by Ex-Warrant Officer Class II Laurie Nicholson, AATTV
456 Office of the Chief of Army OCA/OUT/012/r11994006 dated 20 Sep 2012

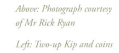

Above: Photograph courtesy of Mr Rick Ryan

Left: Two-up Kip and coins

The Australian Army Training Team – Iraq

The mentoring work of the AATTV has continued with the work of the Australian Army Training Team – Iraq (AATT-I) and the Mentoring Taskforce in Afghanistan.

The Broad Arrow

Perhaps one of the oldest symbols of government and/or ordnance is the mark of the 'broad arrow' to identify Defence-owned property. It has now been embellished by adding two capital letter Ds (for the Department of Defence) to the broad arrow. On some occasions the two capital letters 'WD', for War Department, split by the arrow (W↑D) was used.

This mark has its origins in the Ordnance Service of Britain, the Government Commissaries, Colonial Storekeepers, Military Stores Departments and Ordnance Stores Corps in England and in the Australian Colonies.

The earliest record of the Broad Arrow in connection with munitions was in 1553, when Sir Thomas Gresham[457], the founder of the Royal Exchange, used it when smuggling gunpowder into England so that it appeared to be Government property. It was not until 1687, after the accession of Charles II, that a direct connection between the Office of Ordnance and the 'broad arrow' was established. About this time the broad arrow was also carved into oak trees in the Forest of Dean, which were to be felled for building ships of war in the Royal dockyards. In 1698, the symbol was legalised for the Royal Navy by an Act of King William and Queen Mary, a heavy penalty being imposed for those in unlawful possession of Government stores so branded. An 1806 proclamation defined the marks to be placed on stores of war belonging to the Board of Ordnance and reads as follows:

> 28th July 1806. The Board having been pleased to direct that in future all descriptions of Ordnance Stores should be marked with the broad arrow as soon as they shall have been received as fit for His Majesty's Service; all Storekeepers and Deputy Storekeepers and others are desired to cause this order to be accordingly attended to, in the Department under their direction, reporting to the Board in all cases when articles are received to which this mark cannot be applied.

From that day the broad arrow has been used to stamp or brand just about everything supplied for ordnance capable of bearing such a mark. It is not only a certificate that the article has been examined and found to be fit for the service, but also serves to identify Government property in case of theft or misappropriation.

457 Sir Thomas Gresham; merchant, financier: born London 1519 – died London 21 Nov 1579.

The symbol of the broad arrow is evident in many of the early Government buildings in Australia where the mark has been embossed on every brick used on the site. These bricks were usually handmade and the work of convict labour. The mark of the broad arrow was adopted by the Australian Army Ordnance Department at the beginning of the 20th century and although not as common, the mark is still in use to this day.

Military Slang, Expressions and Terminology

Half of Europe has contributed to the British vocabulary. After every military campaign new expressions and terms were added to the English language, many with no known origins, and therefore their exact meaning and/or source cannot be confirmed, but this short list is included for interest:

- **AWOL** – Absent Without Leave – away from military duties without permission, but without the intention of deserting. Once a member is AWOL for 21 days they then become an Illegal Absentee (IA). Pronounced as an acronym or 'Ack Willy'.

- **Batman**[458] – Originally pronounced bawman, short for bat-horse man (bat being old French for packsaddle), a batman was a person, although not always a soldier, who was allocated to every company on Foreign Service whose primary function was to look after the cooking utensils. Every company also had a bat-horse to carry these utensils; the batman was paid by the Government for his service, and the horse's fodder was also provided at public expense. When the unit was stationed at home the need for this service disappeared, however batmen were often retained as personal servants of the officers.

- **Battalion** – From the Italian Battalia, meaning a battle formation.

- **Boots and Saddle** – This trumpet call comes from the French 'outsell'; literally 'put saddle'.

- **Bugle** – From the Latin 'buculus' (young bull).

- **Chocko/Koala Bear** – Chocko[459] is an abbreviation of the term Chocolate Soldier meaning a soldier who is unwilling to fight. The term comes from a character, in a play by George Bernard Shaw, who carried chocolates in his pack instead of ammunition. It was first used as a derogatory term applied to the soldiers of the 8th Infantry Brigade who arrived in Egypt after the end of the Gallipoli Campaign. During WWII it was used to describe Militiamen or conscripts who could not serve outside of Australia until the Militia Bill was passed in 1943. These men were sometimes referred to as Koalas as

Australia had strict laws protecting its Koalas, prohibiting their hunting, trapping, shooting or their export outside of Australia. The term 'Koala Bear' or just 'Bear' is also applied to members of RASigs employed in the Electronic Warfare environment at Cabarlah, Queensland.

- **Civies/Mufti** – Civilian clothing, any clothing not issued as part of a uniform.

- **Deep Thinker** – A soldier who enlisted or joined the Army, after the first few months of WWII. Most often used as a joking remark to indicate the individual was slow to enlist and therefore not as patriotic as other members of the unit.

- **Dixie** – A mess tin or cooking pot. Taken form the Hindustani 'degchi', first recorded in English in 1879, and commonly used by Diggers since 1916.[460]

- **Digger/Dig** (singular) – An Australian soldier; since its use in WWI it has become synonymous with the Australian soldier. Has also been applied to New Zealand soldiers in WWI.

- **Fill Your Boots** – This term dates back to the 18th century when soldiers' leather water bottles were proofed against leakage with a black tar-like substance. The bottle itself resembled the shape of a boot and was slung via a leather strap for ease of carriage. When departing a location the soldiers would be ordered to 'Fill Your Boots' to prepare for the journey ahead. Although the term has taken on a different meaning in today's modern Army the sentiment is much the same, that is, take or do as much as you can.

- **Furlough** – From the Dutch 'verlof', meaning 'leave'.

- **Furphy** – Is slang for a rumour or other false or suspect information. It was first coined by Australian troops at Gallipoli in 1915 and was later adopted into general use within Australia. The term is derived from the name of a company who manufactured water carts, J. Furphy and Sons Pty Ltd of Shepparton, Victoria. The carts had the name

---

458 Gordon LL. *Military Origins.* New York, A. S. Barnes: 1971, p. 180

459 Dennis P, Grey J, Morris E, Prior R. *The Oxford Companion to Australian Military History (Second Edition). Australia,* Oxford University Press: 2008, p. 131

460 Downing WH, Ramson WS, Arthur JM (editors). *Downing's Digger dialects.* Melbourne, Oxford University Press: 1990, p. 63

of J. Furphy cast into the metal ends. Although there is no evidence that Furphy carts were actually used on Gallipoli the name was a general term used by soldiers to describe all water carts during the period. The drivers of these carts moved freely from areas which included headquarter areas through to the front lines and as such became useful carriers of information, be it gossip or rumour, any news was keenly sought. Shown here is the case end layout of an original Furphy water tank, manufactured by the company from 1898 to 1920.[461]

- **Geek** – A communications and information systems technician or specialist.

- **Goffer** – A soft drink, usually in a can.

- **Grenade** – Comes from the French 'pome grenate' or pomegranate (the fruit), the original grenade being of a similar shape.

- **Gong** – Most commonly used to describe any medal[462] awarded to an individual. Originally it was used to describe only a medal awarded for an act of bravery or distinguished conduct/service, not a campaign or long service medal.

- **Hootchie** – A thin plastic sheet that is used as a sleeping shelter. This term is derived from the Japanese word 'uchi' meaning house. Most likely introduced by the British Commonwealth Occupation Force (BCOF), which served in Japan after WWII and later became the first ground troops committed to the Korean War.

- **Infantry** – One source suggests that this is derived from the Spanish 'Infante'; a knight's page. As pages went on foot, so the term came to mean foot soldiers. The Spanish for foot soldiers in a group was 'Infanteria' and by corruption this has become 'Infantry' in the English language.

- **Kangaroo/Rooster Feathers** – A jovial remark to describe the Emu feathers worn by light horsemen during WWI (see Chapter 3, 'Punch' cartoon – February 1916).

- **Mess** – The word mess originally meant a portion of food, that is, a mess of pottage (mush). Later it came to mean having a meal together followed by a place in which the meal was taken[463] (see Chapter 10).

- **Mixed Dress** – Any item of civilian clothing worn in conjunction with military attire. Not acceptable at any time, although relaxed for some senior officers and most often results in the perpetrator being subject to some form of military discipline.

- **Nasho** – Slang expression for a National Serviceman. National Service has been used a total of four times in Australia since Federation, the last two during the period 1951-1960 and 1964-1972.

- **Picquet** – A reminder of the days of pikes as these were gradually superseded by firearms, a few were still left in the centre of the battalion as a guard for the Colours. It comes from the French picquette, used for a small body of pikemen, and the word afterwards referred to any small force.

- **Platoon** – Comes from the Swedish 'pluton' which was a unit of 48 men which, in turn, came from the French 'peleton' literally meaning 'a ball'.

- **Pogo** – Slang expression – an acronym for 'Personnel On Garrison Orders', or a soldier belonging to a support organisation. The Army is roughly split into two main organisations; 'Forces Command' units or elements that operate within a war zone and non-Forces Command organisations whose job it is to train reinforcements and resupply the field Army, referred to as 'support' units.

- **Retread** – A retired or discharged soldier who, for reasons of his/her own, has chosen to re-enlist in either the Regular or Reserve Forces.

- **Roster** – The likely origin is from the Dutch 'Rooster' meaning a grid iron, because the original lists were drawn up on paper lined like a grid iron. Some old documents in the War Office spell this as Roister, and therefore it may have derived from Roister or Roll.

- **Sergeant Major** – This name is derived from 1639 when the third officer of the Regiment in Cromwell's Army was known as Sergeant Major General. King James II (r. 1685-1688) subsequently called the appointment Major General (see Chapter 2).

- **Soldier** – Soldier is a generic term for any member of the Australian Army. The term 'soldier' comes from ancient Rome, where soldiers were given a handful of salt each day which they could trade.

- **Sotto Voce** – Literally meaning 'under voice' in Italian means to speak under one's breath. Commonly used whilst performing drill at funerals and other solemn occasions. The guard commander gives all orders just loud enough for the guard to hear.

- **Sniper** – The word 'to snipe' when used to describe the action of shooting from a hidden place, originated in the 1770s among British soldiers in India where a hunter skilled enough to kill a snipe (a small long-billed marsh bird) was dubbed a 'sniper'. The term sniper was first used to describe a 'sharpshooter' in 1824.

461 Barnes J, Furphy A. Furphy. *The Water Cart and the Word*. Melbourne, Scholarly Publishing: 2005

462 Fowler HW, McIntosh E. *The Concise Oxford Dictionary of Current English*. Oxford, Clarendon Press: 1975, p. 528

463 Dickson RJ. *Enlivened Anecdotes of Mess Times remembered from a host of one time mess members and the progress of Charles Oswald Littlewart from 2nd Lieutenant to Major General*. Tunbridge Wells, Midis Books: 1973, p. 1

AWM Neg No E01199. A Game of Two-up – WWI

- **Spook/Ghost** – A person from the Army Intelligence Corps. 'Spook' or 'Ghost' refers to their occupation as persons whose job is to go unnoticed whilst gathering information.

- **Trail Arms** – From the old command 'Trayle Your Pike' whereupon the soldier seized his pike just short of the head and allowed the long shaft to trail behind him on the ground.

- **Two-up** – A game of chance played by tossing two, sometimes three, coins into the air and gambling on the outcome. The game is won if the two coins land as either heads or tails upper most and lost if opposing or non-matching sides face up. This game is said to have originated on the Victorian goldfields; however it became a popular form of gambling amongst soldiers. Because of its link to the first ANZACs it is traditionally played on Anzac Day and is the only form of public gambling that can be legally conducted outside a casino on that day.[464]

The Parade Ground

There are many stories and myths associated with the significance and development of parade grounds.

In the 17th and 18th century in Britain, when a regiment marched into a town or any location where they were going to be quartered, a place of assembly was decided upon which may have been a market square, the street outside the senior officer's lodgings or any convenient open patch of ground. If the unit was on active operations and camping in the field, the regiment would form up in front of their tents. This area would be used to draw everyone together in a 'parade', but it would not necessarily be used as a drill square. Once barracks became common in the United Kingdom (very late 18th to early 19th century), the buildings were normally arranged around a square. This open space, which was conveniently situated in the middle of the dwellings, would be used for parades of all sorts; fatigues, drill, pay, punishment, and the assembly of the guards.[465]

The parade ground has been portrayed to generations of soldiers to represent the sanctuary for the unit's fallen soldiers and hence great respect is to be accorded to it. The commonly-held belief has no historical basis. However, given the parade ground's importance, in terms of unit training and discipline, soldiers may not to cross it other than in formed bodies.

464 Dennis P, Grey J, Morris E, Prior R. *The Oxford Companion to Australian Military History (Second Edition)*. Australia, Oxford University Press: 2008, p. 536

465 Terrett LI. *Interview with Andrew Cormack*, Associate Editor, Journal of the Society for Army Historical Research, UK: 2009

Courtesy of DPS Duntroon.
25 Pounder Gun, Parade
Ground – Duntroon

Philanthropic Organisations[467]

The Minister for Defence may engage the services of philanthropic organisations, for the betterment of morale and the well-being of the members of the military. Philanthropic support has been made available by various societies both in Australia and overseas during conflicts, peacemaking, peacekeeping, or normal ADF training activities. Although not always known by the same names, various organisations staffed by volunteers have supported the Army since WWI, as noted by CEW Bean from 1916:

> The (Australian) Comforts Fund established beside the duckwalks near Longueval a coffee-stall, at which the exhausted troops on their way into or out of the line obtained hot coffee or cocoa, served in jam-tins with the lids bent back for handles.[468]

Although these volunteers are classed as non-combatants it was not until the formal recognition of such organisations within the Geneva Convention of 1949 that they were afforded the same protection as medical personnel and chaplains.[469] Members of philanthropic organisations accredited to the ADF are civilians and not members of the ADF. Two aspects of the Geneva Conventions that are particularly applicable to philanthropic organisations are:

- Accredited representatives of philanthropic organisations are not permitted to wear a military uniform or accoutrements except as specifically allowed for within Defence policy.

- Accredited representatives of philanthropic organisations are not permitted to carry personal weapons; however, there may be a Defence obligation to provide philanthropic organisations with personal protection under the Law of Armed Conflict.

The cost of providing philanthropic support to Army is primarily born by the individual philanthropic organisation; however, the limited use of Departmental funds to assist with the delivery of this support has been approved in accordance with Defence policy.

Philanthropic organisations must be authorised to operate within the ADF. The current approved organisations are:

- Australian Red Cross Society (ARCS) (Field Force)

- Everyman's Welfare Service (EWS)

- Salvation Army – Red Shield Defence Services (RSDS)

An ongoing point of discussion has been the issue of the 25 Pounder Artillery Guns on the parade ground at Duntroon which face inwards rather than outwards (outwards, the traditional way of indicating 'holding ground'). There is no known custom or tradition explaining the facing of the guns; the best theory is that the guns have been placed that way for aesthetic convenience (rather than facing a wall and building). Further to this, as both guns are out of service pieces and unmanned, they are therefore not considered to be 'holding ground'.

Holding ground is by definition, 'Troops Keeping the Ground'.[466] On selected unit ceremonial occasions troops are positioned, facing outwards, at the corners of a parade ground to 'Hold Ground'; these troops being equipped with weapons which range from lances to mortars or guns. The symbolism is to afford protection to the unit parading in order to permit it to carry out its ceremonial duties safely.

The tradition stems from the British 'Hollow Square' when a square was formed to defend against an impending cavalry charge. In order to enable troops to rest in place, pickets were posted at sufficient distance from the square to give early warning of an attack. This warning system provided the unit time to 'stand to' and fight off the enemy.

---

466 Unnamed Author (Infantry Centre). *Military Traditions and Customs*, Singleton, Infantry Centre: 7 April 1977, Chap 4, p. 4-14 and para 96

467 Australian Army. *Defence Instruction (General) PERS 42-4 Philanthropic Organisations*: 26 Feb 2004

468 Bean CEW. *The Australian Imperial Force in France, 1916*. St Lucia, Queensland, University of Queensland Press: 1940

469 Geneva Convention. *Protocols Additional, Article 24 and 26*: 12 August 1949

- Young Men's Christian Association (YMCA) – Defence Forces Division

- Young Women's Christian Association (YWCA) – Defence Forces Division

- Returned and Services League of Australia – Australian Forces Overseas Fund (AFOF).

The provision of philanthropic support to augment the welfare needs of ADF members and to complement existing ADF welfare resources has always been appreciated and well accepted.

Soldiers' Army Numbers in the British Army[470]

Prior to Regimental Numbers it is likely that the duplication of surnames of soldiers created a source of confusion in regiments. It was not until 1829 that, in order to identify each man more precisely, the custom of numbering soldiers was introduced in the British Army. It is significant that, in November 1829, British official instructions were issued ordering every soldier to be allotted a 'Regimental Number'. The method was to give the number in accordance with length of service, or, in the words of paragraph 24 of the instruction: '… the soldier of the longest service in the regiment will be registered No 1, the next No 2 and so on to the recruit who last joined the regiment ….'.

In order that the new numbering system would be widely-known among the civil population it was laid down that:

Every soldier is to communicate to his friends the number by which he is known in the regiment and to acquaint them all so that when making enquiries after him whether addressed to the regiment or to the British War Office he could be identified.

This Regimental Numbering system was to last almost a century. The system was simple and would have remained so if it had been extended to the predecessors of the Militia and Territorial Army when those Forces were linked to the Regular Army, but that procedure was not followed; and the Militia and Volunteers were permitted to have their own serial numbering. This subsequently led to confusion as there existed no fewer than four different series of numbers in each Regiment:

- One series for the two regular battalions

- One series for the Militia battalion

- One series for the senior Volunteer battalion

- One series for the junior Volunteer battalion.

It was the function of the Militia to reinforce the regular battalions so it was possible for two men with the same regimental number to serve in the same battalion, thus destroying the distinctive identification of each individual which this system was intended to establish. During WWI the transfer of soldiers from one unit to another within Regiments and Corps became frequent and this led to greater confusion, particularly in those Corps of a decidedly national or clan character where the Christian and surnames were commonly duplicated.

Transfer between Corps was a frequent occurrence necessitating with each transfer the soldier receiving a new number. In some cases, men were transferred as many as six times, receiving a new number on each transfer. In such circumstances it was difficult for men to remember their current number. Such confusion had its lighter side, for on admission to hospital a soldier would sometimes declare the number in the Regiment he favoured, in the hope that on discharge from hospital he would be sent to it.

To overcome these weaknesses in the numbering system, in 1920 a decision was made to introduce a system of Army numbers in place of Regimental Numbers. Under this system all soldiers of the Regular Army and the Auxiliary Forces were allotted Army numbers in one continuous sequential system.

Australian Numbering System[471]

Personal numbers were used in the colonial forces and the early post-Federation Army; however, with the limited information available, it is suggested that the systems used were somewhat haphazard. With the onset of WWI the raising of the AIF required an entirely new and separate numbering system to be created. While not complicated, the AIF system could be confusing. The rules laid down in *AIF Orders* (AIFO) stated that for every infantry battalion, light horse regiment, divisional ammunition column, engineer field company and signal unit, numbering for 'other ranks' (OR) were to start at '1' and continue sequentially; numbers were not allocated to officers. Field artillery brigades (FAB), Australian Army Service Corps (AASC) units and Australian Army Medical Corps (AAMC) units were allotted numbers from a central series commencing at '1' with numbers being allotted from the central list to units, sub-units and individuals as required.

Problems with this system became immediately obvious; because, while a number might be unique to a man, the number itself may not be unique. Take for example the number '1', at the time of the initial raising of the AIF, given that the force consisted of 20 infantry battalions, four light horse regiments, a divisional artillery column, three engineer field companies, a signal company, a signal troop, plus artillery,

---

470 **Authors' Disclaimer:** Every effort has been made to ensure accuracy of information on the evolution of the Regimental Numbering system use by the Australian Army and not all will be captured in this abridged version. This information should be used as a guide only; further research should be conducted on individual Units and organisations to confirm accuracy.

471 http://www.awm.gov.au/research/people/nominal_rolls/first_world_war_embarkation

service Corps and medical units, at least 33 men would have been allotted the number '1'. Research has revealed that, taking into account new formations and units being raised as WWI progressed, a minimum of 107 members of the AIF were allotted the number '1'.

Originally the number '1' was largely reserved for the Regimental Sergeant Major (RSM), all of whom were drawn from the Permanent Military Forces (PMF); however, the practice was not universal. In early 1914, as units were raised and organised, men were generally allotted to sub-units alphabetically and by number; for example, for an infantry battalion of eight companies, the further down the alphabetical list a soldier was, the higher his number.

If a man marched into a unit and it was found that he had the same regimental number as a soldier already serving with the unit, the number would be modified by adding an alphabetic modifier 'A', 'B', etc as a suffix to the number. Two other alphabetic modifiers may be encountered with AIF regimental numbers, namely 'R' for re-enlistment and 'N' for a soldier with prior naval service with the RAN Bridging Train (RANBT).

As the war progressed, the sequential numbering system continued in use for the infantry and light horse; however, for all other Corps the numbering system evolved into a single central number list, starting in 1914, usually at '1'. This explains, for example, the incredibly high regimental numbers allotted to later enlisting artillerymen; the second largest single group in the AIF.

In 1917-1918, when comparing enlistments with earlier years, enlistments had slowed to a trickle and the AIF subsequently commenced a more centralised management of recruitment. From late 1917, while some lower-numbered units, for example the infantry battalions of the 1st Division, continued to receive drafts of specifically-allotted reinforcements; as a broad rule 'General Reinforcements' (GR) were raised and despatched overseas and allocated to units. GR were allotted unique numbers in the range of 50,000-80,000 (the first number issued was 50001). While GR numbers were still referred to as 'regimental numbers', they are the genesis of the Australian Army's 'Army numbers'.

The AIF ceased to exist on 1st April 1921 and AIF regimental numbers ceased to be issued, although they still remained relevant for recording purposes. The AIF aside, while the Army reorganised itself post-war, regimental numbers continued to be issued to the AMF for a short period.

WWI had shown that the 'regimental number' system at that time was inadequate.

Military Order (MO) 524/1921, published on 19th November 1921, finally abolished regimental numbers and laid down the rules for the use of 'Army Numbers.' From that date, the Australian Army never officially used the term 'regimental number'.

From 1921 to 1940, Army Numbers, which started at '1', were issued to formations in blocks of 1000 or multiples of 1000 under authority of MO and *Australian Army Orders* (AAO). Formations were permitted to sub-allot blocks of 100 numbers as required. The first block of numbers, 1–2250, was allotted by AAO 488/1922 to members of the PMF who were then serving.

With the outbreak of WWII, faced with the same restrictions of the *Defence Act 1903* that forbade the overseas deployment of members of the Army during WWI, Australia again opted to raise a separate, all-volunteer force, which was officially named the 2nd AIF.[472] Although the 1921 numbering system continued to be used for both the PMF and Militia until at least 1940, from its beginning the 2nd AIF used its own unique numbering system.

Military Board Instruction (MBI) 59/1939 directed that the 2nd AIF was to be recruited by Military District (MD), that each district's number sequence would commence at '1', and that each district was to prefix an alphabetic modifier to each individual number to identify the MD of enlistment. In addition, the letter 'X', signifying AIF, was to be inserted between the MD letter and the number. The system was:

- 1 MD   (Queensland)   QX1 – upwards
- 2 MD   (New South Wales)   NX1 – upwards
- 3 MD   (Victoria)   VX1 – upwards
- 4 MD   (South Australia)   SX1 – upwards
- 5 MD   (Western Australia)   WX1 – upwards
- 6 MD   (Tasmania)   TX1 – upwards
- 7 MD   (Northern Territory)   DX1 – upwards

The use of the so-called 'index letters' was extended to the Militia. From early 1940 all serving members of the CMF and all new enlistees were allotted numbers from a new system, starting at '1' for each MD, the number modified by the addition of the MD index letter as a prefix. The letter 'X' was not added. The first 2nd AIF number issued for 6 MD (Tasmania) was TX1, while the first CMF number issued for the district was T1.

Prior to August 1942, female enlistees were allocated numbers from the MD sequence, without differentiation; specific blocks of numbers were not, and in fact were never, reserved for female enlistees. In August 1942 orders were issued that all serving female soldiers and all future female enlistees were to have the letter 'F' added to their number immediately after the MD letter. Thus, a serving female member of the 2nd AIF who had enlisted in 4 MD (South

---

472 Military Board Instruction (MBI) No.59 of 18 October 1939

Australia) and been allotted the number SX3450 then had the number SFX3450.

Additional index letters were added as the war progressed. The final list of Army number index letters was:

Q	Queensland (Citizen Military Forces – CMF)
QP	Queensland (Permanent Military Forces – PMF)
QX	Queensland (Australian Imperial Force – AIF)
QF	Queensland (CMF – Female)
QFX	Queensland (AIF – Female)
N	New South Wales (CMF)
NP	New South Wales (PMF)
NX	New South Wales (AIF)
NF	New South Wales (CMF – Female)
NFX	New South Wales (AIF – Female)
V	Victoria (CMF)
VP	Victoria (PMF)
VX	Victoria (AIF)
VF	Victoria Militia (CMF – Female)
VFX	Victoria (AIF - Female)
S	South Australia (CMF)
SP	South Australia (PMF)
SX	South Australia (AIF)
SF	South Australia (CMF – Female)
SFX	South Australia (AIF – Female)
W	Western Australia (CMF)
WP	Western Australia (PMF)
WX	Western Australia (AIF)
WF	Western Australia (CMF – Female)
WFX	Western Australia (AIF – Female)
T	Tasmania (CMF)
TP	Tasmania (PMF)
TX	Tasmania (AIF)
TF	Tasmania (CMF – Female)
TFX	Tasmania (AIF – Female)
D	Northern Territory (CMF)
DP	Northern Territory (PMF – from 1944)
DX	Northern Territory (AIF)
P	Papua (CMF)
PX	Papua (AIF)
PN	Papua Native
NG	New Guinea (CMF)
NGX	New Guinea (AIF)
NGN	New Guinea Native
UKX	United Kingdom (AIF)
R	New Guinea Police (armed constabulary)
B	Accredited Philanthropic Representatives
VBF	British First Aid Nursing Yeomanry (FANY) seconded to AMF.

There were no female enlistments recorded for 7MD/Northern Territory or 8MD/Papua and New Guinea; this is because the white female populations of these territories were evacuated to the southern states of mainland Australia in WWII. Although there were a number of female enlistments recorded that give either 7MD or 8MD as place of birth or place of residence at the time of their enlistment, all enlistments were in the southern states and use the prefixes for those states. In addition, there were no enlistments of 'native' females in either 7 MD or 8 MD. Thus the prefixes DF, DFX, PF, PFX, NGF, NGFX, NGNF, and PNF did not exist.

The FANY was a British female auxiliary organisation, their members wore modified British Army uniforms, providing various unpaid support services to the war effort. A small section of FANY however served as a parent unit for women serving with the top secret and clandestine Special Operations Executive (SOE). The 'VBF' prefix was appended to the existing non-Australian numbers of a small contingent of FANY who were seconded to the Australian Services Reconnaissance Department (SRD) in 1945 for code duties.

Following the end of WWII, numbers with the MD letter and 'X' continued to be allotted to enlistees into both the 2nd AIF and the Interim Army until 1947. The PMF was reinstituted in August 1947 and a short-lived PMF and Supplementary Reserve Army numbering system, which consisted of a straight line of digits without any modifiers, was authorised. This system became obsolete on 30th September 1947 with the raising of the Australian Regular Army (ARA) and the re-raising of the peace-time CMF.

The creation of a new Army also saw the creation of a new numbering system. Under this numbering system, each MD was responsible for issuing numbers, starting from 1, and prefixed by the MD number, followed by an oblique stroke, to denote the State of enlistment, the letter 'P' for PMF was no longer being used. Thus, for example, the 304th ARA soldier enlisted in 2 MD (New South Wales) was issued the number 2/304.

The names of the first persons issued with the new numbers were:

- 1/1   RH Nimmo
- 2/1   JS Whitelaw
- 3/1   EH Cahill
- 4/1   CE Prior
- 5/1   TN Gooch
- 6/1   CA Clowes
- 7/1   Unknown

When recruiting re-commenced in PNG, Army Number 8/1 was issued to J. Davey.

Numbers were allocated in blocks to each MD, with separate blocks for ARA, PMF, RMC cadets, ARA officers not commissioned from RMC, ARA short-service officers, ARA junior trainees, Regular Army Supplementary Reserve (RASR), CMF, AIF still serving and RASR Special Enlistments. As an example, for 1 MD the block 1–6999 was allocated to ARA and 10000–399999 was allocated to CMF.

The introduction of the first National Service (NS) Scheme in 1951 saw the requirement to issue Army numbers to NS enlistees. As NS recruits were members of the CMF, they were issued numbers from the CMF block allocated to their State of enlistment, as follows:

- QLD/1 MD (prefix '1/'):   10000–399999
- NSW/2 MD (prefix '2/'):   50000–399999
- VIC/3 MD (prefix '3/'):   50000–399999
- SA/4 MD (prefix '4/'):   10000–399999
- WA/5 MD (prefix '5/'):   10000–3999999
- TAS/6 MD (prefix '6/'):   5000–399999
- NT/7 MD (prefix '7/'):   2000–399999

Certain specific categories of persons had their numbers modified by alphabetic prefixes. These were:

- PMF Reserve and CMF on Full-Time Duty   A
- Regular Army Emergency Reserve (RAER)   E
- Regular Army Reserve (RAR)   R
- Philanthropic Representatives   B
- Correspondents, Photographers   C

Members of foreign armies attached or seconded to the AMF, for example, students at the Army Staff College, used their own 'national number' prefixed with a particular letter code, as follows:

- United Kingdom   VB
- Canada   VC
- New Zealand   VNZ
- United States   US
- India   VN

In 1950 female enlistments and appointments to the Army were re-introduced and allotments of number blocks were issued for this category of service. As with male enlistments, female numbers started at '1' and were issued to individual MDs in separate blocks for ARA, CMF and former members of the 2nd AIF. Numbers were prefixed by the letter 'F'; thus, for example, 2 MD (New South Wales)

was allocated the block 1–999 for ARA enlistments with the first number issued (to MR Dillon) being F2/1.

In 1961 the Army reviewed and changed the numbering system; the oblique stroke between the 'State number' and the first digit of the Army number was abolished. Thus a person with the number '1/3450' would then have the number '13450'. Secondly, from this date all categories of male enlistments, both ARA and CMF, were issued numbers from the same number blocks. The only exceptions to this were RMC graduates and Army Apprentices, who continued to be issued numbers from their own unique blocks.

The next major change to the Army numbering system occurred in 1965, brought about by the re-institution of NS. To cater for the new intakes of conscripted soldiers, AHQ directed that the 700000 block, previously reserved, be allocated to the Command/MD authorities for issue to NS enlistees. Thus, theoretically, the first NS soldier enlisted in NSW (Eastern Command/2MD) would have been issued the number '2700000', while the one-thousandth soldier enlisted would have been issued the number '2701000'. AHQ directed that in the event a number was unused at intake, for example, a failure to report, then such numbers were to be used for the subsequent intake.

The last major change to the Army numbering system, prior to its abolition, occurred in 1967. Changes included the abolition of letter prefixes for specialised categories of AMF service; abolition of letter prefixes for members of foreign armies; issue of Army numbers to RMC Staff Cadets on enlistment (previously RMC cadets were not allotted a regimental or Army number until graduation); and the decision that a member of the Army was to retain his or her originally-allotted Army number for the entire enlistment, including re-enlistments after break of service.

This change, in particular the decision to issue a single number to accompany a soldier throughout his or her period of military service, regardless of category of service or breaks in service, went a long way to achieving the ideal of 'one soldier, one number'.

The regimental and Army numbering systems served the AMF well for almost a century. However, by 1997, Defence, as an outcome of the Defence Efficiency Review, had recognised the requirement for an integrated personnel management system. The project implemented to enable this shift was titled the 'Personnel Management Key Solution (PMKeyS)'. One of the significant elements of PMKeyS is the 'PMKeyS Number' or 'Employee Identity (ID) Number.' As part of the PMKeyS Project, every member (uniformed and APS) of the ADF was allocated a PMKeyS Number, which effectively replaced the Service number and progressively abolished the Service numbering system. The 'roll out' was a phased operation, with the RAN, the smallest of the Services, being converted to PMKeyS first, in October 2001. The RAAF, the second largest Service, adopted the Army numbering system in February 2002. For the ADF the process was completed with the 'roll out' to Army in July 2002.

The concept of the PMKeyS numbers is simple; the possibility of retaining former numbering systems was entertained but was dismissed as unworkable. Taking into consideration the existing number formats, usage and size, the decision was taken to institute a seven-digit number, starting with the numeral '8'. The 'start at 8' decision permitted up to 2 million people to be registered before the actual number size (the number of digits) would change. It was planned that PMKeyS would continue to progress with numbers being allotted in sequence until such time as numbers reach eight, nine or even higher digits. However, at the start of the process, a seven-digit number was decided on as it would be easier to remember.

The implementation of the PMKeyS ID caused upset among those soldiers who felt their previous service should be recognised by recording their original Army number on any campaign or long service medals awarded. This view was initially supported on individual representation to the Directorate of Honours and Awards.

RMC Staff Cadet Numbers

When a person was appointed to the Corps of Staff Cadets at RMC, he or she was issued with an 'RMC Number'. These numbers started from '1' (issued to SCDT WJ Urquhardt in 1911) and have continued as a straight sequence since that time. Prior to 1921, on graduation, a cadet was not issued with a regimental number but after October of that year every graduating cadet was issued with an Army number (referred to in the case of officers as a 'personal number'). This practice caused problems for the record-keeping organisation if a cadet was discharged prior to graduation as, without an Army number, it was difficult to track and account for the ex-cadet's service. To solve this problem, from 1st January 1967 every RMC cadet was issued with an Army number on enlistment, in addition to the RMC Number. The latter number ceases to have relevance after graduation, except for RMC alumni and 'old boy' purposes.

The Royal Crown

The crowns used on diagrams, engraved on military swords and shown on military badges and accoutrements bear little resemblance to the actual crowns they represent. They are a diagrammatical representation of the crown drawn by the College of Arms, and selected by the Monarch to be used on their Coat of Arms and all other official paraphernalia.

The 'Imperial State Crown' is worn annually by the Queen at the State Opening of the British Parliament. The current Imperial State Crown was manufactured for the coronation of King George VI in 1937, and is an exact replica of the earlier Imperial State Crown manufactured for Queen Victoria, but is of a more lightweight design.

The frames of the old Imperial State Crowns of several British monarchs are kept in the Tower of London. As the most frequently worn Royal crown, the Imperial State Crown has constantly been updated due to age, weight, the personal taste of the monarch or the unavoidable damage that comes with use.

St Edward's Crown is one of the original, and remains one of the senior, British Crown Jewels. It is the official coronation crown used exclusively in the coronation of British monarchs and is the same basic design as the crown made in 1661 for the coronation of King Charles II. This crown was made to replace the original crown destroyed on Oliver Cromwell's order during the English Civil War.

Imperial State or Tudor Crown   *St Edward's Crown*

The design of the St Edward's Crown includes a base with four crosses pattée alternating with four fleurs-de-lis, above which are two arches surmounted by a cross. In the centre is a red velvet cap with an ermine border. The left and right arch has nine pearls and the facing arch shows five (the actual crown has no pearls in the arches). The actual crown is made of solid gold and set with 444 precious stones. Formerly, it was set with jewels hired for the coronation after which the crown was dismantled, leaving only the frame. However, in 1911, the jewels used were set permanently.

Queen Victoria and Edward VII chose not to be crowned with it because it weighs 4lb 12oz. Queen Victoria chose to be crowned with the lighter Imperial State Crown. It was also the crown of choice in the coronation of King George VI on 12 May 1937.

The St Edward's Crown has been used as a symbol of Royal authority since 1953 in the Commonwealth of Nations and can be seen on coats-of-arms, Regimental Guidons, Colours, badges, stamps and swords.

Significant Dates for Army

Following is a list of significant dates in the Australian Army. Many units no longer exist, have had name changes or may have been amalgamated; and many still have associations which maintain traditional links to the original organisations.

Army / Corps Birthdays

Army	01 Mar
Australian Army Aviation	01 Jul
Australian Army Band Corps	02 Aug
Australian Army Catering Corps	12 Mar
Australian Army Legal Corps	30 Sep
Australian Army Psychology Corps	15 Oct
Australian Army Public Relations Service	31 Mar
Australian Intelligence Corps	06 Dec
Corps of Staff Cadets	22 Jun
Royal Australian Armoured Corps	09 Jul
Royal Australian Army Chaplains Department	01 Dec
Royal Australian Army Dental Corps	23 Apr
Royal Australian Army Educational Corps	18 Apr
Royal Australian Army Medical Corps	01 Jul
Royal Australian Army Nursing Corps	01 Jul
Royal Australian Army Ordnance Corps	01 Jul
Royal Australian Army Pay Corps	21 Sep
Royal Australian Artillery	06 Jun
Royal Australian Corps of Military Police	03 Apr
Royal Australian Corps of Signals	12 Jan
Royal Australian Corps of Transport	01 Jun
Royal Corps of Australian Electrical and Mechanical Engineers	01 Dec
Royal Australian Engineers	01 Jul
Royal Australian Infantry Corps	14 Dec

SHORTENED FORMS OF WORDS IN ARMY USE

Acronyms, Initialisms and Abbreviations

Normally shortened forms of words contained within a book are provided so the reader can better understand the entire content; this is especially relevant to books on the military that have developed a verbal culture based on shortened forms of words. Therefore, it would be expected that a casual listener to a conversation between members of the military will be at a loss to understand them because of the flow of acronyms and initialisms. The following list is compiled not only of shortened forms used within this book but also many others which are also included as they too are part of the Customs and Traditions of the Army. The list is not exhaustive and if further information is needed the reader should refer to the AWM internet site at www.awm.gov.au.

#

1ALSG – 1st Australian Logistic Support Group

1ATF – 1st Australian Task Force

1 RAR – 1st Battalion, The Royal Australian Regiment

2IC – Second in Command

2nd AIF – Second Australian Imperial Force

A

AA – Anti Aircraft

AAAvn – Australian Army Aviation Corps

AABC – Australian Army Band Corps

AACC – Australian Army Catering Corps

AAHU – Australian Army History Unit

AALC – Australian Army Legal Corps

AAMC – Australian Army Medical Corps

AAMWS – Australian Army Medical Women's Service

AANS – Australian Army Nursing Service

AAO – Australian Army Order

AAOC – Australian Army Ordnance Corps

AAPRS – Australian Army Public Relations Service

AAPsych – Australian Army Psychology Corps

AASC – Australian Army Service Corps

AASM – Australian Active Service Medal

AASM 45-75 – Australian Active Service Medal 1945-1975

AATnC – Australian Army Transportation Corps

AATT-I – Australian Army Training Team – Iraq

AATTV – Australian Army Training Team Vietnam

AC – Companion of the Order of Australia

ACB – Army Combat Badge

ACFSM – Australian Cadet Forces Service Medal

ACV – Armoured Command Vehicle

AD – Dame of the Order of Australia

AD – Air Defence/Air Dispatch

ADC – Aide-de-Camp

ADF – Australian Defence Force

ADFA – Australian Defence Force Academy

ADFE – Australian Defence Force Ensign

ADJT/Adjt – Adjutant

Admin – Administration or Administrative

ADMS – Assistant Director Medical Services

ADOS – Assistant Director of Ordnance Services

ADS – Advanced Dressing Station

AEME – Australian Electrical and Mechanical Engineers

AFC – Australian Flying Corps

AFG – Australian Federation Guard

AFPO – Armed Forces Post Office

AFS – Army Fire Service

AFV – Armoured Fighting Vehicle

AG – Adjutant General

AGA – Australian Garrison Artillery

AGH – Australian General Hospital

AGRA – Army Group Royal Artillery

AHQ – Army Headquarters

AIC – Australian Instructional Corps

AIF – Australian Imperial Force

AJWE – Australian Joint Warfare Establishment

AK – Knight of the Order of Australia

ALH – Australian Light Horse

ALO – Army Liaison Officer

ALSG – Australian Logistic Support Group

ALTC – Army Logistic Training Centre

AM – Member of the Order of Australia

AM – Albert Medal

Amb – Ambulance

AMCU – Australian Multi-cam Camouflage Uniform or 'MultiCam'

AMF – Australian Military Forces

Ammo – Ammunition

Amph – Amphibious

AMR – Australian Military Regulations

AMR&Os – Australian Military Regulations and Orders

AMS – Army Medical Service/Staff

AN&MEF – Australian Naval and Military Expeditionary Force

ANF – Australian National Flag
ANGAU – Australian New Guinea Administrative Unit
ANZAC – Australian and New Zealand Army Corps
ANZAM – Australia, New Zealand and Malaya
ANZUK – Australia, New Zealand, United Kingdom
ANZUS – Australia, New Zealand and United States
Security Treaty
AO – Order of Australia
AO – Army Order
AOD – Army Ordnance Depot
APC – Armoured Personnel Carrier
APS – Australian Public Service
AQMG – Assistant Quartermaster General
ARA – Australian Regular Army
ARCS – Australian Red Cross Society
ARes – Army Reserve
Armd – Armoured
ARTC – Army Recruit Training Centre
Arty – Artillery
ASC – Army Service Corps (British)
ASCO – Army Services Canteen Organisation
ASEAN – Association of South East Asian Nations
Aslt – Assault
ASM – Active Service Medal
ASM 45-75 – Australian Service Medal 1945-1975
ASOD – Army Standing Orders for Dress
Asst – Assistant
ATF – Australian Task Force
A-Tk [AT] – Anti-Tank
ATO – Ammunition Technical Officer
AUR – Adelaide Universities Regiment
AUSTINT – Australian Army Intelligence Corps
Aux – Auxiliary
Avn – Aviation
AWAS – Australian Women's Army Service
AWE – Australian White Ensign
AWLA – Australian Women's Land Army
AWM – Australian War Memorial
AWOL – Absent Without Leave

B

BASB – Brigade Administrative Support Battalion
BC – Battery Commander
BCOF – British Commonwealth Occupation Force
BCE – Before the Common Era
BCFK – British Commonwealth Force Korea
BDE/Bde – Brigade
BDR – Bombardier
BEM – British Empire Medal

BHC – Battle Honours Committee
BHQ – Battalion Headquarters
Bks – Barracks
BM – Bravery Medal
BM – Brigade Major
BN/Bn – Battalion
BOD – Base Ordnance Depot
BQMS – Battery Quartermaster Sergeant
BRAAC – Brigadier Royal Australian Armoured Corps
BRIG – Brigadier
BSD – Base Supply Depot
BSM – Battery Sergeant Major
Bty – Battery

C

C de G – Croix de Guerre (Awarded by both France and
Belgium)
CA – Chief of Army
CA (AA) – Coast Artillery (Anti-aircraft)
CAC – Commonwealth Aircraft Corporation
CAPT – Captain
CASAC – Chief of Army's Senior Advisory Committee
CASC – Commander Army Service Corps
Casevac – Casualty Evacuation
CAV/Cav – Cavalry
CB – Companion of the Order of the Bath
CB – Confined to Barracks
CBE – Commander of the Order of the British Empire
CCO – Clandestine Communist Organisation
CCRA – Commander, Corps Royal Artillery
CCS – Casualty Clearing Station
CDC – Colonial Defence Committee
CDEME – Commander Division Electrical and Mechanical
Engineers
CDF – Chief of the Defence Force
CDFS – Chief of the Defence Force Staff
CDO/Cdo – Commando
CDR – Commander [RAN]
CDSIGS – Commander Divisional Signals
CDSUP – Commander Divisional Supply
CD-Transport – Commander Divisional Transport
CE – Chief Engineer
CE – Current Era
CER – Combat Engineer Regiment
CES – Complete Equipment Schedule
CGM – Conspicuous Gallantry Medal
CGS – Chief of the General Staff
CHQ – Company Headquarters
C-in-C – Commander-in-Chief

CJOPS – Chief of Joint Operations

CL – Commercial Light (Vehicle)

CMF – Citizen Military Force/Commonwealth Monitoring Force

CMG – Companion of the Order of St Michael and St George

CO – Commanding Officer

COL – Colonel

COMD – Command, Commander, Commanded

COMDT – Commandant

Const – Construction

COY/Coy – Company

CPL – Corporal

CQMS – Company Quartermaster Sergeant

CRA – Commander, Royal Artillery (Divisional)

CRAAOC – Commander Royal Australian Army Ordnance Corps

CRAASC – Commander Royal Australian Army Service Corps

CRAEME – Commander Royal Australian Electrical and Mechanical Engineers

CRE – Commander Royal Engineers (Divisional)

CSC – Conspicuous Service Cross

CSC – Corps of Staff Cadets

CSI – Companion of the Star of India

CSM – Conspicuous Service Medal

CSM – Company Sergeant Major

CSR – Combat Support Regiment

CSSB – Combat Services Support Battalion

CT – Corps Troops/Communist Terrorists

CV – Cross of Valour

CVO – Companion of the Royal Victorian Order

CW – Chemical Warfare

CWGC – Commonwealth War Graves Commission

CWT – Hundredweight (imperial measurement = 112lb) equal to approximately 50.8kg

D

D↑D – Department of Defence

DAAG – Deputy Assistant Adjutant General

DAG – Deputy Adjutant General

DAQMG – Deputy Assistant Quartermaster-General

DB – District Base

DBE – Dame Commander of the Order of the British Empire

DCA – Deputy Chief of Army

DCM – Distinguished Conduct Medal

DCRE – Director Corps Royal Engineers

DDMO – Deputy Director of Military Operations

DDMT – Deputy Director of Military Training

DDS – Director Dental Service

DDS&T – Deputy Director of Supply and Transport

Def – Defence

DEO – Direct Entry Officer

Dept – Department/Depot

Det – Detachment

DFC – Distinguished Flying Cross

DFSM – Defence Force Service Medal

DGMS – Director General Medical Service

DGPERS-A – Director General Personnel – Army

DGPR – Director General Public Relations

DHQ – Divisional Headquarters

DI (A) – Defence Instruction – Army

DI (G) – Defence Instruction – General

DID – Detail Issue Depot

DIV/Div – Division

DLS – Director Legal Service

DLSM – Defence Long Service Medal

DMGO – Deputy Master General of the Ordnance

DMI – Director of Military Intelligence

DMT – Director of Military Training

DMZ – Demilitarised Zone

DOW – Died of Wounds

DP1 – Draft Priority One

DPCU – Disruptive Pattern Camouflage Uniform

DPDU – Disruptive Pattern Desert Uniform

DPS – Defence Publishing Service

DQMG – Deputy Quartermaster General

DRV – Democratic Republic of Vietnam

DSC – Distinguished Service Cross

DSD – District Supply Depot

DSM – Distinguished Service Medal

DSO – Distinguished Service Order

DSU – District Support Unit

DUC – Distinguished Unit Citation

E

Ech – Echelon

ED – Efficiency Decoration

ER – Elizabeth Regina (Queen Elizabeth)

ESB – Engineer Special Brigade

F

FA – Field Artillery

FANY – British First Aid Nursing Yeomanry

FARELF – Far East Land Forces

FCU – Force Communications Unit

Fd – Field

FESR – British Commonwealth Far East Strategic Reserve/
Far East Strategic Reserve

Flt – Flight

FM – Field Marshal

Fmn – Formation

FNQR – Far North Queensland Regiment

FO – Forward Observer

FOC – Freedom of the City

FOE –Freedom of Entry

FOO – Forward Observer Officer

FPDA – Five Power Defence Arrangements

FSB – Fire Support Base/Force Support Battalion

FSD – Field Supply Depot

FUP – Forming Up Point/Place

Fwd – Forward

G

GBE – Knight (or Dame) Grand Cross of the British
Empire

GC – George Cross

GCB – Knight Grand Cross of the Bath

GCI – Good Conduct Increment

GCIE – Knight Grand Commander of the Order of the
Indian Empire

GCM – Good Conduct Medal

GCVO – Knight Grand Cross of the Royal Victorian Order

GD – General Duties

Gd – Guard

GEN – General

G-G – Governor-General of Australia

GHQ – General Headquarters

GL – Ground Liaison

GM – George Medal

GMC – General Motor Company

GMT – Greenwich Mean Time

GOC – General Officer Commanding

Gp – Group

GPMG – General Purpose Machine Gun

GRes – General Reserve

GR – General Reinforcements

GRO – General Routine Order

GS – General Service (Vehicle)

GSO – General Staff Officer

GSW – Gunshot Wound

H

HAA – Heavy Anti-Aircraft

HAG – Heavy Artillery Group

HB – Heavy Batteries

HE – High Explosive

HEIC – Honourable East India Company

HMAS – His/Her Majesty's Australian Ship

HMG – Heavy Machine Gun

HOC – Head of Corps

HOR – Head of Regiment

HOSM – Humanitarian Overseas Service Medal

Hosp – Hospital

How – Howitzer

HQ – Headquarters

HRH – Her/His Royal Highness

HRL – Hunter River Lancers

HSB – Health Support Battalion

HT – Horse Transport

HTM – Heavy Trench Mortar

I

ICAT – International Coalition Against Terrorism

ICB – Infantry Combat Badge

IDC – Imperial Defence Committee

IED – Improvised Explosive Device

IG – Inspector General

IGM – Inspector General Munitions

IGS – Imperial General Staff

IHC – International Harvester Company

Indep – Independent

INF/Inf – Infantry

Instr – Instructor, Instruction

Int – Intelligence

INTERFET – International Force East Timor

ISAF – International Security Assistance Force

J

JAG – Judge Advocate General

JCS – Joint Chiefs of Staff

JG – Jungle Greens (Uniform)

JLU – Joint Logistic Unit

JNCO – Junior Non-Commissioned Officer

JTC – Jungle Training Centre

JTS – Jungle Training School

K

KBE – Knight Commander of the British Empire

KCB – Knight Commander of the Order of the Bath

KCIE – Knight Commander of the Indian Empire

KCMG – Knight Commander of the Order of St Michael
and St George

KCSI – Knight Commander of the Star of India

KCVO – Knight Commander of the Victorian Order

KFF – Khaki Fur Felt (Slouched Hat material)

KG – Knight (of the Order) of the Garter

KIA – Killed in Action

KStJ – Knight of the Most Venerable Order of the Hospital of Saint John of Jerusalem

KT – Knight (of the Order) of the Thistle/Knight Templar

L

L of C – Lines of Communication

L1A1 – Self Loading Rifle

LAA – Light Anti-Aircraft

LAD – Light Aid Detachment

LARC – Lighter Amphibious Resupply Cargo (Vessel)

lb – Pound (imperial weight measurement, 1lb equal to approximately 0.5kg)

LBDR – Lance Bombardier

LCH – Landing Craft Heavy

LCI – Landing Craft Infantry

LCM – Landing Craft Mechanised

LCP – Landing Craft Personnel

LCPL – Lance Corporal

LCT – Landing Craft Tank

LCV – Landing Craft Vehicle

LH – Light Horse

LHQ – Land Headquarters

LMG – Light Machine Gun

LO – Liaison Officer

Loc – Location, Locating

LOG – Logistic, Logistics

LSF – Logistic Support Force

LSG – Logistic Support Group

LSW – Light Support Weapon

LT – Lieutenant/2LT – 2nd Lieutenant

Lt – Light

LTCOL – Lieutenant Colonel

LTGEN – Lieutenant General

LVT – Landing Vehicle Tracked

LZ – Landing Zone

M

MAJ – Major

MAJGEN – Major General

MBE – Member of the British Empire

MBI – Military Board Instruction

MC – Military Cross

MCE – Military Corrective Establishment

MD – Military District

ME – Middle East

Mech – Mechanised, Mechanical

Med – Medium

MFO – Multinational Force of Observers

MG – Machine Gun

MG – Medal for Gallantry

MI – Military Intelligence, Mounted Infantry

MIA – Missing In Action

MID – Mentioned In Despatches

Mil – Military

MLO – Military Liaison Office

MM – Military Medal

MMG – Medium Machine Gun

MO – Medical Officer

Mob – Mobile

Mov – Movement

MP – Military Police

MPH – Miles Per Hour

MSM – Meritorious Service Medal

MT – Motor Transport

Mtd – Mounted

Mtn – Mountain

MUC – Meritorious Unit Citation

Multi – Multiple

MUR – Melbourne University Regiment

N

NATO – North Atlantic Treaty Organisation

NCO – Non-Commissioned Officer

NEM – National Emergency Medal

NG – New Guinea

NGF – New Guinea Force

NGVR – New Guinea Volunteer Rifles

NLF – National Liberation Front (Vietnam)

NORCOM – Northern Command

Norforce – Northern Territory Force

NS – National Service

NSC – Nursing Service Cross

NT – Northern Territory

NVA – North Vietnamese Army

O

OAM – Medal of the Order of Australia

OAWG – Office of Australian War Graves

OBE – Officer of the Order of the British Empire

OC – Officer Commanding

OCS – Officer Cadet School

OCTU – Officer Cadet Training Unit

ODF – Operational Deployment Force

Offr – Officer

OFP – Ordnance Field Park

OIC – Officer in Charge

OM – Order of Merit

OP – Observation Post

Ops – Operations
OPSO – Operations Officer
OR – Other Ranks
ORBAT – Order of Battle
Ord – Ordnance
Org – Organisations
OSB – Operational Service Badge
OSM – Operational Service Medal
OTU – Officer Training Unit

P

Pers – Personnel
PIB – Papua Infantry Battalion
PIR – Pacific Islands Regiment
PJI – Parachute Jump Instructor
PL/Pl – Platoon
PMF – Permanent Military Forces
Pmr – Paymaster
PNG – Papua New Guinea
PNGDF – Papua New Guinea Defence Force
PNGVR – Papua New Guinea Volunteer Rifles
Pnr – Pioneer
POW – Prisoner of War
PR – Public Relations
Pro – Provost (Military Police)
psc – Posted Staff College/Passed Staff College
PT – Physical Training
PTE – Private, soldier
PTE (P) – Private (proficient)
PWLH – Prince of Wales's Light Horse

Q

QM – Quartermaster
QMG – Quartermaster General
QMI – Queensland Mounted Infantry
QMS – Quartermaster Sergeant

R

r. – Reign
RA Inf – Royal Australian Infantry
RA Sigs – Royal Australian Corps of Signals
RA Svy – Royal Australian Survey Corps
RAA – The Royal Regiment of Australian Artillery
RAAC – Royal Australian Armoured Corps
RAAChD/RAACD – Royal Australian Army Chaplains Department
RAADC – Royal Australian Army Dental Corps
RAAEC – Royal Australian Army Educational Corps
RAAF – Royal Australian Air Force
RAAMC – Royal Australian Army Medical Corps

RAANC – Royal Australian Army Nursing Corps
RAANS – Royal Australian Army Nursing Service
RAAOC – Royal Australian Army Ordnance Corps
RAAPC – Royal Australian Army Pay Corps
RAASC – Royal Australian Army Service Corps
RACMP – Royal Australian Corps of Military Police
RACT – Royal Australian Corps of Transport
RAE – Royal Australian Engineers
RAEME – Royal Corps of Australian Electrical and Mechanical Engineers
RAER – Regular Army Emergency Reserve
RAN – Royal Australian Navy
RAP – Regimental Aid Post
RAR – The Royal Australian Regiment
RAR – Regular Army Reserve
RASB – Return from Active Service Badge
RASR – Regular Army Supplementary Reserve
RCT – Regimental Combat Team
Rec – Recovery
Recce – Reconnaissance
Recon – Reconnaissance
Regt – Regiment
Res – Reserve
RFC – Royal Flying Corps
Rfct/Rft – Reinforcement
RFD – Reserve Force Decoration
RFM – Reserve Force Medal
RFSU – Regional Force Surveillance Unit
RGAB – Royal Garrison Artillery Brigade
RGH – Repatriation General Hospital
RMC – Royal Military College
RMC-A – Royal Military College of Australia
RMC-D – Royal Military College – Duntroon
RMO – Regimental Medical Officer
RNSWL – Royal New South Wales Lancers
RNSWR – The Royal New South Wales Regiment
RO/ROs – Routine Order/Routine Orders
RQMS/RQ – Regimental Quartermaster Sergeant
RQR – The Royal Queensland Regiment
RRes – Ready Reserve
RSAR – The Royal South Australia Regiment
RSL – Returned and Services League (previously Returned Services League)
RSM – Regimental Sergeant Major
RSM-A – Regimental Sergeant Major of the Army
RTA – Returned to Australia
RTR – The Royal Tasmania Regiment
RTU – Returned to Unit

RVN – Republic of Vietnam (South)

RVR – The Royal Victoria Regiment

RWAR – The Royal Western Australia Regiment

S

SAA – Small Arms Ammunition

SAFCOL – Special Action Forces Craft, Offshore, Large

SAMR – South Australian Mounted Rifles

SAS – Special Air Service

SAS – Small Arms School

SASR – Special Air Service Regiment

SB – Siege Battery

SC – Star of Courage

SEA – South East Asia

SEATO – South East Asia Treaty Organisation

Sec – Secretary

Sect – Section

SF – Special Forces

SG – Star of Gallantry

SG – State Governor

SGT/Sergt – Sergeant/Serjeant

Sig – Signal

SIG – Signaller

SIS – Special Investigation Service (Military Police)

SM – Security Memorandum

SME – School of Military Engineering

SMG – Sub-Machine Gun

SMLE – .303 inch Short Magazine Lee Enfield

SMO – Senior Medical Officer

SNCO – Senior Non-Commissioned Officer

SNO – Senior Nursing Officer

SO (3), (2) or (1) – Staff Officer (Grade Three, Two or One)

SOPs – Standard Operating Procedures

Spt – Support

SQN – Squadron

SSGT – Staff Sergeant

SSM – Squadron Sergeant Major

SUPO – Supply Officer

SUR – Sydney University Regiment

Svy – Survey

SWPA – South West Pacific Area

T

T – Ton (imperial weight measurement, 2,240lb, equal to approximately 0.984 Tonne)

Tac – Tactical

TAOR – Tactical Area of Operations

TF – Task Force

Tk – Tank

TLC – Tracked Load Carrier

Tn – Terminal

TOS – Taken On Strength

Tps – Troops

Tpr – Trooper

Tpt – Transport

TRG/Trg – Training

Tun – Tunnelling

TW – Tropical Warfare

U

UCG – Unit Citation for Gallantry

UCP – Unit Colour Patch

UN – United Nations

UNCI – United Nations Commission for Indonesia

UNC-K – United Nations Command – Korea

UNCOK – United Nations Commission on Korea

UNIFIL – United Nations Interim Force in Lebanon

UNMOGIP – United Nations Military Observer Group in India and Pakistan

UNSC – United Nations Security Council

UNTSO – United Nations Truce Supervision Organisation

UTS – Universal Training Scheme

UXB – Unexploded Bomb

UXO – Unexploded Ordnance

V

VAD – Voluntary Aid Detachment

VC – Victoria Cross/Victoria Cross of Australia

VC – Viet Cong (Vietnam)

VCGS – Vice Chief of the Defence Staff

VDC – Volunteer Defence Corps

Veh – Vehicle

VMR – Victoria Mounted Rifles

VRD – Vehicle Reception Depot

W

W↑D – War Department

WAAAF – Women's Australian Auxiliary Air Force

WAUR – West Australia University Regiment

WE – War Establishment

WIA – Wounded In Action

Wks – Works

Wksp – Workshops

WO – Warrant Officer

WO1/WOI – Warrant Officer Class One

WO2/WOII – Warrant Officer Class Two

WRAAC – Women's Royal Australian Army Corps

WRAAF – Women's Royal Australian Air Force

WRANS – Women's Royal Australian Naval Service

WWI – First World War/World War One

WWII – Second World War/World War Two

Additional Reading List

Official Publications and Orders

AIF Orders, Order No.2 (vi), dated 26 August 1914

Army. *The Royal Regiment of Australian Artillery – Standing Orders*: 2008

Australia, Commonwealth of. *A History of the 2nd Cavalry Regiment*. Canberra, Department of Defence: 2005

Australia, Commonwealth of. *Australian Flags*. Australia, The McPhersons Printing Group: 1998

Australia, Commonwealth of. *Australian Government Gazette Special 17*. Canberra: 15 January 1993

Australia, Commonwealth of. *Australian Government Gazette Special 28*. Canberra: 17 February 1975

Australia, Commonwealth of. *Australian Government Gazette Special 97*. Canberra: 27 May 1975

Australia, Commonwealth of. *Colour Patch Register 1915-1949*. Canberra, Director Publishing: 1993

Australia, Department of Defence. *A Guide to Customs of the Army Australian*. Canberra, Government Publishing Service: 1984

Australian Army Military Order 135. *Saluting Flag*: 1911

Australian Army Military Order 305/1907. *Establishment Approval Australia Intelligence Corps*: 1907

Australian Army Military Order 58/08. *Australian Ensign*: 1908

Australian Army Military Regulation 68. *Corps and Regimental Seniority*: 1927

Australian Army Order (AAO) 112/1953. *Regimental Marches – Australian Military Forces*: 1953

Australian Army Order (AAO) 132/1927. *Territorial Titles and Mottoes – Regiments and Battalions, Australian Military Forces* : 1927

Australian Army Order (AAO) 175/1937. *Territorial Titles and Mottoes – Australian Military Forces*: 1937

Australian Army Order (AAO) 548/1927. *Regimental Colours and Mottoes – Battalions, Australian Military Forces* : 1927

Australian Army Order (AAO) 91/1953. *Regimental Marches – Australian Military Forces*: 1953

Australian Army Order (AAO) 91-9/3/1927. *Battle Honours – Australian Military Forces*: 1927

Australian Army. Army Ceremonial and Protocol Manual – 2014. Canberra, Defence Publishing Service: 2014

Australian Army. *Army Dress Manual – 1979*. Canberra, Australian Government Printing Service: 1981

Australian Army. *Army Dress Manual – 2013*. Canberra, Defence Publishing Service: 2013

Australian Army. *Army Standing Orders for Dress – 2000, Volume 1 and 2*. Canberra, Defence Publishing Service: 2003

Australian Army. *Aviation Corps, Corps Procedures 2008*: 2008

Australian Army. *Ceremonial Manual – 1977*. Brunswick Victoria, Defence Printing Establishment: 1977

Australian Army. *Ceremonial Manual – 1999 Volume 1 and 2*. Defence Publishing Services, Canberra: 1999

Australian Army. *Ceremonial Manual – 2003 Volume 1*. Canberra, Defence Publishing Services: 2003

Australian Army. *Ceremonial Manual – 2003 Volume 2*. Canberra, Defence Publishing Services: 2003

Australian Army. *Dress Manual – 1963*. Canberra, Australian Government Printing Service: 1963

Australian Army. *Land Warfare Procedures – General LWP-G 3-10-5 Drill 1999*. Puckapunyal, Combined Arms Training and Development Centre: 1993

Australian Army. *Land Warfare Procedures – General LWP-G 7-1-4 Drill 1999*. Puckapunyal, Combined Arms Training and Development Centre: 1999

Australian Army. *Land Warfare Procedures – General LWP-G 7-7-5 Drill 2005*. Puckapunyal, Land Warfare Development Centre: 2005

Australian Army. *The Royal Regiment of Australian Artillery – Standing Orders*: 2008

Australian Army. *The Soldier's Handbook (Amendment No 1) – 1969*. Australian Government Printing Service: 1969

Australian Defence Force. *Minute No. 7/1970 of the Military Board*: 23 January 1970

Australian Military Forces Drill (All Arms) 1953. Richmond, Victoria, Asher & Co. Pty Ltd, Richmond Victoria: 1953

Australian Military Forces Drill (All Arms) Part 1 – Elementary Drill 1958. Army, Melbourne Victoria: 1958

Australian Military Forces Drill Manual 1963. Melbourne Victoria, Army: 1963

Australian Military Forces. *Ceremonial 1958 Australia Provisional*. Military Board, 1 Base Printing Company RAAOC: 1958

Australian Military Forces. *Military Board Instructions, Standing Orders for Dress (Provisional) MBI No 86*. Military Board, Army Headquarters: 1952

Australian Military Forces. *Military Board Instructions, Standing Orders for Dress (Provisional) MBI No 90*. Military Board, Army Headquarters: 1958

Australian Military Forces. *Standing Orders for Clothing, Part 1 Permanent Forces*. Melbourne, Military Board: 1935

Australian Military Forces. *Standing Orders for Vehicle Operation and Servicing (Australia)*. Melbourne, Military Board: 1961

British Army Order (AO) No.287 1916, of April 1916, published under authority of Military Order (MO) No.507 of 1916

British Army Order 70/1915 XIX. *Warrant Officers, Class II*: 1915

Commonwealth Bureau of Census and Statistics (Australia). *Official year book of the Commonwealth of Australia*: 1908

Constitution of Australia

Defence Act 1903 – 1917. *Statutory Rules 1918 N0. 2*: 10 Jan 1918

Defence Honours and Awards Manual. Canberra, Department of Defence: 3 Sep 12

Department of Defence. *1 RAR Official Unit History*: 2007

Department of Defence. *A Guide to Service Customs for Officers, Warrant Officers and Senior Non-Commissioned Officers*. Canberra, Defence Publishing Service: 1994

Department of Defence. *Army Protocol Manual*. Canberra, Defence Publishing Service: 2001

Geneva Convention. *Protocols Additional, Article 24 and 26*: 12 August 1949

Government House. *Commonwealth Government Gazette. The Australian Order of Precedence of Honours and Awards: 15 Jan 1993*

Government House. *Commonwealth Government Gazette. The Australian Order of Precedence of Honours and Awards: 15 Jan 1993*

Great Britain War Office. *The King's regulations and orders for the Army, 1908*. London, H.M.S.O: 1908

Headquarters Training Command. *Australian Army Manual of Land Warfare Part Three – Training – Volume 3 Drill and Ceremonial Pamphlet No.1 Drill 1979*. Brunswick Victoria, Defence Printing Establishment: 1979

Her Majesty's Stationary Office, London. *Dress Regulations for the Officers of the Army (Including the Militia) – War Office, 1900. London,* Harrison and Sons: 1900

His Majesty's Stationary Office, London. *Manual of Ceremonial – 1935*. Melbourne, H.J. Green Government Printer: 1935

Military Board Instruction (MBI) No.59 of 18 October 1939

Military Order 172/1921

Military Order 524 of 1923 and MBI A.120 of 1926

Military Order GO 296/1903: 1903

Military Personnel Policy Manual. Canberra, Department of Defence: October 2013

Ministry of Defence. *Customs of the Army*. WO Code No 9026: August 1964

Ministry of Defence. *Manual of Elementary Drill (All Arms) 1935*. London, HM Stationary Office: 1935

Philanthropic Manual. Canberra, Department of Defence: 6 Dec 13

RAAEC Manual of Army Employment

War Precautions Act: 1920

Defence Instructions

DI(A) ADMIN 12-1	Naming of Army Watercraft
DI(A) ADMIN 26-1	Naming of Army Installations
DI(A) ADMIN 38-3	Administration of Australian Battle Honours
DI(A) PERS 119-1	Army Combat Badge
DI(A) PERS 170-5	Organisation, Role and Responsibilities of the RAACD (interim)
DI(A) PERS 180-1	Royal Australian Army Educational Corps
DI(A) PERS 183-1	The Royal Australian Corps of Military Police
DI(A) PERS 31-3	Army Funerals
DI(A) PERS 47-9	Officer Appointments
DI(A) PERS 97-4	Soldiers Medallion
DI(A) PERS 97-5	Infantry Combat Badge
DI(A) PERS 99-1	Honorary Colonels
DI(G) ADMIN 04-1	Use of the Australian Defence Force Emblem
DI(G) ADMIN 04-1	The Australian Army Emblem
DI(G) ADMIN 12-1	Australian Defence Force Ensign
DI(G) ADMIN 13-1	Use of the Royal Anthem
DI(G) OPS 05-2	Flypasts and Flying Displays
DI(G) PERS 10-7	Promotion in the Australian Defence Force
DI(G) PERS 20-1	Provision of Floral and Non-Floral Tributes
DI(G) PERS 20-6	Death of Australian Defence Force Personnel
DI(G) PERS 20-8	Defence Casualties and Bereavement Support Manual

Letters

Office of the Chief of Army OCA/OUT/012?r11994006 dated 20 Sep 2012

Military Précis and other Articles [473]

Australian Military Forces, *Ceremonial Drill 1-13 Précis.* Ingleburn, Infantry Centre: 1962

Duncan MG. *Customs and Traditions.* Puckapunyal, Headquarters Third Training Group: 1996

Gordon, HB. Précis *Army Customs and Origins:* year unknown

Infantry Centre. *Military Traditions and Customs.* Singleton, Infantry Centre: 7 April 1977

Infantry School, Précis *Formal Dining In.* Fort Benning, USA Infantry School: year unknown

Morrissey P. *Unit History 1st/19th RNSWR*: 2009

Royal Military College Archives. *Traditions and Customs of the Royal Military College, (1998).* Canberra, Royal Military College - Duntroon: 2002

School of Infantry. *Military Traditions and Customs.* Singleton, Infantry Centre: 7 April 1977

The Royal Australian Regiment Association. *The Battalions*: undated

Warrant Officer Wing, School of Infantry. *Customs & Traditions.* Singleton, Infantry Centre: 1975

Warrant Officer Wing, School of Infantry. *Customs & Traditions.* Singleton, Infantry Centre: 1989

---

473 A précis was a locally produced booklet bound by staples. Usually produced in small numbers and had a limited distribution. Revised editions were produced by different training establishments.

Books

Abate FR, Robbins CD, Urdang L. Mottoes: *A Compilation of More Than 9,000 Mottoes From Around the World and Throughout History.* Detroit Michigan, Gale Research Company: 1986

Aelianus T. Bingham J. *The Tactiks of Aelian.* London: 1616. (reprinted by Da Capo Press, 1968)

Alt G. Premier-Leitnant Geschichte der Königl. *Preussischen Kürassiere und Dragoner 1619-1870.* Berlin 1869 (reprinted by Anton Hain KG, Berlin: 1970)

Anderson RC, Laughton LG. *The Mariner's Mirror.* London England, Carr and Perrin WG and Society for Nautical Research: 1911.

Askey MW. *By the Mark Five: A Definitive History of the Participation of Australian Water Transport Units in World War II.* Turramurra NSW, Murray David: 1998

Baker LM (editor). *Pears Cyclopaedia (81st edition).* United Kingdom, Petham Books: 1972

Barnes J, Furphy A. *Furphy: The Water Cart and the Word.* Melbourne, Scholarly Publishing: 2005

Barnes RM. *A History of the Regiments and Uniforms of the British Army.* London, Sphere: 1972

Barret R. *The Theorike and Practike of Moderne Warres.* London, William Ponsonby: 1598

Barton LL. *Australians in the Waikato War, 1863-1864.* Sydney, Library of Australian History: 1979

Bassett J. *The Canadians: John McCrae.* Markham Ontario, Fitzhenry & Whiteside: 1984

Bean CEW. *Official History of Australia in the War of 1914-1918 Volume I.* Sydney, Angus & Robertson: 1941

Bean CEW. *Official History of Australia in the War of 1914-1918 Volume III. The Australian Imperial Force in France 1916.* Sydney, Angus & Robertson: 1941

Bean CEW. *The Australian Imperial Force in France, 1916.* St Lucia Queensland, University of Queensland Press: 1940

Bean CEW. *The Australian Imperial Force in France: During the Allied Offensive.* Sydney, Angus and Robertson: 1942

Beaumont J. *Australian Defence: Sources and Statistics.* Melbourne, Oxford University Press: 2001

Benedictine Monks of St Augustine's Abbey. *The Book of Saints: a Dictionary of Servants of God Canonized by the Catholic Church.* London, A. & C. Black: 1921

Bentley WG. *Trumpet and Bugle Calls for the Australian Army: Including Instructions for Trumpeters and Buglers.* Sydney, Angus and Robertson: 1916

Bezdek RH. *Swords and Sword Markers of England and Scotland.* Colorado USA, Paladin Press: 2004

Blair C, Tarassuk L. *The Complete Encyclopaedia of Arms and Weapons.* London, Batsford: 1982

Bland H. *A Treatise of Military Discipline.* London, Printed D. Midwinter, J. and P. Knapton: 1743

Bomford J. *Soldiers of the Queen.* Australia, Oxford University Press: 2001

Bou J. *Light Horse: A History of Australia's Mounted Arm.* Port Melbourne, Cambridge University Press: 2010

Brumwell S. *Redcoats: The British Soldier and War in the Americas 1755-1763.* New York, Cambridge University Press: 2007

Carlton C. *Going to the Wars: The Experience of the British Civil Wars 1638-1651.* e-Library, Taylor & Francis: 2003

Carman, WY. *A Dictionary of Military Uniforms:* London, B.T. Batsford Limited: 1977

Cassin-Scott J, Fabb J. *Military Bands and their Uniforms.* Poole Dorset, Blandford Press: 1978

Chapman ID, Iven G. *Mackay: Citizen and Soldier.* Melbourne, Melway Publishing: 1975

Charlton P. *The Thirty-Niners.* South Melbourne, Macmillan: 1981

Clark M. *A History of Australia Volume 1.* Carlton, Melbourne University Press: 1962

Clowers W. *General Regulations and Orders for the Army.* London, Horse Guards: 1882

Clugnet L. *"St. Martin of Tours" In The Catholic Encyclopaedia.* New York, Robert Appleton Company: 1910

Collins P. *Strike Swiftly: The Australian Commando Story.* Sydney, Watermark Press: 2005

Cossum JK. *Australian Army Badges: A Collector's Reference Guide – Part 1 1930-1942.* Sunbury Victoria, J.K. Cossum: 1994

Cossum JK. *Australian Army Badges: A Collector's Reference Guide – Part 2 1900-1930.* Sunbury Victoria, J.K. Cossum: 1994

Cossum JK. *Australian Army Badges: A Collector's Reference Guide – Part 3, 1948-1985.* Sunbury Victoria, J.K. Cossum: 1994

Cossum JK. *Australian Army Badges: The Rising Sun Badge.* Sunbury Victoria, J.K. Cossum: 1986

Coulthard-Clark C. *Duntroon – The Royal Military College of Australia, 1911-1986.* Sydney, Allen & Unwin: 1986

Cruso J. *Militarie Instructions for the Cavallrie.* England, University of Cambridge: 1632

Dancocks DG. *Welcome to Flanders' Fields: The First Canadian Battle of the Great War: Ypres 1915.* Toronto, McClelland & Stewart: 1988

Davis BL. *British Army Uniforms and Insignia of World War Two.* London, Arms and Armour Press: 1983

Dennis P, Grey J, Morris E, Prior R. *The Oxford Companion to Australian Military History, Second Edition.* Australia, Oxford University Press: 2008

Dennis P, Grey J, Morris E, Prior R. *The Oxford Companion to Australian Military History.* Australia, Oxford University Press: 1995

Dennys R. *Heraldry and the Heralds.* London, Jonathan Cape: 1982

Dickson RJ. *Enlivened Anecdotes of Mess Times remembered from a host of one time mess members and the progress of Charles Oswald Littlewart from 2nd Lieutenant to Major General.* Tunbridge Wells, Midis Books: 1973

Dorling HT, Purves AA. *Ribbons and Medals.* London, Osprey in association with Spink and Son Ltd: 1983

Downing WH, Ramson WS, Arthur JM (editors). *Downing's Digger dialects.* Melbourne, Oxford University Press: 1990

Duffy C. *The Army of Maria Theresa: The Armed Forces of Imperial Austria 1740-1780.* North Pomfret USA, David & Charles, North Pomfret, VT: 1977

Edwards TJ. *Military Customs.* Aldershot England, Gale and Polden: 1954

Edwards TJ. *Standards, Guidons and Colours of the Commonwealth Forces.* Aldershot England, Gale & Polden: 1953

Fairey E. *The Story and Official History of the 38th Battalion AIF.* Bendigo, 38th Battalion History Committee: 1920

Farmer HG. *The Rise & Development of Military Music.* London, WM Reeves: 1882

Festberg AN. *Australian Army Guidons and Colours.* Melbourne, Allara Publishing: 1972

Festberg AN. *The Lineage of the Australian Army.* Melbourne, Allara Publishing: 1972

Fortescue JW. *A History of the British Army Volume 1.* London, Macmillan: 1910

Fowler HW, McIntosh E. *The Concise Oxford Dictionary of Current English.* Oxford, Clarendon Press: 1975

Franki G, Slatyer C. *Mad Harry: Harry Murray: Australia's*

Most Decorated Soldier. East Roseville NSW, Kangaroo Press: 2003

Franklyn J. *Shield and Crest: An Account of the Art and Science of Heraldry.* London, MacGibbon & Kee: 1961

Gembarewski B. *Wojsko Polskie: Księstwo, Warszawskie 1807-1814.* Warsaw, Genethner I Wolff: 1905

Gentles I. *The New Model Army – In England, Ireland and Scotland 1645-1653.* Oxford, Blackwell Press: 1994

Gladwin M. *Captains of the Soul - A History of Australian Army Chaplains.* Sydney, Big Sky Publishing: 2013.

Glyde K. *Distinguishing Colour Patches of the Australian Military Forces 1915-1951: A Reference Guide.* Claremont Tasmania, DW Thorpe: 1999

Goldsworthy A. *The Complete Roman Army.* London, Thames and Hudson Ltd: 2011

Gordon LL. *British Battles and Medals (7th edition).* Gale Aldershot, Naval and Military Press: 1962

Gordon LL. *Military Origins.* New York, A. S. Barnes: 1971

Grandin R. *The Battle of Long Tan: As Told by the Commanders to Bob Grandin.* Crows Nest NSW, Allen & Unwin: 2004

Grebert R. *The Significance of Ribbon Colours on Medals Worn Since 1815 by Australians.* Dural NSW, Landers Publishing: 2007

Greville PJ. *The Royal Australian Engineers: Paving the Way.* Canberra, Corps Committee of the Royal Australian Engineers: 2002

Grose F. *Military Antiquities Respecting a History of the English Army V2.* London, Kessinger Legacy: 1786

Gush G. *Renaissance Armies 1480-1650.* Cambridge, Stephens: 1975

Hall RJG. *The Australian Light Horse.* Blackburn Victoria, W. D. Joynt: 1968

Harkness A. *The Military System Of The Romans.* New York, D Appleton & Company: 1887

Haythornethwaite PJ. *The Armies of Wellington.* London, Arms and Armour Press: 1994

Heath I. *Armies of the Dark Ages 600-1066.* Worthing, Wargames Research Gp: 1980

Hetherington JA. *Blamey, Controversial Soldier: A Biography of Field Marshal Sir Thomas Blamey, GBE, KCB, CMG, DSO, ED.* Canberra, Australian War Memorial and the Australian Government Publishing Service: 1983

Holweck F. *St. Michael the Archangel. In The Catholic Encyclopaedia.* New York, Robert Appleton Company: 1911

Hopkins RNL. *Australian Armour: A History of the Royal Australian Armoured Corps, 1927-1972.* Canberra, Australian War Memorial and Australian Government Printing Service: 1978

Horne CD. *Salt.* Melbourne, Educational Publications, Army Headquarters: 24 April 1944

Horner DM. *Duty First: The Royal Australian Regiment in War and Peace.* Sydney, Allen & Unwin: 1990

Inglis KS. Sacred Places, War Memorials in the Australian Landscape (3rd edition). Melbourne, Melbourne University Press: 2008

Jobson C. *Royal Regiment of Australian Artillery: Customs and Traditions.* Manly NSW, Directorate of Artillery: 1997

Johnston M, Stanley P. *Alamein: The Australian Story.* South Melbourne Victoria, Oxford University Press: 2005

Joslin EC, Litherland AR, Simpkin BT, Gordon LL. *British Battles & Medals.* London, Spink: 1988

Kent B. *Signal! A History of Signalling in the Royal Navy.* Clanfield United Kingdom, Hyden House: 1993

Kerrigan EE. *American War Medals and Decorations.* New York, Viking Press, New York: 1965

Kirsch JP. *The Catholic Encyclopaedia Volume 2.* New York, Robert Appleton Company: 1907

Kuring I. *Red Coats to Cams: A History of Australian Infantry 1788 to 2001.* Loftus NSW, Australian Military History Publications: 2004

Lacaille F. *Uniformes Naoléoniennes.* Paris, Musée de l'Armée: 2001

Lamont-Brown R. *A Casebook of Military Mystery.* Cambridge, Brown Stephens: 1974

Lawson CCP. *History of the Uniforms of the British Army.* London, Peter Davies: 1940

Leckie N. *Country Victoria's Own.* Loftus NSW, AMH Publications: 2008

Lever GO (editor). *The Australian Army A Brief History, Edition Four.* Sydney, Big Sky Publishing: 2011

Levine B, Weland G. *Knives, Swords, Daggers.* London, Quintet Publishing: 2004

Lilley AB and the Military Historical Society of Australia. *Sydney University Regiment: A description of the Insignia Worn from 1900-1973 by Military Units at the University of Sydney.* Lyneham ACT, Military Historical Society of Australia: 1974

Lindsay N. *Equal to the Task.* Kenmore Queensland, Historia Productions: 1992

Litherland AR, Simpkin BT. *Spink's Standard Catalogue of British and Associated Orders, Decorations and Medals, With Valuations.* London, Spink: 1990

Long G. *Greece, Crete and Syria (1st edition).* Canberra, Australian War Memorial: 1953

Long G. *Australia in the War of 1939-1945, Series 1, Army, Volume I, To Benghazi.* Adelaide, The Advertiser Printing Office: 1961

Lovell-Knight AV. *The Story of the Royal Military Police.* London, Cooper: 1977

Macdonald L. *The Death of Innocence.* London, Headline: 1993

Macquarie University NSW. *The Macquarie Dictionary.* Milton Queensland, The Jacaranda Press: 1987

Maitland G. *Honours and Awards of the Army.* Paddington, NSW, Playbill: 2014

Makepeace-Warne A. *Brassey's Companion to the British Army.* London, Brassey's: 1995

Markham F. *Five Decades of Epistles of Warre.* London, Augustine Matthewes: 1622

Mathieson WD. *My Grandfather's War.* Toronto, Macmillan: 1981

Maton M. *Imperial Honours and Awards to Australians 1901-1992.* St Ives NSW, Michael Maton: 1996

McAulay L. *The Battle of Coral.* Hawthorn Victoria, Hutchinson Australia: 1988

McKay G. *Delta Four: Australian Riflemen in Vietnam.* St Leonards, NSW, Allen & Unwin: 1996

McNab C. *The Roman Army: The Greatest War Machine of the Ancient World.* Oxford England, Osprey Publishing Ltd: 2012.

McNeill IG. *To Long Tan: The Australian Army and the Vietnam War 1950-1966.* St Leonards NSW, Allen & Unwin: 1993

McNicoll R. *The Royal Australian Engineers: The Colonial Engineers.* Canberra, Corps Committee of the Royal Australian Engineers: 1982

Mershman F. *"St. Maurice" In The Catholic Encyclopaedia.* New York, Robert Appleton Comoany: 1911

Michael, M. *The Miracle Flower – The Story of the Flanders Fields Memorial Poppy.* Pittsburgh Pennsylvania, Dorrance Publishing Company: 1941

Ministry of Defence, Great Britain – Army. *Trumpet and Bugle Calls for the Army: With Instructions for the Training of Trumpeters and Buglers.* London, HMSO: 1927

Mollo J. *Military fashion: A Comparative History of the Uniforms of the Great Armies From the 17th Century to the First World War.* London, Barrie and Jenkins: 1972

Moses JA, Davis GF. *Anzac Day Origins.* Canberra, Barton Books: 2013

Norris G. *A Musical Gazetteer of Great Britain & Ireland.* North Pomfret Vermont, David & Charles, Devon: 1981Mershman F. '*St. Maurice' In The Catholic Encyclopaedia.* New York, Robert Appleton Coy: 1911

O'Connor JM. *Australian Airborne: The History and Insignia of Australian Military Parachuting.* Kingsgrove NSW, John O'Connor: 2005

O'Neill RJ. *Australia in the Korean War 1950-1953 Volume 2, Combat operations.* Canberra, Australian Government Publishing Service: 1985

Paget J. *Discovering London Ceremonial and Traditions (2nd edition).* Princes Risborough, Shire Publications: 2003

Paget J. *The Yeomen of the Guard, Five Hundred Years of Service 1485-1985.* Poole, Dorset, Blandford Press: 1984

Pearsall J. (editor) *The Concise Oxford English Dictionary (10th edition revised).* Oxford, Oxford University Press: 2002

Petre C. *Review of Australian Honours and Awards: A matter of honour.* Canberra, Australian Government Publishing Service: 1995

Pietsch P. *Formations und Uniformierungsgeschichte des Paul Preussischen Heeres 1808 bis 1914", Band II, Kavallerie und Artillerie.* Hamburg, Helmut Gerhard Schulz: 1966.

Politics, and Literature, for the Year 1782. London, Pater-Noster-Row: 1797

Robinson G (printed for). *The New Annual Register, or General Repository of History, Robson B. Swords of the British Army: The Regulation Patterns 1788-1914.* London, Arms and Armour Press: 1996

Robson B. *Swords of the British Army: The Regulation Patterns, 1788-1914.* London, Arms and Armour Press: 1975

Sidney L. *Dictionary of National Biography Volume LIII Smith-Stanger.* London, Smith Elder & Co: 1898

Simes, T. *The Military Guide for Young Officers.* London, J. Millan: 1772

Skennerton ID. *British Service Sword and Lance Patterns.* Ashmore City, Queensland, ID Skennerton: 1994

Smythe J. *Certain Discourses.* London, Richard Johns: 1590

Society for Army Historical Research. *Journal of the Society for Army Historical Research – ACI 444.* London: 21 July 1919,

Society for Army Historical Research. *Journal of the Society for Army Historical Research.* London: 1935

Society for Army Historical Research. *Journal of the Society for Army Historical Research.* London: 1936

Sorenson ES. *Life in the Australian Backblocks.* Melbourne, Whitcombe & Tombs Ltd: 1911

St Augustine's Abbey Ramsgate. *The Book of Saints: A Dictionary of Servants of God Canonized by the Catholic Church.* London, A. & C. Black: 1966

Stanley P (editor). *But Little Glory.* Canberra, Military Historical Society of Australia: 1984

Stevens G. *The Originals – The Secret History of the Birth of the SAS in Their Own Words.* London, Random House: 2006

Stirling JF. *The Colonials in South Africa, 1899-1902: Their Record, Based on the Despatches.* Edinburgh, W. Blackwood and Sons: 1907

Strandberg JE, Bender RJ. *The Call of Duty.* San Jose California, R. James Bender Publishing: 1994

Talbot-Booth EC. *The British Army, Its History, Customs, Traditions and Uniforms.* London, Sampson Low, Marston Company: 1937

Taprell Dorling H. *Ribbons and Medals.* London, George Philip and Son Limited: 1963

Taubert S. *Formation Signs and Vehicle Marking of the Australian Army 1903-1984.* Brisbane Queensland, Comtrain Enterprises: 1996

Taylor A. *Discovering Military Traditions.* Aylesbury, UK, Shire Publications: 1972.

Thurston H. "St. George" In The Catholic Encyclopaedia. New York, Robert Appleton Company: 1909

Tsouras P. *Warrior's Words: A Quotation Book: From Sesostris III to Schwarzkopf 1871BC to AD1991.* London, Arms and Armour: 1992

Urdang L, Robbins C. *Mottoes.* Indiana, Gale Research Company: 1986

Van der Essen L. "St. Eligius" The Catholic Encyclopaedia. Vol. 5. New York, Robert Appleton Company: 1909.

Wannan B. *The Australia, Yarns Ballads Legends.* Melbourne, O'Neil Publishers: 1979

Ward R, Marshall W. *Anima'dversions of Warre.* London, John Dawson: 1639

Wheeler W, Liddell Hart BH (editors). *The letters of Private Wheeler, 1809-1828.* London, Michael Joseph Ltd: 1951

White TA. *The History of the Thirteenth Battalion, AIF.* Sydney, Tyrells Ltd: 1924

Wigmore L. *The Japanese Thrust.* Canberra, Australian War Memorial: 1957

Wilkinson F. *Badges of the British Army 1820-1960: An Illustrated Reference Guide for Collectors.* London, Arms & Armour: 1972

Withers H. *The Illustrated Encyclopedia of Swords and Sabres.* North Melbourne, Alto Books: 2008

Wood J. *Chiefs of the Australian Army: Higher Command of the Australian Military Forces 1901-1914.* Loftus NSW, Australian Military History Publications: 2006

Yallop C. (editor). *The Macquarie Dictionary (4th edition).*

Sydney, NSW, Macquarie Dictionary Publishers: 1987

Articles and Journals

Darling Downs Gazette: 24 April 1919

Federal Council of the Military Historical Society of Australia. *The Journal of Proceedings of The Military Historical Society.* Volume XXX Number 2: Apr-Jun 1989

Government House. *Commonwealth Government Gazette. The Australian Order of Precedence of Honours and Awards: 15 Jan 1993*

Gunfire. *Newsletter of the Royal Australian Artillery Association.* NSW: June 2008

Hickmore G. *Origin of In Flanders' Fields.* Ottawa Canada, Public Archives: MG30 EI33

Jones RW. *Australian Infantry Magazine:* January-June 1981, pp. 28-29

Miller G. *The Death of Manfred von Richthofen: Who fired the fatal shot? Sabretache: Journal and Proceedings of the Military History Society of Australia*: 1998, vol. XXXIX, no. 2.

Royal Australian Artillery Association NSW. *Gunfire Newsletter of the Royal Australian Artillery Assoc. (NSW) Inc. Issue 2.* Sydney NSW: June 2008

Society for Army Historical Research. *Journal of the Society for Army Historical Research – ACI 444.* London: 21 July 1919.

Society for Army Historical Research. *Journal of the Society for Army Historical Research. London:* 1936

The Age Newspaper. *The ANZAC Star That Never Shone.* Melbourne, Fairfax Media: 24 April 1990.

The Argus (Melbourne, Victoria: 1848-1957): Thursday 7 April 1927

The Register. Adelaide South Australia: 2 December 1901

The Times. *New Army Rank of Brigadier.* London, News International: 23 December 1997

Internet References

http://en.wikipedia.org/wiki/Edward_George_Honey

http://trove.nla.gov.au/ndp/del/article/74492953

http://www.army.gov.au/Our-history/History-in-Focus/Womens-historical-contribution-recognised-on-Anzac-Day

www.awm.gov.au/atwar/boer.asp

www.awm.gov.au/atwar/korea/

www.awm.gov.au/atwar/structure/one_army.asp

www.awm.gov.au/cms_images/AWM85/2/AWM85-2-12.pdf

www.awm.gov.au/cms_images/AWM85/2/AWM85-2-12.pdf

www.awm.gov.au/encyclopedia/pow/general_info/

www.awm.gov.au/encyclopedia/tobruk/

www.awm.gov.au/encyclopedia/war_casualties/

www.awm.gov.au/research/people/nominal_rolls/first_world_war_embarkation

www.awm.gov.au/research/people/nominal_rolls/pre_first_world_war

www.awm.gov.au/units/event_295.asp

www.catholic.org/saints/patron.php?letter=C

www.defence.gov.au/medals/

www.dva.gov.au/commems_oawg/OAWG/post_war_commemorations/gardens_remembrance/Pages/locations.aspx

www.itsanhonour.gov.au

www.nationalarchives.gov.uk/documentsonline/victoriacross.asp

www.royalengineers.ca/REdressreg57.html

www.tioh.hqda.pentagon.mil/Awards/VIETNAM%20GALLANTRY%20CROSS1.html

Authors Disclaimer: All internet references were correct at time of retrieval; it is not possible to guarantee ongoing currency of these references.

INDEX

About the Authors

Leslie Irvin Terrett

Leslie Irvin (Les) Terrett was born on the 8th April 1957, in Myrtleford, Victoria where he completed his secondary education. He undertook his tertiary education at Melbourne University.

He enlisted into the Australian Regular Army in 1975 and during a successful career in logistics spanning 32 years, achieved the rank of Major. Transferring to the Army Reserve in 2007, he is now posted to the Australian Army History Unit working as a Project Officer with a focus on Oral History and Customs and Traditions.

Les saw active service in Iraq as part of the Coalition Forces in 2003-2004. His family has a long history of military service for Australia, with members having served in the 2nd Boer War, WWI (Gallipoli, Pozieres, Menin Road, Passchendaele, Hangard Wood, Villers-Bretonneux), WWII (Europe and Pacific), Korea, Vietnam and East Timor. Les is proud to have been a Legacy boy. In his civilian career, he works as a Senior Consultant to Government and lives in North Eastern Victoria.

Stephen Craig Taubert

Stephen Craig (Steve) Taubert was born on the 2nd September 1952 in Adelaide, South Australia. After completing his secondary education at Snowtown Area School he moved to Adelaide to undertake an apprenticeship in Fitting and Turning. After completing his qualification he moved to Brisbane, working for a short period within this trade, prior to joining the Australian Regular Army in April 1974. He left the Army in 1994, having achieved the rank of Warrant Officer Class One in a career spanning over 20 years with the Royal Australian Corps of Transport.

Steve is the author of *The History of the First Transport Squadron RACT 1914-1989* (first published 1989) and *Formation Signs and Vehicle Marking of the Australian Army (1997)*. He specialises in high quality graphical images of Military Colours and Badges, many of which are shown throughout this book.